THEMES FROM KAPLAN

Edited by

JOSEPH ALMOG
University of California, Los Angeles

JOHN PERRY
Stanford University

HOWARD WETTSTEIN
University of Notre Dame

With the Assistance of
Ingrid Deiwiks and Edward N. Zalta

New York   Oxford
OXFORD UNIVERSITY PRESS
1989

P
106
T477
1989

Oxford University Press

Oxford   New York   Toronto
Delhi   Bombay   Calcutta   Madras   Karachi
Petaling   Jaya   Singapore   Hong Kong   Tokyo
Nairobi   Dar es Salaam   Cape Town
Melbourne   Auckland

and associated companies in
Berlin   Ibadan

Library of Congress Cataloging-in-Publication Data
Themes from Kaplan/edited by
Joseph Almog, John Perry, and Howard Wettstein.
p.   cm.   ISBN 0-19-505217-X
1. Languages—Philosophy.   2. Kaplan, David, 1933– .
I. Almog, Joseph, 1958– .
II. Perry, John, 1943– .   III. Wettstein, Howard K., 1943– .
IV. Kaplan, David, 1933– .
P106.T477   1989   401—dc 19   88-10027   CIP

2 4 6 8 9 7 5 3 1
Printed in the United States of America
on acid-free paper

Preface

In spring of 1984, a number of philosophers, logicians, linguists, and computer scientists gathered to pay tribute to David Kaplan. The conference was titled "Themes from Kaplan," and was intended as a mid-career affirmation of the importance and influence of Kaplan's ideas.

Papers presented at that conference form the core of the present volume. Some of these papers were in their finished state shortly after the conference ended, and their authors have had a long wait to see their work in print. The editors appreciate their patience.

The final works in the volume are David Kaplan's *Demonstratives* and "Afterthoughts." *Demonstratives* has been circulated in mimeographed form for more than ten years now. The editors appreciate Professor Kaplan's willingness to have this seminal work printed here, and for providing us with his present perspective on the issues discussed in it.

The conference was funded, and the present book prepared for publication, at the Center for the Study of Language and Information (CSLI). This assistance was made possible through a grant from the System Development Foundation (SDF). The editors are grateful to CSLI and to SDF.

The editors wish to express their deep gratitude to Ingrid Deiwiks and Edward Zalta. Deiwiks handled communication with the authors, typed and formatted a number of papers, proofread the entire volume and kept track of innumerable details. Through her tireless efforts, camera-ready copy was prepared at CSLI, which has shortened the time of publication by many months. Zalta assumed many crucial editorial functions, and suggested a number of improvements to individual papers and to the volume as a whole. Deiwiks and Zalta were together responsible for solving many problems involved in adapting the LaTeX computer language to the needs of philosophical and logical prose. In this they were aided by Emma Pease of the CSLI staff.

January 1989   J. A.
                                                            J. P.
                                                            H. W.

Contents

Part II

Contributors

Felicia Ackerman, Professor of Philosophy, Brown University

Robert Merrihew Adams, Professor of Philosophy, University of California, Los Angeles

Joseph Almog, Assistant Professor of Philosophy, University of California, Los Angeles

C. Anthony Anderson, Professor of Philosophy, University of Minnesota

Hector-Neri Castañeda, The Mahlon Powell Professor of Philosophy, Indiana University

Roderick M. Chisholm, Professor of Philosophy, Brown University

Alonzo Church, Professor of Philosophy, University of California, Los Angeles

Harry Deutsch, Professor of Philosophy, Illinois State University

Kit Fine, Professor of Philosophy, University of Michigan, Ann Arbor

David Kaplan, Professor of Philosophy, University of California, Los Angeles

Ruth Barcan Marcus, Professor of Philosophy, Yale University

Julius Moravcsik, Professor of Philosophy, Stanford University

Christopher Peacocke, Professor of Philosophy, University of London

John Perry, Professor of Philosophy, Stanford University

Nathan Salmon, Professor of Philosophy, University of California, Santa Barbara

Scott Soames, Professor of Philosophy, Princeton University

Howard Wettstein, Professor of Philosophy, University of Notre Dame

Edward N. Zalta, Acting Assistant Professor of Philosophy, Stanford University

Part I

1

Introduction

Ruth Barcan Marcus[1]

The first time I saw David Kaplan was across a crowded room at the University of Chicago. I'm no longer sure exactly when that was, except that it was not too long after David had completed his dissertation and was moving like a meteor across our philosophical horizon.

On that occasion, there were several things to be noticed. I'll mention two. What one noticed were those very special abilities of David's, which had been, and would continue to be, appreciated by all of us. First, his extraordinary subtlety, his fine-honed analytical intelligence and technical powers. Also, the very special style of his approach to a philosophical problem. The mode of presentation goes something like this: Here is a philosophical problem. Here is an obvious solution. (One sinks into complacency. For that is the very solution one understands and may even have thought of oneself.) But then, of course, it turns out that isn't the answer at all. It's riddled with flaws. The initially "obvious" solution is a nonsolution, and the issues are unpacked in ways that we hadn't conceived or noticed. He then proceeds to proposals that are dramatically original and permanently influential. Of course, awareness of David's philosophical style has made all of us wary. I learned to stop nodding in approval during stage one, so as not to be undone by stage two. Indeed, that marvelous paper "Bob and Carol and

[1] What follows is the text of my introduction to David Kaplan's talk at the conference "Themes from Kaplan," held at Stanford University, spring 1984.

Ted and Alice" was a response to a puzzle proposed, I believe, in the *Journal of Philosophy*. I was going to submit a solution but refrained, for it seemed to me very likely that if David was going to submit a solution, mine would be some version of the stage-one solution, to be disposed of. And as it turned out, it was.

Another feature of David's work was the freshness of his style: witty, free-wheeling, wild examples that gave vitality to his philosophical presentations. Also, the very special rapport with his audience, which I suspect is unique in philosophical annals. Of course, there is apt to be some fall-out with an audience where he was making his debut. I was in Oxford for the last of his Locke lectures and noticed that directly in front of the podium was a horseshoe of empty seats, except for Joseph Almog. The audience had crowded into the penumbra along the peripheries and in the balcony where their faces hung over like a Daumier etching. I later had occasion to talk to an Oxford philosopher who said how brilliant the lectures were and how much appreciated, except, he confessed, the audience was taken aback by the informality, especially with questions to the audience like "If you don't understand what I just said, raise your hand."

After that first meeting in Chicago, David sent me his dissertation, and I continued to receive drafts of his remarkable work, so much of it still unpublished. One could view it in part as a retreat from Fregeanism, but of course that says very little. For on the way, David turned so many in new directions. The roots of his paper "Quantifying In" are in Frege and Quine. I have read it many times and each time find something that I failed to appreciate in some prior reading. I don't *agree* with some of it, but nevertheless it is a paper of depth and richness, touching on naming and reference, how exactly to refine the notion of opaque context, what if anything "opacity" has to do with problems of substitution, differences between naming and describing, what are the conditions for a name to be scope-neutral, causal theories of naming, and so on. Without the Fregean origins we would also not have had those later fruitful distinctions between content and character that are required for an adequate theory of direct reference, indexicals, or the generalized notion of a context. David's papers "Dthat," "On the Logic of Demonstratives," and the unpublished Locke lectures mark a turn in semantics and epistemology that is new and irreversible. You may see it as a synthesis of Frege and Russell and formal semantics that has raised it to a new plane.

I am pleased and honored to introduce my friend David Kaplan, whose name is incontrovertibly "vivid" to all of us.

2

Content, Character, and Nondescriptive Meaning

Felicia Ackerman[1]

The view of reference that currently has widest acceptance holds that proper names and indexicals are what Kaplan calls directly referential terms, where a singular term is directly referential iff it refers "... directly without the mediation of a Fregean *Sinn* as meaning. If there are such terms, then the proposition expressed by a sentence containing such a term would involve individuals directly rather than by way of ... 'individual concepts' or 'manners of presentation' ...."[2] This view faces

---

[1] I formerly published under the name 'Diana F. Ackerman'. I thank Ernest Sosa and James Van Cleve for helpful discussions of the material in this paper.

[2] David Kaplan, *Demonstratives*, this volume, 483 (italics in original). The version of *Demonstratives* on which this paper is based is draft #2 ©1977, the latest version I have available at the time of this writing. I am conforming to Kaplan's favored terminology in using 'indexical' for terms where "... the referent is dependent on the context of use and ... the meaning of the word provides a rule which determines the referent in terms of certain aspects of the context." (Ibid., 490). A useful way of capturing the notion of a directly referential term comes from Donnellan's explication of Russell's notion of a constituent of a proposition, as follows. If 'Socrates' is a directly referential term, the sentence 'Socrates is snub-nosed' expresses a proposition that can be represented as an ordered pair consisting of Socrates—the actual man, not his name—and the property, being snub-nosed. See Keith S. Donnellan, "Speaking of Nothing," in *Naming, Necessity and Natural Kinds*, ed. Stephen P. Schwartz (Ithaca: Cornell University Press, 1977), 225.

a notorious problem about propositional attitudes. For example, if 'I' and 'she' both directly refer to me, how can I believe

(1)   She looks exhausted

without believing

(2)   I look exhausted

in a context where I do not recognize the exhausted-looking person as myself?

Kaplan's distinction between character and content offers a solution for this problem concerning indexicals, as follows. "The content of a sentence in a given context is what has traditionally been called a proposition,"[3] and the content of an indexical is intuitively supposed to be just the referent itself.[4] "The character of an expression is set by linguistic conventions and, in turn, determines the content of the expression in every context ... it is natural to think of it as *meaning* in the sense of what is known by the competent language user."[5] Content is the object of thought; character is the cognitive significance of the object of thought, the "manner of presentation of a content."[6] Where indexicals are involved, belief (or any other propositional attitude) is not the traditional two-place relation between a conscious being and a proposition. Instead, it is a three-place relation between a conscious being, a proposition (content), and a manner of presentation (character). Thus (1) and (2) can differ in cognitive significance while having the same content and so can true instances of

$$\text{dthat}(D_1) = \text{dthat}(D_1)$$

and

$$\text{dthat}(D_1) = \text{dthat}(D_2)$$

where D_1 and D_2 are coextensive definite descriptions.

Of course, this sort of propositional attitude problem does not arise only for terms Kaplan considers indexical. It also arises for proper names. But Kaplan declines to extend his solution to cases involving proper names. Instead, he says that "Because of the collapse of character, content, and referent [for proper names], it is not unnatural to say

---

[3] Kaplan, *Demonstratives*, 500.
[4] Ibid., 502, 507.
[5] Ibid., 505 (italics in original).
[6] Ibid., 530.

of proper names that they have no meaning other than their referent, ... the informativeness of $\ulcorner \alpha = \beta \urcorner$, with α and β proper names, is not accounted for in terms of differences in either content or character."[7] Thus, as it stands, his view cannot account for the possibility of disbelieving

(3) Hesperus is Phosphorus

while believing

(4) Hesperus is Hesperus.

This not only makes his solution drastically incomplete, but also raises doubts even about the cases where he does apply it. After all, if the problem with proper names has a different sort of solution, one might wonder whether such a solution could be extended for expressions Kaplan considers indexical as well, thereby creating a simpler overall theory. In this paper, however, I will pursue an opposite line. I will show how some of my own work can be extracted from its Fregean framework and adapted to Kaplan's framework in order to provide different cognitive significances for coreferential proper names and thus extend Kaplan's sort of solution to cover these cases as well. The reasons I favor a Fregean approach lie beyond the scope of this paper, where I take a devil's advocate role of assuming that beliefs of the sort in question are three-place relations and seeing how far such an approach can go.

How might coreferential proper names differ in cognitive significance while still being directly referential terms? I will consider three possibilities.

1. *Character as causal chain.* In the final footnote of *Demonstratives*, Kaplan raises the question of whether "the causal chain theory itself" might "constitute a kind of meaning for proper names that is analogous to character for indexicals (but which, perhaps, gives all proper names the same meaning in this sense)."[8] As long as all proper names are taken to have the same character, such a proposal cannot solve the problem. But there are ways of connecting character and causal chain that do not give all proper names the same character. I will suggest several such ways in this paper.

The first is as follows. Let us call the fullest possible a priori specification of the causal chain 'R', leaving open the question of whether this

---

[7] Ibid., 562.
[8] Ibid., footnote 78.

specification itself will involve some recourse to the notion of causally determined reference or will supply a full reductive analysis of this notion.[9] Then one possibility may seem to be that the character of 'Hesperus' will be the character of some description along the lines of 'dthat (the entity bearing R to this very token of 'Hesperus')' and the character of 'Phosphorus' will be the character of some description along the lines of 'dthat (the entity bearing R to this very token of 'Phosphorus')', where in each case the description of the form 'this very token of . . .' refers to the token whose character is at issue. But this particular formulation faces a problem analogous to that of Kaplan's suggestion that 'I' and 'dthat (the person who utters this token)' are "genuine synonyms."[10] 'I' and 'dthat (the person who utters this token)' cannot have the same meaning, since the meaning of the former, but not of the latter, *requires* that the referent is the utterer. Similarly, the meaning of 'this very token of 'Hesperus' ' does not require that the expression refer to the use whose character is at issue. But a new expression, 'this vlery token of 'Hesperus' ' can be introduced and defined so as to require this. The present proposal would thus be revised so as to hold that the character of 'Hesperus' is the same as the character of the description 'dthat (the entity bearing R to this vlery token of 'Hesperus')'. (For simplicity of exposition, I will sometimes talk in terms of such expressions as 'Hesperus' and Phosphorus', where it would be more precise to replace this with references to the particular uses of these expressions.) On this account, the difference in cognitive significance between (3) and (4) would explain how someone could believe that Hesperus is Hesperus without believing that Hesperus is Phosphorus. This account, however, would founder on the following related problem. Consider

---

[9] Both Kripke and Donnellan acknowledge that a full reductive analysis of causally determined reference in terms that make no use of the notion of reference might not be possible. See Donnellan, "Speaking of Nothing," in *Naming, Necessity and Natural Kinds*, ed. Schwartz, 232; and Saul Kripke, *Naming and Necessity* (Cambridge: Harvard University Press, 1980), 94. Of course, the causal chain account of reference can be interesting and informative even if it fails to provide a full reductive analysis of reference, just as it is interesting and informative to claim that knowledge is justified true belief supported by a chain of *known* reasons not essentially involving a falsehood, even though this obviously fails as a full reductive analysis of knowledge.

[10] Kaplan, *Demonstratives*, 522. Kaplan does acknowledge that there are "some subtle complications" with this suggestion. Note that he also says, "For two words or phrases to be synonyms, they must have the same content in every context," (ibid., 521), a condition this suggestion clearly doesn't satisfy.

(5)   Hesperus is dthat (the entity bearing R to this vlery token of 'Hesperus').

It is obviously possible to believe (4) while failing to believe (5). For example, this situation would obtain for a user of (4) who did not accept the causal chain theory of the reference of proper names, either because he had never heard of it or because he was a philosopher who disagreed with it. But if the character of 'Hesperus' is given by the description in question, this description would have to be what was known by competent users of the term (the way competent users of 'I' know that 'I' picks out the speaker) since, as I have indicated, Kaplan identifies character as "*meaning* in the sense of what is known by the competent language user,"[11] and (4) and (5) would have not only the same content, but also the same character. This sort of argument also gives another reason for rejecting Kaplan's above-mentioned suggestion that 'I' and 'dthat (the person who utters this token)' are genuine synonyms, since a competent user with elementary logical acumen may not believe this equivalence. (This is possible even for a philosophically sophisticated user who may, for instance, be unsure of whether 'person' or 'sentient being' should be in the description that is to be a "genuine synonym" of 'I'.)

2. *Character as a given by a description of the form 'dthat (the entity referred to by ...)'.* Few people know (5), but normal users of 'Hesperus' presumably know that

(6)   Hesperus is the entity referred to by 'Hesperus'.

So perhaps the character of 'Hesperus' is the character of the description 'dthat (the entity referred to by this vlery token of 'Hesperus')'. In a related context, Kripke has criticized the view that 'Socrates' could mean 'the man called 'Socrates' '.[12] First he points out that is is hardly "trifling" that Socrates was called 'Socrates'; in fact "it is dubious that the Greeks did call him that."[13] But this criticism does not apply to the current proposal, which identifies the object in question as the referent

---

[11] *Demonstratives*, 505 (italics in original). In ibid., footnote 13, Kaplan says his semantical theory is based on "linguistic rules known, *explicitly or implicitly*, by all competent users of the language" (italics mine). It may seem tempting to say the competent user of 'Hesperus' knows (5) "implicitly." But this move would not help here, since explicit belief would be itself a propositional attitude, and the problem would reappear in that one could believe (4) "explicitly" without believing (5) "explicitly." Whenever I use the terms 'knowledge', 'know', etc., in this paper, I should be taken to be discussing "explicit" knowledge.

[12] See Kripke, *Naming and Necessity*, 68–73.

[13] Ibid., 69.

only of the very name-token under consideration. Second, Kripke argues that this sort of account of reference is circular, for "... if one was determining the referent of a name like 'Glunk' to himself and made the following decision, 'I shall use the term 'Glunk' to refer to the man I call 'Glunk''', this would get one nowhere. One had better have some independent determination of the referent of the word 'Glunk'."[14] But this is circular only as an attempt to analyze the notion of *reference*. There is nothing circular about explicating the character of a name in terms of the notion of reference.

Still, I think this proposal will not work. Consider the following.

(7)   The proposition that Hesperus is visible in the evening is identical with the proposition that Hesperus is visible in the evening.

(8)   The proposition that Hesperus is visible in the evening is identical with the proposition that dthat (the entity referred to by this vlery token of 'Hesperus') is visible in the evening.

It is certainly possible to believe (7) without believing (8). This would be expected, for example, of a philosopher who held the view that 'Hesperus' was not a rigid designator and that being Hesperus was an inessential property of Hesperus. But this poses a problem for the present proposal, which seems to give 'Hesperus' and the corresponding description not only the same content but also the same character.[15]

3. *Character as nondescriptive meaning.* The classical Frege-inspired criterion for the individuation of Fregean senses says that singular terms have the same Fregean sense iff they are interchangeable *salva veritate* whenever used in propositional attitude contexts. I have argued elsewhere that consistent application of such a criterion yields the result that singular terms can be directly referential only if they refer to objects of Russellian acquaintance.[16] Kaplan's approach avoids this con-

---

[14] Ibid., 73.

[15] Of course, it is common to deny, following Mates, that the possibility of believing (7) without believing (8) shows that the singular terms in question do not have the same sense. This is entirely in accord with the present approach provided 'sense' is construed as content. See Benson Mates, "Synonymity," in *Semantics and the Philosophy of Language,* ed. Leonard Linsky (Urbana: University of Illinois Press, 1972), 111–38. But the issue I am considering here is whether (7) and (8) have the same character.

[16] See my paper, "An Argument for a Modified Russellian Principle of Acquaintance," in *Philosophical Perspectives*, vol. 1 (Metaphysics), ed. James Tomberlin (Atascadero, Calif.: Ridgeview Publishing Co., 1987), 501–12.

sequence by not requiring content to be individuated as finely as Frege individuates senses. But the failure of the above two suggestions for the character of proper names suggests that *character* must be individuated finely enough to permit substitutions into propositional attitude contexts; otherwise we will not be able to solve the problem at issue. Elsewhere, I have argued that even Fregeans have not consistently applied the above Frege-inspired criterion for sense individuation and that consistent application of such a criterion leads to the view that proper names to which the causal chain theory of reference applies have what I call nondescriptive connotations, i.e., these names are not directly referential terms; they have Fregean senses that differ from the Fregean sense of any description but have descriptions as their analyses.[17] Some of this material can be adapted to Kaplan's approach as well. I will show how the nondescriptive conceptual element of my view can be separated from my view's Fregean underpinning and used to provide characters for proper names.

I will begin with a sketch of my original Fregean view. My original view uses the above Frege-inspired sense-individuation criterion to argue that if the final a priori test for identifying the referent of a name-token ⌜N⌝ is that it is the entity standing in R to this vlery token of ⌜N⌝, and there is no description that would be interchangeable *salva veritate* with ⌜N⌝ when used in propositional attitude contexts, then ⌜N⌝ has a nondescriptive connotation. My use of 'connotation' corresponds to Kaplan's 'content', which Kaplan points out should be identified with Frege's notion of sense.[18] On this view, in such cases, ⌜the entity standing in R to this vlery token of ⌜N⌝⌝ gives an analysis of name-token ⌜N⌝, in the sense of analysis that 'justified true belief not essentially grounded in any falsehood' gives an analysis of 'knowledge' (on the assumption that this is a correct analysis of 'knowledge'). This is a major type of philosophical analysis, although there are other types of philosophical analysis as well. I will not attempt a full account of this type of analysis here, but some of its aspects are as follows. First, the Frege-inspired

---

[17] See my papers, "Proper Names, Propositional Attitudes, and Nondescriptive Connotations," *Philosophical Studies* 35 (1979): 55–69; "Proper Names, Essences, and Intuitive Beliefs," *Theory and Decision* 11 (1979): 5–26; "Natural Kinds, Concepts, and Propositional Attitudes," in *Studies in Epistemology: Midwest Studies in Philosophy* 5, ed. P. French, T. E. Uehling, Jr., H. K. Wettstein, and R. Fileppa (Minneapolis: University of Minnesota Press, 1980), 467–85; and "Plantinga's Theory of Proper Names," in *Alvin Plantinga*, ed. J. Tomberlin and P. van Inwagen (Dordrecht: Reidel, 1985), 185–96.
[18] Kaplan, *Demonstratives*, 529.

criterion for sense-individuation allows that analysis need not preserve identity of connotation. Thus, the proposition that every instance of knowledge is an instance of knowledge is not identical with the proposition that every instance of knowledge is an instance of justified true belief not essentially grounded in any falsehood, since one can know the first proposition without knowing the second. This result is desirable, as it lets philosophical analyses be informative, and hence is a step toward a solution to the form of the paradox of analysis that asks how philosophical analyses can be both true and informative. Similarly, name token ⌜N⌝ and ⌜the entity standing in R to this vlery token of ⌜N⌝⌝ differ in connotation. Second, on this view, name-token ⌜N⌝ and ⌜the entity standing in R to this vlery token of ⌜N⌝⌝ are necessarily and a priori coreferential.[19]

These two conditions are obviously inadequate to specify the type of *analysans-analysandum* relation in question, since they also apply to such pairs of expressions as '28' and 'second-smallest number equal to the sum of all its divisors excluding itself', and they do not make analysis asymmetrical. To rule out such cases as the foregoing mathematical equivalence, I draw upon what is epistemically significant and peculiar about analyses of the sort in question—the way in which they can be justified and tested for correctness. Thus, my third condition is as follows: the principle that an entity is N iff it is the entity standing in R to this vlery token of ⌜N⌝ can be justified by generalizing from replies that a user of ⌜N⌝ gives to questions about various simple described hypothetical situations, just as the principle that knowledge is justified true belief not essentially grounded in any falsehood can be justified by generalizing from replies to questions about whether various simple described hypothetical test cases would count as cases of knowledge. Fourth, the *analysandum* must express a property that is simpler than the *analysans* in a sense of simplicity that I leave at the intuitive level.

---

[19] In speaking of the analysis of expressions rather than the analysis of concepts, I may seem to be diverging from such philosophers as G. E. Moore. But this way of speaking is just a convenience, since I should always be understood as considering these expressions as having the semantic properties they actually do have. With this proviso, we can say much the same thing about the analysis of expressions in this sense and the analysis of concepts. In fact I will speak of these interchangeably. My use of corner-quotes should be understood in such a way that the fact that 'Socrates' names Socrates is an instance of a name ⌜N⌝ naming N, and the description 'the entity standing in R to Socrates' is an instance of a description of the form ⌜the entity standing in R to ⌜N⌝⌝.

This is just a rough sketch of my original Fregean view, with various complexities omitted both in the discussion of this type of *analysans-analysandum* relation in general, and in the specifics about proper names with nondescriptive connotations.[20] But the basic notion of analysis used here should be familiar enough, as it is the sort of thing that philosophers aim at in giving analyses of such terms as 'knowledge' that are supported and tested by the hypothetical example-and-counterexample method in the way I have indicated. The parallel with 'knowledge' is important here. To count as understanding 'knowledge', English speakers do not have to know its analysis, but their use of the term must be such that generalizations from their replies to questions about simple described hypothetical cases would support the analysis. The same is

---

[20] For example, a natural objection to the view as sketched here is that it is most implausible to suppose that such sentences as 'Socrates is the entity standing in R to this vlery token of 'Socrates'' express necessary truths. But there is also a more complex version of my view that lacks this consequence (but has other problems). Moreover, as Putnam points out in a related context, any consistent reconstruction of the preanalytic notion of "meaning" is bound to have some counterintuitive consequences, since our pretheoretical assumptions about these matters are jointly inconsistent. (See Hilary Putnam, "The Meaning of 'Meaning'," in *Mind, Language and Reality*, vol. 2 of *Philosophical Papers*, ed. Hilary Putnam (Cambridge: Cambridge University Press, 1975), 268–70.) This means that the seriousness of one view's counterintuitive consequences cannot be assessed except in comparison with the counterintuitive consequences of alternative views. I will not try to do this here, since the adaptation I am proposing of my original Fregean view to Kaplan's framework does not have the counterintuitive consequence in question. I discuss my notion of a nondescriptive connotation (including the foregoing problem) in detail in the papers mentioned in footnote 17. For more about the notion of philosophical analysis used here, see my papers, "The Informativeness of Philosophical Analysis," in *The Foundations of Philosophy: Midwest Studies in Philosophy* 6, ed. P. French, T. E. Uehling, and H. K. Wettstein (Minneapolis: University of Minnesota Press, 1981), 313–20; "Essentialism and Philosophical Analysis," in *Studies in Essentialism: Midwest Studies in Philosophy* 11, ed. P. French et al. (Minneapolis: University of Minnesota Press, 1986); and "Analysis and its Paradoxes," in *Proceedings of the 1985 Israel Colloquium for the History, Philosophy and Sociology of Science* (forthcoming). Another oversimplification in the foregoing analysis is illustrated by Kaplan's remarks about the intention to refer to a preconceived individual vs. the intention to follow convention in using a proper name (*Demonstratives*, 558–63). I will not try to remedy this oversimplification here, since the present paper is concerned with the relation between a name's analysis and its sense, content, and character, rather than with details of the analysis itself. But Kaplan's claim that "those who suggest that proper names are merely one species of indexical depreciate the power and the mystery of the causal chain theory" (ibid., 563) seems to overlook the fact that all the relevant complexities of the causal chain theory can be built into the analysis of proper names.

true of names with nondescriptive connotations.

This parallel is also important in rebutting the criticism some philosophers have made that this view of names is ad hoc. Also, some philosophers have called this view obscure. A charge simply that my view is obscure is not precise enough to discuss. Donnellan has independently suggested in conversation that my view is obscure because it is purely negative, that I say what connotations of names with nondescriptive connotations are *not*, but not what they *are*. This objection seems wrong, even granting the distinction between positive and negative properties it presupposes. Comparison with 'knowledge' is useful here. By the Frege-inspired sense-individuation condition, 'knowledge' differs in connotation from any description D such as 'justified true belief not essentially grounded in any falsehood', since there is no such description such that believing that every instance of knowledge is an instance of knowledge entails believing that every instance of knowledge is an instance of D. The "positive" things one can say about the connotation of 'knowledge' deal with the use of and application conditions for 'knowledge' and with whether 'knowledge' is analyzable and, if so, how to analyze it. I have discussed these issues for names with nondescriptive connotations.

I have said in discussions of my original Fregean view that names with nondescriptive connotations are "indefinable" and express "irreducible" properties. I have said indefinable names with different nondescriptive connotations express different irreducible properties, and thus coreferential names can express different irreducible properties. The notions of indefinable term and irreducible property could profit from further explication, but I have used them in an intuitive way, as do most people who object to my original Fregean view. Note one distinction, however. Philosophers often use interchangeably terms like 'indefinable', 'unanalyzable', 'primitive', 'irreducible', etc. But I have argued that T_1 can give an analysis of T_2 while differing in connotation. As I have used 'indefinable' and 'irreducible', an indefinable term does not have the same connotation as any expression that provides an analysis of that term, and indefinable names express irreducible properties. Hence indefinability does not entail unanalyzability. Thus, my original Fregean view has implications beyond semantic questions about names, since it holds that there are many irreducible properties—those expressed by indefinable names with nondescriptive connotations—that philosophers have failed to take account of. This highlights the importance of abandoning the overly narrow and restrictive view of the cognitive side of names that has been held both by the Frege-Russell tradition and by current views. In the papers on my original view, I have used the term 'meaning' (as contrasted with the term 'connotation') so that "... the meaning of [an indexical] term, which is what a competent speaker of the language knows as part of his understanding of the language, determines its connotation in a given context. For example, in the idiolects of different English speakers, 'I' has the same meaning, but different connotations."[21] So I introduced a notion of nondescriptive meaning as well as nondescriptive connotation, as follows. "The analysis of the connotation of a particular use of a [proper name] is given by the description-token that mentions the use in question. Something somewhat analogous for the meaning of a [proper name] is given by the description-type.[22] [Proper names to which the causal chain theory of determining the reference applies] have nondescriptive meanings and particular uses of them have nondescriptive connotations as well."[23]

It is important to see that my original Fregean view that I have sketched above has two independent aspects: reliance on the Frege-inspired sense-individuation criterion of interchangeability whenever used in propositional attitude contexts and abandonment of the overly narrow, overly descriptive view of the cognitive side of proper names held by both the Frege-Russell and Kripke-Donnellan views. If we drop the first of these aspects and combine the second with Kaplan's content-character distinction and the view that proper names are directly referential terms, we get the view that the character of a proper name $\ulcorner N \urcorner$ whose referent is determined by a causal chain is its nondescriptive meaning, whose analysis is the character of $\ulcorner$dthat (the entity standing in R to this very token of $\ulcorner N \urcorner \urcorner$. There are two reasons why this view seems preferable to Kaplan's suggestion that character, context, and referent all collapse for proper names.[24] First, of course, my proposal seems to solve the

---

[21] Ackerman, "Natural Kinds, Concepts, and Propositional Attitudes," 471. This use of 'meaning' seems to correspond to Kaplan's notion of character as linguistic meaning.

[22] I will use such terms as 'analysans', 'analysis', etc., for this sort of case as well.

[23] Ibid., 474.

[24] See Kaplan, *Demonstratives*, 562. Note the extreme oddity of this suggestion in view of the fact that the character is supposed to be cognitive significance or mode of presentation, and the content of a proper name is intuitively supposed to be just the referent itself. How could the mode of presentation of 'Cicero' in my idiolect be simply the man Cicero himself? Note that elsewhere (ibid., 520), Kaplan says, "Insofar as meaning is given by the rules of a language and is what is known by competent speakers [a view he endorses, ibid., 505], I would be more inclined to say in the case of directly referential words ... that their reference is *no* part of their meaning" (italics in original). How is this apparent contradiction

problem at issue by showing how coreferential names can have different characters and permitting a unified treatment of proper names and other expressions Kaplan takes to be directly referential. Second—and this is another reason why this approach is not ad hoc—it draws upon genuine analogies between the nondescriptive meanings of proper names and the characters of other directly referential terms.

For example, as has been mentioned several times, the character of an expression is supposed to be something a competent user knows in virtue of being a competent user of that expression. In what sense does a competent user of 'Socrates' know its nondescriptive meaning? Certainly he need not know that Socrates is dthat (the entity that stands in R to his use of 'Socrates'); that is why the theory of character as causal chain fails. Instead, the relation between the competent user, the term 'Socrates', and the description giving the causal chain is analogous to the relation between the competent user, the term 'knowledge', and the description 'justified true belief not essentially grounded in any falsehood', which for purposes of illustration I assume gives the *analysans* of 'knowledge'. In both cases, the competent user need not and typically will not know the description that gives the *analysans*. But the equivalence between the word and the description can be justified by generalizing from responses the competent user gives to questions about simple described hypothetical situations of the sort I have indicated above.[25] In fact, once this equivalence has been determined, the measure of whether someone counts as a competent user of the term in question—whether he knows its meaning—is whether generalizations from his responses do yield the equivalence, i.e., whether he uses the term in accordance with its analysis. Thus, there is no reason to regard this nondescriptive meaning of a proper name as any more obscure or mysterious than the meaning of 'knowledge'. (The competent speaker is of course not required to know or believe the philosophical theory that the name's meaning is nondescriptive, since 'Socrates' does not mean anything along the lines of 'entity fitting the nondescriptive meaning of this vlery token of 'Socrates' ').

As it stands, however, this proposal can be shown to face the very sort of problem it was designed to solve. Suppose J knows he has gotten the name 'Cicero' from two distinct sources, each of which identifies the referent as an ancient Roman orator. Suppose both sources refer to the same man, but J doubts this, since he suspects that many ancient

---

to be resolved, given that Kaplan also equates character with linguistic meaning?

[25] For more details about this process of justification, see the papers on analysis mentioned in footnote 20, especially "Analysis and its Paradoxes."

Roman orators were named 'Cicero'. Then J may doubt

(9)   Cicero is Cicero

where the two occurrences of 'Cicero' derive from the two different sources. The two occurrences have the same content on Kaplan's view, but they also have the same character on my foregoing proposal. How then can we account for their epistemic inequivalence while retaining the view that proper names are directly referential terms? I will consider two possibilities.

The first rests upon the idea that epistemically inequivalent tokens of 'Cicero' may have irreducible characters that differ qualitatively and whose analyses differ qualitatively in the following sense. The character of the description giving the analysis of any of these name-tokens' irreducible characters does not have any contingently existing entity as a constituent. Instead, the characters of the descriptions giving the analyses of the irreducible characters of epistemically inequivalent name-tokens differ in some other way. For example, the analysis of the character of the second (but not the first) occurrence of 'Cicero' in (9) might be given by a description of the form 'dthat (the entity standing in R to the second occurrence of 'Cicero' in 'Cicero is Cicero' written on a page with such and such characteristics)'. This sort of solution can work as a general strategy only if, for any two coreferential but epistemically inequivalent name-tokens of the same type, there will be some qualitative a priori difference in the way the two name-tokens are identified. For example, one might be the first name-token uttered and the other the second, or one might be to the right of the other, etc. But it is at least questionable whether this sort of condition will inevitably be satisfied.[26]

---

[26] For example, an argument of Max Black's about the identity of indiscernibles might be adapted to argue that two name-tokens that have the form of spheres will be qualitatively indistinguishable to a disembodied mind that views them from no particular spatial perspective. Here I am simply raising this possibility and will not try to evaluate either Black's argument or the plausibility of its application to the present sort of case. For Black's argument, see Max Black, "The Identity of Indiscernibles," in *Universals and Particulars*, ed. Michael Loux (Garden City, N.Y.: Doubleday, 1970), 204–16. Another problem is that even in cases like (9) where the two name-tokens can perhaps be identified in qualitatively different ways, it is questionable whether this should count as part of their cognitive significance, so that the second use of 'Cicero' in (9) would have different cognitive significance if the surrounding sentence has been different. Note also that Kaplan says, "It seems most likely that without indexicals some entities cannot even be uniquely *described*." (*Demonstratives*, 558, italics in original).

If such a condition will not work, a solution might be proposed that has each different name-token itself be a constituent of the cognitive significance of the description giving the analysis of that name-token's irreducible cognitive significance. Thus, irreducible cognitive significances of name-tokens of the same type can count as diverse if the name-tokens are numerically diverse, even if their irreducible cognitive significances do not have qualitatively different analyses.[27] This accords with the intuitive idea that a user of such name-tokens can recognize them as diverse and possibly not coreferential.

But is it really necessary to say that some name-tokens whose cognitive significances have qualitatively identical analyses have different *meanings*? I think not. So far, I have been going along with Kaplan's equation of the two formulations of the notion of character: character as cognitive significance or manner of presentation (in the sense of what is relevant to Frege's problem) and character as linguistic meaning in the sense of what is set by linguistic convention and known by competent users of the language. But the apparent equation of manner of presentation (or cognitive significance—I am using the terms 'cognitive significance' and 'manner of presentation' interchangeably) with linguistic meaning suggested by these two formulations of the notion of character seems wrong. It is easy to come up with contexts in which 'You are you' or 'Then was then' would be informative and thus where the two occurrences of 'you' or 'then', although identical in linguistic meaning, would have different cognitive significances or manners of presentation. Thus, differences in cognitive significance cannot always be accounted for in terms of differences in linguistic meaning. Kaplan says that the fact that "persons could be in the same total cognitive state and still, as we would say, believe different things ... doesn't prove that the cognitive content of, say, a single sentence or even a word is to be identified with its character, but it strongly suggests it."[28] But all this fact shows is that cognitive content is not to be identified with Kaplan's notion of *content*. I suggest that for names with irreducible nondescriptive meanings, all and only those names whose analyses are qualitatively

---

[27] The question might arise here of whether two diverse name-tokens (of the same type or of different types) can ever have the *same* cognitive significance on this approach. I believe this is possible in J's idiolect when he explicitly intends one as an abbreviation or substitute for the other and thinks of it this way. In such cases, the cognitive significance of the description giving the analysis of the cognitive significance of the second token may contain the *first* token as a constituent (and will raise additional problems I will not go into here).

[28] Ibid., 531–32.

identical have the same meaning, regardless of whether these names are identical in cognitive significance.

The view I am suggesting here also can account for how one's general ability to use proper names as part of language enables him to use correctly a name he newly encounters, for example, the name of a historical figure he newly learns about. By contrast Kaplan's suggestion that "unlike indexicals like 'I', proper names are really ambiguous"[29] with character, content, and reference all collapsing into each other seems to face a problem here, since this view makes it unclear how one would learn separate rules for the use of each new name, just as one does not know how to use 'bank' in the sense of 'riverbank' by drawing upon his understanding of 'bank' in the sense of 'commercial bank'. By contrast, although the view I am suggesting gives different meanings to different proper name-types, it makes it clear how their meanings are systematically related and how knowledge of their meanings can be systematically related. Another way to put this kind of problem is as follows: Isn't this sort of learning how to use a word in accordance with the correct rules for its use learning its meaning? Considerations of this sort cast doubt on Kaplan's view that the causal chain theory of reference is "presemantic."[30]

My view also avoids another problem of Kaplan's, which he describes by saying "... a competent speaker knows the character of words. This suggests (even if it does not imply) that if two proper names have the same character, the competent speaker knows that. But he doesn't."[31] On the present proposal, regardless of whether character is taken as linguistic meaning or as cognitive significance, he does, provided he has elementary logical acumen.

Kaplan also says that "What is perhaps even more astounding is that I may introduce a new proper name word [i.e., expression along with its

---

[29] Ibid., 562.

[30] *Demonstratives*, footnote 78. In ibid., 558–63, Kaplan presents a sketch of the role of the intention to refer to a preconceived individual vs. the intention to follow convention in using a proper name, and claims this sketch gives us reason to believe that "assuming the causal chain theory of reference—proper names are not indexicals" (ibid., 562). Why? At most, Kaplan's sketch seems to show that the analysis of a proper name's meaning will be complex (see my remarks in footnote 20 above). Note also Kaplan's remark that "... there is a sense of meaning in which, absent lexical or syntactical ambiguities, two occurrences of the same word or phrase must mean the same. (Otherwise how could we learn and communicate with language?)" (Ibid., 524). How does this bear on Kaplan's suggestion that proper names have no meaning beyond their referents?

[31] Ibid., 562–63.

meaning] and send it on its journey. When it returns to me—perhaps slightly distorted phonologically by its trip through other dialects—I can completely take it into my vocabulary without recognizing it as the very same word [i.e., expression along with its meaning]. Shocking!"[32] On my view, this also will not happen to a person who has elementary logical acumen. Another demonstration of the appropriateness of equating the character (in the sense of linguistic meaning) of a proper name with its nondescriptive meaning can be seen by considering Kaplan's use of the following remarks of Perry.

> Why should we care under what character someone apprehends a thought, so long as he does? ... *We use the manner of presentation, the character, to individuate psychological states, in explaining and predicting action.* It is the manner of presentation, the character, and not the thought apprehended, that is tied to human action. When you and I both have beliefs under the common character of 'A bear is about to attack me', we behave similarly. We both roll up in a ball and try to be as still as possible. Different thought apprehended, same character, same behavior. When you and I both apprehend that I am about to be attacked by a bear, we behave differently. I roll up in a ball, you run to get help. Same thought apprehended, different characters, different behaviors.[33]

These remarks apply to the nondescriptive meanings of proper names as well. Two people J_1 and J_2 who believe that Hesperus is dangerous to behold are apt to behave similarly, but if J_1 believes that Hesperus is dangerous to behold and J_2 believes that Phosphorus is dangerous to behold, J_1 and J_2 may well behave quite differently. Now consider a possible world W^* where J_1 is in the same epistemic situation as in the foregoing example, but where, unknown to J_1, Mars, not Venus, is the referent of 'Hesperus'. On my proposal, 'Hesperus is dangerous to behold' will have the same meaning in J_1's idiolect in W^* as in the actual world, and the content will be different. But J_1's behavior with respect to that sentence will be the same in W^* as in the actual world. Note that

[32] Ibid., 563.

[33] Ibid., 532, quoted from John Perry, "Frege on Demonstratives," *Philosophical Review* LXXXVI (1977): 494. (Italics in Kaplan but not in Perry. Kaplan has also superimposed some of his own terminology onto Perry's views in this quoted passage.)

these remarks will not apply to cognitive significance if it is possible for two name-tokens to have cognitive significances that are epistemically inequivalent (thus diverse) but qualitatively identical.[34]

But even my views so far turn out to need emendation. Examples can be easily constructed to show the possibility of J's perceiving the very same name-token in epistemically inequivalent ways (e.g., by sight and touch), so he does not realize he is perceiving the same token twice. Thus, even individuating cognitive significance by name-tokens is inadequate to solve the Fregean problem. The cognitive significance of the description giving the analysis of the cognitive significance to J of a particular token of 'Cicero' would have to have as a constituent not that name-token itself, but J's particular sensory perception of that token. Such a proposal is quite different from Kaplan's ideas about character. But it preserves two basic aspects of his approach: the view that belief is a three-place relation rather than a two-place one and the view that proper names are directly referential terms and that sentences using them can express propositions that are objects of J's propositional attitudes, even when these propositions include as constituents other people, physical objects and additional such entities that do not meet Russell's criteria for being objects of acquaintance.

---

[34] My views also provide answers to Kaplan's questions in the final footnote (78) of *Demonstratives*, as I will show by listing these questions along with my answers. "Is the work of the causal chain theory presemantic?" No. "Do proper names have a kind of meaning other than reference?" Yes. "Does the causal chain theory itself constitute a kind of meaning for proper names that is analogous to character for indexicals (but which, perhaps, gives all proper names the same meaning in this sense)?" The causal theory gives *analyses* of the meanings and of the cognitive significances of proper names to which the causal theory of reference applies and does not give all proper names the same meaning or the same cognitive significance. "Are proper names words of any particular language?" Yes. Compare 'José' and 'Joseph', for example. "Is there synonymy between proper names that are expressed differently (as there is between 'can't' and 'cannot')?" See footnote 27 of the present paper. "How should we describe the linguistic competence of one who does not know that Hesperus is Phosphorus? Is he guilty of linguistic error?" No. "Should we say he does not know what words he speaks?" No. Affirmative answers to these last two questions would require conditions for lack of linguistic error and for knowing what words one speaks to be either arbitrary or so strong as to be virtually never satisfied for proper names. (See my paper "Plantinga, Proper Names, and Propositions," *Philosophical Studies* (1976)). "Does he know that 'Hesperus' and 'Phosphorus' are different words? Are they?" Yes, they are.

3

Time and Thisness

Robert Merrihew Adams[1]

I have argued elsewhere that there are facts, and possibilities, that are not purely qualitative.[2] In a second paper, however, I have argued that all possibilities are purely qualitative except insofar as they involve individuals that actually exist. In particular, I have argued that there are no thisnesses of nonactual individuals (where the thisness of x is the property of being x, or of being identical with x), and that there are no singular propositions about nonactual individuals (where a singular proposition about an individual x is a proposition that involves or refers to x directly, perhaps by having x or the thisness of x as a constituent, and not merely by way of x's qualitative properties or relations to other individuals).[3] I am also inclined to believe that there are not yet any thisnesses of individuals that will exist but do not yet, nor any singular propositions about future individuals—and, hence, that all possibilities are purely qualitative except insofar as they involve individuals that

---

[1] A draft of this paper was presented to a conference on the thought of David Kaplan, held at Stanford University in March 1984. Terence Parsons responded to the paper. I am indebted to him, and to other participants in the conference, particularly Paul Benacerraf, Kit Fine, and Hans Kamp, for comments that were helpful in revising the paper. I do not pretend to have done justice to all the questions that they have raised.

[2] R. M. Adams, "Primitive Thisness and Primitive Identity," *The Journal of Philosophy* 76 (1979): 5–26.

[3] R. M. Adams, "Actualism and Thisness," *Synthese* 57 (1981): 3–42.

already do exist or have existed (counting timeless individuals, if any, as already existing). This thesis about the relation of time to thisness is the subject of the present paper, in which the conclusions of my previous papers will be presupposed.

I. Some Arguments for the Thesis

A similar view has been maintained by Arthur Prior. "Julius Caesar," he said, "a certain now-identifiable individual, did at a certain time begin to exist. But before that time, the possible outcomes of what was going on did not include the starting-to-exist of *this* individual." What they did include was "the possibility that there should be *an* individual born to these parents" who would have the qualitative properties that Caesar actually had. We may begin by considering an argument Prior offers for this view:

> Suppose there is some person living before the existence of Caesar or Antony who prophesies that there will begin to be a person who will be called "Caesar," who will be murdered, etc., and another person who will be called "Antony," who will dally with Cleopatra, etc. And then suppose this prophet to say, "No, I'm not sure that it *will* be like that— perhaps it is the second of the people I mentioned earlier who will be called 'Caesar' and will be murdered, etc., and the first who will be born later and called 'Antony', etc." This, it seems to me, really would be a spurious switch; and after Caesar and Antony had actually come into being and acted and suffered as prophesied, it would be quite senseless to ask "Are these, I wonder, really the two people he meant?" and if possible more senseless still to ask, "Is it—if either of them— our man's first prophecy, or his suggested alternative, that has now come to pass?"[4]

I think that virtually everyone will feel the intuitive appeal of Prior's contention that these questions are senseless; but the force of the argument needs to be explained.

Prior's explanations of why the questions are absurd, I take it, is that the prophet cannot have made his predictions about either the right or the wrong individuals because he cannot have predicted either that

---

[4] A. N. Prior, "Identifiable Individuals," *Review of Metaphysics* 13 (1960): 690.

Caesar would be called "Caesar" and be murdered or that Antony would be called "Caesar" and be murdered. He cannot have predicted either of these things because to predict them would have been to assert certain singular propositions about Caesar and Antony, and those propositions did not yet exist and, therefore, were not available to be asserted by him at the time of the supposed prophecy. Here we can distinguish two claims:

(1) The prophet could not yet assert any singular proposition about Caesar or Antony.

(2) No singular proposition about Caesar or Antony existed yet.

It is (1) that provides an explanation of the absurdity of the question mentioned by Prior; and that fact will count as evidence for (1), unless a better explanation can be found. I think that Prior's implicit argument is that (1) is explained in turn by (2), and, therefore, the example is evidence for (2) as well as (1).

This is not a very powerful argument for (2). If the prophet was unable to assert any singular propositions about Caesar or Antony, the nonexistence of such propositions would surely not be the only plausible explanation of the fact. There already were such propositions, it might be said, but the prophet was cut off from them because no causal chain could have run from the then future individuals to his thoughts and utterances at that earlier time; Prior's argument has no force against this hypothesis.

Other issues could be raised about the argument. Is (1) true? Or, more generally, are singular propositions about future individuals *available* to us to be asserted, believed, or known now? Does (2) provide an explanation of (1)? Or, conversely, if we can now assert or believe singular propositions about future individuals, does it follow that those propositions already exist? These questions are of interest in their own right, and we will return to them in section IV; but our first order of business is to look at another, and I think better, argument for the thesis that thisnesses of future individuals, and singular propositions about them, do not yet exist.

I was born in 1937. Among the many metaphysically possible continuations of the actual history of the world up until, say, 1935, there are surely some in which I would never have existed. It is plausible to conclude that I could have failed to exist even given everything that existed in 1935, or that had existed before then, or that exists timelessly— and conversely, that all of those things could have existed even if I had never existed. But as I have argued, neither my thisness nor any singular proposition about me exists in any metaphysically possible world in which I never exist; they are not among the things that could have existed even if I had never existed. It follows that they are not among the things that existed in 1935, or before, or that exist timelessly. My thisness, and singular propositions about me, cannot have preexisted me because if they had, it would have been possible for them to have existed even if I had never existed, and that is not possible.

I find this argument persuasive, but I do not want to exaggerate its force. It employs the principle,

(3)   For any beings x and y and time t, if x existed before t or exists timelessly, and y exists contingently and comes into existence at t, then it would be metaphysically possible for x to have existed even if y had never existed.

This principle is plausible. It is natural to think, for example, that it is quite open and undecided what people will come into existence in the future, even given everything that has existed up to now, and everything that exists timelessly; but this principle is not uncontroversial, and there are points at which we may want to raise questions about it.

In 1935, there existed millions of people who were born before I was, but that would not have been true if I had never existed. It may therefore, be objected against (3) that in 1935, there existed something that could not, logically, have existed if I had not later come into existence—namely, a person that was born before I was. The correct reply to this objection is that a person that was born before I was is not, in the relevant sense, something that could not have existed if I never did. Such a person (Montgomery Furth, for example) could perfectly well have existed without my coming along afterward—although in that case, of course, he could not have had the property of being born before I was. What is true in the objection is that the existential generalization "There existed in 1935 a person that was born before I was" is, in fact, true but that it could not have been true (indeed, could not even have existed) if I had never existed. But principle (3) is not concerned with such generalizations. It is concerned, rather, with possibilities *de re* about the existence of beings that instantiate such generalizations in some possible worlds and not in others.

An inventive objector will not be stopped by this reply. It may be suggested, for example, that *Furth's living before Adams was born* is something that did exist in 1935 but that could not have existed if I never had. Some may doubt, of course, whether this is something that is properly said to "exist" at all. But rather than getting into a debate about the criterion for admitting types of entities to the category of "existents," let us allow that *Furth's living in 1935* did exist in 1935. That concession does not undermine principle (3), for Furth's living in 1935 could have existed even if I had not come along later. And, perhaps, *Furth's living* (in 1935) *before I was born* is nothing more nor less than Furth's living in 1935, characterized in terms of a relation that it, in fact, has but that it could have lacked. If Furth's living (in 1935) before I was born is something more than that, a distinct existent, I am inclined to view it as constructed from Furth's living in 1935 and my birth in 1937, and to say that it did not exist before I did. An issue arises here, of the time at which transtemporal relations exist, about which I will have more to say in the next section.

I have mentioned timeless existence in (3) because thisnesses and singular propositions might be classified as abstract objects, and many philosophers think that abstract objects exist timelessly rather than at any time. It may be controversial to apply a principle such as (3) to timeless entities. But it seems to me very odd to classify as timeless a being that, though it may be immune to certain kinds of change, depends metaphysically for its existence on something that occurs at a certain time, so that it has to wait until that time, so to speak, to be assured of existence. Suppose you are considering whether to have children; in such a case you assume that your future children may never exist, in a sense in which it is no longer true that you may never exist. If you agree with me about the metaphysical dependence of thisnesses on individuals, you will also assume that the thisnesses of your future children may never exist, in a sense in which it is no longer true that your thisness may never exist. Would it not be odd to classify as timeless something of which it is first true and later false that it may never exist?

This depends, no doubt, on the sense of 'may'. The sense in which your future children and their thisnesses may never exist is not just that there are possible worlds in which they do not. For it is still true that there are possible worlds in which you and your thisness do not exist, whereas it is not still true, in the relevant sense, that you and your thisness *may* never exist. Those who are most strongly inclined to reject (3), and to hold that thisnesses and singular propositions exist timelessly, may think that the relevant sense of 'may' here cannot be anything but epistemic. *For all you know*, your future children and their thisnesses may never exist, but you know that you and your thisness do exist. I think, however, that there is more to it—that when we say that your future children and their thisnesses may never exist, we (or at any rate I) mean that it is not merely unknown, but metaphysically open and unsettled, whether they will exist. The merely epistemic difference would hardly keep us from thinking of thisnesses as existing timelessly, but something that is first open and later settled, metaphysically, does not seem timeless.

It emerges quite clearly here that my position, like Prior's, rests on an intuition that the future, or an important part of it, is metaphysically open in a way that the present and the past are not. This is a widely shared, but controversial, intuition. Principle (3) can be seen as a partial specification of the way in which the future is to be thought of as metaphysically open. I suspect, myself, that it is too strong a specification. Maybe there are stronger bonds of metaphysical necessity between earlier and later things than it allows. Perhaps, indeed, there must be, if causal determination of later events by earlier events is to be understood. The thesis I am defending, however, is one that appeals mainly to indeterminists, who think that many events, presumably including the coming into existence of most persons, are not causally determined by earlier events. For such events, we want to exclude the sort of bonds of metaphysical necessity that (3) excludes. And to individuals coming into being in such events, the argument based on (3), that their thisnesses do not exist until they do, may be seen as applying.[5]

---

[5] Issues that arise about this argument are in several ways analogous to issues that have arisen in philosophical theology regarding the possibility or impossibility of divine foreknowledge of free human actions. Thus, the question whether *Furth's living before I was born* is something that existed in 1935 corresponds to the question whether it is a *fact* about 1935 that Furth was alive before I was born. Questions of the latter form, in the context of the foreknowledge problem, have given rise to considerable controversy about attempts to distinguish between "hard" and "soft" facts *about* a given time. [All the following articles appeared in *The Philosophical Review*: Nelson Pike, "Divine Omniscience and Voluntary Action," vol. 74 (1965): 27–46; "Of God and Freedom: A Rejoinder," vol. 93 (1984): 599–614; John Turk Saunders, "Of God and Freedom," vol. 75 (1966): 219–25; Marilyn McCord Adams, "Is the Existence of God a 'Hard' Fact?" vol. 76 (1967): 492–503; John Martin Fischer, "Freedom and Foreknowledge," vol. 93 (1983): 67–79.] Likewise, the suggestion that thisnesses and singular propositions may be timeless parallels the famous proposal that the foreknowledge problem could be solved by regarding God as timeless; I regard a solution in terms of timelessness as unpromising in both cases, for reasons that are somewhat similar. Perhaps the problem of the present paper *is* a form of the foreknowledge problem—if thisnesses are God's concepts of individuals. I would want to explore these connections more fully before coming to final conclusions about either problem, but this is not meant to be

II. Thisnesses of Past Individuals

The question naturally arises, whether the same things I am saying about future things that do not yet exist should not also be said about past things that no longer exist. I think not; there is a better case for thisnesses of past than of future individuals.

Perhaps an objector will offer me the mirror image of the argument that I find persuasive against thisness of future individuals. Any example we choose of an individual that exists no longer may be subject to doubts—that it is really immortal, or that it was not really an individual. I choose an example that I believe was an individual that no longer exists: the first pain that I felt on the one occasion when I was stung by a wasp. Let i be that pain (or anything *you* believe was an individual that no longer exists). Now the objector will say, "Surely everything that now exists could still have existed—numerically, and not just qualitatively, the same—even if the history of the world before now had been very different—in particular, even if i had never existed. So if the thisness of i is among the things that exist now, it could have existed even if i had never existed. Since you deny the latter, you should also deny the former." This argument does not persuade me, because I do not believe that the same things could, logically and metaphysically, have existed now no matter what had existed earlier. There is a temporal asymmetry in our modal intuitions here. It is very plausible to say that the existence and identity of anything that exists now cannot depend logically or metaphysically on anything occurring later, but much less plausible to say that it cannot depend on what occurred earlier. Indeed, theses making the identity of individuals depend logically or metaphysically on various facts about their origins or antecedents have great intuitive appeal to many of us. Hence, I have no strong objection to saying that the thisness of i exists now without i existing now, but that if i had not existed earlier, that would have been impossible.

Whatever may be the case regarding future individuals, it seems that thisnesses of past individuals, and more particularly singular propositions about them, are still *available* to us as objects of propositional attitudes. We think that we can entertain, assert, and believe singular propositions about individuals that no longer exist. The possibility of our asserting and believing singular propositions about George Washington and Abraham Lincoln, for example, is not thought to depend in any way on the truth of immortality.

---

a paper about divine foreknowledge.

It is tempting to argue from the present availability of thisnesses of past individuals and singular propositions about them to their present *existence*. If we can entertain, assert, and believe singular propositions about individuals that no longer exist, must not these propositions exist? But I think we must be as cautious about this argument from present availability to present existence as we were about Prior's implicit inference from present *un*availability to present *non*existence. For there certainly are relations that can obtain between things that exist or occur only at different times. For example, a brush fire in September may *cause* a mud slide the following January. Perhaps entertaining, asserting, and believing are relations that can obtain between thoughts or utterances occurring at one time and propositions that exist only at earlier times.

There is a difficulty in this hypothesis of continued availability without continued existence, however. Suppose I am sitting in the dentist's chair, i' is a particular pain I felt five minutes ago, and i'' is a particular pain I am feeling now. Surely I can entertain, and indeed believe, the singular proposition about i' and i'', that i'' is more intense than i'. But when does this proposition exist? If singular propositions can exist after individuals they are about have ceased to exist, then this proposition can exist as soon as i'' begins to exist, although i' no longer exists then. But if singular propositions about an individual exist only when that individual exists, the proposition that i'' is more intense than i' cannot exist at any time, since there is no time at which both i' and i'' exist.

To be sure, this difficulty is analogous to difficulties we cannot escape in any event. If a brush fire in September causes a mud slide in January, when does the causal relation between them exist? If a relation cannot exist at a time when one of the terms it relates does not exist, then this causal relation cannot exist at any time. Perhaps it is a mistake to think of transtemporal relations as existing *at* a time at all; perhaps they do not need a time to exist at. On the other hand, they seem poor candidates for timelessness, since they depend for their existence on things that occur only at certain times, and they must therefore wait until those times to be assured of existence, as I have put it.[6] Maybe they exist—whole in the whole, but not whole in the part—in an extended period of time; on this view, the causal relation between the brush fire

---

[6] This is obviously an adaptation of an argument given in the previous section against the ascription of timelessness to the thisnesses of contingent individuals that come into existence. Principle (3) of the previous section also clearly requires that transtemporal relations not be allowed in general to exist timelessly.

and the mud slide would exist in the period from September to January, but not *at* any instant or *on* any day during the period. Similarly, we could say that singular propositions about individuals that exist only at disjoint times exist in an extended period, but not at any instant within the period. It would be simpler, however, to just allow that singular propositions continue to exist after individuals they are about have ceased to exist.

The one compelling reason for denying that thisnesses of past individuals, and singular propositions about them, still exist would be the belief that the thisnesses and the singular propositions have the individuals themselves as essential constituents. One hesitates to hold it as a universal law that an entity cannot occur at a time when one of its essential constituents does not exist; a performance of a symphony is occurring while the second movement is being performed, even though other essential parts of the performance are not occurring at that time. But we would not expect thisnesses and singular propositions to be related to time in the same way as musical performances. If individuals are constituents of their thisnesses, then presumably there exist thisnesses neither of past nor of future individuals. In that case, the difference between thisnesses of past and of future individuals is not in their existence, but, at most, in their availability. If thisnesses do not have the individuals themselves as constituents, however, I see no convincing argument for denying that thisnesses of past individuals still exist, and some advantage in holding that they do.

III. Existing at a Time

This is a natural point at which to pause for an examination of one of the central concepts of the present discussion, the concept of existing *at* a particular time. My previous essays in actualism have produced no divergence from Quine's dictum, "To be is to be a value of a bound variable." $\ulcorner(\exists y)(y = x)\urcorner$ is equivalent to the one-place propositional function $\ulcorner x \text{ exists}\urcorner$. For actualism, the two-place propositional function $\ulcorner x \text{ exists in } w\urcorner$, where w is a possible world, is not primitive, but is understood as meaning that $\ulcorner(\exists y)(y = x)\urcorner$, or $\ulcorner x \text{ exists}\urcorner$, is included in the world-story[7] of w, or that x would have existed if w had been actual. (Here 'would have existed' is a form of the ordinary one-place

---

[7] The world-story of a possible world w is, roughly, the set of all those propositions that exist in the actual world and that would exist and would be true if w were actual. See my "Actualism and Thisness," 21–22.

predicate 'exists'.) But ⌜x exists at t⌝, where t is a time, is a two-place propositional function for which actualism, as I understand it, provides no such reduction.

A reduction is offered by a view that is sometimes called "presentism" by analogy with "actualism." As the actualist holds that there are no merely possible things, but only things that actually exist, so the presentist holds that there are no merely past or future things, but only things that exist now. For presentism, 'exists' in its sole primitive sense is a one-place predicate equivalent to 'actually exists now', and the presentist's primitive quantifiers range only over things that actually exist now. And as the actualist may say that there are, in the actual world, primitive facts of the form ⌜It could have been the case that p⌝, even though there are no nonactual things that could have existed, so the presentist may say that there are, now, primitive facts of the form ⌜(n years ago) it was the case that p⌝ and/or ⌜(n years from now) it will be the case that p⌝, even though there are no nonpresent things that did or will exist. On this view, ⌜x existed in 1935⌝ can be understood as equivalent to ⌜In 1935, it was the case that $(\exists y)(y = x)$⌝, where 'in 1935' is subject to further reduction.

Presentism complicates the treatment of transtemporal relations. Let us say that x causes* y if and only if x and y exist at disjoint times and x causes y.

(4) $(\exists x)(\exists y)(x$ causes* $y)$

seems to be true; but the presentist cannot accept it as it stands. For by the very meaning of ⌜x causes* y⌝, (4) cannot be true unless its quantifiers range over things that exist at disjoint times; whereas the presentism's quantifiers range only over things that exist at the present time. Presentism's nearest equivalent of (4) will be something like

(5) It was, is, or will be the case that $(\exists y)(\exists \phi)(\sim(\exists x)[y$ is occurring because it was the case that $\phi(x)]$ & y is occurring because it was the case that $(\exists z)(\phi(z)))$.

This complication of transtemporal relations might be acceptable if supported by strong enough metaphysical intuitions. Actualism requires analogous complications in the treatment of modality. But actualism rests, I believe, on strong intuitions to the effect that modal facts must have their whole ontological basis in the actual world, and that the ontological basis of the fact that there could have been, for example, a huge battle fought at Arcola, Illinois, on 18 June 1978, is not something that is or could have been a battle. The corresponding metaphysical basis for presentism would be the view that facts about the past and future must have their whole ontological basis in the present, and that the ontological basis of the fact that an important battle was fought at Waterloo on 18 June 1815, is not something that is or was a battle. This view about time, however, unlike the corresponding view about possibility, seems strongly counterintuitive. Surely the ontological basis of the fact I mentioned about Waterloo is, or includes, something that was a battle and that does not exist now and is not occurring now.

I am therefore inclined to reject presentism and to suppose that our quantifiers should be understood as ranging, at least, over past as well as present things. This leaves us, however, with $\ulcorner x$ exists at (a time) $t\urcorner$ as a primitive two-place propositional function that must be distinguished from $\ulcorner(\exists y)(y = x)\urcorner$.

IV. Names for Future Individuals

I promised to return to the question whether we can assert, believe, or know singular propositions about future individuals that do not yet exist. It has recently been suggested that we can; and the suggestion is couched in terms of the technical concept of a "rigid designator," which must first be explained. In explaining it, I will make use of a distinction I have developed elsewhere between truth *at* and truth *in* a possible world.[8] A singular proposition about an individual x cannot be true *in* a world in which x would not exist, because the proposition also would not exist there. But we can say that it is true *at* such a world if it correctly characterizes that world from our vantage point in the actual world. For instance, the singular proposition that I do not exist is true at, but not in, possible worlds in which I would not exist.

A name or other expression n *rigidly* designates an object x if and only if n designates x at (though not necessarily *in*) every possible world.[9] 'Robert Merrihew Adams', for example, rigidly designates me. I am what it designates at every possible world, including worlds in which I would not have existed. It does this designating, however, in the actual world, and indeed, only in a certain "language" or "dialect." There could possibly, and may actually, be people who use 'Robert Merrihew Adams' as a name of some other person, or perhaps of a lake or a river.

---

[8] R. M. Adams, "Actualism and Thisness," 20–32.

[9] The term 'rigid designator' is due to Saul Kripke, but the interpretation presented here does not claim perfect conformity with any historic precedent.

On the other hand, 'the chairperson of the UCLA philosophy department in 1978' designates me, but not rigidly. There are possible worlds
in which David Kaplan bears the burden of satisfying that particular
description.

There are also indexical and demonstrative expressions, such as 'I'
and 'this', which rigidly designate different individuals in different contexts. On any given occasion of use, they designate the same individual
at all possible worlds; but on different occasions, they designate different
individuals, according to the context.

What proposition a sentence expresses depends on whether its terms
designate rigidly. Thus, it is because 'Robert Merrihew Adams' rigidly
designates me that 'Robert Merrihew Adams does not exist' expresses
a proposition that is true at all and only those possible worlds in which
I would not exist. In order to express a singular proposition about an
individual, a sentence must normally contain a rigid designator for that
individual.

It is widely held that once we have grasped the concept of rigid designation, we can introduce rigid designators simply by giving a description
that is satisfied by exactly one thing and *stipulating* that the name we
introduce is to designate rigidly the thing that in fact satisfies that description. In such a case, the description is said to "fix the reference" of
the name. But, normally, it is not analytically equivalent to the name,
for the name designates its object even at worlds in which the object
would have failed to satisfy the description.

This brings us to the idea that particularly concerns us here, which is
that in this way, we can introduce proper names that rigidly designate
future individuals. In David Kaplan's elegant example, we introduce
the name 'Newman 1' by declaring, "I hereby dub the first human being
to be born in the twenty-first century 'Newman 1'."[10] By assertively
uttering 'Newman 1 will be bald', for instance, we can express, and
assert, a singular proposition about Newman 1, that he or she will be
bald—or so it has been claimed.[11] Here we face two issues: whether
we can indeed express, assert, and believe singular propositions about
future individuals in this way; and whether, if we can, that shows that
there do after all exist singular propositions about future individuals.

---

[10] This is a slightly modified version of an example first introduced by Kaplan in
"Quantifying In," *Synthese* 19 (1968–69): 201. In that paper, Kaplan rejected the
possibility (or at least the propriety) of such a dubbing.

[11] By David Kaplan, in a later paper, "Dthat," in *Syntax and Semantics*, vol. 9,
Pragmatics, ed. Peter Cole (New York: Academic Press, 1978), 241.

Let us begin with the second issue, the one about existence. We have already observed that there are relations that obtain between things that exist at disjoint times. It was this that kept us from regarding the present existence of singular propositions about past individuals as proved by the fact that we entertain, assert, and believe such propositions; and I think it should also keep us from inferring the present existence of singular propositions about future individuals from the fact (if it is a fact) that we can entertain, assert, or believe them. For perhaps the relations of entertaining, asserting, and believing can obtain between thoughts and utterances occurring at one time and propositions existing only at a later time. Maybe an utterance occurring in 1985 could express, and be an assertion of, a proposition that will not exist until 2001. Likewise, it has not been shown that the utterance of a rigid designator in 1985 could not express a thisness that will not come into being until the next century.

If by uttering 'Newman 1 will be bald' now, we express a proposition that will not come into being until fifteen years or so from now, it follows that what proposition, if any, we express now depends on what happens much later. But that is exactly as it should be in this example. Those who think that utterances of 'Newman 1 will be bald' in 1985 express a singular proposition about Newman 1 would certainly agree that what proposition that is depends on obstetrical events at the turn of the twenty-first century.

Those who believe that we can assert and believe singular propositions about future individuals in this way can answer Prior's argument against their opinion. For they have an alternative explanation of why it would be absurd for Prior's prophet to ask whether "perhaps it is the *second* of the people I mentioned who will be called 'Caesar' and will be murdered, etc., and the first who will be born later and be called 'Antony', etc." If we are to make sense of the question at all, or of Prior's argument, we must take it that 'the *second* of the people I mentioned' and 'the first' are meant to be rigid designators (rather like demonstratives) designating the mentioned individuals both at worlds in which they satisfy the descriptions in the order in which they were originally given, and at worlds in which their roles are reversed. Indeed, they presumably designate the same individuals at more widely variant worlds as well; for surely the prophet would be prepared to say, 'It could have been, though it won't be, that both the first and the second of the people I mentioned die of natural causes'. In the actual world, therefore, according to the prophet's intention, 'the second of the people I mentioned' designates the same individual at worlds in which he satisfies either of the two descriptions, or neither of them. It does not follow, however, that the actual world may turn out to be one in which he satisfies the first description instead of the second. For if 'the second of the people I mentioned' is a rigid designator here, its reference is fixed by the second description the prophet gave. According to the convention by which it is introduced, 'the second of the people I mentioned' designates at all possible worlds the individual (if there will be exactly one) who satisfies the prophet's second description in the actual world. That is why the suggestion that perhaps he (actually) will fail to satisfy it is senseless, though it is correct to say that he *could have* failed to satisfy it. This, at any rate, is the answer that ought to be given to Prior by anyone who thinks we can use rigid designators to assert singular propositions about future individuals.

Similar things can be said about 'Newman 1'. Because the reference of 'Newman 1' is fixed by the description 'the first human child born in the twenty-first century', it makes no sense to ask whether perhaps Newman 1 will really be born in the twentieth century. We can know on purely semantical grounds (and, hence, perhaps a priori) that

(6)   Newman 1 will be the first human child born in the twenty-first century

expresses a true proposition, if it expresses any proposition at all, and that

(7)   Newman 1 will be born in the twentieth century

expresses a false proposition if it expresses any proposition at all. But

(8) $\diamond$(Newman 1 will be born in the twentieth century)

expresses a truth if it expresses any proposition at all; for if there will be exactly one first child of the twenty-first century, he or she will doubtless be born only a few seconds after midnight on the first morning of the century, and could surely have been born five minutes sooner.

Keith Donnellan has recently presented a better argument than Prior's against the view that we can assert, believe, or know singular propositions about future individuals. Donnellan deals explicitly with the 'Newman 1' example, focusing on the claim that (6) expresses a truth that we can know a priori. He agrees, in effect, that we could introduce the name 'Newman 1' by stipulating that it rigidly designates the first human being born in the twenty-first century, and that if we did, it would designate that individual, if there turns out to be exactly one such person.

> Let us now imagine that just after midnight on New Century's Eve a child is born who is firmly established to be the first born of the century. He is baptized "John," but those of us who are still around, remembering our stipulation, also call this child "Newman 1." Now it seems to me that it would be outrageous to say that some twenty-five years or so before his birth, we knew that John would be the first child born in the twenty-first century. Suppose one of us, living to a ripe old age, were to meet John after he has grown up a bit. Would it be true to say to John, "I call you 'Newman 1' and Newman 1, I knew some twenty-five years or so before your birth that you would be the first child born in the twenty-first century"?[12]

Donnellan's view of this case is that by virtue of having introduced the name 'Newman 1' in the way described, we can know (perhaps even a priori), that if there will be exactly one first child born in the twenty-first century, the sentence 'Newman 1 will be the first child born in the twenty-first century' expresses a truth, but that we cannot know the truth of what is expressed by the sentence. He suggests that "we are in the somewhat odd position of possessing a mechanism for introducing a name that rigidly designates something, but a mechanism that is not powerful enough to allow us to use the name!"[13] We cannot *use* the name in the sense that having the name in our language does not put us "in a position to have *de re* propositional attitudes toward the entity rigidly designated" by it. It does not enable us to know or believe, nor even to assert, any proposition expressed by means of it. For it would be "just as incorrect to say to ... the first child born in the twenty-first century, 'I believed about you some twenty-five years before your birth ...', etc., as to say to him 'I knew about you some twenty-five years before your birth ...'."[14]

I think it is clear, intuitively, that Donnellan is right in holding that it would not be true to say any of these things to the first child of

---

[12] Keith S. Donnellan, "The Contingent *A Priori* and Rigid Designators," in *Midwest Studies in Philosophy* 2 (Minneapolis: University of Minnesota Press, 1977), 20.
[13] Ibid., 24.
[14] Ibid., 23–24.

the twenty-first century, on the basis of our "use" of 'Newman 1'. But several explanations could be offered of *why* he is right about this. We shall consider four.

(i) Donnellan's own explanation—or partial explanation, as he himself suggests—is that in order for an entity to be an object of a *de re* propositional attitude, "the entity must enter into the 'genetic' account of how the speaker [or thinker] came to acquire the name, the beliefs he would express using the name, etc."[15] Since future entities that do not yet exist cannot enter into such genetic accounts of our present thoughts and utterances, such entities cannot be objects of present propositional attitudes *de re*. Singular propositions about them cannot now be asserted or believed. Donnellan adds,

> Having indicated the direction in which I am inclined to go, I find myself wanting to ask the question, why, if indeed it is true, is one in a position to assert and know *de re* things about an entity when the entity becomes (in the right way) a part of the history of one's use of the name? What does *that* accomplish that allows for this possibility? But perhaps that is a misconceived question. Perhaps the only answer is that that is just when we do ascribe *de re* propositional attitudes.[16]

(ii) It is also possible to offer an explanation that is consistent with the claim that we can have knowledge and beliefs *de re*, and can make assertions *de re*, about future individuals. Suppose there will be exactly one first child of the twenty-first century, and about a month before her birth, her parents will begin to call her "Jan," having decided to call her "Jan" whatever her sex turns out to be. Suppose further that at 11:30 P. M. on the last night of the twentieth century, her parents believe

(9)   Jan will be born in the twentieth century.

At that time, if these suppositions are correct, (9) will certainly express a singular proposition, and one that the parents can believe and assert. As it will turn out (if our suppositions are correct), this singular proposition will also be the proposition expressed by

(7)   Newman 1 will be born in the twentieth century.

[15] Ibid., 25.
[16] Ibid.

Will Jan's parents therefore believe (7)? Certainly not. Being knowledgeable (as we may suppose) about the analytical philosophy of the 1970s and 1980s, they will know, on purely semantical grounds, that (7) expresses a falsehood, if it expresses any proposition at all.

We find ourselves in a familiar situation, which does not always involve future individuals. To take the most hackneyed example, where 'Phosphorus' is a (rigidly designating) name for the Morning Star, and 'Hesperus' for the Evening Star, it seems that many people have known

(10) Hesperus = Hesperus

without knowing

(11) Phosphorus = Hesperus

—even though (10) and (11) express the same singular proposition. Here it is assumed that a singular proposition is constituted by one or more individuals, or their thisnesses, together with one or more qualities or relations, and logical connectives, in such a way that there could not be two distinct singular propositions of exactly the same logical structure in which exactly the same qualities or relations are held to be satisfied by exactly the same ordered n-tuples of individuals.

In order to provide a plausible solution for problems of this sort, I believe we must say that the objects of propositional attitudes *de re* are not always singular propositions in this sense. There are several philosophical theories in the field that could provide us with alternative objects for the attitudes. They are all too complicated to be developed here; perhaps the simplest to mention is the view that the objects of assertion and belief are sentences.[17] Whatever theory is adopted, it ought, I think, to accommodate the following: In some contexts, what people are said to have believed or asserted *de re* depends only on what singular

---

[17] A recent sketch of a version of this view is found in Tyler Burge, "The Content of Propositional Attitudes: Abstract," *Noûs* 14 (1980): 53–58. Another approach is to ascribe different "nondescriptive connotations" to some sentences that differ (for instance) only by containing different proper names for the same individual; see Diana Ackerman, "Proper Names, Propositional Attitudes, and Nondescriptive Connotations," *Philosophical Studies* 35 (1979): 55–69, and "Proper Names, Essences, and Intuitive Beliefs," *Theory and Decision* 11 (1979): 5–26. Alternatively, we might say that what people assert or believe often depends on other facts about the "character" of their thought or utterance, as well as on the proposition (in my sense) that constitutes its "content"; the distinction is drawn, with respect to sentences containing indexical expressions, by David Kaplan, "On the Logic of Demonstratives," *Journal of Philosophical Logic* 8 (1978): 81–98.

proposition (in my sense) is expressed by their thought or utterance. If I say, "I was born in Philadelphia," for instance, and you say, "Robert Merrihew Adams was born in Philadelphia," we will commonly be held to have asserted the same thing. But in other contexts, what people are said to know or believe or assert depends also on other features of their state of mind or utterance or its context. If I were suffering from amnesia and had read a biography of myself without realizing it was about me, I might know that Robert Merrihew Adams was born in Philadelphia without knowing that *I* was born in Philadelphia.[18]

Whatever theory is adopted, it seems likely that it could be used to explain our intuitive data consistently with the doctrine that *de re* assertions, belief, and knowledge about future individuals are possible. If the first child of the twenty-first century will be named "Jan," why wouldn't it be correct for us to say, after her birth, "We knew twenty years ago that Newman 1 would be the first child of the twenty-first century"—and to Jan, "We did not know twenty years ago that *you* would be the first child of the twenty-first century"? And if it would be correct for us to say these things, why wouldn't the three 'that' clauses still express the same singular proposition? After all, there have been people who did not know that Phosphorus = Hesperus, although they knew that Hesperus = Hesperus, and those two sentences express the same singular proposition (in my sense of 'singular proposition').

(iii) Both Donnellan and the position just discussed agree that 'Newman 1' can now be used to express singular propositions about the first child to be born in the twenty-first century, if there will be exactly one such child. The other two views to be considered here deny this. One of them regards 'Newman 1' as expressing not the thisness of an individual but an essence of an individual. If the first child of the twenty-first century will be Jan, then on this view, 'Newman 1' will express not the property of being identical with Jan but some other property necessarily coextensive with it—perhaps the property of being the first human child born in the twenty-first century in α where 'α' rigidly designates the actual world. This, of course, will not keep 'Newman 1' from rigidly designating Jan.

This alternative treatment would be metaphysically interesting if we could suppose that 'Newman 1' expresses a *purely qualitative* essence, but that is doubtful. It is far from clear that 'human', twenty-first

---

[18] This example, and argument, are adapted from John Perry, "Frege on Demonstratives," *The Philosophical Review* 86 (1977): 474–97.

century', and, above all, 'α' have purely qualitative equivalents. Indeed 'α' may introduce worse problems than 'Newman 1'. At least there will be a time when it will be settled which individual, if any, 'Newman 1' designates; but if the actual world will go on forever, will there ever be a time at which it is settled which possible world 'α' designates?

(iv) It is possible to regard 'Newman 1' as a variable bound by an existential quantifier that in most contexts is not expressed. On this view, for example,

(8)   ◇(Newman 1 will be born in the twentieth century)

is an informal abbreviation of

(12)   It will be the case that $(\exists x)(x$ is the first human child born in the twenty-first century & ◇(x is born in the twentieth century)).

And, in general, $\ulcorner \phi$ (Newman 1)$\urcorner$ will be regarded as an informal abbreviation of

(13)   It will be the case that $(\exists x)(x$ is the first human child born in the twenty-first century & ϕ $(x))$.

This treatment of 'Newman 1' does not disturb the point that 'Newman 1' is a rigid designator, for it is well known that variables designate rigidly within any context of use.[19] In (12), for example, it is crucial that within the scope of the existential quantifier, x designates or represents the same individual at the actual world and at all other possible worlds, including one in which that individual is born in a different century. But (12) is a general proposition and is clearly distinct from the singular proposition that the first child of the twenty-first century would express by saying, "I might have been born in the twentieth century."[20]

I am not sure which, if any, of these four accounts of the use of 'Newman 1' is correct. But that is a semantical, rather than a metaphysical, issue. For most metaphysical purposes, the situation is clear enough. If there will be exactly one first child of the twenty-first century, there will be a singular proposition about him or her, that he or she is the first

---

[19] On this Kaplanesque point and its present application, see Nathan U. Salmon, "How *Not* to Derive Essentialism from the Theory of Reference, *The Journal of Philosophy* 76 (1979): 708n.

[20] This treatment of 'Newman 1' is inspired by a similar treatment of proper names in fiction developed by Alvin Plantinga, *The Nature of Necessity* (Oxford: Clarendon Press, 1974), 159–63.

child of the twenty-first century. All of that we already know; and there is nothing more informative that the use of 'Newman 1' can enable us to know or believe now. If we try to express our knowledge in a form that looks more informative (e.g., 'that *you* would be the first child of the twenty-first century'), it becomes clear that in 2015, we could not rightly claim in that form to have known it now. Nevertheless, from the perspective of the twenty-first century, our present knowing and speaking will rightly be seen as standing in some transtemporal relations to the singular proposition that will exist then. Whether some of these relations should be regarded as expression, assertion, belief, and/or knowledge is a question that can be debated in semantics without, I think, affecting the metaphysical picture very much.[21]

---

[21] An analogous treatment of broader issues connected with the truth of statements about "future contingents" is worthy of consideration. (I do not mean that I am prepared to endorse it.) We could think of the meaning of the future tense as consisting largely in the way in which it determines transtemporal relations in which acts of speech or thought performed by means of it will rightly be seen as standing to future events when they have occurred. Among these relations might be *correctly predicting*, or *being verified by*, and, conversely, *being falsified by*. Could this relational understanding of the truth of statements about the future help in resisting the pressure to think of them as timelessly true? This is a pressure we may wish to resist if the timeless truth of such statements seems to us incompatible with a metaphysically open future.

4

Logic and the World

Joseph Almog[1]

I.

Almighty and sublime, purified of any worldly infestation, our idea of logic is laden with allusions to the divine. Thus Russell:[2]

> Pure logic aims at being true, in Leibnizian phraseology, in all possible worlds, not only in this higgledly-piggledly job-lot of a world in which chance has imprisoned us. There is a certain lordliness which the logician should preserve: he must not condescend to derive arguments from the things he sees about him.

And indeed that is how most of us, "professionals," have come to conceive of logic: nothing chains it to the banalities of what things there are and how things are. Logic is free.

As against this lordly vision, a minority of thinkers have felt that nothing could be that free, not even logic. In the very same year in which Russell articulated the lordly vision, Wittgenstein was already asking us pointedly:

---

[1] It is with much admiration of the philosopher and much affection to the man David Kaplan that this paper is written. Many thanks are due to R. Albritton, K. Fine, Y. Gutgeld, M. Gehman, D. Kaplan, and T. Martin.
[2] Bertrand Russell, *Introduction to Mathematical Philosophy* (London: Allen & Unwin, 1919), 192.

If there would be a logic even if there was no world, how could there be a logic given that there is a world?[3]

This question will serve as my staging point from which there is to emerge an alternative to the lordly picture. This alternative approach I call the *worldly* perspective. Its fundamental claim is that logic is concerned with the real world just as truly as zoology, though with its more abstract and general features.

II. The Lordly Tradition

Two opposite pictures then, the worldly and the lordly pictures. Before we plunge into their differences, let me stress a rare but nonetheless critical point of agreement between them. It concerns the objects of which we predicate logical truth: what 'object' are we describing when we describe a truth as a logical truth? The sentence expressing the truth or the truth it expresses? A logical truth is first and foremost a logical *truth*, both sides respond. From this old-fashioned perspective, the modern, that is, post the Tarski and Carnap of 1933–34, fascination of logic with sentences and the linguistic may seem as an aberration. Thus though one may follow more recent customs and inquire which sentences are logically true, in this work I will focus on the more traditional question as to which *truths* are logical.

Our question then is: *which* truths are logical and what *makes* any such truth into a logical one? When we come to characterize the lordly approach to these matters, three fundamental facts about it stand out.

First and foremost, the lordly tradition asserts the doctrine of *logical generalism*: only purely general propositions can serve as logical truths. Like other 'generalistic' doctrines, logical generalism is a *sceptical* doctrine. By nature, a generalist doubts that we can extend to *singular* propositions certain notions he has been happy to apply to general propositions. *Modal* generalism allows handsomely the application of the notion of necessity to general propositions but balks at applying it to singular propositions: to say of a singular proposition, by itself, that *it* is necessary would be meaningless. Similarly, *doxastic* generalism authorizes the notion of belief to apply to general propositions but forbids its application to singular propositions: to say that Pierre believes the singular proposition that-London-is-Pretty by itself is to

---

[3]Ludwig Wittgenstein, *Tractatus Logico-Philosophicus*, trans. D. F. Pears and B. F. McGuinness (London: Routledge & Kegan Paul, 1961), sec. 5.5521.

forget the mode-of-presentation under which he accesses that proposition. In the same vein, *logical* generalism questions our certitude that the singular truth that Quine is red or not red and the truth generated by assigning Quine to the free variable in "Red(x) or not Red(x)" are, in and of themselves, logical truths; for appearances are misleading here. It is only the *source* of these truths, the purely general proposition, *everything is red or not red*, that is a logical truth. The theorems of logic (and assuming soundness and completeness, the *truths* of logic) consist of general propositions only.[4]

This idea that only general propositions belong in logic is one facet of Russell's above quote, i.e., the freedom from the impurities of this higgledly-piggledly job-lot of a world. The second mark of the lordly tradition is also present in Russell's quote: the thesis that all logical truths are *necessary*. At times, Russell, and following him Wittgenstein and Ramsey, even claimed the converse thesis viz. that the only necessity there is is that of logical truths. Be that as it may, they surely all committed themselves to the descriptive claim that all logical truths *are* necessary; furthermore, they have asserted the normative claim that any candidate for the title *should* be necessary. The axiom of reducibility, the axiom of infinity (for individuals) and, for Russell, even the theorem of predicate logic $(\exists x)(x = x)$, all seeming very contingent, were to be banished from the realm of pure logic, stigmatized by Russell as "defects in logical purity."[5] Ramsey, who, as we are about to witness, wanted to keep $(\exists x)(x = x)$, $(\exists x)(\exists y)(x \neq y)$ and their ilk within the province of

---

[4] Some die-hard generalists may even find *everything is red or not red* rather promiscuous: the singularity of the attribute *Red* is as offensive as that of the individual Quine. Only truly general universal closures over both subject and predicate, e.g., *everything is F or not F* would then belong in the province of logic. Call the former position *first-order generalism*, the latter *second-order generalism* (in view of the kind of universal closures they would retreat to, the former to, e.g., $(\forall x)(Red(x) \vee \sim Red(x))$, the latter to, e.g., $(\forall P)(\forall x)(P(x) \vee \sim P(x))$).

One formal manifestation of this flight to (first-order) universal closures is Quine's "generality interpretation" as found, e.g., in *Mathematical Logic*, 80–89. The idea is stated there for open and closed *sentences*; but waving this ontological difference, it is the gambit considered here—only general propositions are asserted as theorems. The idea is anticipated, in its second-order form, in Russell's *Introduction to Mathematical Philosophy*, 196–200 (especially 199). The earliest statement is found in the unpublished "Necessity and Possibility" (1900) and "Recent Work on the Principles of Mathematics," *International Monthly* 4 (1901): 83–101. See also *The Principles of Mathematics*, first ed. (London: Cambridge University Press, 1903), 7–9; and *Our Knowledge of the External World* (London: Allen & Unwin, 1961), 53–54 and 67.

[5] Op. cit., 192–93, 203–4.

logic, felt that he must come up with nothing shorter of a 'proof' that would establish the necessity of such propositions, appearances to the contrary notwithstanding. Either way, Russell's or Ramsey's, at the end of the day, the lordly kingdom of logic was to have only necessary truths as subjects.

Insistent on the necessity of logical truths as these early logicians were, the necessity wasn't built into their definition of the notion of logical truth. However, by the time the main modern notion of validity has emerged, the necessity has been written into the very definition of "logically true" as "true at all models" (of the relevant sort). Originally the models were just ... models, abstract structures with no shred of modality in them. But under the guidance of Carnap, the models have been taken, more and more in the past forty years, to model the (logically) possible ways the world itself could have been. In fact, soon enough the models have even been used not only to analyze the metalevel notion of validity but also to give the truth-conditions of object-level modal locutions like "Necessarily." When the models are made to model modal reality in this way, it becomes inevitable to think of every logical truth, i.e., a truth at all models, as modally necessary.[6]

This modal involvement on the part of the lordly logician should not obscure the third fact about this tradition, its analysis of what makes a truth into a *logical* truth. Cluttered with modal constraints as his analysis might be, the lordly logician has insisted, from time immemorial, on a nonmodal, (clear and) distinct analysis of what makes a proposition logically true, viz. that, other worlds notwithstanding, it is *actually* true solely in virtue of its structure. Even Russell, in the very same pages already quoted[7] presents, very convincingly indeed, logical truth as being primarily "actual truth in virtue of the form of the proposition."

---

[6] As hinted in the above paragraph, the notion of "truth at all models" is not, in and of itself, a modal notion. For the critical question is what do the models model. If we think of each model as reassigning, *in actuality*, extensions to the nonformal components of the claim, or less linguistically, as permuting the constituents of the claim while preserving its form, then the notion involved is "truth in actuality no matter which ("nonlogical") constituents made up this proposition," a notion that doesn't promise the necessity of a logically true proposition. Interestingly enough, a variant of such a notion of validity is given by, e.g., Kripke for none other than ... modal logic. From the original paper in 1959 through the various applications to modal and intuitionistic systems, his notion of validity was that of truth in the *actual* world of every model, not, I insist, truth at all worlds of each model. When the language is enriched appropriately, as ours will be below, Kripke's notion of validity allows for contingent logical truths.

[7] Op. cit., 196–97.

Wittgenstein seconds this with "It is the peculiar mark of logical propositions that one can recognize that they are true from the symbol alone and this fact contains in itself the whole philosophy of logic."[8] And, I should add, this analysis was not confined to philosophical expositions or introductory classes, e.g., the very first formulation of the completeness problem for (first-order) logic, the one given by Hilbert in 1928, relies on this notion, asking us whether all the truths in virtue of form alone are derivable.[9]

I see in this traditional analysis of logical truth as actual truth in virtue of the form of the proposition nothing less than a recognition of the *autonomy* of logic. Logic is logic and not another thing: it is not a branch of the theory of knowledge, nor is it part of the theory of modality. Qua notion, the idea of actual truth in virtue of structure is a distinct notion; distinct from both the modal notion of truth at all *counter*factual, merely possible, worlds and distinct from the epistemological notion of truth ascertained independently of any sensory experience. If it turns out that all the truths in actuality in virtue of structure alone are both necessary and a priori, fine. If not, not.

I conclude from this that we should distinguish virtues and vices in the lordly approach. It is in a disengagement of its third idea, i.e., what *makes* a truth logical, from the first two that lies my own proposal: hold on to the insight that logical truth is truth in *actuality* solely in virtue of structure, but don't follow the lordly philosopher in keeping it only for the perfected general propositions; extend it to *all* propositions.

---

[8] *Tractatus* 6.113.

[9] Hilbert speaks of "the formulas that are not refutable (*widerlegbar*) through any definite stipulation of the suitable predicates. These formulas represent the valid logical propositions." See his "Probleme der Grundlegung der Mathematik," *Mathematische Annalen* 102:1–9. See also the third footnote of K. Gödel's "Die Vollständigkeit der Axiome des Logischen Funktionenkalküls," *Monatshefte für Mathematik und Physik* 37 (1930): 349–60; reprinted with translation in *Kurt Gödel—Collected Works*, vol. I, ed. S. Feferman et al. (Oxford: Oxford University Press, 1986), 103–23, where Gödel uses this notion to settle the problem Hilbert posed. Furthermore and as against popular myths, this notion is contrasted by A. Tarski with the notion of truth at all set-theoretic structures and was held to be the *intuitive* notion of logical validity. See his "On the Concept of Logical Consequence" (1936), in *Logic, Semantics, and Metamathematics* (Oxford: Clarendon Press, 1956), bottom of 410 and 411.

III. Truth in Virtue of the Structural Traits of the World

Consider the run-of-the-mill, singular, nonlogical, truth that Quine is human:

$$P_1 = \langle Quine, \; Human \rangle.$$

Mere analysis of the "internal architecture" of P_1 wouldn't betray its actual truth-value. But though we may remain in the dark as to Quine's humanity, we can extract from such an internal analysis the very existence of Quine: *his* own very lively presence inside P_1 attests for this trait of actuality: there is *that* distinct individual. Quine is. Quine exists.

This last discovery is more than a mere curiosity. For consider this truth:

$$P_2 = \langle Quine, \; Existence \rangle.$$

Begin with its epistemic and metaphysical categorization. If P_2 is accessed in the "standard" way, viz. via the linguistic lens of "Quine exists" or even "he exists," it isn't known a priori (subtleties aside). Perhaps Quine may so know it if he accessed it by way of "I exist"; be that as it may, you and I do not have this access to P_2. As for its 'modal profile', P_2 is modally contingent: Among his imperfections, we note that Quine might not have existed.

The aposteriority and contingency of P_2 notwithstanding, P_2 is a *logical truth*. Or, so I claim. The question is: what is the general source of the difference between *Quine exists* and *Quine is human*? Between *Elizabeth II is identical to Liz* and *Elizabeth II was begat by George VI*?

The key to the answer might seem to rest in the various propositions, but I believe the source of the difference lies at the other end, on the side of the world. Both *Quine is human* and *Quine exists* are fine propositions (sceptics about the latter have leaped, wrongly in my view, from the special *grounds* for the truth of this proposition to its alleged "incoherence"). The critical difference is that while the humanity of Quine is an ordinary, *material* trait of the world, the existence of Quine is a very special trait of the world, what I will call a *pre*fact. Now, what are these '*pre*facts'?

They are *structural* traits of the world. Ordinary worldly facts are not structural; they draw blunt invidious distinctions between the existing worldly building blocks: that Quine is human is a fact; permute him with Mt. Blanc and the fact is gone. The same applies to the factivity of Mt. Blanc's being a mountain when Quine takes over the subject position.

Structural traits, *pre*facts, are very different in this respect. Quine exists, that is a *pre*fact. But replace Quine in it by Kaplan, Mt. Blanc, or the moon, and you still have a prefact on your hands. That is why I believe these prefacts are *structural*: they do not single out a particular constituent of the world and report that it is thus-and-such. They simply specify the very conditions for being such an arbitrary constituent of the world, "a one," in the first place. To be "a one," one has to exist and have its distinct identity.

So much for facts and prefacts. What then makes the *proposition* that Quine exists or that Quine is distinct from Kaplan into a logical truth?

The idea is simple—the prefacts detail structural traits of the world. But if the proposition is about such structural traits, this will already be coded into its own internal 'bowels'. What will be the relevant sign? The structurality of the prefact was reflected in its blindness to particular constituents, in the closure of prefacts under permutations of their subject-constituents. My idea is that if a proposition is about these structural traits, its *truth* will also be closed under permutations of subjects (no wonder that its truth will be permutation-resistant in this way, if what *makes* it true, the prefact, is likewise permutation-resistant).

I will call such propositions, *truths in virtue of the logical structure of the world* (or, for the impatient reader, "structural truths"). I conjecture then for them the following *one*-way conditional:

(L_1) If a proposition is true in virtue of the logical structure of the world, it is permutation-resistant.[10]

IV. Permutation-Resistance as a Sufficient Condition

I myself believe permutation-resistance is not only a necessary but also a sufficient condition for logical truth. But I wanted to separate the innocuous from the controversial: while (L_1) may seem acceptable, its converse would be out of the question to many. Why then has the converse conditional been deemed unacceptable?

Two separate motivations have been operative here. I will begin with the weaker one to get it out of the way. It is often said that there

[10] For a formal definition of the notion of "permutation-resistance" see the appendix at the end of the paper.

might be certain (atomic) properties P that just happen to be true of everything. Hence *Quine is P* would be permutation-resistant. And yet, it is argued, *Quine is P* is surely no logical truth, given the merely *accidental* nature of the truth of $\forall x P x$.

In my view, the objection commits a double error. First, if by "accidental" we mean "contingent," I have already argued that the falsehood of a proposition in a counterfactual situation is no hold against its truth in virtue of the structural traits of this, very actual, world.

Secondly, suppose that the objector discards this modal reading of "accidental" and goes on to say that it isn't the contingency of *Quine is P* that bothers him, it is rather its "accidental nature" in the sense that the P-ness of Quine isn't true of him simply in virtue of his being a thing. Very well then, I concede the point: *Quine is P* isn't true in virtue of his being a being. But, I add, it isn't permutation-resistant either. Similarly, if the objector points to the universal truth of *If x is red, then x is not green* and insists it is no logical truth, I agree but, again, point out that it isn't permutation-resistant either.

All this is quite obvious if we remember to permute not only the individuals but the attributes too. Thus we get, e.g., *Church is British* and *If x is tall, then x is fat*, which would refute, in actuality, the alleged permutation-resistance of the original propositions. Of course, not all attributes (relations) can be freely permuted. Assuming that *Existence* is an attribute and *Identity* is a relation, we see that they cannot be tinkered with. The logicality of *Quine exists* and *Quine is not identical to Church* attests for this.

In view of this favoritism, you may be compelled to claim that we are moving in a circle "defining the attributes that are structural by alluding to the permutation-resistance criterion and at the same time specifying which components are not to be permuted by alluding to the criterion of structurality."

I reject the accusation. For in the first place, I do not conceive of (L_1), when strengthened into a biconditional, as a *definition* or an *analysis* of the notion of "truth in virtue of structural traits of the world." I do think of it as giving necessary-and-sufficient conditions for being such a truth. But this is still a far cry from suggesting that (L_1) "defines" or "analyzes" the notion of "structural trait." What is more, I regard this situation where no "definition" is forthcoming as containing an insight rather than an embarrassment. For, in my view, the last arbiter about the notion of "structural trait of the world" is our intuition about cases. The only way to get hold of the *notion* itself is by intuitions about particular cases as to what is and what is not a trait that beings have simply qua beings; then *given* the notion, we may supply necessary-and-sufficient conditions for belonging in its *extension*. Thus, suppose one would have liked to go here beyond *existence*, *identity*, and other classical candidates, e.g., follow *Tractatus* 2.0251, "space, time and color (being colored) are forms of objects"; the argument, for me, wouldn't come primarily from the permutation-resistance of, e.g., *x is in time*. It would originate with a direct observation about the allegedly special feature of this trait, showing that it is written into the very notion of a being that it be in time.

The other objection to taking permutation-resistance as sufficient for logical truth hits closer to home. The second objector argues that he cannot see why the external *fact* that every being has a property P simply qua being endows the *proposition* that x is P with an *internal* structure that is sufficient to divulge its actual truth.

Let me grant the objector his intended claim: the worldly structure of the fact that, e.g., Quine is P leaves us much freedom as to the parallel structure of the proposition that *Quine is P*. My answer to our objector as to why permutation-resistance is nonetheless a sufficient condition for logical truth is that logic investigates the structural traits of the *world*, rather than the structural traits of propositions representing it.

A truth is made into a logical one by special traits of that which *makes* it true in the first place, i.e., the kind of trait of the *world* in virtue of which this truth is the distinct truth that it is. The structure of propositions, or for that matter of any other truth-bearing "representational" device, is irrelevant at this point. Suppose indeed that I rejected altogether the existence of propositions, let alone their endowment with internal structure. Would my above differentiation of logical from nonlogical truths go by the board?

Not at all. The truth that Quine is human or not human is logical because the worldly *individual* Quine has this attribute in a *way* that is very different from the way he bears *being-human*. If, as I would have it, the explanation of that which is special to the *logical* way of having an attribute alludes to tests like permutation-resistance, then, again, we look at nothing more than individuals in the world and the attributes they possess, i.e., we check whether the attribute is had by every being simply qua being. No mention of propositions is called upon here.

In contrast, the notion of truth in virtue of *propositional* structure focuses on the structure of the relevant representations, the propositions. Philosophers may and actually do differ widely over the structure of such representations. Some think propositions may be as structured as the sentences that express them, some think they are structureless sets of possible worlds and some think they are something in between. Some think necessarily equivalent propositions are identical, some think logically equivalent propositions are identical, some think only "epistemically equivalent" propositions are identical and some (at least myself) think none of these equivalences is sufficient for propositional identity. Be all that as it may, such disputes concern the degrees to which our *representations* of the world are endowed with internal structure. This is a matter which is posterior to unfolding the structure of the world thus represented.

It may very well be the case that the discovery of a trait of the world that holds of every being qua being is not indicative of analogous internal propositional structure. But the discovery of such a permutation-resistant trait of worldly things cannot be similarly detached from the study of the structure of the world itself: to discover a trait things have simply in virtue of being things *is* to unfold the structure of the world.[11]

V. The Worldliness of Attributes

We have encountered above two grades of opposition to my very liberal involvement with worldly items. *First-order* generalism banished individual-involving propositions from the realm of logical truths—*Quine is red or it is not the case that Quine is red* is out, but *everything is either red or not red* is in. In its puritanism, *second-order* generalism made the latter proposition follow the former into exile; only the 'pure', schematic, *everything is F or not F* (i.e., $\forall x(Fx \lor \sim Fx)$), *everything exists* (i.e., $\forall x Ex$), *everything is identical to itself* (i.e., $\forall x(x = x)$) are admissible.

For my own, perversely opposite, reasons I agree with the second-order generalist that *Red* is as unlordly as Quine. For as overtly as Quine, *Red* violates epistemological and modal desiderata the generalists posit on the notion of logical truth: their being (i) a priori and (ii) necessary. How does *Red* create this havoc? The second-order generalist and I agree that it may well satisfy the following epistemological and modal theses:

---

[11] So much for permutation-resistance as a sufficient condition for logical truth, i.e., truth in virtue of the structure of the world. I take up the question whether permutation-resistance of propositions is sufficient for truth in virtue of *internal propositional* structure in footnote 17 below.

(E₁) That the attribute *Being-Red* exists is given a posteriori;

(M₁) That the attribute *Being-Red* exists is merely contingent.

Why would (E₁) and (M₁) be true? The source of both (E₁) and (M₁) traces to a third, more primordial, thesis that is neither epistemic nor modal. It is an ontological thesis about the *actual* existence conditions of the attribute *Red*:

(O₁) The attribute *Being-Red actually* exists only if it *actually* has instances.

Call any attribute having such actual existence-conditions *worldly*. I cannot argue here for the worldliness of *Red*, though I note that my chief lordly opponent, Russell, had, in one of his other moods, admitted that "Logic doesn't know whether there are in fact *N*-adic relations (in intension); this is an empirical question." Be that as it may, I will ask you to meet me half way and grant me the truth of (O₁) for I merely want to establish with it a conditional point: given its truth, interesting logical truths follow.

Assume (O₁) and we are at the origin of (E₁) and (M₁): because of its ontological dependence on worldly generators, we do not know 'without looking' that *Being-Red* exists in actuality; also because of its dependence on such concreta, the attribute *Being-Red* is as modally imperfect as Quine: our world has been blessed with Reds but a world of Browns would not have *Being-Red* among its attributes. Whence (M₁).

We are also in a position to appreciate now how the proposition

P₃   = ⟨*Being-Red, instantiated*⟩

imitates nicely the record of ⟨*Quine, Existence*⟩. Apriority is gone. There is no purely reflective guarantee that the sentence "*Being-Red* is instantiated" signifies a proposition (consider "*Being-Unicorn* is instantiated"). Modal contingency is also unavoidable: P₃ may have been generated in actuality; now that we have it we can take it and evaluate it in a counterfactual Redless world. It cannot be generated over there (cf. ⟨*Quine, Existence*⟩ in a Quineless world); however, given its generation in *actuality*, we have *it* and *it* can be modally evaluated in counterfactual situations where it doesn't exist.

Contingent and a posteriori P₃ may be; and yet, the proposition itself, P₃, is actually true solely in virtue of the structural traits of the world, i.e., the structure (in particular, the existence conditions) of the attribute *Being-Red*. For the very existence of *Being-Red* guarantees that it bears the trait it is ascribed, i.e., that it's instantiated. This is not the case with other traits we may ascribe to it, e.g., that it is my favorite attribute or even the necessary trait that everything that has it has the same color as the actual color of firetrucks. A separate confirmation of this point comes from the fact that the trait of *being instantiated* is permutation-resistant. Any other basic attribute you might care to permute with *Being-Red* would also be actually instantiated, at least on my view of basic attributes. In contrast, permute *Being-Green* with *Being-Red*, and it wouldn't have, in actuality, the trait of being my favorite attribute or be such that everything that bears it has the same color as the actual color of firetrucks.

Finally, the proposition *Red is instantiated* is not only true in virtue of the structural traits of the world; the proposition is also true in virtue of the proposition's internal structure (just like *Quine exists*). Given the assumption that it is the attribute itself that occurs in the proposition, its very presence in the proposition verifies the truth of the predication without any external evaluation. Hence the proposition, though neither a priori nor necessary, is true in virtue of an analysis of its own internal structure.

VI. The Worldliness of Logical Notions

Aware of the unreliability of the attributes, Russell retreated to second-order logical generalism: only *purely* 'logical' propositions will do. At last, a safe haven for logic. But is it? Are the propositions, e.g., *everything is self-identical* and *everything exists* lordly, free of our job-lot of a world?

I doubt it very much. Without any pretense to an informed, let alone scholarly, reading of the text, I am guided here by the early Wittgenstein:

> The 'experience' we need in order to understand logic is not that something or other is the state of things, but that something *is*: that however is not an experience. Logic is *prior* to every experience—that something *is so*. It is prior to the question 'How?', not prior to the question 'What?'[12]

So much for the motif. Here is my own version of the idea. Very much like *Red*, *Existence*, and *Identity* are, on the worldly picture, subject to the ontological thesis:

---

[12] *Tractatus* 5.552.

(O_2) *Existence* and *Identity actually* exist, only if they have *actual*
instances (only if at least one object actually exists)

Aware of the modal and epistemic corollaries induced by the counterpart
thesis (O_1) in the case of *Red*, the lordly logician is quick to point out
that (O_2) would have similar repercussions:

(E_2) That *Existence* and *Identity* actually exist isn't known a
priori

(M_2) That *Existence* and *Identity* exist is merely contingent

Presupposing that all logical truths are a priori and necessary, the
lordly logician looks at (E_2) and (M_2) as the last straw; truths like
$(\forall x)(Exists(x))$ and $(\forall x)(x = x)$, let alone $(\exists x)(Exists(x))$ and $(\exists x)(x =$
$x)$ are going to lack the desired traits and hence wouldn't, in turn, be
logical truths. In a word, a reductio of the worldly view and of (O_2) in
particular. The question is: is the lordly logician right in so arguing?
   Take the most damaging case one can think of:

P_4 $= \langle Existence, Instantiated \rangle$

which is far more precarious than $(\forall x)(x = x)$ and $(\forall x)(Ex)$ (which may
not be a priori but would turn out to be necessary, if the propositions
actually exist in the first place).
   Focusing on epistemological matters, let us "stipulate" that P_4 isn't
known a priori. Cartesian modes of reasoning notwithstanding, pretend
that we may use the *word* 'existence' competently in the *sentence* "Existence has instances" and yet not know whether the attribute *Existence*
has instances. Also, let us pretend that it could have been the case that
no object whatsoever existed. In that apocalyptic counterfactual world,
P_4 is false. Let us suppose this *is* a genuine possibility.
   All this doesn't take away the actual truth of P_4 in virtue of the
structural traits of the world. For assuming that (O_2) does give the
existence-conditions of *existence*, its very being *in* the world guarantees
its having the trait with which it is predicated here. In contrast, its very
being doesn't guarantee that it bears traits like its being Anselm's favorite attribute or being the attribute actually discussed by Moore in "Is
Existence a Predicate?" What is more, assume again (O_2), and assume
that P_4 has the attribute *Existence* itself as constituent, an assumption
about the proposition, not about the world itself. At this point, by a
purely internal analysis of P_4, we can establish that indeed *Existence* is

instantiated. Thus, whether *we* know it a priori or not, whether it would still be true throughout all counterfactual situations, the proposition P_4 is *actually* true in virtue of its own internal structure. Which is also the case of $(\exists x)(x = x), (\forall x)(x = x)$, and $(\exists x)(Exists(x))$.[13]

VII. Logic and Necessity: The Number of Individuals in the World

Qua notion, in and of itself, logical truth seems a distinct notion from the modal idea of necessity. As for the extensions of the two notions, so far my cases of contingent logical truths consisted of *singular* truths, e.g., *Quine exists* and *Redness is instantiated*. There are other examples of this sort: the proposition *If a is F, then some individual is F*, for every such individual existing in actuality. Every being, simply in virtue of being such, has the trait that *if it F's, something F's*. And yet such truths might be contingent: *if Quine is possibly human, then something is possibly human* is an example. Consider a Quineless counterfactual situation *w* in which everything is made of sand. The antecedent *Quine is possibly human* is true at that situation, for actuality provides the required possibility. But the consequent proposition is false at *w*: nothing of *w*, no grain of sand, could have been human. More examples of this sort can be concocted but in analyzing contingent logical truths I would like to focus on one special case of a different sort.

The special case I have in mind originates with Ramsey: true propositions about the number of individuals in the world, e.g., *there are at least two individuals* are not mere truths but rather *logical* truths.

If one presupposes that all logical truths must be necessary, one might be shocked by Ramsey's view: the contingency of our proposition is after all very hard to deny. Ramsey himself avoided the "shock." How? Instead of admitting contingent logical truths, Ramsey preferred

---

[13] A, to me, remarkable anticipation is to be found in Wittgenstein's *Notebooks*, 1914–1916 (transl. from the German by E. Anscombe) (Oxford: Blackwell, 1961), 11e: "If we take '$(\exists x)(x = x)$' it might be understood to be tautological since it could not get written down at all if it were false, but here!"

to bite the bullet and pronounce this proposition *necessary*.[14]

[14] See F. P. Ramsey, "The Foundations of Mathematics," in his *The Foundations of Mathematics* (London: Routledge & Kegan Paul, 1931), 59–61. See also "Facts and Propositions," op. cit., 154–55; and finally "Critical Notice of Tractatus," op. cit., 280–86. Ramsey thought he had two "proofs" for the *necessity* of the number of individuals in the world. The main one, 59–61, I discuss in the text. The additional one, 154–55, can be extracted from the following passage (op. cit., 155):

> ... admit that numerical identity and difference are necessary relations, that ' There is an x such that fx' necessarily follows from 'fa', and that whatever follows necessarily from a necessary truth is itself necessary. If so, their position cannot be maintained; for suppose a, b, c are in fact not everything, but that there is another thing d. Then that d is not identical with a, b, or c is a necessary fact; therefore it is necessary that there is an x such that x is not identical with a, b, or c, or that a, b, c, are not the only things in the world.

The passage is much too coded. I reconstruct from it two separate arguments: one for the claim that there could not have been *fewer* individuals than there are, the other for the claim that there could not have been *more* individuals.

For the first argument assume the *actual* existence of four individuals: a, b, c, d. Let ϕ be: $\phi x \leftrightarrow (x \neq a \land x \neq b \land x \neq c)$. We then have:

(1) $\Box\phi d$ (by necessity of distinctness)

(2) $\phi d \supset \exists x \phi x$ (logical truth)

(3) $\Box(\phi d \supset \exists x \phi x)$ (necessitation)

(4) $\Box(\phi d \supset \exists x \phi x) \supset (\Box\phi d \supset \Box\exists x \phi x)$ (modal logic)

(5) $\Box\exists x \phi x$ (1, 3, 4, *modus ponens*).

Now I, of course, think Ramsey made the fallacious step of moving from the logical truth of a claim to its necessity (step 3). But on top of this, he seems to be involved here in another *faux pas*. Let Ramsey have $\Box\exists x \phi x$. He reads it: "of necessity, there are at least four individuals." I ask: Why? All "$\Box\exists x \phi x$" says is that "of necessity, there exists an individual (e.g., d) that is distinct from a, b, c." That may be true and yet other worlds would have less than four individuals (e.g., they would only have d). From the *truth* of a proposition like "d is distinct from a" at a counterfactual world w, Ramsey infers (fallaciously) the *existence* of d and a *in* that world. Though there cannot be *actual* truth without existence, counterfactual truth without (local) existence is fine (cf. *Quine doesn't exist* in a Quineless world).

The second argument I reconstruct from Ramsey proceeds as follows. Assume there are three individuals: a, b, c. Now grant that there *could* have been a 'new' individual, d. The argument now runs as:

(-1) $\Diamond\exists x \phi x$ (by assumption)

(0) $\Diamond\phi d$ (by what?)

(1) $\Box\phi d$ (by necessity of distinctness)

⋮

Ramsey's main argument (59–61) for the logical truth of claims describing the number of individuals in the world used standard first-order codings of the claims, e.g., that there are at least two individuals, is coded by "$\exists x \exists y (x \neq y)$." But, in addition, he believed quantificational propositions are analyzable in terms of *singular* propositions: existential quantifications are identified with long disjunctions, universal quantifications are identified with long conjunctions. So analyzed, the logical truth of *At least two individuals exist* is inescapable.[15]

VIII. The Flaws in Ramsey's Approach

The problem with Ramsey's argument is that it relies on an identification of a general proposition with its "singular expansion." This seems questionable. Of course, those who (like myself) believe that the identity of structured propositions is fixed by composition from the identity of their constituents, will reject any identification of a general proposition and a complex singular proposition. But in fact general propositions are not necessarily equivalent to their "singular expansion"; so the equivalence fails even the least demanding test of propositional identity.

Let $Dis(F)$ stand for the disjunction of propositions of the form Fa for each existing individual a. We have already seen that the conditional $Dis(F) \supset \exists x F x$ is not necessary. (Take as F, our case of *possibly human*.) In the other direction $\exists x F x \supset Dis(F)$ is not necessary either. How so? We have just seen that the problem for the converse of this conditional, $Dis(F) \supset \exists x F x$, came from *diminishing* domains. The counterexample to the necessity of the present conditional arises from *growing* domains. Let a counterfactual world w have a larger domain

---

(5) $\Box \exists x \phi x$ (as before)

(6) $\exists x \phi x (\Box p \supset p$, modal logic T).

Thus, by (6), the fourth individual, d, already exists in actuality. The procedure can be repeated for any imagined 'new' individual. Thus there can be no 'growing' domains. Note that here Ramsey doesn't merely commit the fallacy of necessitation. He also moves from $\Diamond \exists x \phi x$, a general possibility, to $\Diamond \phi d$, a singular one. He apparently thinks that just because we can evaluate propositions involving actuals in worlds where they don't exist, by symmetry, we have singular propositions involving merely possibles, i.e., d, evaluated here.

[15] For we would identify $\exists x \exists y (x \neq y)$ with the following disjunction involving all pairs of actual individuals: $\langle\langle Kaplan, \ Quine \rangle, \ Distinctness \rangle$, OR $\langle\langle Kaplan, \ Kaplan \rangle, Distinctness \rangle$, OR $\langle\langle a, b \rangle, \ Distinctness \rangle$, OR .... By our own, "modern," lights, the first disjunct is a truth in virtue of logical structure. But then so is the whole disjunction. And hence so is $\exists x \exists y (x \neq y)$.

than the actual domain. Thus there is a new individual of w, for which it is true that it does not actually exist. Hence $\exists x \ Act(Not\text{-}Exist(x))$ is true at w. However, we can generate singular propositions only out of actual individuals (an idea to which Ramsey himself strongly adhered). But then the disjunction

> *Actually (Not-exist (Kaplan))* $\vee$ *Actually (Not-exist (Quine))*
> $\vee$ *Actually (Not-Exist (Mt. Blanc))* $\vee$ ...

is false at w. The same counterexample applies to $Conj(F) \supset \forall x F x$, with *Actually (exists)* used as the offending F. The antecedent conjunction is true at w. The consequent is false at w.[16]

IX. A Neo-Ramseyan Analysis

The irony of it all is that Ramsey does not need to claim that a general proposition is identical to its singular expansion. Nor does he need to claim that they are necessarily equivalent. He only needs to show they logically imply each other. To provide us with an appropriate analysis, let me hitch my wagon to a star and call my own picture "Neo-Ramseyan." It introduces a new relation between propositions, that of *structural implication*. Say that P structurally implies Q iff the material conditional *If P then Q* is a truth in virtue of the structural traits of the world. The insight I extract from Ramsey's work is that a general proposition and its singular support structurally imply each other. Indeed, the conditionals (1)–(2) are both logically true (and, as you can verify, permutation-resistant):

(1)   *If Dis(Happy), then some individual is happy*

(2)   *If some individual is happy, then Dis(Happy)*

---

[16] For Ramsey's view that general propositions are *identical* with complex singular propositions, see op. cit., 34, 41, and especially 59–61. Now suppose that there are infinitely many individuals in the actual world. The propositions $Dis(F)$ and $Conj(F)$ would then involve infinitary disjunctions and conjunctions. To some this may seem unacceptable. I feel no special justification is called for this assumption in the present work if only because the assumption is made in the process of criticizing Ramsey who was *the* one to stress, thirty years before such operations became common, that infinitary logical operations are absolutely innocuous (op. cit., 34, 41, and 74). I also note, and that goes beyond any discussion of Ramsey, that our operations apply to abstract structures, i.e., propositions, not to sentences. Whence the common dismay, justified or not, about "infinitely long sentences" may seem quite inapplicable.

Assume this logical framework. Why would *at least two individuals exist* be logically true? Following Ramsey, we aim to deduce this truth from singular truths. Begin then with the conjunctive singular proposition antecedent, *John exists and Mary exists*. This is a logical truth. The conditional *If John exists and Mary exists, then at least two individuals exist* is also a logical truth. Detach now its consequent and you have what Ramsey sought: the logical truth of *At least two individuals exist*. An alternative route is available to those who persist in questioning the logicality of *Mary (John) exists*. Simply begin with *if John is distinct from Mary, then at least two individuals exist*. Detach the consequent and you are home free.

What individuals there actually are (and hence, how many of them there are) may seem like a trait of the world that does not concern logic. But nothing is quite what it seems. In the way that the structural *Quine exists* differs from the material *Quine walks*, in the way that the structural *Quine is distinct from Church* differs from the material *Quine is younger than Church*, I believe that *At least two individuals exist* differs from *At least two cows exist*. The latter general fact arises from two material singular facts, e.g., *Bossie is a cow* and *Lizzy is a cow*. Two facts about the goings-on *in* the world, about the *state* the world is in.

Not so with *At least two individuals exist*. The latter merely reports what exists and what is identical to what. In so doing, it merely details the multiplicity of subjects the world has, not what the state of these subjects is. It tells us *what* things there are, not *how* they are.[17]

---

[17]Some may agree that the above argument is fine but nonetheless insist that *At least two individuals exist* is not a logical truth. They would point out that the proposition in question is not true in virtue of *its own* internal structure and *because* of that it is no logical truth.

Regarding the general question, I have already argued that, on my view, a truth is made into a logical one by special traits of that which *makes* it true in the first place, i.e., the kind of trait of the *world* in virtue of which it is true. That is why I classify the truth *At least two individuals exist* as logical. Similarly, the question whether Modus Ponens, with the help of which we deduced *At least two individuals exist* from *John exists* and *Mary exists* preserves logical truth should not be confused with the question whether it preserves truth-in-virtue- of-internal-propositional-structure.

Now I also happen to believe that this proposition is true in virtue of its own structure. I take my lead from the *fact* that in order to say that there are at least two individuals, we need to appeal to two separate quantifiers, binding two different variables. (This, of course, would be trivially true on the exclusive interpretation of quantifiers that Wittgenstein seemed to have sympathy for in the *Tractatus*. But my point is that this is true for the normal *inclusive* interpre-

X. Logic and Necessity—A Disengagement

There are then contingent logical truths. The question is: what does this show? One reaction to these findings may consist in the attempt to trace the *source* of this contingency. I know of one hypothesis about this matter, one due to Tony Martin (in conversation). He argued that the *source* of the contingency of the above logical truths is the contingent *existence* of their constituents (individuals, attributes). Stipulate necessary existence for these items and all logical truths would be again necessary.

Read strongly, i.e., "it is sufficient to posit necessary existence for all *actual* individuals and then ...," the hypothesis has already been refuted. Let all actual individuals exist necessarily. The conditional $\exists x F x \supset Dis(F)$ can be refuted in a counterfactual situation with "new," additional, individuals. Read weakly (as Martin intended), i.e., "it is sufficient to posit necessary existence for all individuals, actual or not, ...," the above counterexample wouldn't work. But others would. The truth (and not only the sentence expressing it) that *if actually snow is white, then snow is white* is a contingent logical truth even if all individuals existed necessarily.[18]

---

tation as well.) Of course, I do not pretend to comment here on a whole range of delicate results in definability theory; nor do I pretend to cover the option of avoiding $\exists x \exists y (x \neq y)$ altogether and letting "two" designate directly a number, a second-order property or a set of sets. I simply note that *if* our proposition has the structure of the standard first-order coding, the use of *two* quantifiers, and more important, the use of *two* variables, is inescapable. The question is: why? Why should a quantified proposition bear a trace, not to say a scar, of the kind of singular propositions that would support its truth? Isn't the quantified proposition supposed to be *purely* general?

For me, this much is an indication that our standard assertion that the existence of the form $\exists x \exists y (x \neq y)$ "goes without saying," is very questionable. For it seems that the form codes into itself the kind of singular trait that would make it true. In fact, it seems to present in a schematic way the kind of singular trait from which it was abstracted in the first place. As such, I don't think of it as a *form*, at least not a "platonic form." I think of it as a *kind* of proposition, a kind abstracted from particular instances, a point that would have been clearer in the notation

$$\sum_{i,j} \langle x_i \neq x_j \rangle$$

where it could be *seen* that to get the propositional form (kind) of the quantified proposition, we *operate* on already given *singular* propositions.

[18] This is surely the case if we treat *Actually* in the way I think we should, viz. as attributing to propositions, just like *Necessarily* and *Possibly*, an irreducibly modal property (*Being actually (necessarily, possibly) true*). But even if we followed Lewis and (sometimes) Kaplan and let it introduce the world itself into the propo-

This first type of reaction is content to focus on the "Kantian" question "how are contingent logical truths possible?" One can go beyond this reaction by questioning the implicit presupposition of the "Kantian" formulation viz. why should logical truths be necessary in the first place?

I believe that we find ourselves here in a situation similar to the one created by Kripke's disengagement of the a priori and the necessary. Kripke argues that the latter notions seem to be distinct. Thus if anyone were to show that all a-priori truths must be necessary that would call for a substantive argument rather than a mere trivial observation on the meaning of "a priori." And indeed such a substantive argument has been put forward: if we know about actuality a certain truth P "without looking" at the world itself, then surely P can't depend on any contingent feature of that which we have not looked at. Hence P is necessary. To this Kripke would respond, even before giving his *cases*, that it is precisely because we cognize from within the actual world and *have* to so cognize that we may know of it, without looking, certain truths that would not hold of other situations.

A structurally similar situation holds in our case of the notion of logical truth. Someone may try his hand at the following "bridging argument": if a trait is a *structural* trait of this world, then it must be an *essential* trait of it. For though we may vary the material traits of the world, the "scaffolding" must be fixed for the notion of possibility *for* the world to make sense. Perhaps (something like) such an argument is given in *Tractatus* 2.022, "an imagined world, however different it may be from the real one, must have *something*—a form—in common with it."

Now I myself would respond to such an argument by pointing out that logic focuses on special, structural ("formal"), traits of actuality, traits that may very well be distinct of actuality, that may explain what the actuality of this one and only one real world boils down to. If so, there is no intrinsic reason to expect that such traits would extend to situations which, by their very nature, are *not* actual, are merely possible.

Be all that as it may, the real point of the present work is not so much

---

sition, the result would still hold. For given that propositions are generable from actual building blocks only (an assumption held dear by Russell and Ramsey), the actual world is the only world that can figure in this way in propositions. Hence if a given proposition (e.g., *snow is white*) bears *true-at-W_o*, pure analysis would suffice to show that P is true *tout court*. And yet, the overall proposition *if snow is actually white, then snow is white* is surely contingent, as witnessed by a counterfactual situation with red snow.

to win this debate; it is rather to focus us on two observations which would hold no matter which way the debate would go. The first is that the necessity of logical truths won't come from a trivial observation on the meaning of "logical truth"; one will have to first deny my *cases* of contingent logical truths, and then propose a substantive metaphysical thesis of the order of the above quoted *Tractatus* hypothesis as to why the actual truth of logical truths extends to all possible worlds. Secondly, such a thesis, true or false, would shift the focus of the debate. For so far we were told that the key notion was that of "logical truth," a proper reading of which would establish automatically the necessity of such truths. But if I am right, it's the other way round: it is the notion of *necessity* that is the critical notion here. It will have to be made to satisfy the following thesis: if the world has a given structural trait, it is a modally essential trait of it, a trait it *couldn't* have lacked. And thus, if I am right, we shouldn't build a modal underside to the notion of logical truth; we should rather unfold the structural underside of our modal notions.

Appendix: The Permutation-Resistance of Logical Truths

I define here the permutations with respect to which logical truths are resistant.

A. Rules of Generation for Propositions

(1)   Let there be

   (i)   The domain of existing individuals—D_i

   (ii)   The domain of basic attributes—D_{BA}

   (iii)   A binary relation—*identity*

   (iv)   Complex-attributes formers—*Not*, And*, Nec*, Act**

   (v)   Determiners—*Every, Some, Most, At least one, At least two,* ...

   (vi)   propositional connectives—*Not, And, Nec, Act*

(2)   The domain of (simple and complex) attributes, D_A, is generated by:

   If $P, Q \in D_{BA}$, then $P, Q, Not^* \langle P \rangle, And^* \langle P, Q \rangle, Nec^* \langle P \rangle, Act^* \langle P \rangle \in D_A$

(3)   The domain of propositions, D_P, is generated by:

- (i)   If $x \in D_i$ and $P \in D_A$, then $\langle x, p \rangle \in D_P$

- (ii)   If $x, y \in D_i$, then $\langle\langle x, y \rangle, \text{ } identity \rangle \in D_P$

- (iii) If $P, Q \in D_A$, then $\langle Every\langle P, Q \rangle\rangle$, $\langle Most \text{ } \langle P, Q \rangle\rangle$, $\langle Some \text{ } \langle P, Q \rangle\rangle$, $\langle At \text{ } least \text{ } one \text{ } \langle P, Q \rangle\rangle$, $\langle At \text{ } least \text{ } two \text{ } \langle P, Q \rangle\rangle \in D_P$

- (iv)   if $\phi, \psi \in D_P$, then $\langle Not\langle \phi \rangle\rangle$, $\langle And\langle\langle \phi \rangle, \langle \psi \rangle\rangle\rangle$, $\langle Nec\langle \phi \rangle\rangle$, $\langle Act\langle \phi \rangle\rangle \in D_P$

(4)   Comments on generation rules

- (i) D_{BA} contains *Existence* and *Individual*

- (ii)   I have allowed for an "ambiguous" treatment of *not, and, . . .*, viz. Not* vs. Not, to distinguish the two syntactical roles involved. The philosophical question as to which one is basic is not addressed

- (iii) Similarly, reasons for treating determiners, e.g., *Every*, as *binary* relations (rather than in the Fregean monadic way) are not given here (though note that propositions allowing *Most* can be generated)

B. Permutations

(1)   We have

- (i)   A permutation on individuals—Π_i, a one-one map of D_i onto D_i

- (ii)   A permutation on basic attributes—Π_{BA}, a one-one map of D_{BA} onto D_{BA} such that $\Pi_{BA}(Individual)$ = *Individual*, Π_{BA} (*Existence*) = *Existence*.

(2)   Given the permutation Π_{BA}, a permutation Π_A is induced on D_A, satisfying:

- (i) $\Pi_A(P) = \Pi_{BA}(P)$, for $P \in D_{BA}$

- (ii) $\Pi_A(Not^* \langle P \rangle) = Not^* \langle \Pi_A(P) \rangle$

- (iii) $\Pi_A(And^* \langle P, Q \rangle) = And^* \langle \Pi_A(P), \Pi_A(Q) \rangle$

- (iv) $\Pi_A(Nec^* \langle P \rangle) = Nec^* \langle \Pi_A(P) \rangle$

(v) $\Pi_A(Act^* \langle P \rangle) = Act^* \langle \Pi_A(P) \rangle$

(3) Given a pair of permutations Π_i, Π_A, a permutation Π_P on propositions, a one-one map of D_P onto D_P, is induced, satisfying:

(i) If ϕ is atomic and of the form $\langle x, P \rangle$, then $\Pi_P(\phi) = \langle \Pi_i(x), \Pi_A(P) \rangle$

(ii) If ϕ is atomic and of the form $\langle\langle x, y \rangle, \; identity \rangle$, then $\Pi_P(\phi) = \langle\langle \Pi_i(x), \Pi_i(y) \rangle, \; identity \rangle$

(iii) $\Pi_P(\langle Every \; \langle P, Q \rangle\rangle) = \langle Every \; \langle \Pi_A(P), \Pi_A(Q) \rangle\rangle$

(iv) $\Pi_P(\langle Some \; \langle P, Q \rangle\rangle) = \langle Some \; \langle \Pi_A(P), \Pi_A(Q) \rangle\rangle$

(v) $\Pi_P(\langle Most \; \langle P, Q \rangle\rangle) = \langle Most \; \langle \Pi_A(P), \Pi_A(Q) \rangle\rangle$

(vi) $\Pi_P(\langle At \; least \; two \; \langle P, Q \rangle\rangle) = \langle At \; least \; two \; \langle \Pi_A(P), \Pi_A(Q) \rangle\rangle$

(vii) $\Pi_P(\langle At \; least \; one \; \langle P, Q \rangle\rangle) = \langle At \; least \; one \; \langle \Pi_A(P), \Pi_A(Q) \rangle\rangle$

(viii)$\Pi_P(\langle Not \; \langle \phi \rangle\rangle) = \langle Not \; \langle \Pi_P(\phi) \rangle\rangle$

(ix) $\Pi_P(\langle And \; \langle\langle \phi \rangle, \langle \psi \rangle\rangle\rangle) = \langle And \; \langle\langle \Pi_P(\phi) \rangle, \langle \Pi_P(\psi) \rangle\rangle\rangle$

(x) $\Pi_P(\langle Nec \; \langle \phi \rangle\rangle) = \langle Nec \; \langle \Pi_P(\phi) \rangle\rangle$

(xi) $\Pi_P(\langle Act \; \langle \phi \rangle\rangle) = \langle Act \; \langle \Pi_P(\phi) \rangle\rangle$

C. The Thesis Formalized

(L) ϕ is logically true iff $\Pi_P(\phi)$ is true for all Π_P.

5

Russellian Intensional Logic

C. Anthony Anderson

Alonzo Church has extracted the intensional logic implicit in Russell's *Principles of Mathematics* [PoM] and has provided a formalization of that theory as it would appear in the style of *Principia Mathematica* [PM]. It was found necessary to add a connective '≡' for equality of propositions, taken as synonymous with the defined identity sign of [PM] but allowed to stand between complex well-formed formulas (see [Church 2]). Then, using [PoM] as a guide (especially §500), Church formulates axioms about '≡' which accord with Russell's assertions concerning the identity and distinctness of propositions. The resulting theory appears in [Church 4]. For complete details about the ramified theory of types as it would be used here, consult also [Church 3]. The resulting theory is the most detailed formulation of Russellian intensional logic in print.[1]

In this paper I examine that logic in order to test its adequacy as a codification of reasoning involving intensionality. It is shown that the logic has a feature which is quite desirable from Russell's point of view: the "Axioms of Infinity" are theorems.[2] Unfortunately, a certain para-

---

[1] David Kaplan's unpublished "Russell's Ramified Theory of Types" was written in 1974 and contains an alternative formulation of Russell's intensional logic. I have made use of this paper below in constructing models for the modified Russellian intensional logic proposed here.

[2] The leading idea of the proof appears first in [Bolzano] and again in [Dedekind] No. 66. I showed in my dissertation [Anderson 1] that the axioms for the Fregean version of Church's Alternative (0) have this consequence. The extension of the

dox is derivable in the system (see [Anderson 2] for an informal description of this paradox). The difficulty can be avoided by modifying the notion of a *propositional function*. The modified notion is arguably closer to Russell's ideas (in [PoM]) than the somewhat anachronistic "Ramseyian" propositional functions. In any case the modification avoids the paradox and seems to introduce no unpleasant limitations of its own. Using models constructed in accordance with these ideas, I suggest a reformulation of some of the axioms of Russellian intensional logic. And I offer independent arguments that some of the axioms in Church's formalization are too restrictive—given a certain attractive conception of the role of intensional logic. Finally, I sketch a method for extending the models to accord with this perspective. In an appendix I critically discuss some alternative approaches to Russellian intensional logic.

I. Church's Formalization of Russellian Intensional Logic

The logic employs the ramified theory of types to avoid the "semantical" paradoxes and Russell's paradox about propositions. (See [Church 3] and [Church 4].) The variables are assigned *r-types* (ramified types) corresponding to the domains over which they shall range. There is an r-type i of *individuals* (which may be taken to be any nonempty domain) and for each $n \geq 1$ and r-types $\beta_1, \beta_2, \ldots, \beta_m$, $(\beta_1, \beta_2, \ldots, \beta_m)/n$ is an r-type. If $m = 0$, $(\ )/n$ (abbreviated $0/n$) is the r-type of *propositions* of level (and order) n. Otherwise the r-type is an r-type of *propositional functions* (of level n)—taking m-tuples of entities of r-types $\beta_1, \beta_2, \ldots, \beta_m$, respectively, as arguments and yielding propositions as values. (The r-type $(i, i, \ldots, i)/n$ is abbreviated as m/n, where m is the number of i's occurring.) An r-type $(\alpha_1, \alpha_2, \ldots, \alpha_m)/n$ is *directly lower* than an r-type $(\beta_1, \beta_2, \ldots, \beta_m)/k$ if $\alpha_i = \beta_i$ $(i = 1, 2, \ldots, m)$ and $k > n$. The intent is that r-types shall be cumulative (unlike Russell's own formulation of ramified type theory) in the sense that a domain corresponding to an r-type directly higher than another includes the domain corresponding to the latter.

The *order* of a variable (and of the corresponding r-type) is defined as follows. The order of an individual variable is 0 and the order of a variable of r-type $(\beta_1, \beta_2, \ldots, \beta_m)/n$ is $N + n$, where N is the maximum of the orders that correspond to the r-types $\beta_1, \beta_2, \ldots, \beta_m$ (where $N = 0$

---

argument to the Russellian version formalized by Church is not difficult. Bealer has noticed that this implication holds for his formalization of what he calls "Conception 2"—corresponding to Church's Alternative (0).

if $m = 0$).

As primitive basis take variables of all r-types (with a superscript indicating the r-type), the connectives $\lor$ and $\sim$ of [PM], commas, and parentheses (or brackets). Generally we use p, q, r, s as propositional variables (i.e., as variables of some r-type $0/n$), F, G, H as functional variables and x, y, z as variables of unspecified r-types to be fixed in the context in question. Bold face letters will be syntactical metalinguistic variables and will correspond to the object language variables in an obvious way. The *well-formed formulas* are defined in the usual way except that $\mathbf{f}(\mathbf{x}_1, \mathbf{x}_2, \ldots, \mathbf{x}_m)$ is a well-formed formula whenever $\mathbf{f}$ is of r-type $(\beta_1, \beta_2, \ldots, \beta_m)/n$ and each $\mathbf{x}_i$ $(i = 1, 2, \ldots, m)$ is of r-type α_i, where either $\alpha_i = \beta_i$ or α_i is directly lower than β_i. Also, if $\mathbf{A}$ and $\mathbf{B}$ are well-formed formulas, so is $(\mathbf{A} \equiv \mathbf{B})$. Adopt some standard set of axioms for propositional and functional calculi.[3]

The characteristically intensional part of the logic is given by the axioms for $\equiv$. These are as follows (I add explanatory, but rough, paraphrases into English).

1. $\vdash \mathbf{p} \equiv \mathbf{p}$.
     ("Every proposition is self-identical.")

It is to be understood that these are axioms for every choice of propositional variable $\mathbf{p}$—i.e., for every choice of variable of type $0/n$ for any n. A similar understanding applies to the other axioms below.

2. $\vdash \mathbf{p} \equiv \mathbf{q} \equiv \blacksquare\mathbf{p} = \mathbf{q}$
     ("That $\mathbf{p}$ is identical with $\mathbf{q}$ is the same proposition as that every predicative property of $\mathbf{p}$ is a property of $\mathbf{q}$.")

---

[3] For the record let us take as rules modus ponens and generalization and the axiom schemata for propositional calculus:

P1. $\vdash \mathbf{p} \lor \mathbf{p} \supset \mathbf{p}$

P2. $\vdash \mathbf{q} \supset \blacksquare\mathbf{p} \lor \mathbf{q}$

P3. $\vdash \mathbf{p} \lor \mathbf{q} \supset \blacksquare\mathbf{q} \lor \mathbf{p}$

P4. $\vdash \mathbf{q} \supset \mathbf{r} \supset \blacksquare\mathbf{p} \lor \mathbf{q} \supset \blacksquare\mathbf{p} \lor \mathbf{r}$

where these are axioms for all r-types such that the result is well formed. And for the functional calculus take the schemata:

F1. $\vdash \mathbf{p} \supset_{\mathbf{x}} \mathbf{f}(\mathbf{x}) \supset \blacksquare\mathbf{p} \supset (\mathbf{x})\mathbf{f}(\mathbf{x})$

F2. $\vdash (\mathbf{x})\mathbf{f}(\mathbf{x}) \supset \mathbf{f}(\mathbf{a})$

where these are axioms for all r-types such that the result is well formed, except that in F1 $\mathbf{x}$ is not the particular variable $\mathbf{p}$.

Recall that $\mathbf{p} = \mathbf{q}$ is defined in [PM] to mean $(F)[F(\mathbf{p}) \supset F(\mathbf{q})]$, where F is predicative. In the present notation, this means that if $\mathbf{p}$ and $\mathbf{q}$ are of r-types $0/m$ and $0/n$, respectively, then F is of r-type $(0/k)/1$, where k is the greater of m and n.

3. $\vdash \mathbf{p} \equiv \mathbf{q} \supset \bullet \mathbf{p} = \mathbf{q}$
       ("That $\mathbf{p}$ is identical with $\mathbf{q}$ implies that every predicative property of $\mathbf{p}$ is a property of $\mathbf{q}$.")

4. $\vdash \mathbf{f}(\mathbf{x}_1, \mathbf{x}_2, \ldots, \mathbf{x}_m) \equiv_{\mathbf{x}_1 \mathbf{x}_2 \ldots \mathbf{x}_m} \mathbf{g}(\mathbf{x}_1, \mathbf{x}_2, \ldots, \mathbf{x}_m) \supset \bullet \mathbf{f} = \mathbf{g}$,
       where the variables $\mathbf{x}_1, \mathbf{x}_2, \ldots, \mathbf{x}_m$ are all different.
       ("If two propositional functions agree on all arguments—i.e., they yield the same proposition as value when they are applied to the same arguments in order—then the propositional functions are identical.")

It should be noted that there is really almost nothing at all in [PoM] to suggest that propositional functions be treated in this "extensional" way. Axioms 4 were supplied by Church as a way of making the theory of propositional functions more definite.[4] And we shall find that these axioms are at the heart of the paradox to be discussed below.

5. $\vdash (\exists \mathbf{p}) \bullet \mathbf{p} \equiv \mathbf{P}$, where $\mathbf{p}$ is a propositional variable having no free occurrence in $\mathbf{P}$, the bound variables of $\mathbf{P}$ are all of order less than the order of $\mathbf{p}$ and the free variables and constants of $\mathbf{P}$ are all of order not greater than the order of $\mathbf{p}$.

6. $\vdash (\exists \mathbf{f}) \bullet \mathbf{f}(\mathbf{x}_1, \mathbf{x}_2, \ldots, \mathbf{x}_m) \equiv_{\mathbf{x}_1 \mathbf{x}_2 \ldots \mathbf{x}_m} \mathbf{P}$, where the variables $\mathbf{x}_1, \mathbf{x}_2, \ldots, \mathbf{x}_m$ are all different, the variable $\mathbf{f}$ has no free occurrence in $\mathbf{P}$, the bound variables of $\mathbf{P}$ are all of order less than the order of $\mathbf{f}$, and the free variables and constants of $\mathbf{P}$ are all of order not greater than the order of $\mathbf{f}$.

The axiom schemata 5 and 6 are intensional comprehension schemata for propositions and propositional functions. Axiom (schema) 5 says roughly that to every well-formed formula there corresponds a proposition (of appropriate order so as to conform to the constraints of the ramified theory of types). Axiom (schema) 6 says that for any given well-formed formula $\mathbf{P}$, there is a propositional function (of appropriate order) which, for all arguments, agrees in (propositional) value with $\mathbf{P}$.

---

[4] This is not to suggest that Church thought otherwise about axiom 4. He did not.

7. $\vdash (\mathbf{x})\mathbf{f}(\mathbf{x}) \equiv (\mathbf{y})\mathbf{f}(\mathbf{y})$
   ("Alphabetic change of bound variable does not affect the proposition denoted.")

8. $\vdash\, \sim \mathbf{p} \equiv\, \sim \mathbf{q} \supset \blacksquare\mathbf{p} \equiv \mathbf{q}$
   ("Propositions with identical negations are identical.")

9. $\vdash [\mathbf{p} \vee \mathbf{q}] \equiv [\mathbf{r} \vee \mathbf{s}] \supset \blacksquare\mathbf{p} \equiv \mathbf{r}$
   ("Identical disjunctions have the same first disjuncts.")

It is worth noting that axiom 9 is the first to really distinguish the strict criterion of identity of propositions in [PoM] from weaker criteria, for example, necessary (strict) equivalence.

10. $\vdash [\mathbf{p} \vee \mathbf{q}] \equiv [\mathbf{r} \vee \mathbf{s}] \supset \blacksquare\mathbf{q} \equiv \mathbf{s}$
    ("Identical disjunctions have the same second disjuncts.")

11. $\vdash (\mathbf{x})\mathbf{f}(\mathbf{x}) \equiv (\mathbf{x})\mathbf{g}(\mathbf{x}) \supset \blacksquare\mathbf{f}(\mathbf{x}) \equiv_{\mathbf{x}} \mathbf{g}(\mathbf{x})$
    ("If the universal quantification of two propositional functions are identical, then the functions agree on all values.")

Together with axiom 4 this implies that if the universal quantifications of two propositional functions are identical, then the functions are identical.

12. $\vdash\, \sim \blacksquare \sim \mathbf{p} \equiv (\mathbf{x})\mathbf{f}(\mathbf{x})$
    ("No negation is a universal generalization.")

13. $\vdash\, \sim \blacksquare \sim \mathbf{p} \equiv \blacksquare\mathbf{q} \vee \mathbf{r}$
    ("No negation is a disjunction.")

14. $\vdash\, \sim \blacksquare\mathbf{p} \vee \mathbf{q} \equiv (\mathbf{x})\mathbf{f}(\mathbf{x})$
    ("No disjunction is a universal generalization.")

15. $\vdash\, \sim \blacksquare(\mathbf{x})\mathbf{f}(\mathbf{x}) \equiv (\mathbf{y})\mathbf{g}(\mathbf{y})$, where the variables $\mathbf{x}$ and $\mathbf{y}$ are not of the same type
    ("The proposition that every entity of one r-type is $\mathbf{f}$ is never the same as the proposition that every entity of a different r-type is $\mathbf{g}$.")

In order to reduce mathematics to logic as they desired, Whitehead and Russell found it necessary to add Axioms of Reducibility:

R. $\vdash (\mathbf{f})(\exists \mathbf{g}) \blacksquare \mathbf{f}(\mathbf{x}_1, \mathbf{x}_2, \ldots, \mathbf{x}_m) \equiv_{\mathbf{x}_1 \mathbf{x}_2 \ldots \mathbf{x}_m} \mathbf{g}(\mathbf{x}_1, \mathbf{x}_2, \ldots, \mathbf{x}_m)$,
   where $\mathbf{f}$ is of some r-type $(\beta_1, \beta_2, \ldots, \beta_m)/n$ and $\mathbf{g}$ is of r-type $(\beta_1, \beta_2, \ldots, \beta_m)/1$

The objection against this, that it collapses the hierarchy of orders, has been answered conclusively by [Church 3] and [Myhill 2].[5]

From the point of view of *Principia Mathematica*, this system has the rather pleasant feature that the so-called "Axioms of Infinity," which Russell and Whitehead had to take as hypotheses, are theorems for all types except the type i of individuals.

II. Axioms of Infinity in Russellian Intensional Logic

In giving proofs it is often convenient to have the substitution schemata:

5′ $\vdash (\mathbf{p})\mathbf{A} \supset \check{\mathbf{S}}^{\mathbf{p}}_{\mathbf{B}}\mathbf{A}$ |, where $\mathbf{p}$ is a propositional variable and the bound variables of $\mathbf{B}$ are of order less than the order of $\mathbf{p}$ and the free variables and constants of $\mathbf{B}$ are of order not greater than the order of $\mathbf{p}$.

For the definition of $\check{\mathbf{S}}$ consult [Church 1], 192–93.

6′ $\vdash (\mathbf{f})\mathbf{A} \supset \check{\mathbf{S}}^{\mathbf{f}(\mathbf{x}_1, \mathbf{x}_2, \ldots, \mathbf{x}_m)}_{\mathbf{B}}\mathbf{A}$ |, where $\mathbf{f}$ is an n-ary functional variable, $\mathbf{x}_1, \mathbf{x}_2, \ldots, \mathbf{x}_m$ are distinct variables such that the result is well formed, the bound variables of $\mathbf{B}$ are of order less than the order of $\mathbf{f}$, and the free variables and constants of $\mathbf{B}$ are of order not greater than the order of $\mathbf{f}$.

The schemata 5′ and 6′ follow from 5 and 6, and conversely may replace them as axioms. We sketch the proofs of theorems required to prove the Axioms of Infinity. The proofs will all hold for any arbitrary propositional r-type.

(i) $\vdash \mathbf{p} \equiv \mathbf{q} \supset \blacksquare\mathbf{q} \equiv \mathbf{p}$

Proof. Use axiom 3, the definition of '=', substitution schema 6′ (Hereafter: 'subst'. will be used for applications of 5′ or 6′), axiom 1 and propositional calculus ('P').

(ii) $\vdash \mathbf{p} \equiv \mathbf{q} \supset \blacksquare\mathbf{p} \equiv \mathbf{r} \supset \blacksquare\mathbf{q} \equiv \mathbf{r}$

Proof. Use axiom 3, subst., and P.

---

[5] As Myhill points out, Russell himself was already aware of the objection in [Russell 1] and gave the essentially correct reply. This reply also appears in [Black]. The first really clear statement of the point of which I am aware appears in unpublished correspondence of David Kaplan.

Now define

$$\text{Neg}(\mathbf{P}, \mathbf{Q}) = \blacksquare \sim \mathbf{P} \equiv \mathbf{Q} \ \text{Df}$$

Then we have the following theorems.

(iii) $\vdash \text{Neg}(p, q) \supset \blacksquare \text{Neg}(r, q) \supset p = r$

Proof. Use (ii), generalization ('gen.'), subst., (i), P, axiom 8, axiom 3, and the definition of 'Neg'. (Some of these rules must be applied here more than once.)

(iv) $\vdash \text{Neg}(q, p) \supset \blacksquare \text{Neg}(q, r) \supset p = r$

Proof. Use (ii), gen., subst., P, axiom 3, and the def. of 'Neg'.

(v) $\vdash (\exists q) \, \text{Neg}(p, q)$

Proof. Use comprehension schema 5, (i), gen., subst., P, quantification theory, and the def. of 'Neg'.

(vi) $\vdash (\exists q) \, \text{Neg}(q, p) \supset_p (\exists r) \, \text{Neg}(p, r)$

Proof. From (v), P, and gen.

(vii) $\vdash (\exists p)[(\exists q) \, \text{Neg}(p, q) \blacksquare \sim (\exists r) \, \text{Neg}(r, p)]$

Proof. Use axiom 12, (v), gen., subst., P, familiar laws of quantification theory, and the def. of 'Neg'.

If we think of 'Neg' as corresponding to a relation *Negation* as the comprehension schema 6 will allow us to do, then we have in effect proved that Negation is a one-one function, (iii) and (iv), whose converse domain is included in its domain, (vi), and whose domain contains an element which is not a member of the converse domain, (vii). This establishes that the domain of the relation of Negation is an infinite set, but we go on to connect this up explicitly with the Axioms of Infinity in *Principia Mathematica*.

The definition of *reflexive class* in [PM] is

∗124.01 $\text{Cls refl} = \hat{\rho}\{(\exists R) \blacksquare R \in 1 \rightarrow 1 \blacksquare \mathbf{\Pi}'R \subset D'R \blacksquare \exists! \vec{B}'R \blacksquare \rho = D'R\}$
   Df

Recalling

*93.101 $\vec{B}'P = D'P - \mathbb{C}'P$

The definition *124.01 defines a class to be reflexive if it is the domain (last conjunct) of a one-one relation (first conjunct) whose converse domain is a subset of its domain (second conjunct) and which has something in its domain not in its converse domain (third conjunct).

Then we can prove the Axioms of Infinity for all r-types as follows.

$$F(p,q) \equiv_{pq} \text{Neg}(p,q) \vdash (\exists q)F(p,q) \equiv_p (\exists q)\,\text{Neg}(p,q)$$

by universal instantiation (univ. inst.), distribute the universal quantifier as an existential over the biconditional, and use gen. Hence

$$F(p,q) \equiv_{pq} \text{Neg}(p,q), G(p) \equiv_p (\exists q)F(p,q) \vdash G(p) \equiv_p (\exists q)\,\text{Neg}(p,q)$$

by univ. inst., P, and gen. Hence, by P,

$$F(p,q) \equiv_{pq} \text{Neg}(p,q), G(p) \equiv_p (\exists q)F(p,q) \vdash [G(p) \equiv_p (\exists q)\,\text{Neg}(p,q) \bullet G(p) \equiv_p (\exists q)F(p,q)]$$

So, by existential instantiation ('ex. inst.', see [Church 3]),

$$F(p,q) \equiv_{pq} \text{Neg}(p,q), (\exists G)[G(p) \equiv_p (\exists q)F(p,q)] \vdash (\exists G)[G(p) \equiv_p (\exists q)\,\text{Neg}(p,q) \bullet G(p) \equiv_p (\exists q)F(p,q)]$$

Now, using the comprehension schema 6, some laws of quantification theory, P, and, what is easily proved, the fact that $\equiv$ implies material equivalence:

$$\vdash (\exists G)[G(p) \equiv_p (\exists q)F(p,q)]$$

and, because of the Axiom of Reducibility R, we may take G to be of level 1. Hence, with G predicative,

$$F(p,q) \equiv_{pq}\text{Neg}(p,q) \vdash (\exists G)[G(p) \equiv_p (\exists q)\,\text{Neg}(p,q)\bullet G(p) \equiv_p (\exists q)F(p,q)]$$

Now, applying the contextual definition of [PM]:

*20.01 $f\{\hat{z}(\psi z)\}\blacksquare = \colon(\exists\phi)\colon \phi!x \equiv_x \psi x \colon f\{\phi!\hat{z}\}$ Df.,

(but transcribing into our notation) and the definition of the domain of a relation, we get

(1) $F(p,q) \equiv_{pq} \text{Neg}(p,q) \vdash \hat{p}(\exists q)\,\text{Neg}(p,q) = D'F$

And from (iii), (iv), (vi), and (vii), we can get

(2) $F(p,q) \equiv_{pq} \mathrm{Neg}(p,q) \vdash F(p,q) \supset \blacksquare F(r,q) \supset p = r$

(3) $F(p,q) \equiv_{pq} \mathrm{Neg}(p,q) \vdash F(q,p) \supset \blacksquare F(q,r) \supset p = r$

(4) $F(p,q) \equiv_{pq} \mathrm{Neg}(p,q) \vdash (\exists q)F(q,p) \supset_p (\exists r)F(p,r)$

and

(5) $F(p,q) \equiv_{pq} \mathrm{Neg}(p,q) \vdash (\exists p)[(\exists q)F(p,q)\blacksquare \sim (\exists r)F(r,p)]$

respectively, by familiar laws of quantification theory and P.

Again because of the Axioms of Reducibility, we may take F to be of level 1. Now combining these consequences of the indicated hypothesis and applying ex. inst.:

(6) $(\exists F)[F(p,q) \equiv_{pq} \mathrm{Neg}(p,q)] \vdash \hat{p}(\exists q) \mathrm{Neg}(p,q) \in \mathrm{Cls} \ \mathrm{refl}$

where we used the definition of 'Cls refl' stated above (and, implicitly, the definition *20.02 $x \in (\phi!\hat{x})\blacksquare = \blacksquare\phi!x$ and appropriate Axiom of Reducibility). The hypothesis of (6) follows from the comprehension schema 6, so

(7) $\vdash \hat{p}(\exists q) \mathrm{Neg}(p,q) \in \mathrm{Cls} \ \mathrm{refl}$

From *Principia*,

*124.231 $\vdash \begin{smallmatrix}\bullet\\\bullet\end{smallmatrix}\exists!\mathrm{NC} \ \mathrm{refl}\blacksquare \equiv \blacksquare\exists!\mathrm{Cls} \ \mathrm{refl}$

and

*124.232 $\vdash \begin{smallmatrix}\bullet\\\bullet\end{smallmatrix}\exists!\mathrm{NC} \ \mathrm{refl}\blacksquare \supset \blacksquare \mathrm{Infin} \ \mathrm{ax}$

there follows immediately:

(8) $\vdash \begin{smallmatrix}\bullet\\\bullet\end{smallmatrix}\exists \ !\mathrm{Cls} \ \mathrm{refl}\blacksquare \supset \blacksquare \mathrm{Infin} \ \mathrm{ax}$, by P

Recall,

*24.03 $\exists!\alpha\blacksquare = \blacksquare(\exists x)x \in \alpha$ Df

and infer from (7) and (8)

(9) $\vdash \mathrm{Infin} \ \mathrm{ax}$

The matter is similar for Axioms of Infinity in the r-types of propositional functions except that it is necessary to use as definition,

$$\text{Neg}(\mathbf{f}, \mathbf{g}) = \blacksquare \sim \mathbf{f}(\mathbf{x}_1, \mathbf{x}_2, \ldots, \mathbf{x}_m) \equiv_{\mathbf{x}_1 \mathbf{x}_2 \ldots \mathbf{x}_m} \mathbf{g}(\mathbf{x}_1, \mathbf{x}_2, \ldots, \mathbf{x}_m)$$
Df, where $\mathbf{x}_1, \mathbf{x}_2, \ldots, \mathbf{x}_m$ are all different

and to make use of axiom 4. (We will argue below that this axiom should be rejected.) For these types it is necessary to make use of axiom 13 instead of axiom 12 to prove the analog of (vii).

III. A Paradox in Russellian Intensional Logic

All this is very pleasant, but there lurks a difficulty. According to axiom 4, if propositional functions f and g agree on all arguments, then they are identical. Suppose that the individual domain contains only one individual a, say a human person, and consider some intuitively asymmetrical relation, say x *is taller than* y. This binary propositional function will agree with its converse, y *is taller than* x, on all pairs of values $\langle u, v \rangle$ taken from the domain—there being only one such, namely $\langle a, a \rangle$. It will then follow that the *belief* that for all x and y, x is taller than y if and only if x is taller than y, *is identical with* the belief that for all x and y, x is taller than y if and only if y is taller than x. But the first is a triviality and the second is the belief that *taller than* is symmetrical! It will follow further that if one of these is known a priori, then so is the other—even if the knower in question has no particular information about the cardinality of the domain. Indeed, the two Russellian propositions are identical and hence share all properties.

It is well known that Russell and Whitehead did not conceive of their logic as having an arbitrary domain of individuals. Rather, they supposed that the individuals were to be specified once and for all as entities devoid of complexity or as those things which are neither propositions nor propositional functions. Thus the difficulty outlined does not apply to Russellian intensional logic conceived in that way. But suppose that one has as a goal to construct a workable intensional logic, adequate to deal with intensionalities as they arise in law, science, philosophy, and so on, and taking into account such improvements in the treatment of logic as have been found to be necessary or desirable. Then, it seems, the advocate of the Russellian approach must face this difficulty.

We must show that the thing is really so:

$$(y)[x = y] \vdash F(x, x) \equiv F(z, w)$$

by univ. inst., axiom 1, subst., and the properties of $=$.

$$(y)[x = y] \vdash F(x, x) \equiv F(w, z), \text{ similarly}$$

Hence,

$$(y)[x = y] \vdash F(z, w) \equiv_{zw} F(w, z)$$

by these, the transitivity and commutativity of $\equiv$, and gen. So,

$$(y)[x = y], F(w, z) \equiv_{zw} G(z, w) \vdash F(z, w) \equiv_{zw} G(z, w)$$

by quantification theory and the properties of $\equiv$.

$$\therefore (y)[x = y], F(w, z) \equiv_{zw} G(z, w) \vdash F = G, \text{ by axiom 4}$$

I.e.,

$$(y)[x = y], F(w, z) \equiv_{zw} G(z, w) \vdash (\Phi)[\Phi!(F) \supset \Phi!(G)]$$

$$\therefore (y)[x = y], F(w, z) \equiv_{zw} G(z, w) \vdash [F(z, w) \equiv_{zw} F(z, w)] \equiv [F(z, w) \equiv_{zw} G(z, w)]$$

by subst. $([F(z, w) \equiv_{zw} F(z, w)] \equiv [F(z, w) \equiv_{zw} H(z, w)]$ for $\Phi(H))$ by axiom 1, subst., gen., and P

Now use the deduction theorem, substitute $H(x, y)$ for $F(x, y)$ and $H(y, x)$ for $G(x, y)$, use axiom 1, gen., subst., and P to get:

(10) $(y)[x = y] \vdash [H(z, w) \equiv_{zw} H(z, w)] \equiv [H(z, w) \equiv_{zw} H(w, z)]$

This is already extremely curious. But we go on to dramatize the paradox by eliciting its consequences for the theory of propositions. Using (10), we get

(11) $(y)[x = y], p \equiv [H(z, w) \equiv_{zw} H(z, w)], q \equiv [H(z, w) \equiv_{zw} H(w, z)] \vdash p \equiv q$

by the transitivity and commutativity of $\equiv$. Hence,

(12) $(y)[x = y], p \equiv [H(z, w) \equiv_{zw} H(z, w)], q \equiv [H(z, w) \equiv_{zw} H(w, z)], B(p) \vdash B(q)$

where B is a constant of appropriate type, by (11), axiom 3, and the properties of $=$. Now use the deduction theorem and generalization (twice, in that order) to get

(13) $(y)[x = y] \vdash [p \equiv \blacksquare H(z, w) \equiv_{zw} H(z, w)] \supset_p B(p) \supset \blacksquare[q \equiv \blacksquare H(z, w) \equiv_{zw} H(w, z)] \supset_q B(q)$

Now use ex inst. and the deduction theorem:

$$\vdash (\exists x)(y)[x = y] \supset \blacksquare[p \equiv \blacksquare H(z, w) \equiv_{zw} H(z, w)] \supset_p B(p) \supset$$
$$[q \equiv \blacksquare H(z, w) \equiv_{zw} H(w, z)] \supset_q B(q)$$

The circumlocution is necessary in this last theorem because the syntax does not allow complex expressions to occur in the argument places of a functional variable.

As an example, suppose we take the domain to be specified as containing only the natural number 0 if there are odd perfect numbers and to contain the natural numbers 0 and 1 otherwise. (According to the usual way of speaking about these matters, it has so far not been proved whether or not there are odd perfect numbers.) And let $H(x, y)$ mean that x is less than or equal to y. Finally, let $B(r)$ mean that the proposition r is easy to prove and is obvious to the beginning mathematics student, but is not mathematically interesting. Then our theorem allows us to assert, as a matter of sheer logic, the following surprising proposition: If, as a matter of mathematical fact (now unknown, as one would have said), there are perfect square numbers, then *if* it is easy to prove about our domain of numbers (as specified) that the relation of being less than or equal is self-equivalent therein and this is obvious to the beginning mathematics student, but is not mathematically interesting, *then* it is *also* easy to prove that the relation of being less than or equal to is symmetrical on this domain, and this is obvious to the beginning mathematics student, but of no mathematical interest. But this seems just wrong. The second antecedent is plainly true and the consequent is false as things now stand—and both of these even if there are odd perfect numbers. The symmetry of this relation on this domain so specified clearly implies that there are such numbers so that if such a thing were easily proved or known to beginning students, the answer to this difficult ("open") question of mathematics should be known to us all. Of course if there are no such numbers, then we can alter the specification of the domain to produce a paradoxical theorem corresponding to that possibility.[6]

It might be thought that the difficulty depends essentially upon our assumption that the individual domain contains a single element. If so, one might argue, we can simply restrict the application of Russellian intensional logic to domains containing at least two individuals. If the logic is otherwise satisfactory, then the restriction, though unattractive,

---

[6] See [Anderson 2] for further paradoxical interpretations of this theorem.

may do no significant harm to the overall utility of the logistic system.

It seems very doubtful that such a restriction would be found to be satisfactory, especially if we contemplate extensions of the logic to include modality. But in any case the paradox is generalizable to domains with more than one individual.[7]

Suppose that there are at least two individuals known to be elements of the individual domain, say a and b. Consider the following propositional functions:

$$F_1(x,y) : x \neq y \supset \blacksquare b = b$$

$$F_2(x,y) : a \neq a \supset \blacksquare x = y$$

$$F_3(x,y) : a \neq y \supset \blacksquare x = b$$

$$F_4(x,y) : x \neq a \supset \blacksquare b = y$$

Now we completely define a propositional function $G(x,y)$ by means of the four conditions:

(1) $[x = a \blacksquare y = a] \supset \blacksquare G(x,y) \equiv F_1(x,y)$

(2) $[x = b \blacksquare y = b] \supset \blacksquare G(x,y) \equiv F_2(x,y)$

(3) $[x = b \blacksquare y = a] \supset \blacksquare G(x,y) \equiv F_3(x,y)$

(4) $\sim [x = a \blacksquare y = a] \supset \blacksquare \sim [x = b \blacksquare y = b] \supset \blacksquare \sim [x = b \blacksquare y = a] \supset \blacksquare G(x,y) \equiv F_4(x,y)$

First observe that the value of $G(x,y)$ for any of the pairs $\langle a,a \rangle$, $\langle b,b \rangle$, $\langle b,a \rangle$, $\langle a,b \rangle$ is uniformly the proposition $[a \neq a \supset \blacksquare b = b]$. For all other pairs $\langle u,v \rangle$—if there are any—the value of $G(x,y)$ is $[u \neq a \supset \blacksquare b = v]$. Suppose there is a c in the individual domain distinct from both a and b. Then $G(c,a)$ is the false proposition $[c \neq a \supset \blacksquare b = a]$. And $G(a,c)$ is the true proposition $[a \neq a \supset \blacksquare b = c]$. Hence we know

(*) $(\exists x)[x \neq a \blacksquare x \neq b] \supset \blacksquare \sim [G(x,y) \equiv_{xy} G(y,x)]$

that if there is an individual distinct from both a and b, then $G(x,y)$ is not symmetrical. On the other hand, the following holds:

---

[7] Church has shown (in correspondence) that the argument is generalizable in a certain sense. But the resulting generalization does not seem to me to result in a clearly paradoxical conclusion. It was reflection upon Church's proof that led to the present, somewhat different, generalization.

$$(x)[x = a \lor x = b] \supset [G(x, y) \equiv_{xy} G(y, x)]$$

if a and b are the only two individuals then $G(x, y)$ is symmetrical—the same proposition results in every case. Now by an argument entirely parallel to the original paradox about the unit domain, we can show that any propositional function G satisfying conditions (1)–(4) will be such that

$$(x)[x = a \lor x = b] \supset \blacksquare[G(x, y) \equiv_{xy} G(x, y)] \equiv [G(x, y) \equiv_{xy} G(y, x)]$$

i.e., that if a and b are the only individuals, then that G is self-equivalent is the same proposition as that G is symmetrical. Hence it will follow, as before, that if the first is known by so-and-so, then the second is known by so-and-so. Such a person will then have no trouble deducing from (*) that a and b are the only individuals. So we have the paradoxical conclusion that if there are (perhaps as a matter of contingent fact) only two elements in the individual domain, then this fact can quite easily be known (indeed, a priori) by deduction from the known proposition (*) and another known proposition—that G is symmetrical. Considering the possible ways of specifying the individual domain, this would yield a powerful technique for deciding open questions. The conclusion must be rejected. There is no difficulty in extending the paradox to domains with any finite number of individuals.

As far as I can tell, one cannot actually prove in the present logic the existence of the propositional function defined by the clauses (1)–(4). But according to the conception of a propositional function implicit in the axioms (especially axiom 4), this is (if true) a defect of formulation—to be remedied by supplying further axioms.[8] Indeed, it is that faulty conception of a propositional function which is at the heart of the paradox.

IV. Russellian Propositional Functions

Examination of the proof of our paradoxical theorem reveals that the only suspicious axiom used is axiom 4. As noted above, this is not

---

[8] In the unpublished paper, "The Ramified Theory of Types," of footnote 1, David Kaplan contemplates an axiom (schema) which he calls the "Axiom of Reality." The relevant particular case transcribed into the present system would be:

$$(x)(y)(\exists p)h(p, x, y) \supset (\exists f)[(q \equiv f(x, y)) \supset_{qxy} h(q, x, y)]$$

If this is adopted as an axiom, then the existence of the propositional function specified by conditions (1)–(4) can be proved.

characteristically Russellian. Russell had a number of opportunities to comment on this idea ([Russell 2], [Russell 3], [Russell 4], 123) as it was advocated by Ramsey and he regarded it with suspicion on each such occasion. It is not absolutely clear that it is the "extensional" character of axiom 4 to which Russell would object, for Ramsey's propositional functions were allowed to yield as values any propositions. For example, a propositional function F might be such that F(Socrates) is the proposition that snow is white and F(Plato) is that $2 + 2 = 4$. There are at least two features of this idea to which Russell might object—independently of its taking a propositional function to be a function in extension (i.e., to satisfy axiom 4). In [PoM] Russell insists that the argument must be a "constituent" of the proposition which is the value of the function for that argument ([PoM], 510). But even if we restrict Ramseyian functions to just those, we do not get a notion which Russell would accept as his own. He would not regard a Ramseyian function F which was such that F(Socrates) is the proposition that Socrates is bald and F(Plato) is the proposition that Plato is tall as a propositional function. (See [Anderson 2] for references to appropriate passages in Russell.) Presumably a propositional function must be such that it can at least represent the "meaning" of a predicate. We can satisfy these Russellian constraints by requiring that a propositional function be obtained "by abstraction" from a proposition.[9] A careful study of [PoM] will confirm, I believe, this as (one) interpretation of Russell. And there is some evidence that he may have regarded the order in which the abstraction is performed as being of significance.[10] In the reconstruction of Russellian proposi-

---

[9] This seems to be the basis for Gödel's suggestion in [Gödel 2], 131, footnote 10, that a Russellian propositional function can be represented as a pair consisting of an argument and a proposition.

[10] See [PoM], 94, where Russell says

> If the propositional function $\phi(x, y)$ is to be asserted for all values of x and y, we consider the assertion, for all values of y, of the propositional function $\phi(a, y)$, where a is a constant. This does not involve y, and may be represented by $\psi(a)$. We then vary a, and assert $\psi(x)$ for all values of x. This process is analogous to double integration; and it is necessary to prove formally that the order in which the variations are made makes no difference to the result.

So, one *might* argue, even if we are dealing with a single binary proposition, say $H(a, a)$, one might get $H(x, y)$ by abstracting on the first argument and then the second, but get $H(y, x)$ by abstracting in the reverse order. This is the only relatively clear evidence I find that the Russell of [PoM] might accept the distinction I suggest. It is clear that Russell has in [PoM] an intensional notion of a propositional function, but that observation does not suffice to settle the present question

tional functions which I propose, the order of abstraction is built into the propositional function itself.

Roughly, the suggestion is this. Think of Russellian propositions as structured entities containing in some cases individual things and their attributes. (We do not identify propositional functions with attributes.) These can be represented in a way suggested by the work of David Kaplan [Kaplan]: imagine that the *language* of [PM] (as extended by Church) is supplemented by the addition of the *individuals* themselves (and not merely names for them) and *attributes* to serve as individual constants and primitive predicates. The "well-formed formulas" of such a language will consist of sequences of signs and nonlinguistic entities, but otherwise defined in the usual way. Since we want to allow that alphabetic change of bound variables does not alter the proposition denoted, we may take equivalence classes of these "sentences" under alphabetic variance as representing Russellian propositions. Then to obtain a Russellian propositional function, "abstract" from a proposition by replacing "constants" (e.g., the individuals which are constituents of the propositions) by variables, being careful to specify the order in which the abstraction is made. Formally, we represent such a thing by a *pair* $\langle \, [\![A]\!], f \rangle$, where $[\![A]\!]$ is an equivalence class of well-formed formulas containing one or more variables and obtained from a proposition (representative) as just explained, and f is a function "in extension" whose value for given arguments is always the proposition (representative) which results from **A** by substituting the arguments (yes, the arguments, not their names) for the variables in **A** (taken in a certain fixed order). We do not really need f to be specified separately—it is determined by **A**, but the present construction is a little more intuitive. Now *Russell* would not like to think of the model in the extensional way we have described, but we might use it to reassure someone who understands and trusts set theory. In any case, it seems plausible (to me) that Russellian propositional functions as conceived by him in [PoM] (in so far as that conception is definite) share the relevant formal properties with the suggested model. And the construction provides a sufficiently definite conception to avoid the paradox derived above and to suggest alternative axioms. On these grounds we suggest it as a heuristic guide for the Russellian.

---

of interpretation.

V. Models for Russellian Intensional Logic

The actual details of the models are somewhat tedious, but we include enough detail to see that the thing actually works. Our models will not validate axiom 2. While it is not difficult to make adjustments so as to accomplish this, the complications are not instructive. Further, it should be noted that axiom 2 is nowhere used in any of our proofs. For the present purpose we might simply suppose that identity of propositions, as this is conveyed by the connective $\equiv$, need not be precisely the same notion as the concept of having all predicative properties in common. This is plausible on its face. I do not adopt an axiom asserting this nonidentity since I argue in §VII that such things should not be part of general intensional logic.

Assume given a nonempty set of individuals I and for each predicative r-type $(\beta_1, \beta_2, \ldots, \beta_m)/1$ a set $\mathcal{A}^{\beta_1 \beta_2 \cdots \beta_m}$ of *attributes* of that r-type. We think of the attributes as simply being given and as *not* being propositional functions. We will, in effect, assume that for each set of individuals, there is a predicative attribute of *belonging to that set*. Formally, we secure this by counting '$a \in \alpha$' as a proposition for each individual a and each set of individuals α. In accordance with the informal description above, we take the proposition to just be the sequence consisting of (the individual) a followed by (the expression) '$\in$', followed by (the set) α. And we must make a similar assumption about relations (in extension) among individuals. Similarly, in higher types we will arrange matters so that for every set (or relation) of entities of that type, there is a predicative attribute of belonging to that set. All this is to secure the validity of the Axiom of Reducibility (and ultimately the Axiom of Choice—see footnote 18).

We define domains $\mathcal{D}_\alpha$ corresponding to each r-type α. Proceed by induction on the order corresponding to the r-type.

$$\mathcal{D}_i = I$$

The set $\mathcal{E}_1$ of *propositional expressions of order 1* is defined by induction:

(1_1) A propositional variable $\mathbf{p}^{0/1}$ is a propositional expression of order 1.

(2_1) If $\mathbf{f}$ is a variable of r-type $(i, i, \ldots, i)/1$ (where there are m i's) and $a_1, a_2, \ldots, a_m$ are individuals or individual variables, then $\mathbf{f}(a_1, a_2, \ldots, a_m)$ is a propositional expression of order 1.

(3_1) If $\mathfrak{A}$ is an attribute of r-type $(i, i, \ldots, i)/1$ (where there are
m i's) and $a_1, a_2, \ldots, a_m$ are individuals or individual variables, then $\mathfrak{A}(a_1, a_2, \ldots, a_m)$ is a propositional expression of
order 1.

It is here the sequence consisting of the attribute, followed by '(', followed by the sequence of individuals (or individual variables) separated
in the sequence by commas, followed by ')', which is defined to be a
propositional expression. Evidently 'expression' is being used in a very
general sense.

(4_1) If α is a set of ordered m-tuples of individuals and $a_1, a_2, \ldots, a_m$
are individuals or individual variables, then $\langle a_1, a_2, \ldots, a_m \rangle \in$
α is a propositional expression of order 1.

Again it is the sequence consisting of the actual m-tuple, followed by
the symbol epsilon, followed by the actual set—which is being defined
as a propositional 'expression'.

(5_1) If $\mathbf{A}$ and $\mathbf{B}$ are propositional expressions of order 1 and $\mathbf{x}$
is an individual variable, then $\sim \mathbf{A}, (\mathbf{A} \vee \mathbf{B}), (\mathbf{A} \equiv \mathbf{B})$, and
$(\mathbf{x})\mathbf{A}$ are propositional expressions of order 1.

Since we want "sentences" which differ only by alphabetic change of
bound variables to correspond to the same proposition, we collect propositional expressions into equivalence classes.

The class $[\![\mathbf{A}]\!]_1$ is the class of propositional expressions differing from $\mathbf{A}$ by at most alphabetic change of bound variables.
The set of *propositions* of order 1 is the set of all $[\![\mathbf{A}]\!]_1$ for
closed propositional expressions $\mathbf{A}$ of order 1.

Here the idea of a closed propositional expression is defined in the expected way.

$\mathcal{D}_{0/1} =$ the set of propositions of order 1. The set of *propositional functions* of r-type $(i, i, \ldots, i)/1$ (where there are m
i's) is defined as the set of all ϕ such that $\phi = \langle [\![\mathbf{A}]\!]_1, f \rangle$,
where $\mathbf{A}$ is a propositional expression of order 1 containing
exactly the first m individual variables in alphabetic order,
say $\mathbf{x}_1, \mathbf{x}_2, \ldots, \mathbf{x}_m$, as free variables, f is an m-ary function
belonging to $\mathcal{D}_{0/1}^{I \times I \times \cdots \times I}$, and for each m-tuple of individuals
$a_1, a_2, \ldots, a_m$,

$$f(a_1, a_2, \ldots, a_m) = \mathrm{S}^{\mathbf{x}_1 \mathbf{x}_2 \cdots \mathbf{x}_m}_{a_1 a_2 \cdots a_m} [\![\mathbf{A}]\!]_1 \mid$$

Strictly speaking, the operation of substitution is an operation on syntactical entities. But it is easy to see that there is no problem in extending the idea to sequences of any kind. Indeed, we can extend the idea to apply to our equivalence classes of propositional expressions—and this is what our definition requires. One need only observe that two propositional expressions in a single equivalence class have exactly the same free variables and substituting entities for variables in one such and taking equivalence classes under alphabetic change of bound variables always produces the same result. That is, the value of the function f for the arguments $a_1, a_2, \ldots, a_n$ in order is a certain proposition obtainable from the equivalence class $[\![\mathbf{A}]\!]_1$ of propositional expressions as follows. Consider the propositional expression $\mathbf{A}$ (or indeed any element of $[\![\mathbf{A}]\!]_1$) and substitute the *entities* $a_1, a_2, \ldots, a_n$ for the free occurrences of the variables $\mathbf{x}_1, \mathbf{x}_2, \ldots, \mathbf{x}_n$, respectively. One obtains a closed propositional expression, say $\mathbf{A}^*$, and hence a proposition $[\![\mathbf{A}^*]\!]_1$. The definition is acceptable in the sense that the choice of $\mathbf{A}$ does not matter. Let us use in the metalanguage the notation $\Lambda \mathbf{x}_1, \mathbf{x}_2, \ldots, \mathbf{x}_n [\![\mathbf{A}]\!]_1$ to designate the function f just defined. (Note that we are using the variables $\mathbf{x}_1, \mathbf{x}_2, \ldots, \mathbf{x}_n$ now also in connection with the metalanguage and that the notation requires that they be listed in alphabetic order.) Hence we may assert that the value of this function for the particular arguments $a_1, a_2, \ldots, a_n$ is $[\![\mathbf{A}^*]\!]_1$, i.e., that

$$\Lambda \mathbf{x}_1, \mathbf{x}_2, \ldots, \mathbf{x}_n [\![\mathbf{A}]\!]_1 (a_1, a_2, \ldots, a_n) = [\![\mathbf{A}^*]\!]_1$$

(This notation will actually be little used in the present paper.)

$\mathcal{D}_{(i,i,\ldots,i)/1}$ = the set of propositional functions of r-type $(i, i, \ldots, i)/1$

Suppose defined the propositional expressions of all orders less than k, the propositions of all orders less than k, and the propositional functions of all r-types corresponding to orders less than k. The set $\mathcal{E}_k$ of *propositional expressions of order k* is defined by induction:

(1_k) A propositional variable $\mathbf{p}^{0/k}$ is a propositional expression of order k.

(2_k) If $\mathbf{f}$ is a variable of r-type $(\beta_1, \beta_2, \ldots, \beta_m)/n$ and of order k and $a_1, a_2, \ldots, a_m$ are entities or variables such that a_j

is of type α_j and α_j is either β_j or directly lower than $\beta_j (j = 1, 2, \ldots, m)$, then $\mathbf{f}(a_1, a_2, \ldots, a_m)$ is a propositional expression of order k.

(3_k) If $\mathfrak{A}$ is an attribute of r-type $(\beta_1, \beta_2, \ldots, \beta_m)/1$ and of order k and $a_1, a_2, \ldots, a_m$ are entities or variables such that a_j is of type α_j and α_j is either β_j or directly lower than $\beta_j (j = 1, 2, \ldots, m)$, then $\mathfrak{A}(a_1, a_2, \ldots, a_m)$ is a propositional expression of order k.

(4_k) If α is a set of m-tuples of entities from $\mathcal{D}_{\alpha_1} \times \mathcal{D}_{\alpha_2} \times \ldots \times \mathcal{D}_{\alpha_m}$, already defined, and some d_i is of order $k - 1$, and $\langle a_1, a_2, \ldots, a_m \rangle$ is an m-tuple of entities or variables of the indicated types, then $\langle a_1, a_2, \ldots, a_m \rangle \in \alpha$ is a propositional expression of order k.

(5_k) If $\mathbf{A}$ is a propositional expression of order k, then $\sim \mathbf{A}$ is a propositional expression of order k. If each of $\mathbf{A}$ and $\mathbf{B}$ is a propositional expression and either $\mathbf{A}$ or $\mathbf{B}$ is of order k (and the other is of order k or less), then $(\mathbf{A} \vee \mathbf{B})$ and $(\mathbf{A} \equiv \mathbf{B})$ are propositional expressions of order k. If $\mathbf{A}$ is a propositional expression of order k or less and $\mathbf{x}$ is a variable of order $k - 1$, then $(\mathbf{x})\mathbf{A}$ is a propositional expression of order k. If $\mathbf{A}$ is a propositional expression of order k and $\mathbf{x}$ is a variable of order less than $k - 1$, $(\mathbf{x})\mathbf{A}$ is a propositional expression of order k.

The class $[\![\mathbf{A}]\!]_k$ is the equivalence class of propositional expressions of order k differing from $\mathbf{A}$ by at most alphabetic change of bound variables.

If $[\![\mathbf{A}]\!]_k$ is closed, it is a *proposition of order k*. $\mathcal{D}_{0/k} =$ the set of propositions of order k or less. The set of *propositional functions of r-type* $(\beta_1, \beta_2, \ldots, \beta_m)/n$ and order k is defined as the set of all ϕ such that $\phi = \langle [\![\mathbf{A}]\!]_k, f \rangle$ where $\mathbf{A}$ is a propositional expression of order k containing as free variables exactly the distinct variables $\mathbf{x}_1, \mathbf{x}_2, \ldots, \mathbf{x}_m$, where $\mathbf{x}_1$ is the first variable of r-type β_1 in alphabetic order, $\mathbf{x}_2$ is the first variable of r-type β_2 in alphabetic order not already used, $\ldots$, $\mathbf{x}_m$ is the first variable of r-type β_m not already used, and for each m-tuple of entities $a_1, a_2, \ldots, a_m$ (where a_j belongs to $\mathcal{D}_{beta_j}, j = 1, 2, \ldots, m$), and $f = \Lambda \mathbf{x}_1 \mathbf{x}_2 \ldots \mathbf{x}_m [\![\mathbf{A}]\!]_k$ remains to be defined. To proceed by induction we may

assume that all such functions corresponding to orders less
than k have been defined. For a given m-tuple of entities
$a_1, a_2, \ldots, a_m$ of the indicated orders, we define the value of
f by the equation

$$f(a_1, a_2, \ldots, a_m) = \$_{a_1 a_2 \ldots a_m}^{x_1 x_2 \ldots x_m} [\![A]\!]_k \,|$$

where $\$$ is a (somewhat complicated) substitution operation
to be explained. When a variable, say x_i, is in *argument position* in A (or in any element of A's equivalence class), we
want to substitute the actual *entity* a_i—individual, proposition, or propositional function as the case may be. But if the
variable does *not* occur in argument position, then there are
(only) two cases. (1) The variable x_i is a propositional variable, say p_i, and hence a_i is a proposition, say $[\![B]\!]_n$ (n less
than or equal to k). Then substitute B (or any element of
$[\![B]\!]_n$) for the variable p_i. (2) The variable x_i is a functional
variable, say f_i. For simplicity, let us suppose the object language temporarily extended so as to include as wffs lambda
expressions of the form $\lambda y_1, y_2, \ldots, y_n C$, where C is a wff
and $y_1, y_2, \ldots, y_n$ are distinct variables. Now in the present
case a_i will be a propositional function $\phi = \langle [\![C]\!]_n, g \rangle$ (necessarily of order less than where $g = \Lambda z_1, z_2, \ldots, z_n [\![C]\!]_n$.
Then substitute the expression $\lambda z_1, z_2, \ldots, z_n C$ for the variable f_i and perform lambda contraction—rewriting bound
variables first if necessary to avoid capture. The effect is
that the expression C is substituted for f_i according to the
rule of substitution for functional variables. The result of
performing these operations is a certain expression A^*. The
value of the function f for the indicated arguments is then
$[\![A^*]\!]_k$. So if we write $\Lambda x_1, x_2, \ldots, x_n [\![A]\!]_k$ for the function
f just defined, we may again assert

$$(\Lambda x_1 x_2 \ldots x_n [\![A]\!]_k)(a_1, a_2, \ldots, a_n) = [\![A]\!]_k{}^{11}$$

---

[11] As complicated as this definition is, it is here still somewhat over-simplified.
Strictly the operations involved must be defined inductively as the construction
proceeds. For example, the idea of "lambda contraction" as an operation on propositional expressions is a transformation applied to sequences of entities. We must
show that this function is well defined. Finally, it may be necessary to rewrite C
by alphabetic change of bound variables in different ways in order to avoid capture of variables at different occurrences of x_i. Notice that lambda expressions
are introduced here as a temporary metalinguistic device.

In general then, a propositional function is a pair of the form

$$\langle [\![\mathbf{A}]\!]_k, \Lambda \mathbf{x}_1 \mathbf{x}_2 \ldots \mathbf{x}_n [\![\mathbf{A}]\!]_k \rangle$$

Note that propositions and propositional functions are treated differently when they are "objects" or arguments as opposed to cases when they are asserted or asserted of something. It may be thought that this dual interpretation leads to some difficulty. As far as can now be seen, it does not.

> $\mathcal{D}_{(\beta_1, \beta_2, \ldots, \beta_m)/n}$ = the set of all propositional functions of r-type $(\beta_1, \beta_2, \ldots, \beta_m)/n$ or directly lower r-type.

A *model structure* consists of a nonempty domain of individuals I together with a family $\mathcal{A}$ of sets of predicative attributes. Given such, a *model* is defined by specifying the various domains (based on I and $\mathcal{A}$) as just described and selecting, for each predicative r-type $(\beta_1, \beta_2, \ldots, \beta_m)/1$, a (not necessarily nonempty) set $\mathcal{T}^{\beta_1, \beta_2 \cdots \beta_m}$ of *atomic propositions*, i.e., propositions of the form $[\![\mathfrak{A}(a_1, a_2, \ldots, a_m)]\!]$. The family $\mathcal{T}$ of such sets is regarded as fixing the atomic propositions which are to be true in the model.

An atomic proposition $[\![\mathfrak{A}(a_1, a_2, \ldots, a_m)]\!]$ is *true in* $\mathcal{M} = \langle I, \mathcal{A}, \mathcal{T} \rangle$ if and only if it belongs to $\mathcal{T}^{\beta_1, \beta_2 \cdots \beta_m}$. A proposition $[\![\langle a_1, a_2, \ldots, a_m \rangle \in \alpha]\!]$ is *true in* $\mathcal{M}$ if and only if the indicated m-tuple belongs to the set α. A *negation* proposition $[\![\sim \mathbf{A}]\!]$ is *true* (in $\mathcal{M}$) if and only if $[\![\mathbf{A}]\!]$ is not true (in $\mathcal{M}$). A *disjunction* proposition $[\![\mathbf{A} \vee \mathbf{B}]\!]$ is *true* (in $\mathcal{M}$) if and only if $[\![\mathbf{A}]\!]$ is true (in $\mathcal{M}$) or $[\![\mathbf{B}]\!]$ is true (in $\mathcal{M}$) or both. An *equality* $[\![\mathbf{A} \equiv \mathbf{B}]\!]$ is *true* (in $\mathcal{M}$) if and only if $[\![\mathbf{A}]\!]$ is the same proposition as $[\![\mathbf{B}]\!]$. A *universally quantified* proposition $[\![(\mathbf{x})\mathbf{A}]\!]$ is *true* (in $\mathcal{M}$) if and only if $\$^{\mathbf{x}}_{\mathbf{a}}[\![\mathbf{A}]\!]$ | is true (in $\mathcal{M}$) for every entity a belonging to the domain corresponding to the r-type of the variable $\mathbf{x}$.

Now consider the original language before it is extended so as to include "entities" in the syntax. We wish to define the value of a well-formed formula (of propositional type) for a given assignment of values to its free variables. Let $\mathbf{x}_1, \mathbf{x}_2, \ldots, \mathbf{x}_m$ be the distinct free variables of a well-formed formula $\mathbf{A}$. Then the value of $\mathbf{A}$ for the assignment of entities $\mathbf{a}_1, \mathbf{a}_2, \ldots, \mathbf{a}_m$ (of corresponding r-types) to these variable is:

$$\$^{\mathbf{x}_1 \mathbf{x}_2 \ldots \mathbf{x}_m}_{a_1 a_2 \ldots a_m}[\![\mathbf{A}]\!] \mid$$

And $\mathbf{A}$ is *valid* if its value is a true proposition for every assignment in every model.

These models now invalidate the despised axiom 4. We go on to describe modified axioms which are validated in the models.

VI. Revised Axioms for Russellian Intensional Logic[12]

We leave the syntax and underlying propositional and functional calculi unchanged. The comprehension schemata 5 and 6 are replaced by the schema of substitution 5′, which is unchanged from its formulation above and the following modified version of the schema 6′, respectively.

6* $\vdash (\mathbf{f})\mathbf{A} \supset \breve{S}_{\mathbf{B}}^{\mathbf{f}(\mathbf{x}_1, \mathbf{x}_2, \ldots, \mathbf{x}_m)} \mathbf{A}|$, where $\mathbf{f}$ is an n-ary functional variable, $\mathbf{x}_1, \mathbf{x}_2, \ldots, \mathbf{x}_n$ are distinct variables such that the result is well formed and all occurring as free variables of $\mathbf{B}$, and the bound variables of $\mathbf{B}$ are of order less than the order of $\mathbf{f}$ and the free variables or constants of $\mathbf{B}$ are of order not greater than the order of $\mathbf{f}$.

Note that the difference between this and 6′ is that the variables $\mathbf{x}_1$, $\mathbf{x}_2$, ..., $\mathbf{x}_n$ are all required to occur as free variables of $\mathbf{B}$.

The axiom schemata for $\equiv$ are now axioms 1 and the following in place of axiom 3:

3* $\vdash \mathbf{f}(\mathbf{x}_1, \mathbf{x}_2, \ldots, \mathbf{x}_m) \equiv \mathbf{f}(\mathbf{y}_1, \mathbf{y}_2, \ldots, \mathbf{y}_m) \supset \mathbf{x}_1 = \mathbf{y}_1$

where $\mathbf{x}_1$ and $\mathbf{y}_1$ are individual or propositional variables. In place of axiom 4, we adopt:

4* $\vdash \Pi_{i=1}^{m} [\mathbf{y}_i \neq \mathbf{z}_i \bullet S_{\mathbf{y}_i}^{\mathbf{x}_i} \mathbf{f}(\mathbf{x}_1, \mathbf{x}_2, \ldots, \mathbf{x}_m) \equiv \mathbf{g}(\mathbf{x}_1, \mathbf{x}_2, \ldots, \mathbf{x}_m) |$
$\bullet S_{\mathbf{z}_i}^{\mathbf{x}_i} \mathbf{f}(\mathbf{x}_1, \mathbf{x}_2, \ldots, \mathbf{x}_m) \equiv \mathbf{g}(\mathbf{x}_1, \mathbf{x}_2, \ldots, \mathbf{x}_m) |] \supset \mathbf{f} = \mathbf{g}$, where $\Pi_{i=1}^{m}$ represents the conjunction of all the formulas obtained by setting i successively to be $1, 2, \ldots, m$; $\mathbf{x}_1, \mathbf{x}_2, \ldots, \mathbf{x}_m$ are distinct variables of any types and the $\mathbf{y}_i$ are distinct from one another but of the same types as the corresponding $\mathbf{x}_i$ and the $\mathbf{z}_i$ are distinct from one another but also of the same types as the corresponding $\mathbf{x}_i$.

It requires considerable argumentation to show that this is valid. The basic idea of the proof is the observation that the (equivalence classes

[12] I am indebted to David Kaplan for his instant refutation of another version of 4*. It should be emphasized that Kaplan's ideas have affected parts of the present treatment even at places where there is no explicit acknowledgement.

of) propositional expressions corresponding to two propositional functions will have exactly the same free variable at a given position if they yield the same proposition for two distinct arguments assigned to that variable—all other arguments being held fixed. It is then easy to see that the (classes of) propositional expressions must otherwise also be identical (except for alphabetic change of bound variables). And the idea generalizes to the case where the substitution is for a functional variable in predicate position.

Axioms 5* and 6* are as noted above. We retain axioms 7, 9 , and 10 and replace 11 by

11* $\vdash (x)f(x) \equiv (x)g(x) \supset f = g$

Axioms 12–15 and the Axiom of Reducibility are retained unchanged. So our new list of axioms is 1, 3*, 4*, 5', 6*, 7, 9, 10, 11*, 12, 13, 14, 15, and R. The missing axioms are either provable or invalidated—for example axiom 4 is not valid. Axiom 8 is now provable from axiom 3*.

The paradox of §III is no longer derivable. It will now be a theorem that

$$(\exists x)(\exists y)[x \neq y] \supset \blacksquare f(x, y) \equiv_{xy} g(x, y) \supset \blacksquare f = g$$
(for x and y variables of the same type)

The generalizations of the paradox fail because there are no Russellian propositional functions satisfying the specified conditions (1)–(4) (of §III). Ramseyian extensional propositional functions corresponding to these conditions are not values of the functional variables. The Russellian will of course define such talk contextually.

VII. Generalizing Russellian Intensional Logic

Using these models for guidance, we have reformulated Russellian intensional logic so as to avoid the paradox described in §III. As a bonus, we have validated a principle which Russell seems to accept in [PoM]:

$$f(x) \equiv f(y) \supset x = y$$

and its generalizations (see above, axiom 3*). And this is plausible independently (see [Church 4] and [Anderson 2] for discussion of this principle). This semantical principle of Russell's asserts (roughly) that if x and y differ, then propositions which involve them in the same way will also differ. This construal is of course subject to the limitations imposed by the ramified theory of types.

But it is arguable that we have validated *too much*. Axioms 12, 13, and 14 assert that negations, universal generalizations, and disjunctions are all distinct from one another—and these are valid in our models. While there is little doubt that the Russell of [PoM] would accept this, we may ask independently whether such things should be axioms of intensional logic. I believe that the answer is in the negative.

There are, no doubt, concepts of negation, universal generalization, and disjunction according to which the disputed axioms are correct. But it seems that there are concepts, equally deserving of these designations, which *falsify* axioms 12, 13, and 14. Consider, for example, a formulation of the first-order functional calculus which takes as its primitive operator Church's $|_x$ (from [Church 1], 171). Intuitively $\mathbf{A} \mid_x \mathbf{B}$ means that for every $\mathbf{x}$, not both $\mathbf{A}$ and $\mathbf{B}$—i.e., it is a combination of a universal quantification and a Sheffer stroke. But from the usual point of view, there is no reason why such a thing might not just be taken as a primitive and definitions offered:

$\mathbf{A} = (\mathbf{A} \mid_x \mathbf{A})$ Df, where $\mathbf{x}$ is the first variable not free in $\mathbf{A}$

$(\mathbf{A} \lor \mathbf{B}) = (\mathbf{A} \mid_x \mathbf{A}) \mid_x (\mathbf{B} \mid_x \mathbf{B})$ Df, where $\mathbf{x}$ is the first variable free in neither $\mathbf{A}$ nor $\mathbf{B}$

$(\mathbf{x})\mathbf{A} = (\mathbf{A} \mid_y \mathbf{A}) \mid_x (\mathbf{A} \mid_y \mathbf{A})$ Df, where $\mathbf{y}$ is the first variable not free in $\mathbf{A}$

And on these definitions

$$\sim\sim q \equiv (x)q$$

$$\sim\sim q \equiv \blacksquare q \lor q$$

and

$$(q \lor q) \equiv (x)q$$

contrary, it would seem, to the intent of axioms 12, 13, and 14, respectively. Of course it might be maintained that the concepts involved in these axioms are distinct from those specified by the definitions—as indeed was Russell's intention. Even so, it is worth noticing that we could use in the metalanguage for Russellian intensional logic semantical rules which would interpret $\sim$, $\lor$, and (x) in accordance with the definitions just given. (But, of course, axioms 12, 13, and 14 would not then be validated.) In any case we must ask why a logic, even an intensional logic, should single out some particular concepts of these kinds and treat them, as opposed to others. Even an extreme Platonist, maintaining that there is some special and intuited concept of negation (perhaps that associated with the English word "not"), might agree that this need not and should not be given a special status in intensional logic, as opposed to, say, a metaphysical theory of Forms.[13] It seems to the author that such questions as which concepts are "basic" are best left to metaphysics or, more plausibly, psychology. The more abstract approach here advocated seems to be very much in the spirit of the sort of generality usually associated with the very idea of logic.

If we maintain the "fine-grained" structural criterion of identity of propositions embodied in axioms 8–11 (and generalized in axiom 3* above), we can show that there are indeed concepts of negation, universal generalization, and disjunction which validate the axioms in dispute. Consider a formulation of the first-order functional calculus which adopts $\supset$, the constant falsehood proposition F, and the existential quantifier as primitives.[14] Then nothing but inelegance prohibits the definitions:

$$\sim A = A \supset \blacksquare A \supset F \ \text{Df}$$

$$(A \lor B) = (A \supset B) \supset \blacksquare(\sim B \supset \sim B) \supset B \ \text{Df}$$

$$(x)A = ((\exists x) \sim A \supset (\exists x) \sim A) \supset \blacksquare(\sim (\exists x) \sim A \supset \sim (\exists x) \sim A) \supset \sim (\exists x) \sim A \ \text{Df}$$

Suppose that for some p, q, and r, we had

$$\sim p \equiv \blacksquare q \lor r$$

---

[13] Compare Church's remark [Church 1], 151, footnote 225:

> But in 1906 he [Russell] takes negation as an additional primitive connective on the ground that it would otherwise be impossible to express the proposition that not everything is true—which he holds, is adequately expressed by $\sim (p)p$ but not by $(p)p \supset (s)s$. (To the writer it would seem that Russell's position of 1906 involves the very doubtful thesis that there is *one* indispensable concept of negation, given *a priori*, which it is the business of the logician to reproduce: perhaps not even the extreme realism of Frege would support this.)

[14] It is worth mentioning that $(f)(\exists p)\blacksquare \sim p \equiv (\exists x)f(x)$ is valid in the Russellian logic as originally formulated. This is because the existential quantifier is (in one development in [PM]) defined therein. This asymmetry should give us pause, especially if we plan to apply our intensional logic to the formalization of arguments in the natural language.

i.e.,

$$(p \supset \blacksquare p \supset F) \equiv ((q \supset r) \supset \blacksquare(\sim r \supset \sim r) \supset r)$$

The principle of axioms 8, 9, 10, and 11* requires that identical conditional propositions must have identical antecedents and identical consequents. And we want to preserve this even if $\supset$ is taken as primitive. Hence we will have

$$p \equiv (q \supset r)$$

$$p \equiv (\sim r \supset \sim r)$$

applying the principle twice in the last instance. So further,

$$(q \supset r) \equiv (\sim r \supset \sim r)$$

and from this

$$r \equiv \sim r$$

which is refutable (from our other axioms). We may conclude that no negation is a disjunction. Similar arguments show that no negation is a universal quantification and no disjunction is a universal quantification—as these are defined in the logic under discussion. So there are concepts of negation, universal quantification, and disjunction which falsify axioms 12, 13, and 14 and others which validate them. In this sense, these axioms are not valid, but "contingent" principles of intensional logic.[15]

To the objection that this abstract approach leaves intensional logic without any specific subject matter, I would reply that this is already the case with extensional logic insofar as the domain of individuals (and hence also, in a certain sense, the concept of quantification over that domain) varies from one application to another. And we may add that in a certain sense the *truth functions*, for example negation construed as a function on truth-values, are part of the fixed subject matter of intensional (and extensional) logic. Intensional logic is the logic of concepts of such functions, but with no prejudice as to exactly *which* concepts are selected. It is rather the general principles of all such concepts and of the other logical concepts such as various quantification functions. This last

---

[15]I do not maintain that the theories of *particular* concepts of negation are not worthy of study—in whatever sense this is possible—only that it is best not to specify intensional logic as being about some such.

point of view, it must be admitted, is not literally open to the Russellian since, for example, functions of truth-values (and other extensional entities) must be regarded as abstractive fictions—to be explained away by contextual definition.

One can see in some detail how to alter the models to accommodate these suggestions. Contemplate formulations of the underlying logic which adopt alternative primitive operators and connectives but with the syntax otherwise undisturbed. Imagine that negation, disjunction, and universal quantification are introduced by definition but actually added to the object language. Now require that the synonymy classes corresponding to propositions (and, more generally, propositional expressions) agree with these definitions and use these to construct models for the unextended language—using the scheme described above. We do not attempt to specify these ideas in detail in this place. This is partly because difficulties with the Theory of Descriptions suggest that further modifications may be necessary to produce a completely adequate intensional logic (see [Anderson 2]). Here I urge only that axioms 12, 13, 14 and, for similar reasons, 2 should be omitted.

The resulting logic is rather impoverished. (In particular, the infinity of intensional domains no longer follows.) It appears that other principles of a general structural nature and compatible with the ideas just sketched should be added. In particular some kind of "Axiom of Foundation" for propositions seems valid—asserting that one cannot have an infinite sequence of propositions each involving the next. Such a principle can be formulated and a principle proved which is advocated by [Prior]—that no proposition is a logical complication of itself. The "Axioms of Infinity" again become theorems. But these extensions require further investigation.[16]

VIII. Appendix: Alternative Russellian Approaches

It may have occurred to the reader to suggest that the difficulties all spring from the very idea of a propositional function as a *function*— even as modified along the lines I have suggested. Why not, one may ask, abandon this notion altogether in favor of the idea of a *property* or *attribute*. I will here indicate some drawbacks to this suggestion and, in particular, will point out some defects in two Russellian systems

---

[16]The formation of my ideas about Russell's Ramified Type Theory and about his conception of a propositional function have been greatly influenced by [Goldfarb].

which develop this line: the System IV of [Myhill 1] and the logic T2′ of [Bealer].

The principal flaws in these (and all similar) alternatives is the abandonment of the *rule of substitution for functional variables* and the resulting loss of generality which prevents us from regarding $f(x)$ as an arbitrary proposition about x. We have retained that principle (in a modified form) as axiom 6*. From the present point of view, especially considering the generalization sketched in §VII, quantification over propositional functions (in the Russellian sense) together with the rule of substitution for functional variables enables us to express propositions and to validate inferences not otherwise available. This remark, which may appear somewhat cryptic, will become clearer in the discussion below.

(1) Myhill's System IV

[Myhill 1] is an important but neglected paper which attempts to develop the Russellian viewpoint so as to be adequate for modal and, ultimately, propositional attitude contexts. The reader should consult that paper for complete details of the system. The logic contains a primitive (intensional) abstraction operator λ, which obeys the principle:

(15) $(\lambda x_1 \ldots \lambda x_n)(--x_1-.-\ldots-x_n\ldots)(y_1,\ldots,y_n) \leftrightarrow --y_1-$
$.-\ldots-y_n\ldots$

This enables the logic to develop smoothly since the rule of substitution for functional variables in extensional contexts (and when modality is added, in modal contexts) is a consequence. [Caution: It must not be assumed that the Comprehension Principle and the corresponding Substitution Principle are automatically equivalent. The usual proof of their equivalence is given in *extensional logic* where substitutivity of material equivalence holds. The general principle of substitutivity of '$\equiv$' does not hold in Russellian Intensional Logic as reconstructed above]. The corresponding thing with '$=$' (which Myhill allows between complex expressions) in place of the sign of material equivalence '$\leftrightarrow$':

(9) $(\lambda x_1 \ldots x_n)(--x_1-.-\ldots-x_n\ldots)(y_1,\ldots,y_n) = --y_1-$
$.-\ldots-y_n\ldots$

is rejected.

Now Myhill speaks of the entities denoted by intensional abstraction expressions as "propositional functions." But notice that if these propositional functions are really *functions*, even in the modified sense I propose, and *if juxtaposition means application of function to argument*, then we have no option except to accept the stronger (9). Indeed, even if we think of intensional abstraction expressions as denoting properties—as is suggested by the failure of (9)—there is some difficulty in giving a coherent interpretation. If we read '$(\lambda x)(\ldots x$ - - -)' in some such way as 'the property which is predicated of x when it is asserted that $(\ldots x$ - - -)' and we interpret juxtaposition as *predication*, it is extremely difficult to fix in the mind the distinction between the left and right sides of (9).

I conclude that juxtaposition must be given some other meaning, say corresponding to the formation of an ordered pair, if (9) is to be resisted. In this case it really doesn't matter whether we think of propositional functions as functions or as properties. Given that their being functions plays no formal role in the system, it is just as well to think of Myhill's propositional functions as properties or attributes. This interpretation of juxtaposition has the effect that $f(x)$ can no longer be taken to be an arbitrary proposition about x, but is rather construed as a proposition, intrinsically subject-predicate, which may be thought of as a pair $\langle f, x \rangle$ consisting of the property (or, if you like, the propositional function) f and the individual x.

Although this interpretation would permit the rejection of (9) as invalid, it makes the theorem of System IV:

$$(\exists f)(\exists g)(f \neq g \& [(p)f(p) = (p)g(p)])$$

rather difficult to understand. (See [Myhill 1], 82—and note that a similar argument holds if f and g are of intensional type.)

In any case the rule of substitution for functional variables does not hold in full generality (in particular in contexts involving propositional or property identity or involving propositional attitudes). So, for example, we can no longer express Russell's semantical principle (axiom 3* above) that if x and y are different, then so are propositions which involve them in exactly the same way. (Of course, we can still assert the formula 3* in Myhill's logic, indeed it is valid on the suggested interpretation, but it will not have the required consequences—and so cannot be interpreted as expressing Russell's semantical principle.) And we cannot validate in Myhill's logic the inference:

Jones believes that either Aristotle taught Alexander or Aristotle taught Plato.

∴ Jones has a belief about Aristotle.

The reasoning would go through if we represent the embedded proposition as '$F(a)$', but not if we use the direct symbolization '$A(a) \lor P(a)$'. In the former case, the inference is just existential generalization on 'F', but in the latter, in the absence of (9), the conclusion cannot be drawn. It would be possible, of course, to add a primitive constant expressing the relation between a proposition and what it is "about" and appropriate axioms—one might then hope to deduce the conclusion. But here the superior generality of the propositional function (with substitution for functional variables) appears. It is similar for the inference:

> Whenever Plato believes something about Parmenides, Aristotle believes the same about him.
> Plato believes that if Parmenides was wise, then he was good.
>
> ---
>
> ∴ Aristotle believes that if Parmenides was wise, then he was good.

And the following argument does not seem to be validated in System IV:

> The relation which holds between numbers x and y when either $x < y$ or $x = y$ is the same as the relation which holds between x and y when $x \leq y$.
>
> ---
>
> ∴ The proposition that $2 < 7$ or $2 = 7$ is the same as the proposition that $2 \leq 7$.

The following argument is perhaps not quite as evidently valid, but deserves mention:

> To be bald is (the very same thing as) to be hairless.
>
> ---
>
> ∴ Whoever believes that David is bald, believes that David is hairless.

If we take the premise to be a property identity, then the conclusion seems to follow. But the argument fails in System IV—here again for lack of (9) or the corresponding substitution rule for functional variables.

And if we strengthen (15) to (9) (thus restoring the desired substitution rule) and now attempt to assert Russell's semantical principle (corresponding to our axiom 3*), we once again fall into paradox (see [Anderson 2]).

Finally, I note that if the stronger principle (9) is incorporated into Myhill's logic, there is danger of reinstating the Paradox of the Name Relation.[17]

It seems then that Myhill's System IV is not entirely adequate.[18]

(2) Bealer's Logic T2′

In [Bealer] George Bealer develops an essentially Russellian intensional logic, with a very stringent criterion of identity but without the ramified or even simple theory of types to protect against antinomy. Instead Bealer adopts a primitive predication relation Δ and rejects the Comprehension Principles (and Substitution Principles) in favor of property analogues of the axioms of Zermelo-Fraenkel (or Von Neumann-Bernays) set theory. No use is made of propositional functions.

For ease of comparison we write $\lambda x_1 \ldots x_n(-- x_1 - . - .x_n \ldots)$ for Bealer's intensional abstract $[-- x_1 - . - .x_n \ldots]_{x_1 x_2 \ldots x_n}$ and we write $f(x_1, \ldots, x_n)$ in place of his $\langle x_1, \ldots, x_n \rangle \Delta f$—hence juxtaposition will in our abbreviation express predication. And we generally omit Bealer's square brackets around abstracts which name propositions. For predicate constant F, it is a theorem of T2′ that:

$$(\lambda x F x)(x) \neq F x$$

(See [Bealer], 65, axioms A11 and A12 or [Anderson 3] for details.) This already makes the meaning of intensional abstraction and/or predication somewhat mysterious (see the comments above about interpreting juxtaposition in Myhill's system). Furthermore, in Bealer's logic even the analog of Myhill's (15) fails. One cannot consistently add to T2′ the

---

[17] This point is due to David Kaplan (in conversation). See also [Bealer], 91.

[18] One feature of Myhill's system which seems (to me) to be desirable is the presence of extensional types as well as intensional types. Notice that our models for Russellian Intensional Logic assume the existence of, for example, all classes of individuals. It would be well to make this explicit in the object-language. We can then just identify (some of) the predicative propositional functions with sets—thus validating the Axiom of Reducibility and clearing the way for the Axiom of Choice. Russell was aware of the relationship between the Axiom of Reducibility and the existence of classes (see [PM], 58). The idea of identifying predicative functions with classes is suggested by a number of Gödel's remarks in [Gödel 2] (see especially 140 and 142) and by his identification of the Comprehension Schema with the Axiom of Reducibility in [Gödel 1]. It has also been advocated as an attractive possibility by Church in a lecture at Berkeley, California, 13 February 1981.

Kaplan, in the paper of footnote 1, secures the validity of the Axiom of Reducibility by allowing any (extensional) function from entities to propositions to be a propositional function. But the paradox of §III is derivable in that system.

principle:

(15B)$\lambda x_1 \ldots x_n(--x_1-.-.x_n \ldots)(y_1, \ldots, y_n) \equiv (--y_1-.-.y_n \ldots)$

(Not that Bealer is under any illusions about this particular principle.) This is simply because, in the absence of type theory, (15B) is a principle of abstraction and leads straight to the Russell Paradox (see [Bealer], 95). Nor can one add

(15B$'$)$(\lambda x F x)(x) \equiv F x$

These two are not obviously equally dangerous in T2$'$ in the absence of any principle of substitution and since predicate places are not subject to quantification. But it follows from the fact that one cannot add:

(VB) $(\lambda x F x)(x) \equiv_x (\lambda x G x)(x) \supset \blacksquare F x \equiv_x G x$

Again, because of the peculiarities of the system, the derivation of a contradiction from (VB) is not entirely of a familiar sort. (See [Anderson 3] for details.)

As a consequence of these failures, apparently elementary inferences about properties are not validated. For example,

Aristotle has the property of being wise and Greek.

∴ Aristotle is wise and Aristotle is Greek,

formally,

$(\lambda x(Wx\&Gx))(a)$

∴ $Wa\&Ga$

fails to be valid. So also:

John loves Mary.
Bill loves Carol.

∴ There is a relation which holds between John and Mary and also between Bill and Carol.

Formalized, this is:

Ljm
Lbc

∴ $(\exists r)(r(j, m)\&r(b, c))$

Bealer's T2' does not permit existential generalization on predicates directly. And without (15B) or some substitute, there is no way to infer the existence of the relation r relating the two couples. Because there is no rule of substitution for functional variables the flaws of Myhill's System IV are also present in T2'. In particular the arguments above about Jones and Aristotle and about Aristotle, Plato and Parmenides both fail in the present logic.

The logic T2' incorporates strong principles of nonidentity of concepts corresponding to axioms 12, 13, and 14. As I urged in §VII, these concern particular concepts and should not be part of a general logic of intensions.

Finally we may note that the property-theoretical analogues of the set theoretical axioms which Bealer proposes to prevent paradox are not particularly well-motivated (see [Bealer], 97, 260 note 27, 265 notes 21 and 24). The "iterative conception of sets" may provide some intuitive justification for the currently accepted axioms of set theory, but some of the property analogues seem entirely ad hoc. Especially questionable would be the intensional analog of the Axiom of Choice (which is not discussed by Bealer). It is worth noticing that Russell ultimately rejected the Axiom of Choice—presumably because the principle is implausible when it is intensionally interpreted. (See also [Gödel 2], 151, where the Axiom of Choice is explicitly omitted when the intensional interpretation of [PM] is considered.)

In favor of Bealer's logic, it must be said that the absence of any type structure leaves the syntax pleasantly simple. And it allows, what seems intuitively acceptable, self-predication of properties. But the loss of the validation of the noted inferences seems (to me) to be too high a price to pay for simplicity. And, to reiterate, the failure of (15B) and the like leaves the meaning of the predication symbol and of intensional abstraction obscure.

Bibliography

Anderson, C. Anthony.
[Anderson 1] "Some Models for the Logic of Sense and Denotation with an Application to Alternative (0)." Ph.D. diss., University of California, Los Angeles, 1977.

Anderson, C. Anthony.
[Anderson 2] "Some Difficulties in Russellian Intensional Logic." *Noûs* 20 (1986): 35–43.

Anderson, C. Anthony.
[Anderson 3] "Bealer's *Quality and Concept*." *Journal of Philosophical Logic* 16 (1987): 115–64.

Bealer, George.
[Bealer] *Quality and Concept*. Oxford: The Clarendon Press, Oxford University Press, 1982.

Black, Max.
[Black] *The Nature of Mathematics: A Critical Survey*. Paterson, N.J.: Littlefield, Adams & Co., 1959.

Bolzano, Bernard.
[Bolzano] *Paradoxes of the Infinite*. New Haven: Yale University Press, 1950.

Church, Alonzo.
[Church 1] *Introduction to Mathematical Logic. Vol. 1*. Princeton, N.J.: Princeton University Press, 1956.

Church, Alonzo.
[Church 2] "Russellian Simple Type Theory." In *Proceedings and Addresses of the American Philosophical Association* 47 (1974), 21–33.

Church, Alonzo.
[Church 3] "Comparison of Russell's Resolution of the Semantical Antinomies with that of Tarski." *Journal of Symbolic Logic* 41 (1976): 747–60.

Church, Alonzo.
[Church 4] "Russell's Theory of Identity of Propositions." *Philosophia Naturalis* 21 (1984): 513–22.

Dedekind, Richard.
[Dedekind] *Essays on the Theory of Numbers*. New York: Dover Publications, Inc., 1963.

Gödel, Kurt.
[Gödel 1] "Über formal unentscheidbare Sätze der *Principia Mathematica* und verwandter Systeme I." *Monatshefte für Mathematik und Physik* 38 (1931): 173–98.

Gödel, Kurt.
[Gödel 2] "Russell's Mathematical Logic." In *The Philosophy of Bertrand Russell*, ed. Paul Arthur Schilpp. New York: Tudor Publishing Co., 1944.

Goldfarb, Warren.
[Goldfarb] "Russell's Reasons for Ramification." In *Essays of Bertrand Russell's Metaphysics and Epistemology*, vol. XI of *Minnesota Studies in the Philosophy of Science*, ed. C. Wade Savage and C. Anthony Anderson. Minneapolis: University of Minnesota Press, 1988.

Kaplan, David.
[Kaplan] "Opacity." In *The Philosophy of W. V. Quine*, ed. Lewis Edwin Hahn and Paul Arthur Schilpp. La Salle, Ill.: Open Court, 1986.

Myhill, John.
[Myhill 1] "Problems Arising in the Formalization of Intensional Logic." *Logique et Analyse* 1 (1958): 78–83.

Myhill, John.
[Myhill 2] "A Refutation of an Unjustified Attack on the Axiom of Reducibility." In *Bertrand Russell Memorial Volume*, ed. George W. Roberts. London and New York: Allen & Unwin, 1979.

Prior, Arthur.
[Prior] "Is the Concept of Referential Opacity Really Necessary?" *Acta Philosophica Fennica*, Fasc. XVI (1963): 189–99.

Russell, Bertrand.
[PoM] *The Principles of Mathematics*. Cambridge: Cambridge University Press, 1903.

Russell, Bertrand.
[Russell 1] "Mathematical Logic as Based on the Theory of Types." *American Journal of Mathematics* 30 (1908): 222–62.

Russell, Bertrand.
[Russell 2] Review of *Foundations of Mathematics and other Logical Essays* by F. P. Ramsey. *Mind* XLVI (new series) (1931): 476–82.

Russell, Bertrand.
[Russell 3] Review of *Foundations of Mathematics and other Logical Essays* by F. P. Ramsey. *Philosophy* 7 (1932): 82–86.

Russell, Bertrand.
[Russell 4] *My Philosophical Development.* London: Allen & Unwin, 1959.

Whitehead, Alfred North, and Russell, Bertrand.
[PM] *Principia Mathematica*, vol. 1. Cambridge: Cambridge University Press, 1910.

6

Direct Reference, the Semantics of Thinking, and Guise Theory (Constructive Reflections on David Kaplan's Theory of Indexical Reference)

Hector-Neri Castañeda

> ... A useful semantic theory must reveal both how an episode of thinking can grasp a bit of reality and how an episode of reflective thinking can immediately grasp that grasping. A valuable ontological theory, imposing no limits on empirical or scientific discoveries yet positing the most comprehensive stability of the world, must deliver both the maximum of necessity and the maximum of contingency.
>
> Oscar Thend

> ... just as Mont Blanc with its snowfields [its pieces of solidified lava, its crevices, and underground rodents] is not itself a component of the thought *Mont Blanc is 4000 metres high.*
>
> Gottlob Frege

> ... in spite of all its snowfields Mont Blanc itself is a component
> of what is actually *asserted* in the *proposition* 'Mont Blanc is
> more than 4000 metres high'. We don't assert the thought ... a
> private psychological matter: we assert the *object* of the thought,
> ... a certain complex (an objective proposition, one might say)
> in which Mont Blanc itself is a component part.

Bertrand Russell

I. Introduction: Reference, Semantics and Thinking

In his brilliant monograph *Demonstratives*, David Kaplan has confided
how, beginning in 1966 with "Quantifying In," he has become "more
and more intrigued with problems centering on ... the *semantics of direct reference.*"[1] As a result, he has regaled us with a string of truly
marvelous and rich studies on indexical reference. One fascinating development in these studies is the increasing metaphysication of David's
work. His original concern was with the logic of demonstratives, and
this entailed the production of both formal syntactic systems and corresponding formal-semantic set-theoretical models. But David has evolved
more metaphysical, and has been lately operating with a more profound
notion of semantics, which is independent of both the standard possible-
worlds modelling and the earlier metaphysical "pictures" of the relation
between language and reality. The depth of his concern is revealed
very neatly in his 1977 characterization of direct reference. It is also
manifested in his beautiful diaphilosophical exercise "How to Russell a
Frege-Church,"[2] which continues his work on direct reference.[3]

As I see it, the most profound issue underlying Kaplan's work on
indexical reference is about *mental representation*, namely: whether in
thinking the mind can establish a direct connection with what it thinks,
at least sometimes thinking its objects, so to speak, in *propria persona*,
or whether it must always think its objects through the mediation of conceived or entertained (mentalistic) abstract representations like senses,
concepts, propositions, and their ilk. These entities are conceived to be
typically intersubjective and their mediation consists in that their pres-

---

[1] David Kaplan, *Demonstratives*, this volume, 483. Page references without mention
of bibliographical item are to this volume.

[2] David Kaplan, "How to Russell a Frege-Church," *Journal of Philosophy* 72 (1975):
716–29.

[3] For an elucidation of diaphilosophy, see Hector-Neri Castañeda, *On Philosophical
Method* (Bloomington, Ind.: Noûs Publications, 1980), 14, 19ff, 65, 102ff.

ence to a mind (perhaps also in consciousness) constitutes that mind's thinking of what those mediating entities represent. Of course, this *constitutional mediation* need not be claimed to accompany, much less be grounded in, a *mediated awareness* of the presence of the mediating entities as a means of one's thinking of the represented entities. These mediations are, of course, related to, yet they must be thoroughly distinguished from linguistic mediation. Here *linguistic representation and mediation* are not at issue. We may all agree, at least provisionally, that thinking is symbolic, i.e., carried out (*somehow*) through the production or occurrence of symbolic tokens.

To be sure, Kaplan has not formulated his major topic in precisely those words. For one thing, he has spoken of direct reference, rather than of thinking. Yet the general issue lurks behind his fundamental contention that direct reference occurs without the mediation of Fregean senses. I own that Kaplan has forcefully declared:

> My [David Kaplan's] semantical theory is a theory of word
> meaning, not speaker's meaning. It is based on linguistic
> rules known, explicitly or implicitly, by all competent users
> of the language. (491, footnote 13.)

To the extent that thinking is the tokening of symbols, what the speaker thinks is partially (even sometimes fully) determined by the semantics of the tokened symbols that embody, or constitute, his thinking.

David's notion of reference, because of its assumption of shared rules, may be thought to have a communicational aspect and to shunt private languages. Our concern with thinking has, however, nothing to do with private languages. The private-language issue is certainly the issue whether every system of symbols that is a means of thinking *must* thereby be also a means of communication.[4] Yet we may start off with the assumption that language is not only learned in social interaction, but that it cannot be acquired otherwise,[5] so that all language may fundamentally be a means of communication. On the other hand, we must

---

[4] See Hector-Neri Castañeda, "Private Language Argument," in *The Encyclopedia of Philosophy*, ed. Paul Edwards (New York: Macmillan Company and Free Press, 1967); Saul Kripke, *Wittgenstein on Rules and Private Language* (Cambridge, Mass.: Harvard University Press, 1982); Brian Loar, "Review of *Wittgenstein on Rules and Private Language*," *Noûs* 19 (1985): 273–80; G. P. Baker and P. M. S. Hacker, *Scepticism, Rules and Language* (Oxford: Blackwell, 1984); Paolo Leonardi, "Review of *Scepticism, Rules and Language*," *Noûs* 22 (1988). Of course, see the source of all these discussions, Ludwig Wittgenstein, *Philosophical Investigations* (Oxford: Blackwell, 1953).

[5] This is the most widely held view nowadays, partly due to the influence of Ludwig

also recognize that, in spite of all of that, it is the destiny of each natural language to become, in the possession of a mature speaker, a personal means of thinking. Thus, we must treat the phenomenon of thinking on its own right and the problem it entails, namely: the requisite semantics of a language that functions as a means of thinking.

Of course, crucial constraints permeate a communicational notion of reference that requires that the meaning rules available to, and applied by, hearers in contexts of utterance determine what the speaker is referring to. Yet it clearly is an empirical and contingent matter whether a message or proposition that a speaker thinks and wishes to communicate with her utterance is literally the same as the one that each of her hearers takes her to express. It is indeed an empirical and contingent matter that there are no *Pentecostal Miracles In Reverse*. For Ruth could certainly say, pointing to and looking at David: "He, Paul, lives in Princeton," it being the case that the light and the chemical environment surrounding her and her audience cause each hearer to perceive Ruth's pointing, but subjected to a deflection, and hear the sounds "Paul" she pronounces transformed in his auditory perception into "Charles," "Tyler," "Nathan," etc., respectively, so that one hearer sees her point to, and takes her to be referring to, Charles, another to Tyler, and another to Nathan, etc. To whom did Ruth *actually* refer? Neither the semantic rules nor the pragmatic practice of English can decide. The question seems moot. There is a plurality of references: Ruth's thinking reference (to Paul), and each hearer's thinking reference to his own thought of person.

It is, thus, useful to distinguish from one another:

(i)   the speaker's thinking reference;

(ii)   the speaker's communicational referential intention, i.e., what he intends his hearers to think;

(iii)   each hearer's thinking reference;

(iv)   each hearer's attribution of reference to the speaker; and

(v)   if any, a denotation built into a language or idiolect.

Wittgenstein and his attacks on private language. But this climate has been created by Martin Heidegger, John Dewey, George Herbert Mead, and others. It has its origin in Hegel. Some new clever arguments for a "socialistic" semantics have been propounded by Tyler Burge in "Individualism and the Mental." In *Midwest Studies in Philosophy* 4, ed. P. A. French, T. E. Uehling, Jr., and H. K. Wettstein (Minneapolis: University of Minnesota Press, 1979), 73–121.

Any worthwhile semantic theory of reference must be capable of serving as the foundation for a unified systematic account of *all* the types of reference (i)–(v). Here we limit ourselves, first, to (i) and, second, to indexical reference.

Our task is to examine David Kaplan's Semantic Theory of Direct Indexical Reference from the perspective of thinking reference. Our objective is to enjoy its insights, ascertain to what degree that Semantic Theory illumines thinking indexical reference, and determine what extensions, if any, are necessary to develop it into a comprehensive semantics of thinking, whether indexical or not.

II. Kaplan's Theory of Direct Indexical Reference

1. The Fregean Background

As Kaplan has explained, having been brought up under Frege's semantics he developed his views on direct reference as a drastic revision of that semantics. Now, Frege's semantics is in one respect a very elegant theory of thinking and language, which offers through a thoroughly unified semantics a well-rounded connection of thinking and reality. According to Frege, the very selfsame entity is at once all of the following:

(i)   the *accusative of thinking* (in my terminology), or object, or content, of thought (in other philosophers' terminologies);

(ii) that which constitutes the *cognitive significance* through which acts of thinking and dispositional states of belief can be individuated and distinguished from one another;

(iii) the *meaning* of a complete fact-stating declarative sentence;

(iv) the primary *bearer of truth-values*.

An entity that plays these four roles (i)–(iv) is called by Frege, with a special eye on role (i), a *thought*. In the English-speaking tradition—with a hint of a reduction of thinking to speaking—such an entity has been called a *proposition*.[6] Frege (rightly in my opinion) concentrated on thinking, not on believing.

Frege's semantics provides powerful illumination for a good portion of natural language. To begin with, it applies nicely to mathematical

---

[6] Although G. E. Moore was not a reductionist, his use of the word 'proposition' is perhaps the clearest case in English. See his *Some Main Problems of Philosophy* (London: Allen & Unwin, 1953), lectures given in 1910–1911.

expressions and sentences. But it has a much greater power. It also applies to physical propositions. To illustrate, consider the sentence "The sun shines upon the earth": its meaning is a thought (or proposition) that can be translated into other languages. This proposition is (in my preferred terminology) the accusative of acts of thinking, e.g., the acts of reading the sentence. It is also, among the entities under consideration, the primary possessor of truth. (The sentence itself, or the mental state whose accusative that proposition is, may also be said, but in derivative senses, to be true.) That meaning (= thought or proposition) is what a person cognizes, or merely believes, when he knows, or believes, that the sun shines upon the earth. That person's mental state is different in cognitive content from the state of another person who knows, or believes, say, that the sun illuminates the planet between Venus and Mars. The meaning of the sentence seems to be built into the syntactic and semantic rules of the language. Thus, to think or believe something with that sentence is to think or believe what the sentence means.

To believe something is to be doxastically related to a thought, or a proposition; but it is also to be in a state of mind oriented toward reality and a state in which one takes sides, by positing the truth of the believed proposition, which is thus taken to represent reality. This is Frege's representationalism. And he makes his account of thinking, and of reality, perplexing by postulating one indivisible whole as the reality at which our beliefs and mental acts aim, namely, what he calls *The True*. As has often been remarked, to deal adequately with certain problems of the mind or of semantics, Frege needed a category of *facts*, or, so to speak, *pieces of The True*, which could—whether in a one-one or in a many-one relation—correspond to, and, hence, be represented by the contents of thinking, viz., thoughts or propositions. But we cannot go into this profound issue here.

Frege conceived of The True [The False] as an object all sentences expressing true [false] propositions denote. Thus, complete sentences have for him a two-dimensional semantic structure: on the one hand they possess a meaning or sense (= proposition), on the other hand they denote an object, The True, or The False, as the case may be. This distinction was an extension of his Sense/Referent distinction for singular terms. Consider the sentence "Alonzo Church is the philosophical logician who first publicized Fregean doctrines in the English-speaking world." Its two singular terms 'Alonzo Church' and 'the philosophical logician who first publicized Fregean doctrines in the English-speaking world' differ semantically in expressing different *(first) individual senses* but semantically agree in denoting the same *(primary) referent*, namely, a massive infinitely-propertied chunk in the world. The individual senses *mediate* our thinking of referents, but they can become referents of the same terms in sentences attributing mental states to someone. Thus, in 'David believed that Carnap loved the inventor of the lambda calculus' the terms 'Carnap' and 'the inventor of the lambda calculus' denote their (first) senses. Individual senses are something like properties and they also determine the kind of individual a referent is. "Sense determines reference," he said. Thus, individual senses have a sort of ontic mediation as well as a semantic mediation between language and reference. Many questions arise here, but this is no place to pose them.[7]

What matters for us here is this: That Fregean background is the one Kaplan reacts to, and with good reason as we shall see. The problem of semantic, rather than the one of psychological mediation, concerns him.

2. Basic Characterization of Kaplan's Theory of Direct Reference

Enter indicators: personal pronouns, demonstratives, and their likes. Palpably, a sentence containing one or more of them, e.g., 'I am not the Editor of *Soul*', does not express as a part of the language any truth or falsehood, which both is the meaning of the sentence and must be learned to learn the meaning of the sentence.[8] To account for this phenomenon

---

[7] The preceding summary of Frege's views is standard, and I will not pause to defend it. Even if it is not wholly accurate it does provide a useful foil for our discussion of Kaplan's Theory of Direct Reference for indicators. There is one passage in Frege's "The Thought: A Logical Inquiry," which suggests that he already included piecemeal external targets of thinking in such a way that his ontology is a form of Kantian critical realism. The True and The False would, thus, properly have the indivisibility of Kant's noumenon. The passage was called to my attention by Alberto Coffa. It is this:

'Facts, facts, facts' cries the scientist if he wants to emphasize the necessity of a firm foundation for science. What is a fact? *A fact is a thought that is true.* ... the truth of a thought is timeless.

E. D. Klemke, ed., *Essays on Frege*, (Urbana, Ill.: University of Illinois Press, 1968), "The Thought" (translated by A. M. and M. Quinton), 531.

[8] For this reason perhaps *a* meaning of a declarative sentence is better considered to be a range of (classic, non-Kaplanian) propositions. On this proposal he who knows a meaning of a sentence has a doxastic relationship to a subset of the range constitutive of the meaning in question. A speaker who makes an assertion with a sentence S on a meaning M of S simply chooses one proposition in the subrange of M known to him. See Hector-Neri Castañeda, *Thinking and Doing* (Dordrecht: Reidel, 1975), 35ff.

David Kaplan distinguishes between (a) and (b):

(a)   The *character* of an expression or sentence of a language, which is essentially the expression's or sentence's grammatical meaning, i.e., what a person learns when she learns what the expression or sentence means;

(b)   the *content* which an expression or sentence, given its character, acquires on a *context* of use.

In the case of sentences, Kaplan calls sentential content *propositions*.

Because of (a)–(b) Kaplan's Theory of Direct Reference for indicators (and perhaps for proper names) has a three-tier structure: (i) the *language system*, to which meanings and characters belong; (ii) the *contexts of uses*, through which referents are assigned to expressions, and (iii) the *circumstances of evaluation* at which truth-values are allocated to sentential referents.

With these distinctions in hand, Kaplan has broken Frege's unitary thought, but he continues to maintain some of the Fregean equations:

K-S-1. The grammatical meaning of an expression is still equated with cognitive significance—this is the expression's character.

K-S-2. The possessor of truth-value is still equated with the objects of thought—this is content.

Evidently, there may very well be other theories that, more drastically and presumably in view of *additional* data, break the Kaplanian equations. (Here lie other theoretical forks that open up diaphilosophical projects.)

Other authors have divorced the grammatical meaning of expressions from the expressions' referents, and sentence meanings from the truth-value bearers represented by sentences.[9] But the distinction between character, which combines roles (ii) and (iii) of classical propositions,

---

[9]See, for instance, P. F. Strawson, *Introduction to Logical Theory* (London: Methuen and Company; New York: John Wiley & Sons, 1952); Richard Cartwright, "Propositions," in *Analytic Philosophy*, ed. R. J. Butler (Oxford: Blackwell; New York: Barnes & Noble, 1962). I followed them in "Indicators and Quasi-Indicators," *American Philosophical Quarterly* 4 (1967): 85–100. I introduced there indexical propositions. For quasi-indexical propositions, which depict indexical propositions, see "The [Robert M.] Adams-Castañeda Correspondence," in *Agent, Language, and the Structure of the World*, ed. James E. Tomberlin (Indianapolis: Hackett Publishing Company, 1983). See also Patrick Grim, "Against Omniscience: The Case from Essential Indexicals," *Noûs* 19 (1985): 151–80, and

and content, which combines roles (i) and (iv), is, as far as I know, original with Kaplan. This distinction is a background for his Theory of Direct Indexical Reference.

Kaplan explains the characters of indicators as consisting of their being assigned referents in contexts of use and in their being *directly referential*. This claim that indicators are directly referential involves several important tenets, among which are:

K-DR.1. The referent of an indicator occurring in a sentence S is fixed for all circumstances in which, given a context of use of S, the content of S is evaluated. (493, 506, etc.)

K-DR.2. The referent of an indicator occurring in a sentence S is a constituent of the proposition S expresses in a context of use. Such sentential contents Kaplan calls *singular propositions*. (493ff) We shall refer to them as *Kaplanian* or *Russellian* (singular) propositions.

K-DR.3. The descriptive meaning of a directly referential term t occurring in a sentence S is *not* a component of the propositional content of S: the component part of the content of S, corresponding to t, is simply the referent of t. (497)

K-DR.4. *"Ignorance of the referent does not defeat the directly referential character of indexicals."* (536)

In *Demonstratives* Kaplan seems to maintain the Fregean sense/reference scheme for nonindexical definite descriptions. A definite description containing no indicators denotes its referent through its sense. The

---

also his "Logic and the Limits of Knowledge and Truth," *Noûs* 22 (1988): 341–67. Propositional guises and PROPOSITIONS (or Superpropositions) were introduced in Hector-Neri Castañeda "Perception, Belief, and the Structure of Physical Objects and Consciousness," *Synthese* 35 (1977): 285–351. A very intriguing reaction to the phenomenon of indexicality has been the proposal to take the accusatives of believing (and presumably of thinking) to be, not Fregean-Moorean propositions, but attributes. This has been proposed in David Lewis, "Attitudes *De Dicto* and *De Se*," *Philosophical Review* 88 (1979): 513–43, and by Roderick M. Chisholm, "Review of *Thinking and Doing*," *Noûs* 12 (1979): 385–86, and later developed into a general theory of reference and belief in *The First Person* (Minneapolis: University of Minnesota Press, 1981). A useful discussion of Lewis's view appears in James E. Tomberlin, "Review of David Lewis's *On the Plurality of Worlds*," *Noûs* 23 (forthcoming). Both views are examined in Hector-Neri Castañeda, "Self-Consciousness, Demonstrative Reference, and the Self-Ascription View of Believing," in *Philosophical Perspectives I, Metaphysics*, ed. James E. Tomberlin (Atascadero, Calif.: Ridgeview, 1987) 405–59.

Fregean primary referent of a term being an ordinary massive individual of the world, having infinitely many properties, existing in physical space and time. Indicators, on the other hand, according to Kaplan, refer directly to individuals. Thus, a sentence containing indicators denotes a Russellian singular proposition containing not concepts (senses) of individuals, but *the whole individuals themselves*. This ontological thesis is the core of David Kaplan's Direct Reference View. Thus, it seems that Kaplan also holds:

K-DR.5. The referents of indicators are Frege's primary referents.

As we shall see, K-DR.5 is a most difficult thesis in the Theory of Direct Reference. Not only is it crying out for an elucidation of what an individual is, but it also needs an account of the role the Fregean primary referents play in thinking.

To appreciate the contrast between direct reference (ascribed to indicators and perhaps to proper names) with indirect reference (ascribed to indicator-free definite descriptions), the following crudest picture may be of some help:

The Harpooning Model

A singular referring term in a language L is like a harpooning gun with an aiming device: its character is the aiming device; in the case of indicators the aiming device merely guides the harpoon by indicating the direction in which the harpoon is to be the hurled, but that direction is in no way part and parcel of the harpooned object (if any); in the case of nonindexical terms the aiming device reveals an image of the object to be harpooned and one aims to harpoon the object through piercing the image, which in some respects is like the harpooned object. The content is the object in the former, indexical case, and the image in the other.

Kaplan adds another thesis to his theory:

K-F-1. Characters are functions that map contexts into contents.

This tenet is one among important theses useful in the construction of set-theoretical models suitable for a formal logic of demonstratives. For our purposes here, pertaining to the thinking and making of indexical reference, K-F-1 seems dispensable. However, if we take the 'are' of K-F-1 as identity, then there is a tension between K-F-1 and and K-S-1. For the time being we abstain from K-F-1, and propose that *interpretative functions* like the ones described by K-F-1, which certainly play roles in our thinking and communicational uses of language, must be differentiated both from characters as grammatical meanings and from characters as cognitive (thinkable) content. We discuss the tension between K-F-1 and K-S-1 in the appendix to this essay.

III. Objects, Propositions, and our Thinking of them: Indexical Reference in Perception and Intention

1. Thinking Reference and Semantic Reference

Our purpose is to educate ourselves by reflecting on Kaplan's Direct Reference View with respect to the phenomenon of thinking. Let's start by meditating on tenet K-DR.1. According to it, the referent of a token Oi of a used indicator i is determined by both the meaning (= the cognitive significance) of i and the context of use of Oi. Thus, the actual use of an indicator is irrelevant. Provided that the speaker speaks about some topic or other, the semantic assignment holds. For instance, consider context:

c: John Perry, with no awareness of self, fully absorbed in watching a bird on his lawn, mumbles (thinking) out loud something about birds eating worms.

The meaning of the first-person pronoun (hereafter 'I' for convenience) suffices to assign to Perry's merely *potential* uses of 'I' in *c* a Fregean primary referent, namely: *an* organic massive chunk in the world we think to be, piecewise, the *same* as our beloved author of "The Problem of the Essential Indexical."[10] The reference belongs to 'I', or, rather, to the pair ⟨'I', *c*⟩, regardless of what Perry actually says or thinks.

This bypassing of actual speech acts and linking the referent of an indicator to both the meaning of the indicator and some elements of the speech context seems to shed light on certain ontological and semantic issues. In particular, certain indexical subjunctive statements can be understood in terms of such pairings. For instance, in our current example Perry is undergoing what Sartre used to call unreflective consciousness; yet we may agree that:

---

[10] J. Perry, "The Problem of the Essential Indexical," *Noûs* 13 (1979): 3–21.

(1)   *Had* John Perry at one point in his bird-watching been sud-
       denly inflicted with a sharp bite by a bird, he would have
       become aware of *himself*.

In (1) the locution 'himself' depicts first-person reference, a potential
use of 'I' rather than an actual one. The truth of (1) requires a truth-
making feature in Perry's speech context *c*, and this is the assignment of
a referent to the pronoun 'I' in *c*. This assignment is there in *c* whether
Perry actually thinks of himself or not. Thus, the crucial difference between unreflective and reflective thinking (consciousness) need not, it
seems, require a permanent *I* lurking somewhere behind Perry's statements, which is not the object of reference in unreflective thinking, but
becomes such an object when reflective consciousness inserts itself in
the causal order. The difference may, it seems, be said to consist of the
difference between actual and potential uses of the first-person devices;
but in both cases, a semantic function grounds subjunctive conditionals
about self-consciousness, namely, the function:

(2)   Meaning of 'I' $(c) = x$

But what is x here? Well, Perry himself: he is the speaker in context
c, and the meaning of 'I' is given by this rule:

K-I. In any statement in which it occurs, I designates the speaker of
the statement.

This is an excellent rule for interpreting tokens of sentences with I: a
good rule for the hearer's use of language. K-I gives, therefore, part
of the meaning of the first-person pronoun. However, there appears to
be more to the meaning of I: Rule K-I does not seem to capture the
speaker's use of language. Yet language must be spoken before it is
heard and interpreted. Just two small points.[11] On occasion speaker-
thinkers are caused to call something "A" when confronting an *A* item.
Patently, thinkers think of themselves in the first-person way without
confronting their statements. Further, were Perry to adopt a hearer's
point of view with respect to his own statements, he will not have fully

---

[11] For more discussion on the contrast between speaker's and hearer's rules and the
rule K-I see the exchange between John Perry's "Castañeda on *He* and *I*" and
Hector-Neri Castañeda's "Reply to John Perry: Meaning, Belief, and Reference,"
both in Tomberlin 1983, mentioned above. For language-entry rules see Wilfrid
Sellars, "Some Reflections on Language Games," *Philosophy of Science* 21 (1954):
204–28.

carried out his interpretation of the *I*-statement he is confronting, unless he transcends his identifying John Perry as the person who used *I* and proceeds to think believingly *I am that John Perry* or *I am the one who made that I-statement*. Hence, even from the hearer's perspective, in hermeneutic confrontation with his own statements containing *I* a speaker must introduce an *I*, not as the maker of a statement, but rather as the subject of that hermeneutic confrontation: the speaker must even then think of himself as *himself*. But what is this *himself* that Perry will have to equate with the maker of an I-statement?[12] What is it for Perry to think of *himself*?

Consider what happens later on when Perry's bird-watching comes to a sudden end: a big nasty ant bites him on his nose and he exclaims:

(3)   Damned @#% !x+* ant! But *I* killed you!

In thinking (3) Perry moves up to reflective consciousness. To be sure, in a most important sense, in thinking (3) Perry thinks of Perry himself. Yet he may fail to know that he is Perry, let alone John Perry and all his wonderful biography. It is no great effort of fantasy to imagine that Perry had been so absorbed in bird-watching and was so stunned

---

[12] At this juncture we need the mass of *results* obtained by the studies in the phenomenology of first-person reference, i.e., data that can help us compare and assess theories about indexical reference. The data include both the making of indexical reference and the attributing of indexical reference, not only first-person reference to others through quasi-indexical mechanisms. The first-person quasi-indicator was first studied in Hector-Neri Castañeda, " 'He': A Study in the Logic of Self-Consciousness," *Ratio* 8 (1966): 130–57; then came "Indicators and Quasi-Indicators." The literature on indexicality has grown enormously. *Some* important studies containing crucial data are: John Perry's papers mentioned above and "Frege on Demonstratives," *Philosophical Review* 86 (1977): 464–97; Lynne Rudder Baker, "On Making and Attributing Demonstrative Reference," *Synthese* 49 (1981): 245–73; the letter by Robert M. Adams and the papers by Patrick Grim mentioned in footnote 9 above; Eddy M. Zemach, "*De Se* and Descartes: A New Semantics for Indexicals," *Noûs* 19 (1985): 181–204. Esa Saarinen has provided a useful discussion and comparison of different work on indexical reference in "Castañeda's Philosophy of Language," in *Profiles* 6: *Hector-Neri Castañeda*, ed. James E. Tomberlin, (Dordrecht: Reidel, 1986). A critique of the thesis that first-person is irreducible appears in Stephen Boër and William Lycan in their "Who, Me?" *Philosophical Review* 89 (1980): 427–66. This critique has been mollified in their book *Knowing Who* (Cambridge, Mass.: MIT Press, 1986). To their original critique a response is included in Hector-Neri Castañeda, "Philosophical Refutations" in *Principles of Philosophical Reasoning*, ed. James H. Fetzer (Totowa, N.J.: Rowman and Allanheld, 1984); and to the mollified critique James Tomberlin responds in "Semantics, Psychological Attitudes, and Conceptual Role," *Philosophical Studies* 53 (1988): 205–26.

by the unexpected ant's attack, that during the whole proceedings he had lost all sense of who he was: he was temporarily wholly amnesiac. Thus, in thinking (3) Perry merely thought of *himself, not* of Perry himself. While Perry, Perry himself, the whole of Perry, is an *external* hit or target of the thinker of (3); *himself*, what he calls "I (me)" is an *internal* content or aimed-at target of his thinking (3). The word 'target' for the whole of Perry is not appropriate, for it suggests that he is being aimed at, and clearly for Perry to aim at the whole of Perry he has to have an idea of what he is attempting to hit, and this is what has been ruled out by his temporary ignorance of who he is. Thus, I propose to contrast *a semantic hit* with *an internal content* of a thinking episode. (This contrast corresponds to one of the varied contrasts put forward in the distinction between *de re* and *de dicto* occurrences of terms in psychological sentences.[13])

Our pressing question continues to be: What is it for Perry to think of *himself*, i.e., of himself qua himself? That is: what is the internal content of his thinking in the first-person way, e.g., (3) above?

Of course, we are concerned with the *general question*

(Q)   What are the internal contents of indexical thinking?

Kaplan answers (Q) by means of thesis K-S-1: the cognitive content of an episode of indexical thinking is the grammatical (= syntactico-semantic) meaning of a sentence containing indicators. We must divide this claim into two parts:

K-S-1.A. The (selected) grammatical meaning of an indexical sentence *S* is *part* of the cognitive (internal) content of a piece of thinking embodied in a tokening of *S*.

K-S-1.B. In the case of an *indexical* sentence *S* the grammatical meanings of the indicators in *S* constitute the *whole indexical* cognitive (internal) content of episodes of *thinking* embodied in tokenings of *S*.

The bracketed word 'selected' is intended to single out one relevant meaning out of the several meanings *S* may have if *S* is ambiguous.

Thesis K-S-1.A is a fundamental truth about all sentences, whether they contain indicators or not. It is an analytic truth about languages

---

[13] A detailed discussion of the *de re/de dicto* distinctions and their alleged exhaustiveness and nonoverlappingness appears in Hector-Neri Castañeda, "Reference, Reality, and Perceptual Fields," Presidential Address in *Proceedings and Addresses of the American Philosophical Association* 53 (1980): 763–823.

that function as means of thinking. So functioning requires that thinking reference be anchored to semantic denotation. Given that a tokening of a sentence S counts as a thinking episode, the semantical denotations, or the semantic schemas of denotation, built into S should be *necessary* for the tokener's thinking reference through S to obtain. This much ought not to be controversial. The problem is what to count as grammatical meaning. Further clarification of grammatical meaning is furnished in the appendix, where I argue that the grammatical meanings of indicators, in the sense that they conform to K-S-1.A, cannot be Kaplan's characters conceived as functions mapping contexts into *external semantic hits* of thinking because they cannot be aimed-at (internal) targets.

The issue underlying thesis K-S-1.B has to do with the connections between cognitive content and external hits of thinking. Kaplan's thesis K-DR.3 leaves the cognitive content (= grammatical meaning) of indicators out of the external semantic hits. But the issue also includes whether in experience we need some internal truths, not only the truths of the external hits that Kaplan's K-DR.2 posits exclusively. We will dwell on this issue.

2. Indexical Thinking and the Referential Harpooning of the Unknown

According to tenet K-DR.4, a directly referential term in an uttered sentence S may harpoon an object, even if the speaker of S does not know the object. On page 536 Kaplan comments on K-DR.4 as follows:

> From this it follows that a special form of knowledge of an object is neither required nor presupposed in order that a person may entertain as object of thought a singular proposition involving that object.

And he illustrates this with this intriguing example on page 536:

> A kidnapped heiress, locked in the trunk of a car, knowing neither the time nor where she is, may think 'It is quiet here now' and the indexicals will remain directly referential.

According to the Direct Reference Theory the heiress has got hold directly of the time and the place by using the indicators "now" and "here," respectively. The meanings of the words 'now' and 'here' may have, presumably, guided her in her thinking references, but in the context of her utterance, willy-nilly she simply harpoons a time and a place themselves, and she also harpoons a *singular* Russellian proposition which, on the one hand, does contain the very time and the very place about which she doesn't know anything, and, on the other hand, is wholly beyond her ken because it does not even contain in any way those meanings through which, knowingly, she hurls her referential harpoons successfully into the unknown beyond.

Obviously, the situation is very much like Perry's thinking of himself *as* himself in thinking (3) above. The heiress thinks of a time *as now*, and of a place *as here*. The semantic-thinking force of this 'as' needs elucidation. The heiress, blandly and in full ignorance, asserts:

(4)   It is quiet here now.

Here we have these functions operating:

(5)   the meaning of 'now' (heiress's speech context) = time t; the
       meaning of 'here' (heiress's speech context) = place p.

The heiress by simply being in that speech situation cannot but be in the midst of a harpooning of the unknown time t and the unknown place p.

Thus, her thinking episode does hit *externally* a Russellian proposition of the form:

(4.R) Quiet(p, t).

But what does she think, internally, which she takes to be true and which her so taking it she proclaims by asserting (4)? In what sense can the heiress think (4.R)?

Before tackling the question of internal content, it is of the utmost urgency to acknowledge both a strength and a limitation of the Theory of Direct Indexical Reference. Both are manifested by my Perry example and by Kaplan's heiress illustration.

The strength includes the feature noted above for the contrary-to-fact conditional (1). It is indeed a fundamental property of the indicators 'I', 'here' and 'now' that they possess a *semantic-ontic certainty*: their correct indexical *uses* succeed always in harpooning a real thinker, a real place, a real time in the causal order of the world. We have here the ground for true subjunctive conditionals, like (1) above, about *now* times and *here* places.

Moreover, as Descartes's *cogito* reflection has shown (and Augustin knew) there is in the case of (at least certain uses of) the first-person pronoun a *noumenal certainty*. Here 'noumenal' is used in Kant's sense of a transcendent reality that underlies and is pointed to by all experiences. This certainty is the very little rock that radical skepticism leaves standing. Descartes seems to have glimpsed that *now* has a similar property. To me it seems that all of those indexical mechanisms have a noumenal certainty. That is why I have moved from Kant's transcendental prefix *I think* to the extended transcendental prefix *I think here now that*.[14]

This twofold certainty of the indicators 'I', 'now', and 'here' is nicely accounted for by Kaplan's Theory of Direct Reference. Yet here lies a limitation as well. The twofold certainty permits the investigator of indexical reference to focus exclusively on the property of securely harpooning external semantic hits. But by so focussing one can easily take that external role of some indicators as the only role of indexical reference, leaving out of account the other, internal experiential roles of all types of indexical reference. As has been hinted at in the exegesis of the Perry and heiress examples, direct indexical harpooning is mysterious if it is blind, i.e., if what is harpooned does not connect intimately with the internal, cognitive content of indexical thinking. All of this can be better appreciated by considering an enlarged set of data.

Demonstrative reference of the *this* type lacks the two levels of certainty discussed above. The indicators 'this' and 'that' (and their personal counterparts 'she' and 'he') can err not only metaphysically, as all radical skeptics of sense-perception have argued; it can also err in particular cases. This immediately complicates and expands our data in two important dimensions:

(i)   An unreflective fact intrudes: some of our perceptions can be nonveridical;

(ii)   A most important reflective fact demands account: We may doubt, perhaps incorrectly, our current perceptions.

Let us consider perceptual indexical reference.

3. Perceptual Demonstratives

We are, recall, examining Kaplan's Theory of Direct Reference as an account of, or basis for an account of, thinking reference. To emphasize the centrality of thinking reference let's start from the perspective of a hearer. (Nevertheless, we must not forget that, as remarked at the

---

[14] See Hector-Neri Castañeda, "Metaphysical Internalism, Selves, and the Holistic Indivisible Noumenon," *Midwest Studies in Philosophy* 12 (1988): 129–44.

beginning of this essay, even in dialogue the first-person point of view is unavoidable. Language must be spoken. Even when it is heard it has to be interpreted: a *speaker* has to make sense of what he/she hears.)

3.1 Joseph Calmog's Drowning-Man Adventure

One cloudy morning, hiking near some quarries, Joseph Calmog hears repeatedly the noises "I am drowning." The hearer's point of view seems applicable. The semantical rule K-I above tells Joseph that each use of 'I' denotes its user. Upon hearing the quoted sentence Joseph proceeds to search for the source of the noise. Guided by the noises he hears, or thinks he hears, Joseph comes to what he takes to be a large whole on the ground, full of water, surrounded by a thick mist; he sees something like a man that looks as if he were drowning. Within this background we must distinguish several cases.

(A) Joseph exclaims, thinking out loud, pointing to the vague silhouette behind the mist, expressing his perceptual judgment:

(11)   *That* is a man drowning!

There is in fact a man drowning and Joseph is pointing to him.

(B) Joseph has the same perceptual experience as in case (A), and declares out loud the self-identical perceptual judgment:

(11)   *That* is a man drowning!

This time, however, there is no drowning man; Joseph is hallucinating.

(C) Joseph has exactly the same perceptual field as in case (A), but now he is suspicious about the veridicality of his perceptions, thus, his perceptual judgment is a skeptical one:

(12)   *That* appears to be a drowning man.

In fact Joseph is mistaken about his skepticism. There is in fact a drowning man that he is seeing.

(D) As in case (C), Joseph judges skeptically:

(12)   *That* appears to be [looks like] a drowning man.

This time he is right. He is hallucinating.

The following observations constitute absolutely binding data for any theory of indexical reference and also for any theory of perception:

(I) The indicator *that* has exactly the same meaning in the sentences (11) and (12).

(II) The *thinking referent* of '*that*' is in each assertion the same: an internal perceptual content present to the speaker in his visual field at the time under consideration.

(III) Given that sentences (11) and (12) are used as means of thinking, the tokens of the word '*that*', not only have the same grammatical meaning, but pick out in the context of speech a *strict semantico-pragmatic denotatum* that must be the same as Joseph's thinking referent.

(IV) In cases (A) and (C) there is a Kaplanian referent (= Fregean first-referent) beyond the speaking perceiver's ken. On the Direct Reference Theory this referent is directly harpooned, not so much by the speaker's tokening of '*that*', but, rather, by both his uttering any sentence whatever, including sentence (11), in the context of utterance and the mere abstract pairing of his possible use of '*that*' with a pointing to the Kaplanian referent over and beyond the misty silhouette he sees.

(V) In cases (B) and (D) there is *no* Kaplanian-Fregean referent. This establishes that the strict semantico-pragmatic denotatum of '*that*' in (11) and (12) is not the Kaplanian-Fregean, infinitely propertied existing, first-referent.

(VI) In all four cases the speaker-perceiver expresses a proposition, i.e., a truth-valued content, that commands his assent. It lies *internally* within his perceptual field. He puts it forth noncommittally in sentence (12); but in sentence (11) he formulates that proposition endorsing it as something he believes.

(VII) The nature of the perceiver's perceptual judgment depends both on what he finds in his perceptual field and on the doxastic repertory he marshals. This is clearly evidenced in the twofold contrast between (A)–(B) and (C)–(D).

In cases (A) and (B) the perceiver marshals the same set of beliefs and mobilizes them in exactly the same way. The outcome of that doxastic mobilization is a coming to endorse, or adopt, an existential belief: a positing of a Fregean first-referent, beyond the perceptual experience, in physical space-time and immersed in the causal order of the world. Since this positing is the normal perceptual reaction of our being open to the world, we shall call it the *default doxastic attitude*. The perceiver reveals such a doxastic activity and outcome by means of the existential form of predication, '*is*', he applies to what he calls (a visual) *that*. The difference between cases (A) and (B), between veridical perception and hallucination, cuts the perceiver's doxastic attitude orthogonally: it has to do with the *actual* existence of the Fregean first-referents *beyond* the perceptual field: it is not up to his doxastic powers, but up to nature to determine what really happens.

In contradistinction, in cases (C) and (D) the perceiver marshals different beliefs and ends up by *withholding* judgment about the existence of a Fregean-Kaplanian referent beyond his perceptual field. He cancels the default doxastic attitude and adopts a *neutral posture*, which need not be fully skeptical. He expresses this doxastic neutral posture by applying a different form of predication, '*appears to be [looks like]*', to what in his visual field he identifies demonstratively. Again, as in the subcontrast between (A) and (B), the *actuality contrast* between cases (C) and (D) lies perpendicular to the *doxastic contrast* between (A)–(B) and (C)–(D).

Yet neither the doxastic contrast nor the actuality contrast has anything to do with the referential roles of Joseph Calmog's uses of the demonstrative '*that*' in his perceptual *thinking*. These roles are in fact presupposed by the two contrasts. There is a logical, as well as a psychological, priority in there existing a visual field with certain contents for the perceiver to adopt the default doxastic attitude or the neutral posture. Thus, the appropriate doxastic attitude is naturally signaled by means of a copula (existential *is*, withholding *appears* [*looks*]) applied to an (already) *constituted* subject of predication, picked out and individuated demonstratively as a *that*.

Patently, *the semantics of a language functioning as a means of thinking must itself be neutral with respect to the perceiver's doxastic attitude and posture.*

(VIII) In brief, then, the roles of the Kaplanian-Fregean first-referent, assigned to Joseph's token of '*that*', and the roles of the Russellian-Kaplanian proposition, assigned to Joseph's tokens of sentences (11) and (12), involving such a referent, are neither semantically nor thinkingly referential: they do not pertain to the demonstrative items as such. Those entities enter Joseph's perceptual experience doxastically, through his doxastic attitude, and are posited, or not, through the appropriate form of predication.

We can see that doxastics presupposes semantics, and outpours it. Thus, the standard semantic theories of reference that deal exclusively with the successful default doxastic attitude may be called *doxastic theories* of reference. Such theories restrict the domain of belief unduly by bringing down doxastics to the limits of semantics.

Nota bene 1. During the discussion that followed the presentation of the above at the Kaplan Conference, Rogers Albritton, correctly, pointed out that in case (A), when Joseph's perception is veridical, there is a sense in which he is referring to a real person (which looks like an infinitely-propertied Fregean-Kaplanian referent), and, furthermore, such a referent is the same as what Joseph thinkingly refers to as *"that."* These two points seem to me to be absolutely crucial; the added parenthetical point is not so clear: it depends on one's account of the Fregean first-referents. The sense in which I refer to the external referent is precisely the sense in which I *believe* that there is a physical entity, a person, who is *the same* as what I find in my visual field. Thus, in cases (A) and (B) there is a *doxastic referent* posited within the perceptual judgment, *not* so much through the demonstrative reference carried by the tokening of '*that*', but through the *existential predication* expressed by the copula '*is*'. This mechanism of doxastic reference can be appreciated only if we complicate the data and move away from the successful *default* thinking, which veridically manifests belief, as in case (A). Yet to account for thinking we need a semantics and pragmatics of the means of thinking, regardless of the doxastic attitude the thinking expresses and regardless of the success of that attitude. The sameness involved, which obtains in cases (A) and (C), and is believed to obtain in cases (A) and (B), needs a protracted discussion we cannot carry out here. Nevertheless, we must at least record the following Albritonian:

Perception-theoretical Desideratum. In the case of veridical perception the perceptual individual apprehended as a *that* or a *this* **must** be the same as the physical entity posited in the perceptual judgment of the *is*-type.

Naturally, this desideratum allows of a constrictive as well as of a liberal interpretation. We can interpret the sameness demanded by veridical perception to be strict identity, or, more liberally, we may allow it to be a weaker form of sameness, e.g., one analogous to so-called theoretical identity. In fact, in Guise Theory the sameness in question is simply the general predicational sameness called *consubstantiation*.[15]

---

[15] For a large interdisciplinary collection of data on perception and a Guise-theoretical view of perception see Hector-Neri Castañeda, "Perception, Belief, and the Structure of Physical Objects and Consciousness," *Synthese* 35 (1977): 285–351. This paper abridges a much longer study published in the last two chapters of *Sprache und Erfahrung*, trans. Helmut Pape (Frankfurt: Suhrkamp, 1982).

4. Deliberation, Intentional Action, and Indexical Reference

Let's continue the examination of the above perceptual situations (A)–(D). Patently, the perceptual situation that obtains leads to action. Which action the agent performs depends on the sort of person he is. He may be generally benevolent, or he may now, exceptionally, feel benevolent, or he may be a sadist, etc. Thus, he may be deeply concerned with saving the man he believes to be drowning—or he may decide to enjoy the spectacle of a man drowning. In any case, the agent in the story will proceed from his perceptual beliefs to a course of action. He may act quickly in a type of reflex action, but he may perform his action of attempting to save the man intentionally. He may even engage in deliberation, finding himself bound by conflictive obligations: e.g., the moral obligation to stop a man's suffering, and, giving that he cannot swim, the moral obligation to maintain himself alive for the benefit of his family and of the institutions to which he belongs. Furthermore, he may deliberate about the appropriate means to try to rescue the drowning man he has posited.

Let's extend cases (A) and (B) above to include the agent's deliberation. This requires that Joseph takes his indexical judgment (11) as a *true* premise, *without* engaging in the operations, required by the Direct Reference Theory, of: (i) assigning a referent to his token of 'that' and (ii) testing the resulting Russellian-Kaplanian proposition for truth. We may accept that his *is*-perceptual judgment (11) postulates the existence (or subsistence) of such a proposition, and indeed that his judging (11) posits this proposition as true. Yet Joseph, as agent, will not try to locate that proposition and examine it for truth. We may further agree that the truth of that proposition somehow guides him from the unknown beyond. But the singular proposition that mobilizes his powers of deliberation and action is the indexical truth (11) itself wholly within his grasp.

More generally, when an agent acts intentionally upon an object, she needs to locate in her perceptual experience, through thinking indexical (i.e., experiential) references, the items she is to act upon. To highlight this consider:

4.1 The Quine Award to be Given to Sellars in the Chisholm Auditorium

(13)   The Plantinga-Grunbaum Society for the Philosophy of Mind
has unanimously approved that its President give Wilfrid

> Sellars a special band with an appropriate golden inscription
> and a diploma, both representing the Willard V. O. Quine
> Award for Philosophical Accomplishment. The ceremony is
> to take place at the Roderick Chisholm Auditorium of Brown
> University on 12 May 1988.

This is a perfectly straightforward situation. Let us for convenience assume that proper names are devices available to us to think Fregean-Kaplanian referents, and that sentence (13) expresses a Kaplanian- Russellian singular proposition. (This is actually questionable.[16]) The point here is that *if* we had access to Kaplanian-Russellian singular propositions, they are alone, by themselves, of little value for intentional action. In the situation under consideration, for somebody to be in a position to attempt to act intentionally, it is necessary that he/she moves from the Russellian singular proposition (13) to the *indexical proposition*:

(13∗) *I* ought to give *this* man *this* band and *this* diploma *here* in *this* auditorium *today* right *now*.

To begin with, note the ineliminable, essential first-person reference. The massive individual behind the first-person reference must be taken in, doxastically, through the ineliminable first-person. Next, when ought I to give the award? On some date, of course. But this is not enough for me to act; it is necessary only to the effect that I believing that *today* is the date in question. I mark in the appropriate box on a calendar: "Give Sellars the Quine Award." But when must I act? *Now*, when I believe that today is the day of the ceremony, and now the time in question. To whom ought I to give the award? To Sellars, to be sure—but I can act only if I can identity Sellars as *this man here* or *that man over there*. And I must further think that *these things* in *my* hand are the diploma and the band, or that *this* is the band and *that* is the diploma. (We comment on the status of these identifications below in section 5.) The fundamental episodes of volitional thinking have as contents items of the form, *I to A here now*, where the action variable '*A*' may contain a good number of indexical references.[17]

---

[16] See Saul Kripke, "A Puzzle About Belief," in *Meaning and Use*, ed. A. Margalit (Dordrecht: Reidel, 1979), and Hector-Neri Castañeda, "The Semantics and the Causal Roles of Proper Names," *Philosophy and Phenomenological Research* 46 (1985): 91–113. This paper is part of a paper with the same title that appears in Hector-Neri Castañeda, *Thinking, Language, and Experience* (Minneapolis: University of Minnesota Press, 1988).

[17] For the fully indexical content of volitional thinking see Hector-Neri Castañeda,

Persons, objects, places, and times involved in an agent's obligations enter such obligations through specially deontically relevant properties and relations they possess. One ought to pay debts to creditors, return objects to lenders, help people in distress, etc. In general, the reasons for or grounds of deontic modalities are universalizable. Hence, Russellian-Kaplanian propositions are irrelevant for the *creation* of obligations, duties, interdictions, and prohibitions. Good old internal Fregean propositions and internal Fregean-like practitions (that is, the peculiar internal contents of practical thinking[18]) with full descriptive specification of the relevant properties and relations, seem, not merely to suffice, but to be required by the universalizability underlying deontic status. Now, for the *execution* of obligations, or the violation of prohibitions, we need indexical truths, which, as was illustrated above, identify the persons, objects, places, and times, descriptively conceived as noted, with items *presented* in an appropriate experience. Thus, here again the Russellian-Kaplanian propositions are not merely not needed, but if available must be shunted by the agent in favor of some internal indexical truths. Furthermore, the actual truth of the believed indexical identifications is not required for acting intentionally: it suffices to believe them. Thus, as in the cases (B) and (C) of Joseph Calmog's Drowning-Man Adventure, there may be no true Russellian-Kaplanian proposition underlying (13*). Russellian-Kaplanian propositions just do not seem to have a role to play in practical thinking, practical reasoning, or intentional action.

To hammer this in, let us observe that an agent who recognizes his conflicts of duties and deliberates to find out what to do may be amnesiac. He may, thus, have only his indexical references and a few beliefs about the corner of the world he is at and about some of his obligations. Yet he has all he needs to act deliberately and intentionally. He does not have to search for the Kaplanian propositions having as constituent the unknown Fregean first-referent his uses of 'I' harpoon. Even if he could think of it, he would still have to equate it with *himself* for him to be able to act intentionally. This is precisely the case, in John Perry's

---

Thinking and Doing (Dordrecht: Reidel, 1975), ch. 10, section 3, and "Conditional Intentions, Intentional Action, and Aristotelian Practical Syllogisms," *Erkenntnis* 18 (1982): 239–60.

[18] I have argued on rich data that whereas the contemplative acts and dispositions of the mind have propositions as internal contents, the practical acts and attitudes (e.g., intending, wanting, planning, coming to intend, ordering, commanding, entreating, requesting) take something else, which I have called *practitions* as internal contents. For a layout of the comprehensive argument see *Thinking and Doing*, ch. 6; for data see chs. 2, 4, 6, 7, 10, and 11.

celebrated words, of the essential indexical, which case he claims to have found well established in my papers on indicators and quasi-indicators.

5. Indexical Identities

Intentional and voluntary action hinges on there being indexical internal contents that the agent take to be true. This is what (13*) illustrates. But the success of our intentions and duties requires that we act in one and the same world as we cognize. For this, as remarked above in discussing the connection between (13) and (13*), we need identifications between what we refer to indexically and what is intersubjectively referable. Mixed indexical-nonindexical equations are the bridge between our experiences and the world at large. Let's dwell upon them. Consider some of the identities linking (13) to (13*):

(13*.1) I am the President of the P-G Society.

(13*.2) This here is [you are] Wilfrid Sellars.

(13*.3) This is the Chisholm Auditorium of Brown University.

(13*.4) That is the P-G Society band of the Willard Quine Award.

(13*.5) That is the P-G Society diploma of the Willard Quine Award.

(13*.6) Today is 12 May 1988.

(13*.7) Now is the time of the Award Conferral ceremony.

The agent needs to believe these truths to infer (13*). On the Direct Reference Theory two tenets hold. First, (i) these equations as they belong in the agent's idiolects are essentially propositional functions of the form $x = a$, where the variable 'x' stands for indexical terms awaiting interpretation, and the variable 'a' for singular terms, whatever they may be, if there can be any, that denote Kaplanian-Fregean first-referents. Second, (ii) in speech situations the indicator x receives its interpretations, and, as we remarked earlier when we discussed my Perry example and Kaplan's heiress one, x is supposed to be interpreted as denoting the selfsame Kaplanian-Fregean first-referent that a denotes. Hence, all those equations represent Russellian-Kaplanian propositions of the form:

(13.Kp) $a = a$.

Now, although thesis (i) is trivial, thesis (ii) is controversial. Undoubtedly, once again, such Russellian-Kaplanian propositions are useless for intentional action. In fact, the agent in attempting to ascertain what to do, wants to establish the experiential truths (13∗.1)–(13∗.7). He makes use of a special conception of truth that applies to his internal cognitive contents. He is asking:

(13∗.1?) Am I the P-G Society Secretary?

(13∗.2?) Is this [Are you] Wilfrid Sellars? Etc.

In so asking he is asking something equivalent to:

(13∗.1T?) Is it *true* that I am the P-G Society Secretary?

(13∗.2T?) Is it *true* that this is [you are] Wilfrid Sellars? Etc.

It is of no use to try to enlighten him by saying that the truths he is concerned with are merely some external Russellian-Kaplanian truths of the form $a = a$. Such Russellian truths are indeed less useful than the following, which are not really Russellian:

(13.1f) The P-G Society Secretary is the P-G Society Secretary.

(13.2f) Wilfrid Sellars is Wilfrid Sellars. Etc.

Patently, he can respond by saying:

(13.1.GT) I know that it is true that:

    (i) the P-G Society Secretary is the P-G Society Secretary

    (ii) I am I and that I am me, and

    (iii) the underlying Russellian-Kaplanian propositions of the form $a = a$ are true.
    What I want to know is whether, or not,

    (∗) it is *true* that I am the P-G Society Secretary.
    Please help me ascertain the truth-value of this proposition.

(13.2.GT) On the assumption that sentences with proper names or indicators denote Russellian-Kaplanian propositions, I know that:

    (i) Wilfrid Sellars = Wilfrid Sellars, and

(ii) This man = this man.
   What I don't know is whether, or not:
(*) This man is the same as Wilfrid Sellars. Etc.

The issue is not a mere verbal one about what to call "true" (or "false"), and what to call "proposition." The issue is the very central one of making inferences that, having a valid logical form, by additionally possessing true premises are really sound; the issue is the most serious one of how to move from (13) and (13*) in order to understand the nature of practical thinking and the mechanisms of volition.

The agent insists that there are three types of truths with the following forms: (a) *i is the same as i*, (b) *i is the same as a*, and (c) *a is the same as a*, where 'i' stands for an indexical term and 'a' for a nonindexical one. These internal truths he calls propositions, thus using the word in a traditional Fregean and Moorean sense. (Note that even the thinkable propositions of form (c) are internal to the agent's thinking. This is a point worth attending to in considering what sort of formulation can Russellian-Kaplanian propositions receive.)

Palpably, the agent's retort (13.1G) is perfectly intelligible, and perfectly consistent. But since it contains indicators, the Theory of Direct Reference applies to it. The result is that on that Theory (13.1G) would seem to be contradictory. It would seem to have the agent claiming to know that *a* is the same as *a* and claiming not to know it.

A most important point that emerges is this. The mixed indexical truths, like the series (13*.i), are *de dicto* thinkable empirical truths equating items in experience under indexical reference with other items. This urges the recognition that the grammatical meaning of indexical expressions is part and parcel of those items indexically referred to. This raises a profound question: either the directness of reference to existing physical objects is a fiction, or direct reference does not apply to physical objects.

6. Nota Bene

In the oral discussion of the first version of this paper at the Kaplan Conference there were some valuable questions. It may not be amiss to report them and my answers. The preceding section has been expanded in response to those questions.

(A.) *John Perry* suggested that the agent may act simply because he is so causally wired that his tokening of the sentence '*That* is a drowning man' may cause him to try to help the drowning man—or to refrain from help and become ready to enjoy the spectacle of a man drowning. Thus, we do not have to postulate internal contents that are true or false: the sentence with its mere grammatical meaning may do.

My response was this. Undoubtedly such a causal situation is feasible in principle. But at most it would explain some extreme form of compulsive action. We must, however, explain intentional action, even action based on a deliberation aimed at finding a solution to a conflict of duties. For these we need premises taken to be true and to express a truth that is present to the agent.

(B.) *Robert Moore* suggested that perhaps we can dispense with truth. Perhaps the agent's tokening inferential sequences of sentences, just as we do in logical exercises, may suffice.

My response had two parts. First, in deliberation the agent has to believe his premises and he deliberates in order to elicit a conclusion of the form *I ought, everything relevant being considered, to A*, which he desires to believe. From that conclusion he may go on to infer "Therefore, I shall (will, am going to) A," which he endorses, adopts, as if it were true. (The resolve the agent finally reaches is neither true nor false; it is not really a proposition, but what I have called a *practition*. It has, nevertheless, values analogous to truth-values, which I have called *Legitimacy-values*).[19]

Secondly, believing is a mental state that involves truth. It is of course an error to say that to believe that p is to believe that that p is true. This leads to an unwelcome infinity. But to believe that p is to place the proposition that p on the side of truth. Let me explain the point with a similar case. A child, a machine, that has not got the concepts of *apple* and *pear* may be able to separate the apples and the pears in one basket and place them in different baskets. But a person who has got the two concepts can sort out apples from pears by classifying them. Likewise, to believe that p is not to classify that p as true, but it is, so to speak, to place that p in the truth bin. To believe that that p is true is to classify that p as true. For this one needs a (predicative) concept of truth. This is why above we claimed mere equivalence, not identity, between (13*.1?) and (13*.1T?).

Further discussion of internal truth appears in the preceding section.

---

[19]See *Thinking and Doing*, ch. 4, and the end of ch. 6. A deep criticism of the theory of Legitimacy-values there developed was produced by Michael Bratman in "Castañeda's Theory of Thought and Action," in Tomberlin 1983 cited above. In response the theory of Legitimacy is revised in "Reply to Michael Bratman: Deontic Truth, Intentions, and Weakness of the Will," also in Tomberlin 1983.

C. *Paul Benacerraf* observed that the internal representation of what the agent is to do, i.e., the difference between propositions and practitions, for which I have been arguing for decades, is needed in work in artificial intelligence dealing with the imitation of intentional action.

IV. An Inventory of Gains of the Investigation and the Development of a General Theory of Reference: A Glimpse into Guise Theory

1. Some of the Major Results of the Preceding Investigation

Our reflections on David Kaplan's Theory of Direct Indexical Reference have yielded a good many results recorded in the preceding pages. Some desiderata for any comprehensive and fruitful theory of reference that need special mention are registered below.

Desideratum Ref-1. We need to posit *external "objects of thought"* as the hit targets of thinking in order to account for the connection between thinkers and their world: for the veridicality of most thinking episodes that exercise the default doxastic attitude, for successful existentially *de re* beliefs about the physical world. Such targets may be called facts. Perhaps Kaplanian-Russellian propositions may serve as such targets.

Desideratum Ref-2. We need to posit *internal accusatives* of episodes of thinking in order to account for the contents of the consciousness constitutive of our episodes of (*de dicto*) thinking, for our perceptual claims, our performing intentional actions, our deliberating about what to do, our planning scientific experiments, our dealings with fiction— in brief, for every aspect of human life. Fregean-Moorean propositions, extended to include indexical types, may perhaps serve well for this job.

Desideratum Ref-3. The external targets hit by thinking episodes are *not* real thinking targets: they are *doxastic* targets. Hence, they are not semantically connected with the sentences whose tokenings embody thinking episodes. Kaplanian-Russellian propositions may, thus, perhaps function as doxastic targets and hits, even though they are not genuine semantic hits.

Desideratum Ref-4. The internal cognitive content or accusative of an episode of indexical thinking carried out through the tokening of an indexical sentence S, includes S's grammatical meaning only as a proper part. This meaning is a frame and skeleton fleshed out by the the general pragmatics of indexical reference from materials in the context of thought and speech to produce thought of indexical individuals.

Desideratum Ref-5. The internal cognitive content or accusative of an episode of thinking carried out through the tokening of an indexical sentence is a primary possessor of truth-values.

Desideratum Ref-6. Indexical reference places individuals in experience, especially perceptual fields, as qua experienced in certain ways. Such individuals are in the default doxastic attitude posited as being the same as real individuals (physical objects, persons, physical time, physical space).

Desideratum Ref-7. The external doxastic targets and the internal thinking contents, whether thinking is carried out through the tokening of indexical sentences or not, *must* be closely and systematically connected with each other. These connections must be so pervasive and fundamental so as to undergird the basic unity of world and experience, and to support the representation of the structure of the world by the structure of the language through which the world is experienced.

Desideratum Ref-8. A firm connection between world and experience requires that there be some mechanisms of direct, unmediated semantic reference through which the pragmatico-semantic denotation of some terms be determined directly by linguistic rules and context of speech or thought. And because the semantics of thinking demands a convergence of pragmatico-semantic denotation and thought of referent, there must also be unmediated thought of referents.

Psychological Desideratum. Propositional states are to be individuated by internal accusatives. i.e., units of cognitive significance that are primary possessors of truth-values—they may, in line with good standing philosophical tradition, be called *internal propositions*.

2. Taking Stock of Findings

We have seen that Frege's semantico-inventory for his theory of language and thinking includes:

(1)   Grammatical meanings,

(2)   Informative or cognitive contents,

(3)   Internal accusatives of (*de dicto*) thinking,

(4)   Truth-value possessors.

Of course Frege's inventory also includes:

(-1)   (Declarative) sentence,

(-2)   Ideas, images, and other psychological mechanisms involved in the realization of thinking.

As we have noted above, a little reflection reveals that, independently of indexical reference, we need to enrich the Fregean inventory with a category of:

(5)   *facts*, or *external doxastic targets*.

Frege held the Simplifying View that:

(FV) $(1) = (2) = (3) = (4)$

We have studied how David Kaplan, to account for indexical reference, modified Frege's semantico-ontological inventory by introducing a category like (5), say:

(5′) Kaplanian-Russellian propositions, as semantic hits. There is here a valuable insight. Another powerful insight is that indexical reference breaks Frege's view by rupturing the equation $(1) = (4)$:

sentential indexical grammatical meaning $\neq$ truth-value possessor.

Kaplan still maintains some Fregean equations. Thus, his view includes:

(KV) $(1) = (2) = (3)$, and $(4) = (5')$

Now, the exegesis of the Direct Reference View has shown that the full appreciation of the experiential roles of indexical reference, as well as of the finitude and intensionality of thinking, requires more departures from Frege's equations (FV). Direct reference is important. One must be able to seize some referents as they appear and for what they appear in order to build from them a conception of the world one finds oneself in. But the massive physical objects of the world one believes to exist are too massive to be apprehended in their entirety. It seems, thus, the full benefits of direct reference require thin, manageable *thats* and *thises* whose *esse* consists in their being just *thats* and *thises*. How can this be so?

To produce a general theory of reference, that preserves direct experiential reference, we must, therefore, immediately substitute (5) for (5′). Then to conform to the desiderata spread alongside our discussion engage in the following modifications:

(A)   Segregate within category (4) two subcategories:

>   (4a) Primary possessors of truth-values

>   (4b) Secondary possessors of truth-values

(B)   Distinguish within category (2):

>   (2a) Informational content of a sentence type

>   (2b) Informative content of a thinking episode

(C)   Postulate (to proceed economically at the beginning) the following theses, which may be discarded in the light of challenging new data:

>> (1) = (2a)

>> (2a) is a proper part of (2b)

>> (2a) is a proper part of (3)

>> (3) is a part, often proper, of (2b)

>> (3) = (4a)

>> (4b) = (5)

(D)   Construct a useful connection between (4a) and (4b)

(E)   Eliminate the Fregean referents from the semantic line-up and place them in the realm of doxastics.

These suggestions (A)–(E) deliver only a schema, a framework for theoretical development. Can we execute these suggested modifications?

3. Guise Theory

Interestingly enough, Guise Theory conforms to the desiderata formulated above. It satisfies the preceding schema very snuggly like hand and glove. Unfortunately there is no time now to enjoy the experience of seeing how well Guise Theory fits the above framework. Fortunately, however, there are abundant materials where the theory is expounded.[20] But

---

[20] The first formulation of Guise Theory, although the name was still forthcoming there, appears in "Thinking and the Structure of the World," *Philosophia* 4 (1974): 4–40. The extension of Guise Theory to indexical guises and propositional guises was formally made in "Perception, Belief, and the Structure of Physical Objects and Consciousness." The extension to Ordered Guise Theory was proposed in "Reply to Alvin Plantinga: Method, Individuals, and Guise Theory," in Tomberlin 1983. Interesting summaries and worthwhile issues are

the semantico-ontological schema determined by (A)–(D) is described more fully only in "Perception, Belief, and the Structure of Physical Objects and Consciousness."[21] Here we can only include the following remarks, which may perhaps be a somewhat useful guide for the serious student of reference:

A. The categories in the above ontological inventory correspond to the categories of Guise Theory to their right in the chart below.

The sign '=====' means: *is realized by, corresponds to.*

Needed inventory	**Guise-theoretical inventory**
(1) Grammatical meaning =====	grammatical meaning
(2a) Cognitive significance	
of a singular term =====	individual guise schema
of a sentence =====	propositional guise schema
(3) Internal accusative =====	propositional guise
(4a) Primary bearers of =====	propositional guises
truth-values = internal bearer of truth-values	
(4b) Secondary possessors =====	propositions = Conflational systems of propositional guises
of truth-values	
(4c) Tertiary contingent =====	PROPOSITIONS, or Super-propositions = Consubstantiational and Transubstantiational or Consociational systems of propositions
possessors of truth-values	

N.B. 1. Guise Theory countenances other types of truth than the ones being discussed above because it aims at being a comprehensive

raised in the following papers and Castañeda's respective replies: In Tomberlin 1983: Romane Clark, "Predication Theory: Guised and Disguised," and Alvin Plantinga, "Guise Theory"; in Tomberlin 1986: Jay Rosenberg, "Castañeda's Ontology," David Woodruff Smith, "Mind and Guise," and Jeffrey Sicha, "Castañeda on Plato, Leibniz, and Kant"; in *Synthese* 46 (1984): James E. Tomberlin, "Identity, Intensionality, and Intentionality." Other relevant studies are: Jig-Chuen Lee, "Guise Theory," *Philosophical Studies* 46 (1984): 403–15, and William Rapaport, "Meinongian Theories and a Russellian Paradox," *Noûs* 12 (1978): 153–80, and his "Nonexisting Objects and Epistemological Ontology," *Grazer Philosophische Studien* 25/26 (1984/1986): 61–95.

[21] *Synthese* 35 (1977), part II.

ontology that accounts for all types of human experience. It recognizes several types of predication: internal predication and several types of external predication, these latter are special forms of sameness. They are: Strict Identity, Conflation, Consubstantiation, Transubstantiation, and Consocciations. But the theory is open to the discovery of new types of sameness that are also forms of predication.

N.B. 2. The referents of singular terms are, *roughly*, like Frege's individual senses. They are called *individual guises*. Thus, individual guises can be regarded as the promotion of Fregean individual senses to the role of referents.

N.B. 3. The Fregean first-referents are not in the semantical line-up of singular terms. They are amenable only to *general* reference by means of quantification. They are in the realm of doxastics. The thinkability of individual guises bestows a pervasive transparency to language and to the minds of others. Guise Theory is a fully realist, nonmediational, directly referential view: what exists are systems of guises, and if they are finite they are exactly as they can be thought, exactly as they can appear to consciousness; the facts of the world are nothing but true *propositions*, which are systems of (classical, non-Kaplanian) propositions, which in their turn are systems of propositional guises, which are, if finite, precisely what they can appear to be within thinking, and if they are indexical propositional guises, they are just what can appear in perception.

V. Conclusion

Kaplan's Theory of Direct Indexical Reference is insightful and powerful. Our examination has led us to propose a sequence of modifications. These modifications run along the grain of Kaplan's theory, indeed they merely reinforce and extend the range of direct reference from the semantics of language to the semantics (of the internal contents) of thinking. Since those modifications are already built into Guise Theory, this seems to be a blood kin of David Kaplan's Theory of Direct Indexical Reference.

VI. Appendix: Characters: Meanings vs. Functions from Contexts to Contents

In the preceding investigation into David Kaplan's Theory of Direct Indexical Reference we have considered his characters to be grammatical meanings. This has allowed us sympathetically to consider that theory as a good basis for extension to a semantics of indexical thinking. Thus, we have neglected a part of Kaplan's theory pertaining to so-called formal semantics. The reason is this part of Kaplan's theory seems to interfere with the semantics of thinking. The issues are large and important; they transcend the problems of indexical reference. To this interference we turn here.

The word 'character' is a key expresion in David Kaplan's semantic theory of indexical reference. Among other tenets about characters, the following, formulated with a special reference to thinking, are crucial:

K-S-0. The character of an expression is, roughly, the expression's grammatical (i.e., syntactico-semantical) meaning.

K-S-1. The character of an expression E is the cognitive content the expression contributes to the internal thinking content of an episode of thinking consisting of (or embodied in) a tokening of a sentence containing E.

K-F-1. Characters are functions that map contexts of speech into speech contents.

K-S-00. Speech contents are entities in the world. In the case of sentences they are (external) propositions, i.e., truth-valued entities.

Of these tenets K-S-0 and K-S-00 may be accepted as definitional. They are part and parcel of the stipulations that assign their technical meanings, in Kaplan's theory of direct indexical reference, to 'character' and 'content', respectively. Thus, here only tenets K- S-1 and K-F-1 are major theses of the account offered by that theory.

In the preceding reflexions upon Kaplan's theory, we have seen how right Kaplan is in holding K-S-1. The characters of expressions, not only of indexical expressions, understood *as grammatical meanings must* be *parts* of the internal cognitive contents of thinking episodes carried in tokenings of such expressions. The very functioning of language as a means of thinking hinges on the convergence, or identity, between the contents of linguistically-embodied thinking and consciousness including, and the *semantico-pragmatic* denotata of the embodying tokens of the involved pieces of language. *A fortiori*, the purely semantic meanings are cognitive content. On the other hand, we found the need to recognize internal truth-valued accusatives as cognitive contents of thinking. Hence, the grammatical meanings of sentences containing indicators or other dimensions of contextuality *cannot* be the whole cognitive contents of the thinking episodes embodied in the tokening of such sentences.

K-F-1 is a formal-semantic, not an epistemological or psychological, thesis. It pertains to the formal modellings of language. There are two different subtheses underlying K-F-1:

K-F-1A. In a context C of speech about a certain domain U of entities there is always a function i mapping the set T of singular terms in a piece of language used in C to the entities in the U:

There is a function i: $\langle T, C \rangle \rightarrow U$.

K-F-1B. The function i posited by K-F-1A is constituted by the grammatical meanings of T, thus by K-S-0 and K-S-00:

Each character of t in T: $C \rightarrow U$.

Evidently there is nothing wrong with K-F-1A. And there is nothing wrong with *calling* the function introduced by K-F-1B "character." This character cannot, however, be cognitive content, and to the extent that cognitive content includes grammatical meaning, that function cannot be the same as grammatical meaning.

The function i posited by K-F-1A is actually of the greatest importance. In fact, given that individuals can be parceled out in many different ways in accordance with different principles of ontological parsing, there will always be *many* different interpretative functions at work. (This is the fact that Quine often appeals to in his arguments for the indeterminacy of radical translation.[22]) Thus, K-F-1A is more strongly true than it seems. All those interpretative functions i, posited by the applications of K-F-1A to different ontological parsings of the domain of discourse U, have to do with the veridicality of what one thinks. For this reason the function i may be called semantic, or *interpretative*. Formal semanticists studying truth-conditions in abstract and the general structures of veridicality—just as David Kaplan was doing from the very beginning when he became concerned with indexical sentences (see the beginning of the "Introduction" above)—*correctly* ignore the physical and psychological mechanisms that realize the mappings they are interested in. For philosophers of mind and the functioning of language, on the other hand, those psycho-physical mechanisms are a major

---

[22]See W. V. O. Quine, *Word and Object* (Cambridge, Mass.: MIT Press, 1960, 1964), ch. 2.

concern. Hence, the issue is *not* to reject formal semantics and set-theoretical modelling, but to *locate* our topics in cognitive psychology and in the philosophy of mind within the structures formal semanticists study. We want to understand the phenomena as fully as is possible, and this requires solid interdisciplinary connections and openness to other researchers' results.

Doubtless, such functions i as K-F-1A postulates operate when one is engaged in veridical thinking, whether one knows it or not. That was the case with Joseph Calmog's perceptual judgments in alternatives (A) and (C) of his Drowning-Man Adventure, discussed above in Section III.3. Further, in the case of thinking episodes that rehearse the default doxastic attitude—as in situation A of Joseph Calmog's Adventure—the function i secures the truth of the internal propositions that are the accusatives of such episodes.

Thesis K-F-1B seems to me to work travesty in our understanding of cognitive processes. I propose to replace it with:

C-F∗. The functions i postulated by K-F-1A enter thinking and speaking situations, when they enter them, *causally*. In a thinking (and speaking) situation C there are factors that *cause* the thinker to think, *not* the function itself, but *one* value, the *appropriate functional value*. Interpretative functions i are *external* to the cognitive content of thinking. We need them in a theory of the *processes* of thinking and of veridicality.

Recall that, as we saw in section III.3, a basic interpretative function may fail to operate in the case of hallucinatory experiences. In situations (B) and (D) of the Drowning-Man Adventure, there is no Russellian-Kaplanian proposition that is the external hit, or the internal accusative of Calmog's thinking *That* is [appears to be] *a drowning man*. Yet he thinks demonstratively, even though the functional argument is available: the functional value is missing. Exactly the same happens in nonperceptual thinking about nonexistents.[23] We have so far refrained from discussing them, because we were limiting ourselves to indexical reference.

---

[23] For more discussion on our reference, both singular and general, to nonexisting objects, see Hector-Neri Castañeda, "Objects, Existence, and Reference," *Grazer Philosophische Studien* 25/26 (1985/1986): 3–59; and the exchange: Tyler Burge, "Russell's Problem on Intentional Identity" and Hector-Neri Castañeda, "Reply to Tyler Burge: Reference, Existence, and Fiction," both in *Agent, Language, and the Structure of the World*, ed. James E. Tomberlin (Indianapolis: Hackett Publishing Company, 1983).

Grammatical meanings are sorts of conceptual structure present in the content thought of. This is why grammatical meanings are not literally functions. Just compare (A) and (B) above with this thinkability of grammatical meaning. We may say that they *correspond* to a function, as described above, whose role is thinking-causal not thought-contentual. But correspondence is, normally, not identity.

Let us explore further the logical/epistemico-psychological tension in the notion of character: between K-S-1 and K-F-1B. (Of course, a similar tension would develop were we to introduce a hybrid the notion of character∗ both as the grammatical meanings of indicators and as functions mapping individual guises, or Fregean senses.)

A central issue is to determine what functions are supposed to be here. Let us take functions to be mappings in the mathematical sense, as sets of ordered n-tuples. As far as I can see, we think of mathematical functions in several ways. In the case of a finite function, we can think the ordered pair in *propria persona*. Here is one case: the mapping of the first ten numbers and ten students in a room. We count: ⟨1, Dieter⟩, ⟨2, Hans⟩, ⟨3, Karl⟩, ... Finite or infinite functions we think, not in *propria persona*, but as unified by some property, or set of properties, which are finitely manageably in *propria persona*. For instance: the set of all pairs of the form ⟨man, wife⟩, or the function mapping the class of wives into the class of respective husbands, or, say:

$f : A \rightarrow B$, where A is the class of rational numbers r and B is the class of complex numbers of the corresponding form $r * n + r * i$.

Here we have a complex property *representing* to us the infinite function f. We are thinking a rule for finding pairs of arguments and values of the function, but we are not thinking the function in *propria persona*. We sometimes use a symbolism that in finite means depicts, together with an implicit rule, a finite property; e.g.:

$a1, a2, \ldots, aN$

which is a finite counting mapping if N is finite, but N can be any uncountable ordinal.

Properties *represent* functions. When I think *the quadruple of three is a number* I am normally *not* thinking of a mathematical function conceived as an ordered pair of sets of arguments and values. The notion of set does not enter my mind when I am thinking that 4×3 is a number.

In other words, in the theory of mind and of language as this function in experience, we must distinguish two propositions:

(2)   The quadruple of 3 is a number.

(2.a) $F : N \rightarrow \{y : y = 4 \times x \& x$ is in $N\}$ and $F(3)$ is in N

Here (2) is a purely relational proposition, where the relation is, as the mathematicians say, taken *in intension*. On the other hand, (2.a) is a functional proposition, representing the rule for finding argument/value pairs. The two propositions are equivalent, but not identical. To think (2) is certainly not to think (2.a). Just think how many centuries were required for the equivalence between (2) and (2.a) to become known; consider further how many persons selling in the department stores and the Saturday farm market know (2) but haven't the faintest idea of (2.a).

Let's consider our main topic: indexical reference.

If characters are merely mathematical functions, they are sets of ordered pairs. Obviously these are *not* even parts of what Joseph thinks when he thinks *That is a drowning man*—even if his judgment is veridical. Much less is that function what he thinks when he is hallucinating, or when he thinks *That appears to be [looks like] a drowning man*. For one thing, as we noted, if he is hallucinating, the appropriate value of the function is missing. For another thing, Joseph just can't think those huge ordered pairs in *propria persona*. Third, even if he could, thinking them would interfere with his perceptual experience. Furthermore, to think of that huge ordered pair Joseph would have to think of one interesting member of it, namely, the pair ⟨Joseph Calmog's speech context, what Joseph calls "that"⟩. But this is circular, and excessive.

The function which is the character of 'this' is something like this:

> f : $\{\langle a, B, t, p, s(\text{this}), D\rangle$: where a is a speaker, B the domain of hearers, t the time of utterance of an English sentence s('this'), with the demonstrative 'this', p the place at which a speaks, D a domain of objects referred to by a in his utterance of s('this') lying in the vicinity of $a\} \rightarrow D$.

I am not sure whether this captures the *this*-function as a proximal demonstrative of English. It may be more complex than that. After all, something more has to be said about the speaker's linguistic intentions. Furthermore, we refer demonstratively to fictional persons, institutions, numbers, properties, propositions, practitions, etc.

In any case, the above function f is not what Joseph Calmog thinks when he thinks demonstratively *This is a drowning man*—let alone thinking *This appears to be a drowning man,* or *This seems to be a floating dagger.* It is too complex. It is doubtful that small children can think of such a function whenever they refer to something by calling it "this." In fact, I am not sure of the formulation of the function, yet I have no problem making demonstrative references.

There is a further problem. It is not enough to think of the function. One has to think of its application. One has to think of the items constituting the speech context as argument and then assign the value to that argument. That is, one has to think of the member of D one calls "this." If one conceives of the application as an inferential move, then one has to think of the members of D and assign the value in question. But then one is already thinking of the object. How does one think of the object?

Undoubtedly, as remarked above in connection with K-F-1A, there is a *semantico-pragmatic* assignment of some denotatum to each of one's use of 'this'. There is, clearly, such an interpretative function. But it cannot enter as something thought of. It enters causally, embodied through a psycho-physical set-up. One is in certain situation, opens one's eyes and sees something and calls it "this." In that situation there is no conscious inference from the function and the context to the *this* in question. There need not be any previous identification of the object. The presented *this* is the value of the function, which has entered in the causal process leading to the perceptual judgment *This is F*. The *this* in question is an objectual presentation in the sense of being a subject of predication and also in the sense that in the default doxastic attitude it is taken to be the same as a physical object.[24]

---

[24] This appendix was written at the suggestion of Harald Pilot, whom I also thank for the most fruitful discussions on reference we had on the campus of the University of Heidelberg during June–July 1987.

7

Why Singular Propositions?

Roderick M. Chisholm

I. Introduction

David Kaplan's theory of "direct reference" presupposes the being of certain entities that he calls "singular propositions."[1] According to his theory, there are certain terms that "refer directly without the mediation of a Fregean *Sinn* as meaning"; the sentences in which such terms are used "express singular propositions"; and such propositions "involve individuals directly rather than by way of ... 'individual concepts' or 'manners of representation'" (483). I will express some doubts about such propositions and will suggest a way of avoiding them.

II. The Presuppositions of the Theory of Direct Reference

The theory has both metaphysical and epistemological presuppositions. The *metaphysical* presupposition is that there *are* singular propositions. And the *epistemological* presupposition is that people who use the sentences that purportedly express such propositions can *directly grasp* those propositions. I take it that the "direct" in "direct reference"

---

[1] He makes a clear statement about the nature of these entities in the first few pages of draft #2 of his monograph *Demonstratives: An Essay on the Semantics, Logic, Metaphysics, and Epistemology of Demonstratives and Other Indexicals*, dated March 1977, and privately circulated. References here to Kaplan are to this monograph, published in this volume.

refers, not only to the relation between a singular proposition and the individuals that may be "constituents" of that proposition, but also to the relation between a person and a proposition that his sentence may happen to express. (Kaplan does not use "directly grasp," nor, I believe, does he use any other expression to refer to the relation between the user of a sentence and the singular proposition that his sentence expresses.)

As I interpret the theory, it presupposes that, if there is an individual thing x and if there is the property being F, then there is that singular proposition which is *x being F*. Kaplan notes that "free variables under an assignment of values are paradigms of what I have been calling *directly referential* terms" (484). If x is, say, the tallest man, then you could accept a sentence expressing *x being wise*—that is to say, *the tallest man being wise*—without thereby believing *that* the tallest man is wise. (In the expression, "S accepts a sentence expressing the singular proposition, *the tallest man being wise*," we may substitute, *salva veritate*, any other descriptive phrase that denotes the tallest man—for the sense of the descriptive phrase need not be in any way involved in the singular proposition that the sentence in question expresses.)

But what of this entity which is *x being wise*? If the tallest man is wise, then perhaps there is that *fact* or *event* which is his being wise and he could be said to be a "constituent" of that fact or event or to be "directly involved" in it. Singular propositions, however, are not to be identified with facts or events—unless (what seems to me to be very problematic) there are events that do not occur and facts that are not really factual. But the direct reference theory requires us to say that even if the tallest man is *not* wise, there *is* that singular proposition which is *his being wise* and he—the tallest man, himself—is an actual constituent of it. Surely, we should not feel comfortable about positing such entities. I am reminded of Russell's observation: "Time was when I thought there were propositions, but it does not seem to me very plausible to say that in addition to facts there are also these shadowy things going about such as 'That today is Wednesday' when in fact it is Tuesday."[2]

Nevertheless we should put up with such things—*if* (1) they do what they are supposed to do and *if* (2) there is no plausible alternative. But I think they do not do what they are supposed to do. And I think there is a more plausible alternative.

---

[2]Bertrand Russell, *Logic and Knowledge* (London: Allen & Unwin, 1956), 223.

III. Do Singular Propositions Do What They are Supposed to?

The direct reference theory does not appear to be adequate to Castañeda's distinction between what is expressed by (i) "x judges x to be F" and (ii) "x judges *himself* to be F." The second locution implies the first, but not conversely.[3] Suppose that I am looking at a certain document which, unsuspected by me, is something I had written some time ago. I may conclude that the author of the document was foolish without thereby thinking that *I* was foolish. In such a case I am an x such that x judges x to have been foolish, but I am not an x such that x judges himself to be foolish.

It is clear that, if I am x, there is no distinction between that singular proposition which is x *being foolish* and that singular proposition which is *my being foolish*. It looks, therefore, as though "x judges x to be foolish" and "x judges himself to be foolish" express the same singular proposition. Perhaps the singular proposition theorist could appeal to those "manners of presentation" which Kaplan hopes to dispense with, but I don't know how the details would be worked out.

IV. The Alternative

Let us consider the problem in application to *judging*. What I will say about judging can be applied, *mutatis mutandis*, to other intentional attitudes. What we want to do, then, is to sketch a *nonpropositional* theory of judging.

Judging, according to such a conception, is fundamentally a matter of *attributing* a property to something. Every judgment includes a *direct* attribution of a property to oneself. One takes as undefined "x directly attributes to y the property of being F," and we presuppose that one can *directly* attribute properties only to oneself. In other words, direct attribution is necessarily such that, for every x and y, if x directly attributes anything to y, then x is identical with y.

In attributing a property to himself, a person *may* also happen to attribute a property to another thing; in such a case, the person *indirectly* attributes a property to the other thing. Consider a person who is such that there is just one bearded man who is riding on the bus with him. If that person directly attributes to himself the property expressed

---

[3] See Hector-Neri Castañeda, "He: A Study in the Logic of Self-Consciousness," *Ratio* 8 (1966): 130-57.

by "riding on the bus with a person who is the only bearded man on the bus and who is also an electrician," then he has indirectly attributed the property of being an electrician to the bearded man who is riding on the bus with him. It is not difficult to find, with respect to *anything* to which we attribute a property, some relation which is such that we bear that relation *only* to the thing to which we attribute the property.

The "direct attribution" theory of judgment tells us this:

> x judges y to be F $=_{df}$. There is a relation R such that (a) x bears R to y and only to y and (b) x directly attributes to x a property which is necessarily such that (i) whatever has it bears R to something that is F and (ii) whoever conceives it conceives being-F.

Why the last clause? Otherwise the theory would require us to say that, if I judge you to be an electrician, then I also judge you to be such that all squares are rectangles.[4]

The "he, himself" locution, then, comes to this:

> x judges himself to be F $=_{df}$ x directly attributes to x the property of being-F.

Hence we may say that "x judges himself to be F" implies but is not implied by "x judges x to be F."

We may distinguish between the *object* and the *content* of an attribution and also between the *direct* and the *indirect* objects and contents of attribution. Consider, once again, the example of x judging y to be an electrician. The person x is the *direct object* of his own attribution. The *direct content* will be the property that x directly attributes to himself—that of being a person such that the only bearded man in the bus with him is an electrician. The *indirect object* is the other person y, the man with the beard. And the *indirect content* will be the property that x indirectly attributes to y—namely, the property of being an electrician.

An attribution cannot fail to have a direct object. But it may fail to have an indirect object. If I attribute to myself the property of being sad,

---

[4] We noted what the relation R might be if one person judges another person to be an electrician. What would it be if he simply judges *himself* to be an electrician—if he makes a judgment that could be expressed in English by saying "I am an electrician"? It could be the relation of *being identical with*. (It is important to note that our definition does *not* require us to say that, when one judges oneself to be an electrician, one attributes to oneself the property of *being identical with an electrician*; one needs only to attribute to oneself some property which is necessarily such that whatever has it is an electrician.)

then my attribution has a direct object but no indirect object. In this case, the attribution does not even purport to have an indirect object. (I follow Quine in using "purport" this way.) An attribution may also purport to have an indirect object and yet fail to have such an object. This would happen if there were no bearded man on the bus or if there were more than one. In such a case, the attribution has a direct object, a direct and an indirect content, but no indirect object.

All these distinctions have their analogues in the cases of the other so-called propositional attitudes.

V. Sense and Reference

The linguistic distinction between sense and reference may be explicated by reference to the intentional distinction between content and object. We may analyze the concept of *sense* by making use of the concept of the *content* of thought, and we may analyze the concept of *reference*, or *designation*, by making use of the concept of the *object* of thought.[5]

Here is a definition of the "speaker's sense" of a predicate:

> x uses P with the sense S $=_{df}$ x makes an utterance having P as a part; and P is that part of the utterance which is intended by x to bring it about that S is the content of the thought x thus intends to convey.

If I *intend to convey* something to you, then I intend to cause you to think that *I* am thinking of that something, and I intend to cause you to believe *that* I intend to cause you to think that something.

And here is a definition of what may be called the "speaker's designation" of an expression:

> x uses N to designate y $=_{df}$ x makes an utterance for the purpose of conveying something to someone about y; and N is that part of x's utterance which is intended to bring it about that y is the object of the thought that x thus endeavors to cause.

The concepts of the "hearer's sense" and the "hearer's designation" of a word would be defined analogously and by reference to the hearer's beliefs about the intentions of the speaker.

---

[5] I have worked out these matters in greater detail in "The Primacy of the Intentional," *Synthese* 61 (1984): 89–109.

I would say, then, that we can get along without singular propositions. I have suggested, in the work cited, that this way of looking at meaning may throw some light upon our use of demonstratives. I think it would be good for philosophy if some day David Kaplan were to see what he might accomplish by exploring this point of view.

8

Intensionality and the Paradox of the Name Relation

Alonzo Church[1]

The paradox of the name relation[2] may be illustrated by the now familiar example concerning King George IV and Sir Walter Scott. On a certain occasion, King George wished to know whether Sir Walter was the author of *Waverley*. The *Waverley Novels* (of which *Waverley* was the first) had been published anonymously and at the time there was widespread speculation about the authorship, but it is now known that Scott was indeed the author. Thus in fact Sir Walter Scott = the author of *Waverley*, and by the principle of substitutivity of equality, whatever is true of the author of *Waverley* must be true also of Sir Walter Scott. In particular, one thing true of the author of *Waverley* is that (on the occasion in question) King George wished to know whether Sir Walter Scott was he; and by the principle of substitutivity of equality,

---

[1] The content of this paper was presented as an invited lecture at a joint symposium of the American Philosophical Association and the Association for Symbolic Logic, in Berkeley, California, on 26 March 1983.

[2] Bertrand Russell, "On Denoting," *Mind* 14 (1905): 479–93. Reprinted in *Readings in Philosophical Analysis*, ed. Herbert Feigl and Wilfrid Sellars (New York: Appleton-Century-Crofts, 1949), 103–15; *Logic and Knowledge*, ed. Robert Charles Marsh (London: Allen & Unwin, 1956), 41–56; *Readings in Logical Theory*, ed. Irving M. Copi and James A. Gould (New York: The Macmillan Company, and London: Allen & Unwin, 1967), 93–105; *Intentionality, Mind, and Language*, ed. Ausonio Marras (Urbana: University of Illinois Press, 1972), 362–79.

it follows that King George wished to know whether Sir Walter Scott was Sir Walter Scott. But this last is clearly false, as King George was well acquainted with Sir Walter and therefore certainly knew of his self-identity; moreover, as Russell says,[3] "an interest in the law of identity can hardly be attributed to the first gentleman of Europe."

The term *paradox of the name relation* is taken from Carnap.[4] Indeed Carnap speaks of the "antinomy" of the name relation, but the word "paradox" seems more appropriate, as (without further assumptions) there is no actual contradiction that arises but highly counterintuitive results. For the name relation itself—i.e., the relation between a name and what it is a name of—we shall use also the verb *to denote* and the noun *denotation*. In this we follow J. S. Mill,[5] and Russell from 1905 on,[6] except that we confine the usage to *singular* names, i.e., to names which have as part of their meaning that there is just one denotation. The common names of the natural languages are left out of account as being unnecessary in the formalized language, except to the extent that their place is taken by variables. For variables we prefer the terminology that the variable may *have a value*, chosen within a certain *range* of values that is predetermined as a part of the meaning of the variable.

The paradox of the name relation originated with Frege,[7] who ex-

---

[3] Quoted from "On Denoting."

[4] Rudolf Carnap, *Meaning and Necessity* (Chicago: University of Chicago Press, 1st ed. 1947 and 2d ed. 1956), see §31.

[5] John Stuart Mill, *A System of Logic, Ratiocinative and Inductive*, vol. I, chap. 2 (London: Longmans, Green, and Co., 1884).

[6] Bertrand Russell, "On Denoting," footnote 10. But as to Russell the statement in the text must be qualified by remarking that after his paper of 1905 Russell continues to hold that "denoting phrases never have any meaning in isolation, but only enter as constituents into the verbal expression of propositions which contain no constituent corresponding to the denoting phrases in question." (Quotation from "Mathematical Logic as Based on the Theory of Types," a paper which appeared originally in the *American Journal of Mathematics* in 1908 and has been reprinted in the anthologies of Robert Charles Marsh, op. cit., and of Jean van Heijenoort, *From Frege to Gödel* (Cambridge, Mass.: Harvard University Press, 1967)—see therein section III, objection (2).)

[7] Gottlob Frege, "Über Sinn und Bedeutung," *Zeitschrift für Philosophie und philosophische Kritik* 100 (1892): 25–50; and *Grundgesetze der Arithmetik*, vol. I (Jena: Verlag Hermann Pohle, 1893), IX, 7, 50–51. "Über Sinn und Bedeutung" is reprinted in Gottlob Frege, *Funktion, Begriff, Bedeutung. Fünf logische Studien*, ed. Günther Patzig (Göttingen: Vandenhoeck & Ruprecht, 1962), and rev. ed. (Göttingen: Vandenhoeck & Ruprecht, 1966). English translations of "Über Sinn und Bedeutung" are available in *Translations from the Philosophical Writings of Gottlob Frege*, ed. Peter Geach and Max Black; and in the anthologies of Feigl and Sellars, of Copi and Gould, and of Marras that are cited in footnote

plains the difference in cognitive significance between $a = a$ and $a = b$, even in cases in which $a = b$ holds, on the ground that the names a and b, though having the same denotation, may nevertheless differ in another aspect of their meaning, the sense. For a resolution of the paradox along these lines we must add that:

1. In the natural language, or at least in all the familiar natural languages, there are certain contexts,[8] called indirect contexts, within which names change their meaning in such a way that what would be the sense in an ordinary context becomes the denotation in the indirect context.

2. In a formalized language the semantical irregularity by which the same name has different denotations (and different senses) in different contexts should be abolished by introducing two different names.

In spite of the difficulty in attaching any very precise meaning in general to the distinction between the intensional and the extensional, it seems clear that the entities (*concepts* as we shall call them) which serve as senses of names must be considered intensional. We proceed to show also that Russell's resolution of the paradox of the name relation depends on intensionality.

Russell's resolution of the paradox depends on his well-known theory of descriptions,[9] of which we shall here use the version that appeared in *Principia Mathematica*.[10] To show that it depends also on the intensionality of Russell's propositional functions, as these appear in *The Principles of Mathematics*[11] and in the first edition of *Principia Mathematica*, we may proceed by showing that the paradox is restored if we accept the axioms of extensionality for propositional functions that

---

2; and in *The Philosophy of Language*, ed. A. P. Martinich (New York: Oxford University Press, 1985), 200–12.

[8] Because the contexts in question often involve what, in the grammar of a natural language, is called indirect discourse (or in German, *ungerade Rede*), and because Frege's use of *ungerade* is meant as suggested by this, it seems better to use *indirect* as the English translation—in place of my former use of *oblique* for this.

[9] Contextual definition, first introduced by Russell in connection with descriptions in his paper "On Denoting," came to play an essential role in his theory of knowledge. See his "Knowledge by Acquaintance and Knowledge by Description," and his *A History of Western Philosophy*.

[10] *Principia Mathematica*, 30–32, and *14, 173–86.

[11] *The Principles of Mathematics*, chap. VIII and appendices A and B.

were proposed by Russell in the Introduction to the second edition of *Principia Mathematica*.

According to Russell on page 14 of the Introduction to the first edition of *Principia Mathematica*, if an open sentence, or propositional form, is given in which there occurs a single free variable such as x, there is a corresponding propositional function whose values are obtained by substituting appropriate constants for the variable x (at all free occurrences of x).[12]

At the top of the next page Russell employs 'x is hurt' as an example of an open sentence to illustrate this principle. In reading this passage bear in mind that Frege's systematic use of quotation marks to distinguish mention from use was not adopted by others until much later, and Russell's use of quotation marks here is probably not meant to serve this purpose.[13]

For singular propositional functions Russell writes the principle of extensionality as

$$\varphi x \equiv_x \varphi x \;.\; \supset \;.\; \varphi \hat{x} = \psi \hat{x}$$

This is not assumed in the first edition of *Principia Mathematica*, but it is proposed in the Introduction to the second edition as a possible alternative to the axioms of reducibility, in ramified type theory, and more recently it has been used by others in connection with simple type theory.[14] Using my own notation[15] I prefer to write this principle (or axiom) of extensionality as

$$\varphi x \equiv_x \psi x \supset \varphi = \psi$$

in the lowest type, and analogously in higher types.[16]

---

[12] More accurately "whose value for any argument c of the same type as x is denoted by the result of substituting for the variable x, at all free occurrences of x in the propositional form, a constant denoting c." Generalization to the case of two or more free variables in the propositional form and a corresponding propositional function of two or more arguments is no doubt intended and is implicit in various later passages.

[13] Indeed in "On Denoting" Russell explains that quotation marks are used to distinguish the meaning (i.e., the sense) of a denoting phrase from its denotation. But he simply has no notation or terminology by which conveniently to distinguish a name of the denoting phrase itself from a name of its meaning or sense—although he agrees (see his footnote 10) that, at least in expounding Frege's theory, this distinction must be made.

[14] E.g., by Rudolf Carnap in *Abriß der Logistik* (1929), and in *Logische Syntax der Sprache* (1934).

[15] Alonzo Church, *Introduction to Mathematical Logic* (1956).

[16] *Principia Mathematica*, *9 and *12, explain the device of typical ambiguity, by

Now if we write *Sir Walter Scott is the author of Waverley* as

$$(\imath x)S(x) = (\imath y)A(y,(\imath z)W(z))$$

the result of eliminating the descriptions[17] is:

$$(\exists a) \, . \, S(x) \equiv_x x = a \, . \, (\exists b) \, .$$
$$(\exists c)[W(z) \equiv_z z = c \, . \, A(y,c)]$$
$$\equiv_y y = b \, . \, a = b$$

Thus on Russell's theory of descriptions *King George wished to know whether Sir Walter Scott is the author of Waverley* must be rewritten as:

> *King George wished to know whether*
> $(\exists a) \, . \, S(x) \equiv_x x = a \, . \, (\exists b) \, .$
> $(\exists c)[W(z) \equiv_z z = c \, . \, A(y,c)]$
> $\equiv_y y = b \, . \, a = b$

Here it is not meant that S, W, and A are names of certain propositional functions, but (for example) $S(x)$ is used rather as a convenient abbreviation to represent the full statement that x scottizes, i.e., that x satisfies just those conditions, whatever they are taken to be, which uniquely characterize being Sir Walter Scott. Similarly $W(z)$ is the full statement that z waverlizes, and $A(y,c)$ the full statement that y authors c.

Now if we let φ be the propositional function that corresponds to the propositional form $S(x)$, and ψ the propositional function that corresponds to the propositional form $(\exists c)[W(z) \equiv_z z = c \, . \, A(y,c)]$, the last display becomes:

> *King George wished to know whether*
> $(\exists a) \, . \, \varphi x \equiv_x x = a \, . \, (\exists b) \, . \, \psi y \equiv_y y = b \, . \, a = b$

Then because we know that as a matter of fact $\varphi x \equiv_x \psi x$, there follows by the principle of extensionality for propositional functions and by substitutivity of equality:

> *King George wished to know whether*
> $(\exists a) \, . \, \varphi x \equiv_x x = a \, . \, (\exists b) \, . \, \varphi y \equiv_y y = b \, . \, a = b$

---

which formulas are asserted that have free variables of ambiguous type.

[17] In accordance with the method of *Principia Mathematica*, *14.

This last represents King George as wishing to know something that is logically equivalent to the existence of a unique individual who scottizes. But the fact is that King George's concern was not at all with this, but rather with the authorship of *Waverley*. Indeed the formula in the last display is just the result of eliminating the descriptions from

$$(\imath x)\varphi x = (\imath y)\varphi y$$

and this certainly misrepresents King George's interest in the matter.

Thus Russell's resolution of the paradox of the name relation fails if extensionality is assumed.[18]

Ajdukiewicz's resolution of the paradox was presented to the Twelfth International Congress of Philosophy, at Venice, in 1958.[19]

Ajdukiewicz uses the example "Julius Caesar knew that Rome is situated on the Tiber." The quoted sentence is no doubt true. But the sentence "Rome is the capital of the Popes" is also true,[20] where "is" is the "is" of identity. Does it follow by substitutivity of identity that "Julius Caesar knew that the capital of the Popes is situated on the Tiber"? On the face of it, and taken purely formally, this would seem to follow. Yet the proposed conclusion is seen to be false, on the ground that Caesar had not heard of the Popes or of their capital. This is another instance of the paradox of the name relation, and it might be resolved by Frege's method or by Russell's, but Ajdukiewicz seeks a resolution of the paradox that does not depend on meanings or on intensionalities.

---

[18] This conclusion does not mean that Russell's theory of descriptions is without value. On the contrary, a well-known simplifying feature of Russell's formalized language would be lost by abandoning the theory of descriptions, namely that the argument of a functional variable may be restricted to be a single symbol, either a variable or a primitive constant.

[19] See Kazimierz Ajdukiewicz, "A Method of Eliminating Intensional Sentences and Sentential Formulae," *Atti del* XII *Congresso Internazionale di Filosofia* (Florence, 1960), 17–24. See also Perry Smith's review of this in the *Journal of Symbolic Logic* 37 (1972): 179–80.

[20] The word "true" is here used in Tarski's sense, applying to sentences rather than propositions. Strictly, one should therefore say "true in" a certain language, but the qualification may be omitted when obvious from the context. See Tarski's "Der Wahrheitsbegriff in den formalisierten Sprachen," *Studia Philosophica* 1 (1936): 261–405, and its English translation, with revisions, that appeared in Alfred Tarski, *Logic, Semantics, Metamathematics. Papers from 1923 to 1938*, trans. J. H. Woodger, 2d ed., edited and introduced by John Corcoran (Indianapolis: Hackett Publishing Company, 1983), 152–278.

According to Ajdukiewicz the sentence "Caesar knew that the capital of the Popes is situated on the Tiber" is ambiguous, and it might mean either

(1)   "Caesar knew about the capital of the Popes, about the relation of being situated on, and about the Tiber, that the capital of the Popes is situated on the Tiber"

or

(2)   "Caesar knew about the function capital of, about the Popes, about the relation of being situated on, and about the Tiber, that the capital of the Popes is situated on the Tiber"

and of these two sentences, (1) is true, on the ground that Caesar knew that Rome is situated on the Tiber, and Rome is in fact the capital of the Popes; but (2) is false on the ground that Caesar had not heard of the Popes. Thus substitutivity of identity is preserved.

A modification of Ajdukiewicz's resolution of the paradox is desirable because familiar formalized languages do not provide for abstraction with respect to a constant in the way that Ajdukiewicz's formulation requires. The presumed equivalent in a formalized language of more standard sort is to replace the constant by an appropriate variable, to abstract with respect to this variable, and then separately to supply the constant.

Thus in a formalized language we might try rewriting "Caesar knew that Rome is situated on the Tiber" as

$$K(C, \lambda\Phi\lambda x\lambda y \, . \, \Phi xy, R, a, b)$$

rewriting (1) as

$$K(C, \lambda\Phi\lambda x\lambda y \, . \, \Phi xy, R, f\pi, b)$$

and rewriting (2) as

$$K(C, \lambda\Phi\lambda\psi\lambda\xi\lambda y \, . \, \Phi(\psi\xi)y, R, f, \pi, b).$$

However, once this is done it is seen that the propositional function K, "knew that," appears with five arguments at one place and six arguments at another. Because usual formalized languages do not admit such a thing as a propositional function that may take a varying number of arguments, we amend by taking K, "knew that," to be a binary propositional function of which the second argument may be an ordered quadruple, ordered quintuple, etc.[21] Thus "Caesar knew that Rome is situated on the Tiber" becomes

$$K(C, \langle \lambda\Phi\lambda x\lambda y \,.\, \Phi xy, R, a, b\rangle)$$

while (1) becomes

$$K(C, \langle \lambda\Phi\lambda x\lambda y \,.\, \Phi xy, R, f\pi, b\rangle)$$

and (2) becomes

$$K(C, \langle \lambda\Phi\lambda\psi\lambda\xi\lambda y \,.\, \Phi(\psi\xi)y, R, f, \pi, b\rangle).$$

If

(3)   "Caesar knew that Rome is the capital of the Popes"

is understood in a sense to make it false (on the ground that Caesar had not heard of the Popes), the corresponding ordered n-tuple, or proposition surrogate (see footnote 21), must be

$$\langle \lambda\Phi\lambda x\lambda\psi\lambda\eta \,.\, \Phi x(\psi\eta), I, a, f, \pi\rangle$$

where I is the propositional function, identity, so that Ixy means the same as $x = y$, and as before a is Rome, f is the function *the capital of*, and π is the class of Popes. On the other hand, if (3) is understood in a sense to make it true, the corresponding proposition surrogate must be

$$\langle \lambda\Phi\lambda x\lambda y \,.\, \Phi xy, I, a, f\pi\rangle.$$

This last ordered quadruple, since we know that $a = f\pi$, is demonstrably the same as

---

[21] The ordered n-tuples such as

$$\langle \lambda\Phi\lambda x\lambda y \,.\, \Phi xy, R, f\pi, b\rangle$$

or

$$\langle \lambda\Phi\lambda\psi\lambda\xi\lambda y \,.\, \Phi(\psi\xi)y, R, f, \pi, b\rangle$$

which may thus serve as object of knowledge (belief, assertion, etc.) we shall call proposition surrogates, because it is thought that they may in some respects perform the office of propositions, although conceptually very different from propositions. Indeed the task of finding a satisfactory axiomatic theory of propositions has seemed very difficult in the past, especially in regard to the question of identity of propositions, and it may well be rendered much easier by using proposition surrogates to guide the choice of axioms, and in the end perhaps even to provide a relative consistency proof.

$$\langle \lambda \Phi \lambda x \lambda y \, . \, \Phi xy, I, a, a \rangle$$

and this in turn is therefore the proposition surrogate to be used in analyzing

(4)   "Caesar knew that Rome is Rome."

Following these examples, let us consider more generally the question of the proposition surrogate corresponding to a given sentence of the formalized language *that is in λ-normal form.*[22] If an ordered $(n + 1)$-tuple is to serve as proposition surrogate for such a sentence, its first member must be in the form

$$\lambda x_1 \lambda x_2 \ldots \lambda x_n M$$

where M is in λ-normal form and has as its only free variables exactly one free occurrence of each of the variables $x_1, x_2, \ldots, x_n$—and the remaining n members of the $(n + 1)$-tuple must be, in order, constants $c_1, c_2, \ldots, c_n$ that are of the same types (see footnote 22) as the variables $x_1, x_2, \ldots, x_n$, but are not necessarily all different.

This determines the proposition surrogate uniquely in the case of a given sentence in λ-normal form, and two such sentences will have the same proposition surrogate if and only if they differ only by (1) alphabetic changes and (2) replacements of one constant or one notation by another that is completely synonymous with it. If, however, an analogous definition of the proposition surrogate is used in the case of sentences that are not in λ-formal form, it is difficult to avoid the situation that in some cases in which two sentences are λ-convertible each

---

[22] To avoid antinomy, the formalized language that we use is to obey a simple type theory, and this may conveniently be the type theory of my paper "A Formulation of the Simple Theory of Types," in the *Journal of Symbolic Logic* 5 (1940): 56–68, or (what is the same thing), the type theory of my paper in *Noûs* 7 (1973): 24–33, and *Noûs* 8 (1974): 135–56, with all the intensional types omitted.

Notice that in consequence of the type theory to which the formalized language conforms, every wff has a λ-normal form, to which it can be reduced by λ-conversion.

Then as definition of the ordered pair $\langle A^\alpha, B^\beta \rangle$, where A^α and B^β are wffs of the indicated types, not containing $f^{o\beta\alpha}$ as free variable, we may take $\lambda f^{o\beta\alpha}(f^{o\beta\alpha}A^\alpha B^\beta)$, which is of type $o(o\beta\alpha)$. Thus $\langle A^\alpha, B^\beta \rangle$ is a function whose value with argument $\lambda x^\alpha \lambda y^\beta \, . \, C^\alpha = x^\alpha$ is the truth-value t if $C^\alpha = A^\alpha$ holds, and is otherwise the truth-value f, *and* whose value with argument $\lambda x^\alpha \lambda y^\beta \, . \, D^\beta = y^\beta$ is the truth-value t if $D^\beta = B^\beta$ holds, and is otherwise the truth-value f (this on the assumption that the variables x^α and y^β are so chosen as to have no free occurrences in either C^α or D^β).

to the other, the two corresponding proposition surrogates are the same and in other such cases the two proposition surrogates are different.

As an example of this consider the three sentences,

$$Iaa, (\lambda\Phi\lambda x\lambda y \ . \ \Phi xy)Iaa, (\lambda\Phi\lambda x \ . \ \Phi xx)Ia$$

of which each one is λ-convertible to each of the others. Because I is taken as a primitive (functional) constant and Iaa is in λ-normal form, the corresponding proposition surrogate is, as was found above,

$$\langle\lambda\Phi\lambda x\lambda y \ . \ \Phi xy, I, a, a\rangle.$$

By analogy we might assume that the proposition surrogates for the other two sentences are

$$\langle\lambda\Psi\lambda u\lambda v \ . \ (\lambda\Phi\lambda x\lambda y \ . \ \Phi xy)\Psi uv, I, a, a\rangle$$

and

$$\langle\lambda\Psi\lambda u \ . \ (\lambda\Phi\lambda x \ . \ \Phi xx)\Psi u, I, a\rangle.$$

But by reducing these last two expressions to λ-normal form we find as proposition surrogates for the second and third sentences

$$\langle\lambda\Psi\lambda u\lambda v \ . \ \Psi uv, I, a, a\rangle$$

and

$$\langle\lambda\Psi\lambda u \ . \ \Psi uu, I, a\rangle$$

respectively. Of the three sentences named, we thus find (as at least plausible) that the first two do indeed have the same proposition surrogate, but not the third.

For a sentence not in λ-normal form it will therefore be better to define the proposition surrogate as being the same as the proposition surrogate corresponding to the λ-normal form of the given sentence. As a consequence we will have the situation that two sentences have the same corresponding proposition surrogate (and hence presumably express the same proposition) if and only if they differ only by λ-conversion and by interchange of synonymous constants or other fully synonymous notations. This is the identity criterion that I have called Alternative (1) in my papers about Frege's intensional logic.[23] But the same three

---

[23] See in particular the abstract in the *Journal of Symbolic Logic* 11 (1946): 31, and the paper in *Noûs* that is referred to in footnote 22.

alternatives (0), (1), and (2) may well be considered in connection with Russell's notion of proposition,[24] and in connection with proposition surrogates.

Connectives and quantifiers that occur in a sentence must be treated as being or involving constants—names of functions of appropriate kinds— in order to obtain from the sentence a proposition surrogate that will serve our present purpose.

Consider, for example, Cicero's remark, *If Julius Caesar is a man, then Julius Caesar is mortal.* Putting this into a formalized language, we may write it as

$$Hj \supset Mj$$

where j is an individual constant denoting Julius Caesar, and H and M are functional constants with such meaning that Hx expresses that x is a man and Mx expresses that x is mortal. Then consider the two sentences

$$Hj \supset Mj$$

and

$$Hj \supset Mj \supset Mj \supset Mj.^{25}$$

These sentences are equivalent by propositional calculus, yet someone not well versed in propositional calculus may well believe (what is expressed by) the first one, and yet be in doubt about the second one because it seems to him complicated and not easily analyzed.

Thus the two sentences, though logically equivalent, differ as to possibilities of belief, and the corresponding proposition surrogates must therefore be different. It seems that the best way to deal with this is to use, not the connective $\supset$, but a letter, say, C, as name of the binary propositional function associated with the connective.[26] Then the sentence

$$Hj \supset Mj$$

---

[24] As it appears in the first edition of *Principia Mathematica* and in *The Principles of Mathematics*, after some corrections in at least the latter case.

[25] Brackets and parentheses are omitted under the convention of association to the left.

[26] We must therefore take (unasserted) sentences as names of something, possibly (following Frege) of truth-values, or possibly (following the early Russell) of propositions.

is rewritten as

$$C(Hj)(Mj)$$

and its proposition surrogate is therefore

$$\langle \lambda f \lambda \Phi \lambda x \lambda \Psi \lambda y \ . \ f(\Phi x)(\Psi y), C, H, j, M, j \rangle.$$

Similarly

$$Hj \supset Mj \supset Mj \supset Mj$$

is rewritten as

$$C(C(C(Hj)(Mj))(Mj))(Mj)$$

and so has as its proposition surrogate

$$\langle \lambda f \lambda g \lambda h \lambda \Phi \lambda w \lambda \Psi_1 \lambda x \lambda \Psi_2 \lambda y \lambda \Psi_3 \lambda z \ . $$
$$f(g(h(\Phi w)(\Psi_1 x)(\Psi_2 y)(\Psi_3 z))),$$
$$C, C, C, H, j, M, j, M, j, M, j \rangle.$$

For similar reasons the universal quantifier is best treated as a universality function Π, used together with the abstraction operator λ when and as required. For example, "All men are mortal" becomes in the formalized language $\Pi(\lambda x \ . \ C(Hx)(Mx))$, but "Everything is mortal" may be written simply as ΠM. Something similar applies to the description operator $\imath$ if it is taken as primitive—but here it may be better to adopt Russell's contextual definition.[27]

Proposition surrogates under Alternative (0), as criterion of identity, may be obtained by the following modification of the method of the two preceding sections. Let S be the sentence for which the proposition surrogate is to be found and let there be n occurrences of constants in S, call them $c_1, c_2, \ldots, c_n$ in left-to-right order. Thus $c_1, c_2, \ldots, c_n$ are not necessarily all different when taken as constants rather than as occurrences of constants. Let $x_1, x_2, \ldots, x_n$ be n different variables such that x_i is of the same type as c_i, $i = 1, 2, \ldots, n$, and the replacement of c_i by x_i (at the one place which is the occurrence of the constant that

---

[27] That Russell's contextual definition of descriptions does not resolve the paradox of the name relation without resort to intensional propositional functions does not mean that it may not be used for other purposes (such as economy). And even the use of intensionalities is not in the writer's view ultimately objectionable, it is merely that it ought not to be resorted to without a carefully formulated theory of the particular intensionalities.

is referred to by c_i) will not result in the capture of the variable x_i.[28] Then let $\mathbf{M}$ be the result of replacing each c_i in $\mathbf{S}$ (at the place which is its occurrence in $\mathbf{S}$) by the variable x_i. Then the free variables in $\mathbf{M}$ are x_1, $x_2,\ldots,$ x_n, each with exactly one free occurrence in $\mathbf{M}$. After thus finding $\mathbf{M}$, we find $\mathbf{M}^*$ by replacing every occurrence in $\mathbf{M}$ of the notation $(\mathbf{FA})$, for application of a function $\mathbf{F}$ to an argument A, by the notation $\langle \mathbf{F}, A \rangle$ for the ordered pair of $\mathbf{F}$ and A as this notation is explained in footnote 22. Then the proposition surrogate is

$$\langle \lambda\, x_1 \lambda\, x_2 \ldots \lambda\, x_n\, \mathbf{M}^*,\, c_1,\, c_2,\, \ldots,\, c_n \rangle.\text{[29]}$$

For instance, let $\mathbf{S}_1$ be the sentence

$$\Pi(\lambda x\ .\ C(Hx)(Mx))$$

which was introduced as an example in the last paragraph of the preceding section. Because $\mathbf{S}_1$ is in λ-normal form, the proposition surrogate under Alternative (1) is

$$\langle \lambda F \lambda f \lambda \Phi \lambda \Psi\ .\ F(\lambda x\ .\ f(\Phi x)(\Psi x)), \Pi, C, H, M \rangle$$

and the proposition surrogate under Alternative (0) is

$$\langle \lambda F \lambda f \lambda \Phi \lambda \Psi \langle F, \lambda x \langle f, \langle \Phi, x \rangle, \langle \Psi, x \rangle \rangle \rangle, \Pi, C, H, M \rangle.$$

As a very simple example of a sentence obtained from $\mathbf{S}_1$ by λ-conversion let $\mathbf{S}_2$ be the sentence

$$((\lambda \Phi \lambda \Psi\ .\ \Pi(\lambda x\ .\ C(\Phi x)(\Psi x)))HM).$$

The proposition surrogate of $\mathbf{S}_2$ under Alternative (1) is of course still the same as that of $\mathbf{S}_1$; but the proposition surrogate of $\mathbf{S}_2$ under Alternative (0) is found as follows. First

$$\mathbf{M} \text{ is } (\lambda \Phi \lambda \Psi\ .\ F(\lambda x\ .\ f(\Phi x)(\Psi x)))\Theta\Omega.$$

Hence $\mathbf{M}^*$ is

---

[28] I.e., c_i is not in a wf part of $\mathbf{S}$ of the form $\lambda\, x_i\, \mathbf{W}$.

[29] Another possible determination of the proposition surrogate under Alternative (0) is just to replace every occurrence in $\mathbf{S}$ of the notation $(\mathbf{FA})$ for application of function to argument by the notation $\langle \mathbf{F}, \mathbf{A} \rangle$ for the ordered pair of $\mathbf{F}$ and $\mathbf{A}$. But the definition in the text is preferred because of the closer analogy with the proposition surrogate under Alternative (1), an ordered $(n+1)$-tuple of which the first term shows in a certain sense the form of $\mathbf{S}$, and the other n terms show the constants occurring in $\mathbf{S}$.

$$\langle \lambda\Phi\lambda\Psi\langle F, \lambda x\langle f, \langle\Phi, x\rangle, \langle\Psi, x\rangle\rangle\rangle, \Theta, \Omega\rangle.$$

Therefore the proposition surrogate of S_2 is

$$\langle \lambda F\lambda f\lambda\Theta\lambda\Omega\langle\lambda\Phi\lambda\Psi\langle F, \lambda x\langle f, \langle\Phi, x\rangle, \langle\Psi, x\rangle\rangle\rangle, \Theta, \Omega\rangle, \Pi, C, H, M\rangle.$$

Two defects of the proposal which we have just outlined, to replace propositions by proposition surrogates, must finally be pointed out.

The first of these is the complicated character of the array of types into which the proposition surrogates fall, under our present scheme. In contrast, the propositions of *Principia Mathematica* are distinguished merely as being of first order, of second order, and so on, thus falling into a simply infinite array of types which has the order type ω of the natural numbers. It may be that this is not a defect of major importance, but it also may be that it can be remedied by some change in type theory on which the formalized language is based or by some change in the definition of proposition surrogate or by a combination of the two.[30]

I am indebted to Yoram Gutgeld for calling the second defect to my attention. The formalized language must not have two different primitive constants, say, c_1 and c_2, which denote the same thing but do not have the same sense.[31] For in this case it may well happen that someone who

---

[30] The proposal to avoid the defect by changing to a language based on a set-theoretic approach rather than type-theoretic would seem to be not very significant. For this can be done only at the cost of abandoning Russell's comprehension principle for propositional functions (as it is described above in the second section of this paper). Then if the comprehension principle is restored in the weakened form, that an application of the principle yields an entity of a new sort, a class as distinguished from a set, this is (as well known) the beginning of a new hierarchy of types—as classes cannot, without fear of contradiction, be allowed as members of sets but must rather be members of superclasses, and so on.

[31] Let us call two constants *concurrent* if they denote the same thing, and let us call a class of constants a *concurrent* class if all members of the class denote the same thing.

A now familiar example of two such constants c_1 and c_2 in a natural language is that of the names $\Phi\omega\sigma\phi\acute{o}\rho\sigma\varsigma$ and $\text{'}E\sigma\pi\epsilon\rho\sigma\varsigma$ in ancient Greek. For brevity let us use "c_1" and "c_2" respectively for these two Greek words. Then c_1 is the brilliant white planet which, at times, rises in the east before the sun at an interval which varies from more than three hours down to a fraction of a minute; and c_2 is the brilliant white planet which, at times, is similarly seen in the western sky after sunset. We may suppose that these are primitive constants, although this is never definite in a natural language prior to all formalization. The early Greeks, not knowing that $c_1 = c_2$, used the two different names for the supposedly different planets. After the discovery by Pythagoras that $c_1 = c_2$ became known a third name $\acute{o}$ $\tau\hat{\eta}\varsigma$ $\overset{\prime}{A}\phi\rho\sigma\delta\acute{\iota}\tau\eta\varsigma$ $\overset{\prime}{\alpha}\sigma\tau\acute{\eta}\rho$ (Aphrodite's Star) was introduced for the (in a sense) newly discovered planet that is c_1 and also is c_2.

believes that $c_1 = c_1$ nevertheless fails to believe that $c_1 = c_2$. Yet if we make use of proposition surrogates as objects of belief in the way that we have described in this paper, it will then follow, if x believes that $c_1 = c_1$, that x also believes that $c_1 = c_2$. Or, more generally, if x believes anything about c_1, he must also believe the same about c_2, so restoring the paradox of the name relation.

The most immediate repair of this second defect is as follows. From a given sentence a corresponding ordered n-tuple is first obtained in the way that is described in the three preceding sections, and in the expression of this ordered n-tuple each primitive constant is then replaced by a name of its sense. The resulting expression then denotes an ordered n-tuple which is taken as the proposition surrogate corresponding to the given sentence. In this way the paradox of the name relation is resolved, but not entirely without use of intensionalities—as notwithstanding lack of a general definition of the distinction between what is intensional and what is extensional, the Fregean sense of a name is clearly an intensional entity.

Languages are of course possible within which no two primitive constants denote the same thing. For given any primitive constant we may delete from the language all but one of the class of primitive constants that are concurrent with it (see footnote 31). *Whether it is always effectively possible to cut down the vocabulary of a given language so that no pair of concurrent but non-synonymous primitive constants remains* is an open question. The difficulty lies in a method by which to determine in regard to each pair of primitive constants whether they are concurrent.

9

On Direct Reference

Harry Deutsch[1]

> His ineffable effable
> Effanineffable
> Deep and inscrutable singular Name.

Old Possum's Book of Practical Cats

I. Introduction

I want to draw attention to some central and interesting, yet widely ignored, features of Kaplan's analysis of rigid designation and direct reference in his monograph *Demonstratives* [8]. I have in mind the "two-dimensional" or "double-indexed" nature of Kaplan's analysis, the associated nonstandard criterion of validity, and the resulting failure of the principle of *necessitation* and of what I call the principle of *validation*. It seems to me that neglect of these features of Kaplan's work has led to confusion concerning both the notions of rigid designation and direct reference themselves as well as the variety of technical possibilities for the

[1] I wish to thank my colleague and friend Robert Steinman for helpful discussions on the topic of this paper. The paper was written in a rush to meet an unexpected deadline. Its main ideas, however, occurred to me more than fifteen years ago when I was working on a doctoral dissertation on indexicality at UCLA. This accounts for the "dated" nature of some of the examples. I am very grateful to John Perry for encouraging me to submit a paper for inclusion in this volume.

formulation of quantified modal logic with rigid terms (QML-R). There is now something of a consensus that QML-R should be based on free quantification theory.[2] Such a view derives, I believe, from a mistaken account of rigidity. With the right account in place there is no need for free logic.

There seems also to be a consensus that the double-indexing is relevant only to the treatment of indexical terms and operators, and has no bearing on the semantics of proper names. Kaplan himself has encouraged this view by (1) admitting to doubts as to whether proper names can be fitted into the semantical framework he develops for indexicals, (2) down-playing the role of possible-worlds semantics in the characterization of direct reference, and (3) stressing an analogy between proper names and free variables—as the latter have come to be treated in quantified modal logic. But I will argue that these doubts have to do with the theory of *meaning* Kaplan formulates for indexicals; they do not concern the underlying theory of *reference*—which can and should be applied to the case of proper names. Furthermore, the free-variable model of direct reference obscures—indeed *obliterates*—an essential feature of the concept, namely, what I call its *relativity*. There are, I shall argue, two ways to define rigidity: a single-indexed or *absolute* way and a double-indexed or *relative* way. The former way is inadequate but it is the one central to recent discussions of QML-R and much work in the philosophy of language. Some philosophers have recognized the need for the two-dimensional account,[3] but apparently neither the word nor its import has quite gotten out.[4] To illustrate this, I shall focus on two arguments found in the recent literature. One is an argument given by James Garson in [6] to show that QML-R requires free quantification theory; the other is an argument that arises in the course of a recent debate in the pages of *Mind* concerning "Kaplan-rigidity" versus "Kripke-rigidity." I will start with the latter.

---

[2] 'Consensus' may be too strong a word, but I think [6] speaks at least for a prevailing tendency. See, for example, [4] and [5].

[3] See [16] and especially [2]. One of the themes of the latter is very close to that developed in section III below, but there is an important interpretive difference. See footnote 22 below. [1] might be counted in were it not for the odd fact that its author does not exploit the power of his "truth *at* a world/truth *in* a world" distinction in dealing with the issues he discusses in [1].

[4] A good indication of this—better than the two mentioned in the text below—is the problem to which [18] is devoted and the treatment it receives there. See section VII below.

II. Kaplan-Rigidity versus Kripke-Rigidity

In *Demonstratives*[5] Kaplan characterizes a rigid designator "in the *modified* sense" as "an expression which designates the same thing in *all* possible worlds (irrespective of whether the thing exists in the possible world or not)." Kripke had earlier defined a term to be rigid if it designates the same thing in each world in which that thing exists. Kaplan remarks that his version was Kripke's "intended concept."

> There are two 'definitions' of 'rigid designator' in *Naming and Necessity*, pp. 48–49. The first conforms to what seems to me to have been the intended concept—same designation in *all* possible worlds ....[6]

I do not know whether Kaplan is right about Kripke's intentions,[7] but there are reasons—which I'll come to shortly—to prefer Kaplan's version of rigidity to Kripke's. On the face of it, however, Kaplan's version seems open to the following objection: If an object does not exist in a world w, then it cannot *be* anything in w; it cannot be a mountain or a boy or red. (Such properties might be termed "positive" in contrast to such "negative" properties as not being a mountain, or not existing, and the like.) So let α be a term that rigidly designates an object a at a world w where a does not exist. Then for any predicate P expressing some such positive property, the sentence $P\alpha$ expressing that a has this property is false in w. Hence its negation $\sim P\alpha$ is true in w. Now suppose that everything that does exist in w has this very property. In that event, the sentence $\exists x \sim Px$ is false in w. So it seems that the principle of "existential generalization" (EG) will fail—*even when the term of generalization* (e.g., α) *is rigid*. Robert Steinman raises this objection in [17] and it is seconded by A. D. Smith in [15]. If it were correct, it might appear to be a strong objection to Kaplan-rigidity. In the first place, it would mean that QML-R with Kaplan-rigid terms could not be based on classical quantification theory; it would require instead a free logic. For those of us who find free logic otherwise un-well-motivated, but who accept the notion of rigidity, this would be a reason to reject

---

[5] [8], 497.

[6] [8], 493, footnote 16.

[7] I doubt that he is. Kaplan says: "In spite of the textual evidence, systematic considerations, including the fact that variables cannot be accounted for otherwise, leave me with the conviction that the former notion [Kaplan-rigidity] was intended." Kaplan seems "locked into" the free-variable model of rigidity. But that is no reason to attribute it to Kripke.

Kaplan's approach.[8] Secondly, it is not stretching the truth by much to say that rigid terms were first introduced as part of the solution to the problem of "quantifying in." Rigid terms were supposed to serve as "safe" substituends in the application EG and the substitutivity of identicals. The idea was to have a kind of term that "stuck" to its referent so tenaciously that no contingency could break the connection. For consider a model in which there are only two possible worlds w_1 and w_2, each accessible from the other. Let the term β refer to the object b in w_1 and to a different object c in w_2. Suppose that both b and c (and only b and c) exist in each of these worlds. Suppose also that in w_1, b but not c has the property P, and in w_2, c but not b has P. Then $\Box P\beta$ is true in w_1 (and in w_2) but $\exists x \Box P x$ is false in w_1 (and in w_2). So if a term was fickle like β, an application of EG could easily lead from truth to falsehood even in a constant domain semantics, i.e., a semantics in which each world has the same domain of quantification. The solution was to apply the rule only to terms whose reference does not vary—namely, to rigid designators. If Steinman's argument were correct, it would at least suggest that Kripke-rigidity is to be preferred to Kaplan-rigidity on the grounds that the latter fails to accord with one of the basic reasons for deploying rigid designators in the first place.

A variant of Steinman's argument shows that the use of "negative" properties is not essential.[9] Suppose α is a Kaplan-rigid term whose referent is a. Assume that a exists in w_2 and has the property F therein, but fails to exist in w_1. Let nothing except a have F in any world and assume that w_2 is accessible from w_1. Then $\Diamond F\alpha$ is true in w_1, but $\exists x \Diamond F x$ is false in w_1. Thus, for example, since 'Hitler was a tyrant' is true in the actual world, 'Possibly, Hitler was a tyrant' is true in any world from which the actual world is accessible, including those in which Hitler never existed. If 'Hitler' is "Kaplan-rigid," sentences containing it may have a truth-value whether Hitler exists or not. But conceivably, there may be nothing in some such world w_1, which could even possibly be a tyrant. Perhaps in w_1 there are no sentient creatures at all.

---

[8] Free logic runs roughshod over all the interesting issues concerning the semantics of fictional names. It argues that 'Santa Claus drives a sled with flying reindeer' is true, but 'someone drives a sled with flying reindeer' is false. Yet in the very sense in which the latter is false, the former is false also. And in the very sense in which the former is true (as prefixed by "according to the tale ..."), the latter is also true.

[9] Smith [15] seems to think that Steinman's argument conflates "internal" and "external" negation. It doesn't matter whether it does or not.

What should we make of these arguments? In the first place, as directed against the system of QML-R contained in Kaplan's logic LD of demonstratives, neither argument is strictly correct. In Kaplan's formulation, the quantifiers of LD are *possibilist* quantifiers. An existentially quantified formula of LD such as '$\exists x F x$' holds at a point p in a model if there is some *possible object* belonging to the extension of F at the "world of evaluation" of p. It is not required that the object exist at that world. That is, it is not required that the object fall in the extension of the special LD predicate 'Exists' at the world of evaluation relative to p. Kaplan allows in fact that the extension of 'Exists' might be empty. In Kaplan's semantics, a term can refer to an object that does not exist without bringing down EG (and without calling into being a species of nonexistent objects).[10] Furthermore, Kaplan's semantics allows that an object can possess positive properties at worlds where the object does not exist. An object might belong to the extension of a predicate symbol at a world where that object does not exist. The extension of an ordinary one-place predicate of individuals at a world is an arbitrary subset of the domain U of all possible individuals. There is no additional requirement that any of these objects exist (i.e., belong to the extension of 'Exists' at that world). So in Kaplan's semantics, predication as well as quantification is "possibilist." An object might *be* something at a world in which it does not exist. Steinman's argument (though not the variant of it) founders on this point as well.

Secondly, and more importantly, even if one takes the objections to be directed against an unnamed version of QML-R—one with actualist quantifiers and perhaps even actualist predication[11]—one may be in-

---

[10] I assume in what follows that EG is a principle concerning *quantification* and only indirectly a principle concerning *existence*. In Kaplan's semantics, the inference from 'Fido is a dog' to 'Fido exists' fails. But this has nothing to do with the rigidity of 'Fido' nor with EG. It is due instead to the way in which Kaplan's existence predicate behaves. Thus, similarly, the inference from 'The present King of France is bald' to 'The present King of France exists' fails—even assuming that the description is proper.

EG will fail in Kaplan's semantics if the term of generalization t is *undefined*, i.e., if t denotes the dagger (†), which represents "a completely alien object"—in effect, an impossible object. This object lies outside the range of Kaplan's quantifiers.

It could be argued that Kaplan's metalanguage carries a commitment to the existence of possible but nonactual objects. Perhaps it does and perhaps it doesn't. It depends on the application. One *can* think of the domain of a model as consisting of just actual objects, which exist or don't exist in this or that possible world.

[11] Ever since the publication of Kripke's paper [11], possibilist predication has been a standard feature of quantified modal logic—and with good reason. As Kripke

clined merely to shrug them off. Of course in such a system, EG will fail for Kaplan-rigid terms. After all, if the variables of Kripke's 1963 semantics [11] are the paradigms of direct reference, it should come as no surprise that EG will fail as applied to such terms. In Kripke's semantics, the value of a variable is fixed independently of the framework of possible worlds and their associated domains. In fact, the value of a variable at a world *cannot* be required to be an element of the domain of the world since then the presence of modal operators would make it impossible to state the semantical clause for quantification.

So much, then, for original motivation. Or rather, perhaps the original motivation had less to do with providing safe substituends for EG and more with permitting (and avoiding) the "exporting" of a term from within to without an intensional context. If 'Hitler' is directly referential, we should be able to go gently from 'Necessarily, Hitler was a tyrant' to 'Hitler was such that necessarily he was a tyrant'. Whether the latter entails 'Someone was such that necessarily he was a tyrant' is another question, and one that probably should be answered in the negative. For consider the analogous temporal case: It is true that Hitler was the tyrant who created the Third Reich, i.e., that Hitler was such that he was the tyrant who created the Third Reich. But presumably no one alive now is such that he was the tyrant who created the Third Reich. We are entitled *now* to refer directly, rigidly, to Hitler, although, mercifully, he no longer exists; and the consequent failure of (present tense) EG is equally comforting. Indeed, it is just this sort of example that leads Kaplan from Kripke-rigidity to his "modified" notion, and he takes his inspiration from Kripke:

> In arguing that the object designated by a rigid designator need not exist in every possible world, [Kripke] seems to assert that under certain circumstances what is expressed by 'Hitler does not exist' would have been true, and not because 'Hitler' would have designated nothing (in *that* case we might have given the sentence *no* truth-value) but because what 'Hitler' would have designated—namely Hitler—would

---

points out (note 11), although the actualist alternative is conceptually natural, it leads (in the context of the rest of Kripke's semantics) to a failure of the rule of substitution. For example (in Kripke's notation), although for 'P' a one-place predicate symbol and 'x' a variable, the formula $P(x) \supset \sim (x) \sim P(x)$ would be valid, the formula $\sim P(x) \supset \sim (x) \sim\sim P(x)$ would not be valid. Thus actualist predication gives rise to both a failure of EG and a failure of substitution.

not have existed.[12]

Kaplan infers from this that 'Hitler', as most of us use the name, should designate Hitler in every world, regardless whether Hitler exists therein, though he is quick to remark in effect that the form of the word 'Hitler' could have been used (and in fact is used) to designate things other than Hitler.

Kaplan is firm about the relation between reference and existence: Reference does not entail existence. However, he seems ambivalent about the relation between reference and quantification. In [9] he remarks that "the universe of discourse of a theory need not be limited to the values of the variables ... A theory may afford recognition to ... entities by mentioning them individually, by name or singular term, without quantifying over them." For example, "Though our variable binding discourse be limited to natural numbers, we may wish to drop an occasional reference to an unnatural rational ...." On the other hand, the broad scope of the quantifiers of LD does not permit us to drop such occasional references. I think that when Kaplan came to formulate LD he decided that it would be best to base the system as far as possible on classical quantification theory, and that is why he chose to deploy possibilist quantifiers. I believe Kaplan is right that reference—in particular, direct reference—does not entail existence. But I want to show that given the *right* account of direct reference, there is no need to use possibilist quantifiers in order to preserve the classical rules. This will count as a proper reply to those who think that the doctrine of direct reference conflicts with the principles of classical logic.

Unfortunately, the right account of direct reference is not the one Kaplan has succeeded in communicating. In [8], Kaplan stresses that the referent of a directly referential term is not a function—not even a constant function—of the "passing circumstance" (possible world):

> In actual fact, the referent, in a circumstance, of a directly referential term is simply *independent* of the circumstance and is no more a function (constant or otherwise) of circumstance, than my action is a function of your desires when I decide to do it whether you like it or not.[13]

This may serve to distinguish directly referential terms from de facto rigid terms such as '$\sqrt{2}$'; and it underscores the point Kaplan most

---

[12] [8], 492–93.
[13] [8], 497.

wants to emphasize—that direct reference is not mediated by a concept that, together with a possible world, determines a referent. The trouble is that people have come away from this with the impression that directly referential terms are nothing more than contentless expressions having constant denotation—just like Kripke's 1963 variables. To a logician such as Garson, this just *means* that rigid constants are *primitive* terms whose intensions are constant functions.[14] (And by the way, if my action would remain the same whatever your desires, then my action *is* a trivial (constant) function of your desires. It is only if your single desire would prompt several different acts of mine that my actions would not be a function of your desires!) This impression has only been reinforced by Kaplan's frequently mentioned "picture" of propositions, which contain individuals themselves rather than individual concepts. The picture may help turn our attention from the Frege-Carnap picture: Concept-plus-world determines referent, but I contend that it does not accurately depict the alternative non-Frege-Carnap outlook, and it raises irrelevant questions regarding the existence conditions of such "singular" propositions.[15] The basic difficulty with all these characterizations is that they leave out of account the *relativity* of direct reference.

III. The Relativity of Direct Reference

In [9] Kaplan gives the following definition of denotation for proper names:

> If α is a proper name used on a particular occasion, then
>
> (i) α denotes x if and only if α originated in a dubbing of x and
>
> (ii) for all possible circumstances w, α denotes x with respect to w if and only if α denotes x.[16]

---

[14] See [6].

[15] I would argue that the subject constituents of such singular propositions should not be the individuals themselves but rather "rigid individual concepts"—in the relativistic sense explained below (186). It strikes me as rather odd, if not contradictory, to say that while the singular proposition that Hitler was a tyrant does not now exist (since Hitler does not exist), it is nevertheless a true proposition. If we take the subject constituents to be rigid individual concepts, this problem disappears. The (relatively) rigid concepts are as "abstract" and noncontingent as are the names with which they are associated.

[16] [9], 502.

And he adds: "It is a corollary that if α did not originate in a successful dubbing (one which is a dubbing of *some x*), α nowhere denotes anything."

This is fine if you read it only once and never again. If you read it twice, something could go wrong. When I first read this (in 1970 or so), I had no son named 'Max'. By that time, however, I had resolved to name *a* son of mine 'Max'. So at the time, the name 'Max Deutsch' did not originate in a successful dubbing, and hence I concluded that it "nowhere denotes anything." I now find, after a second reading, that the name does denote something, and that according to Kaplan's definition, it denotes that thing in "all possible circumstances," including those in which I concluded that it "nowhere denotes anything." Notice, though, that Kaplan requires that α be "a proper name used on a particular occasion." This may seem to help: Current uses of 'Max Deutsch' refer rigidly, past (pre-1971) uses fail to refer—and do so equally rigidly. I think this does help, when understood properly, but one has to be careful: What *is* a use of a name? Is it an utterance or other token of it? A speech act or event? (No doubt to use a name is not simply to *employ* it in discourse, but also to *use* it—as opposed to *mentioning* it.) Whatever it is, it might be something that lasts quite a long time. A particular token of 'Max Deutsch' might have lasted the past seventeen years, and if so, the same problem concerning what *it* rigidly designates would arise. The point is that it is not the change of *subject*—from names to uses of names—that helps, but rather the note of change in the semantic properties of the name or of its use. One way to express this change is to use a tensed denotation predicate: At one time (pre-1971), 'Max Deutsch' *denoted* nothing in either 1970 or 1987. It *now denotes* Max Deutsch in 1987 *and* 1970. We should read Kaplan's 'denotes' as being in the present tense and then not forget that time passes, things change, names too change with respect to their semantic properties. But in theoretical semantics, it is not convenient to have a tensed metalanguage; and furthermore, as we will see, names are subject to the same sort of semantic change or variation with respect to *possible worlds*, and the framework of possible worlds possesses no natural underlying ordering analogous to past, present, and future. So instead of using a tensed denotation predicate, we can introduce a second parameter that functions something like a frame of reference. Then we can say, for example, that *relative to 1970*, 'Max Deutsch' denotes nothing in either 1970 or 1987; but *relative to 1987* it denotes Max Deutsch in both 1987 and 1970. Here 'denotes' is untensed.

It seems to me that the need for the frame of reference (or *point of view*, as I sometimes call it) runs deep in the semantics of names, and this need is not satisfied by relatively casual references to "occasions of use." In this connection, names are often confused with indexicals. But in the case of names and unlike indexicals, what matters is not the *orientation* of the context of use itself—the speaker, location, time, possible world, etc., to which the use belongs, but rather the *point of view* invoked by the use. Let's imagine, for example, that time travel is logically possible.[17] So suppose I return to 1970 and assert that Max Deutsch is alive and well in 1987. My act of assertion *takes place in the past*, but its frame of reference is the present. Charitable listeners would regard my statement as a complex prediction about the future; they would have some difficulty adopting to my point of view. These difficulties would be, however, epistemological, not logical. I could very well explain to anyone willing to listen that from the point of view of 1987, my assertion—which takes place in 1970—is straightforwardly true in 1970; although from the point of view of 1970, it is false or lacking in truth-value in 1970. I might even be understood. Yet suppose that upon returning to the past I say *"yesterday* the Dow Jones Industrials declined 508 points." My listeners would rightly take me to be suggesting that the day prior to the day on which my assertion takes place (that is, some time in 1970), the Dow stood at 250 or thereabouts.[18] The point is that the referent of 'yesterday' depends on the actual orientation of the context of use (in particular, it depends on the actual time at which the utterance is produced) in a way that the referent of the name 'Max Deutsch' does not. In general, names *are* "context-dependent" in the sense that what they refer to depends on the frame of reference invoked by the context. Yet, generally, what a name refers to will *not* depend *directly* on the orientation of the context. Of course, sometimes it will. Most names are shared by many things. Hence, to tell which of several things having the same name is under discussion, we must try to determine the intentions of *the speaker*—and *the speaker* is one of the elements of the context's orientation.

Failure to take the frame of reference into account has rather serious consequences. Consider the following two sentences:

(1)   Cassius Clay will develop brain damage.

---

[17] So David Lewis has argued in "The Paradoxes of Time Travel," *American Philosophical Quarterly* 13 (1976): 145–52.

[18] In March of 1970 the Dow was 760 or so.

(2)   Muhammad Ali knocked out Sonny Liston.

I take it that if (1) were used in 1965, it would have expressed a true proposition, and that (2) now expresses a true proposition. But it might be wondered how either (1) or (2) could be true. According to standard tense-logical semantics, (1) is true in 1965 if and only if at some time after 1965 the present-tense sentence

(3)   Cassius Clay develops brain damage

is true. And (2) is true now if and only if at some time prior to now, the present-tense sentence

(4)   Muhammad Ali knocks out Sonny Liston

is true. If one ignores the frame of reference, it is difficult to see how either (3) or (4) could be true at *any* time. Surely neither qualifies as an accurate newspaper headline. Anyone who knew the facts and who read (4) as a headline would have deemed it false (or nonsense); and a similar verdict on (3) should be forthcoming from anyone who knows that to now introduce Muhammad Ali as "Cassius Clay" would not only be dangerously rude but also semantically incorrect.[19]

This difficulty can be resolved by using the notion of the frame of reference: Relative to the present, i.e., the frame of reference of an utterance of (2), the occurrence of 'Muhammad Ali' in (4) refers (rigidly) to Muhammad Ali, and the whole of (4) expresses a proposition that is true at a time t if and only if Muhammad Ali knocks out Sonny Liston at t. Since this proposition is true in 1965, (2), as it should, turns out to be true. But relative to the time at which Muhammad Ali knocked out Sonny Liston, the occurrence of 'Muhammad Ali' in (4) denotes nothing; and the whole of (4) expresses no proposition at all, or in any event not the right one. Relative to *that* time, the occurrence of 'Muhammad Ali' in (4) "nowhere denotes anything." A similar explanation shows why (1) was true in 1965.

It may be objected that there is no need to bring in frames of reference to resolve the problem of the truth of (1) and (2). A simpler solution is available. We can say instead that despite an element of impropriety, (3) *is* true at present, and that in hindsight (4) was true in

---

[19] Actually, Cassius Clay acquired the name 'Muhammad Ali' in 1963 when he became a Black Muslim. As late as the second Clay-Cooper fight in 1966 he was known to the public as 'Cassius Clay'. Since this is a little-known fact, it doesn't affect the force of the example, much less its point.

1965 despite the fact that back then it would have seemed incoherent, or at least quite puzzling. In fact, it might be argued that this very position is a consequence of the doctrine of rigidity: If names are rigid, then once an object acquires a certain name, the name refers to that object through thick and thin. This is sometimes expressed by saying that if a name α denotes x, then necessarily, α denotes x. Such a view seems to be a simple consequence of definitions of rigidity such as Kaplan's. And it is backed up by examples in which α clearly denotes x even though social and legal conventions dictate that x is not *called* α. For example, the occurrence of 'Cassius Clay' in a *present* (true) assertion of

(5)   Cassius Clay knocked out Sonny Liston

denotes Muhammad Ali, although the man is not now *called* 'Cassius Clay'. If it is protested that the relation between a thing and its name is purely contingent, or that a thing can change its name, the reply will be that the *acquisition* of a name is a contingent matter, but once a name is possessed, its continued *possession* is guaranteed. In fact, if, for example, a person acquires a certain name *in the future*, that person possesses that name (in the sense of being its referent) even prior to acquiring it.

Now I think there is a grain of truth in this view, but the rest of it is false. It is true that α might denote x at t, although x is not called α at t—as (5) perfectly well illustrates. My argument that (3) and (4) are not true independently of appropriate frames of reference does not depend on denying this principle. It depends instead on the weaker principle that if contextual orientation and frame of reference *coincide*—as they do when we imagine what it would have been like in 1965 to try to get anything across by uttering (4)—*then* if x is not called α, α does not denote x. The occurrence of 'Cassius Clay' in (5) is "backward looking." It is only relative to certain facts about 1965—that the present use of the name in (5) now denotes Mohammad Ali. It is this that gives (5) its air of historical accuracy as compared with (2). Perhaps the point can be made clearer thus: (5) would have been true even if Muhammad Ali had dropped dead just after the Liston fight. (2), however, would not have been true. In those circumstances, (2) would not have expressed the proposition it does in fact express—which I take to be the same proposition as that expressed by (5). To account for this difference we need to recognize the relativity of rigidity. The idea that despite impropriety and lack of foresight, (3) and (4) are simply true (now, in the case of (3), and in 1965, in the case of (4)) may seem a harmless simplification. But it is not. To suppose that the names x did or will or might acquire, all necessarily denote x in an absolute sense, is like supposing that a nonaccelerating object moves at many different velocities.

Rigidity is relative in modal as well as temporal discourse. Like most people, I have sometimes wondered what the world would have been like had Hitler not existed. Usually in such a reverie I wish away the horrors Hitler's existence brought about. But now, for present purposes, I want to imagine that we were to find out tomorrow that the news of Herr Schicklgruber's existence was an elaborate hoax. No such person ever existed although we all thought "he" did. In this world Hitler is used (at least until tomorrow) as *we* use it. It enters into all the same language games. The inhabitants of this world use 'Hitler' in all the typical ways we use it. But, clearly, from *their* point of view, 'Hitler' does not refer to Hitler. From *their* point of view, the sentence 'Hitler does not exist' is far from straightforwardly true. *Their* difficulties with 'Hitler' are like our difficulties with 'Pegasus'. And however these problems are resolved, it will not turn out that from their point of view, 'Hitler' designates Hitler, however good a match there may be between their *fictional* information about "Hitler" and the actual facts about him. Those inhabitants who have read the Addenda to *Naming and Necessity* may even come to believe that 'Hitler', as they use the term, denotes nothing at all in any possible world.

We, however, describe such a world as one in which *Hitler* does not exist. From *our* point of view, *theirs* is a world in which 'Hitler does not exist' *is* straightforwardly true. From our point of view, 'Hitler' designates Hitler in their world and indeed in any other as well, regardless whether Hitler exists therein.

The foregoing example is a kind of dual of one Kaplan gives in [9]. He considers a world in which there really is a winged horse named 'Pegasus'. He calls such a world an "*M* world":

> But beware the confusion of our language with theirs! If w is an M world, then *their* name 'Pegasus' will denote something with respect to w, and *our* description 'the x such that x is called "Pegasus" ' will still denote the same thing with respect to w, but *our* name 'Pegasus' will still denote nothing with respect to w . . . .

> I do not object to the inhabitants of one of the M worlds remarking that their name 'Pegasus' denotes something with

respect to *our* world that does not exist in our world. But I
reserve the right to retort that *our* name 'Pegasus' does not
even denote with respect to their world.[20]

Kaplan's *M*-worlds play the role played by the actual world in my example. So "ours" and "theirs" are reversed. But the point is the same; or rather, the point would have been the same had Kaplan made it. Kaplan comes within a hair's breadth of the relativity thesis but he doesn't express it. A later remark in [9], and especially those in section XXII of [8], lead me to believe that he doesn't favor the thesis. Kaplan cautions us not to confuse our language with theirs or our names with theirs. How, then, does *our* name 'Hitler' differ from *theirs* in my example? If we discovered that "Hitler" was a hoax, we would no doubt feel fooled. Would we really feel fooled about what language we have been speaking all along? To say that *their* names differ from *ours* seems much like saying that when it appears that the same object is moving uniformly at two different velocities, what is really going on is that there are *two* objects moving at their own distinctive rates!

   This judgment may be too hasty. The section on proper names in *Demonstratives* (section XXII) is one of the most trenchant and interesting parts of that work. There Kaplan declares, with Wittgensteinian force, that "Dubbings create words," and that

> The contextual feature which consists of the causal history
> of a particular proper name expression in the agent's idiolect
> seems more naturally to be regarded as determining what
> word was used than as fixing the content of a single context-
> sensitive word.[21]

Kaplan has immediately in mind the case in which two utterances of 'Aristotle' may refer to two different objects, e.g., Aristotle Onassis and the Greek philosopher: "I am inclined to attribute this difference to the fact that distinct homonymous words were uttered rather than to a context-sensitivity in the character of a single word 'Aristotle'." So he would probably assimilate the examples I have used on behalf of the relativity thesis to the 'Aristotle' case on the ground that the former, like the latter, turn on uses of names with different causal histories.

   I agree that there is a difference between ambiguity—as in the 'Aristotle' case—and the sort of genuine context-sensitivity characteristic of

---

[20][9], 507–8.
[21][8], 562.

indexicals. I agree also that names are not context-sensitive. I have already tried to explain that relativity is not a matter of context-sensitivity of the sort characteristic of indexicals—namely, direct sensitivity to the orientation of the context of use. I could also argue that different causal histories do not spell different names. If Mom and Pop both *independently* decide to name Baby 'Max', have they then come up with *different* names for Baby? I could also point out that none of my examples concern distinct objects with the same name, as in the 'Aristotle' case. I have in fact steered clear of this sort of example. Ambiguity is the effect of several languages at work at once. Relativity is a phenomenon internal to a single reasonably rich language. The more important matter, however, is that the *point* of my examples is not abrogated by the view that "Dubbings create words," even if that view is correct. Nor would this make them bad examples. They were put forward to make a certain phenomenon more visible. They may serve to do that even if the lens is flawed. In any case, there are other ways to bring the phenomenon into focus. Thus, consider this: What makes a world in which Hitler does not exist *even conceivable*? We cannot do this by bearing in mind only *one* world. For either it is a world in which Hitler exists or it is not. If it is the former, then it is irrelevant. If it is the latter, how do we know whereof we speak? To conceive of such a world we must have *two* worlds in mind: One in which Hitler exists and one in which *he* does not exist. We must start with a world in which Hitler exists and then envisage one in which that ingredient—*Hitler*—is left out.[22] This

---

[22] This crucial point is due to Kaplan (see [9]) who adverts to it on behalf of Kaplan-rigidity. It is not clear to me, however, that Kaplan notes, or at any rate, takes seriously, the element of relativity. Joseph Almog in [2] uses the point to argue for a "two-stage" semantic theory—according to which, at the first stage, propositions are generated, which are then, at the second stage, evaluated as to their truth or falsity at various parameters (worlds, times, etc.). He argues that a one-stage theory won't do: "... it takes the name 'Quine', not the man Quine, to the Quineless world." [2], 220. In my estimation, Almog's idea is right on target but a little off-center. It bears some affinity to the relativity thesis, but it is actually closer to absolutism. Almog's first stage—the "generation stage"—is needed only to give us the right propositional constituents, and thereby to generate the right proposition to be evaluated in the second stage. Evaluation itself is one-dimensional—once we have the rigid *entity* to evaluate. To advert again to the analogy with the relativity of motion: The analogue of Almog's view would be the idea that the velocity of an object is absolute, once we have got hold of ("generated") the right object. When it seems that the same object is moving uniformly at two different velocities, in fact there are two different objects moving absolutely at different rates. Analogously, when it appears that the same object—viz., the name 'Quine'—both denotes Quine and denotes nothing in a Quineless world, that is because we are

is relativity. It is only relative to the frame of reference consisting of the first world that the sentence 'Hitler does not exist' is true in the second world. And it helps to add that relative to other frames of reference, this very sentence has a very different status: It is truth-valueless, or false according to some fictional information, or it is sheer nonsense. Perhaps, though, this doesn't help, since it involves identifying "different" words or "different" languages. But then we are in danger of losing sight of the fact that there are *two* worlds involved in conceiving of a world in which Hitler does not exist. It appears, in fact, that this is just what has happened.

I conclude that a name is directly referential only relative to a frame of reference or point of view within which its designatum is fixed once and for all as regards discourse carried on from that point of view. And since the point of view itself may shift, from *theirs* to *ours* or vice versa, this fixing of a designatum should not be represented as an absolute affair—like the assignment of a value to a variable. A more delicate mechanism is required.

IV. Double-Indexing

Kaplan exploits such a mechanism, due originally to Kamp (see [7]), in connection with the analysis of indexicals. In the section on rigid designation in *Demonstratives*, Kaplan stresses the distinction between "possible occasions of *use*—which I call '*contexts*' and 'circumstances of *evaluation*' of what was said on a given occasion of use":

> Possible circumstances of evaluation I call circumstances or, sometimes just *counterfactual situations*. A directly refer- ential term *may* designate different objects when used in different *contexts*. But when evaluating what was said in a given context, only a single object will be relevant to the evaluation in all circumstances.[23]

---

taking semantic measure of two different objects vis-à-vis the Quineless world: the *name* 'Quine' versus the *man* Quine qua constituents of different semantic entities, *sentence* versus *proposition*, undergoing evaluation at the Quineless world. If this criticism seems awkward, it is only because Almog's approach verges so closely on relativity. But if Almog has relativity in mind, why does he insist that the gen- eration stage generates the semantic objects we are next to evaluate? Fixing the frame of reference does not generate the object whose velocity we wish to measure.
[23] [8], 494.

The *context*—which *includes* a possible world c_w (the world of the context)—fixes the referent of a Kaplan-rigid term α to be a certain object, say a. Once we have this "fix" on a, we know what α is to denote in any possible *circumstance*: It is to denote a. Notice that this procedure involves a *pair* of worlds: the world c_w and a world w of evaluation. In general, $c_w \neq w$, and (despite the somewhat misleading notation), c_w is *not* a function of w. (Thus it would be better to write 'w'' for the world of evaluation so as to avoid any suggested necessary relation to c_w.) Now in Kaplan's semantics rigid terms other than the primitive indexicals are formed by attaching the *dthat*-operator to individual constants and definite descriptions. Kaplan's semantical clause for 'dthat α' is this:

$$|\text{dthat } \alpha|_{cftw} = |\alpha|_{cfc_tc_w}$$

Here c is a context, f an assignment of values to variables, and t a time. c_w is a part of c. There are other parts to c—e.g., c_t, the time of the context, and c_A, the agent of the context (the "speaker"). But let us ignore these other parameters, suppressing reference to the assignment and to definite descriptions as well. Then rewriting (and correcting for misleading notation), we have

(6) $|\text{dthat } \alpha|_{c_w,w'} = |\alpha|_{c_w,c_w} = den(\alpha, c_w)$.

We imagine that the individual constant α has already been assigned a denotation, $den(\alpha, w)$, for each world w, and that

$$|\alpha|_{c_w,w'} = den(\alpha, w')$$

for any world w' and individual constant α. Then (6) says that the denotation of 'dthat α' in w' *as fixed in* c_w is the same as the denotation of α in c_w. So the referent of a Kaplan-rigid term in *any* world is fixed to be whatever object the term picks out in the actual world c_w—whatever world happens to be actual (i.e., whatever world c_w happens to be). That is, it follows from (6) that

$$|\text{dthat } \alpha|_{c_w,w'} = |\text{dthat } \alpha|_{c_w,c_w}.$$

I have three suggestions concerning adapting these semantics to the case of names. First, let's stop thinking of 'dthat α' as a demonstrative; think of it instead as a proper name. Names in natural language have no syntactic structure; but in view of relativity, it is reasonable to represent names as having a complex syntactic structure to match that of their semantics. We could get by without this structure, but it is suggestive to have it. Secondly, let's stop thinking of c_w as the actual world or the world in which the utterance takes place, and think of it instead as the frame of reference. For example, c_w might be the world of 1965—which provides the frame of reference for a present utterance of 'Cassius Clay' as in (5).

Third, there is the question of Character. Kaplan objects to giving dthat-terms the status of names. His reason is that the Character of 'dthat α' is not Stable: 'dthat α' may have different Contents in different contexts, and Kaplan holds that a proper name has a Stable Character. He has harsh words for those who would argue that the possibility of ambiguity means that names do not have a Stable Character: "Those who suggest that proper names are merely one species of indexical depreciate the power and the mystery of the causal chain theory."[24] It could also be said that such villains deprecate the power and mystery of meaning. The linguistic meaning of the word 'I' stays constant from context to context, although the term's reference may vary and the contribution it makes to the proposition (content) expressed, may change. In contrast, virtually *nothing* (Kaplan would say *exactly* nothing) stays constant from my use of 'Aristotle' to Jackie's.

Kaplan is right about the Character of 'dthat α'. We should ignore it. It represents nothing. What good is a semantic function that connects Jackie's use of 'Aristotle' with mine? He also observes that variables are the only terms of LD with a Stable Content and Stable Character, but stops short of saying that names are—or might as well be—variables. He says instead that the introduction of names requires "context-indexed definitions," i.e., "definitions" involving dubbings.[25]

Now dubbings are themselves relativistic. In order to dub x, α, I might need to have two worlds in mind: one in which x exists and one in which I exist and do the dubbing. It is *only relative to* the world in which x exists that I succeed in my world in dubbing x, α. This means that in a sense I might succeed in dubbing x, α, without afterwards knowing just what α names. To use a familiar example due to Kaplan: Suppose I now say "Let 'Newman 1' denote the first child born in the twenty-first century." Have I succeeded in dubbing anything 'Newman 1'? Those who take their rigid designation straight will answer affirmatively. They will say that if the description is uniquely identifying,

---

[24] [8], 563.
[25] See Remark 11, page 551 of [8].

then 'Newman 1' picks out just dthat. The contrary intuition is to the effect that 'Newman 1' is a protoname that does not now denote anything despite the properness of the description, but that will eventually come to denote something. The puzzle arises because the absoluteness of definite description combines with the relativity of naming to produce an uneasy tension. My view—made formal below—is that whatever a name α denotes in w *relative to* w must exist in w. It follows that 'Newman 1' relative to the present does not presently denote anything, but relative to the world of the twenty-first century, 'Newman 1' even *now* denotes the first person born in the twenty-first century. This explains why it would be absurd for me to point to Newman 1 after his or her birth and assert that I knew in 1987 that he or she would be the first person born in the twenty-first century. My use of the name 'Newman 1' in 1987—as when I say "Newman 1 will be the first person born in the twenty-first century"—invokes a future frame of reference whose specific content is (of course) obscure to me. In [3], Donnellan marvels at our ability to introduce names like 'Newman 1', names which we cannot then use to express *de re* attitudes towards the things they denote. This would be truly peculiar if rigid reference were absolute—if it were somehow the responsibility of the rigid name itself to put us sufficiently en rapport with its referent. Of course that is not the case, and exotic examples like 'Newman 1' are not required to bring out the point. Any case of dubbing purely "by description" will do. Though I don't know what object is in the box on my desk, if there is just one object in the box, I can dub it α. There is then a sense in which I know that α is in the box and a sense in which I don't. This is sometimes expressed by saying that although I know (even a priori) that the proposition expressed by 'α is the object in the box' is true, I do not know what proposition that is, though I know it to be contingent. I prefer a different characterization. I prefer to say that the sentence 'α is the object in the box', as I use it, is true only relative to a frame of reference consisting of information about the object in the box or consisting of a certain state of affairs—that of such and such an object being in such and such a box. What I lack, then, is information about the relevant frame of reference, i.e., the one relative to which my utterance of the sentence is true. Truth not only corresponds to the facts, it is also relative to them, at least as regards sentences containing rigid designators.

If dubbings are relative, so also must be the Character, such as it is, of a name. This marks the difference between the Characters of indexicals and those of names. The Character of an indexical is transcendent;

it transcends context (= frame of reference, in the case of indexicals).
The Character of a name is immanent and internal to the the frame of
reference. The Character of a name is, in this respect, like the Character,
should we wish to grant it, of *my* use of 'I' or *your* use of it, as opposed
to the Character our respective uses share. So perhaps we can say that
the Character of a name α, at a world w, relative to a frame of reference
invoked by a dubbing in which x is dubbed α, is that function which
associates with each world the object x. We might call such a function,
so obtained, a *rigid individual concept*. It is rigid in virtually the same
way α is rigid. For it is only relative to a given frame of reference that
we can say that the *Character* of α has the value it does in every world,
including those in which x does not exist. (For those who would view
this as a sleight-of-hand trick, a more direct definition involving the
notion of a "rigid function" is possible.) The Character or meaning of
a name is a rigid individual concept, where 'rigid' is understood in the
relativistic sense.

With these stipulations, it seems to me that Kaplan's dthat-operator
(which really *should* be called something more readily pronounced)[26]
provides the means to represent the relativity of direct reference, and
withal, the semantics of names.

V. QML-R: A Proposal

Now I want to argue that we can have Kaplan rigidity without resorting
to possibilist quantification and yet without giving up the classical rules
of quantification. The exercise of developing this argument will bring out
the role of another important and largely neglected feature of Kaplan's
semantics—namely, its nonstandard criterion of validity.

Consider just the nondemonstrative, nontemporal fragment of LD
with *dthat*, and with only monadic predicate symbols (apart from identity) and no functors other than individual constants. For this language
we can describe a new class of structures $M = \langle K, D, g \rangle$, where K is a
nonempty set (of worlds), D is a function defined on K such that for
each $w \in K, D(w)$ is a nonempty set (of individuals), and g is a binary
function such that for each $w \in K$ and predicate F, $g(w, F) \subseteq U =
\bigcup_{w \in K} D(w)$ and for each individual constant a, $g(w, a) \in D(w)$. A pair
$\langle w, w' \rangle$, for $w, w' \in K$ is called a *point* of M; and a point $\langle w, w' \rangle$ satisfying $w = w'$ is called a *good point*. An *assignment* is a function mapping

---

[26]Let's shorten it to 'd'. Cf. [10].

the class of individual variables into the set U. The definitions of denotation and satisfaction are analogous to Kaplan's except that in the semantical clause for quantification, the relevant assignments all have the form f_x^a for $a \in D(w')$, where w' is the second component of the point. Thus we have, e.g.,

$$\models_{f,w,w'} \forall x F x \text{ if and only if } \models_{f_x^a,w,w'} F x$$

for each $a \in D(w')$. (Here I am deviating a bit from Kaplan's notation.)

A formula ϕ is true in M if and only if for any assignment f and any *good* point $\langle w, w \rangle$, we have $\models_{f,w,w} \phi$. A formula ϕ is *valid* if and only if it is true in any structure. A formula ϕ is a *logical consequence* of a set Γ of formulas if and only if for any structure M if each member of Γ is true in M, then ϕ is also true in M. These definitions correspond to those Kaplan gives for LD.

In this system we can reproduce Steinman's argument concerning EG: Let α be an individual constant. Suppose, as is possible, that

$$|\text{dthat } \alpha|_{w,w'} = |\alpha|_{w,w} = g(w, \alpha) \notin D(w').$$

It might also happen that $|\text{dthat } \alpha|_{w,w'} \notin g(w', F)$. So it would then be true that

(i) $\models_{w,w'} \sim F(\text{dthat } \alpha)$.

But suppose further that $D(w') \subseteq g(w', F)$. Then it is false that

(ii) $\models_{w,w'} \exists x \sim F x$.

So the inference from (i) to (ii) fails. Alternatively, we may suppose that $|\text{dthat } \alpha|_{w,w'} \in g(w', F)$ but that $D(w')$ and $g(w', F)$ are disjoint. Then after erasing the negation signs in (i) and (ii), the inference again fails. Does this show that EG as applied to rigid terms is not valid? No, of course not. For notice that the argument depends on the assumption that the point $\langle w, w' \rangle$ is not good. If we assume that this point is good, then $|\text{dthat } \alpha|_{w,w'} \in D(w')$, since $D(w) = D(w')$ and $|\text{dthat } \alpha|_{w,w'} \in D(w)$. Validity in this system (as in effect in LD) is a matter of the preservation of truth through all *good* points (in any model)—though not necessarily through *all* points.

I believe that the foregoing makes a start, anyway, towards a version of QML-R with varying domains (and consequently a genuine theory of quantification), which is based on the classical rules and which gives rigid terms a correct semantics. Of course, the rule of *necessitation* will fail and the classical rules of quantification will be preserved only for closed formulas. These are features the system would share with that of Kripke [11]. The idea is surely at least worth exploring. That is all I am proposing.

VI. Garson's Argument

In his discussion in [6] of the problems involved in formulating a viable quantified modal logic with "world relative" (i.e., varying) domains and genuine terms (rigid or otherwise), James Garson argues that the consequences of combining the classical principles of quantification with rigid terms are "disastrous":

> To appreciate the difficulties in trying to maintain the standard rules, notice first that the sentence $\exists x(x = t)$ is true at a world on a model just in case the extension of t is in the domain of that world. However, $\exists x(x = t)$ is a theorem of first-order logic, and so it follows that every term t of the language must refer to an object that exists in every possible world. This leads to two difficulties. First, there may not be any one object that exists in all the worlds. Second, the whole motivation for the world relative approach was to reflect the idea that objects in one world may not exist in another; but if standard rules are used, we may never have any terms which refer to such objects.[27]

Despite this,

(7) $\exists x(x = t)$

is *valid* in the system suggested in section V; and it is *not* true that every such rigid term must refer to an object that exists in every possible world. Although (7) may fail at some point in a model, it must hold at each good point and thus is valid. The validity of (7) in part reflects the fact that the system has no empty names, though a name can refer to an object that does not exist. I suppose the lack of empty names may seem out of step with the examples of relativity discussed earlier. Can we, for example, represent the point of view of the inhabitants of the Hitlerless world—for whom 'Hitler' "nowhere denotes anything"? I will come back to this question shortly. But representing *their* point of view is not critical. What *is* critical is to see that rigidity is relative to *a* point of view, and that therefore, we need the double-indexed structure. Once this structure is in place, we can see why Garson's argument does not work. He reasons that if *t* is rigid and (7) holds, the referent of *t* must exist in every world. This is like reasoning that since the referent of 'I' must be an existing person, and since the occurrence of 'I' ten lines back is rigid, it follows that I necessarily exist. The absurdity of this argument has nothing to do with the context-dependence of 'I'. Rather, it has to do with the sense in which 'I' is rigid. It is rigid only relative to a frame of reference, which, since it's an indexical, always coincides with some context of use. The same is true of names, except that the frame of reference need not coincide with the context.

When *t* is the indexical 'I' the status of (7) is sometimes explained as follows: Whereas (7) necessarily expresses a true proposition, the proposition it expresses normally will not be necessary. Whoever says 'I exist' expresses a true proposition; but the proposition expressed is usually not *necessarily* true. This explanation is only *almost* right. The sentence 'I exist' does not *necessarily* express a true proposition. There are circumstances in which the sentence expresses no proposition at all— e.g., circumstances in which there are no agents capable of referring to themselves. Furthermore, the sentence invariably expresses a *true* proposition only relative to the very circumstances in which that proposition is "generated" so to speak. If you read in a book the words "I exist," you have no guarantee that the proposition they express is true at the time you read them. Thus, if *t* is 'I', we can expect (7) to express a true proposition only relative to points of the form $\langle c_w, c_w \rangle$, where c_w is a context of use. These are the "good" points whose components are the same context of use. It should be clear, then, why, in a language with indexicals, validity is defined not as truth at every point but as truth at every good point (of a certain kind).

In case *t* is a proper name, the status of (7), and the break between it and

$$\Box \exists x (x = t)$$

is admittedly more problematic. Unlike (7), this formula is not valid. So the rule of *necessitation* (stated semantically: If ϕ is valid, then $\Box\phi$ is valid) fails, just as it does in LD. The problem, however, is not the failure of *necessitation*—that is to be expected in the vicinity of rigidity. The problem is how to interpret the validity of (7) when *t* is a name. For example, is 'Hitler exists' in some sense a truth of logic?

The answer is that the system under discussion is a logic of *denoting* names: names of things actual or possible. It cannot represent the point of view of the inhabitants of the Hitlerless world. For them, 'Hitler' is a nondenoting name. It names nothing actual or possible. Or if it does name some possible object, then *their* world is not a possible frame of reference for 'Hitler' as we use the name. By definition, a frame of reference for a name must be a world in which the referent exists. Let there be given a world w, a name α, and an object x such that x exists in w. Then w is a possible frame of reference for α, and relative to w, α denotes x in every world. By these lights, if α denotes x in w' relative to a frame of reference w for α, and $w = w'$, then x exists in w'. The validity of (7) should thus be interpreted as meaning that it is true in any world w relative to w itself—provided that w is a possible frame of reference for t. If we make the simplifying assumption that any world is a possible frame of reference for any name, then we can omit the condition that w is a possible frame of reference for t. It will follow that from the point of view of the present, 'Hitler exists' is presently true. This does not mean that *Hitler* exists. It means only that 'Hitler' denotes someone or something (e.g., a dog) that exists presently.[28] Generally, features of the context of use will tell us which of several things named 'Hitler' is under discussion. This, perhaps after some research, gives us a frame of reference for our usage. Relative to the frame of reference, our usage is rigid.

VII. Frege's Puzzle

Finally, a word about what has become the bête noire of the so-called New Theory of Reference (NTR)—viz. the problem of identity statements of the form '$\alpha = \beta$', where α and β are distinct names. According to NTR, the two sentences

(8)   Tully is Cicero

(9)   Cicero is Cicero

express the same "singular" proposition, namely, a necessarily true proposition to the effect that a certain object x—Cicero (Tully)—is identical

---

[28] It will be protested that perhaps 'Hitler' denotes nothing at all, perhaps nothing is named 'Hitler'. Perhaps, but so what? The logic in question here is a logic of names as used in *literal* discourse. From this standpoint, occurrences of 'Hitler' in fictional discourse are irrelevant. Similarly, if 'Hitler' is not used as a name at all, it is not something we need to reckon with.

to x. As a corollary, NTR holds that the two sentences

(10) Cicero was an orator

(11) Tully was an orator

express the same proposition. This result is obtained on the basis of the assumption that 'Cicero' and 'Tully' are directly referential and hence (since (8) is true), each contributes nothing more than Cicero (i.e., Tully) to the make-up of the propositions expressed by (8), (9), (10), and (11). The problem is then how to account for the difference in "cognitive significance" between (8) and (9), or between (10) and (11)—the very problem that would have led Frege to claim that (8) and (9) or (10) and (11) express *different* propositions! Certainly a person in full command of the language might readily assent to (10) but not (11), or to (9) but not (8). Yet, according to the NTR, each of these pairs of sentences expresses only one proposition.

One proponent of the NTR, Howard Wettstein, has recently argued that the difference between (8) and (9) or (10) and (11) is not a semantical one, that it is not the business of semantics to explain such differences in cognitive significance.[29] Apparently, Frege was wrong to derive the distinction between sense and reference from examples involving only proper names; better to have derived it from examples involving only definite descriptions (as Frege does also). In response, John Perry, another exponent of the NTR, has argued in [13] that the issue *is* one for semantics to resolve, and he has proposed a solution based on a distinction between (a) the proposition that the truth conditions of an utterance are satisfied, and (b) the proposition expressed by the utterance. According to Perry, "it is the former that fits the conception of the cognitive significance of an utterance that Wettstein has used in his argument." Perry then argues that one might very well believe the singular proposition expressed by an utterance of (8) without believing the proposition that the truth conditions of the utterance of (8) are satisfied. In order to believe the latter, one must believe that 'Cicero' and 'Tully' are coreferential, but this is just what one who fails to assent to (8) most likely fails to believe.

I think Perry's solution is basically right,[30] but I want to point out that from the perspective of the system of QML-R of section V, (8) and

---

[29] See [18].

[30] It may be that, as I have characterized it, Perry's view is not quite right. Must one who fails to assent to (8) have beliefs about utterances, truth conditions, coreference, and names? Must one who *believes* (8) have beliefs about these things?

(9) differ in *logical* status. This means, in effect, that the distinction between the proposition expressed and the proposition "created" (Perry's term for the proposition about truth conditions) by an utterance is *built into* the logic. This fact counts as an argument that the distinction is indeed a *semantical* one, and is not to be relegated to the netherworld of pragmatics, or to a theory of the cognitive heuristics of speech communication.

From the Garsonian point of view, there is *no* semantic difference at all between '$\alpha = \beta$', for rigid α and β, and '$\alpha = \alpha$', provided only that '$\alpha = \beta$' is true. Perhaps this is the very point of view Wettstein has adopted, for it is certainly in accord with his thesis that the difference between (8) and (9) is not a semantic one. To my mind, this is just one further indication that people are working with the wrong account of rigidity, i.e., the "single-indexed" account.

On a double-indexed account, the difference between (8) and (9) emerges quite clearly. Consider the operator V (for 'Validity') defined as follows: $\models_{w,w'} V\phi$ if and only if for each $w'' \in K, \models_{w'',w''} \phi$. (I assume here that '$V\phi$' is not well-formed unless ϕ is a closed formula. So quantifying into $V\phi$ is prohibited.) This says that 'ϕ is valid' is true in w' from the point of view of w if and only if ϕ holds at every good point. It is true that '$V\phi$' has, as Kaplan would say, "hidden quotation marks." Interpretively speaking, V represents a metalinguistic predicate. That is no grounds for denegrating its role here as an operator.[31] The semantical clause defining it is perfectly clear, and the resulting notion is quite useful. For notice that neither (12) nor (13) is valid:

(12) $V\phi \rightarrow \Box\phi$ ("Material" *Necessitation*)

(13) $\Box\phi \rightarrow V\phi$ (*Validation*)

We saw earlier that (12) is not valid, taking ϕ to be (7). The invalidity of (12) reflects the idea that the contingent a priori is possible (as in the

---

It is more likely that the distinctness of the names 'Cicero' and 'Tully' allows, or makes more probable, that one's beliefs project or describe a world in which "Cicero" and "Tully" (note the double quotes) are different *objects*. This idea is like Perry's notion of "internal" reference. (See [13], 20ff.) So it may be that my interpretation of Perry's view given in the text is not right.

[31] Kaplan calls operators such as V "monsters" since whereas syntactically they are operators and not metalinguistic predicates, semantically they do not respect the fact that indexicals (and presumably names) usually force wide-scope readings of operators. In my opinion, it is simply shortsighted to ignore V for this reason. The semantics is flexible enough to permit the representation of metalinguistic predicates as operators in the object language. That's a *nice* feature of the semantics.

Newman 1 case). The invalidity of (13) reflects the idea that, as Kripke has urged in [12], the necessary a posterion is possible. But these are only reflections. In connection with identity statements such as (8), the invalidity of (13) actually encodes a pair of purely *logical* points (which may of course have epistemological implications). These points are, first, that (a) no pair of *distinct* terms must, as a matter of pure logic, be coreferential;[32],[33] this is expressed in the fact that in first-order quantification theory with identity, no formula of the form '$\alpha = \beta$' for distinct terms α and β, is a logical consequence of a (consistent) class of formulas none of which have subformulas of like form.[34] Secondly, (b), identity is a necessary relation among objects; this too is expressed in quantification theory with identity—by the validity of '$\forall x\, x = x$'. Now when α and β are rigid,

$$\alpha = \beta \rightarrow \Box(\alpha = \beta)$$

---

[32] In a Fregean "chosen object" treatment of improper definite descriptions, formulas such as '$\imath x x = x = \imath x x \neq x$' turn out to be theorems of logic. This is obviously a very special case and does not affect the point made in the text—nor likewise does the fact that on any theory of definite descriptions, $\imath x F x = \imath y F y$ should be a theorem.

[33] Similarly, no two occurrences of a single demonstrative pronoun or indexical must, as a matter of pure logic, be coreferential. In [18], Wettstein gives an example in which "synonymous utterances differ in cognitive significance," and concludes that cognitive states cannot be individuated by linguistic meanings. He asks us to imagine two utterances of "He is about to be attacked," where "a single individual is being referred to, but where it is not at all obvious that this is so." In that event, a linguistically competent person might take one of the utterances to be true and the other false. Yet both utterances have the same linguistic meaning. But it is a feature of the semantics of 'he', qua demonstrative, that distinct uses of it need not be coreferential. This logical latitude makes room for a corresponding epistemological gap. Since distinct occurrences of 'he' *can* refer to distinct objects, the way is clear for us to believe, perhaps mistakenly, that they *do* refer to distinct objects. This point I take to be simply a variation on the theme that distinct terms need not in all logic be coreferential. (NB: I do not deny that there are rare cases of analytic identities in which the terms involved are distinct, e.g., 'I am me'. Notice, though, that even this is analytic only on the assumption that it is the same speaker who both begins and ends an utterance of it!)

[34] I do not mean, of course, that the specific formula '$\alpha = \beta$' must occur as a subformula. I mean only that there must be subformulas that are identities involving distinct terms. For example, from premises asserting that objects x and y occupy exactly the same space-time points, it does not follow—as a matter of elementary logic—that x and y are the same object; nor is it a matter of elementary logic that sets having the same elements are the same. Generally, in order to have theorems of the form '$\alpha = \beta$', a theory must provide a criterion of identity.

is valid. Thus if $\alpha = \beta$ holds at a good point in a model, then $\Box(\alpha = \beta)$ also holds (by (b)); but then (by (a)) $V(\alpha = \beta)$ may, in fact, *ought*, to fail. It is interesting that one major source of conflict between the NTR and Fregean theories of reference can be traced to two compatible features of ordinary quantification theory. And if the relativity of direct reference is taken seriously enough to incorporate it into the very formulation of QML-R, we are rewarded with a logical solution to Frege's puzzle about identity statements that fits the NTR like a glove.

References

[1] Robert Merrihew Adams. "Time and Thisness." In *Midwest Studies in Philosophy* 11, ed. P. French, T. Uehling, and H. Wettstein. Minneapolis: University of Minnesota Press, 1986, 315–29.

[2] Joseph Almog. "Naming Without Necessity." *The Journal of Philosophy* 83 (1986): 210–42.

[3] Keith S. Donnellan. "The Contingent *A Priori* and Rigid Designators." In *Midwest Studies in Philosophy* 2. Minneapolis: University of Minnesota Press, 1977.

[4] Kit Fine. "Model Theory for Modal Logic, Part I, The de re/de dicto Distinction." *Journal of Philosophical Logic* 7 (1978): 125–56.

[5] Graeme Forbes. *The Metaphysics of Modality*. Oxford and New York: Clarendon, 1985.

[6] James W. Garson. "Quantification in Modal Logic." In *Handbook of Philosophical Logic*, vol. II, ed. D. Gabbay and F. Guenthner. Dordrecht: Reidel, 1984, 249–307.

[7] Hans Kamp. "Formal Properties of 'Now'." *Theoria* 37 (1971): 227–73.

[8] David Kaplan. *Demonstratives*. This volume.

[9] David Kaplan. "Bob and Carol and Ted and Alice." In *Approaches to Natural Language*, ed. J. Hintikka, J. Moravcsik, and P. Suppes. Dordrecht: Reidel, 1973, 490–518.

[10] David Kaplan. "Dthat." In *Syntax and Semantics* 9, ed. Peter Cole, 221–43. New York: Academic Press, 1978.

[11] Saul A. Kripke. "Semantical Considerations on Modal Logic." *Acta Philosophica Fennica* 16 (1963): 83–94. Reprinted in *Reference and*

Modality, ed. Leonard Linsky. Oxford: Oxford University Press, 1971, 63–72.

[12] Saul A. Kripke. *Naming and Necessity*. Cambridge, Mass.: Harvard University Press, 1980.

[13] John Perry. "Cognitive Significance and the New Theories of Reference." Unpublished manuscript. 1987.

[14] Krister Segerberg. "Two-dimensional Modal Logic." *Journal of Philosophical Logic* 2 (1973): 77–96.

[15] A. D. Smith. "Semantical Considerations on Rigid Designation." *Mind* 96 (1987): 83–92.

[16] Robert C. Stalnaker. "Assertion." In *Syntax and Semantics* 9, ed. Peter Cole. New York: Academic Press, 1978, 315–32.

[17] Robert Steinman. "Kripke-Rigidity versus Kaplan-Rigidity." *Mind* 94 (1985): 369–80.

[18] Howard Wettstein. "Has Semantics Rested on a Mistake?" *The Journal of Philosophy* 83 (1986): 185–209.

10

The Problem of De Re Modality

Kit Fine[1]

I.

Quine has two arguments against quantifying into modal contexts. Each begins in the same way. It is agreed that for a quantified modal statement such as $\exists x \Box x > 7$ to be meaningful, the corresponding notion of objectual satisfaction must be meaningful; it must make sense to say of an object that it satisfies the condition $\Box x > 7$. It is then denied that there is any such notion of objectual satisfaction.

But at this point the two arguments diverge, with each providing a very different ground for the denial. For one, it is taken to be a general requirement on the notion of objectual satisfaction that the variables in a condition to which it is applied should be open to substitution; truth should be preserved upon the substitution of coreferential singular terms. But it is argued that, in the particular case at hand, this requirement is not met and that therefore there is no objectual notion of satisfaction.

According to the other, it is taken to be a consequence of there being an objectual notion of satisfaction for a condition such as $\Box x > 7$ that it makes sense to say of an object that it necessarily fulfill the

---

[1]I should like to thank the members of a seminar on the philosophy of language at the University of Michigan for many helpful discussions on the topics of this paper. Kaplan's two papers on Quine, "Quantifying In" and "Opacity," have greatly influenced me.

corresponding nonmodal condition $x > 7$.[2] But it is argued that this does not make sense—an object does not necessarily fulfill a condition in and of itself, but only relative to a description; and therefore, for this reason, there is no objectual notion of satisfaction.

We may call the problem raised by the two arguments, without discrimination between them, *the problem of de re modality*. The problem raised by the first argument alone may be called *the problem of quantifying in*, or, more specifically, *the problem of quantifying into modal contexts*; and the problem raised by the *distinctive* part of the second argument may be called *the problem of essentialism*. I do not know if this is how other philosophers use these labels; but it is the way I propose to use them here. The rationale for the present division is that the considerations raised by the common part of the two arguments belong most naturally to the first of them.

The difference between the arguments and the problems to which they give rise might be put in the following way. Both arguments constitute an attack on the notion of necessary satisfaction. But, in each case, this notion is understood in a different way. In the case of the first argument, it is understood to be a species of satisfaction; for an object necessarily to satisfy a certain condition $\phi(x)$ is for it to satisfy the corresponding necessity condition $\Box\phi(x)$. The argument is then an attack on the notion of necessary satisfaction as a *species* of satisfaction. In the other case, the notion is understood to be a mode, and not necessarily a species, of satisfaction; for an object necessarily to satisfy a certain condition is for it to satisfy that condition in a certain peculiar way. The argument is then an attack on the notion of necessary satisfaction as a *mode* of satisfaction.

Some further differences between the two arguments should be noted. The first belongs to the general area of the philosophy of language and relates, specifically, to the question of interpreting satisfaction and quantification. The second belongs to the general area of metaphysics and relates, specifically, to the question of how necessity can attach to objects. The arguments therefore raise very different issues and relate to very different areas of philosophy.

The logical argument is operator-indifferent. It applies equally well to any operator which, like the operator of necessity, creates opaque contexts, contexts containing terms not open to substitution. The meta-

---

[2] I am only careful about use-mention conventions when it matters. I use 'condition' sloppily. Sometimes it means open sentence, as here; sometimes it means property; and sometimes it is ambiguous between the two. The context should decide.

physical argument, on the other hand, is operator-specific. Substitute a different operator, such as that for belief, and one gets a different problem.

The focus of the logical argument is on the intelligibility of a certain kind of *expression*. The question is whether there is any meaningful use for free variables within the scope of a modal operator. The focus of the metaphysical argument is on the intelligibility of a certain kind of *idea*. The question is whether it makes sense to say of an object that it necessarily fulfills a condition. One might say that in the one case we are concerned with the intelligibility of a certain kind of expression without regard for what it might express, while in the other case we are concerned with a certain kind of idea without regard for how it might be expressed.

It is perfectly conceivable that one could find the idea of necessary fulfillment intelligible and yet, through acceptance of the logical argument, consider the modal conditions incapable of conveying that idea. Of course, finding the idea of necessary fulfillment *un*intelligible would provide a reason for taking the modal conditions also to be unintelligible. But still, the reason in this case, and in the case of the logical argument, would need to be distinguished. For there is a difference between saying that a form of expression is unintelligible because it is incapable of expressing any idea and saying that it is unintelligible because there is no idea for it to express. In the one case, the fault lies in what one is attempting to say; while, in the other case, it lies in how one is attempting to say it.

Although the two arguments are distinct, they are in a certain way complementary. We can imagine an opponent of Quine attempting to vindicate the notion of *de re* modality in either of two ways. He can appeal either to the thought itself or the language by which it is expressed. He may say: "Can't you just see that the notion of necessary satisfaction is intelligible?" Or he may say: "Doesn't the possibility of quantifying into modal contexts guarantee the intelligibility of the notion?" Quine's two arguments can then be regarded as his response to each of these attempts to vindicate the notion.

What has made it so easy to confuse the two arguments is that the different considerations in either case can often be formulated in very similar terms. Quine's objection to quantified modal logic is often stated in the words: no object necessarily satisfies a condition independently of how it is described. But this may be interpreted either as a problem with the relation of satisfaction, in its application to necessity conditions, or as a problem with the relation of necessary fulfillment, in isolation from its connection with satisfaction.

It may not even help to cite the failure of substitution as the reason why there is no coherent notion of necessary satisfaction. For the failure may be a reason *in general* or a reason in *this special case* for rejecting the coherence of the notion. One may accept as a general principle that the application of the notion of objectual satisfaction requires that the variables in the conditions to which it is applied be open to substitution. Applying this general principle to the particular case of modal conditions, then gives the incoherence of the notion of necessary satisfaction.

On the other hand, one may accept in principle that objectual satisfaction can operate in the presence of substitution failure but have special reasons for thinking that it cannot so operate in this particular case. Presumably these reasons relate to an underlying form of scepticism over the notion of necessary fulfillment. If the application of this notion is relative to a description and if, moreover, the description is given by means of the very term used to refer to the object, then the failure of substitution would show that the relativity mattered, and that an objectual notion of necessary fulfillment was not to be had simply by dropping the reference to the description.

Again, both arguments may appear to be motivated by a common concern. For in both cases, a certain class of statements, the *de dicto* ones, are taken to be unproblematic, and another class of statements, the *de re* ones, are taken to be problematic. The question then is whether the problematic *de re* statements can be "understood" in terms of the unproblematic *de dicto* ones. It is this demand for a reduction that may make it plausible that there can be no notion of satisfaction for modal conditions in the presence of a failure of substitution, and that may likewise make it plausible that any notion of necessary fulfillment should be relative to a description.

But the mechanism of understanding is very different in the two cases. In the logical case, the mechanism is linguistic; it is the functioning of language that is meant to explain how the *de re* is understood in terms of the *de dicto*. In the metaphysical case, the mechanism is ontological; it is not language that carries the reduction, but the facts themselves (if it may be put this way).

The distinction between the *de re* and *de dicto* should also be construed differently in the two cases. For the purpose of the logical argument, it should be taken to be a syntactic distinction: the *de re* statements are those that contain a free variable within the scope of a modal operator. For the purposes of the metaphysical argument, the distinction should be drawn in semantic terms: the *de re* statements are those whose truth-conditions presuppose the intelligibility of the idea of necessary fulfillment.

The critical difference in the two characterizations arises when "genuine" proper names are present in the language. Under the syntactic criterion, simple statements of the form $\Box Fa$, for a genuine proper name, will count as *de dicto*. But under the semantic criterion, such statements will count as *de re*, since presupposed in their truth-conditions is the intelligibility of the idea that an object necessarily fulfills the condition of Fx.

The two arguments are confused or, at least, not clearly distinguished in the earlier work of Quine. A crucial case is to be found in the second section of "Reference and Modality" (Quine [63]). He there writes as if the unintelligibility of quantification into modal contexts were merely another *symptom* of referential opacity. This would be compatible with the failure of substitution being the sole *reason* for finding the modal contexts opaque in the first place. But it seems, from page 149, that Quine wants to put forward another argument for opacity, one that relies on the incoherence of the notion of necessary fulfillment.

Again, it is strange that Quine should think that the physical modalities should call for separate treatment (158). For he has already come by the "sweeping observation" (159) according to which nontruth-functionality and substitution under logical equivalents imply opacity. Now presumably there is no doubt that the physical modalities satisfy the conditions of this observation. So I can only suppose that it is not the logical argument or its conclusion that is in question, but the quite different consideration concerning the notion of necessary fulfillment.

In the later work of Quine, the distinction between the two arguments is at least implicit. For his differential stand on modality and belief compelled him to recognize that there was a problem for the relational idiom of necessity that was not also a problem for belief.

The distinction has been emphasized by Kaplan in his two commentaries on Quine (Linsky [71], 143, and Kaplan [86], 232). But confusion persists. Philosophers are still prone to present one-sided refutations of Quine. So they cite the criticisms of Smullyan, on the one hand, or the criticisms of Kripke, on the other, without realizing that at best only one of Quine's arguments is thereby demolished.

Also, the relevant sense of the *de re/de dicto* distinction or of the mechanism of understanding is not always kept in mind. In Plantinga ([74], 29–43) for example, we find that genuine proper names are used in the *de dicto* statements of a reduction that is directed against the metaphysical sceptic. Or, in Kaplan (Linsky [71]), it is hard not to have the sense that the quest for linguistic understanding in the earlier sections (I–III) has been merged with the quest for ontological understanding in the later sections (IV–XII).

II.

I want now to evaluate Quine's objections to quantified modal logic, dealing first with the metaphysical and then with the logical argument.

I observed before that the metaphysical argument was operator-specific; for different operators it yields different problems. This observation applies as much to different notions of necessity as it does to notions other than necessity. There is not a single problem of essentialism, but a range of problems, that vary according to the notion of necessity in question.

There are perhaps four principal notions of necessity for which the problem arises; these are, respectively, the logical, the analytic, the metaphysical, and the natural. Of these, the most important is undoubtedly the problem for the metaphysical notion. Indeed, not only is this problem of great importance in itself, but it is central, in my opinion, to any attempt to understand the nature of metaphysics.

However, it is not my intention to discuss this problem here. I wish to follow Quine and concentrate my attention on the logical and semantic modalities. The problem for the metaphysical and natural modalities will be discussed in another paper, "The Problem of Essentialism."

Our question then is this: can we make sense of what it is for a condition to be logically or to be analytically true of an object? Before attempting to answer the question, it is worth observing that it is one that naturally arises; it is not just forced upon us by the attempt to interpret quantified modal logic. For those very considerations that lead us to suppose that there is a special analytic or logical mode of truth may equally well lead us to suppose that there is a special analytic or logical mode of satisfaction. If a sentence can be *true* in virtue of its meaning or logical form, then why should a condition not be *true of* an object in virtue of its meaning or logical form?

Not only are the notions ones that naturally arise, they may also have some use. For in logic and semantics, the theses propounded include both closed and open sentences. If it is required that the closed theses should be logically or analytically true, why should it not also be required that the open theses be logically or analytically true of the objects with which they deal? Thus the notions of logical and analytic satisfaction may have the same role in characterizing the aim of these disciplines as the notions of logical and analytic truth.

Quine sometimes talks as if it is the treatment of modality as an operator rather than a predicate that leads us to take the plunge into modality *de re*; for one can only quantify into a sentence that is used, not into one that is mentioned (see Quine [66], 170, 174). But the refusal to countenance any difference in the modal potential of the notions of truth and satisfaction provides another motivation for the plunge, one that in fact applies more naturally to the use of modality as a predicate than as an operator.

Let us now return to our question: does any sense attach to the notions of logical or analytic satisfaction? We may concentrate on the notion of logical satisfaction. For the most part, the considerations concerning the notion of analytic satisfaction will be similar; to the extent that they are not, they may be given separate attention.

If our question itself is to make any sense, then we must be able to say what the putative notion of logical satisfaction is and in a way, of course, that does not already presuppose its intelligibility. It seems to me that the most reasonable way of identifying the notion is as follows. We note that the notion of logical truth is obtained in a certain way from the ordinary notion of truth; there is, if you like, a certain operation that transforms the ordinary notion into the logical notion. The question then is whether this operation yields anything when applied to the notion of satisfaction; is there a notion of logical satisfaction that stands in the same relationship to the ordinary notion of satisfaction as the notion of logical truth does to the ordinary notion of truth?

If asked to explain in general what the operation was, in terms that did not arbitrarily restrict its application, then one would say something like this. Suppose a predicate P of n arguments is given. (Similar considerations apply to expressions of other categories.) Then the operation L (call it "logicizing") delivers a new predicate $L(P)$ which applies to the n arguments $a_1, \ldots, a_n$ exclusively on the basis of their logical form.[3]

---

[3] The transformation L may have an interest that extends beyond its present use. We are all familiar with the problem of characterizing the logical constants. But there is also a problem of characterizing the metalogical terms; these are not the expressions that determine logical form, but the ones whose application is

It is as if the new predicate $L(P)$ operates through a "veil of ignorance," a veil that is opaque to all but logical form.[4] Or one can imagine that there is a mechanism, blind to all but logical form, that surveys the arguments in turn. The predicate L(P) is then one that can only operate on the basis of the information supplied to it by the mechanism.

Our problem, therefore, is what sense if any, attaches to saying: it can be determined that a condition Q is true of the objects $a_1, \ldots, a_n$ on the basis of the logical form of $Q, a_1, \ldots, a_n$ alone. Now when put in this way, a question immediately arises: do the objects $a_1, \ldots, a_n$ themselves contribute to the logical form? Can they be seen through the veil? Or, to put it another way, will our mechanism for discerning logical form even bother to look at them? (I have here presupposed that a uniform decision is made: either the mechanism always looks at the objects or it never does. This is a natural presupposition to make. In terms of the general transformation L, we may suppose that it is determined on the basis of the nature of the predicate P itself which of its arguments are to be looked at.)

Two aspects of logical form need to be distinguished. There is first of all the contribution made by the logical constants themselves. But there is also the contribution that is provided by the pattern of occurrence of the nonlogical constants. This is something that can exist independently of the presence of the logical constants. So it is because of this other aspect that it is taken to be part of the logical form of the sentence 'Nixon admires Nixon' that there are two occurrences of the same singular term 'Nixon'.

The objects $a_1, \ldots, a_n$ will not ordinarily make any contribution to the logical form in the first of these two ways. But it is perfectly conceivable that they might in the second way. Whether or not this is so will depend upon what exactly it is that has logical form. Suppose that logical form is taken, in the standard cases, to be primarily a feature of the physical expression-tokens. Then the pattern of occurrence of the nonlogical constants would be given by the presence of suitable physical

---

determined on the basis of logical form. In terms of L (as extended to expressions of arbitrary category), we may define a metalogical expression E as one for which it is true, or perhaps one should say analytically true, that E has the same extension as L(E). The familiar metalogical predicates, such as those for logical consequence or logical inconsistency, would turn out to be metalogical on this definition. So also would familiar syntactic operations, such as those for negation or disjunction.

[4]My adoption of Rawls's phrase is not intended to be frivolous. There are in fact deep analogies between my use of the veil in characterizing logical notions and his use in characterizing the original position.

similarities among the sub-tokens, and it would presumably not be in the same way that one could talk of pattern of occurrence among the objects of an abstract sequence $a_1, \ldots, a_n$.

Now suppose, as is much more plausible, that logical form, in the standard cases, is primarily a feature of expression-types or of intensions. Then one may still talk of different occurrences of the same sub-expression or of the same constituent. One may say, for example, that there are two occurrences of the sentence-type '$1 = 1$' in the complex sentence-type '$1 = 1 \supset 1 = 1$'. But occurrences in this sense are not tokens (i.e., physical tokens), for no token can occur in a type or intension. They are something as abstract as the types or intensions themselves.

It seems clear that, in this sense of 'occurrence', an object may equally well have different occurrences within a sequence. It would therefore be quite arbitrary, once the pattern of occurrence within an expression-type or intension was taken in, not also to take in the pattern of occurrence within a sequence. (Of course, what an actual physical mechanism would look at in such a case are not the occurrences themselves, which are abstract, but the representatives of them by tokens. It would no more "see" the different occurrences of a symbol-type in an expression-type than it would "see" the different occurrences of the philosopher Socrates in an abstract sequence of objects. But still, the processing of the tokens would merely constitute an indirect means of getting at the logical form of the types.)

It may be noted that one is almost compelled to take this view of logical form on a Russellian conception of propositions. For among the constituents of a proposition will be ordinary objects; and so part of the pattern of occurrence of the nonlogical constituents will be the pattern of occurrence among the ordinary objects. It is then a short step from the pattern of occurrence of ordinary objects in a proposition to the pattern of occurrence of those objects in a sequence.

The position which allowed the objects to make a contribution to logical form would therefore appear to be the more plausible. But let us, in a spirit of neutrality, attempt to work out the conception of necessary fulfillment for either position. In case the mechanism is blind to the objects, this would appear to be straightforward. For upon conducting its search, our mechanism will only report back to "control" on the logical form of the condition; and control is only able to say, on the basis of this information, that the condition is true of the given objects if it is able to say that it is true of those objects whatever they might be. It follows that a condition will be logically true of the given objects just in case its universal closure is a logical truth.

This approach has the interesting consequence that all identities are contingent. For regardless of whether the objects a and b are the same, the condition '$x = y$' will fail to be logically true of those objects, since '$\forall x \forall y(x = y)$' is not a logical truth. On the other hand, all self-identities will be necessary, at least if the identity symbol is a logical constant. For given that '$\forall x(x = x)$' is a logical truth, the condition '$x = x$' will be logically true of any object.

The approach therefore provides some sort of vindication of the contingency theory for identity claims. However, the vindication is not of the usual sort. It is contingently true of 9 and the number of planets that they are the same, not because of some sensitivity to the way the objects are described, but because of a lack of sensitivity to what the objects are.

To the proposed account of logical satisfaction, it might be objected that it is unable to sustain a reasonable interpretation of quantified modal logic. For suppose that we take a condition such as $\Box \phi(x, y)$ to be satisfied by a pair a, b just in case the embedded condition $\phi(x, y)$ is logically satisfied by the pair a, b. Then $\Box x = x$ will be satisfied by the identity pair a, a while $\Box x = y$ will fail to be satisfied by the pair a, a; and so that familiar instance of substitutivity, $\forall x \forall y(x = y \supset (\Box x = x \supset \Box x = y))$, will turn out to be false.

But against this objection, two points need to be made. The first is that it is no requirement on an acceptable conception of logical satisfaction that it should be capable, in the suggested manner, of sustaining an interpretation of quantified modal logic. The other point is that the given conception is, in any case, capable of sustaining such an interpretation. As we shall see later in the paper, by carefully distinguishing between the objectual and referential interpretation of the quantifiers, it is possible to show that the object-blind conception of modality is compatible with the objectual interpretation.

The object-sensitive conception of logical satisfaction is more problematic. For given that the mechanism for discerning logical form actually looks at the objects, we have to determine what it sees.

One question is whether it is aware of which of the objects are the same. Is it a sensitive to relative identity? Perhaps the most reasonable view is that it is. For surely, when it is looking at an expression, i.e., a sequence of symbols, the mechanism will be aware of which of the symbols are the same; and it seems equally plausible that, when looking at a sequence of objects, it should be aware of which of the objects are the same. Identity of occurrence is a matter of logical form, regardless of which entities it is that occur.

On this view, the necessity of identity will hold, in contrast to the previous approach. For if the arguments a_1 and a_2 are the same, then the mechanism will report back to control that they are the same; and so it can then be determined on the basis of the logical form of the condition $x = y$, at least if identity is a logical constant, that the condition is true of the objects.

Even if identity is not a logical constant, a relevant difference between the two approaches will still emerge. For on the object-sensitive approach, a condition of the form '$Fx \supset Fy$' will be logically true of an identical pair of objects; while on the object-blind approach, it will not be, since '$\forall x \forall y (Fx \supset Fy)$' is not a logical truth.

A further question that arises is whether the mechanism, upon looking at the various objects, will be aware of which of them are distinct. Will it be sensitive to relative difference? It needs to be emphasized that this is a separate question from the one concerning relative identity. In the earlier case, we were asking whether the mechanism would provide *positive* information concerning the identity of two of the objects a_i and a_j; in the present case, we are asking whether the mechanism will also provide *negative* information concerning identity. Of course, if it were known that the mechanism provided *all* of the positive information, then the negative information could be gathered from the absence of the corresponding positive information. But the mechanism could *in fact* provide all of the positive information without it being known that it did. It would then be left open which of the objects a_i and a_j about which no information was given were the same and which were distinct. They could all be distinct; they could all be the same, in which case there would only be one object; or some intermediate possibility could obtain.

But although the question is distinct, the answer should be the same; the mechanism should be sensitive to relative difference. For surely it should be sensitive to the occurrence of different symbols in an expression; and it seems equally plausible that it should be sensitive to the occurrence of different objects.

If this is so, then the nonidentity condition '$\sim (x = y)$' will be logically true of distinct objects a_1 and a_2, at least if identity is a logical symbol; for the mechanism will report back to control that the objects are distinct, and then, on the basis of the logical form of the condition, it can be determined to be true of the objects. However, in contrast to the case of relative identity, the distinction between sensitivity and insensitivity to relative difference would not appear to show up when identity is not a logical constant or when identity or its cognates do not appear in the condition.[5]

It is a remarkable fact that, although we expect the mechanism to provide negative information concerning identity of occurrence, this information is not required to show that truth-functionally valid sentences are logically true. To take an example: suppose that χ is a sentence of the form $\phi \supset (\phi \lor \psi)$, where ϕ and ψ are distinct. Then to show that this sentence is true on the basis of its logical form, we need to know that the two occurrences of ϕ are the same, but we do not need to know that ψ is distinct from ϕ.

Whether the same point holds for predicate logic depends upon a subtle question concerning variables. The question might be stated in the paradoxical form: are variables constants? What I mean is: are variables to be given the same status as the logical constants or as the nonlogical constants in the determination of logical form? Do we take such sentences as $\exists x(x = x)$ and $\exists y(y = y)$ to have a different logical form, because of the difference between x and y, or do we take them to have the same logical form, in much the same way that '$0 = 0$' and '$1 = 1$' have the same logical form?

In the former case, there is no essential difficulty in extending our observation to predicate logic. But in the latter case, there is. For consider the sentence $\forall x \forall y(x = y) \supset \forall u \forall v(u = v)$. Then surely it is logically true; and yet in order to show that it is logically true we need to know that the variables x and y are, indeed, distinct.

If such negative information can be relevant, then the possibility is significant both for the characterization and for the representation of logical truth. According to the standard account, endorsed by Quine and many others, a logical truth is a sentence whose truth is preserved under arbitrary substitutions for its nonlogical constants. But apply this account to the sentence $\forall x \forall y(x = y) \supset \forall u \forall v(u = v)$, and we find that it is not a logical truth; for upon substituting x for y, we obtain the sentence $\forall x \forall x(x = x) \supset \forall u \forall v(u = v)$, which is false in a domain of more than one individual.

It would be better, in the account of logical truth, to restrict the

---

[5]In case $\phi(x, y)$ is an identity-free open sentence with two variables x and y, the point can be put in the following way: when $\forall x \forall y(x \neq y \supset \phi(x, y))$ is a logical truth then so is $\forall x \forall y \phi(x, y)$; but when $\forall x \forall y(x = y \supset \phi(x, y))$ is a logical truth, $\forall x \forall y \phi(x, y)$ may not be.

substitutions to those that preserve the exact logical form of the original. Indeed, so much should have already been clear from the intuitive conception of logical truth. For, according to this conception, a logical truth is a sentence that is true in virtue of its logical form. We can therefore expect sentences with *exactly* the same logical form as a logical truth to be true. But we can have no a priori guarantee that sentences with a different logical form, even when obtained by substitution from the original logical truth, should also be true.

These remarks are relevant to the schematic representation of logical form. Suppose we use 'α', 'β', 'γ', ... as schematic letters for variables in much the same way that we use 'p', 'q', 'r', ... as schematic letters for sentences. Then the logical form of $\forall x \forall y (x = y) \supset \forall u \forall v (u = v)$ can be represented by $\forall \alpha \forall \beta (\alpha = \beta) \supset \forall \delta (\delta = \delta)$. But we cannot take the validity of the scheme to consist in the logical truth of all of its concrete instances; for upon substituting x, x, u and v for α, β, γ and δ, we obtain what we have already seen not to be a logical truth. The validity of a scheme should therefore be taken in general to consist in the logical truth of all its "exact" instances; and the class of valid schemes will be closed, not under arbitrary substitutions, but only under those substitutions that preserve exact logical form.

Let me not be misunderstood. I am not actually endorsing a schematic approach to variables or arguing that negative information on logical form is ever relevant to the determination of logical truth. This is a matter for investigation. I am merely pointing out that the very definition of logical truth should not be taken to exclude the possibility. If the class of logical truths are closed under arbitrary substitutions, then this should be treated as a theorem concerning the notion, not as part of its characterization.[6]

One final question remains concerning the concept of logical satisfaction. Do the objects $a_1, \ldots, a_n$ contribute anything else to logical form? When the mechanism looks at them, does it see anything else

---

[6] The issue of negative information is also relevant to the question of characterizing the metalogical terms. For is the negation of a metalogical predicate also metalogical? If there is unrestricted access to the negative information, then it will be. We may say, for example, that a sentence $\phi \lor \sim \psi$ is not a logical truth on the grounds that ϕ and ψ are distinct (and there is no other relevant logical form). However, without the unrestricted access, there is no guarantee that the negative predicate will also be metalogical.

Perhaps there is some interesting way of mathematically exploiting the fact that, in many cases, the application of a metalogical predicate depends only upon positive information.

besides their relative identity and difference? The mechanism is only programmed, if I may put it that way, to detect logical form: and so the question turns, not on the external logical form of the sequence $a_1, \ldots, a_n$ itself, but on the internal logical form of the objects that go to make it up. As we have noted, if they are ordinary concrete objects, they will possess no logical structure and the mechanism will treat them in the same way that it treats the simple symbols of an expression. But the objects may themselves be expressions; and there then seems to be no reason why the mechanism should not be as sensitive to their structure as it is to the structure of the condition itself.

However, even in this latter case, the extra information will be of no use; if the mechanism reports it back to control, it might as well be discarded. For all that we have to go on is the logical form, not the meaning, of the condition; and there is nothing about the logical form of the objects that can help us decide whether a condition of given logical form is true of them. It is therefore, for all intents and purposes, as if no further information were available.

Putting together the three answers, we see that whether a condition is logically true of certain objects depends entirely on their identity type, i.e., on the relative identities and differences among them. Let $\pi(a_1, \ldots, a_n)$ be the statement that says which of $a_1, \ldots, a_n$ are the same and which are distinct. Then the condition $\phi(x_1, \ldots, x_n)$ will be logically true of $a_1, \ldots, a_n$ just in case $\forall x_1 \ldots \forall x_n(\pi(x_1, \ldots, x_n) \supset \phi(x_1, \ldots, x_n))$ is a logical truth.[7] The sensitivity to the objects shows up, if you like, in the presence of the restriction $\pi(x_1, \ldots, x_n)$.

This conclusion needs to be somewhat modified for the concept of analytic satisfaction. In the normal case in which the objects $a_1, \ldots, a_n$ are lacking in semantic structure, we may say, as before, that the condition $\phi(x_1, \ldots, x_n)$ is analytically true of $a_1, \ldots, a_n$ just in case the sentence $\forall x_1, \ldots, \forall x_n(\pi(x_1, \ldots, x_n) \supset \phi(x_1, \ldots, x_n))$ is an analytic truth. But in the case in which some or all of the objects $a_1, \ldots, a_n$ possess semantic structure, this result may not hold. For the "analytic" control sees, not only the logical form, but also the meaning of the condition; and for this reason it is able, in contrast to the "logic" control, to make use of information presented to it concerning the semantic structure of the objects. It is able to determine from the semantic structure of the sentence 'All bachelors are unmarried', for example, that the condition 'x is analytic'

[7]Related principles are discussed in Fine [78] in connection with the elimination of *de re* modality. Similar conceptions of modality have been propounded in Parsons (Linsky [71], 85) and Kaplan ([86], 250–51).

is true of it.

It is to be noted that, even in this case, it is not the meaning of the term used to denote the sentence that is relevant to the determination of analytic satisfaction, but the meaning of the sentence itself. It might plausibly be argued, however, that there is a canonical designation M of the meaning of any sentence, identical or analogous to a Frege-Church structural description of its sense. Relative to such a system of canonical designators, it might then be maintained that a condition $\phi(x)$ is analytically true of ψ just in case the sentence '$\forall x(x$ means $M \supset \phi (x))$' is an analytic truth.

We therefore see that the notions of logical and analytic satisfaction do indeed make sense. Our understanding of logicality and analyticity combines with our understanding of satisfaction to produce intelligible hybrid notions. It might also be remarked that there appears in each case to be a natural reduction of the *de re* to the *de dicto*. This is in itself sufficient, though maybe not indispensable, for establishing intelligibility.

What might be conceded is that these notions are to some extent indeterminate (or perhaps one should say equivocal). There is nothing in our intuitive conception of logical or semantic structure, it might be argued, that will enable one to determine whether the resulting concepts of logical and analytic satisfaction should be object-blind or object-sensitive. But this concession itself is open to question, for it is not clear whether there is a difference of opinion over the application of the concepts or a genuine indeterminacy in the concepts themselves. There is perhaps a similar worry over the logical status of identity. Do conflicts indicate a difference of opinion or a difference in concepts?

But even if the concession is made, the indeterminacy should not be blamed on the notions of logical or analytic *satisfaction*, but on the notions of logical or semantic *structure*. Make it clear what is meant by 'logical' and 'analytic', i.e., by 'logical' and 'semantic' structure, and it then becomes clear what is meant by 'logical' and 'analytic' satisfaction. The difficulty is not over the intelligibility of these notions, but their identity.

In the light of these considerations, Quine's own remarks on the topic are curious. He claims that one can quantify into modal contexts (and here only the meaningfulness of the notion of necessary fulfillment is in question), but at a price. That price is the commitment to "Aristotelian essentialism," by which he means "adopting an invidious attitude toward certain ways of uniquely specifying" an object, seeing these ways, rather than others, "as somehow better revealing its 'essence'" (Quine [63], 155, and [66], 173–74). Others have agreed with Quine on this, even if they have differed from him on the question of whether the price should be paid.

But it does not seem to be true that the price needs to be paid. Certainly, it is not as if the notions of logical or analytic satisfaction have to be *defined* or otherwise *explained* in terms of a class of preferred descriptions. Anyone looking for such a class in the case of our own account will look in vain. (Cf. Kaplan [86], 252.) Even in the very special case in which a condition is analytically true of certain expressions and not others, such descriptions are not presupposed; the condition will simply be true of an expression in virtue of its semantic structure. There will indeed be a description of the expression that is especially revelatory of its semantic structure. But this no more constitutes a preferred description in this case than it does in the standard case of analytic truth.

Quine seems to assume that the explanation of *de re* necessity must take a certain form. With each object a is associated a class of "preferred" conditions Γ in a single free variable, say x (and, similarly, with each n-tuple of objects $a_1, a_2, \ldots, a_n$ is associated a class of preferred conditions Γ in n variables, say $x_1, x_2, \ldots, x_n$). The object a is then said necessarily to satisfy the condition $\phi(x)$ (perhaps we should say $Ex \supset \phi(x)$) just in case the universal sentence $\forall x(\psi(x) \supset \phi(x))$, for $\psi(x)$ a conjunction of conditions from Γ, is necessarily true (and similarly for an n-tuple of objects $a_1, a_2, \ldots, a_n$).[8]

Such an analysis then invites the criticism that it calls for an invidious distinction to be made between those conditions in the relevant variables which belong to Γ and those which do not. Indeed, we seem to have a kind of proof that such a distinction among the descriptions of the objects is required. For not every condition in the relevant variable can belong to Γ on pain of the distinction between the necessary and the contingent collapsing; and some condition, at least in the case of two variables or more, must belong to Γ in order that $x = y$ should be necessarily true of a pair of identical objects a, a.

But from the fact that a class of preferred descriptions always exists, it does not follow that the analysis of *de re* necessity should be given in terms of such a class. Indeed, as we saw in the case of the notions

---

[8]Various subtle questions concerning (i) the presence of constants or modal operators in Γ, (ii) the use of relational descriptions in Γ, and (iii) the possibility of variant analyses have been ignored. I hope to deal more thoroughly with such questions in the projected paper "The Problem of Essentialism."

of logical and analytic necessity, the most natural explanations take another form altogether (although whether this is also true of the notion of metaphysical necessity is a much more difficult question). Even if we insist, somewhat perversely in my opinion, that the explanations take the required form, it will still not be true, at least for the object-blind notion of logical satisfaction, that an invidious distinction among descriptions must be made; for we can simply take the class of preferred conditions to be empty. There will remain a distinction of sorts; for we choose the class to be empty rather than "universal" or something in between. But this is a choice that can be motivated without any regard to the content of the conditions, for a universal class would collapse the modalities and an intermediate one would require an invidious discrimination *among* descriptions. Of course, the resulting notion of logical satisfaction will not make $x = y$ logically true of a pair of identical objects; but the desirability of such a requirement for the purposes of interpreting quantified modal logic is, as we shall see, more problematic than is commonly supposed.

A commitment to Aristotelian essentialism is therefore not necessary for making sense of the *de re* notions of logical and analytic necessity. But neither is it, in the intended sense, *sufficient* for making sense of these notions. For were we to characterize a notion of necessary fulfillment in terms of a nontrivial class of preferred descriptions, we would not thereby obtain a notion of *logical* or *analytic* fulfillment, but some other notion altogether. As Quine himself points out, "essentialism is abruptly at variance with the idea . . . of explaining necessity by analyticity" (Quine [63], 155). Yet our problem just was to make sense of a notion of analytic fulfillment.

But perhaps I am being unfair to Quine. It seems as if he is only interested in the notion of analytic truth, and not in other notions of necessary truth; and this suggests that he is only interested in the notion of analytic fulfillment, and not in other notions of necessary fulfillment. But it is conceivable that he only wishes the notion of necessity to be subject to the requirement that 'Necessarily ϕ' is true iff ϕ is analytic; and this is then compatible with interpreting the notion of necessary fulfillment in terms of privileged descriptions. But this way of viewing the problem is only really appropriate to the logical issue. The constraints that the requirement imposes on a solution to the metaphysical issue are so slight as to be almost worthless.

It appears that Quine and others have conflated two versions of the problem of essentialism: one for the analytic concept of necessity; and the other for the metaphysical concept. They have unwittingly assumed that any *de re* concept of necessity must be a concept of metaphysical necessity. What has perhaps made this conflation so easy is the confusion of subject with source; given that certain objects are the subjects to attributions of necessity, one naturally takes them to be their source. But of course a concept of necessity is none the less intelligible for having no interesting application to objects.

III.

We proceed to an evaluation of the logical argument against quantifying in. This argument may be broken down into five steps. (1) It is argued that occurrences of singular terms within modal contexts are not open to substitution. (2) From this it is inferred that such occurrences are not purely referential. (3) From this it is inferred that the corresponding occurrences of variables are not purely referential. (4) From this it is inferred that the concept of objectual satisfaction is not meaningfully applicable to the conditions formed with the variables. (5) From this it is then inferred that quantification with respect to these variables is incoherent.

This breakdown of the argument may appear excessively minute. But I feel that each step raises significant and independent issues. My discussion of the argument, which will take us to the end of the paper, will be in two major parts. In the first, I shall discuss each of the steps in turn, paying particular attention to the general theoretical issues that they raise. In the second, I shall be concerned to apply the results that will emerge from the first part to the specific question of whether quantification into modal and other problematic contexts is possible.

Step (1): The Failure of Substitutivity

Quine's standard example concerns the number of planets; it is necessary that 9 is greater than 7 and yet not necessary that the number of planets is greater than 7, even though 9 is in fact the number of planets. One small objection against this example is that it is needlessly controversial; for it presupposes the necessity of mathematical truths, and even their analyticity, given that necessity is explained in terms of analyticity. A better example, also used by Quine, concerns identity: it is necessary that $9 = 9$ and yet not necessary that the number of planets $= 9$. But even this example is open to the objection, in case the necessity is logical, that identity is not a logical constant and so '9 = 9' is not necessary. Perhaps the most satisfactory kind of example for avoiding needless controversy is something rather quaint. We may say: it is necessary that if 9 is odd then 9 is odd and yet not necessary that if 9 is odd then the number of planets is odd.

A more serious objection concerns not the status of the condition in the proposed example, but the status of the singular terms. It might be argued that no sentence containing singular terms can be an analytic, let alone a logical truth; for there is nothing about the meaning or logical form of a sentence which will guarantee that the terms have a reference; and it is only if the terms have a reference that a truth-value for the sentence itself is guaranteed. It is not my purpose to discuss this line of reasoning here; it raises large and difficult questions in the philosophy of logic and language. Quine's own views, which would call for a very thorough discussion in themselves, are contained in his paper "Meaning and Inference" (Quine [63]). But we may note that if the reasoning is accepted, then no attempt to find a modal example of substitutivity failure can succeed.

It is hardly satisfactory, however, to fault Quine's argument on such a point, both because it is highly controversial and because the general issue of the transition from substitutivity failure remains. I shall therefore proceed on the assumption that there is indeed a failure of substitution in modal contexts.

Step (2): The Inference to Irreferentiality of Singular Terms

It might be thought that there is no difficulty here; for does not the irreferentiality of an occurrence of a singular term follow by definition from a failure of substitution? But matters are not so simple; and, in fact, our discussion of the step will raise some of the most significant issues that are involved in Quine's argument.

It has to be recognized that there are two concepts of referentiality; one informal and the other technical.

The informal concept of a purely referential occurrence of a term is explained by Quine in the following words (Quine [60], 177): "the term is used purely to specify its object, for the rest of the sentence to say something about." So, within a sentence containing a purely referential occurrence of a singular term, there is a certain division of labor: the term picks out its object; and the rest of the sentence picks out what is said of the object. The sentence as a whole then says the one of the other.

Given this understanding of the concept, the occurrence of '9' in '9 > 7' would appear to be purely referential. For the sentence says of the number 9 that it is greater than 7, with '9' picking out its object, viz. 9, and the rest of the sentence picking out what is said of the object, viz. that it is greater than 7. On the other hand, the occurrence of 'Cicero' in ' 'Cicero' contains six letters' would appear not to be purely referential; for the sentence says nothing of Cicero at all. The occurrence of 'Giorgione' in 'Giorgione was so-called because of his size' has an intermediate status. The sentence does indeed say something of the object Giorgione, but the term 'Giorgione' is not used solely to pick out that object. We might say that the occurrence of the term is referential but not purely referential.

The explanation of the technical concept is rather different. An occurrence of a (referring) singular term in a sentence is purely referential in this sense if truth-value is preserved upon the substitution of coreferential singular terms. Let us be a little more exact. Suppose t is a singular term which occurs in the sentence $\phi(t)$; and let $\phi(s)$ be the sentence which results from $\phi(t)$ upon substituting s for the given occurrence of t. Then the occurrence of t is said to be purely referential if $\phi(t)$ and $\phi(s)$ have the same truth-value whenever the identity sentence $t = s$ is true.

Quine is not careful to distinguish the informal and the technical concepts. We shall be. For the informal concept, we shall reserve the phrase 'purely referential'; though often we shall simply say 'referential' and use 'partly referential' in place of Quine's 'referential'. For the technical concept, we shall use our earlier phrase 'open to substitution'. Our question therefore is whether a failure in being open to substitution implies a failure of pure referentiality.

We could, of course, state the argument without resort to the informal concept of being purely referential; we could attempt to go directly from a breakdown in substitution to an incoherence in the application of the concept of objectual satisfaction. But such a version of the argument could only be as plausible as the one in which the intermediate step was supplied. For our most direct reason for holding objectual satisfaction to be incoherent is that the position of a variable can be occupied by a term that is not purely referential. If, through some freak, substitution could break down and yet the singular term still be purely referential, we would have no reason for supposing objectual satisfaction to be incoherent. There is therefore no advantage to be gained from attempting to avoid the use of the informal concept.

The argument only requires that openness to substitution be a necessary condition for pure referentiality. Quine believes that it is also a sufficient condition, and it is presumably for this reason that he is not careful to distinguish the two notions; one can simply be regarded as a definition of the other.

Considered as a definition, it is from the same mould as the definition of logical truth. In both cases, we have an informal concept that can be expressed in the form: x is F in virtue of x's being G. So the concept of logical truth is that of a sentence being true in virtue of its logical form; and the concept of pure referentiality is that of a sentence saying what it does in virtue of the reference of a singular term occurrence (and whatever else the rest of the sentence does). In both cases, the informal concept is given a definition of the form: feature F is preserved under all transformation that preserve G. So a sentence is said to be a logical truth if its truth is preserved under all transformations that preserve its logical form; and an occurrence of a term in a sentence is said to be purely referential if the truth-value of the sentence is preserved under all substitutions for the term that preserves its reference. (To preserve parity with the definition of logical truth, we should either have 'what the sentence says is preserved' or we should appropriately modify the informal concept. To avoid needless complication, we may leave the informal concept alone and we may take the definition to encapsulate the result that preservation of content is equivalent to preservation of truth-value.)

I am suspicious of all such attempted definitions. For a significant aspect of the informal concept is lost in the process. The informal concept is explanatory; it is required that the presence of the feature G actually explain the presence of the feature F. The defining concept is purely extensional; it is required that the feature F be preserved, but without regard for *why* the feature is preserved. It is plausible that if G explains F then F is preserved under transformations which preserve G; it is possible, though considerably less plausible, that if F is preserved under transformations which preserve G, then G explains F. But even if the implications hold, they should be regarded as consequences of a correct definition of the informal concept and not as constitutive of it.

Of course, general suspicion is no substitute for detailed investigation; and it may be worthwhile to consider further the sufficiency part of Quine's claim, even though it is not strictly relevant to the rest of his argument.

One difficulty in maintaining sufficiency is that there may be grammatical restrictions on which singular terms can be substituted for the given singular term. For all I know, there is no singular term of English which is distinct from and yet coreferential with 'nine' and which can be substituted for 'nine' in the sentence 'Fido is canine' without loss of grammaticality. Yet we would not want to say that, on this account, the given occurrence of 'nine' is purely referential.

A related difficulty is that there may be an impoverishment of terms in a given language. There is no single-letter word of English that is coreferential with 'nine'. Yet we would not want to say, on this account, that the occurrence of 'nine' in ' 'nine' consists of more than one letter of the alphabet' is referential. (A similar example is considered by Lewy [76], 25.)

The first difficulty may be removed by requiring, of a term t that is to be open for substitution in a sentence $\phi(t)$, that not only should the sentence $\phi(s)$ have the same truth-value as $\phi(t)$ whenever s is coreferential with t, but also that $\phi(s)$ should *be* a sentence whenever s is coreferential with t. But this makes for difficulties with the necessity part of Quine's claim; and it does not, in any case, solve the second difficulty. It seems preferable to confine the claim of sufficiency to those languages in which there is no grammatical restriction on the substitution of singular terms and in which any expression whatever can be used to refer to a given object. In so far as a language is not of this sort, it must be suitably related to one that is.

There is a more serious difficulty. Take a sentence ϕ in which it is clear that an occurrence of a singular term is not purely referential. Perhaps 'Giorgione is so-called because of his size' will do; but if it will not, then another example may be chosen. Now form the disjunction of this sentence with '$2 + 2 = 4$'. In the Giorgione example, we obtain 'Giorgione is so-called because of his size or $2 + 2 = 4$'. Then in the resulting sentence, truth is preserved upon substitution of coreferential terms for the given occurrence—indeed, upon substitution of arbitrary terms. Yet the given occurrence is still not purely referential.[9]

This should be intuitively clear in any particular case. It is intuitively clear, for example, that in the sentence 'Giorgione is so-called because of his size or $2 + 2 = 4$', the term 'Giorgione' is not being used solely to pick out an object—or, at least, this is as clear as it is in the original

---

[9]Linsky [67], 100–104, has formulated somewhat similar counterexamples to the sufficiency of Quine's criterion.

sentence 'Giorgione is so-called because of his size'. There is also an argument for this conclusion. For surely the referential status of a term is preserved under disjunction (and the other logical operations). Indeed, if we accepted openness to substitution as both a necessary and sufficient condition, we would be forced to say, in case ϕ contained an irreferential occurrence of a term, that that occurrence remained irreferential in the disjunction $\phi \lor \psi$ when ψ was false but became referential when ψ was true. But surely it is absurd that the referential status of the term should depend upon the nonlinguistic facts in this way.

The general point is that truth-value may be preserved under substitution of coreferential terms for reasons having nothing to do with the referential status of the given occurrence of a term. The occurrence is, if you like, "accidentally" open to substitution.

In this connection, Quine's own example (Linsky [71], 141):

'Giorgione played chess' is true

is of interest. We cannot conclude, simply on the grounds that the occurrence of 'Giorgione' is open to substitution, that it is also referential. Whether it is will depend upon what account we give of the phrase 'is true'. If we regard it as a device of disquotation, analogous in its operation to the erasure or crossing out of the quotation marks, then the occurrence will be referential and, indeed, there will be no difficulty in quantifying into the quotation context, as with:

$\exists x(\text{'}x \text{ played chess' is true})$

If, on the other hand and as is much more plausible, we take 'is true' to be a predicate of sentences and take the quotation-mark expression to be referring, here as elsewhere, to the expression under the quotes, then the occurrence of 'Giorgione' will not be referential and quantification into the quotation context would appear to be impossible.

Presumably, what makes sufficiency so appealing is the thought that if the occurrences of terms t in $\phi(t)$ are generally open to substitution, then the context $\phi(-)$ can be construed as picking out a condition which the individual sentences $\phi(t)$ attribute to the object picked out by t. But although it may be true that the context $\phi(-)$ can be so construed, the actual linguistic composition of the context may prevent it, as we have seen, from being so construed.

The question of sufficiency is not relevant to the *validity* of Quine's argument, but it is relevant to its *scope*. The argument is stated in terms of an example: he shows that substitutivity fails for a particular modal context; and then argues that quantification into that context is not possible. One naturally supposes that what goes for the one case goes for all cases and that there must be a general difficulty over quantifying into modal contexts.

But Quine's own principles rule out this extension of the argument. In the sentence '□ (9 is self-identical)', the occurrence of the term '9' is open to substitution. It therefore follows from sufficiency that the occurrence of the term is referential; and it then follows from his other principles that the context is accessible to quantification. So, by his own lights, Quine should be taken to have shown that quantification into modal contexts is sometimes impossible and that it is sometimes possible![10]

If one held the view, mentioned above, that no necessary truth can contain a singular term, then *all* of the singular terms within modal contexts would be open to substitution and so *all* of the contexts would be accessible to quantification. Indeed, this result would hold good even if the necessity statements were written in explicitly quotational form. It would make sense to say '$\forall x('\phi(x)'$ is analytic)', with the quantifier actually binding the variable under the quotes.

All this is quite absurd and is merely another indication of the implausibility of the substitution test as a sufficient condition for referentiality. If sufficiency is rejected, then the proofs of possibility are blocked and one is thereby free to take a more sensible over-all view of modal contexts. One can hold that all alike are resistant to quantification, even though there is only a partial breakdown, or no breakdown at all, in the substitution of singular terms.

Let us return to the question of necessity. But first, some terminology. In any alleged case of substitution failure, three sentences are used: $\phi(t)$, $t = s$, and $\phi(s)$. These involve two terms t and s, and a context $\phi(-)$. It is interesting to note that the terms and the context each occur twice in the sentences. We call t the *given* and s the *substituted* term. We talk similarly of the given and substituted *occurrences* of those terms. Sometimes we are sloppy, and talk of terms when we should mean occurrences. We call $\phi(t)$ the *given* and $\phi(s)$ the *resultant* or *final* sentence; $t = s$ is called the *identity sentence*. We shall sometimes think of the claim of necessity as providing a *test* for referentiality. If, in a particular case, the given and the identity sentences are true, then we

---

[10] A similar point is made by Baker [78]. He draws the conclusion 'so much the better for quantified modal logic'. I draw the conclusion 'so much the worse for Quine's account of referentiality'.

may talk of a *positive* result from the test if the final sentence is true, and a *negative* result if it is false.

I shall now present a series of counterexamples against the substitution test. In the case of each counterexample, we shall show how the test might be appropriately modified. In this way, we hope eventually to arrive at a correct formulation.

I have tried to find my counterexamples from actually existing languages. But this is merely for dramatic effect. I could, with equal legitimacy, have drawn my examples from artificial languages constructed specifically for the purpose of faulting the test. For I take it that Quine would not want to restrict the scope of his criterion to the languages that happen to exist and would not consider it relevant, in assessing the correctness of the criterion, to engage in a detailed investigation of different languages.

The first counterexample turns on the syntactic status of the given and substituted terms. We note that the sentences 'Eve's elder son was Cain', and 'Eve is the mother of Cain' are true, while the sentence 'The mother of Cain's elder son was Cain' is false. So the result of the test is negative, and yet it is not to be doubted that the occurrence of 'Eve's elder son' in the first sentence is referential.

Such examples are not confined to natural language. An example from arithmetic (with the usual conventions governing the scope of '+' and '.') goes as follows: the sentences '$2.2 = 4$' and '$2 = 1 + 1$' are true; the sentence '$1 + 1.2 = 4$' is false; and yet the given occurrence of '2' in the first sentence is referential.

It seems clear that these counterexamples go against the intended application of the substitution test. What is wrong is that there has been a shift in syntactic function: an expression that originally performed the syntactic function of a singular term is replaced by an expression that no longer does so. A proper formulation of the test is therefore one in which the given and substituted singular terms are required to function *as* singular terms.

The difference in the two formulation of the thesis might be expressed as a difference in the sense of 'occurrence of a singular term'. A *typographic* occurrence has the same shape or appearance as the given singular term; a *syntactic* or *constituent* occurrence must also function as a singular term. On the original formulation, the occurrences of the given and substituted terms were merely taken to be typographic; on the present formulation, they are required to be syntactic.

The distinction between typographic and syntactic occurrence is related to Kaplan's distinction between accidental and vulgar occurrence ([69], 112). Every accidental occurrence is typographic; 'nine' in 'canine', for example, is both. On the other hand, not every purely typographical occurrence is accidental, at least if I correctly understand how Kaplan wishes to use his term. The occurrence of '1 + 1' in '1 + 1.2' is purely typographic. But it is not accidental; it is not, in the relevant sense, a mere accident that we have this combination of symbols. A change in the system of spelling is capable in principle of eliminating all accidental occurrences of singular terms or other meaningful expressions; but it is not in general capable of eliminating all purely typographic occurrences of such expressions.

Quine tends to ignore the distinction between the two kinds of occurrence. He seems to think simply in terms of typographical occurrence. But this has its dangers. As we have seen, it leaves his test open to counterexample. It also leads him to overlook a significant alternative test for irreferentiality; for any purely typographic occurrence of a singular term will, on that count alone, be irreferential. We know, from our discussion of sufficiency, that purely typographic occurrences of singular terms may still be open to substitution; and so we see that this test will genuinely extend the substitution test. A similar point holds in regard to the explanation, as opposed to the test, of irreferentiality. The fact that an occurrence is purely typographic is sufficient by itself to explain its irreferentiality. But in case the occurrence is syntactic, some other explanation must be sought.

There are other difficulties for the substitution test; for even when a substitution preserves the syntactic status of the singular term, it may still induce a syntactic shift in the rest of the sentence. We may suppose that the sentence 'The Smith family leap frogs' is true. The identity sentence 'The Smith family is the same as The Smiths' is presumably also true; and we may take it that the resultant sentence 'The Smiths leap frogs' is false. So the upshot of the test is negative; and yet no one would doubt that the original occurrence of 'The Smith family' was referential.

The shift in the syntax may sometimes be more subtle and may turn on the relationship of the syntax of the predicate-expression to the syntax of the subject-expression. For the purposes of the next example, we must imagine that three men are in a line, with Bill at the back and Fred at the front, and that Fred subsequently leaves. The sentence 'The man behind Fred saw him leave' is presumably true; the identity sentence 'The man behind Fred = The man before Bill' is also true;

and the resultant sentence 'The man before Bill saw him leave' is false. Yet again, no one would doubt that the original occurrence of 'The man behind Fred' was referential.[11]

What has gone wrong in each of these examples is that the syntactic identity of the context has been altered. This is clear in the first two examples. But also it is plausible in the last example. For in the sentence 'The man behind Fred saw him leave', it is part of the syntax of the context ' - saw him leave' that 'him' stands in an anaphoric relationship to 'Fred'. Upon making the substitution to obtain the sentence 'The man before Bill saw him leave', 'him' comes to stand in an anaphoric relationship to 'Bill' and the syntactic identity of the context is thereby altered.

It should therefore be required, in a proper formulation of the substitution test, that the syntactic identity of the context remain the same in the given and resultant sentences. Given this requirement, the previous stipulation concerning singular terms then becomes redundant; for the syntactic identity of the context cannot stay the same without the syntactic status of the occurrences of the singular terms also staying the same.

The difference between the present and the previous formulations might be expressed as a difference in the sense of 'same context'. Again, the difference rests upon the distinction between the typographic and the syntactic. Typographic context is a matter of appearance; as long as the symbols remain the same, the context remains the same. Syntactic context is a matter of analysis; it is only when the syntactic analysis remains the same that the syntactic context can be said to remain the same. Before it was required that the substitution be made within a given typographic context; now it is required that the substitution be made within the same typographico-syntactic context.

Once the test is formulated in this way, it is seen to be entirely incidental that the typographic identity of the context remains the same; all that matters is its syntactic identity. A more general formulation of the test is therefore one in which the contexts are taken to be purely syntactic and in which it is allowed that different instances of the context may be given different typographic realizations. Indeed, so much is already apparent from the actual use we might make of the test; for it

---

[11] Linsky [67], 104, has a similar example involving 'latter'. It should be clear from these examples that I go further than Kaplan in my criticisms of Quine's argument from substitution. For he concedes (Kaplan [86], 235) that if substitution fails then one of the terms is irreferential.

would be taken to be of no consequence, when performing a substitution, that the main verb was modified to agree with the subject or the initial letter of a singular term was capitalized in order to let it head a sentence.

It is hard not to think of these syntactic shifts in occurrence and context as somehow anomalous or irregular; the mechanism for discerning syntax from typography does not take the simplest possible form. We are therefore led to the idea of a syntactically uniform language. Within such a language, these anomalies do not arise: there is agreement both in syntactic and typographic context.

Let us be a little more precise. The requirement on occurrence is a global one. It says that, for any meaningful expression, all syntactic and typographic occurrences of that expression within a larger meaningful expression should coincide. The requirement on context is a local one and may be put in terms of substitution. Any occurrence of a meaningful expression within a larger meaningful expression creates a context, which can be regarded either typographically or syntactically. In requiring these two contexts to agree, we are requiring that the substitutions within them should coincide: any result of making a typographic substitution of a meaningful expression within the typographic context should coincide with the result of making the corresponding syntactic substitution within the syntactic context.

Such a language is, in an obvious sense, completely perspicuous with regard to its syntax: the appearance of an expression is an infallible guide to its syntactic status; and the way it is put together is an infallible guide to its syntactic analysis. The syntax is discerned from the typography in the most straightforward possible way.

It seems reasonable to suppose that the different syntactic anomalies of a language can be ironed out and that it can be converted, upon a suitable adjustment in its notation, to a language that is syntactically uniform. In this way, the underlying syntactic regularities of the language are laid bare. Various familiar devices can be regarded as means to this end. Single-letter spelling, often introduced for purposes of notational economy, also serves to eliminate accidental occurrences of expressions; and bracketing, often introduced for purposes of disambiguation, also serves to eliminate irregular contexts.

Uniformity of language is of great relevance to the substitution test. The original test would appear to apply directly, without qualification, to syntactically uniform languages; for identity of typographic context automatically guarantees identity of syntactic context. But the test also applies *indirectly* to other languages; for we may first convert to a uniform language, and then apply the test to it. In this way, the question of whether the first occurrence of '2' is referential in the sentence '2.2 = 4' of an unbracketed irregular language is reduced to the question of whether the corresponding occurrence of '2' is referential in the corresponding sentence '(2.2) = 4' of a bracketed syntactically uniform language. Conversion also provides a test for purely typographic occurrence: for such occurrences disappear upon conversion; no occurrence in the converted expression corresponds to them.

It should be noted that these indirect tests require us to set up a suitable correspondence between the typographic occurrences of the given and the converted expression; for it is only in terms of such a correspondence that we can say 'what happens' to the given expression. What the correspondence in effect does is to isolate the syntactic (and subsequently, the semantic) contribution of a typographical item. It is not to be taken for granted that this can always be done. We can imagine a code for a language that does not work on compositional principles. Perhaps the sentences of English and of French are independently enumerated and then the n-th French sentence is used as a code for the n-th English sentence. Within the language of the code, the sub-sentential components would not have isolable syntactic or semantic roles. It is against such an example as this that we can appreciate how remarkable it is that isolable roles can be attributed to individual components in ordinary case.

The substitution test is beset not merely by syntactic ills, but also by semantic ills; and again, both subject- and context-expression are equally prone to attack.

Let us deal first with the ills of the subject. Just as the syntactic status of the singular term may shift from the given to the final sentence, so may its reference, notwithstanding the truth of the identity sentence. One kind of case arises from ambiguity. The sentence 'Queen Elizabeth II weighs over a million tons' is true when the subject-phrase refers to the ship. The identity claim 'Queen Elizabeth II = The present queen of England' is true when the subject-phrase refers to the person. The first occurrence of 'Queen Elizabeth II' is clearly referential, and yet the sentence 'The present queen of England weighs over a million tons' is false when the reference of the subject-phrase is again to the person.

A similar kind of case arises from indexicality. At some time before a fateful hour in 1953 it would have been true to say 'The monarch lives' and 'The monarch is King George V'. But at any time after that fateful hour, it would not have been true to say 'King George V lives', even though the first occurrence of 'The monarch' is clearly referential.

I am not sure either of these counterexamples needs to be taken too seriously; I mention them more for the sake of completeness than for their intrinsic interest. They may be avoided by insisting that the test only apply to sentence-types, and not to sentence-tokens. This is not to say that the test has no application to the actual use of language; for instead of talking of the truth-value of a sentence-type, we may talk of the truth-value of a sentence-type in a context which fixes the reference of an indexical or ambiguous term. It then suffices to require that the context remain the same from one sentence to the next.

However, there is a more devious kind of ambiguity, which does raise difficulties at the level of types. With our previous examples, a single occurrence of an expression within a larger expression-type had several 'meanings'. But it is also possible that different occurrences of the same expression should have different meanings, even though each individual occurrence has a single meaning. The first kind of ambiguity might be called *intracontextual*, and the second *extracontextual*. The second is more devious in being less apparent. The detection of intracontextual ambiguity is relatively straightforward and, in many cases, is simply a matter of consulting our intuitions; the detection of extracontextual ambiguity is much more problematic and often calls for a heavy exploitation of semantic theory.

The classic case of inter-contextual ambiguity is provided by Frege's account of oblique contexts. According to Frege, a term may either refer to its standard referent, or, in special contexts, it may refer to a nonstandard referent. The consequence for the substitution test is that it may fail in its application to terms that occur within the special contexts, not because the terms are irreferential, but because the truth of the identity sentence fails to guarantee that the reference of the terms is the same in those contexts.

A somewhat less controversial case than Frege's is provided by the decimal system of notation. Perhaps the most plausible semantical account of this notation is this: a digit denotes according to its position; the dot helps to indicate position; and juxtaposition is used to signify addition.

Consider now the sentences '2.3 = 2.3', '3 = 03', and '2.03 = 2.3'. The first two are true and the third false; and yet it seems clear that the initial occurrence of '3' is referential. If the proposed semantical explanation of the notation is correct, this is because the given occurrence of '3' and the final occurrence of '03' are not coreferential within their respective contexts, notwithstanding the truth of the identity sentence.

These counterexamples raise a subtle issue concerning the intuitive concept of referentiality, one which we have not had to consider until now. Quine says that a referential occurrence of a singular term is used solely to specify its object. But what is "its" object here? Is it the object that the term is used to refer to in the given context? Or is it the object that the term is standardly used to refer to?

It seems advisable to separate the question of whether a term is used to refer to some object or another for the rest of the sentence to say something about from the question of whether this object is the standard referent. Accordingly, we shall henceforth use 'referential' in the weaker noncommittal sense and use 'standardly referential' for the stricter sense (cf. Kaplan [69], 118). (Strictly speaking, it is not a question of whether the referent is standard but of whether the reference-relation is standard. It is possible to imagine that a term might nonstandardly refer to its standard referent. It is perfectly conceivable, for example, that for Frege the referent and the sense of a term might coincide, as in 'the sense of this term'.)

If referentiality is standard, then the counterexamples do not work and no revision to the test needs to be made. Terms in Frege's special contexts and digits after a decimal point will fail to be referential, simply because they do not have their standard reference.

If referentiality is neutral, then the counterexamples stand and a revision to the test does indeed need to be made. A further restriction needs to be placed on the given and resultant occurrences of singular terms. It should not only be required that they have the same syntactic status as singular terms, but also that they should be coreferential.

This restriction differs in an essential way from our previous requirement that the identity sentence be true. For the requirement on the identity sentence concerned the reference of the terms in isolation from the context in which they occurred; while the present restriction concerns the reference of the terms *in situ*. Moreover, given this new condition, the old one should be dropped. For if the occurrences have their standard reference, then the condition on the identity sentence is idle; while if the occurrences fail to have their standard reference, the condition is irrelevant.

However, the new condition is still not enough to protect the substitution test against counterexample. For just as the substitution of a singular term can induce a shift in the syntactic identity of the context, it can also induce a shift in its semantic identity. In one kind of case, a lexical item within the context may change its meaning. An example is provided by languages which have a common notation for arithmetical and Boolean operations. (Some programming languages are like this.) We may suppose that the sign '-' may be used to signify either subtraction or complementation, according as to whether the expression following it is arithmetical or Boolean. We may also suppose that 't' and 'f' are Boolean expressions for the True and the False, that '1' and '0' are arithmetical expressions for 1 and 0, and that the True is identified with 1 and the False with 0. Then the sentence '- $t = f$' is true and the sentence '- 1 = f' is false, even though the occurrences of 't' and '1' in their respective contexts are coreferential. In this case, we cannot even place the blame on the syntactic identity of the context, for it remains the same. What has gone wrong is that the substitution has induced a change in the meaning of the operation-symbol '1'.

Examples from natural language are hard to come by. An example from Hebrew (proposed by Ran Lahav) goes as follows. The word 'TSAFA' can either be the present, third person, feminine form of a verb meaning to float or the past, third person, masculine form of a verb meaning to observe. The word for the moon can either be 'YARE'ACH', which is in the masculine, or 'LEVANA', which is in the feminine. So we see that 'The moon (LEVANA) floats (TSAFA) in the sky (RAKEIA)' is true; and that 'The moon (YARE'ACH) observed (TSAFA) the sky (RAKEIA)' is false, even though the occurrences of 'LEVANA' and 'YARE'ACH' are coreferential. However, this is not a pure example, one in which there is only a semantic shift; for there is also a shift in the syntactic status of the verb 'TSAFA'.

In the case of this example, and others like it, there may be some doubt as to whether the given occurrence of the singular term is genuinely referential. For is the term 'YARE'ACH' being used solely to pick out an object? Is it not also being used to disambiguate the verb 'TSAFA'?

But referentiality is a matter of the direct role of the term in determining what is said. The given sentence says that the moon floats in the sky; and the immediate contribution of the term to this content is its object. This is not to deny that the term may have an indirect role in determining what contribution other expressions make to the content. This is the case with our example, the gender of the subject-term determines the meaning of the verb; but this is no way impugns the referentiality of that term. The term, if you like, performs both off-stage and on-stage; and it is only the on-stage performance that is relevant to referentiality. (Later, we shall have further occasion to be highly discriminating over exactly what role of a term is relevant to its referentiality.)

Another kind of example arises when the substitution induces a shift, not in the meaning of any simple constituent, but in the semantic significance of the syntactic operations by means of which the simple constituents are combined. Again, ordinary arithmetical notation provides an example. The inequality '02 > 1' is true. But upon substituting '(1 + 1)' for '2', we obtain the false inequality '0(1 + 1) > 1'. Here the occurrences of '2' and '(1 + 1)' are coreferential, and even the syntactic identity of the context remains the same. What has happened is that the substitution has induced a change in the semantic significance of juxtaposition; from signifying addition (or perhaps something involving exponentiation), it has come to signify multiplication.

There may also be some doubt as to whether this example is pure; for does not juxtaposition correspond to two distinct syntactic operations in the context '02' and '0(1 + 1)'? More generally, it might be argued that a single syntactic operation should have a single semantic interpretation and that, where this requirement appears to be violated, the syntactic operation should be differentiated according to the different semantic interpretations which it can bear. This point of view raises difficult questions concerning the nature of syntax and its relationship to the semantics. Let me here record my own belief that the relationship between syntax and semantics should not be taken to be as tight as this point of view would have us suppose and that, just as we should be tolerant over a single lexical item bearing several different meanings, so we should be tolerant over a single syntactic construction bearing several different semantic interpretations.

To take care of these counterexamples, the requirement that the syntactic identity of the context remain the same must be strengthened. It must also be required that the semantic identity remain the same. In the simplest case (which, on a certain view, is the most general case), corresponding constituents should have the same meaning, and corresponding syntactic operations should have the same semantic significance.

Again, we may see the difference in the present and the previous formulations of the test as merely a difference in the sense of 'context'. Previously, we took a context to be syntactic; now we take it to be syntactico-semantic.

Considerations of uniformity in language may also be introduced in the same way as before. A uniform language is now one that is completely perspicuous in regard to its syntax and semantics; there is complete coincidence in the application of the typographic, syntactic or semantic concepts of occurrence and context. Syntax is determined from typography and semantics from syntax in the most straightforwardly possible way.

Two varieties of uniformity may again be discerned, one local and the other global. Local uniformity is typified by the occurrences of different expressions having the same syntactico-semantic function in a given context. Global uniformity is typified by the different occurrences of the same expression having the same syntactico-semantic function.

Again, it appears reasonable to suppose that the different semantic anomalies of a language can be ironed out and that it can be converted, upon a suitable adjustment in its notation and possibly its syntax as well, into a language that is both syntactically and semantically uniform. The original test will then apply, without qualification, to such languages; and it will apply indirectly to other languages by means of their conversion to such a language.

Philosophers have tended to be very suspicious of the idea of an "ideal" or uniform language. But there is really no more to this idea than the attempt to be completely systematic about disambiguation. Instead of using one word with two different meanings, we use two words each with a single meaning. Apply this same procedure at the syntactic level and also to the means by which expressions are constructed, and we obtain the general conception of an ideal or uniform language.

A certain form of radical scepticism concerning the concept of uniformity and its application is indeed possible. Perhaps a radical scepticism over the purely syntactic aspect of uniformity could be maintained. But let us here give a partly semantic example (somewhat along the lines of Goodman's 'grue' and Kripke's 'quus'). We suppose that the word 'grun' is used ambiguously; it can mean either 'green' or 'not green'. In any context, the ambiguity is resolved by the number of letters in the subject-expression: if the number is even then the meaning is 'green'; and if the number is odd then the meaning is 'not green'. So sentences of the form ' - is grun' will not be semantically uniform in the sense that I have previously tried to convey.

To this, the sceptic will object that one can, with equal justice, maintain that the ambiguity lies with 'green' rather than 'grun'. 'Grun' is unambiguous; but 'green' means 'grun' when the subject-expression is of even length, and it means 'not grun' when the subject-expression is of odd length. Of course, either hypothesis will require adjustments elsewhere in the semantic analysis of a sentence. But as long as this can be consistently executed, there is no reason to prefer one hypothesis to the other.

I no more have a telling objection to this form of scepticism than I do to any other. But I should like to point out that doubts over the existence of a uniform or ideal language would appear to belong more with these sceptical misgivings than with our natural good judgment.

Granted that there is a coherent concept of uniformity to be used, then our reformulation of the test strikes me as not being merely impervious to counterexample, but also susceptible to some kind of proof. We have that the syntactico-semantic contexts of $\phi(t)$ and $\phi(s)$ are the same. We know that the given occurrence of t is referential and that the substituted occurrence of s is coreferential with it; and we wish to deduce that the truth-values of $\phi(t)$ and $\phi(s)$ are the same.

What is lacking for a demonstration to go through is a precise account of what it is for an occurrence of a term to be referential. Quine's own account in terms of substitution was rejected long ago. But the problem remains; and a solution to it would not only be of great interest in itself, but would help us see what was correct in Quine's original account.

I would like to suggest that an occurrence of a term t in a sentence $\phi(t)$ is referential if there is a semantical analysis of the whole sentence in which the semantic value assigned to the occurrence of a term is its referent. We may imagine a roving semantic eye that picks out whatever is relevant to the given semantical analysis; when it comes to a referential occurrence, it only picks out the referent. It should be noted that this account actually supplied the explanatory factor that was found lacking in Quine's account. It shows the concept of referentiality to be theoretical in nature and to require, for its application, an implicit semantic analysis of the sentence under consideration.

If this is correct, we may assume that our given $\phi(t)$ has a semantical analysis in which the semantic value assigned to the given occurrence of t is its referent. This analysis determines an analysis of the context. This may be compared with the semantical analysis of the context which is meant to be preserved on substitution. If the two are in agreement, it would seem to follow, by some sort of compositionality principle, that the semantic values of $\phi(t)$ and $\phi(s)$ are the same; and from this and the principle that the semantic value of a sentence must always determine its truth-value, it follows that the truth-values of the sentences are the same. On the other hand, if the two analyses are not in agreement, it still seems reasonable to suppose that the analysis of the context will determine an analysis which *is* in agreement with the relevant part of the analysis of the sentence, either because this analysis exists at a lower level (at the level of reference, say, rather than sense) or because it is an alternative, but equivalent, analysis at the same level. The argument may then proceed in the same way as before.

I do not present this reasoning as an actual proof, but it does make clear how a proof might go.

There is a way in which Quine himself concedes the need for something like a uniformity requirement. In a very revealing passage from "Reference and Modality" (Quine [63], 150), he writes:

> Nonsense is indeed mere absence of sense, and can always be remedied by arbitrarily assigning some sense. But the important point to observe is that granted an understanding of the modalities . . ., and given an understanding of quantification ordinarily so-called, we do not come out automatically with any meaning for such sentences as (30)–(31).

But what is lacking in Quine is any explicit acknowledgement of the significance of the requirement for his own argument.

In fact, the presence of the requirement makes an enormous difference to the epistemological status of the test. In unqualified form, the application of the test is completely unproblematic. That one sentence $\phi(s)$ is obtained by substitution from another $\phi(t)$ is a matter for "inspection"; and that the respective sentences involved in the test—the given and final sentences $\phi(t)$ and $\phi(s)$, and the identity sentence $t = s$—have the appropriate truth-values is a matter for ordinary judgment. On the other hand, the application of the qualified test calls for what may be a highly theoretical judgment on the preservation of syntactico-semantic context. We are no longer making straightforward observations about the world, but problematic theoretical claims about the syntax and semantics of language.

It is as if Quine had attempted to state a theoretical truth within the confines of an observation language. In this respect, we might compare his formulation of the substitution test with the commonplace generalization 'Unsupported objects fall'. It may be granted that this generalization holds under conditions of *caeteris paribus*; and yet any proper account of these conditions will have to make use of theoretical terms.

Indeed, what is generally remarkable about Quine's discussion of referentiality is its atheoretical character. Although he was writing at a time when the views of Frege and Russell were already well known, there is no admission, at least in his earlier work, that they had any bearing on the issues at hand. Referentiality was to be decided by a simple 'observational' test; semantical analysis was, at worst, incoherent and, at best, irrelevant.

It might be wondered whether our own formulation of the substitution test not only makes it theoretical in nature, but also makes it useless as a way of testing for irreferentiality. For in any application it must be determined whether the syntactico-semantic context stays the same. And how can this be done unless it has already been determined whether or not the given occurrence of a singular term is referential?

However, the fact remains that we may be able to determine that two syntactico-semantic contexts are the same without knowing what that context is. Indeed, it suffices to determine that the contexts are the same under the hypothesis that the given occurrence of a singular term is referential. For if irreferentiality (something of the form $\neg p$) can be inferred from referentiality (something of the form p), it can be inferred without the benefit of that hypothesis. To take a concrete example, it may be unclear how the name 'Cicero' is functioning in the sentence ' 'Cicero' has five letters'. But it is clear that the name 'Tully' in ' 'Tully' has five letters' is functioning in the same way; and so, under the hypothesis that the original occurrence of 'Cicero' is referential, the two syntactico-semantic contexts will be the same.

If we are testing for standard referentiality, then identity of syntactico-semantic context is enough. We may therefore conclude from the failure of substitution in the example above that the name 'Cicero' in the original sentence is not standardly referential. However, if neutral referentiality is in question, then we also require that the given and resultant occurrences of the singular terms should be coreferential. But whether this is so, even under the hypothesis that the given occurrence is referential, will be highly questionable. For it will always be possible that the given and final terms refer, at their respective occurrences, to themselves; and so it will always be possible that they are not coreferential, except in the uninteresting case in which they are the same.

There would therefore appear to be a significant difference between the amended tests for standard and neutral referentiality: one is of some use; the other is not!

We may conclude this part of the discussion with the consideration of two topics with a more general bearing. As we have seen, the concept of uniformity is required for the proper formulation of the substitution test. This is no accident; it is also required, it seems to me, at many other places in the philosophy of language and logic. An interesting example for us, since it involves referentiality, comes from the attempt to characterize logical truth.

According to the standard account, a logical truth is a sentence whose truth is preserved upon arbitrary substitutions for its nonlogical constants. But on this account (and, indeed, merely on the necessity half of it), the sentence

$$2 = (1 + 1) \supset (2.2 = 4 \supset (1 + 1).2 = 4)$$

is not a logical truth.

For upon substituting '1 + 1' for '(1 + 1)', we obtain the falsehood:

$$2 = 1 + 1 \supset (2.2 = 4 \supset 1 + 1.2 = 4).$$

What is one to make of this argument? One could take the brave step of denying that the original sentence was a logical truth. But although the sentence may not be a logical truth, it can hardly be because the given substitution results in a falsehood, as the proposed account of logical truth would seem to imply. Moreover, the bravery may require one to go too far. For the example generalizes to the extent that one would be forced, on this view, to deny that there were *any* logical truths that significantly involved singular terms.

Another response is to restrict the substitutions to those that preserve the referentiality of the singular terms. But this restriction appears to be completely unmotivated in terms of the original account of logical truth. Moreover, even if it could be motivated, it would still fail to deliver the right results; for referentiality will not guarantee that the syntactico-semantic context remains the same. So Quine ([63], 146) is mistaken in thinking that the principle $\phi(t) \supset \exists x \phi(x)$ will hold when the term t refers and the given occurrences of t are referential (in either the intuitive or technical sense); for, in substituting x for t, the syntactico-semantic context may change.

In this regard, Quine's attitude to the substitutivity principle $t = s \supset (\phi(t) \supset \phi(s))$ is of interest. He takes the failure of the principle merely to be evidence that the given occurrences of the term t are not referential ([63], 140). But in so doing, he denies himself the possibility of making any significant generalization concerning the cases in which the principle holds; he can only say, the principle holds in the cases in which it holds. But it is hard not to believe that such a significant generalization exists, especially when the correct instances are regarded as logical truths.

Surely the proper response to these counterexamples is to require that the substitutions preserve the appropriate syntactico-semantic contest. The counterexamples are then avoided, and in a properly motivated way. We may still abide by the usual schematic representation of logical truths, but we must take the substitution-instances, of which the schemes are representative, to be the result of a syntactico-semantic substitution, and not a purely typographic substitution.

The other general topic concerns the quest for rigor. Quine's discussion of referentiality is typical of much work in the philosophy of logic and language and even in linguistics; it involves very general considerations concerning the nature of language. How should such considerations be formalized? What is the proper framework of concepts and principles within which they should be set?

At the foundation for any such a framework will be a discipline of *universal abstract syntax*. This discipline attempts to formulate the general concepts and principles of syntax, the ones applicable to any possible language, and it attempts to formulate them in the most basic terms. The aim is to get at the idea of syntax as such.

My own conception of this discipline (which I hope to develop more fully elsewhere) differs in two fundamental ways from the orthodox conception, as found in the work of Montague [70] and others. First the discipline is not regarded as an extension of the theory of concatenation. The basic entities of the discipline are not taken to be expressions or strings of symbols, even in a suitably abstract sense. Instead, they are taken to be primitively given and are assumed only to have whatever structure their syntax endows upon them. It is not essential to the idea of syntax that the objects capable of possessing syntactic structure should be strings of symbols. Matrices, diagrams, bodily acts, propositions, even facts, may possess syntactic structure and yet not be, or relevantly taken to be, strings. Thus our discipline might equally well be regarded as the *general theory of constituent structure*.

Second, the basic syntactic structure of the entities is taken to be given, not by certain syntactic constructions, but by the operation of substitution. To be exact, there will be three basic syntactic notions: *occurrence of, occurrence in*, and *substitution*. *Occurrence* of is a two-place relation holding between an occurrence e and the entity of E of which it is an occurrence. *Occurrence in* is a two place relation holding between an occurrence e and another occurrence f within which it occurs. (So we must therefore posit an ontology of occurrences of entities, in addition to the entities themselves.) *Substitution* is a three-place operation: if e is an occurrence and E' and F are entities, then substitution gives the result $F^{E'}/e$ (if any) of substituting E for e in F. Our discipline must lay down the basic principles for these notions. One basic principle, for example, is that if F' is the result of substituting E' for the occurrence e of E within F, then there is an occurrence e' of E' within F' such that the result of substituting any expression E'' for e' within F' is identical to the result of substituting E'' directly for e in F.

I do not wish to dispute the existence of syntactic constructions. It is just that I do not take them as basic. Indeed, if c is any syntactic construction, of two places let us say, then c may be recovered, with the help of substitution, from any one of its instances. For let F be the result of applying c to E_1 and E_2, and let e_1 and e_2 be the corresponding occurrences of E_1 and E_2 in F. Then the result of applying c to any entities E_1' and E_2' is the same as substituting E_1' and E_2' for e_1 and e_2 in F. On the other hand, it is not always clear that the notions of occurrence and substitution are recoverable from the syntactic constructions. I therefore reverse the usual order of definition and take substitution as primitive, rather than the syntactic constructions themselves.

The syntactic structure of a language is given by a domain of entity-types, a domain of occurrences, the relations of occurrence in, and occurrence of, and the operation of substitution. Given such a structure, there is a natural notion of homomorphism. Roughly speaking, a homomorphism is a correspondence between the entities of the two domains which preserves the structure of substitution.

The various notions of interpretation, translation and uniformity should all be explained in terms of the concept of homomorphism. Since we take an abstract view of syntax, the semantic values of an interpretation can themselves be regarded as constituting a syntax. An interpretation may then be regarded as a homomorphism from the syntactic domain of expressions to the semantic domain of semantic values.

Suppose now that f_1 interprets the language L_1 in the semantic domain M_1, and f_2 interprets the language L_2 in the semantic domain M_2. Let g be a homomorphism from M_1 to M_2 which, intuitively speaking, maps each semantic value of M_1 into that aspect of it which the translation should preserve. (In the extreme case, g could be an identity function). Then a translation is a homomorphism h from L_1 to L_2 for which the diagram:

$$M_1 \xrightarrow{\ g\ } M_2$$

$$f_1 \uparrow \qquad\qquad \uparrow f_2$$

$$L_1 \xrightarrow[h]{\qquad} L_2$$

commutes. On this perspective, universal semantic becomes a part of universal syntax.

Finally, let us note that the expressions of a language will usually have a purely typographic structure, which can be specified in terms of suitable concepts of occurrence and substitution. The notions of syntactic and semantic perspicuity can then be defined in terms of the existence of appropriate homomorphisms between the typographic, syntactic and semantic structures. Uniformity, or syntactico-semantic perspicuity, is usually regarded as an all or nothing matter. But it is in fact possible to define various intermediate concepts: the homomorphism may also be isomorphisms; they may or may not be onto; they may only have a local application; and so on.

Two interesting areas of investigation arise within this framework, although they also have an existence outside of it. First, if one takes an abstract view of syntax or semantics then it becomes a definite question to what extent and in what manner a given syntax or semantics can be realized in a given concrete medium, such as the written or spoken word. We therefore have a study of what might be called *syntactic* or *semantic realizability*. Second, philosophers and logicians have concentrated their efforts on *uniform* languages. But most languages that are actually used are not uniform in nature and, indeed, many of their most desirable features would appear to derive from their lack of uniformity. We need to understand not only how a nonuniform language can be transformed into one that is uniform but also how it is that, in the process of transformation, certain desirable features of the original language may be lost.

Universal syntax also provides the natural basis for a completely general theory of abstraction and application. The operation of substitution can be regarded as the combined result of two other operations. Given the occurrence e of an entity E within F, first we remove e. This is the operation of abstraction and it gives us an abstract or form $\lambda e F$. (The notation should not confuse: e here is an occurrence, not a variable; it is abstracted from F and is no part of the resultant entity $\lambda e F$.) We may then insert E' in the gap left by e. This is the operation of application and it gives us a new entity $\lambda e F(E')$. The fundamental law of abstraction then states that the combined effect $\lambda e F(E')$ of these two operations is the same as the result $F^{E'}/e$ of substituting E' for e in F.

Contexts are merely abstracts in the case in which the underlying entities are syntactic; properties (or relations) are merely abstracts in the case in which the underlying entities are semantic. Our previous considerations concerning syntactico-semantic context can therefore be formalized within the general theory of abstraction. It also seems to me, though this is not the place to develop the point, that any satisfactory account of the identity of propositions must be based upon the assumption that abstraction is one of the fundamental operations by means of which they are generated.

We turn to the remaining steps in Quine's argument. Fortunately, we shall not need to be so expansive.

Step (3): From the Irreferentiality of the Singular Term to the Irreferentiality of the Variable

Before the cogency of this step can be evaluated, it must be determined what the concept of referentiality for a variable is. Quine, so far as I know, provides no intuitive account of the concept. It is, however, fairly easy to construct one, by analogy with the account of referentiality for (closed) singular terms.

An occurrence of a singular term is referential if it is used solely to pick out its object. By analogy, we may say that an occurrence of a variable is referential if it is used solely to pick out its value. This account is all right as far as it goes, but we may make it a little more precise. First, we may note that 'value', unlike 'referent', is a relative term. We should therefore say that the role of a referential occurrence of a variable is relative to an assignment of values to the variables, and that, relative to such an assignment, the sole role of the occurrence is to pick out the value of the variable. Second, we may be more explicit about the role. A referential occurrence of a singular term is used to pick out an object for the rest of the sentence to say something about. In the same way, a referential occurrence of a variable is used to pick out a value for the rest of the open sentence to say something about. Finally, we may distinguish, as before, between neutral and standard referentiality. Just as a (closed) term has a standard referent, so a variable has a standardly assumed value, one that is given by an extracontextual specification of the domain. The variable will be standardly referential if it takes the standardly assumed value.

Our question therefore is whether the (standard) referentiality of an occurrence of a variable x in an open sentence $\phi(x)$ implies the (standard) referentiality of the corresponding occurrence of a term t in the sentence $\phi(t)$. We may concentrate on the neutral case of referentiality, since the standard case raises no special problems.

It should be apparent from our previous discussion of the substitution test that a battery of counterexamples might be marshalled against the inference from the referentiality of the variable to the referentiality of the term. Let me here mention just two. First, the occurrence of the variable 'x' in $2.x > 0$' is referential and yet the corresponding occurrence of '1+1' in '$2.1 + 1 > 0$' is not. Indeed, it is not even a syntactic occurrence of a singular term. Second, using Quine's own notation for quasi-quotation, the metalinguistic variable 'α' has a referential occurrence in '$\ulcorner \alpha \urcorner$ is a term', but the corresponding occurrence of the term '0' in '$\ulcorner 0 \urcorner$ is a term' is not referential.

I would like to suggest that, for the inference to go through, it should again be required that the semantic or the syntactico-semantic context remain the same. Even if this requirement were not necessary for the validity of the inference, it might still be necessary for the purposes of the argument of which it is a part. For our aim is to show that, where there is a failure of substitution, there is a hindrance to quantification. But this conclusion could lose its interest if the context into which we could not quantify was not the same, semantically speaking, as the context for which substitution failed.

With the requirement, there appears to be some sort of possibility of proving that the inference goes through. For suppose that an occurrence of a variable x in $\phi(x)$ is referential, where we take this to means that there is a semantical analysis of the open sentence $\phi(x)$ which is such that, relative to an assignment, the semantic value of the occurrence is the value assigned to the variable x. It would then seem to follow, if the semantic contexts remain the same, that the semantic value of t in the corresponding semantical analysis of $\phi(x)$ is its referent. In other words, uniformity would appear to dictate that the role of the value of a variable is the same, though relative to an assignment, as the role of the referent of a singular term, or, to put the matter in quasi-psychological terms, our understanding of the open sentence must be implicit, in the appropriate way, in our understanding of the corresponding closed sentence $\phi(t)$.[12]

---

[12] We have here a response that might be made to Kaplan's alleged refutation of

Although it is not strictly relevant to the evaluation of the argument, it may be of interest to consider the other links that can hold among the referential status of terms. There is, first of all, the remaining cross-categorial link, going from the referentiality of the singular term to the referentiality of the variable. The ordinary symbolism of the predicate calculus suffices to yield a counterexample in this case. For '0' in '$\exists x(x > 0)$' is referential, while the last occurrence of 'x' in '$\exists x(x > x)$' is not referential.

There is then the remaining intracategorial link, going from the referentiality of one variable to the referentiality of another. Again, a counterexample from the predicate calculus may be given. The variable 'x' has a referential occurrence in '$\exists y(x > y)$', but the corresponding occurrence of 'y' in '$\exists y(y > y)$' is not referential.

It is usual to get around these difficulties by requiring that the occurrences of the substituted variables should be free, where the term 'free' is defined in purely typographic terms. But if what we are after is a general principle, then such a restriction is far too narrow and ad hoc. We might have different conventions for the position of the quantifiers; they might be placed at the end of an open sentence, as is common in mathematics, rather than at the front. There are also other ways in which a variable may become bound; the phrase 'the polynomial', for example, binds all of the variables (though none of the parameters) within its scope. It is clear that there is no purely typographic concept which will cover all of these cases.

It again seems advisable to make the links dependent upon a requirement of a semantic or syntactico-semantic uniformity. A similar requirement, we may note, should be placed upon the substitution test that Quine provides for the referentiality of variables. If the given occurrence of 'x' in '$\phi(x)$' is referential, then the sentence '$\forall x \forall y(x = y \supset \phi(x) \supset \phi(y))$' should be true, but only on condition that the syntactico-semantic context is preserved.

Quine's "alleged theorem" (Kaplan [86], section III). The refutation does not go through because it takes no account of the hidden premise concerning uniformity. Kaplan himself responds to the gap he finds in Quine's argument by insisting on a requirement of coherence (238). But it is not clear to me exactly what coherence is or whether it is intended, like uniformity, to constitute a repair to the argument.

Step (4): From the Irreferentiality of the Variable to the Nonobjectuality of Satisfaction

Like the second step, from the failure of substitution to irreferentiality, this step is unlikely to be challenged by the average reader of Quine. But it is again highly problematic, in my opinion, once the critical terms are made clear.

An occurrence of a variable is referential if it is used solely to specify its value. Whether an open sentence containing referential occurrences of variables is satisfied therefore depends only upon the values of those variables. On the other hand, the relation of satisfaction is objectual if it is a relation that holds between an open sentence and an assignment of values to variable.

It is presupposed, in the definition of referentiality, that the corresponding notion of satisfaction is objectual. But the notion of satisfaction may be objectual even though the occurrences of the free variables are not referential; for there is nothing in the idea of satisfaction as a relation between an open sentence and an assignment of values to variables which makes it necessary that the identity of the variables should be of no relevance to whether the relation obtains.

One needs to distinguish between two ways in which an occurrence of a variable may fail to be referential. On the one hand, satisfaction may depend not merely on the value of the variable, but also upon how that value is specified. Call this *external dependency*. On the other hand, satisfaction may depend not merely on the value of variable, but also upon the identity of the variable itself. Call this *internal dependency*.

Referentiality excludes both forms of dependence. Objectuality of satisfaction excludes only the first. It is therefore possible, when only the first is excluded, that satisfaction should be objectual and the variables irreferential.

Quine seems to overlook this possibility in his argument against quantifying into modal contexts. He notes that '$\Box(9 > 7)$' is true but '$\Box$ (The number of planets > 7)' is false. He then supposes that whether an object satisfies '$\Box(x > 7)$' will depend upon the external means by which the object is given. But it is also possible that the satisfaction of the condition should depend upon the internal means by which the object is given, i.e., on the variable 'x' itself.

As far as I know, the possibility of distinguishing in this way between objectual and referential quantification has not previously been noticed. But the possibility should really have been already evident from the comparable case for singular terms. With what is taken to be a partly referential singular term, like 'Giorgione' in 'Giorgione was so-called because of his size', the truth-value of the sentence may depend not only on the referent of the term but also on the term itself. In the same way, the satisfaction of an open sentence containing a free variable may depend not only on the value of the variable but on the variable itself. What goes for the singular term goes equally well for the variable.

The new style of variable, and the quantifier which goes with it, may be called *literalist*, since satisfaction will in general depend not only upon the object but also upon the letter. It is important to appreciate that the literalist quantifiers are not, like the substitutional quantifiers, let us say, an alternative to objectual quantification but are themselves a species of objectual quantification. The form of the satisfaction relation is standard; it is a relation which holds between an assignment of objects from the domain to the variables and an open sentence. The clause for the satisfaction of a quantified open sentence is also standard; an assignment satisfies an existential sentence $\exists x \phi(x)$, for example, just in case an appropriate variant of the assignment satisfies $\phi(x)$.

Indeed, there is something misleading about calling our variables or quantifiers literalist in the first place. We may take it that it is of the essence of the use of variables that the satisfaction conditions for open-sentences be given relative to an assignment of objects from the domain to the variables and that it is of the essence of the use of quantifiers that the satisfaction conditions be given by the standard clauses. So the distinction between literalist and referential quantification may be seen to lie not in the use of the variable or the quantifier but in the choice of the context: some contexts require us to look at the variable sign; others do not. The decision to use only referential variables or quantifiers amounts therefore to a restriction not on the use of the variables or quantifiers but on the contexts in which they may appear.

It seems to me that literalist variables are not a mere theoretical oddity, but may actually be closer to the use of variables outside of logic than the more familiar referential variables. In most programming languages, for instance, we may make assignment statements in which variables occur both on the left and the right; a typical example is '$x := x + 1$'. The evaluation of the expression on the right depends only upon the 'value' of the variable; but the evaluation of the expression on the left depends upon the identity of the variable itself. Or, in ordinary mathematical discourse, we may say 'Let $y = x^2$. Then $dy/dx = 2x$'. Here again, it is the identity of the variables rather than their values which appears to be relevant to the proper evaluation of the term 'dy/dx'. (I do not intend these remarks as a full account of the use of variable signs in ordinary mathematics but merely as a step in the right direction. My own view, which I hope to develop elsewhere, is that variable signs are used in examples like the above to signify variable objects.)

Literalist quantifiers may also be used to modify existing formal languages. We shall assume that the languages contain no individual constants, although our account could be tailored to their presence by allowing them, in the appropriate way, to be partly referential. One example, of immediate interest to us, concerns modality. Let us use the notion of necessity as object-blind in the sense previously explained, so an assignment of values to variables satisfies the open sentence $\Box\phi(x_1, \ldots, x_n)$ just in case $\Box\forall x_1 \ldots \forall x_n \phi(x_1, \ldots, x_n)$ is true. This gives us a perfectly acceptable relation of objectual satisfaction; but one that is literal, not referential; for $\Box x = x$ is satisfied by any assignment of an object to x, but $\Box x = y$ is not satisfied by the assignment of that object to both x and y. The use of literal variables therefore enables us to formulate an appropriate quantified modal logic for such a notion of necessity.

Another example concerns belief. We may wish to express that Ralph is in the situation typified by the case in which he believes that Cicero is Cicero but does not believe Cicero is Tully. It is tempting to suppose that the sentence $\exists x\exists y(x = y \& B_r x = x \& \sim B_r x = y)$ will do. But the logic of referential quantification will not permit it; for the sentence will have $\exists x(B_r x = x \& \sim B_r x = x)$ as a consequence. However, a literalist account of the quantifiers allows us to succumb to temptation with logical impunity. For where $\phi(x_1, \ldots, x_n)$ is an open sentence in which $x_1, \ldots, x_n$ are all of the free variables and are pairwise distinct, we may take $B_r\phi(x_1, \ldots, x_n)$ to be satisfied by the objects $a_1, \ldots, a_n$ just in case there are terms (perhaps appropriate terms) $t_1, \ldots, t_n$ for the objects such that $B_r\phi(t_1, \ldots, t_n)$ is true. On letting x and y both assume Cicero as values, we then see that our sentence is true. It is of course well-known that the sentence can also be made true upon combining nonobjectual quantification with a nonstandard interpretation of identity. But our account is one in which the quantifiers are objectual and identity is standard. It should be noted, however, that the account renders $\exists x(B_r Fx \& B_r Gx)$ equivalent to $\exists x\exists y(x = y \& B_r Fx \& B_r Gy)$. It is the intrabelief, not the cross-belief, connections among terms that get expressed.

Literalist quantifiers may be used for the formalization of classical as well as intensional theories. One example, suggested to me by Allen

Hazen, concerns a many-sorted theory in which the domains associated with the different sorts may overlap. Perhaps we have a sort for numbers and a sort for sets under a logicist construal of numbers as sets. Notwithstanding the overlap of domains, we may wish $x = n$ always to be false when the variables 'x' and 'n' are of different sorts. In such a way, we could permit within the metalanguage ("off-stage") a reduction of numbers to sets and yet not accept within the object-language ("on-stage") that any number was identical to a set. On a referential treatment of the variables such an account is impossible. But on a literalist treatment it offers no special difficulties; for we can take it to be part of the satisfaction conditions for the identity sentence $x = n$ that the variables 'x' and 'n' should be of the same sort.

Another example concerns the theory of truth. We may so use the truth-predicate T that the formula $T\alpha$ is satisfied by an assignment just in case (i) a formula ϕ of the of the object-language is assigned to the metalinguistic variable α, (ii) individuals from the domain of the object-language are assigned to the free variables $x_1, \ldots, x_n$ of ϕ, and (iii) the assignment of those individuals to $x_1, \ldots, x_n$ satisfies ϕ. On a referential treatment of variables, such an interpretation of the truth-predicate is incoherent since the satisfaction of the formula $T\alpha$ does not depend simply upon the formula assigned to α. But on a natural extension of the literalist treatment, under which *any* aspect of the assignment may be relevant to satisfaction, such an interpretation is unproblematic. With this use of the truth-predicate, the metalinguistic formula $T\alpha \supset \forall x T\beta$ is true when the object-language sentence $\forall x F x$, let us say, is assigned to α and the object-language formula $F x$ is assigned to β. For $T\alpha$ is true under this assignment just in case $\forall x F x$ is true; while $\forall x T\beta$ is true under the assignment just in case $T\beta$ is true whenever $F x$ is assigned to β and an arbitrary individual from the object-domain is assigned to x, and this holds, by the interpretation of T given above, just in case $F x$ is true under an assignment of an arbitrary individual to x. Indeed, if we so use metalinguistic terms s that the sentence $T s$ is true under an assignment just in case $T\alpha$ is true under the variant assignment in which the denotation of s is assigned to α, then we may be so bold as to assert $T'\forall x F x' \supset x T$ '$F x$', something which is usually regarded as a blatant case of use-mention confusion. By using such equivalences, we might even give a direct recursive definition of truth, one which made no appeal to an intermediary notion of satisfaction, although the approach would suffer from certain peculiarities of its own.

It is a characteristic feature of the use of literalist variables that the

Leibnizian scheme $\forall x \forall y(x = y \supset (\phi(x) \supset \phi(y)))$ may fail. Our concept of necessity suffices to make the point. For let $\phi(x)$ be the formula $\Box(x = x)$, with the second 'x' designated. Then the resulting instance $\forall x \forall y(x = y \supset (\Box(x = x) \supset \Box(x = y)))$ will be false, at least if there is more than one object in the domain; for, as we have seen, $\Box(x = x)$ will be true under the assignment of an object to x, while $\Box(x = y)$ will be false for the assignment of the same object to x and y. Again, it needs to be emphasized that this is not a failure of the sort familiar from the literature; for the quantifiers are objectual and identity is standard.

It is common to draw a distinction between the substitutivity principle of the above sort for objectual quantification and a substitutivity principle for terms: $s = t \supset (\phi(s) \supset \phi(t))$. It is thought that the second may fail, but that the first must hold. But we see that the one may fail for much the same reason as the other. Of course, this is not to deny that the quantificational principle is valid when the objectual quantifiers are required to be purely referential. But, in this respect, the two principles are on a par; for the principle for terms is equally well valid when the terms are required to be purely referential.

The deviation from the canons of pure referentiality is somewhat greater in the case of our truth theory than in the case of our modal or doxastic logics. For the two logics, it is only the relative identity of the variables that is of any account. As long as one formula is an alphabetic variant of another, its truth-value will remain the same. But for the truth theory, the absolute identity of the individual is also of account. Change a single variable, even when there are no others, and truth-value can change. So even though the statement T '$\forall x F x$'$\supset \forall x T$ '$F x$' is correct, its alphabetic variant T '$\forall x F x$' $\supset \forall y T$ '$F x$' is not. We therefore have a use for the distinction between relative and absolute identity at the level of the variables which is analogous to our previous use of the distinction at the level of the objects.

In addition to the particular object-theories, the metatheory of literalist quantification may be of some interest. We suppose that we are working with a standard first-order language. However, we do not follow the standard semantics in assigning an extension to each predicate and, on this basis, determining which assignments of values to the variables satisfy which atomic predicates. Instead, we simply stipulate which assignments are to satisfy which atomic formulas, as with the truth-predicate T. On the standard semantics, it will follow from the clause for the satisfaction of atomic formulas that satisfaction in this case possesses certain normal properties. For example: it will be *local*—

satisfaction will only depend upon the values of the variables occurring in the atomic formula; and it will be *referential*—change the variables, make a corresponding change in the values, and satisfaction will be preserved. From the other clauses in the definition of satisfaction, it will then follow that these normal properties are preserved under the logical operations.

However, for the literalist semantics, there is no guarantee that even atomic satisfaction will conform to these properties and so there is no basis for an induction. For example, the satisfaction relation for atomic predications of truth will conform neither to locality nor to referentiality. Since these properties are required to validate the standard principles of quantificational logic, there is no guarantee that the literalist semantics will validate these principles.

Instead, we have a minimal logic which corresponds to the case in which no special assumptions are made about atomic satisfaction. We then have a hierarchy of stronger logics corresponding to the various special assumptions that might be made. However, the detailed investigation of these logics is not something which we shall pursue here.

Step (5): From the Nonobjectuality of Satisfaction to the Impossibility of Quantification

Various philosophers have attempted to evade Quine's conclusion by adopting a nonobjectual account of quantification. They have supposed, for example, that the quantifiers are conceptual or substitutional. The question therefore arises as to whether the quantifiers must, in the intended sense, be objectual.

Given our own distinction between the objectual and the referential, it might be thought desirable to miss out the previous step of the argument altogether and to argue directly from the nonreferentiality of the variables to the impossibility of quantification. The question would then be whether the quantifiers must be referential.

There does not appear to be any good reason for insisting upon the objectuality or referentiality of quantification. Quantifiers are not made in heaven, but on earth. Whether they are to be taken one way or another is a matter for stipulation, not discovery.

This is indeed how Quine sometimes regards the matter. Later, we shall give an objective meaning to the question of whether the quantifiers are to be taken to be referential for the purposes of Quine's argument. For the moment, we may note that there appears to be a sense in which the referential quantifiers are basic and so fundamentally the only quantifiers that there are. Although the issue is not strictly relevant to the evaluation of Quine's argument, it may be of some interest to discuss it briefly here. I wish to claim not merely that the *truth-conditions* of the products of nonreferential quantification can be explained in terms of statements involving only referential quantification. This is relatively unproblematic. I also wish to claim that our *understanding* of the one is to be explained in terms of our understanding of the other. If the statement ϕ is the product of a substitutional quantification, let us say, then there must be a statement ψ, formulated in terms of referential quantification alone, which is such that what we understand in understanding ϕ is to be given by what we understand in understanding ψ.

To this, it may be objected that the interplay between quantification and predication reveals a difference in our understanding. Let the product of the substitutional quantification be $\Sigma x F x$. Let the corresponding statement in terms of referential quantification be $\exists x F x$, where x is now the appropriate quantifier over terms and F is taken to be a predicate which is true of a term t just in case Ft (on our original understanding of F) is true. It may now be argued that, in our understanding of $\Sigma x F x$, the meaning of F remains fixed; it has the same meaning in the quantified statement as it has in a simple unquantified statement Ft. However, in our understanding of $\exists x F x$, the meaning of F has changed; it is now metalinguistic.

What is so hard to see, though, is that we have an understanding of $\Sigma x F x$ that does not involve a shift in our understanding of F. I am clear in my own mind that I understand $\exists x F x$, shift and all. But it is completely unclear to me that I have any independent understanding of $\Sigma x F x$. There would appear to be no difference in our understanding of either sentence or perhaps one should say, more cautiously, that any difference would appear to be equally susceptible to explanation in terms of referential quantification.[13]

Similar remarks apply to the conceptual interpretation of the quantifiers, according to which the variables receive 'senses' rather than 'substituends' as values. There are other interpretations of the quantifier to be considered, which differ from the referential account not only in

---

[13] Van Inwagen [81] has experienced similar difficulties in achieving a distinctive understanding of substitutional quantification. It should be noted, in contrast to what his paper suggests, that there is no need for the concept of truth to be involved in our understanding of substitutional quantification; it suffices if the meaning of each primitive predicate appropriately changes.

regard to the status of the values but also in regard to their singularity; the variables may be multivalued, and not merely mono-valued. Perhaps the most famous account of this sort is Carnap's, in which the variables receive both 'referents' and 'senses' as values. There are some treatments of quantification into belief contexts (Kaplan's [71], 138, is an example) which call quite naturally, at the semantic level, for a distinction between two types of values. And even some cases of my own literalist quantifiers could be regarded as a kind of quantification in which both 'referents' and 'expressions' serve as values, but with the expression-value for each variable restricted to the variable itself.

But even quantification of this sort would appear to consist in the simultaneous or 'parallel' use of referential quantifiers. The point is, indeed, a general one. Any explanation of quantification will involve two elements. The first is a specification of the kinds of values that a variable can receive. The second is an account of the role that the different kinds of value play in interpreting an open sentence. By appropriately multiplying the referential quantifiers, and by appropriately tuning the interpretation of the predicates and other parts of speech to accord with the role of the different kinds of values, it would appear that any type of quantification could be seen to consist in the more or less devious application of referential quantification.

It may be wondered, given that there is a genuine indiscernibility in our understanding of the different kinds of quantification, why one rather than another should be taken as basic. I am inclined to think that the answer rests upon two desiderata of semantic explanation: one is the proper disassociation between the sign and what it signifies; the other is the analysis of any particular relationship of signification into its simplest elements. It seems plausible, once these desiderata are pursued to their limit, that only referential quantification should remain.

IV.

Although the preceding critique has been largely negative, two positive conclusions do emerge. The first is that an occurrence of a singular term is irreferential if substitution fails under conditions of uniformity. The second is that referential quantification into a position occupied by an irreferential occurrence of a singular term is impossible, again under conditions of uniformity.

This means that an argument for the impossibility of quantifying in can be recovered from the ruins of our critique. For we may proceed in two steps. First, we may go from the truth of $s = t$, the difference in truth-value between $\phi(t)$ and $\phi(s)$, and the identity of the syntactico-semantic context across $\phi(t)$ and $\phi(s)$, to the irreferentiality of the given occurrence of t in $\phi(t)$ (where referentiality is here taken to be standard). Then we may go from the irreferentiality of t in $\phi(t)$ and the identity of the syntactico-semantic context across $\phi(t)$ and $\phi(x)$ to the unintelligibility of $\forall x \phi(x)$, for $\forall x$ a referential quantifier.

We are therefore not in the position of many of Quine's critics in denying altogether the validity of the considerations he puts forward. If we are to dispute the conclusion of the reconstructed argument, we must dispute one of its premises—either by finding fault with the truth-values attributed to the statements $t = s, \phi(t)$ and $\phi(s)$ or, what is more likely, by finding fault with one of the assumptions of uniformity.

I want now to consider whether this reconstructed argument can be used to show that referential quantification into modal and other such contexts is impossible, dealing with each step of the argument in turn. My main concern is dialectical; I want to see to what extent Quine's argument can be used to establish conclusions concerning irreferentiality or the unintelligibility of quantification. But I also have an interest in the truth; I want to know whether given occurrences of term are irreferential and whether given attempts at quantification are unintelligible.

In considering various alleged examples of irreferential terms or unintelligible quantification, it will sometimes be helpful to be explicit about the languages from which they come. Three main sources may be distinguished. The first, which we call Modalese, is the language of quantified modal logic. It is a first-order language enriched with an operator whose interpretation is given in terms of necessity or belief or some other such intensional notion. The second is an ordinary language such as English, whose quantificational apparatus is given by the appropriate use of determiners and pronouns. The third is a cross between the first two. Ordinary language provides the basic sentences; and logic provides the quantificational apparatus. So in case the ordinary language is English, a typical sentence of the resulting hybrid 'Loglish' would be the sentence '$\exists x(x$ is a spy$)$'. The interpretation and, indeed, the specification of a language such as Loglish is not completely clear; and, to a large extent, the problems raised by Quine can be seen to be problems about just how the specification interpretation should go.

The critical difference between these languages, for our purposes, lies in the degree of control we have over the interpretation of the referential and quantificational apparatus. For English we have no control; the interpretation is simply given to us. For Loglish we have control over the quantificational part, but not the referential part. And for Modalese we have control over both parts.

In the work of Quine, we may note a transition in interest from the more formal languages to the less formal. His initial preoccupation was with first-order modal logic; the question was whether appropriate sense could be made of its symbolism (see especially Quine [47]). But his considerations soon became more general, and took in examples from both semi-formal and informal languages. In some of his work, he switches from one kind of example to another; and often it is not clear whether an example stated in Loglish is merely meant to be a proxy, for the symbol-wary reader, of a purely formal example. Probably, for Quine, the transition is of no great significance; but we, at any rate, will attempt to bear it in mind.

It will be illuminating in the first place to look at the occurrences of terms within unproblematic contexts, what Kaplan has called "vulgar" occurrences (Kaplan [71], 112). If we were going to be completely thorough, we would distinguish cases according as to whether the language was natural or artificial and according to whether the terms were names or description. But it will be sufficient, for our purposes, to concentrate on the case of descriptions from natural language. The main difference between natural and artificial languages here is that hypotheses concerning the use of terms in a natural language may become stipulations concerning their use in an artificial language; and the important differences between descriptions and names may be noted as we go along.

A typical example of a vulgar occurrence of a description is provided by the sentence 'The number of planets is greater than seven'. Is the given occurrence of the description 'The number of planets' referential? Quine would have no hesitation in answering 'Yes'. For truth is preserved under substitution and so it follows, from the very definition of referentiality, that the given occurrence of the description is referential.

But we have already had occasion to observe that the technical and informal concepts of referentiality are to be distinguished and referentiality in the technical sense, i.e., openness to substitution, is not a sufficient condition for referentiality in the informal sense. We therefore do not have this compelling reason for supposing that the occurrence of the description in question is referential.

We may consult the informal explanation of the intuitive concept. Is the description 'The number of planets' used solely to pick out an object? It might appear clear that it is. But here there is a difficulty.

For what is the relevant sense of 'pick out'? There is a sense in which 'A man' in 'A man came to my room last night' may be said to pick out a man. But we would not want to say that, on that account, the given occurrence of 'A man' was referential, or even partly referential.

I have suggested that the relevant sense of 'pick out' is one that relates the role of the term to an account of what a sentence containing it says. The sole contribution of the referential occurrence of a term to the content of the sentence will be its object; the appropriate semantical analysis of the sentence will simply assign the object to the occurrence.

If this is correct, then whether the ordinary occurrences of descriptions are referential will be a theoretical question and will turn on what semantical account is provided of the sentences containing them. If one holds a Russellian view of these sentences, then definite descriptions will function in the same way as indefinite descriptions and it will equally inappropriate, in either case, to say that these descriptions 'pick out' or 'contribute' an object to the content of a sentence. These terms will therefore not be referential. Although their occurrence will be open to substitution, this will be an 'accident' of a kind that was previously considered in connection with counterexamples to the sufficiency of the substitution test. Russell would hold a similar view of names if they were treated as disguised descriptions; but they would be referential if taken to be 'genuine' or 'logically proper'.

On a Fregean view, the matter is more problematic. Frege advocates, not a duality in the category of singular terms, but a duality in the conception of semantic analysis; for it may be conceived to proceed either in terms of sense or in terms of reference. At the level of sense, a description (or name) will not contribute "its object," though at the level of a reference it will. However, it is the analysis at the level of sense that is most naturally taken to disclose what the sentence says. Indeed, it is somewhat odd to think of the rest of the sentence as saying something about the referent of a term that it contains. For unless the levels of analysis are to be crossed, the rest of the sentence will pick out something extensional like a set, rather than something intensional. So on the most plausible view of what a sentence says, its terms will fail to be referential, though on a less plausible view, they will be.

It is curious that the two leading views in the philosophy of language produce results that are not straightforwardly in conformity with our ordinary intuitions on the matter. For one is tempted to follow Quine and to suppose that a sentence containing a vulgar occurrence of a description is used to say something about its referent. Of course, it could be that our intuitions are in error. One would then have the familiar situation in which examples used to illustrate a theoretical concept turn out, upon proper consideration, not to illustrate it at all. But I am inclined to believe that the fault lies with the views and that a more satisfactory account of descriptions could be developed which would indeed provide for a level of analysis at which a description was capable of picking out an object for the rest of the sentence to say something intensional about.

Let us now look at terms that do occur within the problematic contexts. Quine presents a variety of examples, which differ widely in the degree to which they carry conviction. Perhaps the most convincing kind of example is provided by the occurrence of 'nine' in 'Fido is canine'. We have here no hesitation in declaring the occurrence of 'nine' to be irreferential. But the substitution test is of dubious relevance in reaching this conclusion. For we have a much more straightforward reason; the occurrence is not even a meaningful constituent of the sentence.

Another example is provided by quotation. The occurrence of 'Cicero' in ' 'Cicero' contains six letters' is meant to be irreferential. Here we do not have the previous compelling reason for supposing the occurrence to be irreferential; for it is entirely problematic whether the occurrence of 'Cicero' is a meaningful constituent of the sentence. But, as I have already indicated, the substitution test is of some use; for the appropriate assumption of uniformity is relatively unproblematic. However, it needs to be emphasized that the test only entitles us to draw the conclusion that the occurrence of the term is not standardly referential. It is possible, and indeed plausible, that a term under quotes refers to itself (cf. Kaplan [71], 120).

A less convincing example concerns the term 'Giorgione'. In the sentence 'Giorgione is so-called because of his size', this term is not open to substitution; for upon substitution of the coreferential term 'Barbarelli', a truth is converted into a falsehood. But does uniformity hold? Is the term referential?

Quine suggests that the term is partly referential; it is used to pick out its object, but it is not solely so used. He seems to assume that the term makes a double contribution to what the sentence says: it picks out its object; and it also picks out, or 'presents', itself. The rest of the sentence then says of the one that it is called the other because of its size. (We might note that Quine would here appear to be appealing to his intuitions on the matter. For what would a test for partial referentiality, analogous to the substitution test for pure referentiality, look like?)

But there is in fact a much more plausible account of how the sentence functions, one that would make the term referential and consequently lead one to reject the uniformity assumption upon which the application of the substitution test depends. On this alternative account, the term 'Giorgione' is used solely to pick out its referent. However, the expression 'so' in 'so-called' is used to refer to that term. So what the rest of the sentence says of the referent Giorgione is that it is called 'Giorgione' because of its size. The sentence attributes a property to the single thing picked out by the subject-term, not a relation to the two things picked out by the subject-term.

The way 'so' gets to refer to the term is analogous to the way that a demonstrative gets to refer. Indeed, the word 'so' can itself be used just like a demonstrative. We may say 'Giorgione is so-called because of his size', while pointing, at the moment of uttering 'so', to the expression that is to give it its reference. Imagine now that we point to the given occurrence of 'Giorgione' in the sentence and that the pointing becomes implicit. Then we get to something very close to the present use of 'so'.

There is nothing in the given example to favor the one analysis over the other. But consider the following conversation between two people A and B:

A: Giorgione is Italian.

B: Yes, and the man is so-called because of his size.

It is hard to make sense of the conversation on the analysis which requires that reference to 'Giorgione' must already have been made. For where does the reference come from? Surely not from the original occurrence of 'Giorgione', which appears to be straightforwardly referential, and surely not from the subsequent occurrence of 'the man'. On the other hand, the conversation presents no special difficulties for the analysis which requires no antecedent reference to the term.

Of course there is a way, even on the second analysis, in which the term 'Giorgione' performs two roles: for it refers to Giorgione; and it secures a reference for 'so'. But we are not here interested in any role; that a term was used to shock would not make it irreferential. We are only interested in a certain kind of linguistic role. The question is: what does the occurrence of a term inject into the content of a sentence of which it is a part. It is therefore entirely irrelevant to the referential status of a term that is used as the referent of another expression; it plays this role not as an item of language but as an object of the world.

Quine's most contentious examples concern belief and modality. Since the two raise somewhat different issues, let us deal with each in turn. Consider the sentence 'Ralph believes that the man in the brown hat is a spy'. Is the occurrence of the description 'the man in a brown hat' referential or not?

This case is complicated by the fact that there are two readings of the sentence, what we may call the *de re* and the *de dicto* readings. Under the first, it is not necessary that Ralph think of the subject of his belief under the description of being the man in a brown hat; under the second, it is necessary.

In adverting to this difference, I am not attempting to provide any explanation of what it consists in. The suggestion which emerges from the work of Quine strikes me as implausible. He appears to attribute the difference to a lexical ambiguity in the term 'believes' (Quine [60], 146–47, Linsky [71], 103). But the possibility of a dual reading in this case is an instance of a much more general phenomenon, one in which any sentence containing an appropriately embedded description may be given a *de re* or a *de dicto* reading. Since there is no explanation of the general phenomenon in terms of lexical ambiguity, there is no reason to suppose that this is the explanation in the given case.[14] Russell's account in terms of scope avoids this particular difficulty. It also has the advantage of providing readings of intermediate scope. But it is subject to a difficulty of its own; for it can provide no plausible account of the dual reading of such sentences as 'The commissioner is looking for the chairman of the board'.

Given the existence of two readings, the question of referentiality should be considered separately for each. Under the *de dicto* reading, substitutivity may fail. It may be true that Ralph believes that the man in a brown hat is a spy and yet false that he believes that the mayor is a spy, even though the man in a brown hat is the mayor. There is no reason here to suspect a shift in the syntactico-semantic context. We may therefore conclude that the given occurrence of the description is not (standardly) referential.

Under the *de re* reading, the given occurrence of the description will be open to substitution. But we cannot thereby conclude that it is referential. However, it does seem plausible that the present case should

---

[14] Other objections have been levelled against Quine's postulation of a lexical ambiguity; but I find none of them convincing. It should be noted that the present objection still holds if the lexical ambiguity is replaced with a structural ambiguity in the application of a single lexical item of belief.

be assimilated to what we previously called the vulgar use of descriptions. So whatever goes for that case goes for this one too. According to our intuitions on the matter, the descriptions will be referential; on a Russellian view, they will not; and on a Fregean view, they will, though not straightforwardly so.

Similar considerations apply to ordinary names. In particular, there is the possibility of both a *de re* and a *de dicto* reading when names are used in place of descriptions. So on a *de re* reading of the sentences, the truth of 'Ralph believes that Tully is an orator' will follow from the truth of 'Ralph believes that Cicero is an orator'; while on a *de dicto* reading, the implication will not hold. (It would be good to have an account of the different readings that covered the cases of both names and descriptions. This is another reason for not liking the Russellian account in terms of scope, at least when it is combined with an account that makes the names of ordinary language 'genuine' or 'logically proper'.)

The final examples concern modality. A typical case is 'Necessarily, the number of planets is greater than seven'. Is the given occurrence of 'the number of planets' referential? Here it would be tempting to appeal to a difference between the *de re* and *de dicto* reading, just as in the example concerning belief. But Quine would presumably dispute the *de re* reading in this case.[15]

It is important, however, to be clear on the grounds upon which a *de re* reading might be disputed. There is no doubt that the words are capable of bearing a *de re* reading, as much in this case as in the case of belief. The only question is whether this reading is intelligible. The words are capable of carrying the thought, if only the thought is there to be carried. We are therefore back to our old metaphysical worry concerning *de re* modality, which at least in the case of the strict modalities may be allayed by the considerations in the earlier part of the paper.

There might be thought to be a special reason why a *de re* reading is not available when necessity is interpreted as a strict modality. For on such an interpretation, the necessity operator should be subject to the principle that, for any sentence S, 'necessarily, S' is true iff S is necessarily true. But then the behavior of the necessity predicate would seem to preclude a *de re* reading of the sentences containing the necessity operator.

---

[15] In his later work, (Quine [77]), he also disputes the intelligibility of a *de re* reading for the corresponding belief sentences. The two cases therefore become alike.

But once the possibility of a *de re* and *de dicto* reading has been conceded, the principle linking the operator and predicate for necessity should be formulated with more care. For, in case the sentence S contains descriptions (or perhaps names too), we need to ask whether the compound sentence 'Necessarily, S' is to be given a *de re* or a *de dicto* reading. It is then clear that the principle is only plausible for the *de dicto* reading; and so that still leaves open the possibility of a *de re* reading.

Indeed, it would be a mistake to think that necessity was any different from belief in this respect. For the concept of belief is subject to a link principle of its own, one roughly to the effect that, for any sentence S, the sentence 'P believes S' is true iff P is prepared to assent to S. But the existence of a link in this case does not preclude the possibility of a *de re* reading of belief sentences; it only requires that the belief-sentences of the link itself be given a *de dicto* reading.

This completes our survey of the examples. Quine's own substitution test has been replaced by a more sophisticated test, one in which it has been required that there be syntactico-semantic uniformity of context. Using this alternative test, we have been able to find with Quine on some of his examples, and not on others.

In case a term is referential, no further question arises as to how it is being used; it is being used solely to pick out an object. But in case the term is irreferential, this further question does arise. We know the term is *not* being used solely to pick out an object. So how exactly *is* it being used?

Kaplan has noted a tendency on Quine's part to treat all such cases alike: the irreferential (in the technical sense) is assimilated to the accidental (Linsky [71], 113). He himself has a tendency to assimilate the not standardly-referential to the nonstandardly referential (Linsky [71], 119). But our brief survey of some examples would seem to indicate that there should be no general presumption in favor of one kind of explanation rather than another. The phenomenon of substitution failure is too diverse to admit of general explanation. Sometimes the occurrence of the term is not even a constituent; sometimes the context shifts; sometimes the reference of the term shifts. What is required in this area is not presumption, but detailed investigation.

We turn to the question of whether quantification into modal and other such contexts is possible. This question divides up in two separate and independent ways. There is, first of all, the division according to whether the quantifiers are referential or not; and there is, secondly, the division according to whether the use of the quantifiable variables is or is not uniform with the use of singular terms. In this section, we take up the question for referential and nonreferential quantifiers without assuming uniformity; and in the next section, we take up the same question, but under the assumption of uniformity.

The difference between assuming and not assuming uniformity might be put in the following way. Without uniformity, the sense of quantified statements is independent of the sense of their instances; we are therefore free to decide what sense to attach to them. With uniformity, the sense of the quantified statements is already determined by the sense of their instances; we therefore have no freedom to decide what sense they are to have. In the one case, the quantified statements are born with sense; and in the other case, they have it thrust upon them.

Quine is no enemy to the autonomous use of quantifiers; for his own account of quasi-quotation would appear to commit him to it. For in case no variables fall under the quasi-quotes, they are read in the same way as ordinary quotes. But quantification into ordinary quotation contexts is impossible; and so it is only by means of a special convention that any sense can be made of quantification into quasi-quotation contexts. There is also a way in which Quine allows for the autonomous use of quantifiers in connection with the problem of opacity. For he contemplates the possibility of quantifying into modal contexts in the case in which all singular terms have been excised from the primitive notation. The interpretation of the quantified statements is then unconstrained. But the reason is that there exist no instances by which their interpretation might be constrained. Our own perspective is somewhat different. There may be singular terms in the language; substitution may fail; the terms may even be irreferential. It is just that the behavior of the singular terms is not considered relevant to the interpretation of quantification.

Quine is of the opinion that objectual quantification into modal contexts, even of an autonomous sort, is impossible without a commitment to Aristotelian essentialism; certain ways of describing an individual must be taken as preferable to others. It is here that our previous considerations on logical (or analytic) satisfaction may be brought into play; for we may transform our noncommittal account of necessary satisfaction into a noncommittal account of objectual quantification into necessity contexts.

It will be recalled that two concepts of logical satisfaction were distinguished. One was object-blind: the condition $\phi(x, y)$, say, was logically true of individuals a and b just in case $\forall x \forall y \phi(x, y)$ was logically true. The other was object-sensitive: the condition $\phi(x, y)$ was logically true of a and b just in case $\forall x \forall y (x \pi y \supset \phi(x, y))$ was logically true, where π was '=' or '$\neq$' according as to whether $a = b$ or $a \neq b$. Both concepts were seen, in their own way, to be free of essentialist presuppositions.

Let us now interpret the satisfaction of $\Box \phi(x_1, \ldots, x_n)$ in the following way: $\Box \phi(x_1, \ldots, x_n)$ is true of $a_1, \ldots, a_n$ iff $\phi(x_1, \ldots, x_n)$ is logically true of $a_1, \ldots, a_n$. If the concept of logical truth is taken to be object-sensitive, then we obtain a referential reading of the quantifiers; satisfaction depends only upon the values. If the concept of logical truth is taken to be object-blind, then we obtain a 'literal' reading of the quantifiers; satisfaction depends only upon the *assignment* of values. In both cases, the interpretation of the quantifiers is objectual and yet innocent of commitment to essentialism.

The possibility of the first interpretation is not new; it is already implicit in the work of T. Parsons (see Linsky [71], 73–87) and has been underscored by Kaplan and by myself in recent work (Kaplan [86], Fine [84]). But the possibility of the second interpretation would appear to be new. It depends critically on the distinction between objectual and referential quantification; for it is only in terms of that distinction that the usual constraints on objectual quantification can be avoided.

The difference between the two interpretations of the quantifier, though both are objectual, may still appear to be great. It is therefore of interest that there is an account of quantification in which the difference disappears. For we may so interpret the variables that distinct variables assume distinct values (the assignment of values to variables is one-one).

This convention was first proposed by Wittgenstein in the *Tractatus*. It has not turned out to be very useful for logical purposes, though it has been applied both by myself ([78], 297–98) and by Hintikka [56]. It is sometimes to be found in the writings of mathematicians who use '$\{x, y\}$', for example, to refer to a set whose members are distinct.

Under this convention, the literalist and referential readings of the quantifier become indiscernible. For the difference only shows up in the case in which the same individual is assigned to two distinct variables; and, under the convention, this can never happen. If, therefore, the convention had been adopted from the start, the distinctive problems involved in securing a referential reading would never have arisen!

Autonomous interpretations of quantification into belief and other such contexts can also be given. Indeed, Kaplan's 'trick', as propounded in footnote 3 of "Quantifying In," is one such interpretation, of a very general sort. He treats the belief operator as a predicate that holds between the objects picked out by the free variables within its scope and the condition that they help define. Thus the sense of the operator varies with the disposition of the variables.

The possibility of autonomous interpretations of referential quantification is of great relevance to the application of Quine's argument to sentences containing *ordinary language* quantifier phrases. One kind of example is provided by the sentence 'Ralph believes someone is a spy' on a *de re* reading; another kind of example, to which similar considerations apply, is provided by the sentence 'There is someone who is such that Ralph believes that he is a spy'.

The question is: what can the argument from substitution tell us? Given a failure of substitution (using the terms 'the mayor' and 'the man in the brown hat', let us say), does it follow that the quantifier sentences are unintelligible? The issue is complicated by the fact that the sentences to which the substitution test apply could be given a *de re* reading. The argument would not then get off the ground since the sentences would not even change their truth-value. So let us assume, in order to see the argument in its most favorable light, that the sentences are given a *de dicto* reading.

It might then be objected (indeed, often is) that the possibility of the *de re* reading for the test sentences shows that the quantified sentences must be intelligible. This may be so. But it still does not show what, if anything, is wrong with Quine's argument. We still need to know why, if at all, the unintelligibility of the quantified sentences does not follow from the failure of substitution for the test sentences under a *de dicto* reading. To put the point in a particularly graphic form, let us suppose that English never permitted a *de re* reading for sentences containing descriptions. There would then be no possibility of a counterargument to Quine. But the force of Quine's own argument would remain the same.

The weakness of the argument lies, of course, in its implicit assumption of uniformity. For it is always possible that the ordinary language quantifiers should be given an autonomous interpretation. The failure of substitution and, indeed, the general behavior of singular terms would then be irrelevant to the issue of intelligibility.

If it could somehow be assumed that the quantifier constructions were uniform in their interpretation with the use of the terms under a *de dicto* reading, then the argument could get some grip. But it is hard to see how such an assumption might be justified. There is perhaps a general presumption in favor of uniformity. But uniformity with what? It is perfectly conceivable that the quantifier constructions might be uniform in their interpretation with the use of terms on a *de re* rather than a *de dicto* reading. Even if our language was one which, as envisaged above, permitted no *de re* reading, it would still seem more plausible, in the face of a conflict between the direct intuition of the intelligibility of the quantified sentences and a general presumption of uniformity, to give up the presumption, with its highly theoretical character, rather than the intuition. Thus, Quine's argument would still lack force against an opponent for whom there was intuitive evidence of intelligibility.

We have seen that there are no essential difficulties involved in giving an autonomous interpretation of quantification into modal contexts. We must now look at the question of whether a uniform interpretation is possible. In talking of uniformity here, I mean to indicate that the interpretation of a quantified statement such as $\exists x \phi(x)$ is to be uniform with that of its instances, $\phi(t)$; the syntactico-semantic context is to remain the same. The interpretation of the quantified statement must, in this sense, already be implicit in that of its instances.

The second leg of our reconstruction of Quine's argument depends upon the assumption of uniformity. But what reason is there for supposing it to hold? The language of first-order modal logic, it should be appreciated, is one whose interpretation is up to use; its uniformity, or lack of it, is therefore a matter for stipulation. This is equally true of the formal parts of a semi-formal language such as Loglish, though perhaps less likely to be appreciated. It may of course be part of the conventions governing the interpretation of either language that $\forall x$ is to be a universal quantifier and $\exists x$ an existential quantifier. It may even be agreed that the quantifiers are to be referential. But that still leaves open what condition $\phi(x)$ in $\forall x \phi(x)$ or $\exists x \phi(x)$ is to express. The question of uniformity remains undecided.

Although we are always free to adopt an autonomous interpretation of the quantifier, the uniform interpretation is much more natural. It is the one which the quantifiers are naturally assumed to have in the absence of any special explanation. It is the only one to provide a general account of quantification that is of any interest. Moreover, part of the point in setting up an artificial language may be to expose uniformities; the expressions of the language are to bear their interpretation on their face. This purpose is hardly served by tolerating autonomous interpretations. Of course, Loglish will not, in any case, be fully uniform; but it may be seen as a step in the direction of a language that is.

All the same, there may be good reasons for tolerating autonomy. There are clear advantages, for example, in adopting the autonomous interpretation of the quantifier that is required by Quine's account of quasi-quotation. Another example will be given later. But even here, uniformity exerts its pull. For to a large extent, the advantages of these autonomous interpretations derive from the the fact that they simulate a uniform interpretation. Quine's account of quasi-quotation works *as if* Frege were right; it works as if terms under quotation marks did denote themselves and the quantifiers were accordingly interpreted. We may operate such languages and their logics under the illusion of a uniform understanding.

Whatever the reasons for adopting uniformity, its consequence, once adopted, would appear to be straightforward. Referential quantification, as in $\exists x \phi(x)$, is possible only if the occurrences of the singular term t in its instances $\phi(t)$ are referential. We may therefore refer to the results of our earlier section. Given that descriptions within belief or modal contexts are not referential under a *de dicto* reading, it would appear that Quine is vindicated; referential quantification into such contexts is not possible.

But matters are not so simple. For the interpretation of the substituted terms in $\phi(t)$ may not be uniform; and, as a consequence, the term t may be referential in some of the instances $\phi(t)$ and not in others. This can happen in a variety of ways. A sentence containing a given term may be ambiguous, as with the *de re* and the *de dicto* reading of sentences containing embedded descriptions. There may be accidental variations within a given category of expressions, as with the occurrences of '3' and '1 + 1' in '3.2 = 6' and '1 + 1.2 = 6'. Or they may be systematic differences across categories. The most notable example is provided by Russell's theory of descriptions. On this view, there is a radical difference in the interpretation of descriptions and genuine names; and, as a consequence, the description will occur irreferentially, while the names will occur referentially.

In such cases, it seems unreasonable to require that the quantified statement should be interpreted uniformly with all of its instances. To take an extreme case, we would not want to deny a uniform interpretation to the quantifier in $\exists x(x.2 = 4)$' on the grounds that the substituent term '$1 + 1$' occurred irreferentially in '$(1 + 1.2 = 4)$'. The general aim is that the interpretation of a quantified statement should be derivable from its instances. But then it suffices if there is a single instance from which the interpretation might be derived. (In the unlikely event that the interpretation of the quantified statement can be derived from instances which determine different conditions, the quantified statement will be ambiguous.)

The point might be put in terms of a distinction in the meaning of 'instance'. We may take a *substitution* instance of a quantified statement, say $\exists x \phi(x)$, to be the result of making an arbitrary meaningful substitution of a singular term t for x in $\phi(x)$; and we may take a *proper* instance to be a substitution instance which is uniform with the original quantified statement. The point then is that we require, not that a quantified statement be uniform with its substitution instances, but that it have a proper instance.

In the particular case in which the quantifier is to be referential, a uniform interpretation of a quantified statement will be possible just in case there is an instance in which the substituent term is referential. In demonstrating that referential quantification into a modal or other problematic context is impossible, therefore, it does not suffice to show, as Quine would appear to presuppose, that there is an instance in which the substituent term is irreferential. It must be shown that all instances are of this sort.

The idea that the Quinean difficulties might be evaded by discriminating among singular terms is hardly new; it is to be found in the earliest discussion of the problem. But it is important to be clear on what the proposal amounts to and what it will produce. Here the discrimination is on grounds of linguistic function. What we require are instances of the quantified sentence in which the given term is referential. In fact, one such instance will do. But if we have one, we are likely to have many; and if uniformity reigns among the resulting instances, then so will substitutivity. However, this is entirely incidental. Given one proper instance, what we get is a *uniform* interpretation of quantification; for the one instance will determine a condition into which we can quantify.

Contrast this with the proposal that we should select a class of standard names, where being a standard name is a matter, not of linguistic function, but of having the right "core content" for the type of intensional context in question. It is now essential that substitutivity should hold when restricted to the occurrences of the standard names in the relevant contexts. It is also essential that there should be several standard names, indeed one for each object of the domain. However, there is no need for the terms to be referential in the chosen contexts; and given that they are selected on the basis of content, they are unlikely to be so. What we then obtain with such a class of terms is an *autonomous* interpretation of quantification into the chosen contexts: satisfaction is given in terms of the truth of the instances formed with terms from the class; and quantification is explained in terms of satisfaction.

What has perhaps made it so hard to keep the two proposals apart is that the standard terms under the autonomous interpretation behave, in regard to their substitutivity properties, as if they were referential terms in a uniform context. But whatever the reasons, there has certainly been a tendency to confuse the two forms of the proposal. They are lumped together without regard for either the difference in their requirements or the difference in their results. One finds, for example, the following statement in a relatively late work of Quine ([76], 862):

> Instead of bandying a uniquely fulfilled predicate 'G', one may forge a corresponding singular term 'g'. [This presumably would be the description $\iota x G x$.] Here, then, is what Føllesdal called a genuine name, and what Kripke has lately called, more quotably, a 'rigid designator'.

Our own concern at present is with the logical issue. Whether there will indeed be proper instances of the required sort will depend upon what account is given of the referential status of singular terms in the corresponding contexts. If one adopts a Fregean view, then all of the terms in the contexts will fail to be (standardly) referential; and (standardly) referential quantification into such contexts will therefore not be possible. Quite apart from a specifically Fregean view, it follows that if one insists upon the uniform use of all terms, constant or variable, within a modal or similar context and if, also, one permits the use within that context of terms, characteristically descriptions with a *de dicto* reading, for which substitution fails, then standardly referential quantification into the context will not be possible. It is this, it seems to me, that is the main negative conclusion to emerge from the work of Quine. The consequences for quantified modal logic are not indeed damning, but a significant restriction is imposed on the behavior of terms in languages for which uniformity and standard referentiality are desiderata.

It is possible to conceive of a Fregean view, though not of an orthodox sort, that provides for both the *de re* and the *de dicto* readings of descriptions within the problematic contexts (intermediate readings would be somewhat harder to obtain). Descriptions under a *de dicto* reading would refer to their sense, as on the orthodox view. Descriptions under a *de re* reading would refer to their ordinary referent. They would therefore be standardly referential in character. This is, on its own account, a plausible view and, if adopted, would then provide the basis for a uniform interpretation of the standardly referential quantifiers.

On a Russellian view, even the descriptions on a *de re* reading will not be referential and so will not secure a uniform interpretation of the quantifier. This result may appear surprising; for surely the interpretation of the quantified statement is already implicit in what for the Russellian is the wide scope reading of the description. It is, but not in the required way. We have here the uniformity of quantifier to quantifier, not of quantifier to term.

To obtain the requisite uniformity, it must be supposed that the language contains genuine names. The proper instances of the quantified statement will then be obtained, if they exist at all, by substituting the genuine names for the variables. If the language contains no genuine names, then they must be added. But the question then arises as to how the resulting sentences are to be interpreted.

It seems reasonable, especially if uniformity is a consideration, that they should be interpreted in conformity with the *de re* reading of the corresponding sentences with descriptions. We have something like the uniformity requirement in reverse: the interpretation of a quantified sentence, though of a nonorthodox sort, determines the interpretation of its proper instances. These instances then determine the interpretation of the quantified sentences of a more orthodox sort; and so again, the possibility of quantification turns ultimately on the intelligibility of the *de re* readings of the sentences with descriptions.

For the case of the strict modalities, the Russellian will have a natural understanding of the sentences which result from applying the necessity operator to sentences that contain genuine names. For the component sentence will express a singular proposition; and so the compound sentence will say of the singular proposition that it is logically or analytically necessary in the sense that has already been explained. There will not be the usual problems over referentiality, since the objects in the proposition will contribute as much to its logical form as its more intensional constituents.

This understanding of the necessity sentences then automatically yields an interpretation of quantification into necessity contexts. So we have an interpretation of the language of quantified modal logic that is completely uniform, that makes the quantifiers referential, and that construes the modalities as strict. Moreover, this interpretation is one that the Russellian naturally arrives at; it is not one that he need contrive.

But a warning is in order. There is nothing in a language or the set of its truths that enables one to determine whether it is uniform. Uniformity is not a surface phenomenon, but depends upon the underlying semantical analysis. We could imagine a Fregean appropriating the language of quantified modal logic for his own use. He would take closed terms within modal contexts to refer to their standard sense; and he might dispose of free variables within modal contexts by means of Kaplan's 'trick'. In this way, he could simulate the effect of the uniform semantics of the Russellian. But his own semantics would be nonuniform.[16]

The Russellian way out is the best known of the responses to Quine's argument. But it is important to appreciate on what its efficacy rests. It does not simply rest, as we have seen, on the *selection* of terms with desirable substitutivity properties. Nor does it clearly rest, as Quine and others seem to assume, on the *elimination* of terms with undesirable substitutivity properties. For how does that help? How can a sentence be rendered intelligible by the removal of certain terms from the language to which it belongs? Of course, the terms are eliminated in favor of a paraphrase. But the redundancy of the removed terms can hardly make the problematic sentence any the more intelligible. Of course, Quine's argument can no longer be stated once the descriptions are removed from the language. But one does not defeat an argument by refusing to allow one's opponent to use the terms with which it must be stated.

The real efficacy of the Russellian response lies in its differential stand on genuine names and descriptions. Because of the disparity in their semantics, a genuine name can be referential where a description would not be; uniformity can thereby be saved. The relationship of elimination to the differential stand is somewhat problematic. Certainly, elimination is not necessary for the differential stand. The essence of the

---

[16] Kaplan has argued that the Russellian can accommodate the semantical ideas of the Fregean (Kaplan [75]). But the Fregean can also accommodate the semantical ideas of the Russellian. For example, he may treat a singular proposition, along the lines of the "trick," as an ordered pair of an object and a property. Given the possibility of interpreting either theory within the other, there would appear to be a deep sceptical problem as to whether there was a genuine difference between the two theories.

Russellian position is that descriptions are a kind of quantifier phrase. Whether they can be eliminated in favor of other quantifier phrases is a separate and somewhat incidental matter.[17] Elimination may be sufficient, however, for a differential stand; it all depends upon exactly what it is meant to do. If it is intended as a semantical analysis, then it could indeed provide the basis for a differential stand. But if it is intended as something else, as seems to be the case with Quine's own elimination of singular terms, then it is hard to see in what its relevance could consist.

We have so far discussed the question of referential quantification under conditions of uniformity. If the terms within the problematic contexts are referential, then uniformly interpreted quantification into those contexts of a referential sort is possible. But what if the terms are irreferential? Is uniformly interpreted quantification, though of a nonreferential sort, still possible?

The most straightforward case is when the terms within the problematic contexts are referential, but not standardly so. Uniformity then indeed provides a meaning for the quantifiers; for they can be taken to be similarly referential—ranging over the nonstandard, not the standard, referents of the terms. The argument from the failure of substitution fails to get a grip, even under the assumption of uniformity; for what the truth of the identity sentence yields is the identity of the standard referents of the given and substituted terms; yet what is required is the identity of their nonstandard referents.

A specific example of this sort is provided by the Fregean account of modal contexts. The term '9', let us say, in $\Box(9 > 7)$, is taken to refer to its customary sense. So a uniform interpretation of quantification would have us quantifying over the appropriate senses; $\exists x \Box(x > 7)$ would be true simply because $\Box$(the number of planets > 7) is true (under a *de dicto* reading of the description).

This is the interpretation proposed by Church [43] in an early review of Quine's "Notes on Existence and Necessity." Quine originally found it acceptable, scruples over sense aside, but subsequently found reasons to reject it. In evaluating those reasons, it will be important, once again, to distinguish between logical and metaphysical considerations. One can imagine an invidious form of essentialism which allows essential properties to senses or other intensional entities but not to ordinary

---

[17]Kaplan has made a similar point ([72], 214), though in a somewhat different connection.

individuals. To this the radical antiessentialist (and also the radical essentialist) may object that intensional entities and ordinary individuals should be treated on a par. I take it that this is part of the point of Quine's attack on Church: essential attribution to intensions and individuals alike calls for favoritism among descriptions (Linsky [71], 153).

This is an interesting question. But our present concern is with the logical issue. On this, Quine's position is that the modal contexts are equally susceptible to failure of substitution regardless of whether the reference is to intensions or individuals. His example (Linsky [71], 153) is:

$$A = (\iota x)[p.(x = A)]$$

where A is an attribute and 'p' stands for a contingent truth. Substitute one for the other in a modal context and truth-value may change.

But the failure of substitution is no more relevant to the coherence of the quantification in this case than it was in the original case with reference to individuals. For the terms of the identity sentence will refer to the attribute A; but those same terms will refer in a modal context to appropriate "higher-order" intensions. The referents of the terms inside and outside of the context will again pass one another by.

How can Quine have failed to see this? I think he must have been assuming not only the local uniformity of term to variable but also the global uniformity among different occurrences of a term. This entails that the occurrences of a term inside and outside of a modal context must have the same reference, and so an escape from the consequences of a failure of substitution is no longer possible. One is instead led to the kind of systematically disambiguated language that was later proposed by Church [51].

Another case of nonreferential uniformity is when the terms have a double or multiple role. An example, for Quine, is provided by the occurrence of 'Giorgione' in 'Giorgione is so-called because of his size;' for the term both picks out the man and draws attention to itself. Perhaps all linguistic roles should be assimilated to the referential role. If this is done, then these will be the only two possibilities: either the term refers to a single thing, be it a standard or a nonstandard referent; or it refers to several things.

In the present case, it is not completely clear what the requirement of uniformity amounts to. There is the uniformity of variable to term and of term to term. If a term has several roles, is there to be the uniformity of variable to term with respect to all of those roles or only with respect to some of them? We can imagine that the term has several syntactic occurrences, one for each role, though only one typographic occurrence; the several syntactic occurrences coincide in the single typographic occurrence. The variable expression will likewise have several syntactic occurrences. But will it occur *as* a variable in all of these occurrences or in only some of them?

At one extreme is the view that the variable is to serve as a variable in each of its roles or occurrences. The uniform interpretation will then be one in which the variable is multivalued, with as many values as there are roles. For recall, a variable, when uniformly interpreted, will behave just like a term, but relative to an assignment; so each of the roles enjoyed endogenously by the term will be enjoyed exogenously by the variable.

In the case of the Giorgione example, the corresponding uniformly interpreted quantifier will simultaneously range over a pair of values: one an individual, and the other a term for the individual. Under this interpretation, the existential sentence '$\exists x$ (x is so-called because of his size)' will not only be meaningful but true; for when x takes as its values the man Giorgione and his name 'Giorgione', the open sentence '(x is so-called because of his size)' will be satisfied. So even on Quine's construal of the example, uniform quantification into the context will be possible!

A less bizarre example is provided by Carnap's method of extension and intension, as propounded in *Meaning and Necessity* [47]. Carnap takes a singular term to have a double linguistic role: one given by its extension, and the other by its intension. The corresponding interpretation of quantification therefore requires the assignment of both an extension and an intension as a value to a variable. Under this interpretation, the intelligibility of quantification into modal contexts is then guaranteed.

Quine makes the same objection to Carnap's account as to Church's. But the two are not really on a par. We saw that it was essential, if Quine's objection against Church was to be sustained, that the interpretation of different occurrences of the same term should be uniform; the possibility of nonstandardly referential occurrences of terms was then ruled out. But uniformity of this sort creates no difficulties for Carnap. Terms will have the same double linguistic function both inside and outside of modal contexts; it is just that only the extensional aspect of that function is relevant to the outside occurrences.

What makes Quine blind to the resilience of Carnap's account is that he does not take seriously the intended interpretation of Carnap's language. He says (Linsky [71], 153) of the 'curious double interpretation of the variables' that 'this complicating device has no essential bearing and is better put aside'. He treats the variables as referential over intensions instead and then has no difficulty in restating his objection. But if I am right, the 'curious double interpretation' is of the essence of the matter; it is this which renders a fully uniform account of the language possible. Of course, there may be independent objections to the double interpretation, either as an account of ordinary language or as an approach to logical symbolism. But that is another matter.

The other extreme view is that the variable will serve as a variable in only one of its roles, presumably the one that for the term is most unproblematically referential; with respect to the other roles, the variable will function exactly like a term. The variable will therefore be single-valued, though the satisfaction of an open sentence may depend not only on the value assigned to the variable but also on the variable itself. We will have, in fact, the literalist use of the quantifiers.

Now in the case of the Giorgione example, the variable 'x' of 'x is so-called because of his size' will take a single object as value, but will depend for its satisfaction on the identity of 'x' in the same way that an instance of the open sentence depends for its truth upon the identity of the corresponding term. The existential sentence '$\exists x$ (x is so-called because of his size)' is therefore presumably false; for even if there is someone called 'x', it is not likely that he is called 'x' because of his size. Again, a uniform interpretation of quantification into the context is possible!

Similar considerations apply to certain construals of modal discourse. Suppose we so understand the necessity operator that terms within its scope are taken not only to have their standard referents but also to pick out themselves or some feature of themselves. Uniformity will then deliver an appropriate variety of literalist satisfaction and quantification.

It may well be that the concept of necessity is such that 'Necessarily, Cicero = Cicero' is true and 'Necessarily, Cicero = Tully' is false. The concept, in its operation, is object-blind; it is not capable of looking past the terms to the objects which they denote. It is then plausible that the corresponding concept of satisfaction is such that 'Necessarily, $x = x$' is always satisfied and 'Necessarily, $x = y$' is never satisfied. If the identity of the closed terms in 'Cicero = Cicero' can guarantee its necessary truth, then, by parity of reasoning, it would appear that the identity of the variables in '$x = x$' can guarantee its necessary satisfaction; and similarly for the case in which the terms or variables are distinct. In some such way as this, therefore, it should be possible to provide a uniform account of literalist quantification into contexts governed by an object-blind operator for necessity.

This completes our discussion of the possibilities of quantification under conditions of uniformity. I have talked as if it were a matter of decision whether or not the quantifiers were to be referential or not. It is for this reason that I have separately considered the two cases. But the requirement of uniformity actually gives an objective meaning to the question; for the nature of the quantifier will be implicit in the use of the term from which it derives. If it is asked, for this neutral notion of quantification, whether quantification into a given context is possible, then the answer may well be 'Yes', even though no term is capable of occurring referentially within that context.

Quine would be unhappy with this conclusion; for there is a presumption in his work that the quantifiers are referential. This would be understandable if there were an equal presumption that terms are to occur referentially. But there is not. A double standard operates; terms are allowed to be irreferential, but variables are not. It is hard to see what can possibly justify this bias. The proper conclusion to draw from the irreferentiality of a given term is not that the corresponding quantification is impossible but that it is, if possible, similarly irreferential.

Bibliography

Baker, J. R. [78] "Some Remarks on Quine's Arguments Against Modal Logic." *Notre Dame Journal of Formal Logic* XIX (1978): 663–73.

Carnap, R. [47] *Meaning and Necessity*. Chicago: University of Chicago Press, 1947.

Church, A. [43] "Review of Quine's 'Notes on Existence and Necessity'." *Journal of Symbolic Logic* 8 (1943): 45–47.

Church, A. [51] "A Formulation of the Logic of Sense and Denotation." In *Structure, Method, and Meaning: Essays in Honor of Henry M. Sheffer*, ed. Paul Henle, H. M. Kallen, and S. K. Langer. New York: Liberal Arts Press, 1951.

Davidson, D., and Hintikka J., eds. [69] *Words and Objections: Essays on the Work of W. V. O. Quine*. Dordrecht: Reidel, 1969.

Fine, K. [78] "Model Theory for Modal Logic—Part II." *Journal of Philosophical Logic* 7 (1978): 277–306.

Fine, K. [84] "Reference, Essence and Identity." Unpublished manuscript.

Hintikka, K. J. J. [56] "Identity, Variables, and Impredicative Definitions." *Journal of Symbolic Logic* 21 (1956): 225–45.

Kaplan, D. [69], [71] "Quantifying In." In *Words and Objections*, ed. D. Davidson and J. Hintikka. Dordrecht: Reidel, 1969; and in Linsky [71].

Kaplan, D. [72] "What is Russell's Theory of Descriptions?" In *Bertrand Russell*, ed. D. F. Pears. New York: Anchor Books, 1972.

Kaplan, D. [75] "How to Russell a Frege-Church." *Journal of Philosophy* 72 (1975): 716–29; reprinted in Loux [79].

Kaplan, D. [86] "Opacity." In *The Philosophy of W. V. Quine*, ed. L. E. Hahn and P. A. Schilpp. La Salle, Ill.: Open Court, 1986.

Lewy, C. [76] *Meaning and Modality*. Cambridge: Cambridge University Press, 1976.

Linsky, L., ed. [52] *Semantics and the Philosophy of Language*. Urbana: University of Illinois Press, 1952.

Linsky, L. [67] *Referring*. New York: Humanities Press, 1967.

Linsky, L., ed. [71] *Reference and Modality*. Oxford: Oxford University Press, 1971.

Loux, M. J., ed. [79] *The Possible and the Actual*. Ithaca: Cornell University Press, 1979.

Montague R. [70] "Universal Grammar." *Theoria* 36 (1970): 373–98; reprinted in *Formal Philosophy*, ed. R. H. Thomason. New Haven: Yale University Press, 1974.

Parsons, T. [69] "Essentialism and Quantified Modal Logic." *Philosophical Review* LXXVIII (1969): 35–52; reprinted in Linsky [71].

Plantinga, A. [74] *The Nature of Necessity*. Oxford: Clarendon Press, 1974.

Quine, W. V. O. [43] "Notes on Existence and Necessity." *Journal of Philosophy* 40 (1943): 113–27; reprinted in Linsky [52].

Quine, W. V. O. [47] "The Problem of Interpreting Modal Logic." *Journal of Symbolic Logic* 12 (1947): 43–48.

Quine, W. V. O. [53] "Reference and Modality." In *From a Logical Point of View*. Cambridge, Mass.: Harvard University Press, 1953.

Quine, W. V. O. [56] "Quantifiers and Propositional Attitudes." *Journal of Philosophy* 53 (1956); reprinted in Quine [66] and Linsky [71].

Quine, W. V. O. [60] *Word and Object*. Cambridge, Mass.: MIT Press, 1960.

Quine, W. V. O. [63] *From a Logical Point of View*. New York: Harper and Row, 1963; originally printed by Harvard University Press, 1953.

Quine, W. V. O. [66] *The Ways of Paradox*. New York: Random House, 1966.

Quine, W. V. O. [76] "Worlds Away." *Journal of Philosophy* LXXIII (1976): 859–63.

Quine, W. V. O. [77] "Intensions Revisited." In *Midwest Studies in Philosophy* 2. Minneapolis: University of Minnesota Press, 1977.

Van Inwagen, P. [81] "Why I Don't Understand Substitutional Quantification." *Philosophical Studies* 39 (1981): 281–85.

11

Meaning and Explanation

Julius Moravcsik[1]

This essay proposes a new approach to lexical meaning. The key idea underlying the approach is that the meaning of a word 'w' in a natural language will be constituted by key factors that figure in explanations that we would ordinarily give to account for what counts as a w. Thus to understand lexical meaning requires understanding some aspects of explanation. If I know the meaning of a word 'w', then I know how to explain what counts as a w. Explanations may vary from context to context, and they involve a speaker as well as an intended audience. All of this should affect the way we view the structure of lexical meaning. For example, a successful explanation need not involve the ability to give necessary and sufficient conditions for the phenomena under scrutiny. Under normal conditions I can explain to someone what fire is without giving necessary and sufficient condition for this natural phenomenon. This insight is incorporated into the proposal given in this paper. A theory of lexical meaning will be presented according to which the meaning of a term in a natural language does not yield necessary and sufficient conditions for application, and hence does not determine a fixed extension.

The proposal flies in the face of the dominant strains of contemporary

---

[1] I wish to acknowledge my indebtedness for helpful suggestions to John Perry, Ed Zalta, and the circle of linguists in Budapest to whom I read this paper in the summer of 1985, especially Ferenc Kiefer, Katalin Kiss, and Anna Szabolcsi.

semantics. For though these disagree about whether the necessary and sufficient conditions for application can be given in purely qualitative terms, they agree that an adequate semantics should assign to each term a definite fixed extension. It is difficult to think of empirical evidence that people might have offered in favor of this assumption. It is more likely that this dogma arose because of a vague hunch that without this presupposition one could not do compositional semantics; i.e., formulate the rules that enable us to build complexes out of semantically simple elements. We shall see, however, that the new proposal does not threaten compositional semantics.

We shall first outline and illustrate the proposal, and then turn to its theoretical justification.

I. The Four Explanatory Factors as Meaning Structure

If the meaning of an expression provides the key elements of the explanatory schema needed to explain what counts for an entity to fall under it, then we should expect the structure of lexical meaning to contain the key explanatory factors contained in the most general account of explanations. In this essay it will be argued that there are four such factors. This section describes these, and shows why these should be the basic constituents of meaning.

What can we explain? In principle, everything; that is to say, everything that can be named or described in our language. In order to understand an explanation we have to know the conceptual category to which the entity to be explained belongs. Likewise, in order to understand what the range of application of a word is, we must locate the range within a conceptual category. The following is a rough sketch of the basic categories. An entity can be either abstract or spatio-temporal. If it is in space and time, then it is an object, or an event, or an aspect of these. One of the factors that are basic meaning constituents will have to be, then, the factor that tells us in which of these categories the range of application of a given term belongs.

Once we locate a given item in one of these conceptual domains, we want to know what distinguishes it from other items in the same category. This yields the second constituent in a meaning structure; i.e., that which gives us the qualitative distinguishing marks in terms of which the items covered by a given term can be distinguished from other elements in that category, on the basis of the knowledge of the language alone. This characterization is designed to leave a number of issues open. The distinguishing may be only partial or complete and it may be context-dependent or not. It might assume a fund of general knowledge to be shared by the speakers of a language, or it might be relativized to a certain subset of the speakers of the language. Furthermore, we might want to choose different options from among these, depending on the nature of the lexical item.

In their efforts to understand and interact with the environment, humans order experience according to principles of causality. We interpret the spatio-temporal as forming causal chains. It is thus reasonable to assume that just as causal role plays an important part in explanations, so a basic constituent in meaning structures will be the role that an item falling under the word to be explained plays as a cause, or as an effect, or as a part of a causal process. Knowing some of these roles at least, is a part of what it is to understand a given word.

Humans not only observe the world but live in it. This they do typically by setting goals, making plans, and trying to realize their purposes. It is reasonable to suppose that this too affects lexical meaning. We are not only cause-seeking but also function- or purpose-seeking creatures. Hence the fourth basic element in a meaning structure will be that which specifies purposive or functional roles that an item falling under the word plays and that we can know merely by knowing the language to which the word belongs.

The first factor introduced points to what is called in some cases the "matter" of the item to be singled out, while the second gives us the structure combining parts of this "matter." Hence the first two factors will be called the m-factor and s-factor, respectively. The third factor arises because we look for agency in the world of sensory phenomena, while the fourth one reflects our efforts to interpret experience in terms of functional organization. Hence the names of these two factors are the a-factor and f-factor respectively. A complete characterization of the meaning structure thus generated is made up of a relation R combining the four elements m, s, a, and f in the appropriate way. The general schema is therefore: R(m, s, a, f) where the four letters in the parenthesis are property-variables, and in some cases a particular factor, a, or f, may be empty. The actual parts of the meanings of particular words will be properties falling under one of the four key factors.

Having presented this brief sketch, we shall now describe and illustrate each of the key factors. The m-factor has a Kantian philosophic origin. For the main intuition underlying it is that humans interpret reality as either abstract or as in space and time. With respect to the spatial we ascribe dimensions to the phenomena contained therein; the most conspicuous of the classes in this domain is that of a three-dimensional object. We also order things temporally, and elements that receive their primary individuation and specification are events or happenings. Any entity is, then, a configuration of qualities and structure of something abstract, or spatial, or temporal. We know what the m-factor of the term under scrutiny is when we know whether the items within its range are abstract, or events, or material objects. The link between terms and this general location is necessary. Not even in the most outlandish science fiction story can we have an item changing from being abstract to being concrete or from being an event into being a material object without the term changing its meaning.

The abstract, the concrete, the less than two-dimensional, and the category of events are basic domains. They carve up reality into fundamental classes. Given the human perceptual mechanism and its obvious effect on our interpretation of experience, we need to supplement this list. For our perceptual mechanisms present us not only with objects and events, but also with smells, sounds, and tastes. Thus we need to add these to the categories covered by the m-factor.

Two other domains need to be added to what the m-factor covers. One of these will be called transcategorial, and the other the derivative domains. The need for the first one arises because language is used also to single out human artifacts and institutions, as well as a certain way of specifying human cognitive states. We specify certain cognitive states with reference to their objects, and human institutions by reference to participants as well as their material locations. Examples of the transcategorial sort are names for institutions like 'factory', 'university', for artifacts of the relevant kind 'poem', 'symphony', and some of the names of relevant cognitive states are 'hope', 'expectation', or 'approval'. These items exist only because of human practices and ways of organization. They do not have independent metaphysical status.

For example, the m-factor for 'university' includes the various elements from which this institution is constructed; faculty, students, buildings, etc. A university is fundamentally a complex in which these elements are arranged within a certain structure. The same holds for the characterization of an insurance company or a country. The specification of a human institution involves essentially physical objects, certain kinds of humans as well as events. Hence their transcategorial nature. Our hopes and expectations are specified both as mental states and in terms of their typically abstract object or content. Hence the m-factor of these too will be transcategorial.

So far we have not dealt with the m-factor of the meanings of terms whose primary semantic role is that of modifying other elements. In Indo-European languages like English the obvious syntactic categories whose members have this modifying role will be that of adjectives and adverbs, but the class under discussion is primarily a semantically defined class and is not meant to be dependent on the existence of certain syntactic categories across all languages. For example, for an adjective like 'red' the m-factor will be the categories of things that can have this color: objects, surfaces, and other objects of human perception and imagination. The m-factor of an adjective like 'wise' will be the ranges that this adjective can modify: humans, actions, thoughts, and institutions.

Similarly, in the case of adverbs the m-factor specifies what ranges a given adverb can modify. The m-factor for 'slowly' specifies the kinds of entities that can be said to be slow; anything capable of motion as well as different kinds of motions and processes. For 'gently' the m-factor specifies what can be gentle: humans, gestures, actions, and mental processes. ("Gently, he helped him to come to see the errors of his ways.")

This completes the introduction of the m-factor. To find out what the m-factor of a given word is we simply go through the list: abstract, concrete, nonconcrete spatial, event, sensory, transcategorial, derivative, and if so, the nature of the modification involved. Thus there is a procedure for determining the m-factor of any lexical item, and every lexical item that does purport to denote will have to have an m-factor in its lexical meaning structure.

Once we have located the range of application within one of the categories specified by the m-factor, the meaning of an expression should give us general instructions for distinguishing the elements of the range from among the other types of entities within that category. Thus the s-factor of 'number' should tell us how numbers differ from other abstract entities. The s-factor will tell us only about those differences that one can know solely on the basis of the knowledge of the language. From the point of view of a user of English, numbers differ from other abstract entities in the ways in which they enter into orderings of collections according to quantity. This ordering role, then, is the gist of the s-factor specification.

Whereas the instructions for singling out the m-factor, given above, are quite exact, the specification of the s-factor remains purposely vague.

For some lexical items the s-factor enables us to distinguish elements only against a shared fund of background knowledge, while in other cases it might amount to giving necessary and sufficient conditions. Knowing what 'bee' means involves being able to distinguish what bees are from what other insects like wasps or hornets are, but it does not involve telling bees apart from all other actual and possible insect-species. Knowing what 'city' means involves knowing the differences between cities, towns, villages, and family tents. It does not involve being able to tell cities from all other actual and possible forms of human settlement.

An s-factor specification has two aspects. One aspect involves giving conditions for individuation and persistence where these are applicable. Such applicability arises typically in connection with terms that the linguist marks as count plus. In the case of verbs this will involve also giving a number of necessary argument places. In the case of so-called mass terms like 'iron' or 'red', questions of individuation do not arise. But the other aspect is qualitative differentiation, and that does arise for all lexical items with actual or possible ranges of application. Given what we said about the link between lexical meaning and explanations and the contextual nature of the latter, one must not assume that the m- and s-factors jointly will give necessary and sufficient conditions that fully determine a range of application or denotation.

Many lexical items have meanings with only an m- and an s-factor. There are, however, many others whose meaning structures include also a- and f-factors. Turning to the a-factor first, we should note that the meaning of certain terms involves essential reference to their origin. Terms for artifacts are obvious examples. Others include terms for biological species distinguished in terms of modes of propagation. Many human action terms will also have to have an a-factor in their meaning structures, for they are introduced in terms of some of their causal effects. 'Write', 'cut', 'excite', and 'dry out' are obvious examples; we cannot understand these words without understanding certain causal effects that the actions falling under these terms represent and bring about. Not all verbs are of this type. All events form causal chains, but this need not be referred to by the meaning specifications.

Given the human interest in the environment as something practical and utilitarian, it is hardly surprising that many vocabulary items not only have an f-factor in their meaning structures but have this as the dominant factor—in a sense to be spelled out later. For example, once we locate a kind of artifact as concrete and assign to it the origin that shows it to be an artifact, our next question is not about its mechanism but about its characteristic use or function. A good museum of furniture would show that couches have been produced through history in all sizes, shapes, structures, etc.—their common denominator from our point of view of classification is that they play a certain functional role for humans. Another set of obvious examples is provided by verbs describing intentional action. We do not understand such verbs unless we can understand the aim or purpose that is built into the semantics of the words in question. The test for whether the meaning structure of a word contains an f-factor is to see if the applicability of the term could be possible in a conceptual framework that does not allow for teleological notions such as aim, intention, or function. Most of our biological concepts, for example, presuppose a teleological conception of the animal kingdom. This is to be contrasted sharply with a science like geometry. Geometrical terms do not involve reference to how things function but only to structure; hence such terms have no f-factor in their meaning structures.

II. Examples and Elaborations

We shall now consider a variety of examples in order to illustrate how the lexical theory proposed here works. The theory will be called an Aitiational Frame Theory, for its link of meaning and explanation as well as its singling out four key factors recall to one's mind some of the things Aristotle said about an explanatory factor ("aitia"); the reason for calling it a frame theory is that—as we shall see—within this theory denotation is defined only within certain "frames," or ranges of contexts, and not on the meaning structures directly.

Let us consider as an example the noun 'bird'. We check through the list making up the possible m-factors, and assign to this word the category of the concrete. The s-factor is then supposed to distinguish what counts as a bird from all other types of concrete entities. Since 'bird' is a count noun, i.e., admits of genuine pluralization, we can infer that the s-factor contains principles of persistence and individuation. Thus it involves the conditions determining what counts as being the same bird over a period of time, and the conditions on the basis of which we distinguish a number of different birds at any given time. It will include also whatever qualities serve in an explanation under normal circumstances designed to make clear what counts as a bird, in contrast to other types of material objects. Thus it will include being in the animal kingdom, being capable of locomotion, having wings, beak, and a few other salient features. The f-factor contained in the meaning of this term includes the properties of being capable of flight, other forms of locomotion, and the property of having the functions normally associated with living.[2] The a-factor includes the origin and mode of propagation associated with animals. To be sure, birds have many other causal roles, but these are not known to persons solely in virtue of their being speakers of English.

Let us take now a quite different noun, like 'sand'. To be sure, the m-factor will be once more that of being concrete, but the s-factor will not include principles of individuation and persistence, since this term does not divide its reference. The s-factor will include those qualities that we normally invoke when explaining how sand differs from other types of material. Thus it includes being made up of small granules, being a mass, and being made of earth. Since there are no essential functional and causal factors of sand, the f- and a-factors remain empty.

On the other hand, in the case of artifact terms and terms for roles and occupation ('mother', 'lawyer') the f-factor is crucial. For what falls under these terms is defined primarily in terms of how something functions and what it can accomplish or achieve.

Many nouns denote abstract entities. Some of these are singular terms such as 'triangularity', 'justice', 'redness', etc. Since these are singular terms, their semantic function is simply to designate the corresponding properties. We gain insight into what these properties are by looking at the analysis of the related adjectives.

There are, however, abstract general terms such as 'number', 'virtue', 'shape', etc. The m-factor for these will be the property of having an abstract domain. The s-factor will include the features in terms of which we would explain how numbers, virtues, etc., differ from other abstract entities. Thus for 'virtue' the s-factor is: being an outstanding characteristic or feature of elements within a natural kind. These terms have neither f- nor a-factors in their analysis. They cannot have an a-factor, since abstract entities are not linked causally to other elements of reality.

Many terms in English are ambiguous in role as singular abstract terms or general predicates. 'Triangle' and 'two', 'three', etc., are typical examples. The m-factor for 'triangle' construed as a general term will be space, and with obviously no f- or a-factors in the meaning, the s-

---

[2]Though some species do not have the capability of flight, they have parts that seem designed for flight. A creature without any such parts would not be counted as a bird.

factor will include what is involved in distinguishing shapes in general and triangles in particular from other spatial entities.

Turning to verbs we need to recall that the m-factor for this category, whether the items denote events or states, will be time. We can think of what a verb introduces as an entity whose nature we explain by outlining what qualities and structures hold together the different temporal parts within which the events or states in question take place. In the case of nouns, the typical explanation of denotation does not involve much fixed structure, other than persistence and individuation. In the case of verbs, however, the semantics prescribes much more structure. For the principles of individuation and persistence involve also the argument structure and the restrictions on the nature of complements that a given verb can take. The s-factor will have to tell also whether the events denoted by a verb will involve time points or intervals or a combination of these.[3]

'Walk' and 'to be ill' differ in their s-factors, for the former denotes actions while the latter states. For 'walk' the m-factor is time, the f-factor is empty, the a-factor is an animate agent, and the s-factor includes walking taking place in time intervals as well as the qualitative features that play key roles in explanations of how walking differs from what count ordinarily as other modes of locomotion. Other verbs, of course, do have an f-factor in their meaning structures. 'Win' or 'lose' illustrate this nicely. In a world in which there are no aims, goals, etc., there can be no winning or losing.

We would expect of a lexicon to give us the required argument places and complements for a given verb. In AFT this falls out naturally from the conditions of individuation and persistence. For example, in order to talk of the same event of walking through time we need to posit only the identity of the agent and the continuity of the activity. This is why 'walk' is an intransitive verb, even though we can give it an object as in 'walk a mile'. On the other hand, a verb like 'hope' requires, for the persistence of a state of hoping, identity of agent as well as identity of complement. We individuate hopes by the agents as well as by what is hoped for. The s-factor will include this, as well as the property of this being a state of expectation of something desired but without much evidence. Comparisons of s-factors enable us to detect families of verbs such as those of expectation. 'Hope', 'fear', 'expect', and 'wait for' are

---

[3] For a more detailed outline of verb semantics, see Dov Gabbay and Julius Moravcsik, "Verbs, Events, and the Flow of Time," in *Time, Tense, and Quantifiers* ed. C. Rohrer (Tübingen: Niemeyer, 1980), 59–83.

members of this family, and they differ with respect to whether the object is to be desired or avoided, or is neutral in this respect, and again whether there is much or little evidential backing for the state. Verbs like 'wait' and 'trust' are more complex in their meaning since they can have as their object either an individual or something described by a proposition. The agent slot of some of these verbs is crosscategorial. For example, 'express' can have in the agent slot sentences, gestures, or humans.

Some verbs cannot be understood without knowing salient causal roles involved in the events that they denote. The pair 'push' and 'pull' illustrates this. Though these terms are not synonymous, their meanings are closely related. This can be seen within AFT by a comparison of their meaning structures, especially in their s-factors. Both kinds of events involve applying force to an object with the aim of moving it, but the relation in terms of location between agent and object to be moved is different in the two kinds of cases. This example illustrates another strength of AFT; instead of operating with the dichotomy of synonymy and homonymy, we can pair items also if they have, for example, one or more than one of their factors in common.

Let us consider the verb 'persuade'. The meaning of this verb contains an a-factor, for only certain things such as texts, gestures, or humans can do some persuading. How shall we, then, individuate acts of persuasion? Persuasion requires an agent who does the persuading, a patient or intended patient who is the target of the persuasion, and there must be some content; i.e., that of which the intended audience is to become persuaded. Changes in any of these three elements will result in separate acts of persuasion. Hence reflection on conditions of individuation and persistence yields the thesis that 'persuade' requires three argument places; one for the agent, one for the intended audience and one for the content. As we said before, the s-factor contains whatever the basis is for explaining to people how persuasion differs from other acts of communication. Such explanations would describe the relation between speaker and audience, the things that the persuader would normally do, and the expected result in terms of the changed mental state of the intended audience. It is unlikely that such explanations would yield a set of necessary and sufficient conditions for the application of 'persuade'. The contexts and conditions for persuasion are innumerable, and open-ended. We might have to try persuasion with unusual means, or addressing strange creatures from outer space, or getting across unusually complex content. It is much more reasonable to assume that one would start with a conception that fits many typical contexts. As we encounter unusual situations, we use default or nonmonotonic reasoning. That is to say, we do not simply dump our previous explanations, but in systematic ways modify them and adjust them to fit the newly discovered conditions of application.

Certain activities such as walking or eating can take place regardless of whether the agent is a member of a society and social institutions or not. There are other activities that require institutional setting. Paying, buying, and selling can take place only against an institutional background that specifies legitimate modes of exchange and currency. The motions and objects involved in such transactions will vary widely from culture to culture. Nevertheless, a term like 'buy' can apply to actions across cultures. The reason for this is that for a verb like this the f-factor is dominant. It shapes—in a variety of ways—the s-factor. The common denominator among all acts of purchase is not something sensibly given in the motions or objects involved in transaction, but in what is accomplished; thus the functional aspect of the act. There is, furthermore, an intimate semantic relationship between 'buy' and 'sell'—just as we noted this relationship between 'push' and 'pull'. This relationship is difficult to spell out within a semantic theory that operates simply with sameness or difference in meaning. It can be seen, however, with AFT, by a comparing of the respective s-factors of the meanings of the two verbs.

We had occasion to refer to two interesting facts about this lexical representation. First, that not all items have factors of all four types in their meaning structures. A classification of items in terms of which factors they require in their meaning structures could lead to interesting generalizations over semantic categories. Secondly, we mentioned the notion of a factor having a dominant role. A factor F has a dominant role if and only if, once the m-factor has been established, the specification of all of the other factors is subordinate to the specification of F. An illustration of such dominance would be a case where once the f-factor is determined, the a- and s-factors would serve mostly as a means for meeting the requirements of the f-factor. For example, within the meaning structures of artifact terms the f-factor is dominant. This means that we discover what the f-factor is, such as the property of being a thing on which people sit, and then the qualities and structures making up the s-factors are conceived of mostly as means to the specified function. A chair will be whatever artifact is used in a culture to serve as the conventionally assigned object to be used for sitting. There are other cases, such as those of zoological species in which the meaning structure contains an f-factor, but it is not dominant.

It should also be noted that nothing in this theory requires that the meaning specifications must be specifiable explicitly within the vocabulary of the language under investigation. Humans presumably form concepts in the way outlined here, and whether either a concept or some of its parts are explicitly encoded within the language is an open question to be settled by empirical work.

We saw also that the meaning structures posited in this theory are not a set of necessary and sufficient conditions, nor just a bundle of unstructured features with vague boundaries. Rather, they have principles of their own, based on default or nonmonotonic reasoning. The meaning of a term like 'bachelor' presupposes a network of institutional relations involving marriage. If this network behaves in some contexts in unusual way, then exceptions and modifications are noted in the explanation of what it is to be a bachelor. This does not make the term vague, nor leaves it simply as an open-ended nonspecific concept.

The lexical representations are supposed to provide the units over which the rules of compositional semantics operate. Thus it is worth exploring the question of whether under this proposal the lexical meanings are merely additive and remain constant under Boolean operations.[4] That is to say, one might suppose that given a noun with meaning structure $R(m,s,f,a)$ and an adjective with meaning structure $R(m,s)$, within a conjunction one can simply add the factors under each heading and thus obtain the meaning structure of the whole complex. It turns out to be the case, however, that this simple way of composition does not work with every configuration. The following is a partial list of the exceptions.

A problem is raised in connection with predicate negation. The general term 'human' is a count noun; i.e., it divides its reference. But the negation 'not-human' is not a count expression; it carries no principle of individuation. This will be true in the case of each of the general terms that are count plus and are susceptible to negation. Negation changes the structure.

A further problem is raised in connection with dominance. We noted that in the case of an artifact term like 'chair' the f-factor is dominant. This dominance is lost, however, if we add a sufficient number of modi-

---

[4] I am indebted to David Dowty for raising this question and making some suggestions. What follows should convince the reader that AFT analysis on the lexical level is not incompatible with carrying out projects in the formal semantics of natural languages, provided that such projects assume various forms of idealization.

fiers that complicate the s-factor. For example: "wooden chair that can be manufactured on the basis of fifteenth century technology." Not all modifications rob a factor of dominance. A map of when and how this takes place is another area of interesting semantic research.

Finally, an interesting set of exceptions is provided by terms like 'exotic', 'rare', etc. It has been noted in many accounts of the lexicon that some modifiers such as 'fake', 'toy', 'alleged', etc., create complications since in these cases the fakeX (or toyX) etc., is not an X at all. But this is a problem for all theories of semantics. The adjectives listed above create a special problem for adding up features. For an exotic bird, or a rare fish specimen is still a bird and fish, respectively. But one cannot simply take the denotation of the nouns and then construe the adjective as a restriction carving out a subset, as one would in purely denotational semantics. The explanation of an exotic bird or rare kind of bee will be different in terms of s-factor than the one given for the normal healthy specimen. Something exotic may not be merely lacking some of the characteristic features of the species but might have also properties that the normal healthy specimen does not possess. Thus one cannot interpret this term as simply removing some of the qualities constituting the s-factor, but as calling for various changes in that factor. An advantage of AFT is that we can pinpoint the conceptual place at which the modifier 'exotic' will affect meaning, i.e., the s-factor. An exotic bird, toy, etc., will still have the same m-factor and f-factor as the normal species. Once more, the fact that AFT builds more structure into meaning helps us to give more informative analyses of distinctive semantic phenomena.

III. The World From the Agent's Point of View

We have seen now a sketch of AFT and some of its detailed applications. It is time to look at some of its theoretical foundations. Why should giving the meaning of a term be related to explanations? And is there anything special about the explanations whose form shapes the AFT structures?

Recent semantic literature stresses the differences between the layperson's and the expert's grasp of certain terms.[5] Since AFT does not posit necessary and sufficient conditions as meanings, the differences in degrees of informativeness, exactitude, etc., can be accommodated within

---

[5] For an extensive discussion of this matter, see Hilary Putnam, "The Meaning of 'Meaning'," reprinted in his *Mind, Language, and Reality*, vol. 2 (New York: Cambridge University Press, 1975).

this framework. AFT stresses another difference; that of viewing the world as an observer or as an agent that interacts with selected elements of reality. In this section this difference will be defended and the claim presented that the semantics of natural languages incorporates primarily the agential point of view.

Let us consider as examples the concepts one might form of heat or of an animal like a lion. From the point of view of an ideal observer, an adequate concept would involve important qualities that help us to understand why heat functions the way it does, what laws it is subject to, and what its constituency is. Similar descriptions can be given of an adequate concept of a lion from the point of view of an ideal observer. From this point of view, relations between heat and human survival or lions and threat to human life may well be accidental. If, however, we view the task of forming the respective concepts from the point of view of a human agent, these matters will be of key interest. Explaining to a human what counts as heat is to discuss various ways in which heat affects us, can be generated by us, and can be a danger to us. Thus, ferocity, possible uses (skins, etc.) will be parts of the s-factor in the case of 'lion', and various qualities of practical interest will be parts of the s-factor for 'heat'. The two points of view do make a difference.

At this point one might want to minimize the difference in perspective and suggest an expanded conception of the ideal observer; one that would include its noticing and having theories about human interactions with the environment. It is, however, one thing to describe interactions from an outsider's point of view, and another to provide help to the agent. The following remarks illustrate this point.

Let us consider games like baseball or football. For someone who wants a complete explanation of these games from the observer's point of view one should give a list of all of the rules that constitute these respective games. This by itself raises an interesting question. For changing from time to time some of the rules will not change the meaning of 'baseball'. It is a challenge to specify what kinds of rule changes should make us say that the meanings of 'baseball' or 'football' have changed. But in any case, explaining the games to potential players will take a different form. They have to know how to play the game; key features will be those relating to the experience of the player rather than those relating to the experience of the umpire or referee. Explaining baseball to a player will include mention of some rules; but it will not consist of listing all of the rules, and it will include instructions that from the point of view of an observer will seem accidental.

The cognitive roles of observer and participant can be contrasted well also with reference to explanations that we might give of professions such as being a lawyer or a physician. Describing these professions from the observer's point of view involves listing professional qualifications, licensing, rules of operation, and expected accomplishments. This is clearly not what is involved in the meaning of 'lawyer' or 'physician' as used in ordinary English. The meanings of these terms as we understand them are formed from the point of view of the potential client or patient. Thus in the case of 'physician', the s-factor will include the ability to cure, to know conditions of health, and to give competent advice. The f-factor includes basic accomplishments in terms of which we define a physician across cultures. In the case of 'lawyer' the s-factor will include the properties of representing clients in court, giving legal advice, and negotiating with legal authorities. Various conditions that may be essential in the role of the lawyer from the point of view of an ideal observer whose aims include the understanding of the legal system are not included in the client's point of view, and again the other way around.

Still another field that shows the striking differences between the two points of view is that of diseases. Following some suggestions of Putnam one might think that the key problem is that of relating the meanings of names for diseases as used by the expert with the uses of the laypersons.[6] But this is not the main problem confronting lexical semantics in this case. For expert or not, the diagnostician's conception of diseases will be different from that of the potential patient. From the latter point of view how we feel, how a disease curtails our normal functioning, or what kinds of pain we endure will be essential features of meanings of disease terms, while these are not the vital qualities from the point of view of an observer whose main task is to understand how the human body functions.

One might think that everyday usage leaves the fixing of meaning and reference for these terms up to the expert. But while such a move is plausible in connection with terms like 'hydrogen' or 'oxygen', it is implausible in connection with terms denoting a state in which we have direct interest. This is clearest in connection with the more general terms like 'eye problem'. Nobody would be willing to say that this term has whatever extension an expert assigns to it. As patients we know when we suffer pain and impairment of vision. It is up to us to decide

[6] Ibid.

whether we are in this state or not. The explanation for the symptoms need not be a part of the meaning of the term.

Even apart from scientific terms like 'oxygen', there may be terms naming natural kinds with which we do not interact normally. For example, terms like 'beech' and 'elm' might play such a role. The AFT analysis of these will be correspondingly quite thin.

Our first conclusion is, then, that the meanings of many commonly used expressions in a natural language evolve as a result of human interaction with reality. This bears not only on what features will be meaning constituents, but also on why we do not want to represent meanings as necessary and sufficient conditions. For labeling items in the course of interacting with these within certain contexts does not require being able to give necessary and sufficient conditions for the applications of the labels involved. Children learn the meaning of 'mother' in the course of various interactions with their parents. They need no set of necessary and sufficient conditions in order to acquire the uses involved in these activities. Even less do they need to know the biological meaning of 'mother', a layer of meaning that does become a part of the understanding of the adult speaker.

We talked so far in general terms about interacting with reality. It is time to break down this notion into a few typical kinds of cases. What follows is a list of samples.

(1)   How to interact with an entity? This is the concern that shapes the meanings of expressions used in our relations to other human beings as well as to other living things. Our conception of another human is very much in terms of how my actions and thoughts expressed will affect him or her, and how we are affected by the thoughts and actions of other humans. To know a person whose feelings one tries not to hurt is different from having an observer's knowledge of what it is for one person to try not to hurt another. Most of our typical encounters with animals and plants raise the same issues. A hiker and naturalist understands trees and flowers from a different point of view than that of the biologist and botanist. "How can we affect each other; what can we share?" are the concerns that shape many of our concepts of the sentient world.

(2)   How can one use it? This applies to artifacts and other objects that can become in various contexts instruments in

human activities. Our concepts are formed not in the framework of a theoretical classification, but in the course of employing a variety of practices that lead to our intelligent utilization of the environment.

(3)   How to distinguish it from other kinds of items? This concern applies to a wide variety of activities that shape meanings. In our interaction with insects, for example, we want to distinguish the harmful from the useful ones (hornets vs. bees), and in our interaction with fish the ferocious ones from the harmless ones (shark vs. sturgeon). Terms like 'mild' or 'harmless' and 'ferocious' need not have fixed intensions. They are contrast-dependent, and acquire different ranges of denotation in the contexts of uses involved in different human interactions with the environment.

(4)   How to identify observationally? This ability has been given inordinate importance in modern philosophy of language. To be sure, in some contexts this ability plays an important role, but in others it does not. For example, in distinguishing the so-called secondary qualities of color, smell, taste, and sound, sensory acquaintance is at a premium. In many other contexts, however, sensory observation is of little value and importance. For example, to learn terms for institutional roles such as those of lawyer, legislator, judge, etc., sensory observation counts for little since these terms will be defined primarily with the help of functional notions. Similar considerations hold for many terms designating purposive activities. In these cases assumptions about intention, goal, or development are far more important than recognitional capacities. One might have a completely adequate understanding of the meaning of a verb like 'complete' without being good at recognizing sensibly present instances of this kind of *activity*. Sensory observation has been linked to two bad principles in philosophy. One is a form of a verificationist theory of meaning. It says that the meaning of a term consists of the ways in which we can verify the occurrence of an instance via the senses. Fortunately, this view faded as a result of repeated failures to reduce every significant term in the sciences to an observational vocabulary and a vocabulary of explicitly introduced purely theoretical terms. But

a lingering version of this view can be found in the supposition that to know what the extension of a term is consists of knowing how to identify sensibly present instances. Again, terms designating roles and functions are clear counterexamples to such a view. I might know perfectly well what it is to be a banker in Switzerland without being able to identify the bankers scurrying around in the streets of Zürich. Still, the vast exaggeration of the importance of this ability in modern philosophy should not blind us to the fact that in connection with some types of interactions, e.g., those involving colors, this ability is important.

(5)   How to construct it, produce it, or do it? In connection with many terms, this ability is crucial for understanding. For example, we learn typically what a knot is by learning how to tie one. Issues of contrast, use, or identification are of much less significance. We come to understand the meaning of 'knot' in connection with the activity of knot tying, not by observing bulges on a string. Again, there are terms for activities and attitudes, whose meaning involves doing or being in certain states. To learn the meaning of 'approve' is mainly a matter of learning how to approve of things. This involves picking up the rituals associated in any given society with this attitude and act. The same thing is to be said of promising. Given that this is a performative verb, its understanding involves knowing how to promise. It is odd to say: "I know the meaning of 'promise' and I can identify occurrences of promise-making in my environment, but I do not know how to promise." For the matter of identification does not seem crucial while the ability to perform is quite decisive in this case.

This is a very incomplete list. There are many more abilities involved in the variety of ways in which understanding and interactions with reality interact. One might despair at this diversity, and suggest that the meaning of a term is simply a set of routines associated with it, and that the nature of these routines differ, depending on the type of interaction with the environment linked to the characteristic use of any given term. Such an approach is especially congenial to those who want to combine lexical semantics with what is fashionable in artificial intelligence. Nevertheless, such pessimistic thinking should be resisted.

For all of these varieties of interactions contain the element of explaining something to a listener. The understanding presupposed in these interactions has as one of its parts the ability to explain the nature of an item falling under the word in a given context. Thus if we can find some general features of explanations that are relevant to lexical semantics, then we can accommodate variety and still have a general theoretical framework for representing lexical meaning.

IV. Explanations

The vast literature on explanations will not be summarized here.[7] We shall single out, however, a few features of explanations that are relevant to the specification of lexical meaning. First, explanations can be viewed on various levels. For example, one can see these as relations between sentences or propositions, but on another level as the processes involved in person-to-person communication. One can view a state X explaining another state Y under certain idealizations, and in contrast with this, one can interpret explanations also as relative to a certain audience with a specific data base and set of mental attitudes. From our point of view the most important distinction is that between explanations and explanatory factors. For example, in attempting to explain someone's depression we might ask: "Who is making your life miserable?" In answering: "Bill," we not only help to launch an explanation but also single out an agent as a factor within an explanation. Characterizing the main types of explanatory factors involved in all kinds of explanations helps to say something informative about explanations in general, and about explanations as they underlie our various interactions with the environment in particular.

Secondly, while entailment in logic is an all-or-nothing affair, explanations may be more or less complete and adequate. This helps to explain why in AFT meaning specification leads only to a partial fixing of extension.

Thirdly, explanations assume a background of information and context of interest. As the context and shared informational base changes, explanations can be expanded. This helps to link the explanatory factors involved in the AFT analysis of meaning with the kind of nondeductive reasoning that is nonmonotonic, and proceeds by modifying and

---

[7] For interesting recent work, see Nancy Cartwright, *How the Laws of Physics Lie* (Oxford: Clarendon Press, 1983.)

expanding generalizations in the face of new evidence rather than abandon generalizations in the face of a single counterexample. For example, one might explain why cars overheat in hot weather, and then add more clauses as one considers unusual circumstances. This kind of reasoning also underlies the generic use of certain phrases. When we say that beavers build dams, this is meant to apply to the normal case, and added specifications emerge as we move to the unusual case or context. This applies also to verbs denoting events. Statements of the sort: "a walk is ..." will not give criterial conditions to cover all conceivable cases, but to list the factors in terms of which we explain a normal walk, leaving conditions of length, allowance for interruptions, strenuousness of effort, etc., to be filled in by contextual considerations.

These reflections on explanations show that many explanations do not give necessary and jointly sufficient conditions for the phenomena to be accounted for. In most cases explaining what something is consists of partial explanations, with a few key factors in focus. This suggests one of the main claims of this paper, namely that the meaning of a term in a natural language is a partial explanatory structure, in which a few key factors referred to in the explanation are stressed. If this is true, then meanings are intensional in the sense that there is a qualitative structure attached to a word, but not in the sense that these would determine definite extensions.

At this point someone might object by saying that there is nothing new in this proposal. It has been said by others that terms in a natural language are vague or open-textured,[8] and this proposal is simply repeating the same point. There is, however, a difference between vagueness and the indeterminate intensions that this proposal posits. Vagueness is a matter of not being able to specify exactly where the extension of one term ends and where the other starts. Thus color terms are standard examples of vagueness: after all, it is well known that colors shade into each other. Alternately, for a term to be open-textured is for it to be permanently susceptible to further specifications and refinements. The current proposal admits that there may be vague terms and open-textured terms in our languages. But it says something additional about meanings in general. Its says that to understand the meaning of a term is to know not how to specify the extension—be this vague or not—but to be able to give a scheme within which explanations of

---

[8] On this notion, see F. Waismann, "Verifiability," in *Logic and Language*, ed. A. Flew, first series, (Oxford: Blackwell, 1960), 117–44.

samples of what constitutes the extension take place. A term like 'ball' may or may not be vague. Under this proposal its meaning will be a configuration of factors most fundamental in any explanation of what a ball is; i.e., of what it is for us to interact with the environment and in course of this to label some things as balls. This account of meaning is meant to apply even if by some miracle the word 'ball' would become stale in ordinary use and thus not be susceptible to open-texturedness, i.e., further refinements and developments in its meaning and conditions of application. Even if no more balls were ever to be manufactured, the understanding of the meaning structure assigned to 'ball' does not enable us to assign to this term a fixed extension.

In justification of the AFT scheme described and illustrated in the earlier sections it was shown what it is to view the world from the agent's point of view, and how this affects the AFT analysis. In this section we saw that though there are many ways for an agent to interact with reality, all of these involve the ability to explain what an item falling under a given word used is, and that, though there are many different types of explanations, all of these involve certain explanatory factors.

What remains is to show how the key explanatory factors correspond to the four factors involved in the meaning structures generated by AFT. First, in explaining the nature of an entity we indicate the category to which it belongs, and thus also its basic matter or constituents. For example, in explaining what an argument is we point out that it has premises and conclusions as its basic constituents and that these are abstract items. In explaining what a human is we must specify that it is concrete and animate. Thus what was called earlier the m-factor turns out to be also one of the basic factors involved in explanations of all sorts. In a similar way, we can show that what was called the s-factor is also a basic constituent in explanations, namely distinguishing what is explained from other items. In a similar way we can link the a- and f-factors of AFT to basic constituents in explanations. These four factors surface in theoretical as well as practical explanations. They surface whether the items to be explained are abstract or parts of causal networks.

We see, then, that the theoretical justification of the AFT analysis rests on two theses. First, there is a general thesis that there is a set of explanatory factors that are involved in all kinds of explanations. Secondly there is a specific thesis, namely that there are four such factors and that these correlate to the m-, s-, a-, and f-factors of AFT. The general thesis does not depend on the specific one. As AFT develops, the link between meaning and explanation remains a key claim, but the number and nature of the key factors can undergo change and refinement.

V. Concluding Unscientific Postscript

In conclusion we shall survey a couple of philosophical theses that led philosophers to assume that the semantics of words in a natural language must carve out definite extensions. We shall show that there is no logical link between accepting and rejecting these claims on the one hand, and the acceptance of AFT on the other.

One such thesis is that of metaphysical realism. According to this view, reality is a set of elements instantiating certain properties, and the task of human knowledge seeking is to approximate in its conceptualization this objective organization. This view tends to be linked to a strict principle of bivalence; i.e., the view that a given attribute either does or does not apply to any element of reality. According to this thesis there may be vague or indeterminate predicates in a language, but there can be no indeterminate attribute in reality. Needless to say, in this paper we shall not argue for or against metaphysical realism. It suffices here to point out that there is no necessary link between this kind of realism and a principle of strict bivalence. There is nothing self-contradictory in the notion of an indeterminate attribute. Furthermore, the attributes under investigation in AFT are typically complexes of more specific attributes. There is no reason why such complexes should not be organized partly into indeterminate attributes. Let us suppose that we are realist with respect to the attribute of having mass. Such realism can be maintained even if it turns out to be the case that within an ideal account of the world there are many cases with respect to which there is no true-or-false answer to the question of whether the item under scrutiny has or lacks mass. Indeterminate attributes are no more or less of a problem ontologically for the realist than determinate attributes.

The second thesis that might seem to conflict with AFT is scientific realism. According to this view, the organization and elements that a mature science posits correspond to elements and organizations in reality. This view also becomes associated with a principle of strict bivalence. And as in the case of the other type of realism all we need to note is that this view is not a necessary one. Metaphysical and scientific realism do not entail each other. But in either case, linking a thesis of this sort with strict bivalence is a non sequitur. Even if we are realist with regards to the property of being an atom on the ground that this is the very best that science can offer, we need not assume that with regard to every entity we can raise the question: "is this an atom?" and receive a "yes-or-no" answer. Indeterminacy in nature is no more inconceivable than indeterminacy in human conceptualization. In fact, the view that all of nature must be determinate is relatively new. The ancient Greek realists did not embrace it. Plato was, for one, both a metaphysical and scientific realist, but did not think that the fundamental attributes carved out the world into what we would call definite extensions. He thought that in some cases truth was a matter of degrees, and that in certain contexts neither it nor its opposite could be applied. We need not agree with this view; but it would be arbitrary to regard it as self-contradictory.

These brief reflections show that both scientific and metaphysical realism are compatible with the indeterminacy entailed by the AFT analysis. Thus this theory of lexical meaning should not be rejected on such general grounds. It should be judged by its conceptual explanatory power and its ability to account for empirical facts. The previous sections provided the evidence for arriving at a verdict in these matters.

12

Perceptual Content

Christopher Peacocke[1]

David Kaplan has often emphasized the existence of beliefs whose content is to be given by mentioning perceptual experience. In "Quantifying In" he was already committing himself to the view that the senses of words are not adequate to giving the contents of attitudes: "Many of our beliefs have the form: 'The color of her hair is _____', or 'The song he was singing went _____', where the blanks are filled with images, sensory impressions, or what have you, but certainly not with words."[2] A few years later, in "Dthat," Kaplan introduced the notion of a demonstration and indicated its contribution to the determination of cognitive significance.[3] By the time of *Demonstratives*, a canonical form is given for demonstrations, one which highlights the notion of a distinctive type of appearance.[4] In this paper, I will be considering a particular type of content which is intimately related to perceptual experience. Though I will not be discussing Kaplan's writings directly, I hope this paper may still be taken as a tribute to his work: for without the lead given by

---

[1] My thanks to Adrian Cussins, John McDowell, Michael Dummett, and Derek Parfit for helpful comments.

[2] David Kaplan, "Quantifying In," in L. Linsky's reprinting in *Reference and Modality* (Oxford: Oxford University Press, 1971), 142.

[3] David Kaplan, "Dthat," in *Syntax and Semantics* 9, ed. P. Cole (New York: Academic Press, 1978), esp. 230–32. The paper was written for a 1970 Stanford workshop.

[4] David Kaplan, *Demonstratives*, this volume, 514–16, 524–27.

his papers, with their distinctive blend of exuberance and rigor, I would not have realized that any theoretical progress could be made with this intriguing, but seemingly amorphous, subject matter.

I.

Anyone who has bought a house through an estate agent knows that there are two quite different ways in which you can be ignorant of the size of a room. From the agent's handout, you can learn that the sitting room of a prospective purchase is 25 feet long: but this is consistent with your not knowing in another sense how long it is. This ignorance need not be the result of having no idea of how long a foot is: you may have owned a foot ruler since you were a child. You are not in the same kind of situation as you might be if you were told that Oxford is 250 furlongs from Cambridge. What you fail to know about the length of the room is precisely what someone who is in the room is in a position to know: even if he is there for the first time, he can see how long it is. Equally this is consistent with his *not* knowing what you know when you read the handout: he may not know the length of the room in feet. So you and he each know something the other does not. What is it that you do not know from the handout but see to be the case when you enter the room? And what is involved in having the capacity to make judgments with such contents?

Let us call this first example "the example of the room." Here now is a second example which poses parallel questions about contents concerning directions. The knowledge that a certain church is on the horizon 32 degrees counterclockwise of straight ahead is to be distinguished from the knowledge that is gained by looking and seeing it to be in a particular direction. Suppose you know only that the church is 32 degrees counterclockwise, and that you are looking from a distance at a town thick with churches. Asked to direct the beam of a searchlight onto that church, you may well not know in which direction to point the beam.[5] There is a demonstrative way of thinking of a direction such that what you fail to know is anything of this form: that a direction so identified is 32 degrees counterclockwise. Contents of this form are informative and a posteriori. Again, the question arises of what it is you do not know. We can call this "the example of the church." Comparable points

---

[5] An instance of a now very familiar point about demonstratives: see the discussion of the Indispensability Thesis, section II below.

could be made for the perception of velocity and for the perception of the acceleration of a moving body, or again for the perception of the speed with which a piece of music is played. One can know how fast Furtwängler took the slow movement of Beethoven's Seventh Symphony without knowing any metronome marking for his performance.

A third example also concerns directions. In the presence of massive nearby bodies like the earth or the moon, normal humans experience a certain direction as downwards. (The causal basis of such experiences is the operation of gravitationally sensitive mechanisms in the inner ear.) It is tempting to describe this as perception of the gravitational vertical: but strictly we should be careful not to imply that to enjoy such experiences a subject must have the concept of gravitation. It would be an improvement to say just that a certain direction is experienced as downwards. The experience can cause someone to judge that a certain direction, thought of in a distinctive demonstrative way, is downwards. The content is more than just that downwards is downwards, and it is different from the further content that downwards is the direction with certain angular coordinates. Nor is it the content that downwards is the direction of some seen object, since a blind person also experiences a certain direction as downwards. Nor is it a content determined by the direction of bodily surfaces or joints on which sensations of pressure is felt, since the experiences can persist even when the pathways carrying information about pressure are blocked. To capture the content in question, we need both a primitive demonstrative way of thinking of a direction and, apparently, a primitive notion "downwards."

It is not easy, and it may well not be possible at all, to express the distinctive demonstrative contents salient in these examples if we are confined to using the standard apparatus for making statements about distance and direction. Take the case of the room, and, in particular, what you learn about the size of the room on seeing it. The standard apparatus, inherited from Carnap, employs either a three-place predicate, to express a relation between two objects and a number, or a two-place functor.[6] Following the second practice, we might write "$\text{distft}(a, b) = n$" to abbreviate "the distance between a and b in feet is n." The point of the example of the room was that neither your visual experience nor your judgment has as its content that the distance in feet from one end of the room to the other is 25. Nor is the point corrected

---

[6] See W. V. Quine, "Ontological Reduction and the World of Numbers," reprinted in *The Ways of Paradox and Other Essays*, rev. ed. (Cambridge, Mass.: Harvard University Press, 1976), 212–13, and the references therein.

by putting '25' outside the scope of "content that" and saying merely *of* the number 25 that your experience or judgment has the content that it, that number, is the distance in feet. The notion of distance in *feet* ought not to enter a notional specification of the content of your visual experience at all.

Can we do better if we explicitly introduce an ontology of distances? Instead of saying "the distance in feet from a to b is n," we might say: there is some distance D which is the distance from a to b and the measure of D in feet is n—in symbols,

$$\exists D \ (\text{dist}(a, b) = D \ \& \ \text{feetmeasure}(D) = n)$$

Such statements as that the distance from a to b is D can be described as *unit-free*: they do not presuppose any particular unit of distance. It is true of these distances and any points a, b, c, and d that the distance between a and b and the distance between the pair c and d is the same if and only if the measure in feet of the distance between a and b is the same as the measure in feet of the distance between c and d. So someone who uses the notion of distance in feet ought not to find the ontology of distances problematic. It might be said that to express the seen length of the room we need to use this ontology of distances. Of that distance D whose measure in feet is 25, we can say that one end of the room is seen as being distance D from the other: and this does not imply, as it should not, that the distance is seen as 25 feet. A parallel construction could be given for directions from a given origin, and could be used in describing the second and third examples.[7]

However, these considerations do not squarely address our original question. Anyone who draws a distinction between sense and reference should insist that it is modes of presentation of distances, and not distances *tout court*, which enter the contents of judgments. It may well be that there are good grounds for saying that it must be unit-free distances which are thought about in these judgments: but that point does not tell us about the nature of the senses which present them.

The many questions which arise here fall into two broad classes. In the first class are those concerned with what the contents in the examples are, and how they are related to one another. In the second

---

[7] An ontology of distances and directions need not be an irreducible ontology. Our arguments so far have been from requirements of expressibility, not from ontological irreducibility: it is prima facie an open question whether, consistently with these arguments, directions can be identified with something constructed from other geometrical entities.

class are those concerned with what it is to have mental states and events with these contents: they are questions which need to be answered with substantive theories of the contents in question. In this section, I will speak to questions in the first class, more specifically the following. What are the contents of the experiences in these examples? What are the contents of the judgments? And how are the two related?

Let us start with the content of the experiences. It is always tempting in this area to use the idea of the precise direction or distance experienced. Since humans do not have arbitrarily powerful senses, we know that "the precise direction experienced" cannot be exactly the direction from the subject as origin to some three-dimensional coordinate given by real numbers. We also know that it cannot be given by, for instance, a band or sphere with width or diameter of one just noticeable difference around such a point either. This cannot capture "precise direction experienced" either, since directions which are not noticeably different may be associated with different such bands or spheres. This can be so whenever the bands or spheres are separated by less than one noticeable difference along the relevant dimension. In fact the idea of the precise direction experienced is incoherent in a familiar way if it is supposed to conform to the following principle: that the members of a pair of such directions are the same if and only if they seem to be the same. This is just the parallel notion for direction of an incoherent notion of shade in the case of color.[8] For any dimension along which matching (nondiscriminable difference) is nontransitive, contradiction results if we suppose there are shades or precise directions experienced conforming to that principle. If a matches b, b matches c but a does not match c, there is no precise direction experienced coherently assignable to a, since it must both be the same as that of c (by virtue of being the same as that of b, which both a and c match), and different from it (by virtue of a's not matching c). But though we know there is no such coherent notion of precise direction experienced, it seems clear from our three examples that we had nevertheless better make some sense of perceiving something to be in a particular direction, and of perceiving something to be a particular length. It may be that we cannot vindicate all our pretheoretical intuitions if they implicitly use the notion of precise direction experienced: as in many projects which respond to a derivation of a contradiction, there will be elements which reconstruct some but

---

[8] See, for instance, my "Are Vague Predicates Incoherent?", *Synthese* 46 (1981): 121–41, esp. 131. The point that such a notion is incoherent is implicit in Dummett's writings.

not all of our intuitions, and there may not be a uniquely correct way of building such a reconstruction. Still, we cannot simply dismiss our three examples. The experiential phenomena and the judgments based on them seem real enough: and I will argue in a later section that they play an essential part in the psychological explanation of spatial actions. So some construction must be given.

Suppose you perceive the end of one arm of a television aerial to be in a particular direction from you. We can use the notion of the *matching profile* of your experience in respect of the perceived direction of the end of the presented arm. This matching profile is a set of directions: a given direction is in the set if and only if it is not discriminably outside the apparent direction of the end of the perceived arm. For the purposes of this definition, the directions in the set may be arbitrarily finely individuated. In the case of directions, a matching profile could naturally be taken as a particular solid angle, centered on the subject's location at the time of the experience. In the case of perceived distance, the matching profile would be a set of distances. Many refinements could be made to the definition of the matching profile, but the details would not affect the essential uses to which it will be put here. The matching profile of an experience is sensitive to the subject's perceptual acuity in a way Goodman's qualia are not.[9] If two experiences have the same matching profile in respect of perceived direction of an object presented in a given way, it follows that they have the same "direction quale" as determined by Goodman's identity conditions. But the converse condition is not true, as in effect some of Dummett's remarks on Goodman brought out:[10] the size of the matching profile will depend on visual acuity. The matching profile of an experience is not meant to function as the precise perceived direction: we already know that nothing can have such a function. But matching profiles can serve several purposes, the primary one of which is in stating what is required for an experience to be veridical in a given respect. For a perceived object really to be where it seems to be the object itself must be located relative to the subject in roughly the directions contained in the matching profile. On the definition given, these may not be the real directions of the object perceived: the light may be bending, there may be mirrors, or some

---

[9] Qualia of a given kind are distinct if and only if there is something which matches one and not the other (in the respect of the given kind): N. Goodman, *The Structure of Appearance*, 2d ed. (Indianapolis: Bobbs-Merrill, 1966), 272ff.

[10] M. Dummett, "Wang's Paradox," reprinted in *Truth and Other Enigmas* (London: Duckworth, 1978), esp. 267.

patch of the subject's retina may have slipped.[11]

Whenever someone perceives something—an object, a property, a magnitude —he perceives it in a particular way, or, as I shall say, in a particular *manner*. These manners comprise part of the content of perceptual experience, and it is of them that we have to give some account in saying what that content is. To say that these things are perceived in a particular manner is not at all to imply that these things are not themselves perceived. On the contrary: the notion has been introduced here in the context of the phrase "thing perceived in a particular manner."

What properties must these manners have? Suppose we are concerned with the manners in which things of a given kind may be perceived, say distances. We should require that if μ is the manner in which one distance is perceived and μ' is the manner in which a second distance is perceived by the same subject at the same time, and $\mu = \mu'$, then the distances are experienced as the same by that subject. (They match in Goodman's sense.) Anything failing this principle would be too crude to capture the manner of perception of things of the kind in question. We know from the nontransitivity of matching that this necessary condition of identity of manner cannot also be sufficient. For the time being, let us follow Goodman and take matching by exactly the same things as sufficient for identity of manner. That is, if we allow ourselves to slip for brevity's sake into speaking of matching as a relation between the manners themselves: manners μ and μ' are identical if any manner matching either one of them also matches the other. As we saw, we could instead take something more sensitive to perceptual acuity: but let us keep things simple for the present.[12] Let us call the

---

[11] This point means that we could not earlier have introduced the notion of a matching profile for the end of the arm of the TV aerial by saying "a given direction is in the set iff a presented object located in that direction is not discriminably different in direction from the end of the arm." Suppose a book is to the subject's right, but is perceived as straight ahead: and this is so because of slippage in the retina. The slippage could well be of such a sort that the locations of things near to the book are correspondingly misperceived. So the real direction of things not discriminably different from that of the book really will be roughly the same as that of the book; so it would not be correct, on this definition of matching profile, to say "the experience is veridical in respect of perceived direction of the book iff the perceived book really is in the directions in the matching profile." The left hand side of this biconditional would be false, the right true.

[12] Dummett (op. cit.) would point out that, on classical assumptions about space, this will commit us to distinguishing continuum many manners of perception of distance. Is it just absurd to suppose that we need to use such manners in the description of the mental states of finite beings? I would defend the view that use of such manners does not float free of real psychological facts about humans

requirement that identity of manner conforms to these necessary and sufficient conditions 'the first requirement on manners'.

In the case of the particular contents in our examples, those concerning distance and direction, there is a second requirement on the manners. This is the requirement that they be *amodal*, in the sense that the same manner can enter the content of experiences in different sense modalities. When driving, you may hear a squeak as coming from the same direction as that in which you see a particular knob the dashboard: the apparent identity of experienced direction is part of the way your total experience represents the world as being. It also makes sense to say that something feels roughly the same size as it looks.[13]

There is a sense in which manners of perception conforming to these principles and which featured in our initial examples can be described as an *analog*. As a first approximation, a type of manner is analog provided that there is some dimension of variation such that for any pair of distinct points d, d' on that dimension, there are two manners of the given type one of which is a manner of perception of something which is or includes d but not d', and the other of which is a manner of perception of something which is or includes d' but not d.[14] The dimension may be direction or size, but it is neither confined to these, nor to spatial characteristics. One type of nonspatial content falling under this definition is the type of manner in which a note, when played on a violin, is perceived: here the relevant dimension will be a range of pitches. This first approximation, which certainly covers the examples we gave, is slightly too stringent, if we want a criterion to cover all manners of perception. It excludes some conceivable cases of "digitized" vision. We can conceive of our visual experience being digitized in a 1000x1000 matrix of squares. A visually perceived straight line of squares would then be perceived in a distinctive manner. This manner would not be counted as analog under the first approximation, with its requirement about *every* pair of points on the relevant dimension. No doubt there are several legitimate

---

by appealing to the supervenience of statements about the particular manner in which something is perceived on facts about the matching relations sustained by a subject's mental states.

[13] I am making only an existential claim that there are amodal manners of perception of direction and distance: this is not a denial that there may not also be modality-specific manners. But if there are, their relation to the amodal manners is a complex matter.

[14] This "is or includes" formulation is to leave room for the possibility that manners are manners of perception of something with boundaries sufficiently broad that they are in one-one correlation with the matching profiles mentioned earlier.

notions of analog type. If we want to include the case of digitized vision, it would be covered by modifying the criterion to require that there is some way of segmenting the dimension in question such that for points *d* and *d' not in the same segment*, there are manners ...&c. This brings an element of degree into the criterion of analog character of a demonstrative type, since there are ways of dividing a dimension which use only a few segments.

In the recent psychological and philosophical literature the idea of something's being analog has featured prominently. The notion has been applied both to mental representations and to processors on representations.[15] It has been closely linked with Shepard's famous idea of a second-order isomorphism. Shepard wrote:

> isomorphism should be sought—not in the first-order relation between (*a*) an individual object, and (*b*) its internal representation—but in the second-order relation between (*a*) the relations between alternative external objects, and (*b*) the relations among their corresponding internal representations. Thus, although the internal representation for a square need not itself be a square, it should (whatever it is) at least have a closer functional relation to the internal representation for a rectangle than to that, say, for a green flash or the taste of persimmon.[16]

The present paper is not about internal representations, claims about which need experimental investigation, constrained as they should be by their ability to explain empirical psychological phenomena. The present paper is concerned rather with the correct description of some of the more familiar phenomena themselves. But there is a corresponding notion of second-order isomorphism applicable in connection with analog contents. Consider manners of perception of directions. If one such manner is of a direction *d* and another is of a direction *d'*, and *d* is suf-

[15] See, amongst much else, R. Shepard's review of Neisser's *Cognitive Psychology*, in *The American Journal of Psychology* 81 (1968): 258–89; R. Shepard and S. Chipman, "Second-Order Isomorphism of Internal Representations: Shapes of States," *Cognitive Psychology* 1 (1970): 1–17; N. Goodman, *Languages of Art* (Indianapolis: Bobbs-Merrill, 1968), 159–64; D. Lewis, "Analog and Digital," *Noûs* 5 (1971): 321–27; J. Haugeland, "Analog and Analog," in *Mind, Brain and Function*, ed. J. Biro and R. Shahan (Norman, Ok.: University of Oklahoma Press, 1981); N. Block, "Mental Pictures and Cognitive Science," *Philosophical Review* XCII, no. 4 (1983): 499–541.

[16] Shepard and Chipman, op. cit., 2.

ficiently above d', then the perceiver will have the impression that the first direction is above the second direction. In the case of directions, this will hold for a range of relations. Here we have an isomorphism between the relations really holding between what the contents are *of* and the relations of which the subject has the impression that they hold between the perceived objects; in fact formulated that way, in successful perception, it is not just an isomorphism, it is an identity.[17]

I will now argue in support of the claim that these manners of perception constitute a genuine level of content in their own right. They occupy a level distinct from two more familiar levels: the level of the objects in the world which are perceived, and the level of modes of presentation which can enter thought-contents. I will defend the distinctness of these manners of perception from thought-contents even in the case of such perceptually based demonstrative thought-components of the form "that distance" or "that direction." But first for the prima facie irreducibility of manners to that of which are manners of perception. While this part of the irreducibility claim is unlikely to be controversial for the manners of perception of material objects and events, it is less obvious for the analog contents.

Suppose you see two straight lines at oblique angles, one to your right and one to your left. In some such cases, you neither see one line as longer than the other, and nor do you see the lines as of the same length, as matching in length. It follows that the distance between the ends of the one line and the distance between the ends of the other are not presented in the same manner—by the first requirement on manners.[18] Since the lines may in fact be the same length, manners of perception of distance are in a many-one relation to the distances perceived. We cannot avoid this conclusion by trying to identify manners with distances-at-an orientation, or with distances-at-a position. This would rule out the possibility of ever seeing lines at different orientations or positions as matching in length. We often do so: as when we see the arms of a letter V, or a band of parallel straight lines in a rectangular area.

Corresponding points could be developed for the perception of direction, at least when directions are in one-one correspondence with angles

---

[17]I have not said, and it would not be true to say, that whenever analog contents are in question, analog processes operate upon them. I do not know of any evidence this is so in, for instance, moving from one imagined musical tone to another.

[18]Note that this shows that "matches" and "is not discriminably different from" are not equivalent, even when the respect in question is held constant.

from 0 to 360. Two things at very different heights may not appear to be in the same direction, nor do they appear to be in different directions.[19]

These points are of course not a proof that there is no way of identifying manners of perception with something on the level of things perceived: but I do conjecture that the same form of argument just given against particular identifications could be applied to other candidates.

The argument that manners are not modes of presentation is quite different. I will approach the issue obliquely, by considering a puzzle. There is a naive but natural approach to certain demonstrative contents which leads to a contradiction. I will give the intuitive argument first for demonstrative contents about distances. After that, we will be in a position to generalize and state explicitly the principles which lead to contradiction.

Here is the intuitive argument. Suppose you see both a line and a bar on a wallpaper pattern. Suppose too that they look as if they are the same length: they match in respect of apparent length. Now suppose that in fact not merely do they match in this way, but that they are in fact in exactly the same length; and that they are presented in exactly the same manner. We will also assume that once the subject's context is fixed, there is for each distance *presented in a given manner* a unique demonstrative mode of presentation of it of the form "that distance." (We will discuss this assumption later.) Under the suppositions of our example, this implies that the modes of presentation ("m.p.'s") "that distance" used in connection with the line and the bar are identical. Nevertheless, it is consistent with everything in this example so far that you, the perceiver, suspect that the line and the bar are not precisely the same length (and not because your perceptual systems are malfunctioning). You suspect that there could, as things actually are, be objects matching the bar in length which do not match the line in length. For all you believe, a few moments later you may notice something in the wallpaper which matches the bar but not the line in length. So you are not willing to judge, concerning the apparent length of the line and the bar, that the former is identical with the latter. But this is incompatible with the identity of the demonstrative modes of presentation in ques-

---

[19] It may not be possible to make the same point for directions where these are in one-one correspondence with spherical coordinates. The explanation for this seems to be that if two things are in fact in the same direction in this sense, they will be in the same place in the visual field (in the sense of my *Sense and Content* (Oxford: Oxford University Press, 1983)); and it is not clear this is consistent with not seeing them as being in the same direction.

tion, in the presence only of Frege's Principle that if m.p.'s m and m' are identical, the thought that the thing presented by m is identical with the thing presented by m' is uninformative. So we have a contradiction.

There are four principles here which lead to the contradiction. The first is

(1)   Distances are referents of demonstrative distance m.p.'s.

The second, which we can label 'Uniqueness,' is that

(2)   For each distance presented to the subject in a given manner, there is a unique demonstrative m.p. of it of the form "that distance" (once the subject and his context are fixed).

The third is Frege's Principle:

(3)   For any modes of presentation of m and m', if $m = m'$, then the thought that the thing presented by m is identical with the thing presented by m' is uninformative. (Note that the consequent of (3) does not say "it is obvious that m and m' are the same": the thought in question in our examples should be taken to be a ground-level thought, not one *about* m.p.'s.).

Lastly

(4)   There are distinct distances which match.

This can be labeled 'Finitude': for its falsity would imply that there is no upper bound on our powers of perceptual discrimination.

The talk of distances is inessential to reaching the contradiction. There are many notions which could replace "distance" simultaneously in (1), Uniqueness and Finitude, and on which the resulting statements would still be true. One such replacement would be "matching profile," for instance. The argument also generalizes to other types of analog manners.

The argument to the contradiction would also undermine a conception of shades of color and distinctive perceptually based m.p.'s of them which are regarded as conforming to the corresponding versions of (1)–(4). In fact this argument can be seen as a painful elevation—to the level of modes of presentation—of the argument (mentioned earlier) that the notion of a precisely perceived shade/direction/distance is incoherent. It is painful in part because the argument suggests that a problem remains even when the referents of our demonstrative m.p.'s are at least as finely individuated as Goodman's qualia.

It is no solution to say that there are no m.p.'s expressed by suitable utterances of "that distance." It is undeniable that these demonstratives express something with a distinctive cognitive value; their senses on a particular occasion make a distinctive contribution to the information value of the complete content in which they occur. Equally it would be no way out to say that there may be such m.p.'s but that they do not conform to Frege's Principle. It was as conforming to that Principle that modes of presentation were originally introduced. If they are alleged not to conform to it, it is not clear what work they are supposed to do; and we do not have anything else which does the required work of capturing cognitive value.

Scarcely less unattractive is the option of denying that these m.p.'s have referents. The distance, for example, referred to by a distance demonstrative on a particular occasion will need to be mentioned in an account of what it is for an arbitrary thought expressed using the demonstrative to be true. It is hard to know what more could be involved in something's being the reference of the demonstrative. There is also another question, once it is granted that there are truth-evaluable senses containing these demonstrative modes of presentation. The sense, together with the world (and context on some views), determines a truth-value. How is the truth-value determined if not by the requirement that, for a given thought (and context), the object which is the referent of the demonstrative sense have a certain property? Of course this question would be answerable if the apparent reference to distances, directions (etc.) were eliminable, and these demonstratives shown to be merely pseudo-terms translatable away once their surrounding predicational material is specified. But this sort of eliminative view does not necessarily do anything to avoid the contradiction. Perhaps it is the case that (1)–(4) are further analyzable in ways that give them an ontology different from that they superficially appear to have: but it is hard to believe that the logical properties which lead to their incompatibility would not be preserved in any acceptable analysis. If it would be, the problem of contradiction is still with us.

It may fairly be said that it is only to a philosopher that it would occur that there might be something matching the line but not the bar. Is the propounder of the contradiction open to the objection that ordinary, nonphilosophical thought has not been shown—even in the presence of (1)–(4)—to lead to contradiction? It is indeed true that there is an element of rational reconstruction in taking the manners to be manners of perception of finely discriminated magnitudes, in Goodman's fashion. But the argument to the contradiction does not depend on this element. Even if we take the referents to be fuzzy bands on a dimension, the trouble still occurs. A relation of matching for such bands, however wide and however fuzzy, will still be nontransitive, and we will still be able to establish the contradiction. The fact that some discriminably different finely sliced distances, for instance, may ordinarily be counted as in the same roughly individuated distance-band is not enough to block the argument. It seems that any coherent assignment of referents to ana-log contents which cover a continuous dimension will let the argument through.

I take the contradiction to show that (2), Uniqueness, is false. If this is correct, it follows that manners neither are, nor are in one-one corre-lation with, modes of presentation. We have two modes of presentation of a distance when someone rationally wonders whether that length (in connection with the line) is that length (in connection with the bar). But in the content of the subject's experience, there is only one manner of perception of the one distance to which both of these m.p.'s refer—even when we follow Goodman's standards in slicing up manners.

This resolution of course needs independent motivation: we need an account of the individuation of these m.p.'s of distances (and the rest), and of their relation to manners of perception. The account ought to make it clear how and why there are two m.p.'s in the line and bar case.

Consider perceptual modes of presentation of shades of colors. Sup-pose two surfaces which a subject sees match in color, and are in fact of the same Goodmanian shade. The subject may entertain the hypothesis that in fact there is something which would match the one and not the other; and so the m.p.'s of the shade used in the content of the hypoth-esis are distinct. This case seems unproblematic, because the surfaces are perceived as distinct: they apparently occupy different regions of the space around the perceiver. Here it seems right to say that there are two m.p.'s of the one shade because there are two modes of pre-sentation of the form "that surface." The surfaces may really be the same (one surface may have a reflection in an unnoticed mirror), but as long as they are apparently in different regions of space, egocentrically identified, then the subject's hypothesis is epistemically possible.

This simple case has three features which will be shared by the cases in which we are interested. First, to individuate a perceptual m.p. of the shade we need to mention three things: the manner of its perception, the mode of presentation of the surface perceived to have it, and (arguably) the concept *shade*. Second, the conditions leading to the puzzle are not fulfilled because the antecedent of Frege's Principle, (3), is not fulfilled. Third, an m.p. of this type is not to be identified with one of the form "the shade of that surface," i.e., with one which applies a descriptive functor to a perceptual m.p. of a surface. The former m.p. can only be used by a subject who can see (or takes himself to be able to see) the shade in question: whereas the mixed descriptive-demonstrative can be used by someone who, in near darkness, can see the surfaces but cannot see their colors.

Now consider m.p.'s of distances. I suggest that the m.p. "that distance" used in connection with the line is individuated by three things: the manner in which the distance is perceived, the perceptual mode of presentation of the line, and the concept "distance." It is then distinct from the m.p. "that distance" used in connection with the bar, since they differ in respect of the second factor by which they are individuated: the perceptual mode of presentation of the line is distinct from the perceptual mode of presentation of the bar. Contradiction is avoided because the antecedent of Frege's Principle is not fulfilled. Similarly, these m.p.'s are to be distinguished from the mixed descriptive-demonstrative m.p.'s which apply a descriptive functor to a demonstrative m.p. of an object. Perhaps this is clearest in the case of directions. The m.p. "that direction" used in connection with a perceived tree is distinct from the m.p. "the direction of that tree," where "that tree" expresses a demonstrative m.p. of the tree in question. For a person may reasonably think that a tree on the horizon is not in the direction it seems to be. The thought "*That* direction (used in connection with the perceived tree) is not in fact the direction of that tree" is then epistemically possible: indeed, it could be true.[20]

The same points may be made pari passu for demonstrative contents concerning the other magnitudes we considered.

A formal representation of what individuates a perceptual m.p. of a

---

[20] Can we identify "that direction" (used in connection with the perceived tree) with "the apparent direction of the tree"? This is indeed immune to the objections just brought against an identification with "the direction of that tree." But it is one thing for an object to appear to be in a certain direction from a subject, and another for that subject to have the *concept* of apparent direction. A subject who does have that concept may indeed reflect and realize that "that direction is the apparent direction of that tree" is true. But the former demonstrative mode of presentation could be employed without the subject having the conceptual apparatus for so reflecting.

distance, for example, would then be an ordered triple of this form:

$$\langle \mu_D, \; [W, F(\;)_x], \; \text{distance}(\;) \rangle.$$

Here μ is a manner of perception of the distance D to which whole m.p. (individuated by the triple) refers: it is itself indexed by that distance. The second component has the structure of a perceptual mode of presentation of the form "that F," where x is the object presented and W is the way in which it is perceived. Nothing here turns on this particular description of perceptual modes of presentation: others could be used for present purposes. Lastly there is the conceptual component "distance." To say that this ordered triple is an adequate representation of what individuates such a mode of presentation is not to say that such m.p.'s *are* ordered triples, nor is it to be committed to the view that they have the constituents of these triples: any more than saying that a constituent material object is individuated at a given time by its place and kind commits one to saying that the object somehow has that place as a constituent.

This representation by an ordered triple highlights several properties. One point the triplet representation emphasizes is that the question "Are these modes of presentation amodal or not?" must be given a delicate answer. I emphasized that there is a sense in which the first component in what individuates them, the manner in which a distance or direction is perceived, can be amodal: it can enter the content of experiences in several different modalities. But the way W which is one constituent of the second individuating component may well contain modality-specific contents; it will need to do so if it is to capture the required aspects of the contribution to cognitive value of the singular mode of presentation. A second property the triplet representation highlights is the dual role of analog perceptual contents, the manners, in contributing to the individuation of the corresponding modes of presentation of the form "that direction," "that distance," and the rest. They contribute not only in the most obvious way, in the first component of the triple: they also contribute to the individuation of the perceptual mode of presentation in the second component, since they will have to be used in specifying the way W in which the presented object is perceived. The situation can be diagrammed thus, where an arrow from one entry to another means that what is referred to by the former contributes to the individuation of the latter:

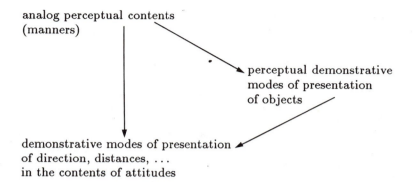

analog perceptual contents
(manners)

perceptual demonstrative
modes of presentation
of objects

demonstrative modes of presentation
of direction, distances, . . .
in the contents of attitudes

We can now consider an objector who acknowledges perceptual demonstrative m.p.'s referring to perceived objects and magnitudes. He also acknowledges that in having a perceptual experience, a subject experiences various relations of matching as holding between the objects and magnitudes he perceives. But the former are at the level of thought constituents, and matching relations hold between the objects themselves. So this objector protests that the manners I have been using are dispensable—there is no need for an ineliminable new level of content. I reply that this objector still has to appeal to manners in individuating his perceptual modes of presentation. Consider, for instance, a demonstrative mode of presentation of a shade ("that shade") admitted by the objector. Suppose the shade represented is, say, a shade of red. Is the demonstrative m.p. he admits individuated in such a way that the content "If I am perceiving properly, that shade is a shade of red" is uninformative? Or is it not so individuated? If it is not, the account is inadequate, since the content *is* uninformative. If it is individuated in such a way as to make the content uninformative, then the demonstrative m.p. "that shade" will not be individuated just by (say) the egocentric location of the surface perceived to have the shade. It has to be individuated by something else in addition. I claim (in conformity with the diagram above) that this additional factor must in general be the manner in which the presented thing or magnitude is perceived. Perhaps in the case of color, the additional factor could for special reasons be the color itself. But in general it must be the manner of perception. Take, for example, a complex pattern of lines, one which may be seen by some as containing a numeral '4', and which may not be so seen by others.[21]

---

[21] For an example of such a pattern, see W. Koehler, *Gestalt Psychology*, reprinting

When the '4' is seen in it, the content "that pattern contains a numeral '4'" is uninformative. A content of a similar demonstrative form, judged when looking at the same pattern, will be informative when the '4' is not seen in the pattern. So it would not be sufficient to have the pattern (type) itself contributing to the individuation of the m.p. "that pattern." The contribution should rather come from a particular manner in which the pattern may be perceived. In sum, then, I would not be disagreeing with this objector over what he says is an adequate means of specifying the content of perceptual experience. But I would be disagreeing when he goes on to say that it makes no use, not even a tacit use, of a distinct level of manners of perception. My thesis is that we need *some* notion of a way in which something is perceived which is distinct from that of a Fregean mode of presentation.

I now consider the relations between the position outlined so far and those found in some recent writers. First, the above discussion strongly supports one feature of Evans' position in *The Varieties of Reference*. He insisted on a sharp distinction between what he called the "nonconceptual" content of experience and the conceptual content of judgment and other propositional attitudes.[22] The contradiction to which (1)–(4) lead and the consequential distinctness of manners of perception from propositional attitude contents emphasize the need for distinguishing the two levels, though the argument I have been giving for distinguishing them has remained neutral on the issue of whether the content of experience is wholly nonconceptual. One might have thought, naively, that at least in the case of perceptual demonstratives of the form "that direction," it ought to be permissible to identify a thought component (or its demonstrative type) with a perceptual content at the level of manners: if what I have been saying is right, it is not possible even in this case. The distinctness of the contents of perception at the level of manners from the contents of attitudes seems ultimately to derive from the different demands made by the two very different notions which individuate the two kinds of content. Individuation of the content of perception is answerable to matters of phenomenology in the first instance, while the content of attitudes is answerable to matters of epistemic possibility—and these two notions can come apart.

A second writer whose aims at least I have been sharing is Dretske. He writes: "If I simply *tell* you, "The cup has coffee in it," this (acoustic)

(New York: Liveright, 1976), 193, fig. 14.

[22] G. Evans, *The Varieties of Reference* (Oxford: Oxford University Press, 1982), 227.

signal carries the information that the cup has coffee in it in digital form. No more specific information is supplied about the cup (or the coffee) than that there is some coffee in the cup. You are not told *how much* coffee there is in the cup, how large the cup is, *how dark* the coffee is [...] If, on the other hand, I photograph the scene and show you the picture, the information that the cup has coffee in it is conveyed in analog form. The picture tells you that there is some coffee in the cup by telling you, roughly, how much coffee is in the cup, the shape, size, and color of the cup, and so on."[23] To capture the distinctive content the picture conveys, and which an experience can also convey, one needs to mention analog contents relating to shape, size, and the rest. Dretske's announced aim is to elaborate the highly intuitive idea that in sensation information is carried in analog form, while in perception it is carried in digital form. But his actual definition of the distinction, however, relates not to the form in which the information is carried, but to the degree of specificity of the information carried by a state relative to the most specific information carried by that state. The state "carries the information that s is F in *digital* form if and only if the signal carries no additional information about s, no information that is not already nested in s's being F"; otherwise, Dretske says, the information is carried in analog form.[24] On this definition, both an experience and a picture may indeed carry the information that an object is red in analog form. But so too may the recording of a particular sentence of the form "John is a bachelor" carry the information that that John is a man in analog form. Dretske's definition captures neither a distinctive type of content, nor a distinctive type of form in which the information is carried. The definition seems to fall short of the strong intuitions underlying the idea that some form of analog/digital distinction can be applied to the content of experience on which the content of some sentences and judgments falls wholly on the nonanalog side.

A consequence for a third writer can be introduced by considering some of the other analog spatial contents of perception. These are by no means exhausted by direction and distance. Visual perception and some other modalities have such contents concerning the two- and three-dimensional shape of surfaces and objects in the environment. When we enter a room, even a room full of abstract sculptures, we perceive things in it as having particular shapes: and there is no question of this

---

[23] F. Dretske, *Knowledge and the Flow of Information* (Cambridge, Mass.: MIT Press, 1981), 137.

[24] Ibid., 137.

requiring that we had in advance concepts of these particular shapes. Here as in the earlier cases we need a distinction between the shape and the manner in which it is perceived. Mach's familiar example illustrates the point as sharply as possible.[25] These two figures

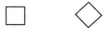

have the same shape. But it does not look to the naive perceiver as if we have here figures of the same shape, the second at 45 degrees to the first. That would be the correct description of this pair

R $\mathcal{R}$

but not of the square and the diamond.

These manners of perception of shapes remain distinct from (neo-Fregean) concepts of shape too.[26] Given that manners have been introduced as capturing ways in which something is perceived, no immediate sense can be made of the idea that unperceived objects are somehow also picked out by these manners. But we can and certainly must make sense of the idea that unperceived objects fall under shape concepts. (A mode of presentation of an object is *not* a way in which something may be judged of an object in the sense in which a manner is a way in which something may be perceived.)

Nevertheless, analog shape contents stand in intimate relations to shape concepts, and the distinctions between analog contents have repercussions on conceptual content. Part of what is involved in mastery of an observational shape concept is possession of this ability: when circumstances are suitable and taken to be normal, to judge without further inference of something presented in an experience with analog content whether it falls under the concept. The vague, observational, nonanalog

---

[25] E. Mach, *The Analysis of Sensations* (Chicago: Open Court, 1914), 106.

[26] I continue to use "concept" in a non-Fregean way, but to a Fregean end: *viz.* for modes of presentation of properties and relations. So these concepts are denizens of Frege's third realm and are constituents of thoughts; they are to be distinguished from the properties and relations they present. It may also be worth noting that I am arguing for the point to which this note is appended without appealing to difference in unsaturatedness.

concepts *square* and *diamond* are distinct by the Fregean test of cognitive significance precisely because this is true: that an experience can have an analog content in circumstances constitutively requiring someone with mastery of the concept to apply *diamond* to the presented object without so requiring him to apply *square* to it; even though of course such an application would be correct.

When we say that an object looks octagonal to a perceiving subject, we are saying something which covers each of two rather different sorts of cases. One is that in which the perceiver has the concept "octagonal," necessarily exercisable whether or not something is presented as octagonal to him, and has a perceptual experience as of something falling under that concept. That experience also has, of course, a more fine-grained analog content. The other case is that in which the subject does not himself have the concept "octagonal" in his repertoire, but in which in a clear sense, he still sees the object as having the same shape as does our first perceiver. Our second perceiver sees the object as having the shape, perceived in a manner given by an analog shape content, which octagonal things present when placed in a certain relation to him. It would be a mistake, not clearly avoided by the author of *Sense and Content*, to assimilate the second case to the first. In particular in chapter 1 of that work, I said that a perceiver must have the concepts used in specifying the representational content of his experiences. That would be true if the 'concepts' are explicitly analog contents: but I gave no examples of these, and used only specifications like 'looks spherical'. A perceiver can have an experience whose representational content has as a component an analog shape content in fact applicable to spheres without having the concept "sphere" in his conceptual repertoire. Perhaps he must be able to introduce it, but that can hardly be the same as already having it. I was probably tempted into trampling on this distinction as a result of a double failure: first, a failure to appreciate that demonstrative thought-contents like "that shape" cannot also be manners of perception, and second a failure to appreciate the significance of the differences between such demonstratives and shape concepts.[27]

---

[27] The distinction between the two cases covered by "looks octagonal" also shows that a certain style of consideration is not sufficient to establish that (say) visual experience has a conceptual content of a given type. This is the consideration that by virtue of his having such experiences, it is correct to say that something looks so-and-so to the subject, where so-and-so is of the type in question. This is not enough to establish the point, because the case may be of the second, and not the first, of our two sorts.

II.

I now turn to a question which falls in the second of the two broad classes distinguished earlier—that is, to a question about what it is to have the capacity for psychological states with particular contents. What is it for an experience to have a particular analog representational content? This is intended as a constitutive question, a correct answer to which must be applicable to any possible experience with a given analog representational content.

The correct answer to this question may have an intrinsic interest as part of the analytical philosophy of folk psychology. But a correct answer will also be relevant to two other areas of inquiry. One such area is the substantive theory of the nonanalog conceptual contents of propositional attitudes. Such a theory must give an account of what it is for a thinker to be capable of judging an individual content. We just saw near the end of the previous section that there are close connections between analog contents and some conceptual contents; and many theories aim to explain the grasp of certain contents, particularly observational contents, by relating that grasp to the content of perceptual experience. Any such theory needs to be complemented by an account of what it is for an experience to have a given analog representational content. Without this complementation, the theory will have elucidated the nature of some contents only in terms of the content of experience, leaving the content of experience itself unelucidated. It is worth noting that such theories are debarred from giving a philosophical elucidation of the content of experience in terms of the content of the judgments they necessarily incline a subject to make: if they do so, they become trapped in a circle, since according to them, the content of some of these judgments is in turn to be explained by their relation to the content of experience.

The second area which needs an account of the content of experience is the philosophy of computational psychology. The first of Marr's three levels of description of an information-processing device is that which states the goal of a (subpersonal) computation, why that computation is appropriate, and the strategy by which it is carried out.[28] The goal of such computations at the early stages of the perceptual process commonly concerns the provision of information of a particular kind about the environment of the perceiver: for instance, what surfaces there are around him, and what their orientation and distances are. That these are correct descriptions of the goals is in part a matter of the relations

---

[28] David Marr, *Vision* (San Francisco: Freeman, 1982), 22ff.

of the subpersonal states identified by computational psychology to experiences with particular representational contents. So the philosophy of computational psychology needs to draw on a theory of the content of experience if it is to say what makes a first-level description of a perceptual mechanism correct.

A theory of what gives experience its content must obviously be defensible for the full, rich range of representational contents that experiences can possess. But the particularly primitive analog contents we have been discussing give a good testing ground for a theory: the manifestation of an experience's having certain analog contents will be relatively simpler than it is for the more sophisticated conceptual contents.

It has become widely accepted, thanks particularly to the writings of Davidson and Dennett, that the ideal of making behavior rationally intelligible should play an essential part in an account of propositional attitude psychology.[29] From such a standpoint, we would expect that for an arbitrary psychological state possessing content, we could say this: its content is one which, as the content of the given state, makes intelligible the actions which that state causes, and would make intelligible the actions the state would cause in counterfactual circumstances. We can call this with refinements to follow, the *Interpretational Account* of the content of a given state. One refinement is immediately called for. We should not be interested in just any old causation, but in cases in which the occurrence of the experience functions as the operative reason for the actions it causes. In addition, a state makes an action intelligible only in the context of various propositional attitudes: what matters is that the occurrence of the experience is an essential component, as things in fact are, in making intelligible the action it causes. This all applies quite smoothly in the case in which the state is that of having a particular kind of perceptual experience.

Thus, seeing something attractive in a particular direction helps to make intelligible the action of reaching out and grasping in that very direction; and it makes the action intelligible under that very description of it. Seeing something as coming from a particular direction, which one can identify as the same direction as that from which one had previously seen something dangerous coming, makes intelligible the action of moving away from it, or taking other defensive measures; and so forth.

---

[29] D. Davidson, *Essays on Actions and Events* (Oxford: Oxford University Press, 1980), and *Enquiries into Truth and Interpretation* (Oxford: Oxford University Press, 1984); D. Dennett, *Brainstorms* (Montgomery, Vt.: Bradford Books, 1978).

In these examples, the actions are made intelligible under descriptions which relate to the spatial directions themselves, and not to directions as identified by some coordinate and metric system. This dovetails with the unit-free character of the referents of analog contents of perception. We also have here an instance of what in earlier work I called the Indispensability Thesis.[30] This Thesis states that no set of attitudes gives a satisfactory psychological [i.e., propositional attitude] explanation of a person's acting on a given object unless the content of those attitudes includes a demonstrative mode of presentation of that object. This still applies when the objects are directions, distances or other magnitudes. Consider the example near the start of this paper, in which an agent has the task of pointing the beam of a searchlight at the church 32 degrees counterclockwise from straight ahead. It is because this agent lacks any knowledge of the form "The church 32 degrees counterclockwise is in *that* direction" that he does not know in any way sufficient for action in which direction to aim the beam. This is a straightforward generalization to the present subject matter of the type of argument used in the case of other kinds of object to defend the Indispensability Thesis.[31]

The Interpretational Account is similar to but distinct from an account based on this idea: that the content of a perceptual experience is that condition on the world which must obtain if the actions, actual and counterfactually possible, which would be caused by the experience in the context of true beliefs are to be successful. (This can be refined in the

---

[30] C. Peacocke, "Demonstrative Thought and Psychological Explanation," *Synthese* 49 (1981): 187–217, at 205–206. This thesis generalizes points made by J. Perry in "The Problem of the Essential Indexical," *Noûs* 13 (1979): 3–21, and further developed in his "Perception, Action and the Structure of Believing," in *Philosophical Grounds of Rationality: Intentions, Categories, Ends*, ed. R. Grandy and R. Warner (Oxford: Clarendon Press, 1986).

[31] Wouldn't an experience plus other attitudes which do not contain any demonstrative content presenting a direction be sufficient for an explanation? And would not this possibility undermine the Indispensability Thesis, since we insisted that demonstrative modes of presentation of directions enter the contents of other propositional attitudes, but not of experience? To this query it may be tempting to reply: "This is no explanation of action on an object unless the experience causes a belief (which requires only a disposition to judge, not an actual conscious judgment): and so the Indispensability Thesis is still true." But matters are more complex. An absentminded person may forget that his beliefs should be overruling the deliverances of his senses in a particular situation in which he finds himself: his experience may influence him to action, and if so, he may well be acting intentionally on the objects in his environment. But we count this case as such because we understand such absentmindedness as a deviation from the ideal of rational psychological explanation: the Indispensability Thesis describes only the ideal.

same ways as the Interpretational Account.) This rival account can make use of the requirement that it is a state with a given, constant content which has a range of causal consequences in different circumstances. But it nevertheless allows in too much as the content of a perceptual experience. Any plausible philosophical theory of mental states with content will have to draw a distinction between circumstances in which a subject's afferent and efferent nerves are properly connected to the outside world, and those in which they are not. It is a substantive question what is the correct principle for drawing the distinction: but some such distinction will be needed by any theory which individuates mental states and their contents at least in part by their relations to their worldly causes and effects.[32] The causes and effects of any state are going to be dependent on how it is, afferently and efferently, connected to the world: it is only when the connections are designated as standard that the individuating environmental causes and effects, possibly conditional on other external circumstances, will be present. But if we restrict ourselves to cases in which the subject is properly connected to the world, afferently and efferently, then this rival of the Interpretational Account lets in too much. Consider a visual experience as of a dog at a certain distance and direction from the subject. For actions based on this to be successful, there must indeed be a dog at the appropriate distance and direction from the subject. But under conditions of proper connection, for the action to be successful there must also be a certain type of retinal stimulation pattern—that type instantiated just whenever there is a dog at the right orientation to and distance from the eye(s): and there must, counterfactually, be certain patterns of stimulation when the eye is at other locations. A similar point holds for cross-sectional properties of the bundle of light rays reaching the eye.

The Interpretational Account avoids this because having the impression that a certain content about one's retinal image obtains does not in general make intelligible, in the context of the subject's other attitudes, the actions which would be caused by an experience of a dog at a given distance and direction. In propositional attitude psychology, these actions are made intelligible under characterizations which relate them to their environment. Some of the most fundamental characterizations are the spatial ones we have been discussing. While an experience as of a fierce dog approaching from a certain direction can contribute to the explanation of action characterized as action in relation to that same di-

---

[32] This is consistent with the theory being partially normative.

rection, attributing an experience whose content concerns retinal states or cross-sections of light has no such rationalizing effect. Of course some subjects do have attitudes about their retinal images—ophthalmologists and psychologists do. But these beliefs are at a level of conceptual sophistication which does not have to be present in everyone who has perceptual experiences of the world: and indeed to explain action on object in the environment, such sophisticated attitudes still have to be connected by inference on the part of the subject with demonstrative analog contents about his surroundings.[33]

There are two competing ways of construing the Interpretational Account. One involves supposing that a statement of what makes it the case that actual and possible actions are intentional under particular descriptions can be given quite independently of what gives experience its content. On this first construal, the Interpretational Account gives the content of experience by relating it to these specifications of intentional action, given independently and in advance. This first construal is not how I intend the Interpretational Account to be read. On the second, intended construal, ascribing content to experience is part of the general enterprise of radical interpretation, in the sense of ascribing contents to the subject's mental states and to his sentences (if any). No content-involving states are available in advance of any others on this reading, not even a specification of which events are intentional actions. On this second reading, the Interpretational Account states a constraint relating the content of experience to the descriptions under which a subject's actions are intentional, a constraint which must be satisfied by any total assignment of content to the subject's mental states and sentences. Someone who accepts the first, rejected, reading, is saddled with the unpromising task of giving an account of what determines the descriptions under which actions are intentional which does not draw upon the content of the subject's experiences.

The enterprise of radical interpretation proceeds under the general rubric of maximizing intelligibility: but can we give more specific con-

---

[33] There may also be a converse problem with some formulations of this rival to the Interpretational Account. An experience may represent something in front of one as being a man. But a man has to have organs and flesh under his skin and a certain physiological and genetic constitution. There will be actual and possible actions which are successful only if a perceived object has these internal properties. But they do not enter the representational content of the experience. Nor do they have to on the Interpretational Account. A parallel point could be developed for the unperceived rear of H. H. Price's tomato (mentioned in his *Perception*, 2d ed. (London: Methuen, 1950)).

straints? One more specific constraint would be this:

> Every feature of the content of an experience is, in some
> circumstances or other, reflected in the content under which
> an action based on it is intentional.[34]

An example of a violation of this constraint would be this. Suppose there
are neurons whose states are sensitive to the direction of the magnetic
north. Perhaps they are also neurons whose states realize the perceptual
experiences of the person in whose brain they are located. If, though,
there are no counterfactually possible circumstances in which these experiences contribute essentially to the rational explanation of an action
intentional under the description "north," then it would be wrong to
take the experiences as representing something to be the case about the
magnetic north. This is a special case of the Tightness Constraint of
Sense and Content specialized to the relation between experience and
action.[35]

III.

The principle that the contents of experience must be reflected in the
descriptions under which actions caused by them are intentional leaves
open a major question, to wit: must spatial contents of experience be reflected in a capacity of the subject for spatial behaviors? An affirmative
answer to this question is returned by Evans. He notes that there is a
distinction between a subject who merely responds differentially to proximal stimuli which are in fact correlated with distal spatial properties
and a subject who has experiences with a spatial representational content; what distinguishes the second subject from the first, he suggests,

---

[34] I use 'intentional under a description' and 'intentional under a content' as stylistic
variants.

[35] Peacocke, *Sense and Content*, chapter 3. A fanatic for symmetry may wonder
whether the content of intentional action is constrained by its relations to the content of experience in precisely the way an experience's content is constrained by
its relation to intentional action. It is not. The symmetrical principle would read
"Every feature of the content under which an action is intentional is one which
enters the content of some experiential state." Even with simultaneous additional
restrictions to actions which are *basic* in the subject's action plan on a particular occasion, and to clearly "nontheoretical" components of content, the quoted
principle is false. One range of examples is given by the competent speaker of a
natural language who is totally deaf. This subject has various intentions to utter
sentences which he cannot, and may not know what it is like to, hear. Nor need
such a subject be able to read.

is that the first subject's stimuli are "not connected to any difference in spatial behaviour."[36] He also writes that terms specifying the content of a subject's perceptions "derive their meaning in part from their complicated connections with the subject's *actions*" (ibid.). This is a weaker claim than the one quoted in the text, for reasons to follow. He also gives another reason for an affirmative answer to the question, a reason which involves something which would be explained if the affirmative answer were correct:

> When we hear a sound as coming from a certain direction, we do not have to *think* or *calculate* which way to turn our heads (say) in order to look for the source of the sound. If we did have to do so, then it ought to be possible for two people to hear a sound as coming from the same direction ... and yet to be disposed to do quite different things in reacting to the sound, because of differences in their calculations. Since this does not appear to make sense, we must say that having spatially significant perceptual information consists at least partly in being disposed to do various things.[37]

Is Evans right that spatial experience requires the capacity for spatial behaviors? If not, what other explanations can there be for the phenomenon he cites in its favor?

There are examples which put pressure on the position that spatial experience requires the capacity for spatial behavior. Consider first a hypothetical organism, which we can call 'The Sphere'. The Sphere lives naturally in a transparent fluid and is, of course, spherical in shape. It has light-sensitive receptors distributed all over its surfaces: the receptors are connected with a complex central processing device. It can change its color, can alter its temperature, and can alter the acidity of its outer layers. But it cannot propel itself, cannot alter its shape, and has no limbs. We can stipulate also that in respect of the nonspatial properties of its surface that it is able to control, it either changes all of its surface in a given respect, or none of it. The Sphere is, then, not capable of any spatial behaviors. But by how much does this conceptually limit the content of its experience?

---

[36] Evans, *The Varieties of Reference*, 155.

[37] Ibid., 155. The point was made earlier by G. Pitcher in *A Theory of Perception* (Princeton, N.J.: Princeton University Press, 1977), 189, as Evans acknowledges in *Collected Papers* (Oxford: Oxford University Press, 1985), 383.

It seems that it would be consistent with the description of The Sphere so far that it has all of the following abilities: (i) the ability to detect a predator at a certain distance from it, together with the ability to change its acidity level accordingly; (ii) the ability to detect a predator as coming towards it with a certain speed, together with the ability to change its acidity rapidly or slowly. In both of these cases, we could have the explanation of continuously varying features of actions by their analog spatial contents; (iii) the ability to change without any spatial behavior in ways determined by where, on an updated cognitive map, the organism takes itself to be as it is moved around in the fluid. The Sphere may react successively in quite different ways to environments which are represented in its experience as having spatial arrays of indistinguishable types, if it has reason to believe that at the successive times it is in qualitatively identical but numerically distinct places, one hostile, the other not. In these circumstances, the ability to react in ways (i) and (ii) to danger cannot be described simply as possession of a noncognitive stimulus-response mechanism. We can even envisage a Sphere which knows of two qualitatively identical regions, at each of which there are two similar organisms. In one region, the organism in one direction may be hostile, while in the other region it is the organism in the other direction. Here then acceptance of the content "That organism is in *that* direction" may enter the explanation of the Sphere's nonspatial behavior.

It seems that we could go on filling out this example in ways which would give a more detailed description of a possible organism which has experiences with spatial contents, but which is not yet capable of spatial behaviors. If The Sphere or some other case to the same point is coherent, then we have to draw a sharp distinction. It is the distinction between (a) an action being intentional under some spatial description, and (b) its being a spatial action, in the sense of being a movement (or a remaining stationary) of some part of the body. Some of the actions of The Sphere *are* intentional under spatial descriptions: one of its actions may be doing something which will protect it when the perceptually presented predator reaches it, or it may be doing something which will benefit it when it is in a room at one particular spatial location rather than in a qualitatively similar room at another. The weaker property (a) of an action is the one which should be used in explaining the sense in which the content of perceptual experiences must be reflected in actions they produce. It is something common to actions of The Sphere and to human spatial behavior.

Dennett has always insisted that the informational content of a state must depend on how that information is *used* (perhaps subpersonally) by the organism. In the description of The Sphere, I have emphasized the reflection of the spatial content of the subject's experience in the descriptions under which its nonspatial behavior is intentional. Dennett further remarked that "The significance an item in the environment can have to a creature is limited by the creature's behavioural repertoire."[38] If we read the phrase "behavioral repertoire" as requiring the capacity for spatial behaviors as a necessary condition of spatial contents, then the possibility of the Sphere counts against the further principle, so construed. If we read the phrase "behavioral repertoire" as picking out the subject's actions intentionally characterized that this principle would be consistent with the possibility of The Sphere; it would then state a constraint on content ascription which I have not been questioning.[39] I should emphasize that I have not at all been operating from a stance according to which only input factors have any constitutive significance for the correct ascription of content.

If we hold that spatial experience does not require the capacity for spatial behavior, we incur an obligation to give another account of the phenomenon which Evans noted would be explained under his hypothesis: that was the phenomenon that we do not have to think or calculate to turn our heads (say) in the direction of a perceived sound. That *some* other account of phenomena of the same general type must exist is suggested when we reflect on some further cases.

Normal English adults, asked to repeat out loud a word spoken to them, do not have to think or calculate in order to comply. We should be extremely reluctant to offer as an explanation of this phenomenon the claim that the ability to hear someone as uttering a particular word requires the capacity on the part of the hearer to be able to utter it himself. We should be reluctant, first because the congenitally dumb

---

[38] D. Dennett, *Content and Consciousness* (London: Routledge, 1969), 75.

[39] On the purely exegetical question, this second reading is strained because Dennett also wrote on the same page that "... for all animals lower than human beings there is no behavioural experiment we could perform that would have ... as its conclusion [that the animals could discriminate circles *as* circles and squares *as* squares], since circles and squares, even under laboratory conditions, could have no bearing *as* circles and squares on the life and activities of the animal." This statement, with its "could have no bearing," does not seem consistent with the reading of the principle defended as true in my text above. So if the true reading was Dennett's intention, we would at least have to regard the passage just quoted as not in fact following from the principle intended.

can hear others as uttering particular words, and second because we can make sense of the claim that normal infants hear and even understand some words that they cannot utter. We ought rather to say about the case of heard and spoken words that for normal humans, there is a concept under which a perceived utterance falls: and the very same concept can be one which enters the content under which one of the subject's utterances is intentionally produced—such as the concept "instance of the word *snow*." Not merely is the utterance intentional under a content containing this concept, but that content is *basic* in the intentions of the speaker: the speaker does not try to produce an utterance of "snow" by doing something else.[40] The subject is also reliably successful in acting on such intentions. An explanation of how this is possible must be in part a matter for an empirical psychological theory. But we can say in advance that it is only when both these conditions are met that the normal English subject does not need to think or calculate when asked to utter "snow." This account is fully consistent with the possibility that there are subjects able to hear events as utterances of "snow" without being able to utter it themselves.

I suggest a parallel account of the phenomenon Evans mentions. One and the same demonstrative component may enter both the content of a perceptual experience and the content under which some piece of spatial behavior is not merely intentional, but basically intentional. This is what happens when a demonstrative component of the form "that direction" enters both a specification of the content of a belief based on an auditory experience, and the reliably successful basic intention with which the subject acts. (The subject does not act just on an intention with a descriptive content to turn his head in whichever direction the sound may be coming from.)

Again, both features are essential for the occurrence of the phenomenon. If the mode of presentation in the content of the intention is not exactly that in the content of the belief, conscious thought or calculation may be necessary before acting upon it, and two subjects may act differently because they reach different conclusions. This would be the case if a subject saw something in a particular direction, and formed the intention to comply with the request to face 120 degrees counterclockwise from the direction of the seen object. The other essential feature would be missing if the mode of presentation in the content of the belief

---

[40] That is, the utterance of "snow" can be teleologically basic in Jennifer Hornsby's sense: see her *Actions* (London: Routledge, 1980), 88 and preceding.

were not one featuring in contents under which the subject is capable of reliably successful basically intentional actions of the sort the agent intends to perform. Thus a billiards player may see the corner of the table as being in a particular direction from him. He may form the intention to hit a given ball in that direction by striking it with a second ball which he hits directly with his cue. Here we have no difficulty in understanding the possibility that two players do different things in trying to fulfill this intention precisely because they have consciously reasoned or calculated in different ways.

Just as the account we gave of the auditory case does not exclude congenital inability to speak, so this account of the phenomenon does not exclude the possibility that some perceivers of spatial properties are not capable of spatial behavior.[41] If the description I have suggested of Evans' phenomenon is right, then a thinker might be in danger of making a now familiar form of fallacious inference. This thinker would start from a correct claim of the impossibility of two adjacent perceivers of a sound doing different things when they both intend to turn their heads in its direction. He then moves to a claim about what it is to have perceptions with spatial contents. But here he moves from a modal claim to a constitutive claim. From the agreed datum that it is impossible for something to be F without being G, it does not follow that being G has to be mentioned in a philosophical account of what it is for something to be F. Any philosophical account at all of what it is to be F which, with some true auxiliary theory, entails that it is impossible to be F without being G, will equally be consistent with the modal datum. Our concern has been with the case in which we replace 'F' with 'is capable of spatial perception' and 'G' with 'displays, if a normal human, what is actually Evans' phenomenon'. On the account I have endorsed, we have yet another illustration of the fact that the constitutive is narrower than the necessary.

IV.

Analog content is a fundamental type of content. It seems impossible to conceive of a subject who perceives and acts in the world and who is not in states with some kind of analog content. The level of analog

---

[41] In particular, it would allow for the intelligibility of the speculation of some developmental psychologists that at certain ages infants are capable of perceiving spatial features which they lack the motor skills for manifesting in their specifically spatial behavior.

content may also be the most primitive level at which a distinction is drawn within folk psychology between what is represented and the way in which it is represented. In recent years, discussions have begun about the relations between informational, teleological, and interpretational accounts of content and mental representation. I suggest that, with its fundamental and relatively primitive character, analog content may be a good starting point for further detailed investigation.

13

Tense and Singular Propositions

Nathan Salmon[1]

I. Information Content

David Kaplan's semantic theory of demonstratives and indexicals is rich and imposing.[2] The theory can be seen, and more importantly *should be* seen, as essentially a modification of the naive theory of cognitive information content against which Frege rebelled in his classic "Über Sinn und Bedeutung."[3]

The primary presupposition of any philosophical theory of cognitive

---

[1] Portions of my book *Frege's Puzzle* (Cambridge, Mass.: MIT Press/Bradford Books, 1986) have been incorporated into the present article with the permission of the MIT Press. Some of the material contained here was read at a conference on Themes from David Kaplan held by Stanford University's Center for the Study of Language and Information in March 1984. The article benefited from the discussion that followed, from written comments by Graeme Forbes, Hans Kamp, and Scott Soames, as well as from discussions with Joseph Almog, Keith Donnellan, Graeme Forbes, Hans Kamp, David Kaplan, Christopher Peacocke, and Scott Soames.

[2] Kaplan's theory is presented in his widely read and discussed manuscript *Demonstratives* (draft #2, UCLA, 1977, published in this volume. References to *Demonstratives* are to this volume.). Certain elements of Kaplan's theory may also be found in "Dthat," and in "On the Logic of Demonstratives," both in *Contemporary Perspectives in the Philosophy of Language*, ed. P. French, T. Uehling, and H. Wettstein (Minneapolis: University of Minnesota Press, 1977), 338–400, 401–12.

[3] In *Zeitschrift für Philosophie und Philosophische Kritik* 100 (1893): 25–50; in English in Frege, 1984, 157–77; also in Frege, 1952, 56–78.

331

content is that the (or at least one) semantic function of declarative sentences is to encode information.[4] I mean the term 'information' in a broad sense to include misinformation—that is, inaccurate or incorrect pieces of information—and even pieces of information that are neither true nor false. A declarative sentence may be said to *contain* the piece of information it semantically encodes, and that piece of information may be described as the *cognitive information content*, or more simply as the *information content*, of the sentence.

Pieces of information are, like the sentences that encode them, abstract entities. Many of their properties can be "read off" from the encoding sentences. Thus, for instance, it is evident that pieces of information are not ontologically simple, but complex. The information that Frege is clever and the information that Frege is busy are both, in

---

[4] A word of clarification is needed concerning my use of the semantic predicates 'encode' and 'information'. Throughout this essay, I am concerned with discrete units of information that are specifiable by means of a 'that'-clause, e.g., the information that Socrates is wise. These discrete units are *pieces of information*. I shall generally use the mass noun 'information' as if it were shorthand for the count noun phrase 'piece of information', i.e., as a general term whose extension is the class of pieces of information. Thus, I write 'information that is such-and-such' to mean "pieces of information that are such-and-such," 'the same information' to mean "the same piece(s) of information," 'different information' to mean "different pieces of information," and so on. I use the verb 'encode' in such a way that an unambiguous declarative sentence encodes (with respect to a given possible context c) a *single* piece of information, which is referred to (with respect to c) by the result of prefixing 'the information that' to the sentence and which is to be called 'the information content' of the sentence (with respect to c). A declarative sentence may encode (with respect to a given context) two or more pieces of information, but if it does so, it is ambiguous. Pieces of information encoded by the proper logical consequences of an unambiguous sentence are not themselves encoded, in this sense, by the sentence. The (piece of) information that snow is white and grass is green is different information (a different piece of information) from the (piece of) information that snow is white, though intuitively the latter is included as part of the former. The sentence 'Snow is white and grass is green' encodes only the former, not the latter. This constitutes a departure from at least one standard usage, according to which the information content of a sentence is perhaps something like a class of pieces of information, closed under logical consequence.

I am not concerned in this essay with a notion of an *amount* of information, which arises in the mathematical theory of communication or information. The information *that snow is white and grass is green and Socrates is Socrates* may be no more or less information than the information *that both snow is white if and only if grass is green and either snow is white or grass is green*. Nevertheless general considerations involving Leibniz's Law strongly suggest that they are numerically distinct pieces of information. For instance, the first concerns Socrates whereas the second does not.

the same way, pieces of information directly about Frege; hence, they must have some component in common. Likewise, the information that Frege is clever has some component in common with the information that Russell is clever, and that component is different from what it has in common with the information that Frege is busy. Correspondingly, the declarative sentence 'Frege is clever' shares certain syntactic components with the sentences 'Frege is busy' and 'Russell is clever'. These syntactic components—the name 'Frege' and the predicate 'is clever'— are separately semantically correlated with the corresponding component of the piece of information encoded by the sentence. Let us call the information-component semantically correlated with an expression the *information value* of the expression. The information value of the name 'Frege' is that which the name contributes to the information encoded by such sentences as 'Frege is clever' and 'Frege is busy'; similarly, the information value of the predicate 'is clever' is that entity which the predicate contributes to the information encoded by such sentences as 'Frege is clever' and 'Russell is clever'. As a limiting case, the information value of a declarative sentence is the piece of information it encodes, its information content.

Within the framework of so-called possible-world semantics, the information value of an expression determines the semantic *intension* of the expression. The intension of a singular term, sentence, or predicate is a function that assigns to any possible world w the *extension* the singular term, sentence, or predicate takes on with respect to w. The extension of a singular term (with respect to a possible world w) is simply its *referent* (with respect to w), i.e., the object or individual to which the term refers (with respect to w). The extension of a sentence (with respect to w) is its truth-value (with respect to w)—either truth or falsehood. The extension of an n-place predicate (with respect to w) is the predicate's semantic characteristic function (with respect to w), i.e., the function that assigns either truth or falsehood to an n-tuple of individuals, according as the predicate or its negation applies (with respect to w) to the n-tuple. Assuming bivalence, the extension of an n-place predicate may be identified instead with the class of n-tuples to which the predicate applies.

Since ordinary language includes so-called indexical expressions (such as 'I', 'you', 'here', 'now', 'today', 'yesterday', 'this', 'that', 'he', 'she', 'there', and 'then'), the information value of an expression, and hence also the semantic intension, must in general be indexed, i.e., relativized, to the context in which the expression is uttered. That is, strictly one should speak of the information value of an expression (e.g., the information content of a sentence) *with respect to* this or that context of utterance, and similarly for the corresponding semantic intension of an expression; the information value and corresponding intension of an expression with respect to one context may be different from the information value and corresponding intension of the same expression with respect to a different context. This generates a higher-level, nonrelativized semantic value for expressions, which Kaplan calls the *character* of an expression. The character of an expression is a function or rule that determines, for any possible context of utterance c, the information value the expression takes on with respect to c. For example, the character of a sentence is a function or rule that assigns to any possible context of utterance c the piece of information that the sentence encodes with respect to c, that is, the information content of the sentence with respect to c.

In addition to the character of an expression, we may consider a related nonrelativized semantic value: the function or rule that determines for any possible context of utterance c the extension (e.g., the referent, the class of application, or the truth-value) that the expression takes on with respect to c. Let us call this the *contour* of an expression. The contour of an expression is fully determined by its character, as follows: Given any context c, the character of an expression determines the information value of the expression with respect to c. This, in turn, determines the intension of the expression with respect to c. Applying this intension to the possible world of the context c yields the extension of the expression with respect to c.[5]

---

[5] I use here, and throughout this essay, a quasi-technical notion of the *context* of an utterance, which is such that, for any particular actual utterance of any expression by anyone, if any facts had been different in any way, even if they are only facts entirely independent of and isolated from the utterance itself, then the context of the utterance would, ipso facto, be a different context—even if the utterance is made by the very same speaker in the very same way to the very same audience at the very same time in the very same place. To put it another way, although a single utterance occurs in indefinitely many different possible worlds, any particular possible context of an utterance occurs in one and only one possible world, so that in every possible world in which the same utterance occurs, it occurs in a new and different context—even if the speaker, his or her manner of uttering, the time of the utterance, the location of the speaker, the audience being addressed, and all other such features and aspects of the utterance remain exactly the same.

There is a very good reason for using the term 'context' in this way: Suppose, for example, that it will come to pass that a Democrat is elected to the presidency in the year 2000, and consider a possible world W that is exactly like the actual world in every detail up to 1 January 1999, but in which a Republican is elected

The systematic method by which it is secured which information is semantically encoded by which sentence is, roughly, that a sentence semantically encodes that piece of information whose components are the information values of the sentence-parts, with these information values combined as the sentence-parts are themselves combined to form the sentence.[6] In order to analyze the information encoded by a sentence into its components, one simply decomposes the sentence into its information-valued parts, and the information values thereof are the

---

to the presidency in 2000. Suppose I here and now utter the sentence

Actually, a Republican will be elected to the U.S. presidency in 2000 A.D.

In the actual world, I thereby assert a piece of information that is necessarily false. In W, on the other hand, I thereby assert a piece of information that is necessarily true. I utter the very same sequence of words of English, with the very same English meanings, in both possible worlds, yet I assert different things. If we were to use the term 'context' in such a way that the context of my utterance remains the same in both worlds, we would be forced to say, quite mysteriously, that the sentence I uttered is such that it would have encoded different information with respect to the context in which I uttered it if W had obtained even though both its meaning and its context of utterance would remain exactly the same. The information content of the sentence would emerge as a function not only of the meaning of the sentence and the context of utterance, but also of the apparently irrelevant question of which party wins the U.S. presidency in the year 2000. Using the term 'context' as I shall throughout this essay, we may say instead that, although I make the very same utterance both in W and in the actual world, the context of the utterance is different in the two worlds. This allows us to say that the sentence I utter takes on different information contents with respect to *different* contexts of utterance, thereby assimilating this phenomenon to the sort of context-sensitivity that is familiar in cases of such sentences as 'A Republican is presently U.S. president'.

[6] The latter clause is needed in order to distinguish 'Bill loves Mary' from 'Mary loves Bill', where the sequential order of composition is crucial. This succinct statement of the rule connecting sentences and their information contents is only an approximation to the truth. A complicated difficulty arises in connection with the latter clause of the rule and with such quantificational locutions as 'someone' in 'Someone is wise'. Grammatically the sentence 'Someone is wise' is analogous to 'Socrates is wise', though logically and semantically they are disanalogous. In 'Socrates is wise', the predicate 'is wise' attaches to the singular term 'Socrates'. This situation is reversed in 'Someone is wise', wherein the restricted quantifier 'someone' attaches to the predicate 'is wise'. Thus, whereas grammatically 'someone' is combined with 'is wise' to form the first sentence in just the same way that 'Socrates' is combined with 'is wise' to form the second sentence, the information values of 'someone' and 'is wise' are combined very differently from the way the information values of 'Socrates' and 'is wise' are combined.

A perhaps more important qualification to the general rule is noted in the next paragraph of the text. Yet another important qualification concerns overlaid quan-

components of the encoded information. In this way, declarative sentences not only encode but also codify information.

One may take it as a sort of general rule or principle that the information value of any compound expression, with respect to a given context of utterance, is made up of the information values, with respect to the given context, of the information-valued components of the compound. This general rule is subject to certain important qualifications, however, and must be construed more as a general guide or rule of thumb. Exceptions arise in connection with quotation marks and similar devices. The numeral '9' is, in an ordinary sense, a component part of the sentence 'The numeral '9' is a singular term', though the information value of the

---

tifiers. It is necessary to distinguish between the information contents of such constructions as:

(A) For everyone x there is someone y such that x loves y

and

(B) For everyone x there is someone y such that y loves x.

One method, due to Alonzo Church and pointed out to me by David Kaplan, employs Russellian propositional functions, i.e., functions from an individual to a singular proposition involving that individual. (Church himself applies the general method in such a way as to invoke only Fregean functions from pure concepts of individuals to Fregean purely general propositions, although the general method can also accommodate anti-Fregean theories by invoking propositional functions.) The information values of the quantifiers 'for everyone' and 'there is someone such that' are certain higher-order properties. (Specifically, they are properties of one-place functions from individuals to truth-values.) Let us designate them by 'Πone' and 'Σone', respectively. Then on this method, the information content of sentence (A) is regarded as having the structure of the following ordered pair:

$$\langle \lambda x \langle \lambda y \langle x,y, \text{ loving} \rangle, \Sigma \text{one} \rangle, \Pi \text{one} \rangle.$$

The information content of sentence (B), on the other hand, is regarded as having the following structure:

$$\langle \lambda x \langle \lambda y \langle y,x, \text{ loving} \rangle, \Sigma \text{one} \rangle, \Pi \text{one} \rangle.$$

(For complete accuracy, the relation of loving should be replaced throughout by the temporally indexed relation of *loving at t*, which may be identified with the ordered pair $\langle loving, t \rangle$—see section VIII below). The first element of the former proposition is the propositional function that assigns to each individual x the proposition made up of the propositional function that assigns to each individual y the proposition that x loves y and the second-order property Σone. The first element of the latter proposition is the appropriate analogue.

A variant of this method replaces these propositional functions with the properties of loving someone (at t) and of being loved by someone (at t), respectively. The information content of sentence (A) may be regarded as the following complex proposition: that the function that assigns truth to an individual x if x loves someone or other, and assigns falsehood otherwise, assigns truth to everyone whatsoever.

former is no part of the information content of the latter. I shall argue below that, in addition to quotation marks, there is another important though often neglected class of operators that yield exceptions to the general rule in something like the way quotation marks do. Still, it may be correctly said of any English sentence free of any operators other than truth-functional connectives (e.g., 'If Frege is clever, then so is Russell') that its information content is a complex made up of the information values of its information-valued components.

II. The Naive Theory

The naive theory is a theory of the information values of certain expressions. According to the naive theory, the information value of a singular term, as used in a possible context, is simply its referent in that context. This is similar to what Gilbert Ryle called the *'Fido'-Fido theory*, according to which the "meaning" or content of a singular term is simply its referent. Elements of this theory can be traced to ancient times. Likewise, the information value of a predicate, as used in a particular context, is identified with something like the semantically associated attribute with respect to that context, that is, with the corresponding property in the case of a monadic predicate or the corresponding n-ary relation in the case of an n-place predicate. On the naive theory, an atomic sentence consisting of an n-place predicate Π and n occurrences of singular terms, $\alpha_1, \alpha_2, \ldots, \alpha_n$, when evaluated with respect to a particular possible context, has as its cognitive content in that context a piece of information, called a *proposition*, which is supposed to be a

---

This powerful method need not assign any information value to an open sentence such as 'x loves y', except relative to an assignment of values to its free variables. Unlike some other possible proposals, it thus generates no counterexamples to a certain principle of compositionality (or interchange) for information value, commonly attributed to Frege, according to which the information value of a compound expression such as (A) or (B) is a function solely of the information values of its information-valued components. (See A. Church, "Intensional Isomorphism and Identity of Belief," *Philosophical Studies* 5 (1954): 65–73, for a similar but more sharply articulated principle.) However, the method does generate counterexamples to a stronger compositionality principle, also attributable to Frege, according to which the information value of a compound expression is a complex made up entirely of the information values of its information-valued components. If the first element of the information content of sentence (A) is the information value of any component of the sentence—for example, the component 'x there is someone y such that x loves y'—then the information value of that component is not made up of the information values of its information-valued components.

complex consisting of something like the attribute referred to by II with respect to that context and the sequence of objects referred to by the singular terms with respect to that context. For example, the cognitive information content of the sentence 'Frege is clever' is to be the singular proposition consisting of Frege and cleverness. On the naive theory, a sentence is a means for referring to its information content by specifying the components that make it up. A sentential connective may be construed on the model of a predicate. The information value of a connective would thus be an attribute (a property if monadic, a relation if polyadic)—not an attribute of individuals like Frege, but an attribute of pieces of information, or propositions. For example, the information value of the connective 'if and only if' might be identified with the binary equivalence relation between propositions having the same truth-value. Similarly, the information value of a quantifier might be identified with a property or properties of individuals. For example, the information value of the unrestricted universal quantifier 'everything' may be the (second-order) property of being a universal (first-order) property, i.e., the property of being a property possessed by every individual. The information value of a sentence, as used in a particular context, is simply its information content, the proposition made up of the information values of the information-valued sentence components.

Within the framework of the naive theory, the *meaning* of an expression might be identified with the expression's character, i.e., the semantically correlated function from possible contexts of utterance to information values. For example, the meaning of the sentence

(1)   I am busy

will be thought of as a function that assigns to any context of utterance c the singular proposition composed of the agent of the context c (= the referent of 'I' with respect to c) and the property of being busy.

III. The Singly Modified Naive Theory

The naive theory is, as its name suggests, a prototheory of information value. For all its naiveté, there is a great deal to be said in its favor. First and foremost, it is a natural and compelling result, perhaps *the* natural result, of a preliminary philosophical investigation into the nature and structure of information. Some of the great thinkers in the philosophy of language, among them Frege and Russell, came to the subject with an initial presupposition of some rudimentary form of the naive theory.

The theory yields a plausible rendering of the claim that the proposition that Frege is clever is information *about* or *concerning* Frege: The proposition is about Frege in the straightforward sense that Frege is an individual constituent of it. The naive theory extends easily to more complex sentential structures involving variables, connectives, quantifiers, and propositional operators. It gives substance to the oft-repeated slogan that to give (or to know) the semantic content (or "meaning," in the sense of information content) of a sentence or statement is to give (know) its truth-conditions. Its notion of information content is exemplary of the kind of notion of proposition that is needed in connection with questions of *de re* modality: If I utter the sentence 'Frege is clever', I assert something that is true if and only if the individual Frege has the property cleverness. Moreover, what I assert is such that it is true with respect to an arbitrary possible world w if and only if that same condition, the very individual Frege having cleverness, obtains in w. It is not enough, for instance, that someone in w who resembles or who represents the actual Frege in a certain way be clever in w, or that someone in w who fits a certain conceptual representation of the actual Frege be clever in w. It must be Frege, the very individual. The naive theory also yields a straightforward notion of *de re* belief, and other *de re* propositional attitudes: To believe p is to believe the proposition p. So to believe *of* or *about* Frege that *he* is clever is to believe the proposition *of* or *about* Frege that *he* is clever, that is, the piece of information consisting of Frege and cleverness. Indeed, these considerations concerning *de re* modality and *de re* propositional attitudes constitute important considerations favoring the naive theory over its principal rival, the orthodox Fregean theory, as well as over the theory of Russell.

Perhaps the most important thing to be said for the naive theory is that it has cogency and intuitive appeal as a theory of assertion. When I utter 'Frege is clever', my speech act divides into two parts: I single someone out (Frege), and I ascribe something to him (cleverness). These two component speech acts, singular reference and ascription, correspond to two components of *what I assert* when I assert that Frege is clever. My asserting that Frege is clever consists in my referring to Frege and my ascribing cleverness to him; so too, that Frege is clever (what I assert) consists of Frege (what I refer to) and cleverness (what I ascribe to him).

Compelling though it is, the naive theory has two fundamental flaws and must be modified if it is to yield a viable theory of information value. The first flaw is that the naive theory is in a certain sense internally inconsistent; the second concerns the eternalness of information. I shall consider each of these problems in turn.

The naive theory rests upon two central ideas. The first is the identification of the information value of a singular term with its referent, i.e., the 'Fido'-Fido theory. By analogy, the referent of a predicate, a connective, or a quantifier is identified with its information value: the semantically correlated attribute of individuals, of propositions, or of properties of individuals, respectively. The second major idea is that the information value of a sentence, as uttered on a particular occasion, is made up of the information values of its information-valued components. Unfortunately, these two ideas come into conflict in the case of definite descriptions. According to the naive theory, the information value of a definite description such as 'the individual who wrote "Thoughts" ' is simply its referent, Frege. Consequently, the sentence 'The individual who wrote "Thoughts" is clever' is alleged to encode the singular proposition about Frege that he is clever. But the definite description is a phrase that, like a sentence, has parts with identifiable information values—for example, the dyadic predicate 'wrote' and the singular term (article title) ' "Thoughts" ', as well as the monadic predicate 'wrote "Thoughts" '. These information-valued components of the definite description are, ipso facto, information-valued components of the containing sentence. If the information value (= information content) of a sentence is made up of the information values of its information-valued components, the information values of these description-components must also go in to make up part of the information that the author of "Thoughts" is clever. And if the information value of a sentence is something made up of the information values of its information-valued components, it stands to reason that the information value of a definite description, which is like a sentence at least in having information-valued components, should also be something made up of the information values of those components. Thus, instead of identifying the information value of 'the individual who wrote "Thoughts" ', as used on a particular occasion, with its referent, one should look instead for some complex entity made up partly of the relational property of having written "Thoughts" (which, in turn, is made up of the binary relation *having written* and the work "Thoughts") and partly of something else—something that serves as the information value of the definite-description operator 'the'. On this modification of the naive theory, the information that the author of "Thoughts" is clever is not the singular proposition about Frege that he is clever but a different piece of information, one that does not have Frege as a component and has in his place something involving the property of authorship of "Thoughts".

Let us call this corrected version of the original theory the *singly modified naive theory*. One extremely important wrinkle in the singly modified naive theory is that a definite description ⌜the ϕ⌝, in contrast with other sorts of singular terms, is seen as involving a bifurcation of semantic values taken on with respect to a context of utterance. On the one hand, there is the description's referent, which is the individual to which the description's constitutive monadic predicate (or open formula) ϕ applies if there is only one such individual and is nothing otherwise. On the other hand, there is the description's information value, which is a complex made up, in part, of the information value of the predicate (or formula) ϕ. By contrast, a proper name or other single-word singular term is seen as involving a collapse of semantic values: its information value with respect to a particular context is just its referent with respect to that context. From the point of view of the singly modified naive theory, the original naive theory errs by treating definite descriptions on the model of a proper name. Definite descriptions are not single words but phrases, and therefore have a richer semantic constitution.

On the singly modified naive theory, any expression other than a simple singular term is, at least in principle, capable of bifurcation of reference and information value. For example, though the information value of a sentence is its information content, sentences might be regarded as referring to something other than their information contents. The singly modified naive theory, as defined so far, is tacit on the question of the referents of expressions other than singular terms (sentences, predicates, connectives, quantifiers, and other operators). However, a familiar argument, due primarily to Alonzo Church and independently to Kurt Gödel, establishes that the closest theoretical analogue of singular-term reference for any expression is its extension.[7] Accordingly, the singly modified naive theory will be understood henceforth to include the thesis that any expression may be thought of as referring, with respect to a given context, time, and possible world, to its extension with

---

[7] See Alonzo Church, "Review of Carnap's *Introduction to Semantics*," *The Philosophical Review* 52 (1943): 298–304 at 299–301; and Kurt Gödel, "Russell's Mathematical Logic," in *The Philosophy of Bertrand Russell*, ed. P. A. Schilpp. The Library of Living Philosophers, Evanston, Illinois (New York: The Tudor Publishing Company, 1944), at 128–29. The general argument is applied to the special case of monadic predicates in my *Frege's Puzzle*, at 22–23, and in greater detail to the special case of common nouns in my *Reference and Essence* (Princeton: Princeton University Press, and Oxford: Basil Blackwell, 1981), at 48–52.

respect to that context, time, and possible world.

IV. Propositions and Proposition Matrices

Kaplan's theory of demonstratives and indexicals is a version of the singly modified naive theory. Although this theory eliminates the inconsistency built into the original naive theory, it retains a second defect of the original theory. This defect is illustrated by the following example: Suppose that at some time $t*$ in 1890 Frege utters sentence (1) (or its German equivalent). Consider the piece of information, or proposition, that Frege asserts in uttering this sentence. This is the information content of the sentence with respect to the context of Frege's uttering it. Let us call this proposition '$p*$' and the context in which Frege asserts it '$c*$'. We may suppose that the piece of information $p*$ is made up of the information value of the indexical term 'I' with respect to $c*$ and the information value of the predicate 'be busy' with respect to $c*$. According to the naive theory, these information values are Frege and the property of being busy, respectively, so $p*$—the information value (= information content) of the whole sentence with respect to $c*$—is a complex abstract entity made up of Frege and the property of being busy, something like the ordered couple ⟨Frege, being busy⟩. Let us call this complex 'Frege being busy', or 'fb' for short. Thus, according to the naive theory, $p* = fb$. But this cannot be correct. If fb is thought of as having truth-value, then it is true if *and when* Frege is busy (if and when Frege has the property of being busy) and false if and when he is not busy. Thus, fb vacillated in truth-value over time, becoming true whenever Frege became busy and false whenever he ceased being busy. (This forces a misconstrual of the intension of sentence (1) with respect to Frege's context $c*$ as a two-place function which assigns to the ordered pair of both a possible world w and a time t a truth-value, either truth or falsehood, according as Frege is busy in w at t or not.) But $p*$, being a piece of information, has in any possible world in which Frege exists a fixed and unchanging truth-value throughout Frege's entire lifetime, and never takes on the opposite truth-value outside his lifetime. In this sense pieces of information are *eternal*.

Not just some; all information is eternal. The eternalness of information is central and fundamental to the very idea of a piece of information, and is part and parcel of a philosophically entrenched conception of information content. For example, Frege, identifying the cognitive information content (*Erkenntniswerte*) of a sentence with what he called the 'thought' (*Gedanke*) expressed by the sentence, wrote:

> Now is a thought changeable or is it timeless? The thought
> we express by the Pythagorean Theorem is surely timeless,
> eternal, unvarying. "But are there not thoughts which are
> true today but false in six months' time? The thought, for
> example, that the tree there is covered with green leaves,
> will surely be false in six months' time." No, for it is not the
> same thought at all. The words 'This tree is covered with
> green leaves' are not sufficient by themselves to constitute the
> expression of thought, for the time of utterance is involved
> as well. Without the time-specification thus given we have
> not a complete thought, i.e., we have no thought at all. Only
> a sentence with the time-specification filled out, a sentence
> complete in every respect, expresses a thought. But this
> thought, if it is true, is true not only today or tomorrow but
> timelessly.[8]

The same sort of consideration is used by Richard Cartwright to
show that the meaning of a present-tensed sentence is not its information content when uttered with assertive intent, or what is asserted by
someone who utters the sentence. Cartwright's argument exploits the
further fact that the truth-value of a piece of information is constant
over space as well as time:

> Consider, for this purpose, the words 'It's raining'. These
> are words, in the uttering of which, people often (though
> not always) assert something. But of course *what* is asserted
> varies from one occasion of their utterance to another. A
> person who utters them one day does not (normally) make
> the same statement as one who utters them the next; and
> one who utters them in Oberlin does not usually assert what
> is asserted by one who utters them in Detroit. But these
> variations in what is asserted are *not* accompanied by corre-
> sponding changes in meaning. The words 'It's raining' retain
> the same meaning throughout ... [One] who utters [these
> words] speaks correctly only if he [talks about] the weather
> at the time of his utterance and in his (more or less) imme-
> diate vicinity. It is this general fact about what the words

[8] G. Frege, "Thoughts," in *Logical Investigations*, ed. P. T. Geach (New Haven:
Yale University Press, 1977), 1–30, at 27–28.

mean which makes it possible for distinct utterances of them to vary as to statement made ... They are used, without any alteration in meaning, to assert now one thing, now another.[9]

Similar remarks by G. E. Moore make essentially the same point about information expressed using the past tense:

As a general rule, whenever we use a past tense to express a proposition, the fact that we use it is a sign that the proposition expressed is *about* the time at which we use it; so that if I say twice over "Caesar was murdered," the proposition which I express on each occasion is a different one—the first being a proposition with regard to the earlier of the two times at which I use the words, to the effect that Caesar was murdered before *that* time, and the second a proposition with regard to the latter of the two, to the effect that he was murdered before *that* time. So much seems to me hardly open to question.[10]

Consider again Frege's "thought" that a particular tree is covered with green leaves. Six months from now, when the tree in question is no longer covered with green leaves, the sentence

(2)   This tree is covered with green leaves

uttered with reference to the tree in question, will express the information that the tree is *then* covered with green leaves. This will be misinformation; it will be false. But that information is false even now. What is true now is the information that the tree *is* covered with green leaves, i.e., the information that the tree is *now* covered with green leaves. This is the information that one would currently express by uttering sentence (2). It is eternally true, or at least true throughout the entire lifetime of the tree and never false. There is no piece of information concerning the tree's foliage that is true now but will be false in six months. Similarly, if the information $p*$ that Frege asserts at $t*$ is true, it is eternally true, or at least true throughout Frege's lifetime and never false. There is no noneternal piece of information concerning Frege that vacillates in truth-value as he shifts from being busy to not being busy.

---

[9] R. Cartwright, "Propositions," in *Analytical Philosophy*, ed. R. Butler, first series (Oxford: Basil Blackwell, 1966), 81–103, at 92–94.

[10] G. E. Moore, "Facts and Propositions," in his *Philosophical Papers* (New York: Collier Books, 1962), 60–88, at 71.

The complex fb is noneternal, neutral with respect to time; hence, it is not a complete piece of information, i.e., it is no piece of information at all, properly so-called.

This is not to say that the noneternal complex fb is not a semantic value of the sentence Frege utters, or that fb has nothing to do with information content. Indeed, fb is directly obtained from the sentence Frege utters in the context $c*$ by taking the individual associated with 'I' with respect to $c*$ and the property associated with 'be busy' with respect to $c*$. Moreover, fb can be converted into something more like a piece of information simply by *eternalizing* it, i.e., by infusing a particular time (moment or interval) t into the complex to get a new abstract entity consisting of Frege, the property of being busy, and the particular time t. One may think of the noneternal complex fb as the matrix of the proposition $p*$ that Frege asserts in $c*$. Each time he utters sentence (1) Frege asserts a different proposition, expresses a different "thought," but always one having the same matrix fb. Similarly, in some cases it may be necessary to incorporate a location as well as a time in order to obtain a genuine proposition, e.g., 'It is raining' or 'It is noon'. A proposition or piece of information does not have differing truth-values at different locations in the universe, any more than it has different truth-values at different times. A proposition is fixed, eternal, and unvarying in truth-value over both time and space.

It has been noted by William and Martha Kneale, and more recently and in more detail by Mark Richard, that this traditional conception of cognitive information content is reflected in our ordinary ascriptions of belief and other propositional attitudes.[11] As Richard points out, if what is asserted or believed were something temporally neutral or noneternal, then from the conjunction,

> In 1971 Mary believed that Nixon was president, and today she still believes that

it would be legitimate to infer

> Today, Mary believes that Nixon is president.

Such an inference is an insult not only to Mary but also to the logic of English, as it is ordinarily spoken. Rather, what we may infer is

---

[11] See William Kneale and Martha Kneale, "Propositions and Time," in *G. E. Moore: Essays in Retrospect*, ed. A. Ambrose and M. Lazerowitz (New York: Humanities Press, 1970), at 235; Mark Richard, "Temporalism and Eternalism," *Philosophical Studies* 39 (1981): 1–13.

Today, Mary believes that Nixon was president in 1971.

The reason for this is that what Mary is said by the first sentence to have believed in 1971 is not the noneternal proposition matrix Nixon being president but the eternal proposition that Nixon is president (at such-and-such time) in 1971. The point is bolstered if 'know' is substituted for 'believe'.[12]

To each proposition matrix there corresponds a particular property of times—or, where necessary, a binary relation between times and places. For example, the time property corresponding to the proposition matrix fb is the property of being a time at which Frege is busy. It is often helpful in considering the role of proposition matrices in the semantics of sentences to think of a proposition matrix as if it were its corresponding property of times (or its corresponding relation between times and places).

V. Information Value and Information-Value Base

Let us call the proposition matrix that a sentence like (1) takes on with respect to a particular context c the *information-content base*, or more simply, the *content base*, of the sentence with respect to c. More generally, we may speak of the *information-value base*, or more simply the *value base*, with respect to a context, of a singular term, a predicate, a connective, a quantifier, etc. The value base of an expression is the entity that the expression contributes to the proposition matrix taken on by (i.e., the content base of) typical sentences containing the expression (where a "typical" sentence containing an expression does not include occurrences of such devices as quotation marks or the 'that'-operator other than those already included in the expression itself).

On the modification of the naive theory described above, the value base of a proper name, a demonstrative, or some other single-word singular term, with respect to a particular possible context c, would simply be the referent of the term with respect to c. The value base of a simple

---

[12]The length of the time interval is a vague matter. For many purposes it may be taken to be the entire year of 1971. It should be noted that when the time interval involved in a proposition is significantly long, the proposition may mimic its noneternal matrix—for example, in contexts like 'Mary once believed that Nixon was a Republican, and she still believes that'—as long as one stays within the boundaries of the time interval in question. Relatively stable properties (such as being a Republican, as opposed to being U.S. president) tend to lengthen the time interval in question. This is similar to a point made by Kneale and Kneale, "Propositions and Time," at 232–33.

predicate, such as 'busy' (i.e., 'be busy') or 'taller than', with respect to a context c, is the attribute—property or relation—semantically associated with the predicate with respect to c, e.g., the property of being busy or the relation of being taller than. The value base of a compound expression with respect to a context c is (typically) a complex made up of the value bases of the simple parts of the compound expression with respect to c, so the value base of a sentence is just its content base. In keeping with the singly modified naive theory, the value base of a definite description, unlike that of a single-word singular term, is not simply its referent but is a complex made up partly of the property associated with the description's constitutive predicate.

Since ordinary language includes indexical expressions such as 'this tree', the value base of an expression is to be indexed to the context of utterance. This generates a new higher-level nonrelativized semantic value for an expression, on the same level as character, which is the function or rule that determines for any possible context c the value base the expression takes on with respect to c. Let us call this new semantic value the *program* of an expression. An indexical expression is precisely one that takes on different value bases with respect to different possible contexts—that is, the expression's program is not a constant function; its value base varies with the context.

The value base of an expression with respect to a context c determines a corresponding function that assigns to any time t (and location l, if necessary), an appropriate information value for the expression. (In fact, the function also determines the corresponding value base.) For example, the proposition matrix fb, which is the content base of 'Frege is busy' with respect to any context, determines a function that assigns to any time t the information about Frege that he is busy at t. (This is the propositional function corresponding to the property of being a time at which Frege is busy.) Let us call the function from times (and locations) to information values thus determined by the value base of an expression with respect to a given context c the *schedule* of the expression with respect to c. In the special case of a single-word singular term, its schedule with respect to any context is always a constant function; however, this need not be true for other sorts of expressions, e.g., sentences. Since the information value of an expression determines its semantic intension, the value base of an expression with respect to a context c also determines a corresponding function that assigns to any time t (and location l, if necessary) the resulting intension for the expression. Let us call this function from times (and locations) to intensions the *superintension* of the expression with respect to *c*. Accordingly, we should speak of the information value, and the corresponding intension, of an expression *with respect to a context c and a time t (and a location l, if necessary)*.

We should also like to speak, as we already have, of the information value of an expression (e.g., the information content of a sentence) with respect to a context *simpliciter*, without having to speak of the information value with respect to both a context *and a time (and a location)*. This is implicit in the notion of the character of an expression, as defined earlier. How do we get from the value base of an expression with respect to a given context to the information value with respect to the same context *simpliciter* without further indexing, or relativization, to a time (and location)?

In the passage quoted above, Frege seems to suggest that the words making up a tensed but otherwise temporally unmodified sentence, by themselves, and even the words taken together with contextual factors that secure information values for indexical expressions such as 'this tree', at most yield only something like what we are calling a 'proposition matrix', i.e., the content base of the sentence with respect to the context of utterance, which is "not a complete thought, i.e., ... no thought at all." He suggests further that we must rely on the very time of the context of utterance to provide a "time-specification" or "time-indication"—presumably a specification or indication of the very time itself—which supplements the words to eternalize their content base, thereby yielding a genuine piece of cognitive information, or "thought." Earlier in the same article, Frege writes:

> [It often happens that] the mere wording, which can be made permanent by writing or the gramophone, does not suffice for the expression of the thought. The present tense is [typically] used ...in order to indicate a time .... If a time-indication is conveyed by the present tense one must know when the sentence was uttered in order to grasp the thought correctly. Therefore the time of utterance is part of the expression of the thought.[13]

On Frege's view, strictly speaking, the sequence of words making up a tensed but otherwise temporally unmodified sentence like (2), even together with a contextual indication of which tree is intended, does not

---

[13] G. Frege, "Thoughts," in *Logical Investigations*, 10.

have cognitive information content. Its information value is incomplete. Presumably, on Frege's view, the sequence of words together with a contextual indication of which tree is intended has the logico-semantic status of a predicate true of certain times—something like the predicate

is a time at which this tree is covered with green leaves,

accompanied by a pointing to the tree in question—except that (2) thus accompanied may be completed by a time, serving as a specification or indication of itself, rather than by a syntactic singular term such as 'now'. Accordingly, on Frege's theory, the information value, or "sense" (*Sinn*), of (2) together with an indication of the intended tree but in isolation from any time would be a function whose values are pieces of cognitive information, or "thoughts" (*Gedanken*).[14] Only the sequence of words making up the sentence *together with* an indication of which

---

[14] On Frege's theory, the domain of this function would consist of senses that determine times, rather than the times themselves.

There is on Frege's theory no reason why the time-indication or time-specification that supplements the incomplete present-tensed sentence could not be verbal, e.g., 'At 12:00 noon on 4 July 1983, this tree is covered with green leaves'. This aspect of Frege's theory allows for a solution to the problem of failure of substitutivity of coreferential singular terms in temporal contexts—a solution very different from Frege's solution to the parallel problem of failure of substitutivity in propositional-attitude contexts. Consider the following example. The expressions 'the U.S. president' and 'Ronald Reagan' refer to the same individual with respect to the time of my writing these words, but the former cannot be substituted *salva veritate* for the latter in the true sentence 'In 1978, Ronald Reagan was a Republican'. Substitution yields 'In 1978, the U.S. president was a Republican', which is false on the relevant reading (the Russellian secondary occurrence or small-scope reading), since in 1978 Jimmy Carter was president and a Democrat. Frege may solve this problem, not implausibly, by noting that the expression 'the U.S. president' is incomplete and requires supplementation by a time-specification, such as may be provided by the time of utterance, before it can refer to an individual. The description 'the U.S. president', supplemented by the time of my writing these words, refers to the same individual as the name 'Ronald Reagan'. Supplemented by the year 1978, or by a verbal specification thereof, it refers to Jimmy Carter. The sentence 'In 1978, the U.S. president was a Republican' includes a verbal time-specification, 'in 1978', which, we may assume, supersedes the time of utterance in completing any expression occurring within its scope in need of completion by a time-specification. This solution is dissimilar from Frege's treatment of substitutivity failure in propositional-attitude contexts. On Frege's theory, a propositional-attitude operator such as 'Jones believes that' creates an oblique context in which expressions refer to their customary information values ("senses") instead of their customary referents. On the Fregean solution to substitutivity failure in temporal contexts presented here, the referent of 'the U.S. president', as occurring within the context 'in 1978, _____', is just its customary referent.

tree is intended and a time-indication or time-specification, as may be provided by the time of utterance itself, is "a sentence complete in every respect" and has cognitive information content.

Now, it is not necessary to view the situation by Frege's lights. Whereas Frege may prefer to speak of the cognitive thought content (or *Erkenntniswerte*) of the words *supplemented by* both a contextual indication of which tree is intended and a "time-indication," one may speak instead (as I already have) of the information content of the sequence of words themselves *with respect to* a context of utterance and a time. The information content of sentence (2) with respect to a context c and a time t is simply the result of applying the schedule, with respect to c, of the sequence of words to t. This is the singular proposition about the tree contextually indicated in c that it is covered with green leaves at t. In the general case, instead of speaking of the information value of an expression supplemented by both a contextual indication of the referents of the demonstratives or other indexicals contained therein and a "time-indication," as may be provided by the time of utterance, one may speak of the information value of the expression *with respect to* a context of utterance and a time (and a location, if necessary). Still, Frege's conception strongly suggests a way of constructing a singly indexed notion of the information value of an expression with respect to (or supplemented by) a context of utterance c *simpliciter*—without further relativization to (or supplementation by) a time (and a location)—in terms of the doubly (or triply) indexed locution: The information value of an expression with respect to a context c (*simpliciter*) is definable as the information value of the expression with respect to both c and the very time of c (and the very location of c, if necessary).

In particular, then, the information content of a sentence with respect to a given context of utterance c is its information content with respect to c and the time of c (and the location of c, if necessary). Consequently, any temporally unmodified sentence or clause encodes different information with respect to different contexts of utterance (*simpliciter*). For example, sentence (2) (or more accurately, the untensed clause 'this tree be covered with green leaves'), encodes different information with respect to different times of utterance, even when pointing to the same tree. Uttered now, it encodes the information about the tree in question that it is covered with green leaves, i.e., that it is now covered with green leaves. Uttered six months from now, it encodes the information about the tree that it is then covered with green leaves. The existence of this linguistic phenomenon is precisely the point made by Frege and echoed by Moore and Cartwright in the passages quoted in section IV above.

Let us call this latest version of the naive theory the *doubly modified naive theory*, abbreviated as simply the *modified naive theory*. The doubly modified naive theory is the singly modified naive theory modified further to accommodate the eternalness of information value.

It follows from our definition of the singly indexed notion of the information value of an expression with respect to a context *simpliciter* that the program of an expression fully determines the expression's character, since, given any context c, the program fully determines the resulting schedule, which together with the time (and location, if necessary) of c fully determines the resulting information value. From this it follows that the program of an expression also determines the expression's contour, as defined earlier. Within the framework of the modified naive theory, the meaning of an expression is better identified with its program, rather than with its character. This allows one to distinguish pairs of expressions like 'the U.S. president' and 'the present U.S. president' as having different meanings, despite their sharing the same character (or at least trivially equivalent characters). More accurately, the program of an expression is the primary component of what is ordinarily called the 'meaning' of the expression, though an expression's meaning may have additional components that supplement the program.[15]

The original and the singly modified naive theories recognize three distinct levels of semantic value. The three primary semantic values are *extension*, *information value* (misconstrued as possibly noneternal), and *character*. In addition, these theories admit two subordinate semantic values. On the same level as, and fully determined by, information value is *intension* (misconstrued as a two-place function from possible worlds and times); on the same level as, and fully determined by, character is *contour*. The various semantic values on the original or the singly modified naive theory, and their levels and interrelations, are diagrammed in figure 1. (Of course, these are not the only semantic values available on the naive theory, but they are the important ones.)

---

[15] For example, the meaning of the term 'table' might include, in addition to its program, some sort of conceptual content, e.g., a specification of the function of a table. If so, it does not follow that this sort of conceptual entity is any part of the information value of the term. Nor does it follow that it is *analytic*, in something like the classical sense, that tables have such-and-such a function. What does follow is that, in order to know fully the meaning of 'table', one would have to know that the things called 'tables' are conventionally believed to have such-and-such a function.

Figure 1: Semantic Values on the
Naive Theory

Top Level:	*character* + context c	$\longrightarrow$	*contour* + context c
	$\downarrow$		
Middle Level:	*information value* with respect to c	$\rightarrow$ *intension* with respect to c + possible world w and time t	$\downarrow$
		$\downarrow$	
Bottom Level:		*extension* with respect to c, w, and t	*extension* with respect to c ($=$ *extension* with respect to c, the possible world of c, and the time of c)

The modified naive theory's notion of the value base of an expression with respect to a given context, and the resulting notion of the program of an expression, impose a fourth level of semantic value, intermediate between the level occupied by Kaplan's notion of the character of an expression and the level of information value. In fact, the introduction of the notion of value base reduces character to the status of a subordinate semantic value. The four primary semantic values, from the bottom up, are *extension*, *information value* (construed now as necessarily eternal), *information value base*, and *program*. In addition, there are a number of subordinate semantic values. Besides intension (construed now as a one-place function from possible worlds), character, and contour, there are *schedule* and *superintension*, both of which are on the same level as, and fully determined by, value base. The various semantic values on this modification of the original naive theory, and their levels and interrelations, are diagrammed in figure 2. (Notice that figure 1 is virtually embedded within figure 2, as its right half.)

Figure 2: Semantic Values on the Modified Naive Theory

	program + context c		*character* + context c		*contour* + context c
	→		→		→
Top Level (Level 4):	program + context c				
Level 3:	information value base with respect to c ↔ schedule with respect to c + time t → superintension with respect to c + time t	↓			
Level 2:	information value with respect to c and t → intension with respect to c and t + possible world w ↓		information value value with respect to c (= information value with respect to c and the time of c) → intension with respect to c (= intension with respect to c and the time of c) + possible world w ↓			↓
Bottom Level:	extension with respect to c, t, and w		extension with respect to c and w (= extension with respect to c, the time of c, and w)		extension with respect to c (= extension with respect to c, the time of c, and the possible world of c)

On the modified naive theory, the extension of an expression with respect to a given context of utterance (*simpliciter*, without further relativization to a time, a place, or a possible world) is the result of applying the intension of the expression with respect to that context—which, in turn, is the result of applying the superintension of the expression with respect to that context to the very time of the context—to the very possible world of the context. Thus, for example, the referent of a singular term—say 'the U.S. president's actual wife'—with respect to a particular context of utterance c is semantically determined in a sequence of steps. First, the program of the expression is extracted from its meaning. This program is then applied to the context c to yield the time-neutral value base of the expression with respect to c. This value base yields the schedule of the expression with respect to c, which assigns to any time t the information value of the expression with respect to both c and t. This schedule is applied to the very time of c itself to give the eternal information value of the expression with respect to c (*simpliciter*). This information value, in turn, yields the expression's intension with respect to c, which assigns to any possible world w the extension of the expression with respect to c and w. The expression's extension with respect to any context c' and possible world w' is the individual who is the wife in the possible world of c' at the time of c' of the individual who is the U.S. president in w' at the time of c'. Finally, this intension is applied to the very possible world of c itself to yield the individual who is the wife in the possible world of c at the time of c of the individual who is the U.S. president in the possible world of c at the time of c. Eureka!

VI. Tense vs. Indexicality

It may appear that I have been spinning out semantic values in excess of what is needed. We needed a singly indexed notion of the information value of an expression with respect to a context, and as a special case, a notion of the information content of a sentence with respect to a context. This led to the original and singly modified naive theories' identification of meaning with character. In the special case of a single-word singular term, what I am calling its value base with respect to a context c is the very same thing as its information value with respect to c, so the program of a single-word singular term is just its character. The only thing that prevents this from holding also for a sentence such as (1) or (2) is that its content base with respect to a context is neutral with respect to time, whereas its information content with respect to the same context is eternal, somehow incorporating the time (and location, if necessary) of the context. It may seem, then, that in the case of a sentence or phrase, what I am calling its 'value base' with respect to a context c is just its information value with respect to c but for the deletion of the time of c (and the location of c), so that the information content of a sentence with respect to a context c is made up of the information values (= value bases) with respect to c of its simple information-valued parts *plus* the time (and location) of c.

If the rule of information-content composition is that information contents are constructed from the information values of the simple information-valued components *together with* the time (and location, if necessary) of utterance, then why bother mentioning those partially constructed pieces of information I have been calling 'proposition matrices'? Singling out content bases as separate semantic values generates the doubly indexed notion of the information content of a sentence with respect to both a context c and a time t, and thereby the nonrelativized higher-level notion of program. What is the point of this doubly indexed notion, and of the resulting notion of program? Are we not interested only in the case where the time t is the time of the context of utterance c (and where the location l is the location of the context c)? Why separate out the time as an independent semantic parameter that may vary independently of the context of utterance? The character of a sentence seems to be meaning enough for the sentence. Semantic theorists heretofore have gotten along fine by indexing the notion of information content once, and only once, to the context of utterance, without relativizing further and independently to times.

For example, in discussing the phenomenon of tense, Frege considers also various indexicals—'today', 'yesterday', 'here', 'there', and 'I'— and suggests a uniform treatment for sentences involving either tense or indexicals:

> In all such cases the mere wording, as it can be preserved in writing, is not the complete expression of the thought; the knowledge of certain conditions accompanying the utterance, which are used as a means of expressing the thought, is needed for us to grasp the thought correctly. Pointing the finger, hand gestures, glances may belong here too.[16]

---

[16] G. Frege, "Thoughts," in *Logical Investigations*, 10–11.

Following Frege, it would seem that we can handle the phenomena of tense and indexicality together in one fell swoop, with tense as a special case of indexicality, by simply relativizing the notion of information value once and for all to the complete context of utterance—including the time and location of the utterance as well as the speaker and his or her accompanying pointings, hand gestures, and glances. Any aspect of the complete context of utterance may conceivably form "part of the expression of the thought," or contribute to the information content. Once information content is relativized to the complete context, including the time of utterance, gestures, and so on, there seems to be no need to relativize further and independently to times.

It has become well known since the middle of the 1970s that the phenomenon of tense cannot be fully assimilated to temporal indexicality, and that the presence of indexical temporal operators necessitates "double indexing," i.e., relativization of the extensions of expressions— the reference of a singular term, the truth-value of a sentence, the class of application of a predicate (or better, the semantic characteristic function of a predicate), etc.—to utterance times independently of the relativization to times already required by the presence of tense or other temporal operators.[17] (Something similar is true in the presence of an indexical modal operator such as 'it is actually the case that' and in the presence of indexical locational operators such as 'it is the case here that'.) Here is an illustration: The present-perfect-tense operator functions in such a way that for any untensed clause S (e.g., 'Frege be busy'), the result of applying the present-perfect-tense operator to S ('Frege has been busy') is true with respect to a time t (roughly) if and only if S is true with respect to some time t' earlier than t. Similarly, the nonindexical operator 'on the next day' + future tense functions in such a way that the result of applying this operator to any untensed clause S is true with respect to a time t if and only if S is true with respect to the day next after the day of t. For example, suppose that at time $t*$, instead of uttering sentence (1), Frege speaks the following words (perhaps as part of a larger utterance):

I will be busy on the next day.

---

[17]The need for double indexing was apparently first noted in 1967 by Hans Kamp in unpublished material distributed to a graduate seminar while Kamp was a graduate student at UCLA. See his "Formal Properties of 'Now'," *Theoria* (1972): 227–73. Kamp's results were reported in A. N. Prior, "'Now'," *Noûs* 2 (1968): 101–19.

This sentence, in Frege's mouth, is true with respect to a time t if and only if Frege is busy on the day next after the day of t—whether or not t is $t*$, and hence even if it is not. Indeed, our primary interest may be in some time t other than $t*$, for example, if Frege's complete utterance at $t*$ is of the sentence

On 24 December 1891 I will be busy on the next day.

On the other hand, the indexical operator 'tomorrow' + future tense functions in such a way that the result of applying it to any untensed clause S is true with respect to a context c and a time t if and only if S is true with respect to c and the day after the day of the time of c, forgetting about the time t altogether. If at $t*$ Frege had uttered the sentence

I will be busy tomorrow

the sentence, in Frege's mouth, would be true with respect to a time t if and only if Frege is busy on the day after the day of $t*$.

Were we to attempt to accommodate 'on the next day' + future tense using relativization only to possible contexts of utterance, without further relativization to times, we would be forced to say that the result of applying this operator to S is true with respect to a context c if and only if S is true with respect to some possible context c' just like c in every respect, e.g., agent, location, etc., except that the time of c' is a day later than that of c. For example, 'I will be busy on the next day' would be regarded as being true with respect to a context of utterance c if and only if its untensed operand

(3)   I be busy

is true with respect to a possible context c' whose day is the day after that of c, but which involves the same agent as c, to preserve the referent of 'I'. Let us assume, for the time being, that an untensed clause such as (3) is a mere surface grammar variation of its present-tensed counterpart, so that (3) and (1) share the very same semantics.

This singly indexed account seems to yield the correct results, until we consider sentences that embed one temporal operator within the scope of another. Consider the following sentence:

(4)   It used to be that the present U.S. president was a Democrat.

This sentence results from applying the temporal operator 'it used to be that' + past tense to the untensed indexical clause

the present U.S. president be a Democrat

in which the phrase 'present U.S. president' resulted from applying the indexical temporal operator 'present' to the phrase 'U.S. president'. According to the singly relativized account, sentence (4) is true with respect to a context of utterance c (roughly) if and only if there is some time t' earlier than the time of c such that the U.S. president at t' is a Democrat at t' (in the possible world of c). But this is the wrong truth-condition for the sentence. In fact, it is the correct truth-condition for the wrong sentence, to wit, the *nonindexical* sentence

(5)   It used to be that: the U.S. president was a Democrat

or more idiomatically,

The U.S. president has been a Democrat

on one of its readings (the Russellian secondary occurrence or small-scope reading). Sentences (4) and (5) differ in their truth-conditions; if both sentences are uttered at a time when the person occupying the presidency is a life-long Republican, though previously the presidency had been held by the Democrats, sentence (4) is false whereas sentence (5) is true. Sentence (4) is true with respect to a context of utterance c (roughly) if and only if there is some time t' earlier than the time of the context c such that the U.S. president *at the time of the context of utterance c*—rather than at t'—is a Democrat *at t'* (in the possible world of c), rather than at the time of c. The temporal operator 'it used to be that ' + past tense directs us to evaluate its operand clause 'the present U.S. president be a Democrat' with respect to times t' earlier than that of the context of utterance c. This clause is true with respect to the same context c and a time t' earlier than that of c if and only if the description 'the present U.S. president' refers with respect to c and t' to something to which the predicate (naked infinitive) 'be a Democrat' applies with respect to c and t'. In computing the referent of the description with respect to c and t', the indexical operator 'present' directs us to seek an object to which its operand phrase 'U.S. president' applies with respect to the very time of the context of utterance c itself, forgetting about the time t'. Thus in evaluating sentence (4) with respect to a time of utterance t (the time of its context of utterance c), we are concerned simultaneously with the extension of 'U.S. president' with respect to t and the extension of 'be a Democrat' with respect to some time t' earlier than t. The truth-value of the whole depends entirely and solely on whether the unique object to which the phrase 'U.S. president' applies with respect to t is something to which the predicate 'be a Democrat' applies with respect to an earlier time t'. It is for this reason that a systematic theory of the extensions of the expressions of a language containing indexical temporal operators requires double indexing, i.e., in general the notion of the extension of an expression (e.g., the truth-value of a sentence) is relativized to both a context and a time, treated as independent semantic parameters. The notion of the extension of an expression with respect to a context c *simpliciter* is then definable as the extension of the expression with respect to the context c and the time of c (and the possible world of c, and if necessary, the location of c).

A systematic singly indexed theory gives the wrong results. Frege's theory, for example, must regard the indexical description 'the present U.S. president' as extensionally semantically equivalent to the nonindexical 'the U.S. president'. Both would be regarded as expressions that are incomplete by themselves (and hence, refer by themselves, in abstraction from any context, to functions), but that when completed by a "time-specification" or "time-indication" (as may be provided by the time of utterance) refer to the individual who is U.S. president at the specified or indicated time. Using extensional semantic considerations alone, Frege's theory is unable to find any difference with respect to truth or even with respect to truth-conditions between sentence (4), taken as uttered at a certain time, and the tensed but nonindexical (5), as uttered at the very same time.[18]

This example illustrates that where an indexical temporal operator

---

[18] This is partly a result of Frege's principle of compositionality (or interchange) for reference. (See footnote 6.) On Frege's theory of tense and indexicality, both 'the U.S. president' and 'the present U.S. president' refer, in abstraction from context, to the function that assigns to any time t the individual who is U.S. president at t—as if they were the functor 'the U.S. president at time _____,—except that the expression may be completed by a time rather than by a verbal time-specification (the time of utterance acting as a self-referential singular term). By Frege's compositionality principle for reference, it follows that any complete sentence built from 'the U.S. president' without using oblique devices (e.g., 'In 1978, the U.S. president was a Democrat'), has the same truth-conditions, and therefore the same truth-value, as the corresponding sentence built from 'the present U.S. president' ('In 1978, the present U.S. president was a Democrat'). See footnote 14.

occurs within the scope of another temporal operator within a single sentence, the extensions of expressions are to be indexed to both the time of utterance and to a second time parameter, which may be other than the time of utterance and other even than a function of the time of utterance. Temporal operators determine which time or times the extension of their operands are determined with respect to. In the special case of indexical temporal operators, the time so determined is a function of the time of the context of utterance. What is distinctive about indexical expressions (such as 'I', 'this tree', or 'the present U.S. president') is not merely that the extension with respect to a context c (*simpliciter*) varies with the context c, or even that the intension or information value with respect to a context c (*simpliciter*) varies with the context c. That much may be true of even a nonindexical expression, such as 'the U.S. president' or 'Frege is busy'. What makes an expression indexical is that its extension with respect to a context c and a time t and a location l and a possible world w varies with the context c, even if the other parameters are held fixed. This is to say that its superintension, and hence its value base, with respect to a context c varies with the context c. It is precisely this that separates 'the present U.S. president' from its nonindexical counterpart 'the U.S. president'.

Though it is less often noted,[19] it is equally important that double indexing to contexts and times (or triple indexing to contexts, times, and locations, if necessary) is required at the level of information value (e.g., with information content) as well as at the level of extension (e.g., with truth-value). For illustration, consider first the sentence,

(6)   At $t*$, I believed that Frege was busy.

By the ordinary laws of temporal semantics, this sentence is true with respect to a context of utterance c if and only if the sentence

I believe that Frege is busy

is true with respect to both c and the time $t*$. This, in turn, is so if and only if the binary predicate 'believe' applies with respect to c and $t*$ to the ordered pair of the referent of 'I' with respect to c and $t*$ and the referent of the 'that'-clause

that Frege is busy

---

[19] See Mark Richard, "Tense, Propositions, and Meanings," *Philosophical Studies* 41 (1982): 337–51, at 346–49. The idea of double-indexing information content to both contexts and times is Richard's.

with respect to c and $t*$. Hence, sentence (6) is true with respect to c if and only if the agent of c believes at $t*$ the piece of information that is the referent of the 'that'-clause with respect to c and $t*$.

What piece of information does the 'that'-clause in (6) refer to with respect to c and $t*$? Obviously, the 'that'-clause refers to the information content of its operand sentence 'Frege is busy', but which proposition is that?

If information content is to be singly indexed to context alone, it would seem that the 'that'-clause 'that Frege is busy' refers with respect to c and $t*$ to the information content of 'Frege is busy' (or of 'Frege be busy') *with respect to c* (forgetting about $t*$ altogether). This is the proposition that Frege is busy at t, where t is the time of c. However, this yields the wrong truth-condition for sentence (6). This would be the correct truth-condition for the sentence

At $t*$, I believed that Frege would be busy now.

Sentence (6) ascribes, with respect to c, a belief at $t*$ that Frege is busy *at $t*$*. Assuming that information content is singly indexed to context alone, we are apparently forced to construe the 'that'-operator in such a way that a 'that'-clause $\ulcorner$that $S\urcorner$ refers with respect to a context c and a time t' not to the information content of S with respect to c but to the information content of S with respect to a (typically different) context c' exactly like c in every aspect (agent, location, etc.) except that its time is t'. (The contexts c and c' would be the same if and only if t' were the time of c.) This yields the desired result that the displayed sentence is true if and only if the agent of c believes at $t*$ the information that Frege is busy at $t*$.

This account appears to yield exactly the right results until we consider a sentence that embeds an indexical temporal operator within the 'that'-operator, and embeds the result within another temporal operator. Consider the following:

(7)   In 1989, Jones will believe: that the present U.S. president is the best of all the former U.S. presidents.

This sentence is true with respect to a context c if and only if Jones believes in 1989 the piece of information referred to by the 'that'-clause

that the present U.S. president is the best of all the former U.S. presidents with respect to c and the year 1989. On the singly indexed account of information content, sentence (7) comes out true if and only if Jones believes in 1989 that the U.S. president in 1989 is the best of all the U.S. presidents before 1989. But this is the wrong truth-condition for sentence (7). It is the right truth-condition for the wrong sentence:

> In 1989, Jones will believe: that the then U.S. president is the best of all the former U.S. presidents.

Sentence (7) ascribes, with respect to c, a belief that the U.S. president at t (the time of c) is the best of all the U.S. presidents before 1989. In order to obtain this result, the 'that'-clause in (7) must be taken as referring with respect to c and the year 1989 to the proposition that the U.S. president at t is the best of all the U.S. presidents prior to 1989 (or to some proposition trivially equivalent to this). This cannot be accommodated by a singly indexed account; it requires seeing information content as doubly indexed: to the original context c (so that the ascribed belief concerns the U.S. president at t rather than in 1989) and the year 1989 (so that the ascribed belief concerns the class of presidents before 1989 rather than those before t).

VII. Temporal Operators

The example just considered illustrates the need for the double indexing of information content that is generated by the modified naive theory's notion of the content base of a sentence. In addition to this, there is an important semantic function for the content base of a sentence, a function that cannot be fulfilled by its information content. To see this, it is important to look more closely at the semantics of temporal operators.

Consider the temporal operator 'sometimes' + present tense, which attaches to an untensed clause S to form a new sentence. An appropriate extension for this operator would be a function from some aspect of the operand clause S to a truth-value. What aspect of S?

Two sorts of operators are very familiar to philosophers of language. An *extensional* operator is one that operates on the extensions of its operands, in the sense that an appropriate extension for the operator itself would be a function from *extensions* appropriate to the operands (as opposed to some other aspect of the operands) to extensions appropriate to the compounds formed by attaching the operator to an appropriate operand. An extensional sentential connective (such as 'not' or 'if ... , then - - -') is truth-functional; an appropriate extension would be a function from (n-tuples of) truth-values to truth-values, and hence an appropriate information value would be an attribute (property or relation) of truth-values—for example, the property of being falsehood, or the following relation: either u is falsehood or v is truth. An *intensional* or *modal* operator is one that operates on the intensions of its operands. An appropriate extension for a modal connective like 'it is necessarily the case that' or 'if it were the case that ..., then it would be the case that - - -' would be a function from (n-tuples of) sentence intensions (functions from possible worlds to truth-values) or propositions to truth-values, and an appropriate information value would be an attribute of intensions or propositions—for example, the property of being a necessary truth.

Now, is the 'sometimes' operator extensional? Certainly not. With respect to my actual present context, the sentences 'It is cloudy' and '$2 + 2 = 5$' are equally false, though 'Sometimes it is cloudy' is true whereas 'Sometimes $2 + 2 = 5$' is false. Thus, 'sometimes' + present tense is not truth-functional, and hence not extensional. Nor is the 'sometimes' operator intensional, in the above sense. With respect to my actual present context, the two sentences

> The senior senator from California is a Republican

and

> The present senior senator from California is a Republican

have precisely the same intension—indeed, they have (very nearly) the same information content—though

(8)   Sometimes the senior senator from California is a Republican

on the relevant reading (the Russellian secondary occurrence or small-scope reading), is true whereas

(9)   Sometimes the present senior senator from California is a Republican

on either of its two readings (Russellian small-scope vs. large-scope), is false. Thus, 'sometimes' + present tense is neither an extensional operator nor an intensional or information-content operator. What, then, is it?

Let us try the following theory: suppose that 'sometimes' + present tense operates on the contour of its operand clause, its function from contexts of utterance to truth-values. The result of applying this operator to an untensed clause S would be true with respect to a context c if and only if there is some context c' that coincides exactly with c in every aspect (agent, location, etc.) other than time and such that S is true with respect to c'. Thus, for example, on this theory the sentence,

(10)   Sometimes this tree is covered with green leaves

is true with respect to a context of utterance c if and only if there is some time, which may be other than the time of the context c, at which the tree indicated in c is covered with green leaves. Similarly, the sentence

(11)   Sometimes I am busy

is true with respect to Frege's context $c*$ if and only if there is some time at which Frege is busy. Sentence (10) would be regarded as encoding, with respect to a context c, the information about the contour of the untensed operand clause

this tree be covered with green leaves

that it yields the value truth for some context or other (not necessarily c) which includes the same contextual indication of a tree as c (e.g., the same agent pointing to the same tree in the same way, to preserve the referent of 'this tree') and the same possible world as c but which may have a different time from c. Similarly, sentence (11) would be regarded as encoding with respect to a context c the information about the contour of its untensed operand clause (3) that it yields the value truth for some context or other which includes the same agent and the same possible world as c, but which may have a different time from c. On this theory, then, the information value of 'sometimes' + present tense varies with the context of utterance. Its information value with respect to a context c is always a property of functions from contexts to truth-values, to wit, the property of yielding the value truth for some context or other that coincides exactly with c in every aspect other than time. In general, on this theory, all temporal operators—such as 'present', 'sometimes' + past tense, 'today' + present tense, 'yesterday' + past tense, 'in 1989' + future tense, and various tense operators such as present perfect tense—operate on the contours of their operands, so that the extension of a sentential temporal operator is a function from sentence contours to truth-values, and its information value is a property of sentence contours.

Here again, this theory seems to yield exactly the correct results until we embed an indexical temporal operator within the scope of another temporal operator. Consider again the sentence:

(9) Sometimes the present senior senator from California is a Republican.

Here the indexical operator 'present' is embedded within the operator 'sometimes' + present tense. According to the theory under consideration, sentence (9) contains with respect to a context of utterance c the information about the contour of the operand clause

the present senior senator from California be a Republican

that it yields the value truth for some context or other exactly like c in every aspect other than time. Thus, according to the theory, sentence (9) is true with respect to a context c if and only if there is some time t', which need not be the time of c, such that the senior senator from California at t' is a Republican at t' (in the possible world of c). This is the wrong truth-condition for sentence (9), and the correct truth-condition for the nonindexical sentence

(8) Sometimes the senior senator from California is a Republican

on one of its readings (the Russellian secondary occurrence or small-scope reading). Sentence (9) is true with respect to a context c if and only if there is some time t' such that the senior senator from California *at the time of the context c*—rather than at t'—is a Republican at t' (in the possible world of c)—rather than at the time of c.

In fact, the theory that a temporal operator such as 'sometimes' + present tense is a contour operator is simply the singly indexed theory all over again. In order to obtain the correct results, one must regard a sentential temporal operator such as 'sometimes' + present tense as operating on some aspect of its operand clause that is fixed relative to a context of utterance (in order to give a correct treatment of such temporally modified indexical sentences as (9)) but whose truth-value typically varies with respect to time (so that it makes sense to say that it is *sometimes* true, or true at such-and-such time). On the original and singly modified naive theories' three-tiered array of semantic values (as diagrammed in the right half of figure 2 in section V above), once it is acknowledged that information content is eternal, there simply is no such semantic value of a sentence. Nothing that is fixed relative to a context is also time-sensitive in the required way. In order to find an appropriate semantic value for temporal operators such as 'sometimes' + present tense to operate on, one must posit a level of semantic value intermediate between character and information content. This strongly suggests that the objects of sentential temporal operators—the things operated on by sentential temporal operators such as 'sometimes' + present tense—are something like proposition matrices, or perhaps sentence superintensions. The 'sometimes' operator is neither an extensional operator nor an intensional (i.e., modal) operator, nor is it even a contour operator. Instead, 'sometimes' + present tense is a superintensional operator.[20] That is, an appropriate extension for 'sometimes' + present tense with respect to a context c, a time t, and a possible world w, would be a function from the superintension (or, equivalently, from the schedule or content base) of its operand clause (with respect to c) to a truth-value—namely, the function that assigns truth to a proposition matrix (or to its corresponding schedule or superintension) if its value for at least one time (the resulting proposition or sentence intension) itself yields truth for the world w, and which otherwise assigns falsehood to the proposition matrix (or the corresponding schedule or

---

[20] Modal operators on the so-called branching worlds (or "unpreventability") interpretation emerge as superintensional operators.

The burden of Richard's article cited in the previous footnote is to show that one can consistently hold that propositions are eternal while temporal sentential operators operate on noneternal semantic values of sentences, by holding that temporal sentential operators operate on two-place functions from contexts and times to eternal propositions. These two-place functions are similar to (and determined by) sentence programs. Indeed Richard calls his two-place functions the 'meanings' of sentences. However, the claim that temporal operators operate on the "meanings" of expressions is misleading. When each of Richard's two-place functions is replaced by its corresponding one-place function from contexts to one-place functions from times to eternal propositions—i.e., the corresponding function from contexts to schedules—it emerges that temporal operators operate on something at the level of schedule rather than operating on something at the level of program.

Richard also apparently misconstrues to some extent what Kaplan (and others) mean in saying that an operator "operates on" such-and-such's. In general, to say that a given operator operates on the such-and-such of its operand is to say that an appropriate extension for the operator would be a function from such-and-such's appropriate to expressions that may serve as its operand to extensions appropriate to the compounds formed from the operator together with the operand. For example, to say that a modal sentential operator operates on the information content or on the intension of its operand sentence (the correlated function from possible worlds to truth-values) is to say that an appropriate extension for a modal operator would be a function from propositions or from sentence intensions to truth-values (that is, to the appropriate extensions for sentences).

superintension). In general, temporal operators—such as 'sometimes', tense operators (including complex ones such as present perfect and future perfect), indexical temporal operators (e.g., 'present'), and even nonindexical specific time indicators (e.g., 'on 24 December 1989' + future tense or 'when Frege wrote "Thoughts" ' + past tense)—may all be seen as superintensional operators.

The result of applying 'sometimes' + present tense to an untensed clause S may be regarded as encoding, with respect to a given context c, information concerning the content base of the operand clause S with respect to c. For example, sentence (11) contains, with respect to Frege's context $c*$ (or any other context in which Frege is the agent), the information about the proposition matrix fb that it is sometimes true. Accordingly, an appropriate information value for a temporal operator such as 'sometimes' + present tense would be a property of proposition matrices—in this case, the property of being true at some time(s).

It is in this way that temporal operators such as 'sometimes' + present tense provide a place for proposition matrices in temporal semantics, and thereby generate a doubly indexed notion of the information value of an expression (e.g., the information content of (1) or (2)) with respect to both a context c and a time t that may be other than the time of c. Just as it is the information content of its operand that a modal operator says something about (e.g., that it is a necessary truth), so it is the information content base of its operand that a temporal operator says something about.

VIII. Predicates and Quantifiers

An important point about predicates, quantifiers, and certain other operators emerges from the four-tiered modified naive theory, and from the distinction between information value and value base in particular: The value base of a predicate such as 'be busy', with respect to a given context of utterance c, is an attribute, i.e., a property or relation. This, together with a time t, determines the information value of the predicate with respect to c and t. In turn, the information value of a predicate with respect to c and t, together with a possible world w, determines the extension of the predicate with respect to c, t, and w. It follows that the information value of a predicate such as 'be busy' with respect to a context c and a time t is not just the property of being busy (or anything similar, such as the function that assigns to any individual x the proposition matrix, x being busy). The property of being busy together with a possible world w cannot determine the extension of 'be busy' with respect to both the world w and the time t. The property of being busy together with a possible world w determines only the class of (possible) individuals who are busy *at some time* in w, or, at most, the function that assigns to any time t the class of (possible) individuals who are busy at t in w. The information value of 'be busy' with respect to a given time t must be such as to determine for any possible world w the class of (possible) individuals who are busy *at the given time* t in w. Only some sort of complex consisting of the property of being busy *together with the given time* t is such as to determine for any possible world w the extension of 'be busy' with respect to both w and t. Thus, the information value of 'be busy' with respect to a given time t is not merely the property of being busy but a complex consisting of this property and the time t. This, it may be assumed, is a *temporally indexed attribute*—in this case, the temporally indexed property of *being busy at* t.

In general, the information value of a predicate with respect to a time t (and a location l, if necessary) is not the same attribute as the value base of the predicate but is the temporally (and, if necessary, spatially) indexed attribute that results from taking the value base of the predicate together with the time t (and location l, if necessary). Exactly analogous remarks apply to quantifiers, other second-order predicates, the definite-description operator 'the', and certain other operators.

This heretofore unrecognized fact about the information values of predicates allows us to retain, at least as a sort of general guide or rule of thumb, the principle that the information value of a compound expression, such as a sentence or phrase, is a complex made up solely and entirely of the information values of the information-valued components that make up the compound. In particular, the information content of sentence (1), or of clause (3), with respect to a context of utterance c may be thought of as made up of the agent of the context c and the property of being busy at t, where t is the time of c. There is no need to introduce the time t as a third and separate component; it is already built into the information value of the predicate.

Since the information value of an expression with respect to a context c *simpliciter* is the information value with respect to both c and the time of c (and the location of c, if necessary), it follows that the information value of a typical predicate with respect to a context c *simpliciter* varies with the context c—whether or not the predicate is indexical (such as one possible reading of 'current', as in 'current journal issue'), and hence even if it is not, such as 'be busy'. It is this previously unnoticed feature of predicates that accounts for the fact that a nonindexical temporally unmodified clause, e.g., 'Frege be busy', or the sentence 'Frege is busy', takes on not only different truth-values but also different information contents when uttered at different times, even though the expression is not indexical. It is also this feature of predicates that accounts for the fact that certain noneternal (i.e., temporally nonrigid) definite descriptions, such as 'the senior senator from California', take on not only different referents but also different information values when uttered at different times, though the description is not indexical. Recall that the distinctive feature of an indexical like 'I' or 'the present senior senator from California' is that it takes on different information-value bases in different contexts. The predicate 'be busy', the definite description 'the senior senator from California', and the sentence 'The senior senator from California is busy' all retain the same value base in all contexts. Their information value varies with the context, but not their value base.

The account presented here of the information values of temporal operators as properties of proposition matrices (or other value bases) makes for an important but usually unrecognized class of exceptions to the general principle that the information value of a compound expression is made up of the information values of its information-valued components. Where T is a monadic temporal sentential operator, e.g., 'sometimes' + present tense or 'on 4 July 1968' + past tense, the information content of the result of applying T to a clause S, with respect to a context c, is made up of the information value of T with respect to c together with the information-content *base* of S with respect to c, rather than the information content of S itself. In general, if T is a temporal operator, the information value with respect to a context c of the result of applying T to an expression is a complex made up of the information value of T with respect to c and the value base, rather than the information value, of the operand expression with respect to c. Ordinarily, the information value of an expression containing as a part the result of applying a temporal operator T to an operand expression is made up, in part, of the value base of the operand expression rather than its information value. (For complete accuracy, the notion of information value with respect to a context, a time, and a location, for a language L should be defined recursively over the complexity of expressions of L.)[21]

---

[21] The value base of the result of attaching an information content operator (such as 'necessarily' or the 'that'-operator) to a sentence is a complex made up of the value base of the operator and the content base of the sentence, rather than its

IX. Information-Value Base vs. Kaplan's Content

The notion of value base, and the attendant notion of program, are analogous in certain respects to the notion of information value and Kaplan's notion of character, respectively. In particular, the notion of value base is highly reminiscent of Kaplan's use of what he calls the 'content' of an expression in his seminal work on the logic and semantics of indexicals, *Demonstratives*. In fact, I came upon the notions of program and value base in musing over Kaplan's distinction between character and what he calls 'content', and over the work of Mark Richard on the relations between sentence meanings, tense operators, and propositions. (See footnotes 18 and 19 above.) In order to avoid confusion with my use of the term 'content' in the phrase 'information content', I shall use the expression 'kontent' as a term for Kaplan's notion. That is, I shall use the word 'kontent' as a general term for all and only those things that fit Kaplan's notion of what he calls a 'content', and I shall use the phrase 'kontent of' as a term for the semantic binary many-one relation (or the semantic one-place function) between anything that fits Kaplan's notion of what he calls the 'content of' an expression and the expression itself. Thus, the kontent of an expression with respect to a given context is the thing that fits Kaplan's notion of what he calls the 'content' of the expression in that context.

Kaplan defines[22] the kontent of a sentence, in a given context, to be *what is said* in uttering the sentence in the given context, adding that the kontent of a sentence "is what has traditionally been called a proposition," and that Frege used the word 'thought' (*Gedanke*) for the kontent of a sentence. Kaplan also claims that a modal operator, such as 'it is necessary that' or 'it is possible that', operates on the kontent of its

---

information content. Thus, for example, the value base of the 'that'-clause 'that Frege is busy' with respect to any context c does not involve the information content of 'Frege is busy' with respect to c, which is the proposition that Frege is busy at t, where t is the time of c. Instead, it is something like the ordered pair of two elements: (1) A certain abstract entity, analogous to a property, which is the operation of assigning any proposition to itself (this operation—call it 'O_p'— is the value base of the 'that'-operator with respect to any context); and (2) the proposition matrix fb. Thus the value base of 'that Frege is busy' has the following structure: $\langle O_p, \langle \text{Frege, being busy} \rangle \rangle$. The information content of 'Sometimes Frege believes that he is busy' has the following structure, where 'Σtimes' designates the property of proposition matrices of being true at some time(s):

$$\langle\langle \text{Frege}, O_p, \langle \text{Frege, being busy} \rangle, \text{believing} \rangle, \Sigma\text{times} \rangle.$$

For further details see appendix C of my *Frege's Puzzle*, op. cit.

[22] *Demonstratives*, this volume, 500–501.

operand sentence. On the basis of Kaplan's definition, together with his accompanying remarks, it would seem that the kontent of a sentence is indeed simply its information content, the piece of information asserted by someone who utters the sentence, and in general, that the kontent of an expression, in a given context, is just its information value, with respect to that context. But Kaplan goes on to claim[23] that temporal operators and modal operators alike operate on kontents. He adds that if sentence kontents were eternalized by the infusion of particular times,

> thus ... making [kontents] *specific* as to time ..., it would make no sense to have temporal operators. To put the point another way, if *what is said* is thought of as incorporating reference to a specific time ..., it is otiose to ask whether what is said would have been true at another time .... Temporal operators applied to ... sentences [whose kontents] incorporate a specific time ... are redundant.

Kaplan elaborates in a footnote to the passage containing these remarks:

> Thus we think of the temporally neutral 'proposition' [i.e., sentence kontent] as changing its truth-value over time. Note that it is not just the noneternal sentence ... that changes its truth-value over time, but the 'proposition' itself .... An alternative (and more traditional) view is to say that the verb tense in [a tensed sentence] S involves an implicit temporal indexical, so that S is understood as synonymous with [⌜It is now the case that S⌝] .... Technically, we must note that [temporal] operators must, if they are not to be vacuous, operate on [kontents] which are neutral with respect to [time]. Thus, for example, if we take the [kontent of a sentence] to be [an eternal, time-specific proposition rather than a noneternal, temporally neutral proposition matrix], the application of a temporal operator to such a [kontent] would have no effect; the operator would be vacuous.[24]

Continuing this line of thought in the text, he writes:

> This functional notion of the [kontent] of a sentence in a context may not, because of the neutrality of [kontent] with

---

[23] Ibid., 503.
[24] Ibid., 503–4, footnote 28.

respect to time and place, say, exactly correspond to the classical conception of a proposition. But the classical conception can be introduced by adding the demonstratives 'now' and 'here' to the sentence and taking the [kontent] of the result.[25]

Claiming that the temporal sentential operators operate on sentence kontents, and having already defined the kontent of a sentence as the information asserted by someone who utters the sentence, or *what is said*, Kaplan is forced to construe the information content of a sentence—what is said—as something that may take on different truth-values with respect to different times, and in some cases even with respect to different places. But we saw in section IV above that this is incorrect. As Frege, Moore, and Cartwright correctly pointed out—and as Kaplan seems to acknowledge—propositions do not vacillate in truth-value over time or space. Moreover, as Kneale and Kneale and Richard point out, *what is said* in uttering a sentence is similarly eternal, temporally and spatially fixed. This is precisely because what is asserted in uttering a sentence is a piece of information, an eternal proposition. The truths truthsayers say and the sooths soothsayers soothsay—these all are propositions fixed, eternal, and unvarying. Eternal are the things asserters assert, the things believers believe, the things dreamers dream. Eternal also are the principles we defend, the doctrines we abhor, the things we doubt, the things we cannot doubt. The truths that are necessarily true and those that are not, the falsehoods that are necessarily false and those that are not—these are one and all eternal propositions.

It does not follow, as Kaplan argues, that temporal sentential operators become redundant or vacuous, so that it makes no sense to have them. It is true that a temporal sentential operator, if it is not to be vacuous, must operate on some aspect of its operand sentence that yields different truth-values with respect to different times—something that is time-neutral or noneternal. What follows from this is that, contrary to Kaplan, temporal operators do not operate on information contents. In fact, we have already established this much in section VII above with the two sentences

The senior senator from California is a Republican

and

The present senior senator from California is a Republican

---
[25] Ibid., 504.

which, if uttered simultaneously, yield the same (or at least trivially equivalent and very nearly the same) information content, but whose temporal existential generalizations (sentences (8) and (9), respectively), if uttered at the time of my writing these words, yield very different information contents and even different truth-values. Since they are not generally vacuous or redundant, temporal operators must operate on some aspect of their operands other than the information content, something other than *what is said* in uttering the operand. What we have already seen is that temporal operators are superintensional operators. The extension of a sentential temporal operator is a function from proposition matrices or from sentence superintensions (i.e., from functions from times to eternal propositions) to truth-values, and its information value may be thought of as a property of proposition matrices or of sentence superintensions.

Kaplan's notion of what he calls the 'content' of an expression is in fact a confused amalgamation of the information content and the information-content base. On the one hand, Kaplan defines the kontent of sentence (1) with respect to Frege's context $c*$ to be *what is said* by Frege in $c*$, the information he asserts. This is the eternal singular proposition $p*$ about Frege that he is busy at $t*$. It is precisely this proposition $p*$ that is said to be possible (possibly true) in 'It is possible that Frege is busy', when uttered at $t*$. On the other hand, the kontent is also supposed to be something that is noneternal and neutral with respect to time; it is supposed to be that which is said to be sometimes the case in 'Sometimes Frege is busy'. This is the content base, the proposition matrix fb. But fb is not $p*$; it is only the matrix of $p*$. Kaplan mistakenly assumes at the outset—and indeed explicitly asserts (without argument)—that both modal and temporal operators operate on the very same semantic value of their operand sentences. This semantic value is what kontents are supposed to be. In fact, Kaplan's intended notion would have been better captured by defining the kontent of a sentence S to be what is operated on by both a modal operator, as in ⌜It is possible that S⌝, and a temporal operator as in ⌜Sometimes S⌝.

Kaplan is aware of the tension between his notion of what he calls 'content' and the eternalness of information, and he attempts to accommodate the "traditional" or "classical" conception of a proposition by identifying the traditional proposition expressed, with respect to a given context, by a sentence such as (1) with the kontent of the result of inserting 'now' in an appropriate position—that is, with the content base of

(12) I am busy now

with respect to the same context. This clever proposal exploits the fact that the content bases of temporally modified sentences are eternal and time-specific rather than noneternal and time-neutral. But it also obscures the equally important fact that what is said by Frege in uttering (1) at $t*$ is the eternal proposition $p*$, and not just its matrix fb— a fact that Kaplan fails to recognize. He comes tantalizingly close to recognizing this latter fact when he shows (p. 500) that what is said in uttering a temporally indexical sentence such as (12) at different times is different. His argument for this is that if such a sentence is uttered by me today and by you tomorrow, then

> [if] what we say differs in truth-value, that is enough to show that we say different things. But even if the truth-values were the same, it is clear that there are possible circumstances in which what I said would be true but what you said would be false. Thus we say different things.

This is indeed correct. But the same argument could equally be made for a nonindexical tensed sentence. Thus it is not surprising to find the following analogous argument given earlier by G. E. Moore:

> It seems at first sight obvious that, if you have a number of judgements [i.e., utterances] with the same content, if one is true the rest must be.

> But if you take a set of judgements [i.e., utterances] with regard to a given event A, [using words to the effect] either that it is happening, or that it is past, or that it is future, some of each set will be true and some false, which are true and which false depending on the time when the judgement [i.e., utterance] is made.

> It seems a sufficient answer to say that a judgement [i.e., an utterance of a sentence of the form] "A is happening" made at one time never has the same content as the judgement [i.e., an utterance of the sentence] "A is happening" made at another.[26]

---

[26] G. E. Moore, "The Present," Notebook II [c. 1926], in *The Commonplace Book 1919–53*, ed. C. Lewy (New York: The Macmillan Company, 1962), 89.

Consider the sentence 'Frege is busy'. Mimicking Kaplan, and following Moore, one may argue that if it is uttered at $t*$ and again on the next day, and if what are said on the two occasions of utterance differ in truth-value (across time), as indeed they may, that is enough to show that different things are said. This is precisely because it is known in advance that what is asserted is not the sort of thing that can switch in truth-value from one moment to the next. Of course, the very same content base is expressed with respect to the two occasions. Since what is said or asserted on the one occasion is different from what is said or asserted on the other, it is not the content base that is said or asserted.

Once it is acknowledged that the information contents of sentences—what is said or asserted—are eternal propositions rather than proposition matrices, it emerges that a simple proposal to identify the traditional proposition expressed by a sentence S with the content base of the result of attaching the 'now'-operator to S is inadequate. This proposal delivers the wrong result, for example, with a sentence such as (6) or the following:

> Although I cannot claim to be wealthy today, in ten years I
> will be able to assert truly (the proposition, as traditionally
> conceived) that I am wealthy.

Kaplan's proposal delivers only the singly indexed notion of the ("traditionally conceived") proposition expressed by 'I am wealthy' with respect to a context c. As we have seen (sections VI and VII), what is needed in order to deal adequately with this construction is a more general, doubly indexed notion of the information content of 'I am wealthy' with respect to both a context c and a time t that may be other than the time of c.

In general, the kontent of an expression is a confused amalgamation of the information value and the value base. Kaplan's notion of what he calls the 'character' of an expression is defined and understood in terms of his notion of what he calls 'content'—roughly, as a function from contexts to kontents. Consequently, the former is correspondingly a confused amalgamation of program and what I am calling 'character'. I have chosen to follow Kaplan's explicit definition of the kontent of a sentence as the thing asserted, or *what is said*, in defining character as a function or rule that assigns information values, rather than value bases, to contexts—although one would be equally justified in using Kaplan's term 'character' for what I am calling the 'program' of an expression. If the truth be told, there simply is nothing that is the kontent of sentence (1) with respect to a context c, for nothing is both *what is said* (the proposition asserted) in uttering (1) in c, and also what is said to be sometimes the case in sentence (11) (the proposition matrix). Likewise, nothing is the *karacter* of sentence (1); that is, there is nothing that exactly fits Kaplan's notion of what he calls the 'character' of (1).

It is instructive to look at how the four-tiered modified naive theory treats a simple, untensed clause, such as (3) as well as various complex sentences built from it. The program of (3) is given by the following rule:

> For any context c, the value base of (3) with respect to c is the proposition matrix *A being busy*, where A is the agent of c. This proposition matrix is made up of A (the value base of 'I' with respect to c) and the property of being busy (the value base of 'be busy' with respect to c).

The schedule of (3) with respect to a given context c is thus given by the following rule, where A is the agent of c:

> For any time t, the information value of (3) with respect to c and t is the singular proposition about A that he or she is busy at t, which is made up of A (the result of applying the schedule of 'I' to t) and the property of being busy at t (the result of applying the schedule of 'be busy' to t).

The information value of (3) with respect to a context c *simpliciter* is therefore the singular proposition about the agent of c that he or she is busy at t, where t is the time of c itself.

We may contrast this with the indexical sentence (12). Its program is given by a rule something like the following:

> For any context c, the content base of (12) with respect to c is the higher-order singular proposition made up of the following two things, where A is the agent of c and t is the time of c: (i) the proposition matrix *A being busy* (the value base of (3) with respect to c); and (ii) the property of proposition matrices of obtaining (or being true) at t (the value base of 'now' + present tense with respect to c).

This rule reveals the fact, exploited by Kaplan, that the content base of the eternal sentence (12) is in fact already a full-fledged, eternal proposition, rather than a noneternal proposition matrix. The schedule of (12) with respect to a context c is thus a constant function from times to the higher-order proposition about the proposition matrix A *being busy* that it obtains at t. The information content of (12) with respect to a context c *simpliciter* is this same higher-order singular proposition, whereas the information value of the simpler (3) with respect to c is the singular proposition about A that he or she is busy at t. Now, obviously, A is busy at t if and only if A *being busy* obtains at t. Consequently, the information values of (3) and (12) with respect to any context of utterance are trivially equivalent. If we assume that sentence (1) is merely a surface transformation of (3), then *what is said* by uttering either (1) or (12) at the same time is very nearly the same, as long as the speaker is the same. Still, the content bases are very different. With respect to any context c, the content base of (1) is noneternal, neutral with respect to time, whereas the content base of (12) is eternal. As Kaplan notes, only the former can be felicitously operated upon by temporal operators.

Contrary to Kaplan, since the information contents, *what is said*, are trivially equivalent, the function of 'now' cannot be primarily to affect what is said in context. Its effect on information content is in fact negligible, virtually nil. Rather, the function of 'now' is primarily to affect the content base of its operand, eternalizing it and thereby sealing it off from the influence of external occurrences of temporal operators. For example, applying the 'sometimes' operator to sentence (1), whose content base with respect to any context is noneternal, aptly yields sentence (11), whose content base is eternal. By contrast, 'sometimes' is at best superfluous in

Sometimes I am busy now.

Compare also the role of the 'present' in sentences (4) and (9).

Analogously, the schedule of such a sentence as

I will be busy tomorrow

as uttered by someone A at time t, is the constant function that assigns to any time t', the eternal proposition about the proposition matrix A *being busy* that it obtains on d^+, where d^+ is the day after the day of t. The schedule of the sentence

I will be busy on the next day

with respect to the same context, on the other hand, is a nonconstant function that assigns to any time t', the proposition about A *being busy* that it obtains on the day next after d', where d' is the day of t'. The information contents of the two sentences with respect to any context (*what are said*) are very similar, though the schedules are very different, and only the latter sentence may be felicitously operated upon by temporal operators. Consider: 'On 24 December 1989 I will be busy on the next day' vs. 'On 24 December 1989 I will be busy tomorrow'.

X. Pure Tenses

A considerably richer semantic theory of temporal operators may be obtained by drawing a three-way distinction among *quantificational* or *general* temporal operators, *specific* or *singular* temporal operators, and *pure tense* operators such as simple past or future tense. Quantificational or general temporal operators include such operators as 'sometimes', 'always', present perfect tense (as in 'I have been busy' in the sense of 'I have sometimes been busy'), 'it will always be that' + present tense, and 'twice before' + past tense, etc. Specific or singular temporal operators include 'it is now the case that', 'on 24 December 1989' + future tense, 'when Frege wrote "Thoughts" ' + past tense, etc. (Compare: 'possibly' vs. 'actually'.) The difference between these two sorts of temporal operators lies in their accompanying semantics. Very roughly, a specific sentential temporal operator T is one such that there is some specific time t semantically associated with T, with respect to a context (and a time and a possible world), in such way that the result of applying T to a sentence S is true with respect to a time t' if and only if S is true with respect to t, and t stands in some appropriate temporal-order relation to t'. For example 'On 24 December 1989 I will be busy' is true with respect to a context c and the year 1983 if and only if both of the following conditions obtain: (i) clause (3) (or sentence (1)) is true with respect to c and 24 December 1989, and (ii) 1989 is later than 1983. A general sentential temporal operator T is a nonspecific temporal operator such that there is some specific property P of classes of times semantically associated with T (with respect to semantic parameters) in such a way that the result of applying T to a sentence S is true with respect to a time t' if and only if the class of times with respect to which S is true and which stand in some appropriate temporal-order relation to t' has P. For example, in the case of the present perfect tense, the property P is that of being nonempty, and the appropriate temporal-order relation is the earlier-than relation.[27]

Consider now ordinary past or future tense, as in

Frege was busy

or 'Frege will be busy'. Past tense is sometimes treated by philosophers as though it were a quantificational temporal operator, so that the displayed sentence is regarded as being true with respect to a time t if and only if 'Frege be busy' (or 'Frege is busy') is true with respect to some time t' earlier than t. (See, for example, the quote from G. E. Moore in section IV above.) While a simple past-tensed sentence might sometimes be used in this way (roughly, as equivalent to the corresponding present-perfect-tensed sentence), it generally is not. Ordinarily, when a simple past-tensed sentence such as 'Frege was busy' is used, it is used with implicit reference to a specific (though perhaps vaguely delineated) time, so that if Frege was not busy at the relevant time, then what is said is false even if Frege was busy at some time or other prior to the utterance. Consider: 'I asked Frege to come along, but he was busy' vs. 'I have sometimes asked Frege to come along, but he has sometimes been busy'. Analogous remarks apply to future tense.

Moreover, most simple temporal operators other than tense operators seem to require, in idiomatic English, an appropriate adjustment in the tense of the operand. For example, if I wished to apply the temporal operator 'at 3:00 P.M. on 4 December 1983' to sentence (1), at the time of my writing these words—which happens to be 2:55 P.M. on 4 December 1983—I should use the sentence

At 3:00 P.M. on 4 December 1983 I will be busy.

---

[27] These explications of the notions of specific and general temporal operators cannot be regarded as strict definitions, and are intended only to convey a general idea. The operator 'when Frege wrote "Thoughts"' + past tense is to count as a specific temporal operator even if it should turn out that Frege did not write "Thoughts." Also, given a sufficiently liberal notion of a property of a class, some precaution must be taken if a specific temporal operator is to be precluded from being a general temporal operator. It may be appropriate to define a general temporal operator as a *nonspecific* temporal operator of a certain sort. (A similar difficulty is encountered in defining ordinary quantifiers in such a way as to preclude ordinary singular terms.) More importantly, the explications provided here are appropriate for what I shall call 'complete' temporal operators below, although the terminology of 'specific' or 'singular' and 'quantificational' or 'general' temporal operators will be used also for the components of these which I shall call 'incomplete' temporal operators below, e.g., 'when Frege wrote "Thoughts"' *without* an accompanying tense operator. These various notions can be made precise, though it is preferable to leave them at an intuitive, informal level in motivating the account under consideration here.

That is, in addition to affixing the operator, I would shift from present to future tense. If I waited six minutes and forever thereafter, I must instead use the sentence

At 3:00 P.M. on 4 December 1983 I was busy.

These adjustments in tense seem to be required, although the content base of each sentence is eternal, and the same proposition (or at least trivially equivalent, and very nearly the same, propositions) would be asserted at each time. It is as if it is insufficient merely to indicate the particular time; one must also indicate the temporal direction of the indicated time—either earlier or later—relative to the time of utterance. The simple specific temporal operator 'at 3:00 P.M. on 4 December 1983' is, in a sense, an *incomplete* temporal operator; it applies to a tensed but otherwise temporally unmodified sentence such as 'I will be busy' to form a new sentence. Indeed, one might also regard simple past tense (or simple future tense) as another sort of incomplete temporal operator, one that modifies an untensed, temporally unmodified clause such as (3) to form a sentence that may now be modified by an incomplete specific or incomplete general temporal operator. It is as if the tense operator primes the atomic clause for the application of a specific or general (incomplete) temporal operator. An incomplete specific or general temporal operator combines with a pure tense operator to form a *complete* temporal operator; the complete temporal operator applied to (3) is 'at 3:00 P.M. on 4 December 1983' + future tense. And of course, the extension of a complete temporal operator is a function from sentence superintensions to truth-values.

In light of these facts, it is instructive to regard ordinary past tense as a superintensional operator with the following distinguishing property: its extension with respect to a time t and a possible world w is the function that assigns to any sentence superintension f (i.e., to any function from times to sentence intensions) not a truth-value, but the class of times t' earlier than t and for which the value of f yields truth for the world w (or equivalently, the characteristic function of this class of times). An analogous construal is possible for the future tense operator, replacing 'earlier' by 'later'. A past-tensed or future-tensed but otherwise temporally unmodified sentence would thus have as its extension not a truth-value, but a class of times (or the corresponding characteristic function from times to truth-values).

For example, the extension of the simple past-tensed sentence

(13) I was busy

with respect to a context c, a time t, and a possible world w would be the class of times t' earlier than t and such that its component untensed clause (3) is true with respect to c, t', and w. An unmodified past tense sentence such as (13) might be represented formally as

$Past\ Tense[Busy(I)]$.

Such a sentence is essentially *incomplete*, standing in need of completion by an incomplete temporal operator, either specific or general, in order to achieve genuine truth-value.

The extension (with respect to a context, a time, and a possible world) of an incomplete specific temporal operator, such as 'at 3:00 P.M. on 4 December 1983', may be taken to be simply the indicated time, rather than the corresponding function from sentence superintensions to truth-values. Indeed, even the information values of certain incomplete specific temporal operators , such as 'now' and 'at 3:00 P.M. on 4 December 1983', may plausibly be regarded as simply the indicated time, rather than the corresponding property of proposition matrices of being true at that time. In the case of an incomplete descriptive specific temporal operator, such as 'when Frege wrote "Thoughts" ', its information value may plausibly be regarded as analogous to that of the corresponding definite description 'the earlier time at which Frege writes "Thoughts" '. The word 'when' in such constructions may be regarded as the temporal analogue of the definite-description operator 'the'.

Where T is any incomplete specific temporal operator, without an accompanying tense operator, the result of applying T to a past-tensed sentence such as (13) is representable formally as

$T(Past\ Tense[Busy(I)])$.

This is a *complete* sentence, one whose extension is a truth-value. The sentence is true (with respect to semantic parameters) if and only if the extension (with respect to those parameters) of T is an element of the extension (with respect to those parameters) of the operand past-tensed sentence (13). It is thus as if the past-tense operator in (13) transformed its operand clause (3) into the corresponding predicate

is an earlier time at which I am busy.

An incomplete specific temporal operator such as 'at 3:00 P.M. on 4 December 1983' attaches to the tensed sentence as if the operator were a singular term to which a monadic predicate attaches. Hence the complete temporal operator 'at 3:00 P.M. on 4 December 1983' + future tense is a one-place connective, whose extension may be regarded as a function from proposition matrices (or from sentence schedules or superintensions) to truth-values.

In ordinary use, a past-tensed but otherwise temporally unmodified sentence such as (13), standing alone as a declarative sentence in a piece of discourse, may be regarded as involving an implicit, specific, demonstrative temporal operator 'then', or 'at that time', in order to obtain a complete sentence,

I was busy then.

This ordinary sort of use of (13) would thus be represented formally as

$Then(Past\ Tense[Busy(I)])$

and would be taken to mean something very much like 'That time is an earlier time at which I am busy'. If the time implicitly designated in an utterance of (13) (standing alone as a declarative sentence in a piece of discourse) is not one at which the speaker is busy, what is said is false even if the speaker has been busy at other times prior to the utterance. Analogous remarks apply to the future-tensed 'I will be busy'.[28]

Since the extension of an incomplete specific temporal operator such as 'at 3:00 P.M. on 4 December 1983', without an accompanying tense operator, is simply the indicated time, in order to obtain a complete sentence whose extension is a truth-value from an incomplete specific temporal operator and an untensed clause as operand, a tense operator *must be* supplied as a bridge connecting the superintension of the operand clause with respect to a time t (e.g., the time of utterance) to the extension of the temporal operator with respect to t, thereby achieving truth-value. Which tense operator is appropriate will depend on the direction of the indicated time, earlier or later, relative to the time t. This account thus accommodates the fact that the appropriate complete temporal operator typically shifts its constitutive tense from future to past with the passage of time.

Just as an incomplete specific temporal operator may be plausibly treated as a singular term, so an incomplete quantificational temporal operator may be plausibly treated as a corresponding quantifier. The extension of 'sometimes', for example, may be taken to be the class of all

---

[28] Cf. W. V. O. Quine, *Word and Object* (Cambridge, Mass.: MIT Press, 1960), at 170–71.

nonempty classes of times (or equivalently, the characteristic function of this class), and its information value may likewise be taken to be the corresponding higher-order property of being a nonempty class of times. A quantificational temporal operator thus also requires an accompanying tense as a bridge connecting the superintension of its operand clause to its own extension. The result of applying a quantificational temporal operator to a tensed sentence is true if and only if the extension of the tensed sentence (which is not a truth-value, but a class of times) is an element of the extension of the quantificational temporal operator. Thus, for example, the sentence

Sometimes Frege was busy

is true with respect to a time t if and only if the class of times earlier than t at which Frege is busy (the extension of 'Frege was busy' with respect to t) is nonempty, i.e., if and only if some time t' is a time earlier than t at which Frege is busy. (The complete quantificational temporal operator 'sometimes' + past tense provides a roughly correct, albeit somewhat strained, definition of one use of the present perfect tense, as in 'Frege has been busy', as well as of philosophers' alternative use of simple past tense.) Incomplete quantificational temporal sentential operators such as 'sometimes', 'always', 'twice before', etc., are thus regarded as attaching to tensed sentences in the way that quantifiers such as 'something', 'everything', and 'exactly two smaller things' attach to monadic predicates, whereas incomplete specific temporal operators such as 'on 4 December 1983', 'when Frege wrote "Thoughts" ', etc., are regarded as attaching to tensed sentences in the way that singular terms are attached to by monadic predicates.[29]

---

[29] A problem for this account arises in connection with such constructions as 'Frege always was busy', which does not mean that every time is a past time at which Frege is busy. The sentence seems to mean instead that every past time is a time at which Frege is busy. But on the account proposed here, the past-tense operator operates on the value base of the untensed clause 'Frege be busy' and the incomplete operator 'always' attaches to the result (i.e., to the past-tensed 'Frege was busy'), apparently resulting in the incorrect former reading for the sentence. The alternative, latter reading would seem to require seeing the past-tense operator as somehow modifying the 'always' rather than the untensed clause.

Whereas the latter reading of the sentence is closer to the actual meaning than the former (which is clearly a misreading), it also does not seem exactly correct. The sentence in question generally is not used with this meaning (although, of course, it *can be* so used). As with a simple past-tensed sentence, a sentence such as 'Frege always was busy' is ordinarily used with implicit reference to a particular (perhaps vaguely delineated) period or interval of time in mind, so that what is

There are complications involved in extending this account of temporal operators to cases in which temporal operators such as 'sometimes', 'always', 'now', and 'today' are applied directly to present-tensed sentences, as in any of the examples (8)–(11). The account would suggest that such instances of present tense be regarded as instances of a pure tense operator, analogous to past or future tense except that its extension with respect to a time t and a possible world w, is the function that assigns to any sentence superintension f the class of times t'—whether earlier than, later than, or overlapping with t—for which the value of f yields truth for the world w (or equivalently, the characteristic function of this class of times). Such an operator is required, on the account being considered here, in order to prime a temporally unmodified clause such as (3) for an operator such as 'sometimes' or 'today', to bridge the superintension of the unmodified clause with the extension of the incomplete specific or general temporal operator.

Consider now the simple present-tensed sentence (1). Strictly speaking, this probably should not be regarded as the atomic sentence formed by attaching the temporally unmodified predicate corresponding to the naked infinitive phrase 'be busy' to the term 'I', as represented formally by

$Busy(I)$.

What this represents is the English clause (3) or 'me be busy' (as in 'One can see me be busy'). Although (3) is not a grammatical sentence of English, it is complete in itself. Its extension (with respect to appropriate semantic parameters) is a truth-value; it is true with respect to a context c, a world w, and a time t if and only if the agent of c is busy at t in w. What, then, becomes of such a sentence as (1)?

On the account of temporal operators under consideration, the result of applying present tense to (3), represented formally as

---

said is true as long as Frege is busy throughout that period even if at some other times he is not busy. This feature of such constructions can be accommodated on the present account by taking incomplete quantificational temporal operators, such as 'always', to involve implicit reference to a particular period or interval—very much in the manner of implicitly relativized uses of quantificational constructions in English (as, for example, the 'everything' in 'Everything is in order' or the 'everyone' in 'Is everyone here?'). A sentence such as 'Frege always was busy', standing alone as a declarative sentence in a piece of discourse, may thus be taken to mean something like the following: Every time during *that period* is an earlier time at which Frege is busy (with reference to a contextually indicated period of time).

Present Tense[Busy(I)]

is not a complete sentence of English, capable of truth-value standing alone. Its extension is a class of times rather than a truth-value. Yet surely one who wishes to assert what is encoded by a simple, atomic clause such as (3) uses a tensed sentence, (1). How are we to accommodate the fact that a simple, present-tensed sentence such as (1) is capable of achieving truth-value when standing alone as a declarative sentence without an additional temporal operator?

On this theory, such uses are regarded as involving an implicit use of a specific, indexical temporal operator such as 'now'. For example, sentence (1) standing alone would be seen as elliptical for (12), represented formally as

Now(Present Tense[Busy(I)]).

This account of simple present tense is exactly analogous to the treatment suggested above of simple past tense according to which a simple past-tensed sentence such as (13) or 'Frege was busy', standing alone as a declarative sentence in a piece of discourse, is elliptical for a temporally indexical completion, e.g., 'Frege was busy then'. We may call this *the ellipsis theory of present tense.*[30]

---

[30] One alternative to the ellipsis theory of present tense is the theory that the English construction represented by '*Busy(I)*' is simply sentence (1). Indeed, it is commonplace in most discussions concerning logical form to assume that this English sentence is, at least as typically intended, an atomic sentence constructed from the singular term 'I' and the simple predicate 'am busy', while regarding the present tense of the latter not as a separate component of the sentence but as somehow built into the predicate. In an effort to facilitate understanding of the general theory of temporal operators presented here, much of the preceding discussion was based on the presumption of some such theory. However, if verb tenses are to be taken seriously in accordance with the general theory of temporal operators presented here—as semantically significant contributions to sentences in themselves—this alternative theory ultimately requires the postulation of a systematic semantic ambiguity in the present tense, so that a simple, present-tensed sentence such as (1) is ambiguous between the complete

Busy(I)

and the incomplete (in need of supplementation by an incomplete specific or general temporal operator)

Present Tense[Busy(I)].

The first would be an instance of the *tenseless* use of present tense, the second of the *tensed* use of present tense. The tenseless (1) has a truth-value for its extension and would be an appropriate operand for any complete temporal operator, whereas the tensed (1) would be the result of applying a certain tense operator (viz., present

It is not my purpose here to fill out the details of the ellipsis theory of present tense or to cite linguistic evidence either in favor of or against this general account of the simple tenses. I offer the theory in order to provide an indication of the richness of the apparatus of the modified naive theory for dealing with complete and incomplete temporal operators.[31]

It is interesting to note that on the ellipsis theory of present tense suggested here, a present-tensed sentence such as (2) is taken to be an incomplete sentence standing in need of completion, much as if it were the corresponding predicate 'is a time at which this tree is covered with green leaves'. At the level of information value, the present-tense operator thus converts the content base of its untensed operand clause into something like its corresponding property of being a time at which the particular tree in question is covered with green leaves. In a sense, this theory of the pure tenses partially vindicates Frege's construal of a present-tensed sentence as standing in need of completion or supple-

---

tense qua tense operator) to the tenseless (1). The more complex logical form of the latter would have to be regarded on this theory as going entirely unrepresented in the surface grammar. We may call this *the ambiguity theory of present tense*.

Certain general considerations tend to favor the ellipsis theory over the ambiguity theory of present tense. In general, when attempting to explain apparently divergent uses of a single expression or locution, if an ellipsis account is available, it is to be preferred over the postulation of a systematic semantic ambiguity— although, of course, some third alternative may be preferable to it. See Saul Kripke, "Speaker's Reference and Semantic Reference," in *Contemporary Perspectives in the Philosophy of Language*, ed. P. French, T. Uehling, and H. Wettstein (Minneapolis: University of Minnesota Press, 1979), 6–27, especially 19.

[31] It is probably important for a full theory of the simple tenses to take account of the fact that the proper operands of tenses in English seem not to be whole clauses but simple predicates (or, more accurately, verbs). Since tenses are to be treated in any case as superintensional operators, it is largely a simple problem of formal engineering to transform the theory of pure tenses presented here into a theory of tenses as operators on the value bases of simple predicates rather than on the value bases of whole clauses. For example, in accordance with the spirit of the general theory of tenses presented here, a past-tensed predicate such as 'was busy'—which results from applying the past tense operation to the simple predicate (naked infinitive) 'be busy'—may be regarded as having for its extension, with respect to a possible world w and a time t, not a class of individuals (or its corresponding characteristic function from individuals to truth-values) but the function that assigns to each (possible, past, present, or future) individual i the class of times before t at which i is busy in w.

It may also be important to recognize that the 'that'-operator, which transforms a sentence into a singular term (typically) referring to the sentence's information content, may be attached in English to a tensed but apparently otherwise temporally unmodified sentence, e.g., 'When Frege wrote "Thoughts," he knew that he was busy'. It may be necessary to regard such 'that'-clauses as involving an implicit 'then' or 'now' operator. See footnote 21 above.

mentation, typically provided by the time of utterance. Frege's theory works remarkably well as a theory of tense. Unfortunately, as we saw in sections VI and VII above, it fails as an account of temporal indexicality.

Selected Bibliography

Blackburn, S., ed. "The Identity of Propositions." In *Meaning, Reference and Necessity*. Cambridge: Cambridge University Press, 1975, 182–205.

Cappio, J. "Russell's Philosophical Development," *Synthese* 46 (1981): 185–205.

Carnap, R. *Meaning and Necessity: A Study in Semantics and Modal Logic*. Chicago: University of Chicago Press, 1947.

Cartwright, R. "Propositions." In *Analytical Philosophy*, ed. R. Butler. First series. Oxford: Basil Blackwell, 1966, 81–103.

Church, A. "Review of Carnap's *Introduction to Semantics*," *The Philosophical Review* 52 (1943): 298–304.

Church, A. "On Carnap's Analysis of Statements of Assertion and Belief," *Analysis* 10 (1950): 97–99; also in *Reference and Modality*, ed. L. Linsky. Oxford: Oxford University Press, 1971, 168–70.

Church, A. "A Formulation of the Logic of Sense and Denotation." In *Structure, Method and Meaning: Essays in Honor of Henry M. Sheffer*, ed. P. Henle, H. Kallen, and S. Langer. New York: Liberal Arts Press, 1951, 3–24.

Church, A. "Intensional Isomorphism and Identity of Belief," *Philosophical Studies* 5 (1954): 65–73; also in *Propositions and Attitudes*, ed. N. Salmon and S. Soames. Oxford: Oxford University Press, 1988, 159–68.

Church, A. "Outline of a Revised Formulation of the Logic of Sense and Denotation," Part I, *Noûs* 7 (1973): 24–33; Part II, *Noûs* 8 (1973): 135–56.

Donnellan, K. "Reference and Definite Descriptions," *The Philosophical Review* 75 (1966): 647–58.

Donnellan, K. "Proper Names and Identifying Descriptions." In *Semantics of Natural Language*, ed. D. Davidson and G. Harman. Dordrecht: Reidel, 1972, 356–79.

Donnellan, K. "Speaking of Nothing," *The Philosophical Review* 83 (1974): 3–31; also in Schwartz, 1977, 216–44.

Evans, G. "Pronouns, Quantifiers, and Relative Clauses (I)." In *Reference, Truth, and Reality*, ed. M. Platts. London: Routledge and Kegan Paul, 1980, 255–317.

Fine, K. "Properties, Propositions, and Sets," *Journal of Philosophical Logic* 6 (1977): 135–92.

Frege, G. "Begriffsschrift." In English in Frege's *Conceptual Notation and Related Articles*. Oxford: Oxford University Press, 1972; also in Frege, 1952, 1–20.

Frege, G. "Function und Begriff." In English in Frege, 1984, 137–56; also in Frege, 1952, 21–41.

Frege, G. "Über Sinn und Bedeutung," *Zeitschrift für Philosophie und Philosophische Kritik* 100 (1893): 25–50; in English in Frege, 1984, 157–77; also in Frege, 1952, 56–78.

Frege, G. "Über Begriff und Gegenstand." In English in Frege, 1984, 182–94; also in Frege, 1952, 42–55.

Frege, G. *Translations from the Philosophical Writings*, trans. P. Geach and M. Black. Oxford: Basil Blackwell, 1952.

Frege, G. "Der Gedanke." In English in Frege, 1984, 351–72; also in Frege, 1977, 1–30; also in Salmon and Soames, 1988, 33–55.

Frege, G. *Logical Investigations*, ed. P. T. Geach. New Haven: Yale University Press, 1977.

Frege, G. *Posthumous Writings*, ed. H. Hermes, F. Kambartel, and F. Kaulbach, trans. P. Long and R. White. Chicago: University of Chicago Press, 1979.

Frege, G. *Philosophical and Mathematical Correspondence*, ed. G. Gabriel, H. Hermes, F. Kambartel, C. Thiel, and A. Veraart, abr. B. McGuinness, trans. H. Kaal. Chicago: University of Chicago Press, 1980.

Frege, G. *Collected Papers on Mathematics, Logic, and Philosophy*, ed. B. McGuinness, trans. M. Black, V. H. Dudman, P. Geach, H. Kaal, E. H. W. Kludge, B. McGuinness, and R. H. Stoothoff. Oxford: Basil Blackwell, 1984.

French, P., Uehling, T., and Wettstein, H., eds. *Contemporary Perspectives in the Philosophy of Language*. Minneapolis: University of Minnesota Press, 1979.

Gödel, K. "Russell's Mathematical Logic." In *The Philosophy of Bertrand Russell*, ed. P. A. Schilpp. The Library of Living Philosophers, Evanston, Illinois. New York: The Tudor Publishing Company, 125–53.

Kamp, H. "Formal Properties of 'Now'," *Theoria* 37 (1972): 227–73.

Kaplan, D. "Dthat." In *Syntax and Semantics 9: Pragmatics*, ed. P. Cole. New York: Academic Press, 1978, 221–43; also in French et al., 1979, 383–400.

Kaplan, D. "On the Logic of Demonstratives." In French et al., 1979, 401–12; also in Salmon and Soames, 1988, 66–82.

Kaplan, D. *Demonstratives*, draft #2, Department of Philosophy, UCLA, 1977; also in this volume.

Kaplan, D. "Opacity." In *The Philosophy of W. V. Quine*, ed. L. E. Hahn and P. A. Schilpp. La Salle, Ill.: Open Court, 1986, 229–89.

Kneale, W., and Kneale, M. "Propositions and Time." In *G. E. Moore: Essays in Retrospect*, ed. A. Ambrose and M. Lazerowitz. London: Allen & Unwin, 1970, 228–41.

Kripke, S. "Identity and Necessity." In *Identity and Individuation*, ed. M. Munitz. New York: New York University Press, 1971, 135–64; also in Schwartz, 1977, 66–101.

Kripke, S. *Naming and Necessity*. Cambridge, Mass.: Harvard University Press, and Oxford: Basil Blackwell, 1972, 1980; also in *Semantics of Natural Language*, ed. D. Davidson and G. Harman. Dordrecht: Reidel, 1972, 253–355, 763–69.

Kripke, S. "Speaker's Reference and Semantic Reference." In French et al., 1979, 6–27.

Montague, R. "The Proper Treatment of Quantification in Ordinary English." In Montague, 1974, 247–70; also in *Formal Philosophy*, ed. R. Thomason. New Haven: Yale University Press, 1974.

Moore, G. E. *The Commonplace Book 1919–53*, ed. C. Lewy. New York: The Macmillan Company, 1962.

Moore, G. E. "Facts and Propositions." In *Proceedings of the Aristotelian Society, Supplementary Vol. 7*, 1927; also in Moore, *Philosophical Papers*. New York: Collier Books, 1962, 60–88.

Perry, J. "Frege on Demonstratives," *The Philosophical Review* 86 (1977): 474–97.

Perry, J. "The Problem of the Essential Indexical," *Noûs* 13 (1979): 3–21; also in Salmon and Soames, 1988, 83–101.

Perry, J. "Belief and Acceptance." In *Midwest Studies in Philosophy V: Studies in Epistemology*, ed. P. French, T. Uehling, and H. Wettstein. Minneapolis: University of Minnesota Press, 1980, 533–42.

Perry, J. "A Problem About Continued Belief," *Pacific Philosophical Quarterly* 61 (1980): 317–32.

Prior, A. N. *Past, Present, and Future*. Oxford: Oxford University Press, 1967.

Prior, A. N. "'Now'," *Noûs* 2 (1968): 101–19.

Prior, A. N. *Papers on Time and Tense*. Oxford: Oxford University Press, 1968.

Prior, A. N. *Objects of Thoughts*. Oxford: Oxford University Press, 1971.

Putnam, H. "Meaning and Reference," *Journal of Philosophy* 70 (1973): 699–711; also in Schwartz, 1977, 119–32.

Putnam, H. "The Meaning of 'Meaning'." In *Minnesota Studies in the Philosophy of Science VII: Language, Mind, and Knowledge*, ed. K. Gunderson. Minneapolis: University of Minnesota Press, 1975; also in Putnam, *Philosophical Papers II: Mind, Language, and Reality*. Cambridge: Cambridge University Press, 1975, 215–71.

Quine, W. V. O. *Mathematical Logic*. New York: W. W. Norton and Company, 1940.

Quine, W. V. O. "Quantifiers and Propositional Attitudes," *Journal of Philosophy* 53 (1956): 177–87; also in Quine, *The Ways of Paradox*. New York: Random House, 1966, 183–94; also in Linsky, 1971, 101–11.

Quine, W. V. O. *Word and Object*. Cambridge, Mass.: MIT Press, 1960.

Richard, M. "Temporalism and Eternalism," *Philosophical Studies* 39 (1981): 1–13.

Richard, M. "Tense, Propositions, and Meanings," *Philosophical Studies* 41 (1982): 337–51.

Richard, M. "Direct Reference and Ascriptions of Belief," *Journal of Philosophical Logic* 12 (1983): 425–52; also in Salmon and Soames, 1988, 169–96.

Russell, B. *Principles of Mathematics*. New York: W. W. Norton and Coompany, 1903.

Russell, B. "On Denoting," *Mind* 14 (1905): 479–93; also in Russell, 1956, 41–56; also in Russell, 1973, 103–19.

Russell, B. "Knowledge by Acquaintance and Knowledge by Description," chapter X of Russell's *Mysticism and Logic and Other Essays*. London: Longmans, Green and Company, 1911, 209–32; also in Salmon and Soames, 1988, 16–32.

Russell, B. *The Problems of Philosophy*. Oxford: Oxford University Press, 1912.

Russell, B. "Descriptions," chapter 16 of Russell's *Introduction to Mathematical Philosophy*. London: Allen & Unwin, 1919, 167–80.

Russell, B. *The Analysis of Mind*. London: Allen & Unwin, 1921.

Russell, B. "The Philosophy of Logical Atomism." In Russell, 1956, 177–281.

Russell, B. *Logic and Knowledge*, ed. R. C. Marsh. London: Allen & Unwin, 1956.

Russell, B. "Mr. Strawson on Referring," *Mind* 66 (1957): 385–89; also in Russell, 1973, 120–26.

Russell, B. *Essays in Analysis*, ed. D. Lackey. New York: Allen & Unwin, 1973.

Salmon, N. *Reference and Essence*. Princeton: Princeton University Press, and Oxford: Basil Blackwell, 1981.

Salmon, N. "Assertion and Incomplete Definite Descriptions," *Philosophical Studies* 42 (1982): 37–45.

Salmon, N. "Fregean Theory and the Four Worlds Paradox," *Philosophical Books* 25 (1984): 7–11.

Salmon, N. *Frege's Puzzle*. Cambridge, Mass.: Bradford Books/MIT Press, 1986.

Salmon, N. "Reflexivity," *Notre Dame Journal of Formal Logic* 27 (1986): 401–29; also in Salmon and Soames, 1988, 240–74.

Salmon, N. "Illogical Belief." In *Philosophical Perspectives 3*, ed. J. Tomberlin. Atascadero, Calif.: Ridgeview, forthcoming.

Salmon, N. "Reference and Information Content: Names and Descriptions." In *Handbook of Philosophical Logic IV*, ed. D. Gabbay and F. Guenthner. Dordrecht: Reidel, forthcoming.

Schwartz, S. *Naming, Necessity, and Natural Kinds*. Ithaca: Cornell University Press, 1977.

Whitehead, A. N., and Russell, B. *Principia Mathematica*, 2d ed. Cambridge University Press, 1927.

14

Direct Reference and Propositional Attitudes

Scott Soames[1]

I.

If it weren't for propositional attitudes, direct reference would probably be uncontroversial. Conversely, if it weren't for direct reference, propositional attitudes might seem far more tractable. It is the combination that many people find problematic. Nevertheless, both are real, and both must be accounted for in an adequate semantic theory.

It is helpful to begin with propositional attitudes. One reason for this is that natural languages contain propositional attitude constructions.

---

[1] This paper is a condensed version of a longer work written in the summer and fall of 1984, "Direct Reference, Propositional Attitudes, and Semantic Content," *Philosophical Topics* 15, no. 1 (1987), reprinted in *Propositions and Attitudes*, ed. Nathan Salmon and Scott Soames (Oxford: Oxford University Press, 1988). This shortened version is the result of talks given at the University of Illinois, the Pacific Division Meetings of the American Philosophical Association, and North Carolina State University in the winter and spring of 1985. The points presented here, and developed in greater detail in the longer article, grew out of work originating in my critique, "Lost Innocence," *Linguistics and Philosophy* 8, no. 1 (1985): 59–71, of Jon Barwise and John Perry, *Situations and Attitudes* (Cambridge, Mass.: MIT Press, 1983). I am indebted to Joseph Almog, David Kaplan, and Nathan Salmon for extensive discussion and correspondence that was helpful in developing several of these points. I have also profited from discussion with Ali Akhtar Kazmi, Julius Moravcsik, and Mark Richard.

Thus, conclusions about the nature of semantic information needed to account for these constructions are important for developing adequate semantic theories for these languages. However, there is another, more fundamental, reason for connecting semantic information with propositional attitudes. Imagine a language lacking propositional attitude constructions, but nevertheless used by speakers to represent and convey information. Although such a language lacks the means of reporting the propositional attitudes of others, it still can be used by speakers to make assertions and to express their own beliefs.

How so? Presumably in the following way: Sentences are vehicles for encoding information relative to contexts of use. In standard cases, someone who assertively utters a sentence asserts, perhaps among other things, the information encoded by the sentence in the context. Similarly, someone who is prepared to accept a sentence in a context believes that which the sentence encodes in the context. Thus a semantic theory, even for a language lacking propositional attitude constructions, will play a central role in characterizing the beliefs and assertions of speakers. If the conception of semantic information utilized by the semantic theory gives rise to incorrect characterizations of speakers' beliefs and assertions, then the theory must be rejected, even if there are no propositional attitude sentences it has characterized incorrectly.

This leads to a conception of semantics in which the fundamental task of a semantic theory is to tell us what sentences say in various contexts of utterance. On this view, the meaning of a sentence can be thought of as a function from contexts to what is said by the sentence in those contexts. The crucial question then becomes: What sort of things are in the range of this function? In other words, what is semantic content, or information?

One familiar answer to this question is that the semantic content of a sentence consists in its truth-conditions. On this conception, a semantic theory amounts to a recursive characterization of a three-place predicate—'S is true with respect to a context C and circumstance E'. Contexts can be thought of as different possible situations in which the sentence might be uttered. Circumstances are different possible situations in which the sentence might be evaluated as true or not. A theory that defines the three-place truth predicate just mentioned will also define two derivative notions—truth-conditional content, and truth-conditional character, à la Kaplan.[2]

---

[2] David Kaplan, *Demonstratives*, this volume. Also "The Logic of Demonstratives,"

(1)   *The truth-conditional content of a sentence S* with respect
      to a context *C* is the set of all circumstances *E* such that *S*
      is true with respect to *C* and *E*.

(2)   *The truth-conditional character of a sentence S* is a func-
      tion from contexts *C* to truth-conditional contents of *S* with
      respect to *C*.

Strict truth-conditional semantics can be seen as claiming that the information semantically encoded by a sentence in a context is its truth-
conditional content in the context; and that the meaning of a sentence
is its truth-conditional character.

It is precisely this conception of semantics that I wish to challenge.
Truth-conditional content cannot be identified with semantic content.
The reason it can't is that truth-conditional content lacks the structure
needed to play the role of that which is said by sentences, and asserted
or believed by speakers. The truth-conditional content of a sentence is
just an unstructured set. Moreover, there is no way for this approach to
prevent sentences with fundamentally different syntactic structures from
being assigned the same truth-conditional content. In contrast to this, I
will argue that the objects of propositional attitudes must encode much
of the syntactic structure of the sentences used to express and report
them.

The way to accomplish this encoding is, I think, to revive a conception of information due in large part to Bertrand Russell. On this
conception, the information encoded by a sentence is a structured proposition, which is a nonlinguistic object built up from the semantic contents
of the sentence's constituents. The strategy is to take Russell's leading
ideas and put them in the form of a two-stage semantic theory. The
first stage consists of a recursive assignment of structured propositions
to sentences. The second stage is a recursive characterization of truth
relative to a circumstance, for structured propositions. Meaning is then
a function from contexts to propositions, which in turn determine, but
are not determined by, sets of truth-supporting circumstances.

My argument for this conception will consist of three main parts.
First, I will use assumptions about propositional attitudes and direct
reference to show that semantic content cannot be identified with truth-
conditional content, and semantic theories cannot be simply theories of

in *Contemporary Perspectives in The Philosophy of Language*, ed. Peter A. French,
Theodore E. Uehling, Jr., and Howard K. Wettstein (Minneapolis: University of
Minnesota Press, 1979), 401–10.

truth. Second, I will outline the positive, Russellian alternative. Finally, I will return to direct reference and propositional attitudes, and explain why I think this conception can withstand familiar doubts about substitution in propositional attitude constructions.

II.

Let us begin with the basic negative argument against strict truth-conditional semantics. It takes the form of a reductio ad absurdum of a set of four assumptions, the first three of which are as follows.

A1   Semantic content is identical with truth-conditional content. The semantic content of a sentence (with respect to a context C and assignment f of values to variables) is the set of all circumstances in which it is true (with respect to C and f).

A2   Propositional attitude sentences report relations to the semantic contents of their complements. An individual i satisfies $\ulcorner x$ v's that $S \urcorner$ (with respect to C and f) iff i bears R to the semantic content of S (with respect to C and f).

A3   Many propositional attitude verbs, including 'say', 'assert', and 'believe' distribute over conjunction. If i satisfies $\ulcorner x$ v's that $P\&Q \urcorner$ (with respect to C and f), then i satisfies $\ulcorner x$ v's that $P \urcorner$ and $\ulcorner x$ v's that $Q \urcorner$ (with respect to C, f).

Even without the fourth assumption, which I will use in giving the reductio, A1–A3 have some interesting, and potentially problematic, consequences. The first of these is a consequence of A1 and A2.

Consequence One

Truth-conditional equivalents are substitutable in propositional attitude sentences. If $\ulcorner x$ v's that $P \urcorner$ is true (with respect to C and f), and if the truth-conditional content of P (with respect to C and f) is identical with the truth-conditional content of Q (with respect to C' and f'), then $\ulcorner x$ v's that $Q \urcorner$ is true (with respect to C' and f').

Adding A3 produces consequences two and three.

Consequence Two

Propositional attitudes (corresponding to A3) are closed under truth-conditional consequence. If $\ulcorner x$ v's that $P \urcorner$ is true (with respect to C,

f), and if the truth-conditional content of P (with respect to C, f) is a subset of the truth-conditional content of Q (with respect to C', f'), then $\ulcorner x$ v's that $Q\urcorner$ is true (with respect to C', f').

Consequence Three

To assert (believe) a truth-conditional impossibility is to assert (believe) everything. If the truth-conditional content of P (with respect to C, f) is the empty set, then $\ulcorner x$ v's that $P\urcorner$ is true (with respect to C, f) only if $\ulcorner x$ v's that $Q\urcorner$ is too, for every Q.

Exactly how problematic these consequences are depends on what sort of things are chosen to play the role of truth-supporting circumstances. Standardly, circumstances have been thought of as ways the world might have been, alternative total states of the world, or possible worlds for short. Sentences that express claims that would have been true no matter what the world was like—for example, mathematical truths—are assigned the set of all possible worlds as truth-conditional content. Sentences that express claims that would have been false no matter what—for example, mathematical falsehoods—are assigned the empty set. Sentences that express contingent truths or falsehoods are assigned the subset of worlds in which they are true.

It should be evident, however, that with possible worlds as truth-supporting circumstances, Consequences One–Three lead to severe difficulties. Corresponding to Consequence One we have the result that anyone who believes or asserts what is expressed by one mathematical truth thereby believes or asserts that which is expressed by each mathematical truth. Corresponding to Consequence Two we have the result that anyone who believes or asserts something believes or asserts every necessary consequence of that thing. Corresponding to Consequence Three we have the result that no one has ever believed or asserted a mathematical falsehood, since no one has ever (simultaneously) believed and asserted everything.

These results are unacceptable. However, this doesn't mean that the truth-conditional conception of semantics and semantic content has been refuted. It hasn't been refuted, even if one accepts assumptions A2 and A3. The defender of truth-conditional semantics may simply choose a different sort of object to play the role of circumstances in which sentences are evaluated for truth or falsity. In fact, he has available a range of candidates which, in principle, allow for finer and finer semantic discriminations.

One can think of these candidates roughly as follows. Let L be a language, D be the set of individuals the language is used to talk about, and B be the set of properties expressed by simple predicates of L plus their complements (where the complement of a property P is the property of not having P). By a *state description* I will mean a set each of whose members consists of an n-place property from the set B of basic properties plus an n-tuple of objects drawn from the domain D. A state description is *consistent* iff no two of its members are negations of one another—i.e., iff no two of its members are identical save for the fact that one contains a property P and the other contains its complement. A state description is *complete* iff it contains a complete assignment of objects to properties—i.e., iff for every n-place property P in the set B of basic properties, and every n-tuple of objects drawn from the domain D, either P plus the n-tuple is a member of the state description, or the complement of P plus the n-tuple is a member of the state description. Finally, a state description is *metaphysically possible* only if it is metaphysically possible for the objects in the state description to jointly instantiate the properties they are paired with.

Complete, consistent, metaphysically possible state descriptions approximate *metaphysically possible worlds*. State descriptions which are merely complete and consistent, but not metaphysically possible, can be thought of as representing *logically possible worlds*. These are much more finely grained than standard possible worlds. For example, different mathematical truths are true in different logically possible worlds; and similarly for mathematical falsehoods. Thus, the difficulties created by Consequences One–Three are alleviated, at least in part, by thinking of circumstances of evaluation as *logically* possible, rather than metaphysically possible.

One can go further in this direction by dropping the requirements that state descriptions be complete and consistent. By dropping completeness one moves from logically possible worlds to *logically possible facts*, thereby distinguishing among the semantic contents of logically equivalent sentences. For example, the content of (3a) is distinguished from the content of (3b) in that the former includes "facts" that are, so to speak, silent about radioactivity, whereas the latter does not.[3]

---

[3] The semantic content of (3a) on this account is the set of consistent state descriptions D such that $\langle L, \langle$ Plymouth Rock, Massachusetts$\rangle\rangle$ is a member of D (where L is the relation of being located-in). The content of (3b) is the set of consistent state descriptions D' such that $\langle L, \langle$ Plymouth Rock, Massachusetts$\rangle\rangle$ is a member of D' *and* either $\langle R, \langle$ Plymouth Rock$\rangle\rangle$ is a member of D' or $\langle$ non-$R, \langle$ Plymouth

(3a) Plymouth Rock is in Massachusetts.

(3b) Plymouth Rock is in Massachusetts & it is radioactive or it isn't.

This is significant, since a person lacking the concept of radioactivity might believe or assert something about Plymouth Rock without believing or asserting anything having to do with radioactivity.

We can go still further by dropping the requirement that state descriptions be consistent. This allows the construction of "inconsistent facts," which can be used in building up contents for contradictory beliefs and assertions. With each relaxation of a requirement on state descriptions, the difficulties posed by Consequences One–Three become less and less severe. So much so that when we relax all the requirements, we reach a position that may appear to avoid the difficulties entirely.

Essentially this position is developed and defended by Jon Barwise and John Perry in their book *Situations and Attitudes*.[4] Their *abstract situations* are very much like state descriptions that don't have to be complete, consistent, or metaphysically possible. The system they present retains assumptions A1–A3, while taking abstract situations rather than possible worlds to be the circumstances that support the truth of sentences.[5]

Although this approach is initially attractive, I have come to believe that it doesn't really provide a solution to the problems posed by Con-

---

Rock⟩⟩ is a member of D' (where R is the property of being radioactive, and non-R is its complement). These sets are not the same, since the state description whose only member is ⟨L, ⟨Plymouth Rock, Massachusetts⟩⟩ is a member of the semantic content of (3a), but not the semantic content of (3b). (On this account, the semantic content of a conjunction is the intersection of the semantic contents of the conjuncts, the semantic content of a disjunction is the union of the semantic contents of the disjuncts, and the semantic effect of negating an atomic sentence is to replace the property expressed by the predicate with its complement.)

[4] Barwise and Perry, *Situations and Attitudes*.

[5] I should indicate that although this is a fruitful way of looking at the system in *Situations and Attitudes*, there are other perspectives that might be taken. Certainly, Barwise and Perry have their own foundational concerns that are used to motivate situations, and these can be developed systematically in more than one way. Moreover, situation semantics has undergone changes since the publication of the book designed to rectify a number of important problems, including some of those noted below. (See Jon Barwise and John Perry, "Shifting Situations and Shaken Attitudes," *Linguistics and Philosophy* 8, no. 1 (1985): 105–61.) Nevertheless, the semantic system presented in *Situations and Attitudes* has its own integrity, and is useful in illuminating the limits of a strict truth-conditional approach in which fine-grained truth-supporting circumstances are substituted for possible worlds.

sequences One–Three. In order to show this I will make some further assumptions.

First, I take for granted certain corollaries of assumption A1 that arise from familiar recursive clauses in the characterization of truth with respect to a context and circumstance. These principles specify the semantic contents of compound sentences on the basis of the contents of their constituents.[6]

Corollaries of A1

(4a) The semantic content of a conjunction (with respect to a context C and assignment f) is the intersection of the contents of the conjuncts (with respect to C, f).

(4b) The semantic content of a disjunction (with respect to C, f) is the union of the contents of the disjuncts (with respect to C, f).

(4c) The semantic content of an existential quantification, $\ulcorner \exists x\ Fx \urcorner$, (with respect to C, f) is the set of circumstances E such that for some object o in E, o "is F" with respect to E (and C, f).[7]

---

[6]The corollaries in (4) are consequences of A1 together with the following standard clauses in a recursive characterization of truth with respect to a context and a circumstance:

(a)   A conjunction is true with respect to a context C, assignment f, and circumstance E iff each conjunct is true with respect to C, f, and E.

(b)   A disjunction is true with respect to C, f, and E iff at least one of its disjuncts is true with respect to C, f, and E.

(c) $\ulcorner \exists x\ Fx \urcorner$ is true with respect to C, f, and E iff there exists an object o in E such that Fx is true with respect to C, f', and E, where f' differs at most from f in assigning o to x.

(d) $\ulcorner F[\text{an } x\colon Gx] \urcorner$ is true with respect to C, f, and E iff there exists an object o in E such that both Gx and Fx are true with respect to C, f', and E, where f' is as in (c).

(e) $\ulcorner F[\text{the } x\colon Gx] \urcorner$ is true with respect to C, f, and E iff there exists exactly one object o in E such that Gx is true with respect to C, f', and E, where f' is as in (c), and, in addition, Fx is true with respect to C, f', and E.

[7]Barwise and Perry don't provide an explicit account of simple existential quantifications in *Situations and Attitudes*. However, (4c) is in the spirit of the leading ideas presented there. The other corollaries in (4) are explicitly adopted.

(4d)   The semantic content of $\ulcorner F[\text{an } x\colon Gx]\urcorner$ (with respect to C, f) is the set of circumstances E such that for some object o in E, o "is G" and o "is F" with respect to E (and C, f).

(4e)   The semantic content of $\ulcorner F[\text{the } x\colon Gx]\urcorner$ (with respect to C, f) is the set of circumstances E such that for exactly one object o in E, o "is G" with respect to E (and C, f); and, moreover, o "is F" with respect to E (and C, f).

The invariance of these principles across different choices of truth-supporting circumstances reflects the fact that no matter what one's conception of circumstances, the circumstances that make a conjunction true are those that make the conjuncts true; the circumstances that make a disjunction true are those that make either disjunct true; and so on. I will take this invariance to be part of the very idea of what truth-supporting circumstances are. It is also inherent in the widespread conception of semantic theories as theories of truth with respect to a circumstance.[8]

Another principle used in the reductio that might well be regarded as a corollary of A1 is the following limited version of compositionality.

C   The semantic content of a nonintensional sentence (with respect to a context C and assignment f) is a function of the syntactic structure of the sentence plus the semantic contents of its constituents (with respect to C, f). Thus, if S and S' have the same syntactic structure and differ only in the substitution of constituents with the same semantic contents (with respect to C and f), then the contents of S and S' will be the same (with respect to C and f).

The principle is to be understood as applying to sentences that are free of quotation and all opacity-producing operators. Although it could easily be extended to a much larger class of sentences, the limited version is all that will be used in the reductio. This version is presupposed in standard versions of truth-conditional semantics, and is incorporated in familiar clauses like those in (4).

---

[8] Although Barwise and Perry do not put their theory in this form, the basic system in *Situations and Attitudes* could be formulated as a characterization of truth with respect to a context and an abstract situation. Complications would arise in the case of sentences containing definite descriptions. However, these don't affect the points at issue here. For a critical discussion of the treatment of definite descriptions in situation semantics see my "Incomplete Definite Descriptions," *The Notre Dame Journal of Formal Logic* 27, no. 3 (1986): 349–75.

The final principle used in the reductio is an assumption, A4, about direct reference.

A4   Names, indexicals, and variables, are directly referential; the semantic content of such a term (with respect to a context C and assignment f) is its referent (relative to C, f).

The treatment of variables as directly referential is semantically orthodox. In recent years, a number of arguments have been given for extending this treatment to names and indexicals.[9] Although this extension is not strictly required for the reductio, it is both useful and, in my opinion, well motivated. Thus, I will adopt A4.

Later, I will say a bit about how it might be defended against objections based on problematic substitutions in propositional attitude ascriptions. For now, I simply want to register the fact that very often such substitution works in favor of direct reference analyses, and against familiar descriptive alternatives. For example, suppose John looks at me, shakes his head, and utters the words "Scott is making a mess." This can be correctly reported in a variety of ways.

(5a)   John said that I was making a mess. (Said by me)

(5b)   John said that you were making a mess. (Said to me)

(5c)   John said that he (pointing at me) was making a mess.

(5d)   John said that Scott was making a mess.

(5e)   John said that Soames was making a mess.

(5f)   The author of "Direct Reference and Propositional Attitudes" is such that John said that he was making a mess.

A significant virtue of the direct reference thesis, A4, is that an explanation of these legitimate substitutions is forthcoming from it, together with natural subsidiary assumptions (C and A2). This is something that cannot be said for classical descriptive alternatives.

---

[9] See Saul Kripke, "Naming and Necessity," in *Semantics of Natural Language*, ed. Donald Davidson and Gilbert Harman (Dordrecht: Reidel, 1972), 254–355; and "A Puzzle About Belief," in *Meaning and Use*, ed. A. Margalit (Dordrecht: Reidel, 1979), 239–83; David Kaplan, *Demonstratives*, this volume; John Perry, "Frege on Demonstratives," *The Philosophical Review* LXXXVI, no. 4 (1977): 474–97; and "The Problem of the Essential Indexical," *Noûs* 13 (1979): 3–21; Barwise and Perry, *Situations and Attitudes*; and Nathan Salmon, *Frege's Puzzle* (Cambridge, Mass.: MIT Press, 1986).

III.

We are now ready for the reductio. There are many different ways in which it can be constructed. I will sketch three.

First, imagine the following situation. Professor McDuff, looking through the class yearbook says (and I quote), "He (pointing to a picture of a student) is a brilliant mathematician and he (pointing to a picture of a football player) is the best athlete in school." On the basis of this, we assertively utter (6).

(6)   Professor McDuff said (believes) that he (pointing to a picture of a student) is a brilliant mathematician and he (pointing to a picture of a football player) is the best athlete in school.

Suppose further that, unknown to the professor and his audience, the mathematician is the athlete. Thus, in fact, the professor has pointed to two pictures of the same individual.[10] Someone overhearing the conversation who was aware of this might report the professor's praise to the student-athlete, in the manner indicated in (7a).

(7a)   Professor McDuff said (believes) that you are a brilliant mathematician and you are the best athlete in school. (Said addressing the student-athlete)

On the basis of this, the student-athlete could correctly respond as follows:

---

[10] The use of pictures to provide different appearances of the same individual is convenient, but not necessary. For example, after overhearing The Ancient Babylonian utter (a) and (b), Venus could correctly report (c) and (d).

(a)   That (pointing in the morning to Venus) is a star seen in the morning.

(b)   That (pointing in the evening to Venus) is a star seen in the evening.

(c)   The Ancient Babylonian said that I am a star seen in the morning.

(d)   The Ancient Babylonian said that I am a star seen in the evening.

If we could get The Ancient Babylonian to speak slowly enough, we could get him to say:

(e)   That (pointing in the morning to Venus) is a star seen in the morning and that (pointing in the evening to Venus) is a star seen in the evening.

Venus could then correctly report:

(f)   The Ancient Babylonian said that I am a star seen in the morning and I am a star seen in the evening.

A reductio could then be constructed using (f) that paralleled the one in the text that uses (7b).

(7b) Professor McDuff said (believes) that I am a brilliant mathematician and I am the best athlete in school.

Not only do these reports seem perfectly correct, they follow from (6) by A4, A2, and compositionality in the complement. Thus, they have to be accepted.

However, now consider (8).

(8)   Professor McDuff said (believes) the following: that a brilliant mathematician is the best athlete in school and I am a brilliant mathematician and I am the best athlete in school. (Said by the student-athlete)

Here, we have simply added a conjunct to the complement sentence in (7b). Since the conjunct that is added is a truth-conditional consequence of the complement to which it is added, corollaries (4a) and (4d) of A1 (for conjunction and indefinite descriptions) ensure that the complements of (7b) and (8) have the same semantic content. But then, A2 allows us to derive (8) from (7b). Finally, (9) is derived by invoking distribution of 'say' and 'believe' over conjunction (as specified in A3).

(9)   Professor McDuff said (believes) the following: that a brilliant mathematician is the best athlete in school.

It should be noted that the descriptions in these examples are understood to be inside the scope of the propositional attitude verbs. Thus, (9) is tantamount to the claim that professor McDuff said the following: that some mathematician or other is the best athlete in school. The problem, of course, is that when (8) and (9) are understood in this way, they may be false when (6) is true. Thus, at least one of the principles used in the derivation has to be given up.

The same point is illustrated by the second reductio.

(10) $(\exists x : Px \land Mx)(\exists y : Py \land Ey)[a \text{ believed that } (Mx \land Ey)]$
There is a planet x seen in the morning sky and a planet y seen in the evening sky and the ancients believed that x was seen in the morning sky and y was seen in the evening sky.

(11) $\imath x(Px \land Mx) = \imath y(Py \land Ey)$
The planet seen in the morning sky is the planet seen in the evening sky.

We know from the semantics of quantification that (10) is true iff there is an assignment f of values to variables which associates a planet seen in the morning sky with the variable x and a planet seen in the evening sky with the variable y, such that the open belief sentence is true with respect to f. From (11) it follows that the referents of x and y with respect to f must be identical. The assumptions, A4, that variables are directly referential, A2, that propositional attitudes have a relational semantics, and C, compositionality, give us (12).[11]

(12) $(\exists x : Px)$ [a believed that Mx and Ex]
There is a planet x such that the ancients believed that x was seen in the morning sky and x was seen in the evening sky.

We can now pull the same trick as before, using A2, A3, and corollaries (4a) and (4c) of A1 (for conjunction and quantification) to derive (13) and (14).

(13) $(\exists x : Px)$[a believed that $((Mx \land Ex) \land \exists z(Mz \land Ez))$]

(14) a believed that $\exists z(Mz \land Ez)$
The ancients believed there was something that was seen both in the morning sky and in the evening sky.

In effect, we have used assumptions A1–A4, to drive the quantifier inside. But then, since (13) and (14) may be false while (10) and (11) are true, at least one of the these assumptions must be rejected.

The third version of the reductio involves (15) and (16).

(15)   Mark Twain = Herman Melville and Samuel Clemens = Stephen Crane.

(16)   Mark Twain = the x such that Mark Twain = x.

---

[11] In appealing to compositionality, I am assuming that '$Mx \land Ey$' has the same syntactic structure (in the sense relevant to C) as '$Mx \land Ex$'. Although this could be debated, the outcome of the debate would not affect the reductio—since the reductio can be recreated without this assumption. The examples (13′) and (14) follow directly from (10) and (11) by A1–A4 without the need for (12) as an intermediary. (Similar points hold for other versions of the reductio.)

(13′) $(\exists x : Px \land Mx)(\exists y : Py \land Ey)$[a believed that $((Mx \land Ey) \land \exists z(Mz \land Ez))$]

This does not mean that intermediaries like (12) are questionable, given A1–A4. On the contrary, with A1–A4 there is no blocking them. There are, however, certain weakenings of these assumptions that allow the conclusions of the reductios to be drawn even when intermediary steps analogous to (12) are blocked. Examples of this involving weakenings of A2 are given in section 4 of my "Direct Reference, Propositional Attitudes, and Semantic Content."

(15) is an embarrassment to standard treatments of the attitudes in which truth-supporting circumstances are taken to be metaphysically possible worlds. Since its semantic content in such systems is the empty set, everything is a semantic consequence of it. Since no one can say or believe everything, such systems implicitly predict that it expresses something that cannot be believed or asserted.

One virtue of systems that relax constraints on truth-supporting circumstances is that they avoid this embarrassment. In such systems, the semantic content of (15) is a nonempty set of circumstances in which three distinct individuals are identified. Although such circumstances are metaphysically impossible, they are semantically legitimate, and so are available for the construction of semantic contents. Thus, such systems make it perfectly possible to believe or assert that which is expressed by (15).

Belief or assertion of that which is expressed by (16) is unproblematic on any account. However, now consider their conjunction, (17).

(17)   Mark Twain = Herman Melville and Samuel Clemens = Stephen Crane and Mark Twain = the x such that Mark Twain = x.

From the conjunction corollary (4a) of A1, it follows that a circumstance E is a member of the semantic content of (17) only if E is a member of the semantic content of each conjunct. From the assumption that names are directly referential (plus the coreferentiality of 'Mark Twain' and 'Samuel Clemens', and the noncoreferentiality of the other pair), it follows that E is a member of the semantic content of the first two conjuncts only if, in E, Mark Twain is identified with two distinct individuals. But then, E cannot be a member of the semantic content of the third conjunct, since, by the description corollary (4e) of A1, that conjunct requires that Mark Twain be identified with exactly one individual in E. The semantic content of (17) is, therefore, the empty set. Thus, if assumptions A1–A4 are retained, then the problems posed by (15) for possible world semantics are recreated by (17) for theories that eliminate such worlds in favor of finer-grained truth-supporting circumstances.

A variant of this point is made by each reductio. What they show is that the problems posed by propositional attitudes for standard possible world semantics cannot be solved by substituting fine-grained circumstances for possible worlds. Instead, something in the basic structure of the theory must be changed. I suggest that the assumption to be given up is the one that identifies semantic content with truth-conditional content.

IV.

But why, one might ask, do I choose to reject this assumption rather than A2, about propositional attitudes, or A4, about direct reference? There are several reasons for this, which I have time (and space) only just to mention.[12]

First, if one sees direct reference as the source of the problem, then one must banish it entirely. Eliminating it in the case of names would not be enough; directly referential indexicals and variables would also have to go. It seems doubtful that one could allow for even the possibility of introducing directly referential terms by explicit stipulation (since otherwise the reductio could be recreated). Such radical elimination is, in my opinion, too extreme.

Second, eliminating direct reference is not *sufficient* to block the construction of reductios of the type we have been considering. In each case, the assumption of direct reference allowed us to substitute one coreferential term for another in a propositional attitude ascription. Following Kripke, we can get the same result without direct reference, from normal practices of ascribing beliefs and assertions.[13] The example involves Kripke's Pierre, who is proficient in English and French, understands both 'London' and 'Londres', but fails to realize that the latter is a translation of the former (and that the two are, therefore, coreferential). Imagine Pierre calling from London to talk to a friend in Paris. During the course of the conversation he assertively (and sincerely) utters, "Londres est jolie." After hanging up the phone he assertively (and sincerely) utters, "London is not pretty" in response to a visitor who asks his opinion of the city he lives in. What has Pierre said? Clearly, he has said both that London is pretty (to his friend on the phone) and that London is not pretty (to the visitor). By extending the case further, one can use results analogous to this to eliminate reliance on direct reference in the earlier reductios.[14]

Third, in some cases the substitution of one singular term for another is unproblematic anyway. In the McDuff case, the professor says, "He (pointing to a picture of a student) is a brilliant mathematician and he

---

[12] For more extended discussion see sections 4 and 5 of "Direct Reference, Propositional Attitudes, and Semantic Content."

[13] Saul Kripke, "A Puzzle About Belief."

[14] Section 4, "Direct Reference, Propositional Attitudes and Semantic Content."

(pointing to a picture of a football player) is the best athlete in school."
The reports (7a) and (7b) of this remark are perfectly acceptable. Unlike
some other examples, these do not involve attributing conflicting statements (or beliefs) to an otherwise rational agent; nor do they give rise to
the suspicion that we are being forced to accept counter-intuitive results
on the basis of adherence to otherwise plausible principles. Whatever
semantic analysis of propositional attitude ascriptions turns out to be
correct, these reports are ones that we want, pretheoretically, to come
out true.[15] But once we have this, the reductio can be recreated without
further reliance on direct reference.

Analogous points can be made in defense of the role of the relational
assumption, A2, in the derivations. There are two leading ideas behind
this assumption. The first is that propositional attitudes like saying, asserting, and believing are relations to things that are said, asserted, and
believed. The second is that these things are the information contents
semantically encoded by sentences (relative to contexts and assignments
of values to variables).

The first of these ideas is supported by the existence of overtly relational ascriptions, such as (18).

(18a) Jones asserted (believed) several propositions that Ed denied.

(18b) Jones asserted (believed) the proposition expressed at the
top of page 96.

(18c) Jones asserted (believed) the proposition that the earth is
round.[16]

---

[15] The same, I think, is true of the reports (c), (d), and (f) by Venus in footnote 9,
and the report (12) in the second version of the reductio.

[16] It should be noted that (i)–(ii) entail (iii)–(iv), and that (i), (iv) entail (ii)–(iii).

(i)   The proposition expressed at the top of page n = the proposition that S.

(ii)   Jones asserted (believed) the proposition expressed at the top of page n.

(iii) Jones asserted (believed) the proposition that S.

(iv)   Jones asserted (believed) that S.

This strongly suggests that if examples like those in (18) have a relational semantics, then examples of the form (iii)–(iv) do, too.

Overtly relational ascriptions can also be used to reconstruct the reductios without relying on ascriptions of the form (iv). If the two leading ideas behind A2 are
correct, then this can be done directly, in terms of *what sentences say*, or indirectly,
using (v)–(vi) to derive conclusions about *what speakers say*.

The second idea is supported by the fact that two individuals may say (believe) the same thing even though they utter different sentences, as in (19), or sentences with different meanings, as in (20).

(19a) Florence is a beautiful city.

(19b) Firenze é una bella città.

(20a) I won the lottery. (Said by Jones)

(20b) You won the lottery. (Said by Mary to Jones)

This is reflected by the fact that what is asserted or believed can be *reported* in indirect discourse using sentences that differ in form or meaning from those uttered or accepted by the agent. Indeed, in some cases this is the only way in which such reports can be made. Thus, corresponding to (19b) and (20b) we have (21).

(21a) Giovanni said that *Florence is a beautiful city*.

(21b) Mary said that *I won the lottery*. (Said by Jones)

(21c) There is someone such that Mary said that *he won the lottery*.

   What is preserved in all these cases is not the sentences themselves, or their meanings, but their contents relative to their respective contexts (and assignments to pronoun/variables). Since this strongly supports assumption A2, it is not a likely candidate for rejection.[17] As a result,

---

(v)   A sincere, reflective, competent speaker who assertively utters S in a context C says or asserts, perhaps among other things, what S says (expresses) in C.

(vi) If x says (or asserts) that which is said (expressed) by a conjunction in a context C, then x says (or asserts) that which is said (expressed) by each conjunct in C.

Using these principles, one can derive the incorrect conclusion that x has asserted that which is expressed by ⌜For some y Ryy⌝ from the premise that x has assertively uttered ⌜R London, Londres⌝ or ⌜R this (pointing at o from one perspective), that (pointing at o from a different perspective)⌝.

[17] Even if A2 could be rejected, it is not clear that doing so would help with the reductios. In section 4 of "Direct Reference, Propositional Attitudes, and Semantic Content," I show that the reductios can be recreated using weakenings of A2 in which objects of the attitudes consist not just of truth-conditional contents, but of contents plus characters plus reference-fixing properties. In light of this, the most reasonable approach is to find another assumption to reject.

the only plausible strategy that remains for dealing with the reductios is to give up the assumption, A1, that semantic content is truth-conditional content.[18]

V.

Let us, then, reject that assumption and try to construct an alternative account of semantic content that will block the problematic derivations. Two things are needed for this—a characterization of the facts in virtue of which ascriptions of beliefs and assertions are true, and a new semantic theory.

With regard to the former, I think of beliefs as arising from certain kinds of mental states, together with their causal relations to objects in the environment.

(22a) ⌜x believes that S⌝ characterizes the agent as being in a mental state whose information content is identical with the semantic content of S in the context of the report. (Where mental states have internal structure, with the contents of at least some of their constituents determined by causal relations to objects in the environment.)

If we restrict attention to cases in which the agent is a competent speaker of a language, we can use (22b) as a heuristic to approximate (22a) by letting dispositions to assent to sentences play the role of mental states.

(22b) If i is a sincere, reflective, and competent speaker, then i satisfies ⌜x believes that S⌝ with respect to C, f, iff i is disposed to assent to some sentence S' whose semantic content in the context of assent = the semantic content of S relative to C and f.[19]

The account of assertion is similar.

---

[18] The ineffectiveness of rejecting A3 is discussed both in section 4 of "Direct Reference, Propositional Attitudes, and Semantic Competence," and in "Lost Innocence," *Linguistics and Philosophy* 8, no. 1 (1985): 59–71.

[19] Although this principle is a useful heuristic, it should not be regarded as an analysis of belief. Its most obvious limitation is that it does not apply to believers who are not language users. Even when applied to language users it must be restricted to cases in which the agent, i, the sentence S', and its semantic content (in the context of assent) stand in a certain (as yet not fully analyzed) recognition relation. I have in mind examples like 'Newminister 1' in which a proper name is introduced by a reference-fixing description 'the first Tory Prime Minister of Britain elected in the twenty-first century'. (For discussion of a similar example

(23a) An individual i satisfies $\ulcorner x$ asserts that $S\urcorner$ with respect to C, f if i is a competent speaker who assertively utters some sentence S' whose semantic content in the context of i's utterance = the semantic content of S with respect to C, f.

To convert this to a biconditional we need to recognize that one can assert a proposition without uttering a sentence that expresses it. This happens when one's commitment to the proposition can readily be inferred from one's utterance in the context. It would seem, then, that $\ulcorner x$ asserts that $S\urcorner$ should be true just in case the semantic content of S in the context of the report matches the content of some sentence that can readily be inferred from a sentence assertively uttered by the agent.[20]

(23b) $\ulcorner x$ asserts that $S\urcorner$ characterizes the agent as having assertively uttered a sentence S' in an associated context C', such that for some S'' that can be readily inferred from S', the content of S'' in C' = the content of S in the context of the report.

With these characterizations in mind, imagine that an agent assertively utters (24a).

(24a) $R(\text{Peking, Beijing})$

Let us assume, for the sake of this argument, that 'Peking' and 'Beijing' are directly referential. (The particular examples aren't crucial; other pairs of directly referential terms would work as well.) Suppose further that the agent refuses to assertively utter, and indeed dissents from, (24b)–(24d).

---

see Keith Donnellan, "The Contingent A Priori and Rigid Designators," in *Contemporary Perspectives in the Philosophy of Language*, ed. P. French, T. Uehling, and H. Wettstein (Minneapolis: University of Minnesota Press, 1977).) In such a case, the sentence 'Newminister 1 will be conservative' may express a singular proposition involving a certain individual. However, assent to the sentence by a competent speaker is not sufficient for belief in that proposition. Intuitively, the manner in which the sentence presents the proposition to the agent is too indirect for assent to indicate belief.

It should be noted that the cases discussed in the text ('Hesperus'/'Phosphorus', 'London'/'Londres', etc.) are not like this. In these cases, the agents are acquainted with the referents, they associate names with them, and they grasp the propositions expressed by sentences containing the names. What they do not do is recognize that the same referents are associated with different names, and that the same propositions are expressed by different sentences. But that is not required in order for assent to the sentences to indicate belief in the propositions they express.

[20] I will not here try to analyze the nature of this inference. One example of the kind of inference I have in mind is that from a conjunction to its conjuncts.

(24b) R(Peking, Peking)

(24c) $[\lambda x R(x, x)]$, Peking—i.e., Self-R(Peking), R(Peking, itself)

(24d) $\exists x R(x, x)$

   Direct reference, compositionality, and characterizations (22) and (23), of belief and assertion, allow one correctly to describe the agent in either of two ways: as believing (and asserting) that Peking bears R to Beijing, or as believing (and asserting) that Peking bears R to Peking. There are, I think, pragmatic reasons for preferring the first of these reports to the second. Still, on the semantic analysis I am suggesting, both are true—it is true that the agent believes (and has asserted) that Peking bears R to Beijing, and it is true that the agent believes (and has asserted) that Peking bears R to Peking. This is not to say that the agent believes, or has asserted, that Peking bears the relational property of self-R-ing, that Peking bears R to itself, or that at least one thing self-R's (or bears R to itself). In order to account for this, we need a new theory of content in which the content of (24b) differs from that of (24c) and (24e), even though they are true with respect to exactly the same truth-supporting circumstances.

(24e) R(Peking, Peking) $\wedge \exists x R(x, x)$

   In constructing this theory, we need to define a notion of semantic content that is sensitive to the different structures of (24b)–(24e). In effect, we must encode at least some of the syntactic structure of sentences into their semantic contents. Since there is more than one way to do this, I will summarize, in what follows, the one that seems to me to be the most promising.[21]
   The approach embodies an essentially Russellian conception of semantics and semantic content. It can be illustrated by considering an elementary first-order language with lambda abstraction, a belief operator, and a stock of semantically simple singular terms, all of which are directly referential. On the Russellian account, the semantic content of a variable relative to an assignment is just the object assigned as value of the variable; the semantic content of a closed (directly referential) term, relative to a context, is its referent relative to the context. The contents of n-place predicates are n-place properties and relations. The

---

[21] See sections 6 and 7 of "Direct Reference, Propositional Attitudes, and Semantic Content" for the development and evaluation of two different approaches.

contents of '∧' and '¬' are functions, CONJ and NEG, from truth-values to truth-values.

Variable-binding operations, like lambda abstraction and existential quantification, can be handled by using propositional functions to play the role of complex properties corresponding to certain compound expressions.[22] On this approach, the semantic content of $\ulcorner[\lambda x Rx, x]\urcorner$ is the function g from individuals o to propositions that attribute the relation expressed by R to the pair $\langle o, o \rangle$. $\ulcorner[\lambda x Rx, x]t\urcorner$ can then be thought of as attributing the property of bearing-R-to-oneself to the referent of t; and $\ulcorner\exists x Rx, x\urcorner$ can be thought of as "saying" that g assigns a true proposition to at least one object.

The recursive assignment of propositions to sentences is given in (25).

(25a) The proposition expressed by an atomic formula $\ulcorner Pt_1, \ldots, t_n \urcorner$ relative to a context C and assignment f is $\langle\langle o_1, \ldots, o_n \rangle, P* \rangle$, where $P*$ is the property expressed by P, and o_i is the content of t_i relative to C and f.

---

[22] Although this Russellian method is, I think, essentially on the right track, it does lead to certain technical problems in special cases. For example, as Nathan Salmon has pointed out to me, Russellian propositional functions must be defined on possible, as well as actual, individuals, in order to assign correct extensions to expressions in different possible worlds. This means that these functions cannot be thought of as set-theoretic constructions involving only actually existing objects. Another problem involves nonwellfoundedness. As Terence Parsons has observed, in order for the self-referential, but unparadoxical, (i) and (ii) to have their intended interpretations, the propositional functions corresponding to the matrices in these examples must be defined on the propositions expressed by (i) and (ii).

(i) (x) (I assert $x \rightarrow$ I believe x)

(ii) (x) (I assert x today $\rightarrow x$ is expressible in English)

This is impossible, if the set-theoretic conception of propositions and propositional functions is maintained.

These problems can, I believe, be avoided by taking the semantic contents of compound expressions to be complex attributes rather than propositional functions. For example, the content of $\ulcorner[\lambda v S]\urcorner$, with respect to a context C and assignment f, might be taken to be the property P of being an object o such that dthat [the proposition expressed by S with respect to C and an assignment f' that differs from f at most in assigning o to v] is true. The extension of P at a world w will then be the set of objects o such that the relevant propositions containing them are true with respect to w (provided that a proposition has the one-place property of being true, at a world w, iff the two-place relation of being true-with-respect-to holds between it and w).

Other ways of assigning attributes to compound predicates may also be found. For present purposes, I will leave the final resolution of this issue open, and continue in the text to use familiar Russellian propositional functions as contents of compound predicates.

(25b) The proposition expressed by a formula $\ulcorner[\lambda v S]t\urcorner$ relative to C and f is $\langle\langle o\rangle, g\rangle$, where o is the content of t relative to C and f, and g is the function from individuals o' to propositions expressed by S relative to C and an assignment f' that differs from f at most in assigning o' as the value of v.[23]

(25c) The propositions expressed by $\ulcorner\neg S\urcorner$ and $\ulcorner S \wedge R\urcorner$ relative to C and f are $\langle$NEG, Prop $S\rangle$ and $\langle$CONJ, $\langle$Prop S, Prop $R\rangle\rangle$ respectively, where Prop S and Prop R are the propositions expressed by S and R relative to C and f, and NEG and CONJ are the truth functions for negation and conjunction.

(25d) The proposition expressed by $\ulcorner\exists v\ S\urcorner$ relative to C and f is $\langle$SOME, $g\rangle$, where SOME is the property of being a nonempty set, and g is as in (b).

(25e) The proposition expressed by $\ulcorner t$ believes that $S\urcorner$ relative to C and f is $\langle\langle o$, Prop $S\rangle, B\rangle$, where B is the belief relation, o is the content of t relative to C and f, and Prop S is the proposition expressed by S relative to C and f.

(25f) The proposition expressed by a sentence (with no free variables) relative to a context C is the proposition it expresses relative to C and every assignment f.

On this approach, the meaning of an expression is a function from contexts to propositional constituents. The meaning of a sentence is a compositional function from contexts to structured propositions. Intensions (and extensions) of sentences and expressions relative to contexts (and circumstances) derive from intensions (and extensions) of propositions and propositional constituents. These, in turn, can be gotten from

---

[23] Nathan Salmon has suggested to me the possibility of using this lambda construction to distinguish the proposition expressed by (i)–(iii) from those expressed by (iv)–(v).

(i)   London is both pretty and not pretty.

(ii)   London is nonself-identical.

(iii) London is not identical with itself.

(iv)   London is pretty and London is not pretty.

(v)   London is not identical with London.

This suggestion has significant consequences, touched on below, for the semantics of propositional attitude ascriptions.

a recursive characterization of truth with respect to a circumstance, for propositions.

For this purpose, we let the intension of an n-place property be a function from circumstances to sets of n-tuples of individuals that instantiate the property in the circumstance; we let the intension of an individual be a constant function from circumstances to that individual; and we let the intension of a one-place propositional function g be a function from circumstances E to sets of individuals in E that g assigns propositions true in E. Extension is related to intension in the normal way, with the extension of a proposition relative to a circumstance being its truth value in the circumstance, and its intension being the set of circumstances in which it is true (or, equivalently, the characteristic function of that set). Truth relative to a circumstance is defined in (26).

(26a) A proposition $\langle\langle o_1, \ldots, o_n \rangle, P* \rangle$ is true relative to a circumstance E iff the extension of $P*$ in E contains $\langle o_1, \ldots, o_n \rangle$.

(26b) A proposition $\langle\langle o \rangle, g \rangle$ is true relative to E (where g is a one-place propositional function) iff o is a member of the extension of g in E (i.e., iff $g(o)$ is true relative to E).

(26c) A proposition $\langle \text{NEG}, \text{Prop } S \rangle$ is true relative to E iff the value of NEG at the extension of Prop S in E is truth (i.e., iff Prop S is not true relative to E).
A proposition $\langle \text{CONJ}, \langle \text{Prop } S, \text{Prop } R \rangle\rangle$ is true relative to E iff the value of CONJ at the pair consisting of the extension of Prop S in E and the extension of Prop R in E is truth (i.e., iff Prop S and Prop R are true relative to E).

(26d) A proposition $\langle \text{SOME}, g \rangle$ is true relative to E (where g is as in (b)) iff the extension of g in E is nonempty (i.e., iff $g(o)$ is true relative to E for some o in E).

(26e) A proposition $\langle\langle o, \text{Prop } S \rangle, B \rangle$ is true relative to E iff $\langle o, \text{Prop } S \rangle$ is a member of the extension of B in E (i.e., iff o believes Prop S in E).

According to this theory, if R is a simple two-place predicate, the propositions expressed by (24a)–(24e) are given in (27a)–(27e).

(27a) $\langle\langle o, o \rangle, R* \rangle$[24]

---

[24] $R*$ = the property expressed by R and o = Peking (the city).

(27b) $\langle\langle o, o\rangle, R*\rangle$

(27c) $\langle\langle o\rangle, g\rangle$ [25]

(27d) $\langle\text{SOME}, g\rangle$ [26]

(27e) $\langle\text{CONJ}, \langle(27a), (27d)\rangle\rangle$

It is easy to see that the sentences in (24) express propositions that encode their different syntactic structures. Thus, we no longer have the result that anyone who believes or asserts what is expressed by (24a)–(24b), thereby believes or asserts that which the others express. This is just what is needed to block the reductios discussed earlier.

It is important to emphasize that in achieving this result we have not abandoned a semantic account of truth-conditions. Rather, we have supplemented the account with a theory of structured propositions. The end result is a two-part conception of semantics. First, there is an assignment of propositions to sentences relative to contexts. Second, there is a recursive theory of truth-in-a-circumstance for propositions. The chief virtue of this two-part conception is that it combines the structure needed in objects of propositional attitudes with the truth-conditions needed to explicate the manner in which information encoded by a sentence represents the world.

VI.

Finally, a word should be said about direct reference and substitution in propositional attitude constructions. The positive theory I have outlined has the consequence that if $t1$ and $t2$ are directly referential terms that refer to the same thing, then the proposition expressed by the sentence (formula) $\ulcorner t1$ bears R to $t2\urcorner$ will be the same as the proposition expressed by the sentence (formula) $\ulcorner t1$ bears R to $t1\urcorner$. Thus, anyone who believes or asserts the former believes or asserts the latter. How problematic this is depends in part on whether $t1$ and $t2$ are variables, indexicals, or names. Some feel uneasy with all three, and many find the result in the case of names intolerable. I do not.

---

[25] g is the propositional function that assigns to each object o the proposition that o bears $R*$ to o.

[26] Russell thought of SOME as the property of being a propositional function that "is sometimes true"—i.e., of being a function that assigns a true proposition to at least one object.

One reason I don't is that I distinguish the proposition expressed by the sentence ⌜$t1$ bears R to $t1$⌝ from the proposition expressed by the sentences ⌜$t1$ bears the property of Self-R-ing⌝ and ⌜$t1$ bears R to itself⌝.[27] Thus, I account for the fact that someone can believe or assert the proposition expressed by ⌜$t1$ bears R to $t2$⌝ without believing or asserting the proposition expressed by ⌜$t1$ bears the property of Self-R-ing⌝—even where $t1$ and $t2$ are both coreferential and directly referential. Blocking the move to (28c) takes much of the sting out of the move from (28a) to (28b).[28]

(28a) x believes/asserts that $R(t1, t2)$

(28b) x believes/asserts that $R(t1, t1)$

(28c) x believes/asserts that Self-$R(t1)$ [or $R(t1, \text{itself})$]
    ($t1$, $t2$, coreferential and directly referential)

Additional reluctance to move from (28a) to (28b) may be attributed to pragmatic factors. This is something that has been argued at length by Nathan Salmon, and by Jon Barwise and John Perry.[29] The basic idea in the Salmon formulation is quite simple. Propositional attitude ascriptions of the form

(29) x verbs that S

report a relation between an agent and the proposition expressed by the complement sentence. The relation in question is the existential

---

[27] I am here letting the propositions in (i) go proxy for those in (ii).

(ia) $t1$ bears R to $t1$

(ib) $t1$ bears the property of self-R-ing

(ic) $t1$ bears R to itself

(iia) $R(t1, t1)$

(iib)   Self-$R(t1)$

(iic) $R(t1, \text{itself})$

These propositions differ in that the former consist of the relation of bearing plus a sequence of arguments; whereas the latter consist of the relation of R-ing, or the relational property of Self-R-ing, plus arguments. However, with respect to the point at issue, the two groups of propositions are completely comparable.

[28] The distinction between the propositions expressed by ⌜$R(t1, t1)$⌝ and ⌜Self-$R(t1)$⌝ seems to me to be evident. The suggestion that ⌜$R(t1, \text{itself})$⌝ be assimilated to the latter is due to Nathan Salmon.

[29] In *Frege's Puzzle* and *Situations and Attitudes*.

generalization of a three-place relation between an agent, a sentence (or other mode of presentation) and the proposition expressed by that sentence (or mode of presentation). That existential generalization is given in (30).

(30)   There is a sentence (or mode of presentation) S' such that x bears a certain attitude toward S' and S' expresses the proposition P.

The essential semantic requirement is that the complement sentence S in (29) express the same proposition, in the context of the report, that the agent's sentence S' expresses in the situation reported. Often, there are several different sentences that express the same proposition in the reporter's context as S' does in the agent's context. Thus, the reporter can choose to satisfy the *semantic* requirement in a number of different ways.

However, he is also expected to satisfy the *pragmatic* requirement of making his remark maximally informative to his audience. This requires selecting a complement sentence in (29) that both expresses the correct proposition and most closely parallels, or suggests, the agent's sentence S'. The reluctance to move from (28a) to (28b) in a case in which the agent assertively uttered a sentence containing two names rather than one is due in part to this pragmatic requirement. Since an utterance of (28b) will suggest to one's audience that the agent himself used one name rather than two, (28b) should not be used in a case in which one believes, or suspects, that this suggestion is false.

Still, a residual uneasiness may remain. We do, I think, ordinarily suppose that it is possible to believe and assert that Cicero bears R to Tully without believing or asserting that Cicero bears R to Cicero. This intuition may well remain even after the facts about reflexives and pragmatics have been accommodated. If it does, then the positive view I have outlined will not account for all of our linguistic intuitions.

This is a serious matter. The best evidence in semantics comes from the settled intuitions of competent speakers. Any semantic theory ought to try to capture as many of these as possible; and no semantic theory can be correct if it leads to widespread conflict with such intuitions. However, these intuitions are not infallible; competent speakers can be wrong about some of the semantic features of their language.

In some cases this is transparent, as when common intuitions about the predicate 'is true' and Tarski's schema T lead demonstrably to error. In other cases, like the one at hand, it is not. Nevertheless, I maintain that the intuition that the truth-values of (28a) and (28b) may vary independently of one another is mistaken. As I see it, semantic facts about English are not always fully accessible to simple introspection by competent speakers. Thus to discover these facts we need to construct the best theory of the language we can. If one tries to do this, one will, I think, be driven to accept substitution of coreferential names, indexicals (relative to a context), and variables (relative to an assignment). Although a theory incorporating this result may conflict with some of our intuitions, it will, I believe, prove to be truer to the whole range of basic semantic evidence and intuitions than any alternative account.

15

Cognitive Significance Without Cognitive Content

Howard Wettstein[1]

Imagine how it must appear to the Martian making his first visit to earth. Let us suppose that he too is an intelligent being whose intelligence has, however, evolved without the mediation of language, but rather, say, through the development of ESP. So he is something like the angels who, according to St. Thomas, can see things directly in their essences and communicate thought without language. What is the first thing he notices about earthlings? That they are forever making mouthy little sounds—clicks, hisses, howls, hoots, explosions, squeaks—some of which sounds name things in the world and are uttered in short sequences which say something about these things and events in the world.

Instead of starting out with such large, vexing subjects as soul, mind, ideas, consciousness, why not set forth with language, which no one denies, and see how far it takes us toward the rest.

From "The Delta Factor," by Walker Percy.

[1] This paper appeared in *Mind* 97 (1988) and appears here with the permission of the editor of that journal. Talks based upon this paper were given at the University of Notre Dame; the University of California, San Diego; the Center for Advanced Study in the Behavioral Sciences, Stanford; and the University of California, Los Angeles. I am grateful for the helpful comments I received on these occasions. For reactions to earlier drafts I wish to thank Laird Addis, Arthur Collins, Aron Edindin, Alasdair MacIntyre, Philip Quinn, Kenneth Sayre, Lawrence Simon, and Zeno Vendler. Special thanks indeed are owed to Thomas Blackburn, Richard Foley, David Kaplan, Ernest LePore, Genoveva Marti, and especially Joseph Almog.

I. Introduction: Two Conceptions of Semantics

In the beginning, there was Frege who approached the philosophical study of language with his gaze firmly fixed upon one of those "large, vexing subjects," the "eternal structure of thought."[2] Michael Dummett attributes the following three theses to Frege.

> ...first, that the goal of philosophy is the analysis of the structure of *thought* [that is, the objective and eternally existing contents of thought]; second, that the study of *thought* is to be sharply distinguished from the study of the psychological process of *thinking*; and, finally, that the only proper method for analyzing thought consists in the analysis of *language*.[3]

A central aim of semantics, for Frege, is thus the elucidation of how language expresses thought contents. 'Hesperus is Phosphorus', maintained Frege, expresses a significant piece of information, a nontrivial thought content. Our semantic account of names must explain how this is so. Frege concluded that the contribution of the two names to the thought content must be different.

Frege's sense-reference approach not only explains the contributions of names to thought contents, it does so in a way that respects what I will call the "intentionality intuition." This is the powerful traditional idea that in order to be thinking about something, one must have a *cognitive fix* on it, that something in one's thought must correctly distinguish the referent from everything else in the universe.[4] 'Hesperus'

---

[2] I borrow the phrase from Tyler Burge, "Sinning Against Frege," *Philosophical Review* 88 (1979): 398–442. The quotation is from page 398.

[3] M. Dummett, *Truth and Other Enigmas* (London: Duckworth, 1978), 458.

[4] Russell, giving voice to this intuition, maintains that in order to be genuinely thinking about an object, or making a judgment about it, one must know *which thing is in question*. The "cognitive fix" requirement can be understood in a number of ways, some requiring an extremely strong cognitive relation to the referent, some requiring a more modest relation. Russell himself was quite a fanatic about intentionality (in the sense of "aboutness"). He required, or at least there was a strong tendency in his thought to require, that to really be thinking about an object, one must be *directly acquainted* with it. Otherwise, one would not know which thing was in question, even if one possessed a definite description that denoted the object. Frege maintained a weaker requirement, that one possess an individuating sense. Weaker still is is a tendency in, for example, Keith Donnellan's thought, according to which some special sort of causal connection to a thing is enough to establish a cognitive fix. See the latter's "Rigid Designators and the Contingent A Priori," in *Contemporary Perspectives in the*

and 'Phosphorus', then, not only contribute differently to the thought content, but, holds Frege, what each name contributes is its distinctive mode of presentation, its own cognitive fix on the referent. That a semantic account of a name must make plain the cognitive perspective on the referent that is associated with the name is another crucial feature of the Fregean perspective, one intimately related to Frege's emphasis on thought.

Frege's outlook on the business of semantics thus eliminates semantical accounts like Mill's "pure denotation" view of proper names, recently championed by many of us. Millian accounts make the semantics of the two names the same, and so will not be able to explain what Frege took to be the very datum, that sentences like 'Hesperus is Phosphorus' express nontrivial thought contents. The Millian approach to names, moreover, fails to explain the speaker's cognitive fix on the referent. Even worse, that approach, at least as it's been recently developed, implies that the speaker need not have much of a cognitive fix, perhaps none at all. Kripke, to mention one prominent example, takes it to be plain that one can refer by proper name even if one has very little information about the referent—not nearly enough to individuate it.[5] So much the worse, from Frege's point of view, for cognitively insensitive Millian accounts.

One might, though, approach the philosophical study of language in a radically different spirit, that suggested by Walker Percy's remarks. Let's focus for a moment not upon language vis-à-vis thought, but upon language vis-à-vis the realm of things language is used to talk about, or, even better, vis-à-vis our practices of talking about things.

The social practices that constitute natural language are, after all, pretty fascinating in and of themselves. Articulated speech is indeed distinctively human, the first thing that Percy's Martian notices about us. And thought is one of Percy's "large, vexing subjects," one that might better be approached a bit later—which is not to say that the two subjects are not, in the end, intimately related. My semanticist thus fixes his gaze upon language as a social, institutional arrangement, and upon speakers as participants in a social practice.

Speaking, it occurs to him, like other kinds of practical mastery, does not presuppose theoretical understanding of the practice. We are

---

Philosophy of Language, ed. P. French, T. Uehling, and H. Wettstein (Minneapolis: University of Minnesota Press, 1979), 45–60.

[5] Indeed, argues Kripke, typical speakers may not know any more about Cicero than that he was "a Roman orator," hardly individuating knowledge, and yet they are still perfectly competent with the name.

indeed fortunate—God, so to speak, has been good to us—that articulable insight is not necessary, for it is extremely difficult to attain. Indeed, speakers, and other practitioners, may well find their own practices theoretically impenetrable. Adequate theoretical characterizations of one's practices will typically not be available to introspection. Nor will competent practitioners typically be able even to select some correct characterization from a list of fairly plausible candidates.[6]

The semanticist thus sees himself as engaging in an anthropological study of the institutional arrangements that constitute natural language.[7] His charge, more specifically, is to provide an account of the semantics of our linguistic practices. Which features of the total communication situation do our practices count as determining the references of proper names? What, as our practices go, links up a particular name (or utterance) with a particular referent? This is the sort of question in which he is interested.[8]

---

[6] The point I am making about the typical inaccessibility of the "rules" that characterize our practices is perhaps easy to see for the case of proper names, where just about everyone seems confused about the matter. The point, however, is quite generally applicable. Consider, for example, the kind of example in which one might well suppose, and it has indeed been supposed, that the rules are much closer to consciousness. In the case of the first-person pronoun, for example, typical speakers may have a better *rough idea* of the semantic character of our practices than they do with proper names. This is not to say, however, that they can discern an adequate general characterization—as opposed to a rough idea—by introspection, or even that they can select such an adequate characterization from a list of subtly different candidates. Consider Kaplan's candidate rule: the reference of the first-person pronoun is the agent of the context. Notice that "agent of the context" is a technical term for Kaplan. For technical reasons having to do with contexts in which no one is speaking, Kaplan doesn't understand 'the agent' to mean the same as 'the speaker'. The typical competent speaker, I submit, will not find Kaplan's "agent" idea the obvious one. See also pages 202–3 of my paper "Has Semantics Rested on a Mistake?," *Journal of Philosophy* 83 (1986): 185–209; also in *Has Semantics Rested on a Mistake?, and Other Essays* (Stanford: Stanford University Press, forthcoming), for further discussion.

[7] It is indeed tempting, following the suggestions of both Walker Percy and David Kaplan in his 1982 Pacific APA response to John Searle, to characterize semanticist as a Martian anthropologist. Don't look into the speaker's head, Kaplan advised, for an account of our practices, but import an alien who has the advantage of distance from our practices. Making the anthropological semanticist a Martian—that is, one who is not a participant in our, or perhaps any linguistic practices—raises its own problems that, for the present, I'd rather avoid.

[8] My anthropological semanticist is not looking for anything like an analysis of the notion of "reference." He, and I—following Kripke in *Naming and Necessity* (Cambridge, Mass.: Harvard University Press, 1980)—take this notion to be a kind of primitive (*for the time being*). Ultimately, I believe, we must say something more substantive about the fundamental notion of "reference," but such a study

Frege's sense-reference account might be seen as providing an answer to this latter question. Contemporary anti-Fregeans have argued that Frege's is not a good answer. It fails to accurately reflect the character of our practices. Perfectly competent speakers often fail to have available the sort of information required of them by Frege's account. They often lack anything like purely qualitative individuating beliefs about the referents of the names that they use. The beliefs that they do have, moreover, often correctly apply to individuals other than the referents of the relevant names, and so on.

Frege, moreover—and this is a point of importance for distinguishing the two conceptions of semantics—does not put forth his sense-reference account as an answer to our anthropological semanticist's question: "What, according to actual linguistic practice, determines the reference of proper names?" Frege's picture provides, inter alia, an answer to this question, but this is not his focus at the beginning of "On Sense and Reference."[9] His primary concern is with explaining the contribution of names to thought contents. If we use 'semantics' in the second, and non-Fregean way, we can say that Frege's interest wasn't primarily semantical.

One with a Fregean conception of semantics, on the other hand, might well wonder about the very relevance to semantics—in his sense— of Millian-style accounts of names. The thesis that the reference of a name depends upon, as Donnellan and Kripke urge, a historical chain of communication, even if this thesis formulates some yet-to-be-classified kind of truth about our practices with proper names, fails to answer the specifically "semantic" questions about the contribution of names

---

should not be thought of as preliminary to the study described in the text, nor have anti-Fregeans yet had virtually anything to say about it (excluding for the moment the minority who have been interested in the physicalistic reduction of the notion of "reference," and who, unlike Kripke himself, claim to see in Kripke's work the makings of such a reduction). A tentative suggestion: If we take seriously the idea that natural language is an institutional arrangement, it would seem natural to see the notion of reference as an "institutional notion," not any more reducible to something physical or psychological than is, say, the notion of "ownership" in some legal system. I find Searle's remarks on institutional facts suggestive here. (See John Searle, *Speech Acts* (London: Cambridge University Press, 1969).) Perhaps it is an "institutional fact" that a certain term refers to something, a fact comparable to the fact that someone owns something, or that someone stole third base. I will pursue this theme elsewhere.

[9] G. Frege, "On Sense and Reference." In *Translations from the Philosophical Writings of Gottlob Frege*, ed. P. Geach and M. Black (Oxford: Blackwell, 1966). I owe this point to Joseph Almog.

to thought contents, and about the cognitive fix involved in the use of names. If, as we are sometimes told, a theory of meaning is a theory of understanding, then it is far from clear that Mill, or the Donnellan-Kripke approach, tells us anything about meaning.

Mill's contemporary sympathizers have indeed often been attacked for the alleged cognitive insensitivity of their view. Millians have not been conscious of deep differences between their conception of semantics and Frege's, and so they have often been embarrassed by the apparent failure of their semantics to yield illumination of the sort demanded by Frege. Alternatively, they have twisted and turned to show that *their* semantic apparatus can be pressed into cognitive service.[10]

The anthropological conception of semantics yields a natural response on behalf of the Millian. The aim of the anthropological semanticist is not, after all, to solve Frege's problems. Nor does the anthropological semanticist presume that his work will yield such solutions. It is not at all obvious that elucidating the social reference-determining conditions will explain the cognitive dimension, for example, the informativeness of 'Hesperus is Phosphorus'. The explanation of the latter may well turn upon, in Putnam's terms, what's in the head of the speaker. Reference, on the other hand—at least if the Millian is correct—has little to do with the head of the speaker. The anthropological semanticist, however, need not assume that his work will be of no help in illuminating the cognitive dimension. He can adopt, as they say, a "wait-and-see" attitude.

Philosophic debates in which the adversaries argue at cross purposes, as have Fregeans and their opponents, are typically fueled by deep, unarticulated differences. The divergence in philosophic outlook between Fregeans and anti-Fregeans is not exhausted, I will argue, by this difference in conception of the semantic enterprise. My central aims here are to call attention to still deeper differences, and to draw some implications for the area of intersection of philosophy of language and philosophy of mind in which Frege and his followers have been so interested.

The anti-Fregean view, it turns out, is far from cognitively insensitive. That view, seen in the context of the broad outlook to be proposed here, does provide a most natural way of thinking about the cognitive dimension. Mill's remarks on names—and those of Donnellan and Kripke as well—do fail to provide for the sort of account of the cognitive di-

---

[10]See "Has Semantics Rested on a Mistake?" for a criticism of various attempts, most notably that of David Kaplan and John Perry.

mension that Frege sought. Their not providing for such an account is indeed a virtue, for a Frege-style account, I will argue, presupposes a Cartesian perspective that we have reason to reject.

II. Frege's Cartesianism

Frege, like his recent critics, never does formulate—or even gesture towards—a comprehensive philosophical outlook. His semantical work, at the same time, is grounded in strong intuitions about intentionality, the contents of thought, and related matters in metaphysics, epistemology, and the philosophy of mind. There is, I submit, a big picture lurking in the wings. I see in Frege's work the deep influence of the Cartesian tradition. I have in mind here not so much specific Cartesian doctrines, as a tendency of mind, a way of approaching the philosophy of language and the philosophy of mind. Frege's sense-reference perspective, his emphasis on the connections between language and objective thought contents accessible to the mind, rather than on, say, the connections between language—thought of as a public, social institution—and the world, bespeaks this Cartesian influence.[11]

Frege might well seem, however, a most unlikely neo-Cartesian. Frege himself, as Michael Dummett emphasizes, has played a crucial role in the twentieth-century anti-Cartesian revolution. Frege's own revolutionary contribution, as Dummett notes, consisted in making the philosophical study of meaning, rather than skepticism and the theory of knowledge, the starting point in philosophy. Frege, moreover, emphasized what we might call "the publicity of thought content," the idea that the thoughts we express with language are not in principle private to the minds of individual thinkers, but are in the public, albeit a nonphysical, domain.

Consider, however, the Fregean semantic perspective vis-à-vis the Cartesian "mirror-of-nature" tradition in the philosophy of mind. That tradition, it is often noted, sees the mind as set against nature, as the

---

[11] The widespread feeling that the Fregean conception of semantics is inevitable— that semantics cannot be divorced from questions about thought and about cognitive significance—owes much, I believe, to a lingering Cartesian influence. This is not to say that contemporary neo-Fregeans are all fundamentally, or equally, Cartesian, or that they all exhibit the influence of that tradition in the same respects. They, under a number of anti-Cartesian influences—most notably that of Wittgenstein—depart in various and sundry ways both from the letter of Frege's law, and the Cartesian spirit that I see as inspiring it. One can, however, see in such contemporaries the strong influence of the Cartesian picture, or so it seems to me.

repository of images and conceptual representations of things. Pieces of language become meaningful by being associated with the conceptual representations. Leaving aside the question of images, and the probably related Fregean "ideas," isn't this picture at least a very close relative of Frege's?

One difference, already noted, is Frege's antipsychologistic platonism, his insistence that senses do not reside in the mind, but rather in a third, objective realm. Still, there is for Frege a realm of representations, distinct from the things represented and accessible to the mind, and linguistic expressions become meaningful only by being associated with these representations.[12]

Frege's making the representations abstract and therefore public entities may obscure, moreover, an important individualistic strain in his view. The reference of a proper name depends, for Frege, not upon anything like the role of the name in the public language, but rather upon the individual's associating a particular sense with the name.[13,14]

Frege's view shares other characteristic features of a Cartesian orientation. It is, Frege tells us, the representations, senses, and not words, that refer in the primary instance.[15] The reference of words is thus

---

[12] The interpretation of Frege is becoming an increasingly tricky business. My reading of Frege makes him an arch-representationalist, and emphasizes the distance between his picture of language and thought and that of someone like the later Wittgenstein. I think that this is in line with a naive, straightforward reading of the text, but this is, of course, controversial. In any case, many philosophers have expressed agreement with the philosophical views of "my" Frege, and we can thus speak of the "Fregean tradition," even if, contrary to my view, Frege never did maintain this sort of outlook. Kaplan remarks that when he presented a similar reading of Frege at Oxford, the response was that first, Frege never held any such thing, and second, if he did he would have been correct.

[13] Similarly, the thought content of a sentence that contains indexical expressions depends upon which sense the speaker attaches to the indexical. In the case of indexicals, however, it may appear that Frege is no more individualistic than anyone else. Doesn't the reference of a demonstrative, e.g., depend upon something quite individual? Even here, I believe that a more social picture is available. The reference of a demonstrative, I argue in "How to Bridge the Gap Between Meaning and Reference," *Synthese* 68 (1984): 63–84, depends not upon the individual's preferred descriptions, nor more generally upon his intentions to refer, but rather upon socially available cues, typically—but not exclusively—pointing gestures and things of the sort.

[14] I am speaking here of Frege's own view. One Neo-Fregean variation consists in socializing Frege's view, and attempting to retrieve the sense of a name not from the individual's associations but from a kind of social poll. Such a view would be continuous with the representationalist aspect of the Cartesian heritage, but would depart from its individualism. See footnote 41 below.

[15] "The regular connexion between a sign, its sense, and its reference is of such a

derivative from the reference of senses.[16]   Proponents of a Cartesian orientation also characteristically emphasize the clarity and distinctness of the representations, and make mathematical concepts the paradigm, and again, Frege is no exception.

So much for Frege's Cartesian perspective on individual terms and the conceptual representations with which they are associated. The same themes reappear—perhaps more strikingly—when we consider Frege's treatment of language at the level of whole sentences.   Just as the vitality—to use Wittgenstein's metaphor—of individual expressions derives from their association with senses, so the vitality of whole sentences derives from their association with sentential senses. Just as the senses of singular terms, rather than the terms themselves, are the things that refer in the most basic sense, so sentential senses—the thought contents—are the primary bearers of truth and falsity. Fregean thoughts, like their constituent senses, are well defined and eternally existing. They constitute, Frege tells us, the "common treasure of mankind."

Frege, although his focus is directed towards Plato's heaven and not towards social practice, would acknowledge the platitude that natural language is a social, institutional arrangement. That particular sentences get correlated with particular thought contents is, he would surely agree, an artifact of human institutional arrangements. Frege would insist, however, that one's thinking a certain thought content is no matter of human convention, institutional arrangement, or anything of the like. It is a matter of one's mind grasping an objectively existing content. More important, then, at least in a sense more important, than the fact that sentences express such "thoughts" is the fact that by uttering sentences we assert them, we give voice to the thought contents that we are thinking. The traditional Fregean account of the "propositional attitudes," for example the idea that belief consists in a relation between a person and a thought content, emerges directly.

---

kind that to the sign there corresponds a definite sense and *to that in turn* [italics added] a definite reference...." From G. Frege, "On Sense and Reference."

[16] Indeed, as Joseph Almog pointed out to me, Frege may be seen as offering a reductive analysis of the reference of terms, reducing the latter to the satisfaction of descriptively articulated conditions. Josef Stern offered the complementary observation that to speak of linguistic reference is not really to speak of the same relation as the "reference" of a sense.

III. A Social, Naturalistic Alternative

Frege, we might say, puts forth a thought-driven picture of language.[17] Language, if we overlook its imperfections, is thought externalized. Frege's conception contrasts dramatically with the one I want to develop, the one I see rationalizing the work of Frege's recent critics. My picture shares much with, and owes a great deal to, that of Wittgenstein.[18] Wittgenstein, although some Fregeans are fond of claiming him for their own, gives voice to a radically different perspective, one less representationalist, and arguably more naturalistic. I don't want here to engage in Wittgenstein interpretation, an even trickier business than Frege interpretation. So let me just sketch my alternative.

The approach I have in mind, in stark contrast to the Cartesian tradition, denies that pieces of language become meaningful by being associated with representations, mental or objective. It is here that the connections between Wittgenstein and contemporary anti-Fregeans emerge most clearly. Consider Putnam's slogan, slightly adapted: Meaning ain't in, nor is it available to, the head. Indeed, a central lesson of Wittgenstein's *Philosophical Investigations*[19] is that there is less available to the head than one might have supposed, and further that whatever is intellectually available is less relevant to philosophers' questions about language (and even thought) than one might have supposed.

If the vitality of linguistic expressions is not a function of associated representations, of what is it a function? The broadly Wittgensteinian answer is that the significance of a piece of language is a function of its embeddedness in social, linguistic practice. The problem for those of us—virtually everybody—brought up Cartesian is to make this more concrete, to somehow allow us to get a feel for how meaningfulness could be a function of anything other than representations.

The Donnellan-Kripke historical chain picture—whether or not it provides the last word on its subject matter[20]—can be pressed into ser-

---

[17] Having made the distinction, crucial to Frege's account, between the psychological process of thinking and its objective content, I will not always be careful to observe it, at least where there is no danger of confusion. I thus take not only Frege's view, but also views according to which thought contents are *mental*, to be "thought-driven." I want to emphasize how much all such Cartesian-spirited views have in common, despite differences about the ontological status of the contents.

[18] The seminal work of Strawson should also be mentioned in this connection.

[19] L. Wittgenstein, *Philosophical Investigations*, trans. G. E. M. Anscombe. New York: Macmillan Publishing Co., Inc., 1953.

[20] As anything more than a picture which provides direction to our thinking, it is

vice here as suggesting a model of how significance might depend upon social practice, and not upon representations. An introductory philosophy student, quite ignorant about Aristotle and his accomplishments, asks, "Who was Aristotle? Was he the one who believed that everything was water?" The name 'Aristotle' as it occurs in the student's questions, surmises, and assertions, makes reference to Aristotle, our Aristotle, in virtue of—as the Donnellan-Kripke sketch goes—a historical chain of communication that stretches back to something like an original baptism. Notice that the Donnellan-Kripke account gives the name a role in the *public language*; it functions as part of a public, name-using practice. The name, as uttered on these occasions, has a *conventional* referent.[21] The name connects to the referent, then, in virtue of a communal practice of using this name as a name for him, and not in virtue of conceptual associations.[22]

Wittgenstein, in the service of a social practice picture, sometimes appears to urge that we drop talk of "meaning" in favor of talk of "use." I don't know that we need follow this advice strictly, but there is surely something to be said for his idea. Talk of "meaning" tends, for one thing, to suggest the very representationalist picture we are at pains to supplant. It tends to conjure up images of "grasping meanings," when there are—think about names from Millian perspective—no meanings to grasp. And thinking about linguistic competence in terms of grasping meanings encourages us to emphasize the theoretical knowledge involved in competence, to think in terms of *knowing that* as opposed to the more appropriate *knowing how*.

It is natural enough, moreover, to speak of "meaning" both in connection with communal linguistic practice *and* in connection with individual speakers' conceptual associations. So meaning-talk, instead of

---

surely inadequate. The sketch it provides, moreover, may well be questioned, even by the anti-Fregeans. Kaplan, in *Demonstratives*, this volume; and Joseph Almog in "Semantical Anthropology," in *Midwest Studies in Philosophy* 9, ed. P. French, T. Uehling, and H. Wettstein (Minneapolis: University of Minnesota Press, 1984), 479–90, suggest that although historical chains need to be brought into the total picture of our practice with names, the chains are not to be brought into the semantics, per se. That is, contrary to the suggestion of Donnellan's and Kripke's original remarks, the historical chains do not, strictly speaking, determine reference. Kripke himself recently suggested a similar view in conversation.

[21] See footnote 38 below for a brief discussion of the so-called ambiguity of proper names.

[22] 'Conceptual' here is not intended to invoke anything like Fregean senses, or Cartesian concepts. What I have in mind, for example, is the fact that I associate being a philosopher with the name 'Bertrand Russell'.

helping us keep these topics distinct, encourages conflating them. Keeping them distinct is, of course, absolutely crucial from the point of view taken here.[23]

The moral I want to draw is not that we need to banish all talk of meaning, but that we handle it with care. Wittgenstein himself at times appears to urge not that we drop talk of meaning in favor of talk of use, but that we identify meaning with use. It seems too strong, however, to suggest that there isn't *anything* more to meaning, in any of its manifestations, than communal linguistic practice. We might settle for the more modest methodological exhortation that insofar as we do talk of meaning, we give pride of place to the social, specifically to communal practice, rather than to individual, or even community-wide, representations. Even when we turn to the Fregean's favorite questions about individual cognition—and we ought not do this too quickly, so the methodological sermon continues—our prior study of meaning *as* use will be focal. It is to court disaster to look first toward what is available to the individual consciousness for the clarification of virtually anything that comes under the rubric "meaning."

Crucial to the outlook that I am recommending, then, is its rejection of Frege's thought-driven conception of language.[24] One implication of the latter conception, an implication noted above, is that it is the conceptual representations rather than their linguistic embodiments that, in the first instance, refer. The real action, as it were, takes place at a good distance from our social practices. This would seem to lead to the thought that the first step towards understanding how words refer is to understand how thoughts do so.[25] Nothing could be farther from the truth according to our new picture. What we semanticists study is not thought, but our social practices of talking about things. Indeed, it

---

[23] Kaplan has remarked that talk of linguistic meaning, even descriptive meaning, seems more at home when we turn our attention from proper names to, for example, indexicals. Even here, however, talk of "meaning" has probably done more harm than good, again encouraging representationalist tendencies, and leading us away from the proper emphasis on the use of language as a kind of practical mastery. Kaplan's account of indexicals (in *Demonstratives*), ground-breaking as it was, had a strong representationalist flavor, a point to which I'll return in the final section below.

[24] See chapter 2, "Russell and More Frege," of my forthcoming book, *The Magic Prism: An Essay in the Philosophy of Language*, for a more detailed look at Frege's representationalism. Russell's position on this question, as noted and explored there, is complicated.

[25] It is interesting that one who looks for illumination on this apparently fundamental question fails to get much help from, say, Frege.

becomes tempting, although it is no doubt too simple, to construe silent thought on the model of internal utterance.

So far we have the bare bones of the more socially sensitive, naturalistic picture that I want to recommend. I will soon turn to implications for the area of intersection of the philosophy of language and the philosophy of mind to which Fregeans have riveted our attention. First, however, I want to more fully sketch my picture. The additional features of my view that I will mention are important to the overall perspective, but they do not figure directly in the account of the cognitive dimension that I will offer. I thus want to mention and motivate them here, but a full discussion will not be possible.

(1) Clarity and Distinctness

Frege attributes to the third realm entities that he takes to stand behind language, entities like senses and thought contents, an extreme, perhaps even absolute, refinement; they are necessarily clear and distinct. Think here of Frege's comment, for which he took some chiding from Wittgenstein,[26] that a concept without boundaries is no concept at all.

Frege, of course, is not alone here. There is a deep tendency in the representationalist tradition to attribute such purity to the representations, a tendency that has consequences for one's conception of language. The ways in which the conception of language may be affected are various. Philosophers have sometimes seen language, or at least its more "respectable" parts, as itself possessing a kind of clarity and distinctness—as being associated, for example, with clear criteria that specify necessary and sufficient conditions of application. Alternatively, language may be seen as a mere dim reflection of the pristine realm, and the messiness of language attributed to our all-too-human ways of getting at the clear and distinct concepts.[27] Either way, the background conception of perfectly refined representations plays a dominating role.

Rejecting the representationalist picture may open the door to a different way of thinking about linguistic practice. It is here that we anti-Fregeans have most to learn from Wittgenstein. A truly social, antirepresentationalist picture will not merely reject the ontology of ob-

---

[26] See section 71 of the *Philosophical Investigations*.

[27] Think here about the tendency to see an important task of philosophy as "explicating" sloppy ordinary talk and replacing it with more precise, scientifically acceptable forms of speech.

jective or mental concepts. It is not even enough to embrace the idea that meaningfulness is to be cashed out ultimately in terms of linguistic practice. One might go this far, but remain in the grip of a picture of practice and its governing rules (or *RULES*) that derives from the rejected Cartesian perspective. One might well presuppose, and see semantics as the attempt to uncover—as indeed we anti-Fregeans have—a kind of rigidity on the part of the phenomena, a fixedness that the phenomena may in fact fail to exhibit.

A detailed look at actual practice is out of the question here, but it will stand us in good stead to remind ourselves that our practices with words do not evolve from the attempt to capture in words, or communicate to others, preexistent concepts that, almost by definition, possess the required refinement.

In the beginning—if the reader will indulge me one more time—there were the primitive brutes, bumping into each other and grunting, by way of indicating to their fellows salient features of the environment. Linguistic practice, on this impressionistic picture, gets more articulated, more refined, as suits the practical, social, and, eventually, intellectual needs of the brutes and their successors. The crucial point is that whatever precision, articulation, refinement does evolve is a result of pressures of the sorts mentioned, and not a result of the desire to capture in words some absolutely precise Cartesian concepts. The precision achieved is thus never "absolute," whatever that might mean, nor is there any absolute standard—like the Cartesian concepts—by which we might assess the precision of usage.

To the extent one thinks that such a sketch roughly represents the way things really go, to that extent one will be skeptical of philosophers' tendency to impute clarity and distinctness to usage, or to usage-when-it-is-up-to-snuff. And to that extent, one will be sympathetic even to Wittgenstein's more radical "lack-of-regimentation" claims.

Consider, for example, the putative "family resemblance" phenomenon. Reflection upon actual linguistic practice with many general terms, 'game' for example, fails to reveal—urges Wittgenstein—what the traditional picture led us to expect: a set of features common to all games, features that are individually necessary and jointly sufficient for something to be a game. Given our new picture, Wittgenstein's claims don't seem outlandish. Why indeed can't there be terms the utility of which don't depend upon there being something substantive shared by the things to which the term applies? Might there well not be utility to having a term that collects a range of things that are roughly similar to one another, things that fail to share any single feature, but that share a kind of family resemblance?[28,29]

Consider a related "lack of refinement" phenomenon, vagueness, the fact that, for example, there are no sharp boundaries separating games from nongames. The Cartesian can try to account for vagueness in any number of ways,[30] but, to be sure this phenomenon does not fit like hand-in-glove with the Cartesian picture, and something will have to be said.

Far from being a source of pressure to our more naturalistic, social account, vagueness is entirely to be expected. Remember, we don't start with preexistent, sharply demarcated concepts, the common treasure of personkind.[31] Our practices with words are only as refined as they are, and there is no external standard (like how well they capture our conceptual representations) by which to measure them. If there are cases that in practice rarely occur, for example, borderline cases of the

---

[28] Perhaps you will think: But how could someone ever *learn* to apply a general term, if not by somehow picking up, even if not totally consciously, which features count as the, so to speak, essential ones? This question, however, presupposes a "definition-based" picture of concept acquisition, as opposed to what we might call a "paradigm-based" picture. Having been exposed to a certain number of cases, and been perhaps corrected on a number of occasions on the application of the term, one gets the feel for what is to count as a genuine application of the term, somewhat like the way one gets the feel for how to serve in tennis. The topic of definition-based, as opposed to paradigm-based, pictures of concept acquisition deserves more attention than it has received in the philosophic literature. For an interesting discussion see chapter 5 of Stephen Stich's *From Folk Psychology to Cognitive Science* (Cambridge, Mass.: MIT Press, 1983).

[29] I am merely scratching the surface here. As Stephen Stich points out, there may be various kinds of cases in which the traditional picture of predicates-and-properties fails, and there may be very different reasons why it fails, not all having to do with family resemblances. See his paper, "Are Belief Predicates Systematically Ambiguous?" in *Belief*, ed. R. J. Bogdan (Oxford: Clarendon Press, 1986). Nor is this notion of family resemblance sufficiently clear. For example, is Wittgenstein advancing what has come to be known as a "cluster theory," or is his point about family resemblance terms, as I suspect, a more radical one?

[30] He might, for example, modify his picture of concepts so that the concepts themselves—or the properties—can somehow be vague. Alternatively, he might attribute vagueness only to language and not to concepts, and go on to lament the great gap between the two. Finally, he might understand the "master's" inability to decide borderline cases as a lack of total, theoretical mastery of the relevant nonvague expression.

[31] This last word seems just right, not only because it avoids the masculine form, but because it would apply even to angels (if there were any). Fregean thoughts are the common treasure of all rational beings. Again, the real action, as noted above, takes place at a great remove from social practice.

applicability of a term, then it is likely that even a master of the term will not be able to say that the term either clearly does, or clearly does not, apply. This inability reflects not a lack of mastery, but rather reflects the fact that, as Wittgenstein says, the borders have not yet been drawn.[32]

An important component of the antirepresentationalist picture is thus its expectation that usage will turn out to be considerably less regimented than we have supposed. This is not to say that we can expect Wittgenstein's family resemblance picture to provide a generally applicable model. The primitive brutes and their successors, after all, can become attuned to relatively stable aspects of their natural environments—for example, the water that they drink and bathe in—and come to have terms that apply in an at least somewhat, and perhaps dramatically, less open-ended way. Even pieces of language that seem more deeply institutional than do natural kind terms like 'water' may presumably vary widely in the degree of regimentation they exhibit. Perhaps we should expect a continuum here. The point, though, is that we cannot simply proceed as we have, taking Kaplan's

> The reference of the first-person pronoun is the agent of the context

as the model of what the semanticist should aim to uncover.[33]

---

[32] These Wittgensteinian reflections suggest a more fundamental criticism of Fregeanism than that typically urged by the anti-Fregeans, namely that *there can be no Fregean sense of terms like 'game'*. The sense of this term, for one thing, was supposed to consist in a specification of those features, common to all games, that are necessary and sufficient for the application of the term. Wittgenstein's point, though, is that there are no such common features. Games, moreover—and this emphasizes from another side why there *cannot be* a sense that has the class of games as its extension—do not constitute a determinate kind, the sort of thing that might be determined by a Fregean sense. Games rather constitute loose, open-ended assortment.

[33] Another Wittgensteinian theme to be pursued elsewhere: It has been often assumed that there is a single notion, "reference," that provides the master key to the connection between words and things. But it seems far from obvious that the semantics of predicates is best understood in terms of the notion of reference. That is, it isn't obvious—perhaps especially in light of the Wittgensteinian discussion of "is a game"—that the final semantical word on predicates is that they refer to properties. Nor is it even obvious that indexicals like 'now' *refer* to times. (What are times?) What I see as the core of Kaplan's idea about 'now' was that the truth-values of utterances that contain 'now' depend not upon anything like a Fregean sense that has a time as reference, but simply upon a feature of the context of utterance, namely, when the sentence was uttered. This need not incline us to say that 'now' *refers* to the time of utterance.

(2) Propositional Content

Propositions, it is often noted, have been wanted as the bearers of truth, and as the "objects of propositional attitudes." Frege's representationalist picture makes it natural to let the sentence-level representations, the Fregean thoughts, play these roles. What, though, if we reject representationalism in favor of the kind of perspective I am advocating? What becomes of propositions?

The topic is, however, gigantic. I can only sketch what I take to be the natural response, that a truly social and naturalistic conception will want to do without propositions. I will briefly mention two sorts of considerations that seem to me to militate against propositions.

(a) Naturalism

Kaplan has recently objected to the Platonistic conception of the individuation of words. We suppose, he argues, that the distinction between word tokens and abstract types is the basis of the individuation of words. Not so! What makes your utterance of 'Aristotle' and mine two occurrences of the same word is not the supposed fact that both occurrences stand in a relation to some abstract stereotype that they instantiate, or are members of, an abstract type that inhabits Frege's third realm. The worldly occurrences need to be linked in some more naturalistic way; their being occurrences of the same word must be a function of our social, linguistic interactions.[34]

I want to reject, in this same spirit, the notion that thought, belief, and assertion, for example, consist in relations to abstract entities. The anti-Fregeans' "singular propositions" may appear to be more innocuous than Fregean thoughts, for singular propositions are abstract entities that have been, so to speak, brought down to earth. Among their constituents, after all, are things like you and me. Even such propositions, however, seem to me objectionable from a naturalistic point of view. Had we anti-Fregeans not started with Fregean thoughts and then made the appropriate amendments—replacing Frege's propositional constituents, senses, with referents—would it have seemed natural to construe thought, belief, and assertion as involving relations between minds (or even persons) and abstract entities? The very idea that thought, et al., involves such relations may well be a legacy of the Fregean/Cartesian

---

[34] Kaplan's positive suggestion is to link them in terms of the Donnellan-Kripke chains of communication.

picture.

(b) The Messiness of Linguistic Practice

How does the propositions picture—explicated in terms either of Fregean thoughts or singular propositions—comport with that other implication of our social orientation, the fact that usage often fails to be sharply bounded, that usage is only as clear as it needs be? Assume, for a moment, that Wittgenstein was correct, and that 'game' is a family resemblance term. What proposition is expressed by 'That is a game'? What, specifically, are we to make of the predicate constituent? The idea that the predicate constituent is the property of being a game surely doesn't comport well with our "family resemblance" account.

My question is whether the apparatus of propositions is compatible in spirit with the social orientation. There is no question that it can be made compatible. One might insist that the proposition does contain the property of being a game (or the sense of 'game'), it's just a fuzzy property (or sense), or something of the like. Surely we can hang onto the notion of a proposition, if we want to. The question is whether the most natural way to work out a socially sensitive conception of language involves the notion of a proposition.

These remarks raise many questions, of course, questions about how, without propositions, we are to do the work traditionally assigned to them. Are we to try to do without truth bearers? If not, what will play that role? How are we to construe belief, if not as involving a relation to a proposition? I cannot, of course, begin to deal with these questions here, but I will do so elsewhere.[35]

IV. Intentionality: The Missing Cognitive Fix

I turn now to the problems bequeathed to us by Frege that have seemed to make life so difficult for anti-Fregeans. Let's begin with what may appear to be the anti-Fregean's most severe headache, the Cartesian intuition concerning intentionality, the problem of the missing cognitive fix. The Cartesian idea that reference requires discriminating knowledge initially looks unassailable. Indeed, I have heard it said that this alone disqualifies the anti-Fregean's semantical views. The Cartesian

---

[35] In "Bringing Belief Down to Earth," a chapter in my forthcoming book, *The Magic Prism: An Essay in the Philosophy of Language*, I attempt to develop an account of belief that is sensitive to the points made here.

intentionality intuition takes on a very different look, however, when reconsidered from the vantage point of our more social, naturalistic picture.

If we look at our actual practices, as Wittgenstein urged, rather than think about them, the "cognitive fix" requirement immediately begins to look suspicious, perhaps just plain wrong. People often simply don't have much of a fix on the things to which they refer. For one thing, as has been pointed out time and again, the beliefs that a speaker has about the referent of a name that he is using may be very far off the mark, and yet his reference is not affected.[36] A philosophy student may mistakenly associate with 'Aristotle' the properties of having taught Plato and having died of hemlock poisoning, and yet his utterances of the name, say, on an exam, count as references to Aristotle, our Aristotle.

There are many cases, moreover, in which a competent speaker doesn't begin to possess the sort of information about his referent that would single out that referent, that would distinguish the latter from many other things. Felipe Alou, I know, was a major-league baseball player. I don't know much else about him, surely not enough to individuate him in any serious way from many others, and yet I can use his name to say things about him. Similarly, as Kripke points out, all that many people know about Cicero is that he was *a Roman orator*.[37] Consider also Kripke's Gell-Mann and Feynman example in which a speaker competent with two names associates precisely the same (meager) information with each. Such a speaker refers to Gell-Mann when he uses the latter's name, and to Feynman when he utters 'Feynman', despite the fact that the only salient thing he knows about either of them is that

---

[36] Here, as elsewhere throughout this paper, it is "semantic reference," the conventional reference of the name, as opposed to the "speaker's reference," roughly the individual that the speaker has in mind, that is under discussion, unless otherwise indicated. For the distinction between semantic reference and speaker's reference see Kripke's paper, "Speaker's Reference and Semantic Reference," in *Contemporary Perspectives in the Philosophy of Language*, 6–27.

[37] Fregeans sometimes appeal to the fact that we also know that he was called "Cicero." This metalinguistic move has, for me at least, the flavor of an ad hoc response to save the theory. Independently, however, it is far from unproblematic. To mention one problem, the names we use often name many different people, and so, in general, the metalinguistic move, unless further supplemented, will often not provide individuating descriptions. To mention another, Cicero wasn't called "Cicero" by his fellows. That's our name for him. So this approach certainly needs refinement. Cf. Stephen Schiffer's remarks (110–11) in "The Real Trouble with Propositions," in *Belief: Form, Content, and Function*, ed. R. J. Bogdan (Oxford: Clarendon Press, 1986), 83–117.

each is *a leading theoretical physicist*. Putnam makes the same point with the natural kind terms 'elm' and 'beech'.

Reference in the absence of an accurate cognitive fix looks miraculous, I submit, only to the Cartesian, or the residual Cartesian strain in us. If pieces of language refer only in virtue of their being associated with representations, then it is miraculous that someone should refer to something in the absence of an appropriate representation. This sense of miraculousness fades fast, however, when we bring the conception of a public language into sharp focus, a conception suggested by the sorts of examples mentioned above. What connects the student's utterance to Aristotle is not the student's cognitive fix on Aristotle. What connects utterance to referent is rather the fact that the student is using a linguistic device that, as our social practices go, refers to Aristotle. Linguistic expressions, as parts of a public practice, attain a kind of life of their own. One who uses a name participates in a public practice, and refers to the name's *conventional* referent.[38] Indeed, so from there being an epistemological requirement of the sort supposed by the traditional picture, it rather seems that one of the crucial functions of proper names is to allow us to bridge great cognitive gulfs, to allow us to make things subjects of discourse even when they are epistemically far removed from us. The public language thus makes it possible for us to speak about things even when our beliefs about them are very scanty, confused, even badly mistaken. The examples that seem to show that reference does not require discriminating knowledge should not, then, seem astounding, or indeed at all surprising, at least not on our social picture.[39]

---

[38] More accurately, proper names, as used on particular occasions, have conventional referents. The name 'Aristotle' can be used to refer to any one of the people so called. On particular occasions of use, however, only one of these will be the conventional referent. This fact about our practices will make life difficult for the anthropological semanticist. He will want to inquire as to what subtle factors determine which individual called "Aristotle" is in question on particular occasions. It is sometimes suggested that this so-called ambiguity of names is evidence for the Fregean picture. It is far from obvious, however, that the answer to the semantical anthropologist's question will pertain exclusively to the beliefs of the speaker. It is very far from obvious that such considerations should convince us that speakers need to have *individuating* conceptions of their referents. Perhaps their beliefs can be far off the mark, but something very different makes it the case that it is this Aristotle that is in question, perhaps some features of the context, or perhaps something about the historical chain of communication. Or perhaps, to allude to the more radical Wittgensteinian tack suggested at the end of section III above, there is no one simple formula, a theory that will neatly apply to every case.

[39] Taking seriously that proper names are elements of the public language does not,

One with Cartesian intuitions might admit that underscoring the social and institutional character of natural language is the best way for the anti-Fregean to proceed:

> Emphasizing that proper names are part of a public, institutional practice might well seem to make sense of the idea that a speaker need not have much of a cognitive fix on the things about which he speaks. The effect of the anti-Fregean proposal, though, is to make speech and thought radically discontinuous—for such a cognitive fix is surely indispensable to *thought*—and such a radical discontinuity is just not acceptable. If, in the Aristotle-Socrates case above, for example, it is clear that the descriptions the speaker would offer really do take us to Socrates, then he surely was *thinking* about Socrates. If, moreover, a speaker uses a name in the absence of a cognitive fix, then he really can't be *thinking* about anyone.

So much in philosophy depends upon which phenomena one takes to be fundamental, where one starts. The anti-Fregean focus has admittedly not been on thought, but on language, public language. The Cartesian, believing as he does that this is the wrong place to begin, might well conclude that notwithstanding the apparent counterexamples drawn from actual communicative practice, linguistic reference, unless it is to be divorced from thought, *must* require discriminating knowledge.

Alternatively, if one with Cartesian intuitions is impressed enough with the social and institutional character of natural language *and* with the anti-Fregeans' counterexamples, he might be willing to endorse the alleged discontinuity between thought and speech.[40] "I'll give you speech," we might imagine him saying, "but thought is quite another

---

on the other hand, *entail* that the references of names does not depend upon the properties that individual speakers associate with the name. Nor does the public-language picture entail that reference surely doesn't require a cognitive fix. Perhaps a practice might evolve in which the references of certain sorts of linguistic expressions were dependent solely upon the properties that the speaker associates with the expression. I think that although we cannot rule out this possibility a priori, it is not at all surprising, given the public-language picture, that names do not function in this way.

[40] The general approach discussed in this paragraph, although not all of the details, was endorsed by John McDowell (in conversation) and by Gareth Evans in *The Varieties of Reference* (Oxford: Clarendon Press, 1982). Evans writes,

> The abandonment of the principle of identification [the "cognitive fix" requirement] at the level of saying is a trivial consequence of the distinc-

thing." The idea is that the correct interpretation of speech is perhaps, in the final analysis, in the public domain. It is a matter of the conventions of the linguistic community, and really not a matter of what's in the head of the speaker. What one *thinks*, on the other hand, is very much a matter of what's in (or available to) the head of the thinker. An utterance of 'Aristotle wrote the *Ethics*', say, in a philosophy class, counts as a reference to Aristotle, but if the speaker takes Aristotle to be the teacher of Plato, etc., his *thought* is directed upon Socrates. What about one whose beliefs about Aristotle are so indefinite that they fail to discriminate anyone? Perhaps such a speaker fails to be thinking about anyone.[41]

Emerging here again is the deep difference between a broadly Cartesian orientation, and the more social, naturalistic view. It is no accident, no mere oversight, that anti-Fregeans have tended to begin with the study of public practices of communication, practices that we tend to see as, so to speak, relatively out in the open. Thought seems to us, or at least to me, a much more difficult and elusive topic, one with which we might do better had we some grip on our public communicative practices.

It thus makes good sense that the Cartesian would worry that we anti-Fregeans have distanced speech from thought in an extreme way. My worry, on the other hand, is that the Cartesian, on the basis of his philosophical picture of thought, either denies what seems plain about

---

tion between what one says and what thought one intends to express. Its abandonment at the level of *belief* or *thought* would be an extremely significant move. What has happened is that the former has been mistaken for the latter. (76, footnote 18)

[41] Another Fregean variation involves insisting that reference does require individuating knowledge, but not on the part of the individual speaker or thinker. Kripke, in *Naming and Necessity*, discusses a socialized description theory of names, an attempt to defeat anti-Fregean criticisms by socializing Frege's approach. One might, in this spirit, try to retrieve the sense of a name not from the individual speaker, but somehow from the linguistic community. Such an approach would be more socially sensitive than Frege's, but it would still over-intellectualize language (and, to anticipate, thought), at least from the point of view taken here. The distinction that needs emphasis is that between an approach that makes reference depend upon the beliefs of the community, and one that makes it depend only upon the community's practice. Couldn't it be, for example, that our current beliefs about a historical individual have become all fouled up, but that the continuity of usage secures reference nevertheless? Our remarks about *him* are, in such a case, mistaken, but there remains an individual about whom we are talking, and about whom we are mistaken.

speech (for example, that reference does not require a cognitive fix), or else grants the latter, but insists on distancing thought from speech. I don't believe that there is any such radical discontinuity between thought and speech, or that the approach taken here suggests such a discontinuity. What seems dubious to me is what the Cartesian takes to be so obvious, the idea that if we restrict our attention to the question of about whom the speakers are *thinking*, it is clear that the background descriptions provide the decisive answer.

Let's begin with examples in which speakers fail to have any sort of real cognitive fix, examples in which the background descriptions fail to individuate. Someone says, "Cicero was a Roman orator," and can't identify Cicero much further. It seems very far-fetched, indeed altogether ad hoc, to suppose that such a perfectly competent and sincere speaker who fails to believe very much about Cicero, ipso facto fails to be thinking about the latter. Surely, in the example above, I was thinking about Felipe Alou. The phenomenon of reference in the absence of individuating information is so pervasive that the supposition in question would deny thought content to an extremely wide range of sincere utterances produced by reflective people. This surely seems like the proverbial philosopher's view, as opposed to what seems plain to just about everyone.[42] Thinking about something, it would seem, no more requires a cognitive fix than does speaking about something.

Let's turn to the case of the speaker who has "mistaken beliefs," whose background descriptions fit not the referent of the uttered name, but rather someone else. Consider the Aristotle-Socrates case above. There are, no doubt, examples of this sort with respect to which it will be perfectly natural to say that the speaker was thinking about the denotation of the background descriptions. The question is whether this is necessarily so, whether the simple fact that the background descriptions take us to Socrates itself establishes that the speaker was thinking about Socrates. It seems pretty clear, at least if we take our cue from our ordi-

---

[42] One might, of course, insist that it can't be that speakers are so cognitively impoverished, that contrary to what the Kripke-Putnam examples suggest, we somehow *must* have available some individuating description. If the Fregean can make good on such an insistence, and do so in a natural way—a tall order—then these counterexamples lose their force. Evans and McDowell, impressed by the Cartesian intuition, but also by the social character of language *and* by the anti-Fregean counterexamples, grant that we often don't have such information when we use, for example, historical names. They thus insist that in such cases, speakers, although their words refer, and their sentences have truth-values, fail to express thought.

nary judgments, that the background descriptions do not play any such decisive role. We would ordinarily say, after all, in many such cases, that the speaker expressed a mistaken *belief*, even a mistaken *thought*, about Aristotle.[43]

Let's turn from our ordinary judgments, and get philosophical. The Fregean, in making the background descriptions decisive, gives a kind of cognitive priority to descriptions over names. This is natural enough, given the Fregean outlook, including the cognitive fix requirement, modes of presentation that are supposed to capture the cognitive perspective, and so on. The question is, however, whether *we* ought to accept this inegalitarian treatment of names vis-à-vis descriptions.

The situation, after all, is that the speaker actually uttered a name that, as our practices go, names *Aristotle*. If queried about of whom he was speaking, it is true, our speaker would have provided a description that fits Socrates. How does this make it the case that he was thinking of Socrates? Why not say instead that he was thinking about the person named by the name that he used, that is Aristotle, and the background descriptions merely reveal his (in this case false) beliefs about that person. In any case, the uttered name takes us to one person, the to-be-uttered-if-asked descriptions to another. What, other than the disputed Cartesian picture, makes it so obvious that we should favor the latter?

My point here, as already indicated, is not that we ought always to give priority to the uttered name over the background descriptions, or that, more generally, whatever singular term is uttered should furnish the key to the referent-in-thought. Sometimes, we ought indeed to privilege unuttered, background terms. One might, for example, utter the name 'Jones' as a mere slip of the tongue, while thinking about, and intending to say something about, Smith. Alternatively, one might mistakenly take 'Brown' to be the name of Harris, and, thinking about and intending to say something about Harris, one might use the name 'Brown'. So a name other than the uttered name may deserve priority, and so may a background description. Someone might, for example, be thinking about "the most ugly, and nasty, professional wrestler, who-

---

[43] Again, the Fregean can insist that if the speaker really has a mistaken belief that is about Aristotle, then the descriptions must fit the latter. One way to make this work would be to come up with descriptions other than the obvious ones, and argue that these are really available to the speaker. I am again skeptical about the prospects for a natural-seeming answer along these lines, but I do not here explore the matter further.

ever that is." Thinking that the person in question is none other than Brutus Beefcake, the speaker may make a remark mentioning the latter by name. If B.B. does not really fit the description, however, there may well be circumstances in which it would be appropriate to say that the speaker was really thinking of "the most ugly, and nasty, professional wrestler, whoever that is," or even that he was thinking about the Iron Sheik, if the latter is indeed uglier and nastier than any other.

We should not, then, expect a simple formula in answer to the question of how, in general, we are to determine which item it was about whom someone was thinking.[44] My point here was not to provide such an answer, one that favors, say, uttered names over background descriptions. It was merely to dispel the illusion that at least cognitively—if not semantically—names must be backed up by individuating concepts, and that the question of about whom someone is thinking when he utters a name is to be resolved by reference to such a background concept. Whatever we do, in the end, with the thorny problem of reference in thought, it is far from clear that the Cartesian spirited Fregean idea, the contention that the descriptions-to-be-uttered-if-asked must be decisive, has much merit.[45]

I will conclude this section with some remarks on the implications of my view for another topic that deserves book-length treatment, that of silent thought. It is sometimes supposed that the Cartesian intentionality intuition has a kind of obvious plausibility when it comes to

---

[44] Indeed, it may be that in many cases, there is no one thing thought about. Even some of the cases briefly described in the last paragraph may be more appropriately described as cases in which the agent is thinking to some extent of one person, and to some extent of another. I discuss this question in more detail in "How to Bridge the Gap Between Meaning and Reference." Cf. S. Kripke, "Speaker Reference and Semantic Reference."

[45] My own view, elaborated in "Bringing Belief Down to Earth," is that ascription of reference in thought, like ascription of belief, depends upon subtleties involving not only the situation of the thinker, but also the situation of the reporter, the one who is ascribing the reference-in-thought or the belief. In other words, "about whom he was thinking" depends not only upon considerations having to do with the thinker, but also upon what is relevant or important to the discussion in which the reporter is engaged. Quine, in *Word and Object* (Cambridge, Mass.: MIT Press, 1960), emphasized this sort of context-sensitivity of "attitude reports," and I discuss this in "Bringing Belief Down to Earth." My view is thus doubly anti-Cartesian. First, I certainly don't think that the question of reference in thought is to be resolved by looking exclusively to the speaker's concepts. Second, and more radically, I think that there are factors that, on the more traditional picture, ought to have nothing to do with the question of reference in thought, that are really extremely germane, the "pragmatic" factors mentioned above.

silent thought episodes; that somehow silent thought, as opposed to overt speech, is a most natural candidate for the Cartesian picture. Consider again someone who, although ignorant of Cicero's accomplishments (say other than being a Roman orator), uses the name pretty much as we all do. We are ordinarily willing to ascribe thoughts about Cicero to such a person when he says things like "I know who Cicero was. He was a Roman orator." Isn't it equally clear that he is in a position to have silent thoughts about Cicero? Surely it's not the verbalization that makes thought about Cicero possible.

Being a participant in a name using practice, specifically, being competent with 'Cicero', our speaker is in a position to use the name not only in overt speech episodes, but also in silent thought. Do names, then, actually occur in silent thought episodes? Are there at least some such episodes that amount to internal utterance? My point does not depend on positive answers to these questions. Whether or not his silent thought that Cicero was an orator amounts to his silently rehearsing this sentence—indeed however we understand silent thought episodes— his competence with the name, his participation in the practice, puts him in a position to have the thought that he would express, were he to put it into words, as "Cicero was an orator." Not only does the reference of an utterance not depend upon one's cognitive fix, the reference of one's silent thought similarly does not depend upon "what's in the head." This will, of course, seem preposterous from a Cartesian point of view.

V. How Puzzling Is Frege's Puzzle?

Frege's discussion of cognitive significance, at the beginning of "On Sense and Reference," is focused upon his famous puzzle about informative identity sentences. How, Frege wants to know, are we to explain the difference in "cognitive value" between the trivial 'Hesperus is Hesperus' and the informative 'Hesperus is Phosphorus', that fact that these sentences formulate different thoughts?

Frege's focus on identity-sentences is not altogether salutary, for contrary to its suggestion, the fundamental problem about the cognitive dimension of language with which Frege was centrally concerned has nothing special to do with identity. Frege's fundamental problem was that of accounting for the fact that a mere change of one coreferring name for another can affect a change, indeed a very significant change, in the thought content of a sentence. Frege might well have avoided identity, with all its attendant perplexities, and have asked for the explanation of the difference in cognitive value between 'Hesperus is a planet' and the corresponding "Phosphorus" sentence.[46]

Frege's discussion—let's focus on the two sentences just mentioned—draws attention to what I'll call "Frege's data," to cognitive phenomena of undeniable importance: One might understand both sentences, for example, but be willing to assert only one of them, even emphatically deny the other. Alternatively, one might find, say, the "Hesperus" sentence old hat, but the "Phosphorus" sentence highly informative. Finally, one might behave quite differently depending upon which of these sentences one accepts.

Frege's data are both uncontroversial and uncontroversially important, but the lessons Frege would have us learn from them are far from uncontroversial. The most notorious lesson, quite obviously controversial, is Frege's sense-reference approach to semantics. There is, however, a more subtle, prior message that Frege takes the cognitive phenomena to convey, a putative implication that can be made to seem almost like a datum itself. Notice that in formulating Frege's puzzle in the first two paragraphs of this section, I gloss "difference in cognitive value," as "difference in thoughts expressed." Frege's contention that the two sentences express different thoughts, distinct propositional contents—a natural enough contention given Frege's thought-oriented approach—is far from uncontroversial.

One might, for example, insist, in the spirit of the Russell-Kaplan singular-propositions picture, that 'Hesperus is a planet' and 'Phosphorus is a planet' express the same proposition. Alternatively, one might, in the spirit of the naturalistic approach I've been advocating, try to make do without propositions, without unified things that are, as Strawson once put it, the upshots of assertive utterances. Frege's quasi-datum is surely contestable. What we cannot contest, however, and what I want to explain, are what I've dubbed "Frege's data," the cognitive phenomena that, for Frege, made it plain that different thought contents were indeed expressed by the respective sentences.

Let's keep in mind that our project is not to make good on the alleged cognitive failures of the anti-Fregean semantic approach. Having made the distinction between semantics, on the anthropological conception, and the study of cognitive significance, the anti-Fregean ought not to be

---

[46] Focusing the discussion on the identity case may well induce a solution that fails to apply to the general case. Frege's metalinguistic *Begriffsschrift* account is a case in point.

embarrassed that, say, Mill's remarks on names (or those of Donnellan and Kripke) do not immediately address Frege's data. At the same time, the output of anthropological semantics ought to cohere with a more general account of language and thought, one that must address Frege's data. How, then, might one approach the cognitive phenomena if one takes a broadly Millian approach to the semantics of proper names?

It is striking that even those who have led the revolt against the Fregean orientation have approached the explanation of the cognitive phenomena in a way more suited to the Fregean, representationalist picture. To the representationalist, the obvious and only way to explain differences in the cognitive roles of expressions is in terms of differences in associated representations. Kaplan, to mention a prominent example, tries to account for the difference in cognitive roles of indexical expressions, by resurrecting modes of presentation, not Fregean senses mind you, but more kosher "ways in which agents represent the references of their terms."[47]

The appeal of the representationalist picture, here as before, is a function of the fact that we are its captives. It is difficult to so much as conceive an alternative, even in bare outline. If 'Hesperus is a planet' differs cognitively for an agent from the corresponding "Phosphorus" sentence, doesn't this have to be because he is thinking of the referent in two different ways, because he is employing two different cognitive perspectives. If someone finds 'Hesperus is Phosphorus' informative,

---

[47] John Perry, especially in "Frege on Demonstratives," *Philosophical Review* 83 (1974): 3–32, embraced a similar view. The Perry-Kaplan idea was to retrieve modes of presentation from the "characters" of the indexicals, that is, from the rules that determine their references. 'I' and 'he' have very different characters, and this is so even when the expressions are used to refer to the same thing (and thus induce the same propositional constituent on the Kaplan singular propositions picture). This difference in character means, according to Perry and Kaplan, that 'I' and 'he' take us to their single referent (in the case we are imagining) in different ways, by means of different cognitive perspectives. 'I' presents me as (roughly) "the speaker," and this "mode of presentation" is, of course, very different than that associated with 'he'. The two sentences, 'I am about to be attacked' and 'He is about to be attacked' thus differ in cognitive significance. They can express the same proposition, but, even when they do so, each presents that proposition in a distinctive way, by means of a distinctive cognitive perspective. Notice that the Perry-Kaplan modes of presentation, unlike Fregean senses,

(a) determine a reference only relative to a context of utterance,

and

(b) do not enter into the propositions expressed.

doesn't this have to be because he associates a different way of thinking (or mode of presentation or cognitive perspective) with the left hand side of the equation than he does with the right hand side? How else might we begin to explain the obvious cognitive differences?

I have argued elsewhere against the Perry-Kaplan approach to the cognitive significance of indexicals.[48] While I stressed there the Fregean flavor of that approach,[49] I was not sufficiently focused upon what I now see as, especially in Kaplan's case, the most striking similarity with Frege, Kaplan's representationalism. He, no less than Frege, explains cognitive differences between expressions as differences in their associated modes of presentation.[50] Here I want to urge that we abandon representationalism even in the study of the cognitive significance phenomena. Modes of presentation, no matter how liberalized and attenuated, remain spiritual descendants of the Fregean approach. Reflection on some of the anti-Fregean discussions of proper names, moreover, should convince at least the discussants that no such representationalist approach, no matter how benign its representationalism, has any hope.

I have in mind here Kripke's Gell-Mann-Feynman case, and Putnam's Elm-Beech story. The original point of these examples was to show that reference does not depend upon what's in the head.[51] What I want to take from these examples is the fact that two names can play cognitively inequivalent roles for a speaker despite the fact that the associated "conceptual files" are identical. The same phenomenon can occur with coreferring names. Someone might acquire the names 'Cicero' and 'Tully', associating with them precisely the same information, say, "a famous Roman." Still the names may differ in "cognitive value." It may never strike the speaker that only one person may be in question, and so he may react very differently to sentences that contain one name, that to those that contain the other. The anti-Fregean explanation of the cognitive difference between 'Cicero' and 'Tully', then, given our

---

[48] See "Has Semantics Rested on a Mistake?"

[49] Kaplan, following Frege, wanted his semantical apparatus to yield an explanation of the cognitive significance phenomena. Kaplan's "characters," like Fregean senses, (1) are in the head, (2) determine reference (although only relative to a context), and (3) explain cognitive significance.

[50] Note, in this connection, that Kaplan's approach to indexicals, while it rejects Frege's version of the cognitive fix requirement, does not reject the requirement. What is needed, according to Kaplan, is a context-relative sort of fix. Relative to a context in which I am speaking, the Kaplanian character of 'I' provides an individuating concept of me.

[51] See pages 439–40 above for a brief discussion of these examples.

own examples, better not rely upon necessary differences in associated information, that is upon different modes of presentation.[52]

My proposal, then, is that we forget modes of presentation, and take a fresh look at the data to which Frege drew our attention. I urged in the last section that the Cartesian intentionality intuition—remember how unassailable it seemed at first—takes on a very different look when considered from the vantage point of our more social, naturalistic picture. The same can be said for the highly-plausible-if-you've-been-brought-up-on-Frege idea that to explain a difference in the cognitive roles of expressions one must appeal to a difference in cognitive perspectives.

Let's begin with the reflection that the more epistemology one builds into linguistic competence with names, that is, the more of a cognitive fix one requires, the more it will seem that Frege's data present not merely interesting and important phenomena to be explained, but a prima facie problem, a *puzzle*. Why is this? The thesis that linguistic competence with names requires mental apprehension of the referent induces a tension between two names coreferring, and their being cognitively inequivalent. If in using each of the two names one must focus upon their single

---

[52]My point here is that a mode-of-presentation type account of the cognitive dimension is very strongly out of step with the anti-Fregean approach. This doesn't mean, of course, that one couldn't try to make the mode-of-presentation type analysis work. Indeed, given the dominant sense that there can be no other way to explain cognitive differences between expressions, it is not surprising that one sees anti-Fregeans searching for some way, compatible with the anti-Fregean approach to semantics, to make it work. One hears in discussion, for example, the idea that the conceptual files in the Cicero-Tully case are distinct, for the speaker associates "being called 'Cicero'" with the name 'Cicero', and "being called 'Tully'" with 'Tully'. Note first that this is just the sort of move that anti-Fregeans fight vigorously when it is used in defense of a Fregean approach to *semantics*. Note second, however, that it seems plausible to suppose that there might be examples in which the same name is in question. One might pick up the name "Paderewski" in two different contexts with the same associated information, e.g., "a famous Polish musician." The speaker may have forgotten where he picked up the names, but he may well remember that there were two such occasions and that he assumed that two different people were in question, and he may begin to wonder whether there are indeed two different people, or whether Paderewski is none other than Paderewski.

There are many other ways to try to work out such a Frege-inspired approach to cognitive significance. My point here is that the spirit of the anti-Fregean outlook should strongly discourage the very attempt. Cf. Kaplan's remarks in "Dthat," in *Contemporary Perspectives in the Philosophy of Language*, on the attempt to find a way to make Fregean semantics work: "I don't deny that on a phenomenon by phenomenon basis we can (in some sense) keep stretching Frege's brilliant insights to cover. With a little ingenuity we *can* do that. But we shouldn't."

referent, how can this identity of reference have escaped notice?

Indeed, if one raises the epistemic stakes enough, it will be impossible to have coreferring names that differ cognitively. Imagine, to take a fanciful example, that we required that a name user be omniscient about the referent. It would then be impossible to be competent with two coreferring names without realizing that only one referent was in question. Coreferring names could then not differ in cognitive significance.

Let's go to the other extreme. Although for present purposes we can consider this another fanciful example, anti-Fregeans have sometimes suggested a "no-epistemology" picture of linguistic competence. One might, on this view, possess *radically* mistaken beliefs about the referent of a name, or virtually no beliefs at all, and still be in a position to use the name as a name for its socially determined referent. Smith, on the periphery of a conversation between mathematicians in which the name 'Joan' is used as a name for a theorem, mistakenly takes Joan to be a woman. Alternatively, Smith comes away completely unsure of who or what Joan is. In either of these cases, on the no-epistemology view, one may still be in a position to say things about the referent, that is the theorem, by using the name. One might, for example, speculate about Joan's properties, or ask who or what Joan is.

If one thus doesn't need to know virtually anything about the referent, it is very easy to see how one could pick up two coreferring names, and not know that they had a single referent. The no-epistemology theorist, since he doesn't think that competence requires mental apprehension of the referent, will thus not see Frege's data as presenting a serious and difficult problem, a real puzzle. Indeed, the explanation of the fact that 'Cicero' and 'Tully' might play different cognitive roles— and not much of an explanation is really needed—would involve simply pointing out that competence with two names does not put one in a position to know whether or not the names corefer. How could it, given that competence requires no knowledge of the referent?

Frege advanced a view intermediate between "omniscience" and "no-epistemology," that a name user need attach to the name a purely qualitative concept that he takes to single out a referent. This is, of course, far from requiring omniscience—much farther, say, than Russell's direct acquaintance requirement[53]—and it allows for a cognitive difference be-

---

[53] Russell required, in effect, that the name user have the referent smack up against his mind. He concluded that coreferring names, used concurrently, could not differ cognitively—if they were really names, that is. If two expressions look like names, but clearly differ cognitively, 'Cicero' and 'Tully', for example, this shows,

tween coreferring names. Like the omniscience view, however, it demands a substantive cognitive fix—something intellectually available to the speaker must mentally focus him on the referent. A consequence is that, compared to the no-epistemology view, a more substantive explanation of two coreferring names differing cognitively is required. If one is really mentally focused on the same thing twice, why doesn't he know it? Frege's view yields a natural answer, of course. One might not know that a single thing is in question because his focus is not direct, so to speak, as it was for Russell, but is mediated by a concept. If he is focused upon the same thing twice, but by means of different concepts, he may well not realize that the same thing is in question.

We are now in a position to see how the perspective I've been outlining in this paper yields a very different way of thinking about the cognitive phenomena. While I have not plumbed the depths of how little need be in the head in order to use a name—I have not subscribed to the no-epistemology view—the use of a name, on my account, emphatically does not involve a substantial cognitive fix, the mental apprehension of a referent. Indeed, one of the functions of names is to allow a speaker (or thinker) to bridge great cognitive gaps, to allow one to speak of, say, Cicero, despite one's lack of anything like an individuating conception of Cicero. A consequence is that, just as on the no-epistemology view, the cognitive phenomena no longer have the air of paradox. The use of a name doesn't require mental apprehension of its referent, and so there is no puzzle, no special problem, about how a speaker might be competent with coreferring names and yet not know that they corefer. Given how little one needs to know (or even believe) about the referent to be competent with a name, there is no presumption that a speaker will know of two coreferring names in his vocabulary, that they corefer.

I have been emphasizing the fact that the more social conception I have been advocating dispels the sense of mystery concerning Frege's data. What seems equally important is that we have introduced a new form of explanation of Frege's data, one radically different from that suggested by the traditional representationalist account. The powerful grip of the latter led us to suppose that the only way to explain a cognitive difference was in terms of a difference in mode of presentation. Anti-Fregeans, laboring under this supposition, have been raking the leaves, as it were, to somehow retrieve such representational differences.

---

concluded Russell, that they were not really functioning as names, but were definite descriptions disguised.

Notice that cognitive perspectives, modes of presentation have no role in our new form of explanation. We don't look into the speaker's head and find two different conceptual files, in terms of which we can now see why 'Cicero' and 'Tully' play different cognitive roles for him. We rather reflect upon the fact that given how little needs to be in his head, his mere competence with the names puts him in no position to decide the question of whether or not these names corefer. Indeed, as noted above, were we to look inside his head, we might find identical conceptual files for each of two *cognitively distinct* names. We might, of course, find different conceptual files, say "being a famous Roman orator," associated with 'Cicero', and "being a famous Roman politician" with 'Tully'. Such a difference, however, does not affect our explanation of what makes it possible for him to wonder whether Cicero was Tully. Such wonder is not rendered more intelligible by the difference in conceptual files. A competent speaker, given how little he need know or even believe about the references of names, might well raise the question even if both files had included merely "is a famous Roman."[54]

I began this essay with the distinction between two conceptions of semantics, Fregean and anthropological. The attention of the anthropological semanticist, I argued, is not focused upon the cognitive dimension that, under Frege's influence, has seized center stage. If it turns out that the anthropological semanticist's work fails to provide much help in the explication of the cognitive phenomena, so be it. Much to our surprise,

---

[54] The form of explanation I am employing applies to cases that involve indexicals as well. The approach favored by Kaplan and Perry individuated cognitive perspectives by linguistic meanings. A problem for that approach, fatal I have argued, is presented by cases in which the same indexical, with the same linguistic meaning, plays different cognitive roles. How, for example, can we explain the fact that one might react very differently to two utterances of 'That is the battleship Enterprise'? One might, I suppose, look to the visual perspectives—in the case of "perceptual demonstratives," for a way of discriminating the cognitive perspectives. Such a speaker may, however, be faced with qualitatively identical scenes, and may still wonder whether the same ship is in question. We could, at this point, try stretching a bit further to recover a difference in cognitive perspective. The natural explanation, I submit, bypasses the need for such stretching. The speaker's knowledge, or beliefs, about the relevant referents is incomplete enough so that he cannot decide the question of whether there is one thing in question or two. The properties he takes the referent of 'that' to possess in the first context, and those he takes the referent of 'that' to possess in the second, neither conclusively indicate that a single thing is in question, nor that two are. The relevant properties can be different (for example, if the scenes look very different) as they will be in many cases, or they can be the same.

however, the anti-Fregean semantical outlook, at least when embedded in the sort of broader perspective I have been recommending, yields a most natural approach to the cognitive dimension. Central to this approach is the outright rejection, argued for in section IV above, of the Cartesian intentionality intuition. To put the point in a more positive way, linguistic contact with things—reference, that is—does not presuppose epistemic contact with them. Underscoring this deep lesson of the anti-Fregean revolution leads, as we have just seen, to a radically non-Fregean account of the Fregean's favorite topic, the cognitive significance of language.

16

Singular Propositions, Abstract Constituents, and Propositional Attitudes

Edward N. Zalta[1]

Consider an apparent conflict between Frege's ideas in [1892] and Kaplan's ideas in [1977] (this volume). From Frege, we learn that the cognitive significance of coreferential names may be distinct. But Kaplan identifies the cognitive significance of a word or phrase with its character ([1977], 531). The character of an expression is a function from context to content, and the content of a proper name is its denotation. Consequently, unambiguous, coreferential names, which have the same denotation from context to context, must have the same "constant" character. Hence, they must have the same cognitive significance, contrary to Frege. The difference in cognitive value between '$a = a$' and '$a = b$', where 'a' and 'b' are names, is still puzzling for Kaplan, something which he acknowledges in [1977] (562).

The present paper offers a resolution of this conflict between Frege

---
[1] I'd like to thank John Perry, Chris Menzel, and Chris Swoyer for encouraging me to write this paper. The research was conducted at the Center for the Study of Language and Information, with funds supplied, in part, from the System Development Foundation. In this paper, italic is used for emphasis, for the introduction of terms, and for symbolic expressions that are part of a formal language. Boldface is used to express notions that are part of the semantics of the formal language.

and Kaplan. We substantiate Frege's suggestion that the cognitive significance of unambiguous, coreferential names may be distinct. However, we preserve the following views of Kaplan: (a) that names are directly referential, in the sense that no intermediate entities, such as senses, are required to secure or determine their denotation, (b) that the content (or denotation) of a simple sentence in a given context is a Russellian, singular proposition, and (c) that there is a distinction to be drawn between the character and content of indexicals. In addition, we validate two of Kaplan's predictions, the first recent and the second not so recent: (1) that there is a way to view belief as a three-place relation which relates a person to a proposition under a mode of presentation ([1977], 532), and (2) that there are intermediate entities which play a role in belief and which account for the deviant logical behavior of propositional attitude contexts ([1971], 119).

The paper is structured as follows. In section 1, a logical system is described, and an analysis of the propositional attitudes is sketched. In section 2, we show that this framework preserves important ideas of both Frege and Kaplan. Also, some comparisons are drawn to other theories. In section 3, we distinguish the content, character, and *cognitive character* of a term, the latter being a new semantic notion that helps to make our framework more precise. These distinctions allow us to state the costs involved in reconciling the views of Frege and Kaplan. Also, some special flexibility in the theory is discussed. Finally, in section 4, some of the outstanding puzzles about indexicals are explained. We develop a Fregean explanation of the substitutivity puzzles about indexicals while preserving most of the basic insights of Kaplan's philosophy of language.

I.

The system we use to resolve the differences between Frege and Kaplan was developed in [1983].[2] It is based upon a conception of Russellian propositions, the truth or falsity of which is basic. Such propositions are "complexes" that result by "plugging" objects into all of the gaps of properties and relations. In addition, a metaphysical counterpart to the syntactic operation of quantification may bind the gaps in relations, and whenever a propositional complex has this operation binding a gap of the relation involved, it is a "quantified" proposition. There are molecular and modal complexes of both singular and quantified propositions. For

---

[2]Readers familiar with [1983] may skip this section.

simplicity, we regard all names and descriptions are rigid designators. Descriptions do not get Russellian eliminations, they contribute only their denotation to the proposition denoted (in effect, they operate as if they were prefaced by Kaplan's 'dthat' operator).

Here is a more formal characterization. A simple, atomic sentence of the form 'Rab' denotes a proposition that could be described semantically as follows: $\mathbf{PLUG}_1(\mathbf{PLUG}_2(\mathbf{d}(R), \mathbf{d}(b)), \mathbf{d}(a))$, where $\mathbf{d}(\tau)$ is the denotation of term τ and where the relativization of the denotation function to an interpretation and assignment to the variables has been ignored.[3] The extension of this proposition at a world $\mathbf{w}$ is the truth-value T iff $\langle \mathbf{d}(a), \mathbf{d}(b) \rangle$ is an element of the extension of the relation $\mathbf{d}(R)$ at $\mathbf{w}$. If the description '$(\imath x)\phi$' replaces 'b' in 'Rab', the resulting formula '$Ra(\imath x)\phi$' denotes the singular proposition: $\mathbf{PLUG}_1(\mathbf{PLUG}_2(\mathbf{d}(R), \mathbf{d}((\imath x)\phi)), \mathbf{d}(a))$. The two singular propositions described so far will be identical whenever 'b' and '$(\imath x)\phi$' denote the same object. The compound and modal sentences $\sim \phi$, $\phi \rightarrow \psi$, and $\Box \phi$, denote the complex propositions $\mathbf{NEG}(\mathbf{d}(\phi))$, $\mathbf{COND}(\mathbf{d}(\phi), \mathbf{d}(\psi))$, and $\mathbf{NEC}(\mathbf{d}(\phi))$, respectively. And a quantified sentence such as $(\forall x)\phi$ denotes the complex proposition $\mathbf{UNIV}_1(\mathbf{d}([\lambda x\ \phi]))$.[4] The truth-value (extension) of these complex propositions at a world will depend on the truth-value of their parts at that world (and other worlds as well, in the case of modal propositions). This kind of system, even when modified so that sentences denote propositions relative to a context, embodies what Salmon calls the "naive theory of information content" ([1986], 17).

The question immediately faced by such a naive theory is whether it can represent the difference in semantic information between sentences such as "Socrates is wise" and "The son of Phaenarete is wise." For the former is represented as 'Ws' and the latter is represented as '$W(\imath x)Sxp$'. Given that 'Socrates' and 'the son of Phaenarete' denote the same individual, it follows that these two representations denote the same singular proposition. But if the semantic information of a sentence is identified with the proposition it denotes, the two sentences embody the same semantic information. The analysis of propositional attitude constructions suggests that this semantic information should be located

---

[3] Many philosophers represent the denotation of 'Rab', as the ordered triple $\langle \mathbf{d}(R), \mathbf{d}(a), \mathbf{d}(b) \rangle$. But since propositions are not sets, we prefer to use $\mathbf{PLUG}$. It is metaphysically more neutral.

[4] For further details concerning these logical operations, one may consult Parsons [1980], my [1983], McMichael and Zalta [1980], Bealer [1982], and Menzel [1986]. These operations are the metaphysical counterparts to the syntactic operations Quine describes in [1960].

somewhere at the level of propositions, for such constructions appear to relate persons to the propositions denoted by the embedded sentence. By representing the difference in semantic content between "Socrates is wise" and "The son of Phaenarete is wise" at the level of propositions, one can account for the apparent consistency of "K believes that Socrates is wise" and "K doesn't believe that the son of Phaenarete is wise." So how can we represent the difference in semantic content of these two sentences if we keep our "naive" picture of language?

Before we answer this question, let us consider what would happen were we to build the difference in information content between the name and the description into the propositions denoted by the two sentences. Suppose that "Socrates is wise" were to denote a singular proposition but that "The son of Phaenarete is wise" were to denote some complex involving the property of being wise and the property of being the son of Phaenarete (where the latter property is a complex resulting from the application of a uniqueness operation to the result of plugging Phaenarete into the second place of the *son of* relation).

This modification would have several undesirable results which stem from rejecting the simple picture. For one thing, our understanding of propositional truth would be complicated, since the truth of propositions would no longer be basic. The truth of the proposition denoted by "The son of Phaenarete is wise" would have to be *evaluated*, in terms of whether certain objects stand in certain relations. Moreover, the method of evaluating the *sentence* "The son of Phaenarete is wise" would differ from the way in which "Socrates is wise" is evaluated, for the two sentences are no longer both treated as atomic. But worst of all, the move would still fail to account for the apparent consistency of propositional attitude constructions in which the embedded sentences differ only by the appearance of coreferential proper names. For example, "K believes that Mark Twain is an author" and "K doesn't believe that Samuel Clemens is an author" are consistent, and this modified semantic account wouldn't help us to understand why.

Examples such as this suggest that it is not the semantic information of the embedded sentences that is relevant to the analysis of attitude contexts, since that seems to be the same for "Twain is an author" and "Clemens is an author." Rather, the *cognitive* content of the embedded sentences seems to be relevant to the analysis. The cognitive content of "Twain is an author" and "Clemens is an author" may be distinct since the cognitive content of the two names may be distinct. Similarly, the cognitive content of "Socrates is wise" and "The son of Phaenarete is wise" may be distinct, since the cognitive content of 'Socrates' and 'the son of Phaenarete' may be distinct. It seems that we need to build the cognitive content of the name (or description, as the case may be) into what is semantically signified by the sentence when it is embedded in attitude constructions. By regarding the semantic content as constructed somehow out of the cognitive content, we could explain the apparent consistency of both pairs of attitude reports considered above, as well as the associated inference failures involving identity.

Let us, then, reconsider the simple picture of language with which we began, in which "Socrates is wise" and "The son of Phaenarete is wise" denote the same proposition. The question before us is, how, in the context of this simple picture, can we build the difference in the cognitive content of these two sentences into a difference of semantic content? Can we then do the same for "Twain is an author" and "Clemens is an author"? What, then, will be the explanation of why someone can believe that Socrates is wise without believing that the son of Phaenarete is wise, or believe that Mark Twain is an author without believing that Samuel Clemens is an author?

To answer these questions, we propose: (1) that there are Russellian singular propositions with abstract constituents that encode the cognitive content of names and descriptions, and (2) that such propositions serve as the secondary significance of sentences embedded in propositional attitude contexts. In [1983], an axiomatized theory of abstract individuals, abstract properties, and abstract relations was developed. Abstract individuals are of the same logical type as ordinary individuals and their distinguishing feature is that they encode properties that ordinary individuals typically exemplify. Abstract properties (relations) are of the same logical type as ordinary properties (relations) and their distinguishing feature is that they encode properties that ordinary properties (relations) exemplify. Two abstract entities are the same iff they encode the same properties.

This is all you really need to know about abstract entities to understand our solution to the puzzles of propositional attitude reports. In virtue of the fact that abstract individuals, properties, and relations encode properties of ordinary individuals, properties and relations (respectively), the former can respectively *represent* the latter. In virtue of the fact that abstract individuals, properties, and relations are of the same logical type as ordinary individuals, properties, and relations (respectively), new singular and complex propositions may be obtained by replacing their ordinary constituents with abstract ones. The entities that result are entitled to be called "propositions" because they are structured complexes in which relations (ordinary or abstract) have all of their gaps filled. It is important that one not confuse our understanding of "proposition" with other notions (such as, "the meaning of a sentence").

It seems reasonable to think that attitude reports are ambiguous. Sometimes, the embedded sentences signify what they ordinarily denote. On these *de re* readings, the truth of the report is unaffected by the intersubstitution of coreferential terms in the embedded sentence. But at other times, the embedded sentences signify something else. On these *de dicto* readings, the truth of the report *is* affected by such substitutions. By proposing that the embedded sentences of *de dicto* reports signify singular propositions with abstract constituents, we could explain why these substitutions fail. The idea is that the terms of the embedded sentence signify the abstract constituents of these propositions. Such a view identifies the cognitive content of a sentence as its semantic significance in *de dicto* attitude reports.

The *de re* reading of an attitude report can be analyzed in a simple manner—the embedded sentence denotes the proposition with ordinary constituents that it usually denotes. The *de re* reading of the report "K believes that Socrates is wise" can be represented as '$B(k, Ws)$'. In this representation, 'B' denotes a two-place relation, 'k' denotes person K, and 'Ws' denotes the proposition $\mathbf{PLUG_1}(\textbf{being wise, Socrates})$. This representation regards the English proper names as directly referential. The *de re* reading of "K believes that the son of Phaenarete is wise" is represented as: $B(k, W(\imath x)Sxp)$. Given that the denotations of 'Socrates' and 'the son of Phaenarete' are identical, this representation relates K to the same proposition as before. This explains why substitutivity preserves truth in *de re* readings of these reports. So let us turn to the *de dicto* readings, which by definition, are the ones for which substitutivity fails.

The *de dicto* readings of attitude reports involve the same two-place relation between persons and propositions, except that in these cases, the propositions signified contain abstract rather than ordinary constituents. These propositions are the intermediate objects of belief, entities that can be grasped and that represent propositions with ordinary constituents. They are propositional modes of presentation that contain individual modes of presentation as constituents. Consider person K in the example above. Even though it is directly referential, the name 'Socrates' has a cognitive significance for K. It may be identified as an abstract individual that encodes properties. This abstract individual encodes the properties that K associates with the name 'Socrates'. Socrates need not exemplify any of these properties. In fact, some other individual might even uniquely exemplify them. But that doesn't matter for our purposes, for it will still be accurate to identify the cognitive significance of the sentence "Socrates is wise" for K with a proposition having, instead of Socrates himself as a constituent, the abstract individual that encodes the properties K associates with 'Socrates'. Note that if we were to require that the abstract individual associated with 'Socrates' for K encoded not only properties Socrates exemplified, but ones which are uniquely exemplified by Socrates, such individuals would do what Fregean senses are supposed to do, namely, determine the denotations of the names with which they're associated. But we shall not suppose that language works quite the way Frege says it does, and in particular, we do not think that the sense of a name for a given individual has to "determine" or "secure" the denotation of the name with which it is associated.

So now let us consider the *de dicto* reading of the report, "K believes that Socrates is wise." If we let '$\underline{s}_k$' denote the abstract individual that K associates with 'Socrates,' our representation of this report is: $B(k, W\underline{s}_k)$, which represents the report as being true just in case K stands in a certain relation to a singular proposition with an abstract constituent. The semantic description of the proposition to which K is related is: $\mathbf{PLUG}_1(\text{being wise}, \underline{\text{Socrates}}_k)$.[5] On this analysis, it is important to distinguish the truth of this belief *report* from the truth of the *belief* reported. The belief *report* is made true by the fact that K bears an appropriate relation to a singular proposition with an abstract constituent.[6] The singular proposition with an abstract constituent serves to represent for K the ordinary singular proposition that has Socrates himself as a constituent. But it is upon this latter, ordinary proposition that the truth of K's *belief* depends. We can take advan-

---

[5] There are also singular propositions that are obtained by replacing ordinary properties with abstract properties (abstract properties encode properties of properties). Such singular propositions will play a role in explaining substitutivity failures with respect to property denoting expressions ([1983], 140ff). However, in this paper, we shall be concerned only with the substitutivity failures of singular terms. So we are not going to discuss propositions having abstract properties as constituents.

[6] If you want to know what relation this is, the answer will have to be in ambiguous English: it is the relation that holds between K and this singular proposition just in case K believes that Socrates is wise.

tage of the directly referential character of our representing language to define the notion of "truly believes" so that one is forced to examine the truth of ordinary propositions to determine the truth of the belief reported: x *truly believes* ϕ iff both $B(x, \phi)$ and ϕ^*, where ϕ^* is the result of removing all of the underlines and subscripts from ϕ. If we're given '$B(k, W\underline{s_k})$' as the *de dicto* reading of the English report, then the truth of the belief reported depends on the truth of 'Ws' (i.e., ϕ^*). Since 'Ws' is true, it follows that K believes truly.

Consider next the *de dicto* reading of "K believes that the son of Phaenarete is wise." On our analysis, the person denoted by 'K' will be related to a singular proposition with an abstract constituent by the the relation denoted by 'B'. However, this time, we can say a little more about which abstract object is a constituent of the intermediate proposition. It will be one that encodes the property of being a unique son of Phaenarete. In this way, the constituent of the intermediate proposition encodes the semantic information embodied in the description. This is the reason why we need not adopt the modification of the naive theory of information value that Salmon describes ([1986], 21). The sentence "The son of Phaenarete is wise," strictly speaking, denotes the proposition that has Socrates plugged into the property of being wise. But in intensional contexts of the kind we're considering, this sentence may alternatively signify a proposition that is an intermediate representation. This representation not only has the same logical structure of the proposition represented, but also (has a constituent that) encodes the information embodied in the definite description as well.

A certain misplaced focus might make our analysis seem unusual on first encounter. Singular propositions with abstract constituents prove to be useful because they have several important characteristics—they are of the same logical type as ordinary propositions (so they can serve as the second argument of two-place attitude relations), and they have constituents that represent ordinary objects and relations (so they can represent ordinary propositions). But because they are the same logical type as ordinary propositions, they have one other feature which, from our point of view, should simply be ignored. And that is their truth-value. It may be thought odd that the truth-value of the intermediate propositions involved in the *de dicto* readings of belief reports will typically be false. For instance, in the *de dicto* reading of the examples considered so far, the singular propositions with an abstract constituent that make the reports true have an abstract object plugged into the property of being wise. The extension of this proposition will be the value

F, since we may assume that no abstract objects are in the extension of the property of being wise. This fact, however, is of no importance, for the intermediate propositions don't have to *be* truths, they only have to *represent* truths. Such propositions have the right logical form for representing ordinary propositions, but it is the truth-values of the latter that we are really interested in. Given the definition of true belief, the judgment that K believes truly rests essentially on the truth-value of the ordinary proposition represented, not the intermediate proposition.[7]

We may now straightforwardly answer the question of how someone can believe that Socrates is wise without believing that the son of Phaenarete is wise even though Socrates just is the son of Phaenarete. The answer is that the *de dicto* readings of "K believes that Socrates is wise" and "K doesn't believe that the son of Phaenarete is wise" are consistent. Unlike the *de re* readings, where the same ordinary proposition is signified by distinct embedded sentences, distinct intermediate propositions are signified by the distinct embedded sentences in the *de dicto* readings. On the *de dicto* readings, "K believes that Socrates is wise" will be true just in case K bears a certain relation to the proposition that has the cognitive significance of 'Socrates' for K plugged into the property of being wise, whereas "K doesn't believe that the son of Phaenarete is wise" will be true just in case K fails to bear this relation to a different proposition, one that has the cognitive significance of 'the son of Phaenarete' (for K) plugged into the property of being wise. The significance of 'Socrates' for K will be a distinct object from the significance of 'the son of Phaenarete' for K, if this is really a case where K believes that Socrates is wise without believing that the son of Phaenarete is wise.

Symbolically, we get the following representations of the English re-

---

[7] It may also be objected that our analysis of *de dicto* reports does not distinguish *de dicto* beliefs about ordinary objects from *de re* beliefs about abstract objects. It may be asked, "How do you distinguish the *de dicto* reading of "K believes that Socrates is wise" from the *de re* reading of "K believes that that abstract object which serves as the sense of 'Socrates' for K is wise"? However, this question is based on a misunderstanding of what the data is. The proper response to make here is that "K believes that the abstract object which serves as the sense of 'Socrates' for K is wise" is not a piece of data that requires an analysis. It is expressed with a mixture of ordinary words from the target English language and technical expressions from the purely formal object language. Genuine data, however, is expressed in *nontechnical* English. An analysis can be given for sentences containing expressions that happen to be technical terms of our theory as long as we represent these expressions as having the ordinary meaning that they have in nontechnical English.

ports, where '$\underline{s}_k$' denotes the abstract object that serves as the cognitive significance of 'Socrates' for K, and '$(\imath x)Sxp$' denotes the abstract object that serves as the cognitive significance of 'the son of Phaenarete' for K:

(1) K believes that Socrates is wise

     a) $B(k, Ws)$ (re)

     b) $B(k, W\underline{s}_k)$ $(dicto)$

(2) K doesn't believe that the son of Phaenarete is wise

     a) $\sim B(k, W(\imath x)Sxp)$ (re)

     b) $\sim B(k, W\underline{(\imath x)Sxp})$ $(dicto)$

(3)   Socrates is the son of Phaenarete

     a) $s = (\imath x)Sxp$

Given (3a), (1a) and (2a) are inconsistent, by a simple application of the law of substitutivity of identicals. But no such inconsistency may be derived using (3a) from (1b) and (2b).[8]

    A similar answer explains how someone can believe that Mark Twain is an author without believing that Samuel Clemens is. In this case, the cognitive significance of "Mark Twain" for the individual in question must be different from the significance of "Samuel Clemens." Distinct abstract objects represent the cognitive significance of the names, and *de dicto* readings of "K believes that Twain is an author" and "K doesn't believe that Clemens is an author" can be given along the same lines as those described for the previous case.

II.

The system just described preserves one of Kaplan's central philosophical ideas: names are directly referential. No intermediate senses secure or determine their denotation. However, we regard names as ambiguous. In *de dicto* contexts, they have a secondary significance. What they signify

---

[8] For further details of the logical system in which these representations are a part, the reader should consult chapters V and VI of [1983]. In (3a), the symbol '=' signifies the standard relation of identity between ordinary objects. Two ordinary objects are identical iff necessarily, they exemplify the same properties. Identity between abstract objects is defined differently.

in such contexts does not secure or determine the denotation of the name either. In a world of perfect information, the objects signified would encode only properties exemplified by whatever the name denotes. But in our world, misinformation frequently creeps in, and in some bizarre cases, there is perfect misinformation (these are the cases where the properties featured in a name-learning situation individuate something other than what the name denotes). So though our abstract entities play many of the roles Fregean senses are supposed to play in the philosophy of language, such as the cognitive significance of terms, and the semantic significance of terms in *de dicto* contexts, they do not play all of these roles.[9]

Another important characteristic of Kaplan's work is preserved: singular propositions are the denotations of simple atomic sentences, no matter whether they are outside or inside belief contexts. So even though an atomic sentence inside a *de dicto* belief context has a secondary significance, this secondary significance is still couched in a singular proposition. Though the proposition involved has abstract constituents, it is structurally isomorphic with the proposition ordinarily denoted by the sentence. The value of utilizing singular propositions with abstract constituents is that they can bind up all of the information needed to individuate distinct beliefs with the same propositional object, without sacrificing any of the compositional rules for building up the structure of the proposition from the structural components of the embedded sentences. The simple theory of language is complicated only by the occasional ambiguity of names and descriptions in belief contexts.

Moreover, we have validated two of Kaplan's predictions. The first is that there is a belief relation which relates an individual to a proposition by way of some third thing (though we differ with Kaplan somewhat on

---

[9] See Burge [1977], 358–61, and Salmon [1981], 12ff, for good discussions of the various roles Fregean senses may play in the philosophy of language. One of Burge's conclusions, however, is that no entity simultaneously can be the cognitive significance of a term and be its denotation in belief contexts. This conclusion can be undermined by our distinction between the truth of the belief report and the truth of the belief reported. Burge bases his argument on cases where we want to say that different individuals A and B have the "same belief," even though the cognitive significance of the names involved in the report differs for these individuals. On our understanding of *de dicto* reports, however, "having the same belief" does not mean that the intermediate proposition with abstract constituents has to be the same for both individuals. It just means that the proposition represented by these intermediate propositions has to be the same. Since that is the proposition in virtue of which both may be said to believe truly, we would argue, this is the proposition in virtue of which both may be said to "have the same belief."

what this third thing is). Although we employ a two-place belief relation as basic, a full account of true belief for *de dicto* reports requires that we refer to a person, an intermediate representation which is propositional in structure, and an ordinary proposition towards which the belief is directed and upon which the truth of the belief rests. Though Kaplan identifies the intermediate representation both as the cognitive significance and character of the sentence embedded in the belief report, we identify it only as the cognitive significance of the embedded sentence.

The second prediction of Kaplan's we've validated appears in his seminal article [1971]. And that is that there are intermediate entities which can play a role in explaining the deviant logical behavior of terms in belief contexts. Although Kaplan has changed his views somewhat since the publication of this article, and is no longer convinced that Fregean entities are required, it should be clear that the quasi-Fregean theory we've adopted is consistent with some of Kaplan's recent views. We've given up the Fregean principles that are incompatible with Kaplan's present position by denying that the sense of a term determines its denotation and that the denotation of a sentence is a truth-value.

It is instructive here to draw some comparisons to the work of others besides Kaplan. Our analysis has elements that flesh out a recent proposal by Salmon ([1986], 111). Salmon suggests that the problematic nature of belief reports can be explained by using the primitive *three*-place relation of belief *BEL*, an existential generalization of which may be used to define the more familiar two-place relation. Salmon defines: K believes that p iff $(\exists x)(K$ grasps p by means of x & $BEL(K, p, x))$. The idea is that the third relatum of the BEL relation is something like a mode of presentation for propositions, though, at the end of his book, he notes that a more complete account of these things needs to be developed ([1986], 126). Such an account may be provided by the present theory, for it seems reasonable to suggest that the third relatum of Salmon's BEL relation is nothing other than a singular proposition with abstract constituents. These propositions seem to have the features Salmon's proposal requires (they can be grasped, they can represent ordinary propositions, and so forth). If this is right, it becomes interesting to think about the differences between his analysis and the present one.

The most obvious difference is that our analysis employs a two-place relation of belief as primitive. Abstraction principles then guarantee that there is a relation that works like the three-place relation BEL.[10]

---

[10] These abstraction principles are developed in [1983], 122–23.

In contrast, Salmon's analysis takes *BEL* as primitive and regards the two-place belief relation as constructed. The present theory, therefore, provides a slightly more direct explanation of why, in the logic of belief reports, it appears that the belief predicate is a two-place predicate. From our point of view, the *BEL* relation is not needed for the analysis of the truth of the belief report, though in *de dicto* cases, it is needed for the analysis of the truth of the belief reported. In these cases, the definition of "true belief" relates a believer, an intermediate proposition with abstract constituents, and the represented proposition with ordinary constituents.[11]

Another difference between the two analyses is this: although Salmon's analysis requires that there be certain intermediate entities that play a role in belief, these entities are not directly utilized in the semantics of belief reports. His proposal, which involves existential generalization, requires that such entities be part of his ontology. Consequently, they might be signified by of pieces of language. But on Salmon's proposal, they are not signified by any piece of language. Our semantic theory, however, exploits the fact that there are such entities. They play a role in explaining the mysterious ambiguity that attitude reports exhibit.

There may also be a connection between our analysis and Perry's triadic view of belief. Perry's major conclusion in [1979] is that one has to distinguish between belief states and the objects of belief—the former are not to be individuated by the latter. The objects of belief, for Perry, are essentially the ordinary propositions, and an individual may believe one of these propositions in virtue of being in a certain belief state. Different belief states may all be belief states having the same propositional object. A given belief state may, as the circumstances vary, have different propositional objects (these are typically cases of "indexical belief"). A connection between this view and ours is the following: our singular propositions with abstract constituents could be used to individuate belief states. To see this, consider again the *de dicto* readings of (1) and (2). We could say, using Perry's terminology, that (1b) reports that K is in a certain belief state while (2b) reports that K fails to be in another belief state. But both belief states in question are states with the same

---

[11] It may be that singular propositions with abstract constituents are still involved in the beliefs reported by *de re* reports as well. But, given the way such reports behave, we are not justified in making any inferences about the nature of the intermediate propositions involved. That's another reason for not taking the three-place *BEL* relation as basic. For the semantics of *de re* reports, it is unnecessary, and by postulating that it is involved in the analysis of such reports, we would go beyond the evidence presented by the data.

object, namely, the ordinary proposition that has Socrates plugged into the property of being wise. For it is this latter proposition that determines whether the state in question is felicitous (i.e., is a case of true belief). This seems to fit nicely with Perry's analysis, and demonstrates how singular propositions with abstract constituents may be useful for individuating belief states.

III.

Our work suggests that one new semantic function should be added to the semantic apparatus—the *cognitive character* function. In the semantics for the formal language, assume that there is a set **C** of contexts. The *cognitive character* function maps a proper name, relative to an individual **i** and a context **c**, to the abstract individual that serves as the cognitive significance of the name for **i** in **c**. It maps a property (relation) name, relative to **i** and **c**, to the abstract property (abstract relation) that serves as the cognitive significance of the name for **i** in **c**. Finally, it maps a description of the form $(\imath y)\phi$, relative to **i** and **c**, to the abstract entity that encodes the property of being the unique ϕ.

Unambiguous coreferential names such as 'Mark Twain' and 'Samuel Clemens' have the same character, for Kaplan's 'character' function maps each name to its content (or denotation) in each context **c**. But the cognitive character of these two names may differ. So the major difference between our approach to language and Kaplan's is that the cognitive significance of a term is not identified with its character, but rather with its cognitive character. The reason for doing this brings us back to our original point of departure, namely, the conflict between Frege's views and Kaplan's views. The cognitive significance of coreferential names 'a' and 'b' may differ, and this can account for the difference in cognitive significance between 'a = a' and 'a = b'. It also accounts for the difference in cognitive significance between "Twain is an author" and "Clemens is an author," and between other similar pairs of sentences that differ only by coreferential proper names. For Kaplan, however, the characters of these sentences are the same, and if cognitive significance is identified with character, even a three-place relation of belief of the kind Kaplan posits will not explain how someone can believe that Twain is an author without believing that Clemens is.

So the resolution of the incompatibility between the ideas of Frege and Kaplan comes at the cost of giving up two Fregean principles (that sense determines reference, and that sentences denote truth-values) and giving up Kaplan's idea that cognitive significance of an expression is to be identified with its character.

In the two previous sections, we denoted the value of the cognitive character function for name n with respect to individual i by underlining the name and subscripting i's name to it (this ignores context, but it will be temporary). To denote the value of this function for a description, we underlined the description. The underlining operation is not to be iterated, for it is not necessary to worry about the cognitive significance of these special terms. They are not part of the data, which is expressed solely in nontechnical English. The analysis of iterated belief reports will not require us to iterate the cognitive character function, though a complete discussion of this will be reserved for another occasion.[12]

This new semantic function of cognitive character plays the central role in interpreting the underline (and subscript) notation. The notation makes it possible to construct complex formal names of singular propositions with abstract constituents. By defining the cognitive character function on the names and descriptions of the language, our treatment of the attitudes becomes more flexible than Frege's. Frege seems to think that every term inside an intermediate context automatically denotes its sense. This forces attitude reports to be *de dicto*. But not only do we want the flexibility to regard some reports as *de re*, we also want the flexibility to regard some reports as mixed *de re/de dicto*. In certain reports, some embedded terms seem to be in *de re* position while others seem to be in *de dicto* position. Consider (4):

(4)   Irwin hopes that the strongest man in the world beats up the man who just insulted him.

(4) has readings on which it says something true in each of the following situations:

(A)   Dmitri is the strongest man in the world and is a friend of Irwin, though Irwin doesn't know of his distinction. While Dmitri is standing next to Irwin at a party, Dashiell, someone Irwin and Dmitri have been talking to at this party, insults Irwin. As Irwin looks first at Dmitri and then at Dashiell, he fervently imagines the first man beating up the second.

(B)   Dmitri, the strongest man in the world, is not an acquaintance of Irwin, nor does the latter know who the strongest

---

[12] No special maneuvers are necessary to analyze iterated beliefs, however.

man in the world is. Dmitri is not at the party in question, and so is not around when Dashiell insults Irwin face to face. Irwin immediately relieves his "cognitive dissonance" by fantasizing this particular guy being beaten up by the strongest man in the world, whoever he may be.

(C)   Dmitri, the strongest man in the world, is an acquaintance of Irwin (again, Irwin is unaware of Dmitri's distinction), and while together at a party, the two are told that some man has uttered an insulting remark about Irwin. Irwin notes Dmitri's size and fantasizes this big guy beating up the man who just insulted him, whoever he may be.

(D)   Dmitri, the strongest man, is not an acquaintance of Irwin's, nor does Irwin know who the strongest man is. Dmitri is not at the party in question, and is nowhere near when Irwin is told that some man insulted him (Irwin). Irwin then fantasizes the strongest man in the world, whoever he is, beating up the man who just insulted him, whoever he is.

Now the point of this example is to suggest that, for each context (A)–(D), there is a *different preferred* reading of (4). The preferred reading of (4) in context (A) takes both descriptions as *de re*, for this seems to be a case where substitutions of coreferential terms for either description will preserve truth (the way Irwin is cognizing these men is not important for the truth of (4) in this situation). The preferred reading of (4) in context (B) takes the first description as *de dicto* and the second as *de re*, for it seems that substitution only on the second description preserves truth (the way Irwin is cognizing Dmitri is important to the truth of (4) in this situation, whereas the way he is cognizing Dashiell is not). The preferred reading of (4) in context (C) takes the first description as *de re* and the second as *de dicto*, for it seems that substitutions only on the first description preserves truth (the way Irwin is cognizing Dashiell is important to the truth of (4) in this situation, whereas the way he is cognizing Dmitri is not). And the preferred reading of (4) in context (D) takes both descriptions as *de dicto*, since it seems that no substitution for the descriptions would preserve truth (the way Irwin is cognizing both Dmitri and Dashiell is crucial to the truth of (4) in this situation).

Formally speaking, the four different representations of (4) we're now considering are as follows, where 'i' denotes Irwin, 'B' denotes the *beat up* relation, 'S' denotes the property of being the strongest man in the world, 'I' denotes the *insults* relation, and '$(\imath x)\phi$' denotes the abstract object that encodes the property of being something that uniquely exemplifies ϕ:[13]

(4a) $H(i, B((\imath x)Sx, (\imath y)Iyi))$ *re/re*

(4b) $H(i, B(\underline{(\imath x)Sx}, (\imath y)Iyi))$ *dicto/re*

(4c) $H(i, B((\imath x)Sx, \underline{(\imath y)Iyi}))$ *re/dicto*

(4d) $H(i, B(\underline{(\imath x)Sx}, \underline{(\imath y)Iyi}))$ *dicto/dicto*

(4a) is the preferred reading of (4) in (A), and so forth.

This example shows that the significance of an embedded sentence (relative to a context) may be of mixed character, composed partly from the cognitive character of some of its constituent terms (relative to the subject of the attitude and to the context) and partly from the denotation of some of its constituent terms (relative to that context). (4a)–(4d) give us the means to discriminate among four different types of hope states of the kind which will be satisfied iff the singular proposition having Dmitri and Dashiell themselves appropriately plugged into the relevant relation is true. The example also shows why it is neither necessary nor useful to extend the definition of the cognitive character function to cover sentences as well as names and descriptions. This flexibility in our logic is still consistent with the idea that, relative to a given context and individual, a sentence may have a unique (cognitive) significance that is composed out of what is (cognitively) signified by each of the parts of the sentence.

IV.

With the discussion of context and the addition of the cognitive character semantic function to Kaplan's distinction between character and content, the way is open for a treatment of indexicals. Unlike names, indexicals do not have constant character. But the present picture suggests that in addition to their character (which yields a content for them for each context), they have a cognitive character as well. However, the notion of cognitive character for indexicals is not quite the same as that for proper names. The cognitive significance of a proper name in a given attitude report is closely tied to the historical encounters between the subject

---

[13] For simplicity, we'll take 'him' in the second description to be a name for Irwin.

of the report and the name itself. This is not the case with indexicals. The cognitive character of an indexical does not reflect such encounters, but rather reflects that, relative to context c, the subject of the report cognizes the entity denoted by the indexical in c in a certain way.[14] An indexical not only has a denotation relative to c, but it also signifies something intimately related to the mind of the subject of the report. This secondary significance plays the crucial role in the explanation of substitutivity failures.

To capture this secondary significance formally, we extend the cognitive character function: it is now to be defined on indexicals (context-dependent names) as well as (noncontext-dependent) names and descriptions. It is still indexed to individuals and contexts. The value of the function for a given indexical, relative to an individual and a context, is the abstract entity that objectifies the way the individual cognizes the denotation of the indexical in that context. The abstract entities we've postulated can serve as the objectifications of these ways of cognizing, since they can encode the properties involved in the content of the cognition. Of course, the properties involved in the cognizings need not be exemplified by the object of the cognition.

Now the semantics of attitude reports containing indexicals will work essentially the same way as those discussed above. Relative to a context, the report will have a pure *de re* reading in which all the indexicals signify their content in that context (as given by their character). Then, depending on the complexity of the report, there will be various *de dicto* readings in which the indexicals alternatively signify their cognitive character.

Consider the following case, adapted from Soames [1989] (this volume). Professor K, looking through a class yearbook, points to a picture of a student and says "I believe he is a scholar," and then points to a picture of a football player in full uniform and says, "I don't believe he is a scholar." Unknown to the professor, he has pointed to two different pictures of the class valedictorian, Alex Jones. Now consider K's two reports:

(5)   I believe he is a scholar (pointing to the first picture)

---

[14]One possibility we haven't discussed is that the cognitive significance the names and indexicals have for the *author* of the report is involved in the *de dicto* readings, rather than the cognitive significance the names and indexicals have for the subject of the report (i.e., the person who bears the attitude). Typically, this will not be a factor when considering the truth of such reports, though they may play a role in iterated reports. This is a topic for some other occasion, however.

(6)   I don't believe he is a scholar (pointing to the second picture)

The *de re* readings of (5) and (6), relative to the contexts in question, are inconsistent. On the *de re* reading, (5) is true iff Professor K is related in a certain way to the proposition that results by plugging the individual denoted by 'he' (relative to the context c in which (5) is uttered) into the property denoted by 'is a scholar'. (6) asserts that Professor K is not so related to the proposition that results by plugging the individual denoted by 'he' (relative to the context c' in which (6) is uttered) into the property denoted by 'is a scholar'. However, 'he' denotes Alex Jones in both c and c'. So the propositions in question are identical, and (5) and (6), therefore, are inconsistent.

Formally speaking, we get the following representations of the *de re* readings of (5) and (6):

(5a) $[B(I, S(he))]_c$ (*re*)

(6a) $[\sim B(I, S(he))]_{c'}$ (*re*)

In these representations, each formula is surrounded with brackets and then relativized to a context. We assume that (6) is uttered in a new context c', since the professor is pointing to a new picture. However, no term in (5a) changes its denotation from context c to context c'. Since none of the terms are underlined, we process this representation semantically by taking only the denotation of each term relative to the context in question. Clearly, then, (5a) and (6a) are inconsistent.

But the *de dicto* readings of (5) and (6) are consistent. The *de dicto* reading of (5) asserts a relation between K and the proposition that results by plugging the abstract object which objectifies the way K is cognizing Alex (relative to the context in which (5) is uttered) into the property of being a scholar. The abstract object involved here is what is signified by the indexical in this context, and this object will be the value of the cognitive character function for the indexical 'he', relative to K and the context of (5). Formally speaking, we may represent the *de dicto* reading of (5) as follows:

(5b) $[B(I, S(\underline{he}_I))]_c$ (*dicto*)

In this formula, '$\underline{he}_I$' denotes, relative to context c, the abstract individual that objectifies the way Professor K is cognizing Alex when looking at the first picture. To process this representation compositionally, the denotations of the (special) terms relative to context c are used. Thus,

(5b) represents (5) as being true just in case K is related in a certain way to a proposition with an abstract constituent. In Perry's terminology, this proposition individuates K's belief state.

The *de dicto* reading of (6) is consistent with this reading of (5). It may be represented formally as follows:

(6b) $[\sim B(I, S(\underline{he}_I))]_{c'}$ (*dicto*)

In this representation, '$\underline{he}_I$' denotes something different than what it denoted in (5b). That's because in the context in which (6) is uttered, K is looking at a different photograph, and is cognizing Alex in a different way. The cognitive character of the indexical 'he' has a different value in this context, and so the singular proposition signified by the embedded sentence in (6b) will have a different abstract constituent from the one had by the singular proposition signified by the embedded sentence in (5b). Since the facts of this case allow us to assume only that $[he]_c = [he]_{c'}$, and not that $[\underline{he}_I]_c = [\underline{he}_I]_{c'}$, we cannot deduce that the truth of (5b) is inconsistent with the truth of (6b).

These readings account not only for the truth of the belief reports, but for their logical behavior as well. In particular, the *de dicto* readings show why names and/or descriptions that have the same denotation as the English indexical may not be substituted for the indexical preserving truth. The indexical is not contributing its denotation in those contexts, but rather its cognitive content (as given by its cognitive character). It is still important to observe the distinction between the truth of the belief report and the truth of the belief reported. This distinction, and the definition of "truly believes," carry over into the system enriched with indexicals (with everything being relativized to context). For the *de dicto* readings, the truth of the belief reported depends not on the intermediate proposition that makes the report true, but on the ordinary proposition represented by the intermediate one. Thus, the particular belief state (5b) describes is a felicitous (true) one, since Alex is indeed a scholar (in this case, $[\phi^*]_c$ is $[S(he)]_c$, and this latter expression denotes the proposition that has Alex plugged into the property of being a scholar). And for this same reason, the particular belief state (6b) describes is not felicitous.

Consider next the case of the shopper who accepts (7) and (8) because he is ignorant of (9) (Perry [1979]):

(7)   I believe that the shopper with a torn sack is making a mess

(8)   I don't believe that I am making a mess

(9)   I am the shopper with a torn sack

On our analysis, there are two readings for both (7) and (8) and a single reading for (9):

(7a) $[B(I, M(\imath x)\phi)]_c$ (*re*)

(7b) $[B(I, M(\underline{\imath x)\phi}))]_c$ (*dicto*)

(8a) $[\sim B(I, M(I))]_c$ (*re*)

(8b) $[\sim B(I, M(\underline{I}_I))]_c$ (*dicto*)

(9a) $[I = (\imath x)\phi)]_c$

The belief states reported by (7a) and (8a) do not help us understand the facts of the case. They are inconsistent reports about the subject's mental state. The denotation of 'I' in context **c** is the same as that of the definite description. But (7b) tells us that the subject is in one belief state, while (8b) tells us that the subject fails to be in some other belief state.[15] Despite the fact that the two belief states in question have the same felicity conditions (i.e., have the same ordinary proposition as object), they are distinct states, and they are individuated by using singular propositions with abstract constituents.

Relative to a context, the word 'I' has a cognitive significance for the person using it. It is not required that the abstract object serving as the cognitive significance of 'I' encode properties that the subject uniquely exemplifies. The subject may be mistaken about who he is (he may be deluded or an amnesiac). The abstract object in question encodes only those properties that the subject associates with himself in the context in question. No puzzles arise should these properties be uniquely exemplified by some other person, since this representation plays a role only in identifying the subject's mental state and *not* in identifying the ordinary proposition which is the object of that state and upon which the felicity conditions of the state depend. We leave Frege's claim, that everyone is presented to himself in a unique and primitive way, an open question. The theory requires at most an abstract object that encodes a general concept of the self. This suffices to distinguish the cognitive significance of 'I' from the cognitive significance of any other name or description. But it is to be emphasized that this concept is not

---

[15] In (8b), '$\underline{I}_I$' denotes relative to context **c**, what the indexical 'I' cognitively signifies for the person denoted by the indexical in **c**.

incorporated into the ordinary propositions that are the objects of the states.[16]

This analysis of attitude reports containing indexicals will, we believe, handle the puzzling cases that have appeared in the recent literature (Castañeda [1966], [1967]; Perry [1977], [1979]; Lewis [1979], and Stalnaker [1981], and Richard [1983], among others). In each of these cases, it is important to remember: (a) that attitude reports receive both *de re* and *de dicto* readings, (b) that the *de dicto* readings involve abstract representations which do not intrinsically determine in any way the objects which they represent, and (c) that the truth of the belief reported by the *de dicto* report will depend on the ordinary propositions that have the objects represented as constituents.

For our present concerns, however, the conclusion to be drawn is that the system just outlined preserves Kaplan's much of Kaplan's analysis of indexicals even though it has a quasi-Fregean outlook on the propositional attitudes. The resolution of the conflict between Frege's work and Kaplan's in our system with indexicals rejects the idea that the character of an indexical is its cognitive significance. This theoretical identification is the only thesis of Kaplan's that needs to be refined. A new semantic function, which distinguishes the cognitive character of a name or indexical from its ordinary character, proves useful in solving the outstanding puzzles about the attitudes. The abstract objects that serve as values of this cognitive are crucial. By postulating such a realm of entities and revising some of Frege's ideas, we've been able to assimilate many of the fundamental intuitions about metaphysics and the philosophy of language that have been the cornerstones of Kaplan's

---

[16]Note that we are also following Perry in "breaking the connection between senses and thoughts" ([1977], 493). Here, Perry conceives of "thoughts" as information, and these seem to be ordinary propositions with ordinary constituents.

One place where we may differ from Perry is the following. As we understand him, two people can be in the *same* belief state when both of them are sitting and think to themselves "I am sitting." From our point of view, this *sameness* might amount to the following: they are both in the state that is individuated by the proposition that has the cognitive significance of 'I' plugged into the property of sitting. Now this description applies to both individuals, relativized to the cognitive significance of 'I' for each person, and this is one reason for thinking they are in the same state. But it may be the case that their conceptions of themselves differ, in which case we have distinct objects which serve as the cognitive significance of 'I' for these individuals. So, if the propositions with these abstract constituents individuate belief states, we may also want to say that, strictly speaking, they are not in the exact same "individual" state, though they may be in the same "general" state.

work.[17]

Bibliography

Bealer, G.
[1982] *Quality and Concept*. London: Oxford University Press.

Burge, T.
[1977] "Belief De Re." *Journal of Philosophy* 74 (June): 338–62.

Castañeda, H.
[1966] "'He': A Study in the Logic of Self-Consciousness." *Ratio* 8: 130–57.
[1967] "Indicators and Quasi-Indicators." *American Philosophical Quarterly* 4: 85–100.

Frege, G.
[1892] "On Sense and Reference." In *Translations of Frege's Philosophical Writings*, ed. Geach and Black. Oxford: Blackwell, 1970, 56–78.

Kaplan, D.
[1977] *Demonstratives*. This volume.
[1971] "Quantifying In." Reprinted in *Reference and Modality*, ed. Linsky. London: Oxford University Press, 112–44.

Lewis, D.
[1979] "Attitudes De Dicto and De Se." *The Philosophical Review* 88: 513–43.

McMichael, A., and Zalta, E.
[1980] "An Alternative Theory of Nonexistent Objects." *Journal of Philosophical Logic* 9: 297–313.

Menzel, C.
[1986] "A Complete, Type-Free, "Second Order" Logic and its Philosophical Foundations." Report No. CSLI–86–40, Center for the Study of Language and Information, Stanford University.

---

[17] A more complete description of our logical system, which incorporates contexts and indexicals, is developed in the appendix to [1988].

Parsons, T.
[1980] *Nonexistent Objects*. New Haven: Yale University Press.

Perry, J.
[1977] "Frege on Demonstratives." *The Philosophical Review* 86: 474–97.
[1979] "The Problem of the Essential Indexical." *Noûs* 13: 3–21.

Quine, W. V. O.
[1960] "Variables Explained Away." In *Selected Logical Papers*. New York: Random House, 227–35.

Richard, M.
[1983] "Direct Reference and Ascriptions of Belief." *Journal of Philosophical Logic* 12: 425–52.

Salmon, N.
[1986] *Frege's Puzzle*. Cambridge, Mass.: The MIT Press.
[1981] *Reference and Essence*. Princeton: Princeton University Press.

Soames, S.
[1989] "Direct Reference and Propositional Attitudes." This volume.

Stalnaker, R.
[1981] "Indexical Belief." *Synthese* 49: 129–52.

Zalta, E.
[1983] *Abstract Objects: An Introduction to Axiomatic Metaphysics*. Dordrecht: Reidel.
[1988] *Intensional Logic and the Metaphysics of Intentionality*. Cambridge, Mass.: The MIT Press.

Part II

17

Demonstratives

An Essay on the Semantics, Logic, Metaphysics, and Epistemology of Demonstratives and Other Indexicals

David Kaplan[1]

---

[1] This paper was prepared for and read (with omissions) at a symposium on Demonstratives at the March 1977 meetings of the Pacific Division of the American Philosophical Association. The commentators were Paul Benacerraf and Charles Chastain. Much of the material, including the formal system of section XVIII, was originally presented in a series of lectures at the fabled 1971 Summer Institute in the Philosophy of Language held at the University of California, Irvine. © 1977 by David Kaplan.

Table of Contents

Preface

In about 1966 I wrote a paper about quantification into epistemological contexts. There are very difficult metaphysical, logical, and epistemological problems involved in providing a treatment of such idioms which does not distort our intuitions about their proper use and which is up to contemporary logical standards. I did not then, and do not now, regard the treatment I provided as fully adequate. And I became more and more intrigued with problems centering on what I would like to call the *semantics of direct reference*. By this I mean theories of meaning according to which certain singular terms refer directly without the mediation of a Fregean *Sinn* as meaning. If there are such terms, then the proposition expressed by a sentence containing such a term would involve individuals directly rather than by way of the "individual concepts" or "manners of presentation" I had been taught to expect. Let us call such putative singular terms (if there are any) *directly referential terms* and such putative propositions (if there are any) *singular propositions*. Even if English contained no singular terms whose proper semantics was one of direct reference, could we determine to introduce such terms? And even if we had no directly referential terms and introduced none, is there a need or use for singular propositions?

The feverish development of quantified modal logics, more generally, of quantified intensional logics, of the 1960s gave rise to a metaphysical and epistemological malaise regarding the problem of identifying individuals across worlds—what, in 1967, I called the problem of "Trans-World Heir Lines." This problem was really just the problem of singular propositions: those which involve individuals directly, rearing its irrepressible head in the possible-world semantics that were then (and are now) so popular.

It was not that according to those semantical theories any sentences of the languages being studied were themselves taken to express singular propositions, it was just that singular propositions seemed to be needed in the analysis of the nonsingular propositions expressed by these sentences. For example, consider

(0) $\exists x(Fx \wedge \sim \Box Fx)$.

This sentence would not be taken by anyone to express a singular proposition. But in order to evaluate the truth-value of the component

$\Box Fx$

(under some assignment of an individual to the variable 'x'), we must first determine whether the *proposition* expressed by its component

$$F x$$

(under an assignment of an individual to the variable 'x') is a necessary proposition. So in the course of analyzing (0), we are required to determine the proposition associated with a formula containing a *free* variable. Now free variables under an assignment of values are paradigms of what I have been calling *directly referential* terms. In determining a semantical value for a formula containing a free variable we may be given a *value* for the variable—that is, an individual drawn from the universe over which the variable is taken to range—but nothing more. A variable's first and only meaning is its value. Therefore, if we are to associate a *proposition* (not merely a truth-value) with a formula containing a free variable (with respect to an assignment of a value to the variable), that proposition seems bound to be singular (even if valiant attempts are made to disguise this fact by using constant functions to imitate individual concepts). The point is, that if the component of the proposition (or the step in the construction of the proposition) which corresponds to the singular term is determined by the individual and the individual is directly determined by the singular term—rather than the individual being determined by the component of the proposition, which is directly determined by the singular term—then we have what I call a singular proposition. [Russell's semantics was like the semantical theories for quantified intensional logics that I have described in that although no (closed) sentence of *Principia Mathematica* was taken to stand for a singular proposition, singular propositions are the essential building blocks of all propositions.]

The most important hold-out against semantical theories that required singular propositions is Alonzo Church, the great modern champion of Frege's semantical theories. Church also advocates a version of quantified intensional logic, but with a subtle difference that finesses the need for singular propositions. (In Church's logic, given a sentential formula containing free variables and given an assignment of values to the variables, no proposition is yet determined. An additional assignment of "senses" to the free variables must be made before a proposition can be associated with the formula.) It is no accident that Church rejects *direct reference* semantical theories. For if there were singular terms which referred directly, it seems likely that Frege's problem: how can $\ulcorner \alpha = \beta \urcorner$, if true, differ in meaning from $\ulcorner \alpha = \alpha \urcorner$, could be reinstated, while Frege's solution: that α and β, though referring to the same thing, do so by way of different senses, would be blocked. Also: because of the fact that the component of the proposition is being determined by the individual rather than vice versa, we have something like a violation of the famous Fregean dictum that *there is no road back* from denotation to sense [propositional component]. (Recently, I have come to think that if we countenance singular propositions, a collapse of Frege's intensional ontology into Russell's takes place.)

I can draw some little pictures to give you an idea of the two kinds of semantical theories I want to contrast.

Fregean Picture

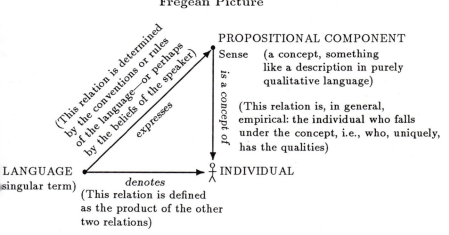

Direct Reference Picture

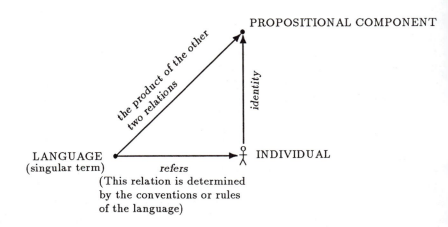

(These pictures are not entirely accurate for several reasons, among them, that the contrasting pictures are meant to account for more than just singular terms and that the relation marked 'refers' may already involve a kind of Fregean sense used to fix the referent.)

I won't go into the pros and cons of these two views at this time. Suffice it to say that I had been raised on Fregean semantics and was sufficiently devout to wonder whether the kind of quantification into modal and epistemic contexts that seemed to require singular propositions really made sense. (My paper "Quantifying In" can be regarded as an attempt to *explain away* such idioms for epistemic contexts.)[2]

But there were pressures from quarters other than quantified intensional logic in favor of a semantics of direct reference. First of all there was Donnellan's fascinating paper "Reference and Definite Descriptions."[3] Then there were discussions I had had with Putnam in 1968 in which he argued with respect to certain natural kind terms like 'tiger' and 'gold', that if their Fregean senses were the kind of thing that one grasped when one understood the terms, then such senses could

---

[2]David Kaplan, "Quantifying In," *Synthese* 19 (1968): 178–214; reprinted in *The Philosophy of Language*, ed. A. P. Martinich (Oxford: Oxford University Press, 1985).

[3]Keith Donnellan, "Reference and Definite Descriptions," *Philosophical Review* 75 (1966): 281–304; reprinted in Martinich, op. cit.

not determine the extension of the terms. And finally Kripke's Princeton lectures of spring 1970, later published as *Naming and Necessity*,[4] were just beginning to leak out along with their strong attack on the Fregean theory of proper names and their support of a theory of direct reference.

As I said earlier, I was intrigued by the semantics of direct reference, so when I had a sabbatical leave for the year 1970–71, I decided to work in the area in which such a theory seemed most plausible: demonstratives. In fall 1970, I wrote, for a conference at Stanford, a paper "Dthat."[5] Using Donnellan's ideas as a starting point, I tried to develop the contrast between Fregean semantics and the semantics of direct reference, and to argue that demonstratives—although they *could* be treated on a Fregean model—were more interestingly treated on a direct reference model. Ultimately I came to the conclusion that something analogous to Donnellan's referential use of a definite description could be developed using my new demonstrative, "dthat." In the course of this paper I groped my way to a formal semantics for demonstratives rather different in conception from those that had been offered before.

In spring 1971, I gave a series of lectures at Princeton on the semantics of direct reference. By this time I had seen a transcript of *Naming and Necessity* and I tried to relate some of my ideas to Kripke's.[6] I also had written out the formal semantics for my Logic of Demonstratives. That summer at the Irvine Philosophy of Language Institute I lectured again on the semantics of direct reference and repeated some of these lectures at various institutions in fall 1971. And there the matter has stood except for a bit of updating of the 1971 Logic of Demonstratives notes in 1973.

I now think that demonstratives can be treated correctly only on a direct reference model, but that my earlier lectures at Princeton and Irvine on direct reference semantics were too broad in scope, and that the most important and certainly the most convincing part of my theory is just the logic of demonstratives itself. It is based on just a few quite

---

[4] Saul Kripke, "Naming and Necessity," in *Semantics of Natural Language*, ed. G. Harman and D. Davidson (Dordrecht: Reidel, 1972); revised edition published as a separate monograph, *Naming and Necessity* (Oxford: Basil Blackwell, 1980). References are to the revised edition.

[5] David Kaplan, "Dthat," in *Syntax and Semantics*, vol. 9, ed. P. Cole (New York: Academic Press, 1978); reprinted in Martinich, op. cit.

[6] Although the central ideas of my theory had been worked out before I became familiar with *Naming and Necessity*, I have enthusiastically adopted the 'analytical apparatus' and some of the terminology of that brilliant work.

simple ideas, but the conceptual apparatus turns out to be surprisingly rich and interesting. At least I hope that you will find it so.

In this work I have concentrated on pedagogy. Philosophically, there is little here that goes beyond the Summer Institute Lectures, but I have tried, by limiting the scope, to present the ideas in a more compelling way. Some new material appears in the two speculative sections: XVII (Epistemological Remarks) and XX (Adding 'Says'). It is my hope that a theory of demonstratives will give us the tools to go on in a more sure-footed way to explore the *de re* propositional attitudes as well as other semantical issues.

I. Introduction

I believe my theory of demonstratives to be uncontrovertable and largely uncontroversial. This is not a tribute to the power of my theory but a concession of its obviousness. In the past, no one seems to have followed these obvious facts out to their obvious consequences. I do that. What is original with me is some terminology to help fix ideas when things get complicated. It has been fascinating to see how interesting the obvious consequences of obvious principles can be.[7]

II. Demonstratives, Indexicals, and Pure Indexicals

I tend to describe my theory as 'a theory of demonstratives', but that is poor usage. It stems from the fact that I began my investigations by asking what is said when a speaker points at someone and says, "He is suspicious."[8] The word 'he', so used, is a demonstrative, and the accompanying pointing is the requisite associated demonstration. I hypothesized a certain semantical theory for such demonstratives, and then I invented a new demonstrative, 'dthat', and stipulated that its semantics be in accord with my theory. I was so delighted with this methodological sleight of hand for my demonstrative 'dthat', that when I generalized the theory to apply to words like 'I', 'now', 'here', etc.— words which do *not* require an associated demonstration—I continued to call my theory a 'theory of demonstratives' and I referred to these words as 'demonstratives'.

That terminological practice conflicts with what I preach, and I will try to correct it. (But I tend to backslide.)

The group of words for which I propose a semantical theory includes the pronouns 'I', 'my', 'you', 'he', 'his', 'she', 'it', the demonstrative pronouns 'that', 'this', the adverbs 'here', 'now', 'tomorrow', 'yesterday', the adjectives 'actual', 'present', and others. These words have uses other than those in which I am interested (or, perhaps, depending on how you individuate words, we should say that they have homonyms in which I am not interested). For example, the pronouns 'he' and 'his' are used not as demonstratives but as bound variables in

---

[7]Not everything I assert is part of my theory. At places I make judgments about the correct use of certain words and I propose detailed analyses of certain notions. I recognize that these matters may be controversial. I do not regard them as part of the basic, obvious, theory.

[8]See "Dthat," p. 320 in Martinich.

> For what is a man profited, if he shall gain
> the whole world, and lose his own soul?

What is common to the words or usages in which I am interested is that the referent is dependent on the context of use and that the meaning of the word provides a rule which determines the referent in terms of certain aspects of the context. The term I now favor for these words is 'indexical'. Other authors have used other terms; Russell used 'egocentric particular' and Reichenbach used 'token reflexive'. I prefer 'indexical' (which, I believe, is due to Pierce) because it seems less theory laden than the others, and because I regard Russell's and Reichenbach's theories as defective.

Some of the indexicals require, in order to determine their referents, an associated demonstration: typically, though not invariably, a (visual) presentation of a local object discriminated by a pointing.[9] These indexicals are the true demonstratives, and 'that' is their paradigm. The demonstra*tive* (an expression) refers to that which the demon*stration* demonstrates. I call that which is demonstrated the 'demonstratum'.

A demonstrative without an associated demonstration is incomplete. The linguistic rules which govern the use of the true demonstratives 'that', 'he', etc., are not sufficient to determine their referent in all contexts of use. Something else—an associated demonstration—must be provided. The linguistic rules assume that such a demonstration accompanies each (demonstrative) use of a demonstrative. An incomplete demonstrative is not *vacuous* like an improper definite description. A demonstrative *can* be vacuous in various cases. For example, when its associated demonstration has no demonstratum (a hallucination)—or the wrong kind of demonstratum (pointing to a flower and saying 'he' in the belief that one is pointing to a man disguised as a flower[10])—or too many demonstrata (pointing to two intertwined vines and saying

---

[9]However, a demonstration may also be opportune and require no special action on the speaker's part, as when someone shouts "Stop that man" while only one man is rushing toward the door. My notion of a demonstration is a theoretical concept. I do not, in the present work, undertake a detailed 'operational' analysis of this notion although there are scattered remarks relevant to the issue. I do consider, in XVI below, some alternative theoretical treatments of demonstrations.

[10]I am aware (1) that in some languages the so-called masculine gender pronoun may be appropriate for flowers, but it is not so in English; (2) that a background story can be provided that will make pointing at the flower a contextually appropriate, though deviant, way of referring to a man; for example, if we are talking of great hybridizers; and (3) that it is possible to treat the example as a *referential use* of the demonstrative 'he' on the model of Donnellan's referential use of a definite description (see "Reference and Definite Descriptions"). Under the referential use

'that vine'). But it is clear that one can distinguish a demonstrative with a vacuous demonstration: no referent; from a demonstrative with no associated demonstration: incomplete.

All this is by way of contrasting true demonstratives with pure indexicals. For the latter, *no associated demonstration is required, and any demonstration supplied is either for emphasis or is irrelevant.*[11] Among the pure indexicals are 'I', 'now', 'here' (in one sense), 'tomorrow', and others. The linguistic rules which govern *their* use fully determine the referent for each context.[12] No supplementary actions or intentions are needed. The speaker refers to himself when he uses 'I', and no pointing to another or believing that he is another or intending to refer to another can defeat this reference.[13]

Michael Bennett has noted that some indexicals have both a pure *and* a demonstrative use. 'Here' is a pure indexical in

I am in here

and is a demonstrative in

In two weeks, I will be here [pointing at a city on a map].

---

treatment we would assign as referent for 'he' whatever the speaker *intended* to demonstrate. I intended the example to exemplify a failed demonstration, thus, a case in which the speaker, falsely believing the flower to be some man or other in disguise, but having no particular man in mind, and certainly not intending to refer to anything other than that man, says, pointing at the flower, "He has been following me around all day."

[11] I have in mind such cases as pointing at oneself while saying 'I' (emphasis) or pointing at someone else while saying 'I' (irrelevance or madness or what?).

[12] There are certain uses of pure indexicals that might be called 'messages recorded for later broadcast', which exhibit a special uncertainty as to the referent of 'here' and 'now'. If the message: "I am not here now" is recorded on a telephone answering device, it is to be assumed that the time referred to by 'now' is the time of playback rather than the time of recording. Donnellan has suggested that if there were typically a significant lag between our production of speech and its audition (for example, if sound traveled very very slowly), our language might contain two forms of 'now': one for the time of production, another for the time of audition. The indexicals 'here' and 'now' also suffer from vagueness regarding the size of the spatial and temporal neighborhoods to which they refer. These facts do not seem to me to slur the difference between demonstratives and pure indexicals.

[13] Of course it is certain intentions on the part of the speaker that make a particular vocable the first person singular pronoun rather a nickname for Irving. My semantical theory is a theory of word meaning, not speaker's meaning. It is based on linguistic rules known, explicitly or implicitly, by all competent users of the language.

III. Two Obvious Principles

So much for preliminaries. My theory is based on two obvious principles. The first has been noted in every discussion of the subject.

Principle 1 *The referent of a pure indexical depends on the context, and the referent of a demonstrative depends on the associated demonstration.*

If you and I both say 'I' we refer to different persons. The demonstratives 'that' and 'he' can be correctly used to refer to any one of a wide variety of objects simply by adjusting the accompanying demonstration.

The second obvious principle has less often been formulated explicitly.

Principle 2 *Indexicals, pure and demonstrative alike, are directly referential.*

IV. Remarks on Rigid Designators

In an earlier draft I adopted the terminology of Kripke, called indexicals 'rigid designators', and tried to explain that my usage differed from his. I am now shying away from that terminology. But because it is so well known, I will make some comments on the notion or notions involved.

The term 'rigid designator' was coined by Saul Kripke to characterize those expressions which designate the same thing in every possible world in which that thing exists and which designate nothing elsewhere. He uses it in connection with his controversial, though, I believe, correct claim that proper names, as well as many common nouns, are rigid designators. There is an unfortunate confusion in the idea that a proper name would designate nothing if the bearer of the name were not to exist.[14] Kripke himself adopts positions which seem inconsistent with this feature of rigid designators. In arguing that the object designated by a rigid designator need not exist in every possible world, he seems to assert that under certain circumstances what is expressed by 'Hitler does not exist' would have been true, and not because 'Hitler' would have designated nothing (in *that* case we might have given the sentence *no* truth-value) but because what 'Hitler' would have designated—namely

---

[14] I have discussed this and related issues in "Bob and Carol and Ted and Alice," in *Approaches to Natural Language*, ed. J. Hintikka et al. (Dordrecht: Reidel, 1973), especially appendix X.

Hitler—would not have existed.[15] Furthermore, it is a striking and important feature of the possible world semantics for quantified intensional logics, which Kripke did so much to create and popularize, that variables, those paradigms of rigid designation, designate the same individual in *all* possible worlds whether the individual "exists" or not.[16]

Whatever Kripke's intentions (did he, as I suspect, misdescribe his own concept?) and whatever associations or even meaning the phrase 'rigid designator' may have, I intend to use *'directly referential'* for an expression whose referent, once determined, is taken as fixed for all possible circumstances, i.e., is taken as *being* the propositional component.

For me, the intuitive idea is not that of an expression which *turns out* to designate the same object in all possible circumstances, but an expression whose semantical *rules* provide *directly* that the referent in all possible circumstances is fixed to be the actual referent. In typical cases the semantical rules will do this only implicitly, by providing a way of determining the *actual* referent and no way of determining any other propositional component.[17]

We should beware of a certain confusion in interpreting the phrase 'designates the same object in all circumstances'. We do not mean that the expression *could not have been used* to designate a different object.

---

[15] Kripke, *Naming and Necessity*, p. 78.

[16] The matter is even more complicated. There are two 'definitions' of 'rigid designator' in *Naming and Necessity*, pp. 48–49. The first conforms to what seems to me to have been the intended concept—same designation in *all* possible worlds—the second, scarcely a page later, conforms to the more widely held view that a rigid designator need not designate the object, or any object, at worlds in which the object does not exist. According to this conception a designator cannot, at a given world, designate something which does not exist in that world. The introduction of the notion of a *strongly* rigid designator—a rigid designator whose designatum exists in all possible worlds—suggests that the latter idea was uppermost in Kripke's mind. (The second definition is given, unequivocally, on page 146 of "Identity and Necessity," in *Identity and Individuation*, ed. M. K. Munitz (New York: New York University Press, 1971).) In spite of the textual evidence, systematic considerations, including the fact that variables cannot be accounted for otherwise, leave me with the conviction that the former notion was intended.

[17] Here, and in the preceding paragraph, in attempting to convey my notion of a directly referential singular term, I slide back and forth between two metaphysical pictures: that of possible worlds and that of structured propositions. It seems to me that a truly semantical idea should presuppose neither picture, and be expressible in terms of either. Kripke's discussion of rigid designators is, I believe, distorted by an excessive dependence on the possible worlds picture and the associated semantical style. For more on the relationship between the two pictures, see pages 724–25 of my "How to Russell a Frege-Church," *The Journal of Philosophy* 72 (1975): 716–29.

We mean rather that given a *use* of the expression, we may ask of *what has been said* whether *it* would have been true or false in various counter-factual circumstances, and in such counterfactual circumstances, which are the individuals relevant to determining truth-value. Thus we must distinguish possible occasions of *use*—which I call *contexts*—from possible circumstances of *evaluation* of what was said on a given occasion of use. Possible circumstances of evaluation I call circumstances or, sometimes, just *counterfactual situations*. A directly referential term *may* designate different objects when used in different *contexts*. But when evaluating what was said in a given context, only a single object will be relevant to the evaluation in all circumstances. This sharp distinction between *contexts of use* and *circumstances of evaluation* must be kept in mind if we are to avoid a seeming conflict between Principles 1 and 2.[18] To look at the matter from another point of view, once we recognize the obviousness of both principles (I have not yet argued for Principle 2) the distinction between contexts of use and circumstances of evaluation is forced upon us.

If I may wax metaphysical in order to fix an image, let us think of the vehicles of evaluation—the what-is-said in a given context—as propositions. Don't think of propositions as sets of possible worlds, but rather as structured entities looking something like the sentences which express them. For each occurrence of a singular term in a sentence there will be a corresponding constituent in the proposition expressed. The constituent of the proposition determines, for each circumstance of evaluation, the object relevant to evaluating the proposition in that circumstance. In general, the constituent of the proposition will be some sort of complex, constructed from various attributes by logical composition. But in the case of a singular term which is directly referential, the constituent of the proposition is just the object itself. Thus it is that it does not just *turn out* that the constituent determines the same object in every circumstance, the constituent (corresponding to a rigid designator) just *is* the object. *There is no determining to do at all.* On this picture—and this is *really* a picture and not a theory—the definite description

(1)   The $n[(\text{Snow is slight} \land n^2 = 9) \lor (\sim\text{Snow is slight} \land 2^2 = n + 1)]$[19]

---

[18]I think it likely that it was just the failure to notice this distinction that led to a failure to recognize Principle 2. Some of the history and consequences of the conflation of Context and Circumstance is discussed in section VII.

[19]I would have used 'snow is white', but I wanted a contingent clause, and so many

would yield a constituent which is complex although it would determine the same object in all circumstances. Thus, (1), though a rigid designator, is not directly referential from this (metaphysical) point of view. Note, however, that every proposition which contains the complex expressed by (1) is *equivalent* to some singular proposition which contains just the number three itself as constituent.[20]

The semantical feature that *I* wish to highlight in calling an expression *directly referential* is not the *fact* that it designates the same object in every circumstance, but the *way* in which it designates an object in any circumstance. Such an expression is a *device of direct reference*. This does not imply that it has no conventionally fixed semantical rules which determine its referent in each context of use; quite the opposite. There are semantical rules which determine the referent in each context of use—but that is all. *The rules do not provide a complex which together with a circumstance of evaluation yields an object. They just provide an object.*

If we keep in mind our sharp distinction between contexts of use and circumstances of evaluation, we will not be tempted to confuse a rule which assigns an object to each *context* with a 'complex' which assigns an object to each *circumstance*. For example, each context has an *agent* (loosely, a speaker). Thus an appropriate designation rule for a directly referential term would be:

(2)   In each possible context of use the given term refers to the agent of the context.

But this rule could not be used to assign a relevant object to each circumstance of evaluation. Circumstances of evaluation do not, in general, have agents. Suppose I say,

(3)   I do not exist.

Under what circumstances would *what I said* be true? It would be true in circumstances in which I did not exist. Among such circumstances are those in which no one, and thus, no speakers, no agents exist. To search a circumstance of evaluation for a speaker in order to (mis)apply rule (2) would be to go off on an irrelevant chase.

---

people (possibly including me) nowadays seem to have views which allow that 'snow is white' may be necessary.

[20] I am ignoring propositions expressed by sentences containing epistemic operators or others for which equivalence is not a sufficient condition for interchange of operand.

Three paragraphs ago I sketched a metaphysical picture of the structure of a proposition. The picture is taken from the semantical parts of Russell's *Principles of Mathematics*.[21] Two years later, in "On Denoting,"[22] even Russell rejected that picture. But I still like it. It is not a part of my theory, but it well conveys my conception of a directly referential expression and of the semantics of direct reference. (The picture needs *some* modification in order to avoid difficulties which Russell later noted—though he attributed them to Frege's theory rather than his own earlier theory.)[23]

If we adopt a possible worlds semantics, all directly referential terms

---

[21] Bertrand Russell, *The Principles of Mathematics* (London: Allen & Unwin, 1903).

[22] Bertrand Russell, "On Denoting," *Mind* 14 (1905): 479–93.

[23] Here is a difficulty in Russell's 1903 picture that has some historical interest. Consider the proposition expressed by the sentence, 'The centre of mass of the Solar System is a point'. Call the proposition, '*P*'. *P* has in its subject place a certain complex, expressed by the definite description. Call the complex, 'Plexy'. We can describe Plexy as "the complex expressed by 'the center of mass of the solar system'." Can we produce a directly referential term which designates Plexy? Leaving aside for the moment the controversial question of whether 'Plexy' is such a term, let us imagine, as Russell believed, that we can directly refer to Plexy by affixing a kind of *meaning marks* (on the analogy of quotation marks) to the description itself. Now consider the sentence '^{m}the center of mass of the solar system^m is a point'. Because the subject of this sentence is directly referential and refers to Plexy, the proposition the sentence expresses will have as its subject constituent Plexy itself. A moment's reflection will reveal that this proposition is simply *P* again. But this is absurd since the two sentences speak about radically different objects.

(I believe the foregoing argument lies behind some of the largely incomprehensible arguments mounted by Russell against Frege in "On Denoting," though there are certainly other difficulties in that argument. It is not surprising that Russell there confused Frege's theory with his own of *Principle of Mathematics*. The first footnote of "On Denoting" asserts that the two theories are "very nearly the same.")

The solution to the difficulty is simple. Regard the 'object' places of a singular proposition as marked by some operation which cannot mark a complex. (There always will be some such operation.) For example, suppose that no complex is (represented by) a set containing a single member. Then we need only add $\{...\}$ to mark the places in a singular proposition which correspond to directly referential terms. We no longer need worry about confusing a complex with a propositional constituent corresponding to a directly referring term because no complex will have the form $\{x\}$. In particular, Plexy $\neq$ {Plexy}. This technique can also be used to resolve another confusion in Russell. He argued that a sentence containing a nondenoting directly referential term (he would have called it a nondenoting 'logically proper name') would be meaningless, presumably because the purported singular proposition would be incomplete. But the braces themselves can fill out the singular proposition, and if they contain nothing, no more anomalies need result than what the development of Free Logic has already inured us to.

will be regarded as rigid designators in the *modified* sense of an expression which designates the same thing in *all* possible worlds (irrespective of whether the thing exists in the possible world or not).[24] However, as already noted, I do not regard all rigid designators—not even all strongly rigid designators (those that designate something that exists in all possible worlds) or all rigid designators in the modified sense—as directly referential. I believe that proper names, like variables, are directly referential. They are not, in general, strongly rigid designators nor are they rigid designators in the original sense.[25] What is characteristic of directly referential terms is that the designatum (referent) determines the propositional component rather than the propositional component, along with a circumstance, determining the designatum. It is for this reason that a directly referential term that designates a contingently existing object will still be a rigid designator in the modified sense. The propositional component need not choose its designatum from those offered by a passing circumstance; it has already secured its designatum before the encounter with the circumstance.

When we think in terms of possible world semantics this fundamental distinction becomes subliminal. This is because the style of the semantical rules obscures the distinction and makes it appear that directly referential terms differ from ordinary definite descriptions only in that the propositional component in the former case must be a *constant* function of circumstances. In actual fact, the referent, in a circumstance, of a directly referential term is simply *independent* of the circumstance and is no more a function (constant or otherwise) of circumstance, than my action is a function of your desires when I decide to do it whether you like it or not. The distinction that is obscured by the style of possible world semantics is dramatized by the structured propositions picture. That is part of the reason why I like it.

Some directly referential terms, like proper names, may have no semantically relevant descriptive meaning, or at least none that is specific: that distinguishes one such term from another. Others, like the indexicals, may have a limited kind of specific descriptive meaning relevant to the features of a context of use. Still others, like 'dthat' terms (see below), may be associated with full-blown Fregean senses used to fix the referent. But in any case, the descriptive meaning of a directly referential term is no part of the propositional content.

---

[24] This is the *first sense* of footnote 16.
[25] This is the *second sense* of footnote 16.

V. Argument for Principle 2: Pure Indexicals

As stated earlier, I believe this principle is uncontroversial. But I had best distinguish it from similar principles which are false. I am *not* claiming, as has been claimed for proper names, that indexicals lack anything that might be called 'descriptive meaning'. Indexicals, in general, have a rather easily statable descriptive meaning. But it is clear that this meaning is relevant only to determining a referent in a context of use and *not* to determining a relevant individual in a circumstance of evaluation. Let us return to the example in connection with the sentence (3) and the indexical 'I'. The bizarre result of taking the descriptive meaning of the indexical to be the propositional constituent is that what I said in uttering (3) would be true in a circumstance of evaluation if and only if the speaker (assuming there is one) of the circumstance does not exist in the circumstance. Nonsense! It *that* were the correct analysis, what I said could not be true. From which it follows that

It is impossible that I do not exist.

Here is another example to show that the descriptive meaning of an indexical may be entirely *inapplicable* in the circumstance of evaluation. When I say,

I wish I were not speaking now.

The circumstances desired do not involve contexts of *use* and *agents* who are not speaking. The *actual* context of use is used to determine the relevant individual: *me*—and time: *now*—and then we query the various circumstances of evaluation with respect to *that* individual and *that* time.

Here is another example, not of the inapplicability of the descriptive meaning to circumstances but of its irrelevance. Suppose I say at t_0, "It will soon be the case that all that is now beautiful is faded." Consider what was said in the subsentence,

All that is now beautiful is faded.

I wish to evaluate that content at some near future time t_1. What is the relevant time associated with the indexical 'now'? Is it the future time t_1? No, it is t_0, of course: the time of the context of use.

See how rigidly the indexicals cling to the referent determined in the context of use:

(4)   It is possible that in Pakistan, in five years, only those who are actually here now are envied.

The point of (4) is that the circumstance, place, and time referred to by the indexicals 'actually', 'here', and 'now' are the circumstance, place, and time of the *context*, not a circumstance, place, and time determined by the modal, locational, and temporal operators within whose scope the indexicals lie.

It may be objected that this only shows that indexicals always take *primary* scope (in the sense of Russell's scope of a definite description). This objection attempts to relegate all direct reference to implicit use of the paradigm of the semantics of direct reference, the variable. Thus (4) is transformed into,

> The actual circumstances, here, and now are such that it is possible that in Pakistan in five years only those who, in the first, are located at the second, during the third, are envied.

Although this may not be the most felicitous form of expression, its meaning and, in particular, its symbolization should be clear to those familiar with quantified intensional logics. The pronouns, 'the first', 'the second', and 'the third' are to be represented by distinct variables bound to existential quantifiers at the beginning and identified with 'the actual circumstance', 'here', and 'now' respectively.

(5) $(\exists w)(\exists p)(\exists t)[w=$the actual circumstance $\wedge\ p=here \wedge t=now$
$\wedge \Diamond$ In Pakistan In five years $\forall x(x$ is envied $\rightarrow x$ is located at p during t in $w)]$

But such transformations, when thought of as representing the claim that indexicals take primary scope, do not provide an *alternative* to Principle 2, since we may still ask of an utterance of (5) in a context c, when evaluating it with respect to an arbitrary circumstance, to what do the indexicals 'actual', 'here', and 'now' refer. The answer, as always, is: the relevant features of the context c. [In fact, although (4) is equivalent to (5), neither indexicals nor quantification across intensional operators is dispensable in favor of the other.]

Perhaps enough has been said to establish the following.

(**T1**) *The descriptive meaning of a pure indexical determines the referent of the indexical with respect to a context of use but is either inapplicable or irrelevant to determining a referent with respect to a circumstance of evaluation.*

I hope that your intuition will agree with mine that it is for this reason that:

(**T2**) *When what was said in using a pure indexical in a context* c *is to be evaluated with respect to an arbitrary circumstance, the relevant object is always the referent of the indexical with respect to the context* c.

This is just a slightly elaborated version of Principle 2.

Before turning to true demonstratives, we will adopt some terminology.

VI. Terminological Remarks

Principle 1 and Principle 2 taken together imply that sentences containing pure indexicals have two kinds of meaning.

VI. (i) Content and Circumstance

What is said in using a given indexical in different contexts may be different. Thus if I say, today,

> I was insulted yesterday

and you utter the same words tomorrow, what is said is different. If what we say differs in truth-value, that is enough to show that we say different things. But even if the truth-values were the same, it is clear that there are possible circumstances in which what I said would be true but what you said would be false. Thus we say different things.

Let us call this first kind of meaning—what is said—*content*. The content of a sentence in a given context is what has traditionally been called a proposition. Strawson, in noting that the sentence

> The present king of France is bald

could be used on different occasions to make different statements, used 'statement' in a way similar to our use of *content of a sentence*. If we wish to express the same content in different contexts, we may have to change indexicals. Frege, here using 'thought' for content of a sentence, expresses the point well.

> If someone wants to say the same today as he expressed yesterday using the word 'today', he must replace this word with 'yesterday'. Although the thought is the same its verbal expression must be different so that the sense, which would otherwise be affected by the differing times of utterance, is readjusted.[26]

I take *content* as a notion applying not only to sentences taken in a context but to any meaningful part of speech taken in a context. Thus we can speak of the content of a definite description, an indexical, a predicate, etc. It is *contents* that are evaluated in circumstances of evaluation. If the content is a proposition (i.e., the content of a sentence taken in some context), the result of the evaluation will be a truth-value. The result of evaluating the content of a singular term at a circumstance will be an object (what I earlier called 'the relevant object'). In general, the result of evaluating the content of a well-formed expression α at a circumstance will be an appropriate extension for α (i.e., for a sentence, a truth-value; for a term, an individual; for an n-place predicate, a set of n-tuples of individuals, etc.). This suggests that we can represent a

---

[26] From "The Thought: A Logical Inquiry," *Mind* 65 (1956): 289–311. If Frege had only supplemented these comments with the observation that indexicals are devices of direct reference, the whole theory of indexicals would have been his. But his theory of meaning blinded him to this obvious point. Frege, I believe, mixed together the two kinds of meaning in what he called *Sinn*. A *thought* is, for him, the *Sinn* of a sentence, or perhaps we should say a *complete* sentence. *Sinn* is to contain both "the manner and context of presentation [of the denotation]," according to "Über Sinn und Bedeutung" (*Zeitschrift für Philosophie und philosophische Kritik* 100 (1892); trans. as "On Sense and Nominatum," in *Contemporary Readings in Logical Theory*, ed. Copi and Gould (Macmillan, 1967); mistrans. as "On Sense and Meaning," in Martinich, op. cit.). *Sinn* is first introduced to represent the cognitive significance of a sign, and thus to solve Frege's problem: how can $\ulcorner \alpha = \beta \urcorner$ if true differ in cognitive significance from $\ulcorner \alpha = \alpha \urcorner$. However, it also is taken to represent the truth-conditions or *content* (in our sense). Frege felt the pull of the two notions, which he reflects in some tortured passages about 'I' in "The Thought" (quoted below in XVII). If one says "Today is beautiful" on Tuesday and "Yesterday was beautiful" on Wednesday, one expresses the same thought according to the passage quoted. Yet one can clearly lose track of the days and not realize one is expressing the same thought. It seems then that thoughts are not appropriate bearers of cognitive significance. I return to this topic in XVII. A detailed examination of Frege on demonstratives is contained in John Perry's "Frege on Demonstratives," *Philosophical Review* 86 (1977): 474–97.

content by a function from circumstances of evaluation to an appropriate extension. Carnap called such functions *intensions*.

The representation is a handy one and I will often speak of contents in terms of it, but one should note that contents which are distinct but equivalent (i.e., share a value in all circumstances) are represented by the same intension. Among other things, this results in the loss of my distinction between terms which are devices of direct reference and descriptions which *turn out* to be rigid designators. (Recall the metaphysical paragraph of section IV.) I wanted the content of an indexical to be just the referent itself, but the intension of such a content will be a constant function. Use of representing intensions does not mean I am abandoning that idea—just ignoring it temporarily.

A *fixed content* is one represented by a constant function. All directly referential expressions (as well as all rigid designators) have a fixed content. [What I elsewhere call a *stable* content.]

Let us settle on *circumstances* for possible circumstances of evaluation. By this I mean both actual and counterfactual situations with respect to which it is appropriate to ask for the extensions of a given well-formed expression. A circumstance will usually include a possible state or history of the world, a time, and perhaps other features as well. The amount of information we require from a circumstance is linked to the degree of specificity of contents, and thus to the kinds of operators in the language.

Operators of the familiar kind treated in intensional logic (modal, temporal, etc.) operate on contents. (Since we represent contents by intensions, it is not surprising that intensional operators operate on contents.) Thus an appropriate extension for an intensional operator is a function from intensions to extensions.[27] A modal operator when applied to an intension will look at the behavior of the intension with respect to the possible state of the world feature of the circumstances of evaluation. A temporal operator will, similarly, be concerned with

---

[27] As we shall see, indexical operators such as "It is now the case that," "It is actually the case that," and "dthat" (the last takes a term rather than a sentence as argument) are also intensional operators. They differ from the familiar operators in only two ways: first, their extension (the function from intensions to extensions) depends on context, and second, they are directly referential (thus they have a fixed content). I shall argue below (in section VII: Monsters) that all operators that can be given an English reading are 'at most' intensional. Note that when discussing issues in terms of the formal representations of the model-theoretic semantics, I tend to speak in terms of intensions and intensional operators rather than contents and content operators.

the time of the circumstance. If we built the time of evaluation into the contents (thus removing time from the circumstances leaving only, say, a possible world history, and making contents *specific* as to time), it would make no sense to have temporal operators. To put the point another way, if *what is said* is thought of as incorporating reference to a specific time, or state of the world, or whatever, it is otiose to ask whether what is said would have been true at another time, in another state of the world, or whatever. Temporal operators applied to eternal sentences (those whose contents incorporate a specific time of evaluation) are redundant. Any intensional operators applied to *perfect* sentences (those whose contents incorporate specific values for all features of circumstances) are redundant.[28]

---

[28] The notion of redundancy involved could be made precise. When I speak of building the time of evaluation into contents, or making contents specific as to time, or taking what is said to incorporate reference to a specific time, what I have in mind is this. Given a sentence S: 'I am writing', in the present context c, which of the following should we take as the content: (i) the proposition that David Kaplan is writing at 10 A.M. on 3/26/77, or (ii) the 'proposition' that David Kaplan is writing? The proposition (i) is specific as to time, the 'proposition' (ii) [the scare quotes reflect my feeling that this is not the traditional notion of a proposition] is neutral with respect to time. If we take the content of S in c to be (ii), we can ask whether it would be true at times other than the time of c. Thus we think of the temporally neutral 'proposition' as changing its truth-value over time. Note that it is not just the noneternal sentence S that changes its truth-value over time, but the 'proposition' itself. Since the sentence S contains an indexical 'I', it will express different 'propositions' in different contexts. But since S contains no *temporal* indexical, the time of the context will not influence the 'proposition' expressed. An alternative [and more traditional] view is to say that the verb tense in S involves an implicit temporal indexical, so that S is understood as synonymous with S': 'I am writing now'. If we take this point of view we will take the content of S in c to be (i). In this case *what is said* is eternal; it does not change its truth-value over time, although S will express different propositions at different times.

There are both technical and philosophical issues involved in choosing between (i) and (ii). Philosophically, we may ask why the temporal indexical should be taken to be implicit (making the proposition eternal) when no modal indexical is taken to be implicit. After all, we *could* understand S as synonymous with S'': 'I am actually writing now'. The content of S'' in c is not only eternal, it is perfect. Its truth changes neither through time nor possibility. Is there some good philosophical reason for preferring contents which are neutral with respect to possibility but draw fixed values from the context for all other features of a possible circumstance whether or not the sentence contains an explicit indexical? (It may be that the traditional view was abetted by one of the delightful anomalies of the logic of indexicals, namely that S, S', and S'' are all logically equivalent! See Remark 3, p. 547.) Technically, we must note that intensional operators must, if they are not to be vacuous, operate on contents which are neutral with respect

What sorts of intensional operators to admit seems to me largely a matter of language engineering. It is a question of which features of what we intuitively think of as possible circumstances can be sufficiently well defined and isolated. If we wish to isolate location and regard it as a feature of possible circumstances we can introduce locational operators: 'Two miles north it is the case that', etc. Such operators can be iterated and can be mixed with modal and temporal operators. However, to make such operators interesting we must have contents which are locationally neutral. That is, it must be appropriate to ask if *what is said* would be true in Pakistan. (For example, 'It is raining' seems to be locationally as well as temporally and modally neutral.)

This functional notion of the content of a sentence in a context may not, because of the neutrality of content with respect to time and place, say, exactly correspond to the classical conception of a proposition. But the classical conception can be introduced by adding the demonstratives 'now' and 'here' to the sentence and taking the content of the result. I will continue to refer to the content of a sentence as a proposition, ignoring the classical use.

Before leaving the subject of circumstances of evaluation I should, perhaps, note that the mere attempt to show that an expression is directly referential requires that it be meaningful to ask of an individual in one circumstance whether and with what properties it exists in another circumstance. If such questions cannot be raised because they are regarded as metaphysically meaningless, the question of whether a particular expression is directly referential (or even, a rigid designator) cannot be raised. I have elsewhere referred to the view that such questions are meaningful as *haecceitism*, and I have described other metaphysical manifestations of this view.[29] I advocate this position, although I am

---

to the feature of circumstance the operator is interested in. Thus, for example, if we take the content of S to be (i), the application of a temporal operator to such a content would have no effect; the operator would be vacuous. Furthermore, if we do not wish the iteration of such operators to be vacuous, the content of the compound sentence containing the operator must again be neutral with respect to the relevant feature of circumstance. This is not to say that no such operator can have the effect of *fixing* the relevant feature and thus, in effect, rendering subsequent operations vacuous; indexical operators do just this. It is just that this must not be the general situation. A content must be the *kind* of entity that is subject to modification in the feature relevant to the operator. [The textual material to which this note is appended is too cryptic and should be rewritten.]

[29] "How to Russell a Frege-Church." The pronunciation is: "Hex̄-ee-i-tis-m." The epithet was suggested by Robert Adams. It is not an accident that it is derived from a demonstrative.

uncomfortable with some of its seeming consequences (for example, that the world might be in a state qualitatively exactly as it is, but with a permutation of individuals).

It is hard to see how one could think about the semantics of indexicals and modality without adopting such a view.

VI. (ii) Character

The second kind of meaning, most prominent in the case of indexicals, is that which determines the content in varying contexts. The rule,

'I' refers to the speaker or writer

is a meaning rule of the second kind. The phrase 'the speaker or writer' is not supposed to be a complete description, nor it is supposed to refer to the speaker or writer of the *word* 'I'. (There are many such.) It refers to the speaker or writer of the relevant *occurrence* of the word 'I', that is, the agent of the context.

Unfortunately, as usually stated, these meaning rules are incomplete in that they do not explicitly specify that the indexical is directly referential, and thus do not completely determine the content in each context. I will return to this later.

Let us call the second kind of meaning, *character*. The character of an expression is set by linguistic conventions and, in turn, determines the content of the expression in every context.[30] Because character is what is set by linguistic conventions, it is natural to think of it as *meaning* in the sense of what is known by the competent language user.

Just as it was convenient to represent contents by functions from possible circumstances to extensions (Carnap's intentions), so it is convenient to represent characters by functions from possible contexts to contents. (As before we have the drawback that equivalent characters are identified.[31]) This gives us the following picture:

---

[30] This does not imply that if you know the character and are in first one and then another context, you can *decide* whether the contents are the same. I may twice use 'here' on separate occasions and not recognize that the place is the same, or twice hear 'I' and not know if the content is the same. What I do know is this: if it was the same person speaking, then the content was the same. [More on this epistemological stuff later.]

[31] I am, at this stage, deliberately ignoring Kripke's theory of proper names in order to see whether the revisions in Fregean semantical theory, which seem plainly required to accommodate indexicals (this is the 'obviousness' of my theory), can throw any light on it. Here we assume that aside from indexicals, Frege's theory

Character: Contexts ⇒ Contents

Content: Circumstances ⇒ Extensions

or, in more familiar language,

Meaning + Context ⇒ Intension

Intension + Possible World ⇒ Extension

Indexicals have a *context-sensitive* character. It is characteristic of an indexical that its content varies with context. Nonindexicals have a *fixed* character. The same content is invoked in all contexts. This content will typically be sensitive to circumstances, that is, the non-indexicals are typically not rigid designators but will vary in extension from circumstance to circumstance. Eternal sentences are generally good examples of expressions with a fixed character.

All persons alive in 1977 will have died by 2077

expresses the same proposition no matter when said, by whom, or under what circumstances. The truth-value of that proposition may, of course, vary with possible circumstances, but the character is fixed. Sentences with fixed character are very useful to those wishing to leave historical records.

Now that we have two kinds of meaning in addition to extension, Frege's principle of intensional interchange[32] becomes two principles:

---

is correct, roughly, that words and phrases have a kind of descriptive meaning or sense which at one and the same time constitutes their cognitive significance and their conditions of applicability.

Kripke says repeatedly in *Naming and Necessity* that he is only providing a picture of how proper names refer and that he does not have an exact theory. His picture yields some startling results. In the case of indexicals we do have a rather precise theory, which avoids the difficulty of specifying a chain of communication and which yields many analogous results. In facing the vastly more difficult problems associated with a theory of reference for proper names, the theory of indexicals may prove useful; if only to show—as I believe—that proper names are not indexicals and have no meaning in the sense in which indexicals have meaning (namely a 'cognitive content' which fixes the references in all contexts). [The issues that arise, involving token reflexives, homonymous words with distinct character, and homonymous token reflexives with the same character are best saved for later—much later.]

[32] See §28 of Rudolf Carnap's *Meaning and Necessity* (Chicago: University of Chicago Press, 1947).

(F1) The character of the whole is a function of the character of the parts. That is, if two compound well-formed expressions differ only with respect to components which have the same Character, then the Character of the compounds is the same.

(F2) The Content of the whole is a function of the Content of the parts. That is, if two compound well-formed expressions, each set in (possibly different) contexts differ only with respect to components which *when taken in their respective contexts* have the same content, then the content of the two compounds *each taken in its own context* is the same.

It is the second principle that accounts for the often noted fact that speakers in different contexts can say the same thing by switching indexicals. (And indeed they often *must* switch indexicals to do so.) Frege illustrated this point with respect to 'today' and 'yesterday' in "The Thought." (But note that his treatment of 'I' suggests that he does not believe that utterances of 'I' and 'you' could be similarly related!)

Earlier, in my metaphysical phase, I suggested that we should think of the content of an indexical as being just the referent itself, and I resented the fact that the representation of contents as intensions forced us to regard such contents as constant functions. A similar remark applies here. If we are not overly concerned with standardized representations (which certainly have their value for model-theoretic investigations) we might be inclined to say that the character of an indexical-free word or phrase just *is* its (constant) content.

VII. Earlier Attempts: Index Theory

The following picture seems to emerge. The meaning (character) of an indexical is a function from contexts to extensions (substituting for fixed contents). The meaning (content, substituting for fixed characters) of a nonindexical is a function from circumstances to extensions. From this point of view it may appear that the addition of indexicals requires no new *logic*, no sharp distinction between contexts and circumstances, just the addition of some special new *features* ('contextual' features) to the circumstances of evaluation. (For example, an *agent* to provide an interpretation for 'I'.) Thus an enlarged view of intension is derived. The intension of an expression is a function from certain factors to the extension of the expression (with respect to those factors). Originally such factors were simply possible states of the world, but as it was noticed that the so-called tense operators exhibited a structure highly analogous to that of the modal operators the factors with respect to which an extension was to be determined were enlarged to include moments of time. When it was noticed that contextual factors were required to determine the extension of sentences containing indexicals, a still more general notion was developed and called an "index." The extension of an expression was to be determined with respect to an index. The intension of an expression was that function which assigned to every index, the extension at that index.

> The above example supplies us with a statement whose truth-value is not constant but varies as a function of $i \in I$. This situation is easily appreciated in the context of time-dependent statements; that is, in the case where I represents the instant of time. Obviously the same statement can be true at one moment and false at another. For more general situations one must not think of the $i \in I$ as anything as simple as instants of time or even possible worlds. In general we will have
>
> $$i = (w, t, p, a, \ldots)$$
>
> where the index i has many *coordinates*: for example, w is a *world*, t is a *time*, $p = (x, y, z)$ is a (3-dimensional) *position* in the world, a is an *agent*, etc. All these coordinates can be varied, possibly independently, and thus affect the truth-values of statements which have indirect references to these coordinates. [From the *Advice* of a prominent logician.]

A sentence ϕ was taken to be logically true if true at every index (in every 'structure'), and $\Box\phi$ was taken to be true at a given index (in a given structure) just in case ϕ was true at every index (in that structure). Thus the familiar principle of modal generalization: if $\models \phi$, then $\models \Box\phi$, is validated.

This view, in its treatment of indexicals, was technically wrong and, more importantly, conceptually misguided.

Consider the sentence

(6)   I am here now.

It is obvious that for many choices of index—i.e., for many quadruples $\langle w, x, p, t \rangle$ where w is a possible world history, x is a person, p is a place, and t is a time—(6) will be false. In fact, (6) is true only with respect to those indices $\langle w, x, p, t \rangle$ which are such that in the world history w, x is located at p at the time t. Thus (6) fares about on a par with

(7)   David Kaplan is in Portland on 26 March 1977.

(7) is empirical, and so is (6).

But here we have missed something essential to our understanding of indexicals. Intuitively, (6) is deeply, and in some sense, which we will shortly make precise, universally, true. One need only understand the meaning of (6) to know that it cannot be uttered falsely. No such guarantees apply to (7). *A Logic of Indexicals* which does not reflect this intuitive difference between (6) and (7) has bypassed something essential to the logic of indexicals.

What has gone wrong? We have ignored the special relationship between 'I', 'here', and 'now'. Here is a proposed correction. Let the class of indices be narrowed to include only the *proper* ones—namely, those $\langle w, x, p, t \rangle$ such that in the world w, x *is* located at p at the time t. Such a move may have been intended originally since improper indices are like impossible worlds; no such contexts *could* exist and thus there is no interest in evaluating the extensions of expressions with respect to them. Our reform has the consequence that (6) comes out, correctly, to be logically true. Now consider

(8)   □ I am here now.

Since the contained sentence (namely (6)) is true at every proper index, (8) also is true at every proper index and thus also is logically true. (As would be expected by the aforementioned principle of modal generalization.)

But (8) should not be *logically* true, since it is false. It is certainly *not* necessary that I be here now. But for several contingencies, I would be working in my garden now, or even delivering this paper in a location outside of Portland.

The difficulty, here, is the attempt to assimilate the role of a *context* to that of a *circumstance*. The indices $\langle w, x, p, t \rangle$ that represent contexts must be proper in order that (6) be a truth of the logic of indexicals, but the indices that represent circumstances must include improper ones in order that (8) *not* be a logical truth.

If one wishes to stay with this sort of index theory and blur the conceptual difference between context and circumstance, the minimal requirement is a system of *double* indexing, one index for context and another for circumstance. It is surprising, looking back, that we (for I was among the early index theorists) did not immediately see that double indexing was required, for in 1967, at UCLA, Hans Kamp had reported his work on 'now'[33] in which he had shown that double indexing was required to properly accommodate temporal indexicals along with the usual temporal operators. But it was *four* years before it was realized that this was a general requirement for (and, in a sense, the key to) a logic of indexicals.

However, mere double indexing, without a clear conceptual understanding of what each index stands for, is still not enough to avoid all pitfalls.

VIII. Monsters Begat by Elegance

My liberality with respect to operators on content, i.e., intensional operators (any feature of the circumstances of evaluation that can be well defined and isolated) does not extend to operators which attempt to operate on character. Are there such operators as 'In some contexts it is true that', which when prefixed to a sentence yields a truth if and only if in some context the contained *sentence* (not the content expressed by it) expresses a content that is true in the circumstances of that context? Let us try it:

(9)   In some contexts it is true that I am not tired now.

For (9) to be true in the present context it suffices that some agent of some context not be tired at the time of that context. (9), so interpreted, has nothing to do with me or the present moment. But this violates Principle 2! Principle 2 can also be expressed in more theory laden way by saying that indexicals always take primary scope. If this is true—and it is—then no operator can control the character of the indexicals within its scope, because they will simply leap out of its scope to the front of the operator. I am not saying we could not construct a language with such operators, just that English is not one.[34] And such operators *could not be added to it*.

There *is* a way to control an indexical, to keep it from taking primary scope, and even to refer it to another context (this amounts to changing its character). Use quotation marks. If we *mention* the indexical rather

---

[33]Published in 1971 as "Formal Properties of 'Now'," *Theoria*.

[34]Thomason alleges a counterinstance: 'Never put off until tomorrow what you can do today'. What should one say about this?

than *use* it, we can, of course, operate directly on it. Carnap once pointed out to me how important the difference between direct and indirect quotation is in

> Otto said "I am a fool."
> Otto said that I am a fool.

Operators like 'In some contexts it is true that', which attempt to meddle with character, I call *monsters*. I claim that none can be expressed in English (without sneaking in a quotation device). If they stay in the metalanguage and confine their attention to sentences as in

> In some contexts "I am not tired now" is true

they are rendered harmless and can even do socially useful work (as does, 'is valid' [see below]).

I have gone on at perhaps excessive length about monsters because they have recently been begat by elegance. In a specific application of the theory of indexicals there will be just certain salient features of a circumstance of evaluation. So we may represent circumstances by indexed sets of features. This is typical of the model-theoretic way. As already indicated, all the features of a circumstance will generally be required as aspects of a context, and the aspects of a context may all be features of a circumstance. If not, a little ingenuity may make it so.[35]

---

[35] Recall that in a particular formal theory the features of a circumstance must include all elements with respect to which there are content operators, and the aspects of a context must include all elements with respect to which there are indexicals. Thus, a language with both the usual modal operators '$\Diamond$', '$\Box$', and an indexical modal operator 'It is actually the case that' will contain a possible world history feature in its circumstances as well as an analogous aspect in its contexts. If a circumstance is an aspect of a context, as seems necessary for the definition of truth, then we only need worry about aspects of contexts that are not features of circumstances. The most prominent of these is the *agent* of the context, required to interpret the indexical 'I'. In order to supply a corresponding nonvacuous feature to circumstances we must treat contents in such a way that we can ask whether they are true for various agents. (Not *characters* mind you, but contents.) This can be done by representing the agent by a *neutral*—a term which plays the syntactical role of 'I' but gets an interpretation only with respect to a circumstance. Let a be a special variable that is not subject to quantification and let b be a variable not in the language. Our variable a is the neutral. We wish to introduce content operators which affect the agent place and which can be iterated. Let R be a relation between individuals, for example 'aRb' for 'b is an uncle of a'. Then we may interpret the operator $O^R\phi$ as $(\exists b)[aRb \wedge (\exists a) (b = a \wedge \phi)]$. If ϕ is 'a walks', $O^R\phi$ comes to 'an uncle of a walks'. The indexical 'I' can be represented by an operator O^I for which 'aRb' is just 'I=b'. The result should be that $O^I\phi$ is equivalent to replacing the neutral a by the indexical 'I'.

We could then represent contexts by the same indexed sets we use to represent circumstances, and instead of having *a logic of contexts and circumstances* we have simply *a two-dimensional logic of indexed sets*. This is algebraically very neat and it permits a very simple and elegant description of certain important classes of characters (for example, those which are true at every pair $\langle i, i \rangle$, though the special significance of the set is somehow diminished in the abstract formulation).[36] But it also permits a simple and elegant introduction of many operators which are monsters. In abstracting from the distinct conceptual roles played by contexts of use and circumstances of evaluation the special logic of indexicals has been obscured. Of course restrictions can be put on the two-dimensional logic to exorcise the monsters, but to do so would be to give up the mathematical advantages of that formulation.[37]

IX. Argument for Principle 2: True Demonstratives

I return now to the argument that all indexicals are directly referential. Suppose I point at Paul and say,

He now lives in Princeton, New Jersey.

Call *what I said*—i.e., the content of my utterance, the proposition expressed—'Pat'. Is Pat true or false? True! Suppose that unbeknownst to me, Paul had moved to Santa Monica last week. Would Pat have then been true or false? False! Now, the tricky case: Suppose that Paul and Charles had each disguised themselves as the other and had switched places. If that had happened, *and* I had uttered as I did, then the proposition I *would have* expressed would have been false. But in that possible context the proposition I *would have* expressed is not Pat. That is easy to see because the proposition I *would have* expressed, had I pointed to Charles instead of Paul—call this proposition 'Mike'—not only *would have* been false but actually is false. Pat, I would claim, would still be true in the circumstances of the envisaged possible con-

---

[36] See, for example, Krister Segerberg, "Two-dimensional Modal Logic," *Journal of Philosophical Logic* 2 (1973): 77–96. Segerberg does metamathematical work in his article and makes no special philosophical claims about its significance. That has been done by others.

[37] There is one other difficulty in identifying the class of contexts with the class of circumstances. The special relationship between the indexicals 'I', 'here', 'now' seems to require that the agent of a context be at the location of the context during the time of the context. But this restriction is not plausible for arbitrary circumstances. It appears that this approach will have difficulty in avoiding the problems of (6) and (8) (section VII).

text provided that Paul—in whatever costume he appeared—were still residing in Princeton.

IX. (i) The Arguments

I am arguing that in order to determine what the truth-value of a proposition expressed by a sentence containing a demonstrative *would be* under other possible circumstances, the relevant individual is not the individual that *would have* been demonstrated had those circumstances obtained and the demonstration been set in a context of those circumstances, but rather the individual demonstrated in the context which *did* generate the proposition being evaluated. As I have already noted, it is characteristic of sentences containing demonstratives—or, for that matter, any indexical—that they may express different propositions in different contexts. We must be wary of confusing the proposition that would have been expressed by a similar utterance in a slightly different context—say, one in which the demonstratum is changed—with the proposition that was actually expressed. If we keep this distinction in mind—i.e., we distinguish Pat and Mike—we are less likely to confuse what the truth-value of the proposition *actually* expressed would have been under some possible circumstances with what the truth-value of the proposition that *would have been* expressed would have been under those circumstances.

When we consider the vast array of possible circumstances with respect to which we might inquire into the truth of a proposition expressed in some context *c* by an utterance *u*, it quickly becomes apparent that only a small fraction of these circumstances will involve an utterance of the same sentence in a similar context, and that there must be a way of evaluating the truth-value of propositions expressed using demonstratives in counterfactual circumstances in which no demonstrations are taking place and no individual has the exact characteristics exploited in the demonstration. Surely, it is irrelevant to determining whether what I said would be true or not in some counterfactual circumstance, whether Paul, or anyone for that matter, *looked* as he does now. All that would be relevant is *where he lives*. Therefore,

(**T3**) the relevant features of the demonstratum *qua demonstratum* (compare, the relevant features of the x Fx *qua the x Fx*)—namely, that the speaker is pointing at it, that it has a certain appearance, is presented in a certain way—cannot be the essential characteristics used to identify the relevant individual in counterfactual situations.

These two arguments: the distinction between Pat and Mike, and consideration of counterfactual situations in which no demonstration occurs, are offered to support the view that demonstratives are devices of direct reference (rigid designators, if you will) and, by contrast, to reject a Fregean theory of demonstratives.

IX. (ii) The Fregean Theory of Demonstrations

In order to develop the latter theory, in contrast to my own, we turn first to a portion of the Fregean theory which I accept: the Fregean theory of demonstrations.

As you know, for a Fregean the paradigm of a meaningful expression is the definite description, which picks out or denotes an individual, a unique individual, satisfying a condition *s*. The individual is called the *denotation* of the definite description and the condition *s* we may identify with the *sense* of the definite description. Since a given individual may uniquely satisfy several distinct conditions, definite descriptions with distinct senses may have the same denotation. And since some conditions may be uniquely satisfied by no individual, a definite description may have a sense but no denotation. The condition by means of which a definite description picks out its denotation is *the manner of presentation* of the denotation by the definite description.

The Fregean theory of demonstratives claims, correctly I believe, that the analogy between descriptions (short for 'definite descriptions') and demonstrations is close enough to provide a sense and denotation analysis of the 'meaning' of a demonstration. The denotation is the demonstratum (that which is demonstrated), and it seems quite natural to regard each demonstration as presenting its demonstratum in a particular manner, which we may regard as the sense of the demonstration. The same individual could be demonstrated by demonstrations so different in manner of presentation that it would be informative to a competent auditor-observer to be told that the demonstrata were one. For example, it might be informative to you for me to tell you that

> That [pointing to Venus in the morning sky] is identical with
> that [pointing to Venus in the evening sky].

(I would, of course, have to speak very slowly.) The two demonstrations—call the first one 'Phos' and the second one 'Hes'—which accompanied the two occurrences of the demonstrative expression 'that' have the same demonstratum but distinct manners of presentation. It is this difference between the sense of Hes and the sense of Phos that accounts, the Fregean claims, for the informativeness of the assertion.

It is possible, to pursue the analogy, for a demonstration to have no demonstratum. This can arise in several ways: through hallucination, through carelessness (not noticing, in the darkened room, that the subject had jumped off the demonstration platform a few moments before the lecture began), through a sortal conflict (using the demonstrative phrase ⌜that F⌝, where F is a common noun phrase, while demonstrating something which is not an F), and in other ways.

Even Donnellans's important distinction between referential and attributive uses of definite descriptions seems to fit, equally comfortably, the case of demonstrations.[38]

The Fregean hypostatizes demonstrations in such a way that it is appropriate to ask of a given demonstration, say Phos, what *would* it have demonstrated under various counterfactual circumstances. Phos and Hes might have demonstrated distinct individuals.[39]

We should not allow our enthusiasm for analogy to overwhelm judgment in this case. There are some relevant respects in which descriptions and demonstrations are disanalogous. First, as David Lewis has pointed out, demonstrations do not have a syntax, a fixed formal structure in terms of whose elements we might try to define, either directly or recursively, the notion of sense.[40] Second, to different audiences (for example, the speaker, those sitting in front of the demonstration platform, and those sitting behind the demonstration platform) the same demonstration may have different senses. Or perhaps we should say that a single performance may involve distinct demonstrations from the perspective of distinct audiences. ("Exactly like proper names!" says the Fregean, "as long as the demonstratum remains the same, these fluctuations in sense are tolerable. But they should be avoided in the system

---

[38] I have written elsewhere, in appendices VII and VIII of "Bob and Carol and Ted and Alice," of these matters and won't pursue the topic now.

[39] It could then be proposed that demonstrations be individuated by the principle: $d_1 = d_2$ if and only if, for all appropriate circumstances c, the demonstratum of d_1 in c = the demonstratum of d_2 in c. An alternative principle of individuation is that the same demonstration is being performed in two different contexts if the standard audience can't determine, from the demonstration alone, whether the contexts are distinct or identical. This makes the individuation of demonstrations more epistemological than the metaphysical proposal above.

[40] Although recent work on computer perception has attempted to identify a syntax of pictures. See P. Suppes and Rottmayer, "Automata," in *Handbook of Perception*, vol. 1 (New York: Academic Press, 1974).

of a demonstrative science and should not appear in a perfect vehicle of communication.")

IX. (iii) The Fregean Theory of Demonstratives

Let us accept, tentatively and cautiously, the Fregean theory of demonstrations, and turn now to the Fregean theory of demonstratives.[41]

According to the Fregean theory of demonstratives, an occurrence of a demonstrative expression functions rather like a place-holder for the associated demonstration. The sense of a sentence containing demonstratives is to be the result of replacing each demonstrative by a constant whose sense is given as the sense of the associated demonstration. An important aim of the Fregean theory is, of course, to solve Frege's problem. And it does that quite neatly. You recall that the Fregean accounted for the informativeness of

That [Hes] = that [Phos]

in terms of the distinct senses of Hes and Phos. Now we see that the senses of the two occurrences of 'that' are identified with these two distinct senses so that the ultimate solution is exactly like that given by Frege originally. The sense of the left 'that' differs from the sense of the right 'that'.

IX. (iv) Argument Against the Fregean Theory of Demonstratives

Let us return now to our original example:

He [Delta] now lives in Princeton, New Jersey

where 'Delta' is the name of the relevant demonstration. I assume that in the possible circumstances described earlier, Paul and Charles having disguised themselves as each other, Delta would have demonstrated Charles. Therefore, according to the Fregean theory, the proposition I just expressed, Pat, would have been false under the counterfactual circumstances of the switch. But this, as argued earlier, is wrong. Therefore, the Fregean theory of demonstratives though it nicely solves Frege's problem, is simply incorrect in associating propositions with utterances.

Let me recapitulate. We compared two theories as to the proposition expressed by a sentence containing a demonstrative along with an asso-

---

[41] The Fregean theory of demonstrations is not a part of my obvious and uncontroversial theory of indexicals. On the contrary, it has the fascination of the speculative.

ciated demonstration. Both theories allow that the demonstration can be regarded as having both a sense and a demonstratum. My theory, the direct reference theory, claims that in assessing the proposition in counterfactual circumstances it is the actual demonstratum—in the example, Paul—that is the relevant individual. The Fregean theory claims that the proposition is to be construed as if the sense of the demonstration were the sense of the demonstrative. Thus, in counterfactual situations it is the individual that *would* have been demonstrated that is the relevant individual. According to the direct reference theory, demonstratives are rigid designators. According to the Fregean theory, their denotation varies in different counterfactual circumstances as the demonstrata of the associated demonstration would vary in those circumstances.

The earlier distinction between Pat and Mike, and the discussion of counterfactual circumstances in which, as we would now put it, the demonstration would have demonstrated nothing, argue that with respect to the problem of associating propositions with utterances the direct reference theory is correct and the Fregean theory is wrong.

I have carefully avoided arguing for the direct reference theory by using modal or subjunctive sentences for fear the Fregean would claim that the peculiarity of demonstratives is not that they are rigid designators but that they always take primary scope. If I had argued only on the basis of our intuitions as to the truth-value of

> If Charles and Paul had changed chairs, then he (Delta) would not now be living in Princeton

such a scope interpretation could be claimed. But I didn't.

The perceptive Fregeans among you will have noted that I have said nothing about how Frege's problem fares under a direct reference theory of demonstratives. And indeed, if 'that' accompanied by a demonstration is a rigid designator for the demonstratum, then

> that (Hes) = that (Phos)

looks like two rigid designators designating the same thing. Uh Oh! I will return to this in my Epistemological Remarks (section XVII).

X. Fixing the Reference vs. Supplying a Synonym[42]

The Fregean is to be forgiven. He has made a most natural mistake. Perhaps he thought as follows: If I point at someone and say 'he', that occurrence of 'he' must refer to the male at whom I am now pointing. It does! So far, so good. Therefore, the Fregean reasons, since 'he' (in its demonstrative sense) means the same as 'the male at whom I am now pointing' and since the denotation of the latter varies with circumstances the denotation of the former must also. But this is wrong. Simply because it is a rule of the language that 'he' *refers* to the male at whom I am now pointing (or, whom I am now demonstrating, to be more general), it does not follow that any synonymy is thereby established. In fact, this is one of those cases in which—to use Kripke's excellent idiom—the rule simply tells us how to *fix the reference* but does not supply a synonym.

Consider the proposition I express with the utterance

He [Delta] is the male at whom I am now pointing.

Call that proposition 'Sean'. Now Sean is certainly true. We know from the rules of the language that any utterance of that form must express a true proposition. In fact we would be justified in calling the *sentence*

He is the male at whom I am now pointing.

almost analytic. ('Almost' because of the hypothesis that the demonstrative is *proper*—that I am pointing at a unique male—is needed.)

But is Sean necessary? Certainly not, I might have pointed at someone else.

This kind of mistake—to confuse a semantical rule which tells how to fix the reference to a directly referential term with a rule which supplies a synonym—is easy to make. Since semantics must supply a meaning, in the sense of content (as I call it), for expressions, one thinks naturally that whatever way the referent of an expression is given by the semantical rules, that *way* must stand for the content of the expression. (Church [or was it Carnap?] says as much, explicitly.) This hypothesis

---

[42] I use Kripke's terminology to expound the important distinction he introduces in *Naming and Necessity* for descriptive meaning that may be associated with a proper name. As in several other cases of such parallels between proper names and indexicals, the distinction, and its associated argument, seems more obvious when applied to indexicals.

seems especially plausible, when, as is typical of indexicals,

> the semantical rule which fixes the reference seems to exhaust
> our knowledge of the meaning of the expression.

X. (i) Reichenbach on Token Reflexives

It was from such a perspective, I believe, that Reichenbach built his inge-
nious theory of indexicals. Reichenbach called such expressions 'token-
reflexive words' in accordance with his theory. He writes as follows:

> We saw that most individual-descriptions are constructed by
> reference to other individuals. Among these there is a class
> of descriptions in which the individual referred to is the act
> of speaking. We have special words to indicate this refer-
> ence; such words are 'I', 'you', 'here', 'now', 'this'. Of the
> same sort are the tenses of verbs, since they determine time
> by reference to the time when the words are uttered. To
> understand the function of these words we have to make use
> of the distinction between *token* and *symbol*, 'token' mean-
> ing the individual sign, and 'symbol' meaning the class of
> similar tokens (cf. §2). Words and sentences are symbols.
> The words under consideration are words which refer to the
> corresponding token used in an individual act of speech, or
> writing; they may therefore be called *token-reflexive* words.
>
> It is easily seen that all these words can be defined in terms
> of the phrase 'this token'. The word 'I', for instance, means
> the same as 'the person who utters this token'; 'now' means
> the same as 'the time at which this token was uttered'; 'this
> table' means the same as 'the table pointed to by a gesture
> accompanying this token'. We therefore need inquire only
> into the meaning of the phrase 'this token'.[43]

But is it true, for example, that

(10)   'I' means the same as 'the person who utters this token'   ?

It is certainly true that

> I am the person who utters this token.

---

[43] H. Reichenbach, *Elements of Symbolic Logic* (New York: Macmillan, 1947), p. 284.

But if (10) correctly asserted a synonymy, then it would be true that

(11) If no one were to utter this token, I would not exist.

Beliefs such as (11) could make one a compulsive talker.

XI. The Meaning of Indexicals

In order to correctly and more explicitly state the semantical rule which the dictionary attempts to capture by the entry

>   I: the person who is speaking or writing

we would have to develop our semantical theory—the semantics of direct reference—and then state that

(D1) 'I' is an indexical, different utterances of which may have different contents

(D3) 'I' is, in each of its utterances, directly referential

(D2) In each of its utterances, 'I' refers to the person who utters it.

We have seen errors in the Fregean analysis of demonstratives and in Reichenbach's analysis of indexicals, all of which stemmed from failure to realize that these words are directly referential. When we say that a word is directly referential are we saying that its meaning *is* its reference (its only meaning is its reference, its meaning is nothing more than its reference)? Certainly not.[44] Insofar as meaning is given by the rules of a language and is what is known by competent speakers, I would be more inclined to say in the case of directly referential words and phrases that their reference is *no* part of their meaning. The meaning of the word 'I' does not change when different persons use it. The meaning of 'I' is given by the rules (D1), (D2), and (D3) above.

---

[44] We see here a drawback to the terminology 'direct reference'. It suggests falsely that the reference is not mediated by a meaning, which it is. The meaning (character) is directly associated, by convention, with the word. The meaning determines the referent; and the referent determines the content. It is this to which I alluded in the parenthetical remark following the picture on page 486. Note, however, that the kind of descriptive meaning involved in giving the character of indexicals like 'I', 'now', etc., is, because of the focus on context rather than circumstance, unlike that traditionally thought of as Fregean sense. It is the idea that the referent determines the content—that, contra Frege, there *is* a road back—that I wish to capture. This is the importance of Principle 2.

Meanings tell us how the content of a word or phrase is determined by the context of use. Thus the meaning of a word or phrase is what I have called its *character*. (Words and phrases with no indexical element express the same content in every context; they have a fixed character.) To supply a synonym for a word or phrase is to find another with the same *character*; finding another with the same *content* in a particular context certainly won't do. The content of 'I' used by me may be identical with the content of 'you' used by you. This doesn't make 'I' and 'you' synonyms. Frege noticed that if one wishes to say again what one said yesterday using 'today', today one must use 'yesterday'. (Incidentally the relevant passage, quoted on page 501, propounds what I take to be a direct reference theory of the indexicals 'today' and 'yesterday'.) But 'today' and 'yesterday' are not synonyms. For two words or phrases to be synonyms, they must have the same content in every context. In general, for indexicals, it is not possible to find synonyms. This is because indexicals are directly referential, and the compound phrases which can be used to give their reference ('the person who is speaking', 'the individual being demonstrated', etc.) are not.

XII. Dthat[45]

It would be useful to have a way of converting an arbitrary singular term into one which is directly referential.

Recall that we earlier regarded demonstrations, which are required to 'complete' demonstratives, as a kind of description. The demonstrative was then treated as a directly referential term whose referent was the demonstratum of the associated demonstration.

Now why not regard descriptions as a kind of demonstration, and introduce a special demonstrative which requires completion by a description and which is treated as a directly referential term whose referent is the denotation of the associated description? Why not? Why not indeed! I have done so, and I write it thus:

dthat[α]

where α is any description, or, more generally, any singular term. 'Dthat' is simply the demonstrative 'that' with the following singular term func-

---

[45] Pronunciation note on 'dthat'. The word is not pronounced dee-that or duh-that. It has only one syllable. Although articulated differently from 'that' (the tongue begins behind the teeth), the sounds are virtually indistinguishable to all but native speakers.

tioning as its demonstration. (Unless you hold a Fregean theory of demonstratives, in which case its meaning is as stipulated above.)

Now we can come much closer to providing genuine synonyms.

> 'I' means the same as 'dthat [the person who utters this token]'.

(The fact that this alleged synonymy is cast in the theory of utterances rather than occurrences introduces some subtle complications, which have been discussed by Reichenbach.)

XIII. Contexts, Truth, and Logical Truth

I wish, in this section, to contrast an *occurrence* of a well-formed expression (my *technical* term for the combination of an expression and a context) with an *utterance* of an expression.

There are several arguments for my notion, but the main one is from Remark 1 on the Logic of Demonstratives (section XIX below): I have sometimes said that the content of a sentence in a context is, roughly, the proposition the sentence would express if uttered in that context. This description is not quite accurate on two counts. First, it is important to distinguish an *utterance* from a *sentence-in-a-context*. The former notion is from the theory of speech acts, the latter from semantics. Utterances take time, and utterances of distinct sentences cannot be simultaneous (i.e., in the same context). But in order to develop a logic of demonstratives we must be able to evaluate several premises and a conclusion all in the same context. We do not want arguments involving indexicals to become valid simply because there is no possible context in which all the premises are uttered, and thus no possible context in which all are uttered truthfully.

Since the content of an occurrence of a sentence containing indexicals depends on the context, the notion of *truth* must be relativized to a context.

> If c is a context, then an occurrence of ϕ in c is true iff the content expressed by ϕ in this context is true when evaluated with respect to the circumstance of the context.

We see from the notion of truth that among other aspects of a context must be a possible circumstance. Every context occurs in a particular circumstance, and there are demonstratives such as 'actual' which refer to that circumstance.

If you try out the notion of truth on a few examples, you will see that it is correct. If I now utter a sentence, I will have uttered a truth just in case *what I said*, the content, is true in *these* circumstances.

As is now common for intensional logics, we provide for the notion of a *structure*, comprising a family of circumstances. Each such structure will determine a set of possible contexts. Truth in a structure, is truth in every possible context of the structure. Logical truth is truth in every structure.

XIV. Summary of Findings (so far): Pure Indexicals

Let me try now to summarize my findings regarding the semantics of demonstratives and other indexicals. First, let us consider the non-demonstrative indexicals such as 'I', 'here' (in its nondemonstrative sense), 'now', 'today', 'yesterday', etc. In the case of these words, the linguistic conventions which constitute *meaning* consist of rules specifying the referent of a given *occurrence* of the word (we might say, a given token, or even utterance, of the word, if we are willing to be somewhat less abstract) in terms of various features of the context of the occurrence. Although these rules fix the referent and, in a very special sense, might be said to define the indexical, the way in which the rules are given does not provide a synonym for the indexical. The rules tell us for any possible occurrence of the indexical what the referent would be, but they do *not* constitute the content of such an occurrence. Indexicals are directly referential. The rules tell us what it is that is referred to. Thus, they *determine* the content (the propositional constituent) for a particular occurrence of an indexical. But they are not a *part* of the content (they constitute no part of the propositional constituent). In order to keep clear on a topic where ambiguities constantly threaten, I have introduced two technical terms: *content* and *character* for the two kinds of meaning (in addition to extension) I associate with indexicals. Distinct occurrences of an indexical (in distinct contexts) may not only have distinct referents, they may have distinct meanings in the sense of *content*. If I say "I am tired today" today and Montgomery Furth says "I am tired today" tomorrow, our utterances have different contents in that the factors which are relevant to determining the truth-value of what Furth said in both actual and counterfactual circumstances are quite different from the factors which are relevant to determining the truth-value of what I said. Our two utterances are as different in content as are the sentences "David Kaplan is tired on 26 March 1977" and

"Montgomery Furth is tired on 27 March 1977." But there is another sense of meaning in which, absent lexical or syntactical ambiguities, two occurrences of the *same* word or phrase *must* mean the same. (Otherwise how could we learn and communicate with language?) This sense of meaning—which I call *character*—is what determines the content of an occurrence of a word or phrase in a given context. For indexicals, the rules of language constitute the meaning in the sense of *character*. As normally expressed, in dictionaries and the like, these rules are incomplete in that, by omitting to mention that indexicals are directly referential, they fail to specify the full content of an occurrence of an indexical.

Three important features to keep in mind about these two kinds of meaning are:

1.   Character applies only to words and phrases as types, content to occurrences of words and phrases in contexts.

2.   Occurrences of two phrases can agree in content although the phrases differ in character, and two phrases can agree in character but differ in content in distinct contexts.

3.   The relationship of character to content is something like that traditionally regarded as the relationship of sense to denotation, character is a way of presenting content.

XV. Further Details: Demonstratives and Demonstrations

Let me turn now to the demonstratives proper, those expressions which must be associated with a demonstration in order to determine a referent. In addition to the pure demonstratives 'that' and 'this' there are a variety of demonstratives which contain built-in sortals: 'he' for 'that male', 'she' for 'that female',[46] etc., and there are demonstrative phrases built from a pure demonstrative and a common noun phrase: 'that man drinking a martini', etc. Words and phrases which have demonstrative use may have other uses as well, for example, as bound variable or pronouns of laziness (anaphoric use).

I accept, tentatively and cautiously, the Fregean theory of demonstrations according to which:

---

[46]'Male' and 'female' are here used in the grammatical sense of gender, not the biological sense.

(1)   A demonstration is a way of presenting an individual.

(2)   A given demonstration in certain counterfactual circumstances would have demonstrated (i.e., presented) an individual other than the individual actually demonstrated.

(3)   A demonstration which fails to demonstrate any individual might have demonstrated one, and a demonstration which demonstrates an individual might have demonstrated no individual at all.

So far we have asserted that it is not an essential property of a given demonstration (according to the Fregean theory) that it demonstrate a given individual, or indeed, that it demonstrate any individual at all. It is this feature of demonstrations: that demonstrations which in fact demonstrate the same individual might have demonstrated distinct individuals, which provides a solution to the demonstrative version of Frege's problem (why is an utterance of 'that [Hes] = that [Phos]' informative?) analogous to Frege's own solution to the definite description version. There is some theoretical lattitude as to how we should regard such other features of a demonstration as its place, time, and agent. Just to fix ideas, let us regard all these features as accidental. (It may be helpful to think of demonstrations as *types* and particular performances of them as their *tokens*). Then,

(4)   A given demonstration might have been mounted by someone other than its actual agent, and might be repeated in the same or a different place.

Although we are not now regarding the actual place and time of a demonstration as essential to it, it does seem to me to be essential to a demonstration that it present its demonstrata from some perspective, that is, as the individual that looks thusly *from here now*. On the other hand, it does not seem to me to be essential to a demonstration that it be mounted by any agent at all.[47]

---

[47] If the current speculations are accepted, then in the original discussion of Pat and Mike the emphasis on the counterfactual situation in which the same agent was doing the pointing was misguided and that feature of counterfactual situations is irrelevant. It is the agent of course who focuses your attention on the relevant local individual. But that needn't be done *by* anyone; we might have a convention that whoever is appearing on the demonstration platform is the demonstratum, or the speaker might take advantage of a natural demonstration of opportunity: an explosion or a shooting star.

We now have a kind of standard form for demonstrations:

The individual that has appearance A from here now

where an appearance is something like a picture with a little arrow pointing to the relevant subject. Trying to put it into words, a particular demonstration might come out like:

The brightest heavenly body now visible from here.

In this example we see the importance of perspective. The same demonstration, differently located, may present a different demonstratum (a twin, for example).

If we set a demonstration, δ, in a context, c, we determine the relevant perspective (i.e., the values of 'here' and 'now'). We also determine the demonstratum, if there is one—if, that is, in the circumstances of the context there is an individual that appears that way from the place and time of the context.[48] In setting δ and c we determine more than just the demonstratum in the possible world of the context. By fixing the perspective, we determine for each possible circumstance what, if anything, would appear like that from that perspective. This is to say, we determine a *content*. This content will not, in general, be fixed (like that determined by a rigid designator). Although it was Venus that appeared a certain way from a certain location in ancient Greece, it might have been Mars. Under certain counterfactual conditions, it *would* have been Mars that appeared just that way from just that location. Set in a different context, δ, may determine a quite different content or no content at all. When I look at myself in the mirror each morning I know that I didn't look like that ten years ago—and I suspect that nobody did.

The preceding excursion into a more detailed Fregean theory of demonstrations was simply in order to establish the following structural features of demonstrations:

1.   A demonstration, when set in a context (i.e., an *occurrence* of a demonstration), determines a content.

---

[48] Since, as remarked earlier, the speaker and different members of the audience generally have different perspectives on the demonstration, it may appear slightly different to each of them. Thus each may take a slightly different demonstration to have been performed. Insofar as the agent and audience of a given context can differ in location, the location of a context is the location of the agent. Therefore the demonstratum of a given demonstration set in a given context will be the individual, if any, thereby demonstrated from the speaker's point of view.

2.   It is not required that an occurrence of a demonstration have a fixed content.

In view of these features, we can associate with each demonstration a *character* which represents the 'meaning' or manner of presentation of the demonstration. We have now brought the semantics of demonstrations and descriptions into isomorphism.[49] Thus, I regard my 'dthat' operator as representing the general case of a demonstrative. Demonstratives are incomplete expressions which must be completed by a demonstration (type). A complete sentence (type) will include an associated demonstration (type) for each of its demonstratives. Thus each demonstrative, d, will be accompanied by a demonstration, δ, thus:

$$d[\delta]$$

The character of a *complete* demonstrative is given by the semantical rule:

> In any context c, $d[\delta]$ is a directly referential term that designates the demonstratum, if any, of δ in c, and that otherwise designates nothing.

Obvious adjustments are to be made to take into account any common noun phrase which accompanies or is built-in to the demonstrative.

Since no immediately relevant structural differences have appeared between demonstrations and descriptions, I regard the treatment of the 'dthat' operator in the formal logic LD as accounting for the general case. It would be a simple matter to add to the syntax a category of 'nonlogical demonstration constants'. (Note that the indexicals of LD are all logical signs in the sense that their meaning [character] is not given by the structure but by the evaluation rules.)

XVI. Alternative Treatments of Demonstrations

The foregoing development of the Fregean theory of demonstrations is not inevitable. Michael Bennett has proposed that only places be demonstrata and that we require an explicit or implicit common noun phrase to accompany the demonstrative, so that:

---

[49] We should not, of course, forget the many disanalogies noted earlier nor fail to note that though a description is associated with a particular character by linguistic *convention*, a demonstration is associated with *its* character by *nature*.

> that [pointing at a person]

becomes

> dthat [the person who is there [pointing at a place]].

My findings do not include the claim that the—or better, a—Fregean theory of demonstrations is correct. I can provide an alternative account for those who regard demonstrations as nonrepeatable nonseparable features of contexts. The conception now under consideration is that in certain contexts the agent is demonstrating something, or more than one thing, and in others not. Thus just as we can speak of agent, time, place, and possible world history as features of a context, we may also speak of first demonstratum, second demonstratum, ... (some of which may be null) as features of a context. We then attach subscripts to our demonstratives and regard the n-th demonstrative, when set in a context, as rigid designator of the n-th demonstratum of the context. Such a rule associates a character with each demonstrative. In providing no role for demonstrations as separable 'manners of presentation' this theory eliminates the interesting distinction between demonstratives and other indexicals. We might call it the *Indexical theory of demonstratives*. (Of course every reasonable theory of demonstratives treats them as indexicals of some kind. I regard my own theory of indexicals in general, and the nondemonstrative indexicals in particular, as essentially uncontroversial. Therefore I reserve *Indexical theory of demonstratives* for the controversial alternative to the Fregean theory of demonstrations—the Fregean theory of demonstra*tives* having been refuted.)

Let us call my theory as based on the Fregean theory of demonstrations the *Corrected Fregean theory of demonstratives*. The Fregean theory of demonstrations may be extravagant, but compared with its riches, the indexical theory is a mean thing. From a logical point of view, the riches of the Corrected Fregean theory of demonstratives are already available in connection with the demonstrative 'dthat' and its descriptive pseudodemonstrations, so a decision to enlarge the language of LD with additional demonstratives whose semantics are in accord with the Indexical theory need not be too greatly lamented.

If we consider Frege's problem, we have the two formulations:

> that [Hes] = that [Phos]

and

> $that_1 = that_2$

Both provide their sentence with an informative character. But the Fregean idea that that very demonstration might have picked out a different demonstratum seems to me to capture more of the epistemological situation than the Indexicalist's idea that in some contexts the first and second demonstrata differ.

The Corrected Fregean theory, by incorporating demonstration types in its sentence types, accounts for more differences in informativeness as differences in meaning (character). It thereby provides a nice Frege-type solution to many Frege-type problems. But it can only forestall the resort to directly epistemological issues, it cannot hold them in abeyance indefinitely. Therefore I turn to epistemological remarks.

XVII. Epistemological Remarks[50]

How do content and character serve as objects of thought? Let us state, once again, Frege's problem

(FP) How can (an occurrence of) $\ulcorner \alpha = \beta \urcorner$ (in a given context), if true, differ in cognitive significance from (an occurrence of) $\ulcorner \alpha = \alpha \urcorner$ (in the same context)?

In (FP) α, β are arbitrary singular terms. (In future formulations, I will omit the parentheticals as understood.) When α and β are demonstrative free, Frege explained the difference in terms of his notion of sense. A notion which, his writings generally suggest, should be identified with our *content*. But it is clear that Frege's problem can be reinstituted in a form in which resort to contents will not explain differences in 'cognitive significance'. We need only ask,

(FPD) How can $\ulcorner \text{dthat}[\alpha] = \text{dthat}[\beta] \urcorner$ if true, differ in cognitive significance from $\ulcorner \text{dthat}[\alpha] = \text{dthat}[\alpha] \urcorner$?

Since, as we shall show, for any term γ,

$\ulcorner \gamma = \text{dthat}[\gamma] \urcorner$ is analytic

the sentence pair in (FP) will differ in cognitive significance if and only if the sentence pair in (FPD) differ similarly. [There are a few assumptions built in here, but they are O.K.] Note, however, that the *content* of $\ulcorner \text{dthat}[\alpha] \urcorner$ and the *content* of $\ulcorner \text{dthat}[\beta] \urcorner$ are the same whenever $\ulcorner \alpha = \beta \urcorner$

---

[50] This section has benefited from the opportunity to read, and discuss with him, John Perry's paper "Frege on Demonstratives."

is true. Thus the difference in cognitive significance between the sentence pair in (FPD) cannot be accounted for in terms of content.

If Frege's solution to (FP) was correct, then α and β have different contents. From this it follows that $\ulcorner\text{dthat}[\alpha]\urcorner$ and $\ulcorner\text{dthat}[\beta]\urcorner$ have different characters. [It doesn't really, because of the identification of contents with intensions, but let it pass.] Is character, then, the object of thought?

If you and I both say to ourselves,

(B)   "I am getting bored"

have we thought the same thing? We could not have, because what you thought was true while what I thought was false.

What we must do is disentangle two epistemological notions: *the objects of thought* (what Frege called "Thoughts") and the *cognitive significance of an object of thought*. As has been noted above, a character may be likened to a manner of presentation of a content. This suggests that we identify objects of thought with contents and the cognitive significance of such objects with characters.

E. Principle 1 *Objects of thought (Thoughts) = Contents*

E. Principle 2 *Cognitive significance of a Thought = Character*

According to this view, the thoughts associated with $\ulcorner\text{dthat}[\alpha] = \text{dthat}[\beta]\urcorner$ and $\ulcorner\text{dthat}[\alpha] = \text{dthat}[\alpha]\urcorner$ are the same, but the thought (not the denotation, mind you, but the *thought*) is *presented* differently.

It is important to see that we have not *simply* generalized Frege's theory, providing a higher order Fregean sense for each name of a regular Fregean sense.[51] In Frege's theory, a given manner of presentation presents the same object to all mankind.[52] But for us, a given manner of presentation—a character—what we both said to ourselves when we both said (B)—will, in general, present different objects (of thought) to different persons (and even different Thoughts to the same person at different times).

---

[51] According to Church, such higher order Fregean senses are already called for by Frege's theory.

[52] See his remarks in "On Sense and Nominatum" regarding the "common treasure of thoughts which is transmitted from generation to generation" and remarks there and in "The Thought" in connection with tensed sentences, that "Only a sentence supplemented by a time-indication and complete in every respect expresses a thought."

How then can we claim that we have captured the idea of cognitive significance? To break the link between cognitive significance and universal Fregean senses and at the same time forge the link between cognitive significance and character we must come to see the *context-sensitivity* (dare I call it ego-orientation?) of cognitive states.

Let us try a Putnam-like experiment. We raise two identical twins, Castor and Pollux, under qualitatively identical conditions, qualitatively identical stimuli, etc. If necessary, we may monitor their brain states and make small corrections in their brain structures if they begin drifting apart. They respond to all cognitive stimuli in identical fashion.[53] Have we not been successful in achieving the same cognitive (i.e., psychological) state? Of course we have, what more could one ask! But wait, they believe different things. Each sincerely says,

> My brother was born before I was

and the beliefs they thereby express conflict. In this, Castor speaks the truth, while Pollux speaks falsely. This does not reflect on the identity of their cognitive states, for, as Putnam has emphasized, circumstances alone do not determine extension (here, the truth-value) from cognitive state. Insofar as distinct persons can be in the same cognitive state, Castor and Pollux are.

E. Corollary 1 *It is an almost inevitable consequence of the fact that two persons are in the* same *cognitive state, that they will* disagree *in their attitudes toward some object of thought.*

The corollary applies equally well to the same person at different times, and to the same person at the same time in different circumstances.[54] In general, the corollary applies to any individuals x, y in different contexts.

My aim was to argue that the cognitive significance of a word or phrase was to be identified with its character, the way the content is presented to us. In discussing the twins, I tried to show that persons

---

[53] Perhaps it should be mentioned here, to forestall an objection, that neither uses a proper name for the other or for himself—only 'my brother' and 'I'—and that raising them required a lot of environmental work to maintain the necessary symmetries, or, alternatively, a lot of work with the brain state machine. If proper names are present, and each uses a different name for himself (or, for the other), they will never achieve the same *total* cognitive state since one will sincerely say, "I am Castor" and the other will not. They may still achieve the same cognitive state in its relevant part.

[54] The corollary would also apply to the same person at the same time in the same circumstances but in different places, if such could be.

could be in the same total cognitive state and still, as we would say, believe different things. This doesn't prove that the cognitive content of, say, a single sentence or even a word is to be identified with its character, but it strongly suggests it.

Let me try a different line of argument. We agree that a given content may be presented under various characters and that consequently we may hold a propositional attitude toward a given content under one character but not under another. (For example, on March 27 of this year, having lost track of the date, I may continue to hope to be finished by this March 26, without hoping to be finished by yesterday.) Now instead of arguing that character is what we would ordinarily call cognitive significance, let me just ask why we should be interested in the character under which we hold our various attitudes. Why should we be interested in that special kind of significance that is sensitive to the use of indexicals; 'I', 'here', 'now', 'that', and the like? John Perry, in his stimulating and insightful paper "Frege on Demonstratives" asks and answers this question. [Perry uses 'thought' where I would use 'object of thought' or 'content', he uses 'apprehend' for 'believe' but *note that other psychological verbs would yield analogous cases.* I have taken a few liberties in substituting my own terminology for Perry's and have added the emphasis.]

> Why should we care under what character someone apprehends a thought, so long as he does? I can only sketch the barest suggestion of an answer here. *We use the manner of presentation, the character, to individuate psychological states, in explaining and predicting action.* It is the manner of presentation, the character and not the thought apprehended, that is tied to human action. When you and I have beliefs under the common character of 'A bear is about to attack me', we behave similarly. We both roll up in a ball and try to be as still as possible. Different thoughts apprehended, same character, same behavior. When you and I both apprehend that I am about to be attacked by a bear, we behave differently. I roll up in a ball, you run to get help. Same thought apprehended, different characters, different behaviors.[55]

Perry's examples can be easily multiplied. My hope to be finished by a certain time is sensitive to how the content corresponding to the

---

[55] John Perry, "Frege on Demonstratives," p. 494.

time is presented, as 'yesterday' or as 'this March 26'. If I see, reflected in a window, the image of a man whose pants appear to be on fire, my behavior is sensitive to whether I think, 'His pants are on fire' or 'My pants are on fire', though the object of thought may be the same.

So long as Frege confined his attention to indexical free expressions, and given his theory of proper names, it is not surprising that he did not distinguish objects of thought (content) from cognitive significance (character), for that is the realm of *fixed* character and thus, as already remarked, there is a natural identification of character with content. Frege does, however, discuss indexicals in two places. The first passage, in which he discusses 'yesterday' and 'today' I have already discussed. Everything he says there is essentially correct. (He does not go far enough.) The second passage has provoked few endorsements and much skepticism. It too, I believe, is susceptible of an interpretation which makes it essentially correct. I quote it in full.

> Now everyone is presented to himself in a particular and primitive way, in which he is presented to no one else. So, when Dr. Lauben thinks that he has been wounded, he will probably take as a basis this primitive way in which he is presented to himself. And only Dr. Lauben himself can grasp thoughts determined in this way. But now he may want to communicate with others. He cannot communicate a thought which he alone can grasp. Therefore, if he now says 'I have been wounded', he must use the 'I' in a sense that can be grasped by others, perhaps in the sense of 'he who is speaking to you at this moment', by doing which he makes the associated conditions of his utterance serve for the expression of his thought.[56]

What is the particular and primitive way in which Dr. Lauben is presented to himself? What cognitive content presents Dr. Lauben to himself, but presents him to nobody else? Thoughts determined this way can be grasped by Dr. Lauben, but no one else can grasp *that* thought determined in *that* way. The answer, I believe, is, simply, that Dr. Lauben is presented to himself under the character of 'I'.

A sloppy thinker might succumb to the temptation to slide from an acknowledgement of the privileged *perspective* we each have on ourselves—only I can refer to me as 'I'—to the conclusions: first, that

---

[56] Gottlob Frege, "The Thought: A Logical Inquiry," p. 298.

this perspective necessarily yields a privileged *picture* of what is seen (referred to), and second, that this picture is what is intended when one makes use of the privileged perspective (by saying 'I'). These conclusions, even if correct, are not forced upon us. The character of 'I' provides the acknowledged privileged perspective, whereas the analysis of the content of particular occurrences of 'I' provides for (and needs) no privileged pictures. There may be metaphysical, epistemological, or ethical reasons why I (so conceived) am especially *important* to myself. (Compare: why *now* is an especially important time to me. It too is presented in a particular and primitive way, and this moment cannot be presented at any other time in the same way.)[57] But the phenomenon noted by Frege—that everyone is presented to himself in a particular and primitive way—can be fully accounted for using only our semantical theory.

Furthermore, regarding the first conclusion, I sincerely doubt that there is, for each of us on each occasion of the use of 'I', a particular, primitive, and incommunicable Fregean self-concept which we tacitly express to ourselves. And regarding the second conclusion: even if Castor were sufficiently narcissistic to associate such self-concepts with his every use of 'I', his twin, Pollux, whose mental life is qualitatively identical with Castor's, would associate the *same* self-concept with *his* every (matching) use of 'I'.[58] The second conclusion would lead to the absurd result that when Castor and Pollux each say 'I', they do not thereby distinguish themselves from one another. (An even more astonishing result is possible. Suppose that due to a bit of self-deception the self-concept held in common by Castor and Pollux fits neither of them. The second conclusion then leads irresistibly to the possibility that when Castor and Pollux each say 'I' they each refer to a third party!)

The perceptive reader will have noticed that the conclusions of the sloppy thinker regarding the pure indexical 'I' are not unlike those of the Fregean regarding true demonstratives. The sloppy thinker has adopted a *demonstrative theory of indexicals*: 'I' is synonymous with 'this person' [along with an appropriate *subjective* demonstration], 'now' with 'this time', 'here' with 'this place' [each associated with some demonstration], etc. Like the Fregean, the sloppy thinker errs in believing that the

---

[57] At other times, earlier and later, we can know it only externally, by description as it were. But now we are directly acquainted with it. (I believe I owe this point to John Perry.)

[58] Unless, of course, the self-concept involved a bit of direct reference. In which case (when direct reference is admitted) there seems no need for the whole theory of Fregean self-concepts. Unless, of course, direct reference is limited to items of direct acquaintance, of which more below.

sense of the demonstration is the sense of the indexical, but the sloppy thinker commits an additional error in believing that such senses are in any way necessarily associated with uses of pure indexicals. The slide from privileged perspective to privileged picture is the sloppy thinker's original sin. Only one who is located in the exact center of the Sahara Desert is entitled to refer to that place as 'here', but aside from that, the place may present no distinguishing features.[59]

The sloppy thinker's conclusions may have another source. Failure to distinguish between the cognitive significance of a thought and the thought itself seems to have led some to believe that the elements of an object of thought must each be directly accessible to the mind. From this it follows that if a singular proposition is an object of thought, the thinker must somehow be immediately acquainted with each of the individuals involved. But, as we have seen, the situation is rather different from this. Singular propositions may be presented to us under characters which neither imply nor presuppose any special form of acquaintance with the individuals of the singular propositions. The psychological states, perhaps even the epistemological situations, of Castor and Pollux are alike, yet they assert distinct singular propositions when they each say 'My brother was born before me'. Had they lived at different times they might still have been situated alike epistemologically

---

[59] So far, we have limited our attention to the first three sentences of the quotation from Frege. How are we to account for the second part of Frege's remarks?

Suppose Dr. Lauben wants to communicate his thought without disturbing its cognitive content. (Think of trying to tell a color-blind person that the green light should be replaced. You would have to find another way of communicating what you wanted to get across.) He can't communicate *that* thought with *that* significance, so, he himself would have to attach a nonstandard significance to 'I'. Here is a suggestion. He points at his auditor and uses the demonstrative 'you'. If we neglect fine differences in perspective, the demonstration will have the same character for all present and it certainly will have the same demonstratum for all present, therefore the demonstrative will have the same *character and content* for all present. The indexical 'now' will certainly have the same character and content for all present. Thus 'the person who is speaking to you [points] now' will have a common character and content for all those present. Unfortunately the content is not that of 'I' as Dr. Lauben standardly uses it. He needs a demonstrative like 'dthat' to convert the description to a term with a fixed content. He chooses the demonstrative 'he', with a relative clause construction to make clear his intention. Now, if Dr. Lauben uses 'I' with the nonstandard meaning usually attached to 'he who is speaking to you [points] now' he will have found a way to communicate his original thought in a form whose cognitive significance is common to all. Very clever, Dr. Lauben.

[Perhaps it is poor pedagogy to join this fanciful interpretation of the second part of the passage with the serious interpretation of the first part.]

while asserting distinct singular propositions in saying 'It is quiet here now'. A kidnapped heiress, locked in the trunk of a car, knowing neither the time nor where she is, may think 'It is quiet here now' and the indexicals will remain directly referential.[60]

E. Corollary 2 *Ignorance of the referent does not defeat the directly referential character of indexicals.*

From this it follows that a special form of knowledge of an object is neither required nor presupposed in order that a person may entertain as object of thought a singular proposition involving that object.

There is nothing inaccessible to the mind about the semantics of direct reference, even when the reference is to that which we know only by description. What allows us to take various propositional attitudes towards singular propositions is not the form of our acquaintance with the objects but is rather our ability to manipulate the conceptual apparatus of direct reference.[61]

The foregoing remarks are aimed at refuting *Direct Acquaintance Theories of direct reference*. According to such theories, the question whether an utterance expresses a singular proposition turns, in the first instance, on the speaker's *knowledge of the referent* rather than on the *form of the reference*. If the speaker lacks the appropriate form of acquaintance with the referent, the utterance cannot express a singular proposition, and any apparently directly referring expressions used must be abbreviations or disguises for something like Fregean descriptions. Perhaps the Direct Acquaintance theorist thought that only a theory like his could permit singular propositions while still providing a solution for Frege's problem. If we could *directly* refer to a given object in nonequivalent ways (e.g., as 'dthat[Hes]' and 'dthat[Phos]'), we could not—so he thought—explain the difference in cognitive significance between the appropriate instances of $\ulcorner \alpha = \alpha \urcorner$ and $\ulcorner \alpha = \beta \urcorner$. Hence, the objects susceptible to direct reference must not permit such reference in inequivalent ways. These objects must, in a certain sense, be wholly local and completely given so that for any two *directly* coreferential terms

---

[60] Can the heiress plead that she could not have believed a singular proposition involving the place p since when thinking 'here' she didn't *know* she was at p, that she was, in fact, unacquainted with the place p? No! Ignorance of the referent is no excuse.

[61] This makes it sound as if an exact and conscious mastery of semantics is prerequisite to having a singular proposition as object of thought. I will try to find a better way to express the point in a succeeding draft.

α and β, $\ulcorner \alpha = \beta \urcorner$ will be uniformative to anyone appropriately situated, epistemologically, to be able to use these terms.[62] I hope that my discussion of the two kinds of meaning—content and character—will have shown the Direct Acquaintance Theorist that his views are not the inevitable consequence of the admission of directly referential terms. From the point of view of a lover of direct reference this is good, since the Direct Acquaintance theorist admits direct reference in a portion of language so narrow that it is used only by philosophers.[63]

I have said nothing to dispute the epistemology of the Direct Acquaintance theorist, nothing to deny that there exists his special kind of object with which one can have his special kind of acquaintance. I have only denied the relevance of these epistemological claims to the semantics of direct reference. If we sweep aside metaphysical and epistemological pseudo-explanations of what are essentially semantical phenomena, the result can only be healthy for all three disciplines.

Before going on to further examples of the tendency to confuse metaphysical and epistemological matters with phenomena of the semantics of direct reference, I want to briefly raise the problem of *cognitive dynamics*. Suppose that yesterday you said, and believed it, "It is a nice day today." What does it mean to say, today, that you have retained *that* belief? It seems unsatisfactory to just believe the same content under any old character—where is the *retention*?[64] You *can't* believe

---

[62] For some consequences of this view with regard to the interpretation of demonstratives see "Bob and Carol and Ted and Alice," appendix VII.

[63] There is an obvious connection between the fix in which the Direct Acquaintance Theorist finds himself, and *Kripke's problem*: how can $\ulcorner \alpha = \beta \urcorner$ be informative if α and β differ in neither denotation nor sense (nor, as I shall suggest is the case for proper names, character)?

[64] The sort of case I have in mind is this. I first think, "His pants are on fire." I later realize, "I am he" and thus come to think "My pants are on fire." Still later, I decide that I was wrong in thinking "I am he" and conclude "His pants were on fire." If, in fact, I *am* he, have I *retained* my belief that my pants are on fire simply because I believe the same content, though under a different character? (I also deny that content under the former, but for change of tense, character.) When I first thought "My pants are on fire," a certain singular proposition, call it 'Eek', was the object of thought. At the later stage, both Eek and its negation are believed by me. In this sense, I still believe what I believed before, namely Eek. But this does not capture my sense of *retaining a belief*: a sense that I associate with saying that some people have a very rigid cognitive structure whereas others are very flexible. It is tempting to say that cognitive dynamics is concerned not with retention and change in what is believed, but with retention and change in the characters under which our beliefs are held. I think that this is basically correct. But it is not obvious to me what relation between a character under which a belief is held at one time and the set of characters under which beliefs are held at a later

that content under the same character. Is there some obvious standard adjustment to make to the character, for example, replacing *today* with *yesterday*? If so, then a person like Rip van Winkle, who loses track of time, can't retain any such beliefs. This seems strange. Can we only *retain* beliefs presented under a fixed character? This issue has obvious and important connections with Lauben's problem in trying to communicate the thought he expresses with 'I have been wounded'. Under what character must his auditor believe Lauben's thought in order for Lauben's communication to have been successful? It is important to note that if Lauben said 'I am wounded' in the usual meaning of 'I', there is no one else who can report what he said, using *indirect* discourse, and convey the cognitive significance (to Lauben) of what he said. This is connected with points made in section VIII, and has interesting consequences for the inevitability of so-called *de re* constructions in indirect discourse languages which contain indexicals. (I use 'indirect discourse' as a general term for the analogous form of all psychological verbs.)

A prime example of the confusion of direct reference phenomena with metaphysical and epistemological ideas was first vigorously called to our attention by Saul Kripke in *Naming and Necessity*. I wish to parallel his remarks disconnecting the *a priori* and the *necessary*.

The form of *a priority* that I will discuss is that of logical truth (in the logic of demonstratives). We saw very early that a truth of the logic of demonstratives, like "I am here now" need not be necessary. There are many such cases of logical truths which are not necessary. If α is any singular term, then

$$\alpha = \text{dthat}[\alpha]$$

is a logical truth. But

$$\Box(\alpha = \text{dthat}[\alpha])$$

is generally false. We can, of course, also easily produce the opposite effect.

---

time would constitute retaining the original belief. Where indexicals are involved, for the reasons given below, we cannot simply require that the very same character still appear at the later time. Thus the problem of cognitive dynamics can be put like this: what does it mean to say of an individual who at one time sincerely asserted a sentence containing indexicals that at some later time he has (or has not) *changed his mind* with respect to his assertion? What sentence or sentences must he be willing to assert at the later time?

$\Box(\text{dthat}[\alpha] = \text{dthat}[\beta])$

may be true, although

$\text{dthat}[\alpha] = \text{dthat}[\beta]$

is not logically true, and is even logically equivalent to the contingency,

$\alpha = \beta$

(I call ϕ and ψ logically equivalent when $\ulcorner \phi \leftrightarrow \psi \urcorner$ is logically true.) These cases are reminiscent of Kripke's case of the terms, 'one meter' and 'the length of bar x'. But where Kripke focuses on the special epistemological situation of one who is present at the dubbing, the descriptive meaning associated with our directly referential term dthat[α] is carried in the semantics of the language.[65]

How can something be both logically true, and thus *certain*, and *contingent* at the same time? In the case of indexicals the answer is easy to see.

E. Corollary 3   *The bearers of logical truth and of contingency are different entities. It is the* character *(or, the sentence, if you prefer) that is logically true, producing a true content in every context. But it is the* content *(the proposition, if you will) that is contingent or necessary.*

As can readily be seen, the modal logic of demonstratives is a rich and interesting thing.

---

[65] A case of a seemingly different kind is that of the logical equivalence between an arbitrary sentence ϕ and the result of prefixing either or both of the indexical operators, 'it is actually the case that' (symbolized 'A') and 'it is now the case that' (symbolized 'N'). The biconditional $\ulcorner(\phi \leftrightarrow AN\phi)\urcorner$ is logically true, but prefixing either '$\Box$' or its temporal counterpart can lead to falsehood. (This case was adverted to in footnote 28.) It is interesting to note, in this case, that the parallel between modal and temporal modifications of sentences carries over to indexicals. The foregoing claims are verified by the formal system (sections XVIII and XIX, see especially Remark 3). Note that the formal system is constructed in accordance with Carnap's proposal that the intension of an expression be that function which assigns to each circumstance, the extension of the expression with respect to that circumstance. This has commonly been thought to insure that logically equivalent expressions have the same intension (Church's Alternative 2 among principles of individuation for the notion of sense) and that logically true sentences express the (unique) necessary proposition. Homework Problem: What went wrong here?

It is easy to be taken in by the effortless (but fallacious) move from certainty (logical truth) to necessity. In his important article "Three Grades of Modal Involvement,"[66] Quine expresses his scepticism of the first grade of modal involvement: the sentence predicate and all it stands for, and his distaste for the second grade of modal involvement: disguising the predicate as an operator 'It is necessary that'. But he suggests that no new metaphysical undesirables are admitted until the third grade of modal involvement: quantification across the necessity operator into an open sentence.

I must protest. That first step let in some metaphysical undesirables, falsehoods. All logical truths are analytic, but they can go false when you back them up to '□'.

One other notorious example of a logical truth which is not necessary,

>I exist.

One can quickly verify that in every context, this character yields a true proposition—but rarely a necessary one. It seems likely to me that it was a conflict between the feelings of contingency and of certainty associated with this sentence that has led to such painstaking examination of its 'proofs'. It is just a truth of logic!

Dana Scott has remedied one lacuna in this analysis. What of the premise

>I think

and the connective

>Therefore   ?

His discovery was that the premise is incomplete, and that the last five words

>up the logic of demonstratives

had been lost in an early manuscript version.[67]

---

[66] *Proceedings of the XI International Congress of Philosophy* 14, 65–81; reprinted in W. V. Quine, *The Ways of Paradox* (New York: Random House, 1966).

[67] Again, it is probably a pedagogical mistake to mix this playful paragraph with the preceding serious one.

XVIII. The Formal System

Just to be sure we have not overlooked anything, here is a machine against which we can test our intuitions.

The Language LD

The *Language* LD is based on first-order predicate logic with identity and descriptions. We deviate slightly from standard formulations in using two sorts of variables, one sort for positions and a second for individuals other than positions (hereafter called simply 'individuals').

Primitive Symbols

Primitive Symbols for Two Sorted Predicate Logic

0. Punctuation: (,), [,]

1. Variables:

    (i)   An infinite set of individual variables: $\mathcal{V}_i$

    (ii) An infinite set of position variables: $\mathcal{V}_p$

2. Predicates:

    (i)   An infinite number of m-n-place predicates, for all natural numbers m, n.

    (ii) The 1-0-place predicate: Exist

    (iii) The 1-1-place predicate: Located

3. Functors:

    (i)   An infinite number of m-n-place i-functors (functors which form terms denoting individuals)

    (ii) An infinite number of m-n-place p-functors (functors which form terms denoting positions)

4. Sentential Connectives: $\land$, $\lor$, $\neg$, $\rightarrow$, $\leftrightarrow$

5. Quantifiers: $\forall$, $\exists$

6. Definite Description Operator: the

7. Identity: $=$

Primitive Symbols for Modal and Tense Logic

8.   Modal Operators: $\Box$, $\Diamond$

9.   Tense Operators:
      F (it will be the case that)
      P (it has been the case that)
      G (one day ago, it was the case that)

Primitive Symbols for the Logic of Demonstratives

10.   Three 1-place sentential operators:
      N (it is now the case that)
      A (it is actually the case that)
      Y (yesterday, it was the case that)

11.   A 1-place functor: dthat

12.   An individual constant (0-0-place i-functor): I

13.   A position constant (0-0-place p-functor): Here

Well-formed Expressions

The *well-formed expressions* are of three kinds: formulas, position terms (p-terms), and individual terms (i-terms).

1.   (i)   If $\alpha \in \mathcal{V}_i$, then α is an i-term
      (ii) If $\alpha \in \mathcal{V}_p$, then α is a p-term

2.   If π is an m-n-place predicate, $\alpha_1, \ldots, \alpha_m$ are i-terms, and $\beta_1, \ldots, \beta_n$ are p-terms, then $\pi\alpha_1 \ldots \alpha_m \beta_1 \ldots \beta_n$ is a formula

3.   (i)   If η is an m-n-place i-functor, $\alpha_1, \ldots, \alpha_m$, $\beta_1, \ldots, \beta_n$ are as in 2., then
            $\eta\alpha_1 \ldots \alpha_m \beta_1 \ldots \beta_n$ is an i-term
      (ii) If η is an m-n-place p-functor, $\alpha_1, \ldots, \alpha_m$, $\beta_1, \ldots, \beta_n$ are as in 2., then
            $\eta\alpha_1 \ldots \alpha_m \beta_1 \ldots \beta_n$ is a p-term

4.   If ϕ, ψ are formulas, then $(\phi \wedge \psi)$, $(\phi \vee \psi)$, $\neg\phi$, $(\phi \rightarrow \psi)$, $(\phi \leftrightarrow \psi)$ are formulas

5.   If ϕ is a formula and $\alpha \in \mathcal{V}_i \cup \mathcal{V}_p$, then $\forall\alpha\phi$ and $\exists\alpha\phi$ are formulas

6. If ϕ is a formula, then

    (i) if $\alpha \in \mathcal{V}_i$, then   the $\alpha \ \phi$ is an i-term

    (ii) if $\alpha \in \mathcal{V}_p$, then   the $\alpha \ \phi$ is a p-term

7. If α, β are either both i-terms or both p-terms, then $\alpha = \beta$ is a formula

8. If ϕ is a formula, then $\Box\phi$ and $\Diamond\phi$ are formulas

9. If ϕ is a formula, then $F\phi$, $P\phi$, and $G\phi$ are formulas

10. If ϕ is a formula, then $N\phi$, $A\phi$, and $Y\phi$ are formulas

11. (i) If α is an i-term, then dthat$[\alpha]$ is an i-term

    (ii) If α is a p-term, then dthat$[\alpha]$ is a p-term

Semantics for LD

LD Structures

Definition: $\mathfrak{A}$ is an LD structure iff there are $\mathcal{C}$, $\mathcal{W}$, $\mathcal{U}$, $\mathcal{P}$, $\mathcal{T}$, and $\mathcal{I}$ such that:

1. $\mathfrak{A} = \langle \mathcal{C}, \mathcal{W}, \mathcal{U}, \mathcal{P}, \mathcal{T}, \mathcal{I} \rangle$

2. $\mathcal{C}$ is a nonempty set (the set of contexts, see 10 below)

3. If $c \in \mathcal{C}$, then

    (i) $c_A \in \mathcal{U}$ (the *agent* of c)

    (ii) $c_T \in \mathcal{T}$ (the *time* of c)

    (iii) $c_P \in \mathcal{P}$ (the *position* of c)

    (iv) $c_W \in \mathcal{W}$ (the *world* of c)

4. $\mathcal{W}$ is a nonempty set (the set of *worlds*)

5. $\mathcal{U}$ is a nonempty set (the set of all *individuals*, see 9 below)

6. $\mathcal{P}$ is a nonempty set (the set of *positions*, common to all worlds)

7. $\mathcal{T}$ is the set of integers (thought of as the *times*, common to all worlds)

8. $\mathcal{I}$ is a function which assigns to each predicate and functor an appropriate *intension* as follows:

   (i)   If π is an m-n-predicate, $\mathcal{I}_\pi$ is a function such that for each $t \in T$ and $w \in \mathcal{W}$, $\mathcal{I}_\pi(t, w) \subseteq (\mathcal{U}^m \times \mathcal{P}^n)$

   (ii) If η is an m-n-place i-functor, $\mathcal{I}_\eta$ is a function such that for each $t \in T$ and $w \in \mathcal{W}$, $\mathcal{I}_\eta(t, w) \in (\mathcal{U} \cup \{\dagger\})^{(\mathcal{U}^m \times \mathcal{P}^n)}$ (Note: $\dagger$ is a completely alien entity, in neither $\mathcal{U}$ nor $\mathcal{P}$, which represents an 'undefined' value of the function. In a normal set theory we can take $\dagger$ to be $\{\mathcal{U}, \mathcal{P}\}$.)

   (iii) If η is an m-n-place p-functor, $\mathcal{I}_\eta$ is a function such that for each $t \in T$ and $w \in \mathcal{W}$, $\mathcal{I}_\eta(t, w) \in (\mathcal{P} \cup \{\dagger\})^{(\mathcal{U}^m \times \mathcal{P}^n)}$

9. $i \in \mathcal{U}$ iff $(\exists t \in T)(\exists w \in \mathcal{W})(\langle i \rangle \in \mathcal{I}_{\mathrm{Exist}}(t, w))$

10. If $c \in \mathcal{C}$, then $\langle c_\mathrm{A}, c_\mathrm{P} \rangle \in \mathcal{I}_{\mathrm{Located}}(c_\mathrm{T}, c_\mathrm{W})$

11. If $\langle i, p \rangle \in \mathcal{I}_{\mathrm{Located}}(t, w)$, then $\langle i \rangle \in \mathcal{I}_{\mathrm{Exist}}(t, w)$

Truth and Denotation in a Context

We write: $\models^{\mathfrak{A}}_{cftw} \phi$ for ϕ, when taken in the context c (under the assignment f and in the structure $\mathfrak{A}$), *is true with respect to* the time t and the world w.

We write: $|\alpha|^{\mathfrak{A}}_{cftw}$ for   *The denotation of α,* when taken in the context c (under the assignment f and in the structure $\mathfrak{A}$), *with respect to* the time t and the world w

In general we will omit the superscript '$\mathfrak{A}$', and we will assume that the structure $\mathfrak{A}$ is $\langle \mathcal{C}, \mathcal{W}, \mathcal{U}, \mathcal{P}, T, \mathcal{I} \rangle$.

Definition: *f is an assignment* (with respect to $\langle \mathcal{C}, \mathcal{W}, \mathcal{U}, \mathcal{P}, T, \mathcal{I} \rangle$) iff:

$$\exists f_1 f_2 (f_1 \in \mathcal{U}^{\mathcal{V}_i} \ \& \ f_2 \in \mathcal{P}^{\mathcal{V}_p} \ \& \ f = f_1 \cup f_2)$$

Definition: $f_x^\alpha = (f \sim \{\langle \alpha, f(\alpha) \rangle\}) \cup \{\langle \alpha, x \rangle\}$
(i.e., the assignment which is just like f except that it assigns x to α)

Definition: For the following recursive definition, assume that $c \in \mathcal{C}$, f is an assignment, $t \in \mathcal{T}$, and $w \in \mathcal{W}$:

1.   If α is a variable, $|\alpha|_{cftw} = f(\alpha)$

2. $\models_{cftw} \pi\alpha_1 \ldots \alpha_m \beta_1 \ldots \beta_n$ iff $\langle |\alpha_1|_{cftw} \ldots |\beta_n|_{cftw} \rangle \in \mathcal{I}_\pi(t, w)$

3.   If η is neither 'I' nor 'Here' (see 12, 13 below), then

$$|\eta\alpha_1 \ldots \alpha_m \beta_1 \ldots \beta_n|_{cftw} = \begin{cases} \mathcal{I}_\eta(t,w)(\langle |\alpha_1|_{cftw} \ldots |\beta_n|_{cftw} \rangle), \\ \quad \text{if none of } |\alpha_j|_{cftw} \ldots |\beta_k|_{cftw} \\ \quad \text{are } \dagger; \\ \dagger, \text{ otherwise} \end{cases}$$

4.   (i) $\models_{cftw} (\phi \wedge \psi)$ iff $\models_{cftw} \phi \ \& \models_{cftw} \psi$

       (ii) $\models_{cftw} \neg\phi$ iff $\sim \models_{cftw} \phi$
       etc.

5.   (i)   If $\alpha \in \mathcal{V}_i$, then $\models_{cftw} \forall\alpha\phi$ iff $\forall i \in \mathcal{U}$, $\models_{cf_i^\alpha tw} \phi$

       (ii)   If $\alpha \in \mathcal{V}_p$, then $\models_{cftw} \forall\alpha\phi$ iff $\forall p \in \mathcal{P}$, $\models_{cf_p^\alpha tw} \phi$

       (iii)   Similarly for $\exists\alpha\phi$

6.   (i)   If $\alpha \in \mathcal{V}_i$, then:

$$|\text{the } \alpha \ \phi|_{cftw} = \begin{cases} \text{the unique } i \in \mathcal{U} \text{ such that } \models_{cf_i^\alpha tw} \phi, \text{ if} \\ \quad \text{there is such;} \\ \dagger, \text{ otherwise} \end{cases}$$

       (ii)   Similarly for $\alpha \in \mathcal{V}_p$

7. $\models_{cftw} \alpha = \beta$ iff $|\alpha|_{cftw} = |\beta|_{cftw}$

8.   (i) $\models_{cftw} \Box\phi$ iff $\forall w' \in \mathcal{W}$, $\models_{cftw'} \phi$

       (ii) $\models_{cftw} \Diamond\phi$ iff $\exists w' \in \mathcal{W}$, $\models_{cftw'} \phi$

9.   (i) $\models_{cftw} F\phi$ iff $\exists t' \in \mathcal{T}$ such that $t' > t$ and $\models_{cft'w} \phi$

       (ii) $\models_{cftw} P\phi$ iff $\exists t' \in \mathcal{T}$ such that $t' < t$ and $\models_{cft'w} \phi$

       (iii) $\models_{cftw} G\phi$ iff $\models_{cf(t-1)w} \phi$

10.   (i) $\models_{cftw} N\phi$ iff $\models_{cfc_Tw} \phi$

       (ii) $\models_{cftw} A\phi$ iff $\models_{cftcw} \phi$

       (iii) $\models_{cftw} Y\phi$ iff $\models_{cf(c_T-1)w} \phi$

11. $|\mathrm{dthat}[\alpha]|_{cftw} = |\alpha|_{cf\,c_{\mathrm{T}}c_{\mathrm{W}}}$

12. $|\mathrm{I}|_{cftw} = c_{\mathrm{A}}$

13. $|\mathrm{Here}|_{cftw} = c_{\mathrm{P}}$

XIX. Remarks on the Formal System

Remark 1:   Expressions containing demonstratives will, in general, express different concepts in different contexts. We call the concept expressed in a given context the *Content* of the expression in that context. The Content of a sentence in a context is, roughly, the proposition the sentence would express if uttered in that context. This description is not quite accurate on two counts. First, it is important to distinguish an *utterance* from a *sentence-in-a-context*. The former notion is from the theory of speech acts, the latter from semantics. Utterances take time, and utterances of distinct sentences cannot be simultaneous (i.e., in the same context). But to develop a logic of demonstratives it seems most natural to be able to evaluate several premises and a conclusion all in the same context. Thus the notion of ϕ *being true in c and* $\mathfrak{A}$ does not require an utterance of ϕ. In particular, c_{A} need not be uttering ϕ in c_{W} at c_{T}. Second, the truth of a proposition is not usually thought of as dependent on a time as well as a possible world. The time is thought of as fixed by the context. If ϕ is a sentence, the more usual notion of the proposition expressed by ϕ-in-c is what is here called the Content of $N\phi$ in c.

Where Γ is either a term or formula,

we write: $\{\Gamma\}_{cf}^{\mathfrak{A}}$ for   The Content of Γ in the context c (under the assignment f and in the structure $\mathfrak{A}$).

Definition:

(i)   If ϕ is a formula, $\{\phi\}_{cf}^{\mathfrak{A}} = $ that function which assigns to each $t \in \mathcal{T}$ and $w \in \mathcal{W}$, Truth, if $\models_{cftw}^{\mathfrak{A}} \phi$, and Falsehood otherwise.

(ii)   If α is a term, $\{\alpha\}_{cf}^{\mathfrak{A}} = $ that function which assigns to each $t \in \mathcal{T}$ and $w \in \mathcal{W}$, $|\alpha|_{cftw}$.

Remark 2: $\models^{\mathfrak{A}}_{cftw}\phi$ iff $\{\phi\}^{\mathfrak{A}}_{cf}(t,w) = $ Truth. Roughly speaking, the sentence ϕ taken in context c is *true with respect to t and w* iff the proposition expressed by ϕ-in-the-context-c would be true at the time t if w were the actual world. In the formal development of pages 544, 545, and 546, it was smoother to ignore the conceptual break marked by the notion of *Content in a context* and to directly define *truth in a context with respect to a possible time and world*. The important conceptual role of the notion of Content is partially indicated by the following two definitions.

Definition: ϕ *is true in the context c* (in the structure $\mathfrak{A}$) iff for every assignment f, $\{\phi\}^{\mathfrak{A}}_{cf}(c_{\mathrm{T}}, c_{\mathrm{W}}) = $ Truth.

Definition: ϕ *is valid in* LD ($\models\phi$) iff for every LD structure $\mathfrak{A}$, and every context c of $\mathfrak{A}$, ϕ is true in c (in $\mathfrak{A}$).

Remark 3: $\models(\alpha = \mathrm{dthat}[\alpha])$; $\models(\phi \leftrightarrow AN\phi)$; $\models N(\text{Located I, Here})$; $\models$ Exist I. But, $\sim\models \Box(\alpha = \mathrm{dthat}[\alpha])$; $\sim\models \Box(\phi \leftrightarrow AN\phi)$; $\sim\models \Box N(\text{Located I, Here})$; $\sim\models \Box(\text{Exist I})$. Also, $\sim\models F(\phi \leftrightarrow AN\phi)$.

In the converse direction (where the original validity has the form $\Box\phi$) we have the usual results in view of the fact that $\models(\Box\phi \rightarrow \phi)$.

Definition: If $\alpha_1, \ldots, \alpha_n$ are all the free variables of ϕ in alphabetical order then *the closure of $\phi = AN\forall\alpha_1 \ldots \forall\alpha_n\phi$*.

Definition: ϕ *is closed* iff ϕ is equivalent (in the sense of Remark 12) to its closure.

Remark 4: If ϕ is closed, then ϕ is true in c (and $\mathfrak{A}$) iff for every assignment f, time t, and world w, $\models^{\mathfrak{A}}_{cftw}\phi$.

Definition: Where Γ is either a term or a formula, *the Content of Γ in the context c (in the structure $\mathfrak{A}$) is Stable* iff for every assignment f, $\{\Gamma\}^{\mathfrak{A}}_{cf}$ is a constant function (i.e., $\{\Gamma\}^{\mathfrak{A}}_{cf}(t,w) = \{\Gamma\}^{\mathfrak{A}}_{cf}(t',w')$, for all t, t', w, and w' in $\mathfrak{A}$).

Remark 5:   Where ϕ is a formula, α is a term, and β is a variable, each of the following has a Stable Content in every context (in every structure): $AN\phi$, dthat$[\alpha]$, β, I, Here.

If we were to extend the notion of Content to apply to operators, we would see that all indexicals (including N, A, Y, and dthat) have a Stable Content in every context. The same is true of the familiar logical constants although it does not hold for the modal and tense operators (not, at least, according to the foregoing development).

Remark 6:   That aspect of the meaning of an expression which determines what its Content will be in each context, we call the *Character* of the expression. Although a lack of knowledge about the context (or perhaps about the structure) may cause one to mistake the Content of a given utterance, the Character of each well-formed expression is determined by rules of the language (such as rules 1–13 on pages 545 and 546, which are presumably known to all competent speakers. Our notation '$\{\phi\}^{\mathfrak{A}}_{cf}$' for the Content of an expression gives a natural notation for the Character of an expression, namely '$\{\phi\}$'.

Definition: Where Γ is either a term or a formula, *the Character of* Γ is that function which assigns to each structure $\mathfrak{A}$, assignment f, and context c of $\mathfrak{A}$, $\{\Gamma\}^{\mathfrak{A}}_{cf}$.

Definition: Where Γ is either a term or a formula, *the Character of* Γ *is Stable* iff for every structure $\mathfrak{A}$, and assignment f, the Character of Γ (under f in $\mathfrak{A}$) is a constant function (i.e., $\{\Gamma\}^{\mathfrak{A}}_{cf} = \{\Gamma\}^{\mathfrak{A}}_{c'f}$, for all c, c' in $\mathfrak{A}$).

Remark 7:   A formula or term has a Stable Character iff it has the same Content in every context (for each $\mathfrak{A}$, f).

Remark 8:   A formula or term has a Stable Character iff it contains no essential occurrence of a demonstrative.

Remark 9:   The logic of demonstratives determines a sublogic of those formulas of LD which contain no demonstratives. These formulas (and their equivalents which contain inessential occurrences of demonstratives) are exactly the formulas with a Stable Character. The logic of demonstratives brings a new perspective even to formulas such as these.

The sublogic of LD which concerns only formulas of Stable Character is not identical with traditional logic. Even for such formulas, the familiar Principle of Necessitation (if $\models \phi$, then $\models \Box\phi$) fails. And so does its tense logic counterpart: if $\models \phi$, then $\models (\neg P\neg\phi \wedge \neg F\neg\phi \wedge \phi)$. From the perspective of LD, validity is truth in every possible *context*. For traditional logic, validity is truth in every possible *circumstance*. Each possible context determines a possible circumstance, but it is not the case that each possible circumstance is part of a possible context. In particular, the fact that each possible context has an agent implies that any possible circumstance in which no individuals exist will not form a part of any possible context. Within LD, a possible context is represented by $\langle \mathfrak{A}, c \rangle$ and a possible circumstance by $\langle \mathfrak{A}, t, w \rangle$. To any $\langle \mathfrak{A}, c \rangle$, there corresponds $\langle \mathfrak{A}, c_T, c_W \rangle$. But it is not the case that to every $\langle \mathfrak{A}, t, w \rangle$ there exists a context c of $\mathfrak{A}$ such that $t = c_T$ and $w = c_W$. The result is that in LD such sentences as '$\exists x$ Exist x' and '$\exists x \exists p$ Located x, p' are valid, although they would not be so regarded in traditional logic. At least not in the neotraditional logic that countenances empty worlds. Using the semantical developments of pages 543–46, we can define this traditional sense of validity (for formulas which do not contain demonstratives) as follows. First note that by Remark 7, if ϕ has a Stable Character,

$$\models^{\mathfrak{A}}_{cftw} \phi \quad \text{iff} \quad \models^{\mathfrak{A}}_{c'ftw} \phi$$

Thus for such formulas we can define,

ϕ *is true at* t, w *(in* $\mathfrak{A})$ iff for every assignment f and every context c, $\models^{\mathfrak{A}}_{cftw} \phi$

The neotraditional sense of validity is now definable as follows,

$\models_T \phi$ iff for all structures $\mathfrak{A}$, times t, and worlds w, ϕ is true at t, w (in $\mathfrak{A}$)

(Properly speaking, what I have called the neo-traditional sense of validity is the notion of validity now common for a quantified S5 modal tense logic with individual variables ranging over possible individuals and a predicate of existence.) Adding the subscript 'LD' for explicitness, we can now state some results.

(i)   If ϕ contains no demonstratives, if $\models_T \phi$, then $\models_{LD} \phi$

(ii) $\models_{LD} \exists x$ Exist x, but $\sim \models_T \exists x$ Exist x

Of course '$\Box \exists x$ Exist x' is not valid even in LD. Nor are its counterparts, '$\neg F \neg \exists x$ Exist x', and '$\neg P \neg \exists x$ Exist x'.

This suggests that we can transcend the context-oriented perspective of LD by generalizing over times and worlds so as to capture those possible circumstances $\langle \mathfrak{A}, t, w \rangle$ which do not correspond to any possible contexts $\langle \mathfrak{A}, c \rangle$. We have the following result:

(iii) If ϕ contains no demonstratives,
$$\models_T \phi \quad \text{iff} \quad \models_{LD} \Box(\neg F \neg \phi \wedge \neg P \neg \phi \wedge \phi).$$

Although our definition of the neotraditional sense of validity was motivated by consideration of demonstrative-free formulas, we could apply it also to formulas containing essential occurrences of demonstratives. To do so would nullify the most interesting features of the logic of demonstratives. But it raises the question, can we express our new sense of validity in terms of the neotraditional sense? This can be done:

(iv) $\models_{LD} \phi \quad \text{iff} \quad \models_T AN\phi$

Remark 10: Rigid designators (in the sense of Kripke) are terms with a Stable Content. Since Kripke does not discuss demonstratives, his examples all have, in addition, a Stable Character (by Remark 8). Kripke claims that for proper names α, β it may happen that $\alpha = \beta$, though not a priori, is nevertheless necessary. This, in spite of the fact that the names α, β may be introduced by means of descriptions α', β' for which $\alpha' = \beta'$ is not necessary. An analogous situation holds in LD. Let α', β' be definite descriptions (without free variables) such that $\alpha' = \beta'$ is not a priori, and consider the (rigid) terms dthat[α'] and dthat[β'] which are formed from them. We know that:

$$\models (\text{dthat}[\alpha'] = \text{dthat}[\beta'] \leftrightarrow \alpha' = \beta').$$

Thus, if $\alpha' = \beta'$ is not a priori, neither is dthat[α'] = dthat[β']. But, since:

$$\models (\text{dthat}[\alpha'] = \text{dthat}[\beta'] \rightarrow \Box(\text{dthat}[\alpha'] = \text{dthat}[\beta']))$$

it may happen that dthat[α'] = dthat[β'] is necessary. The converse situation can be illustrated in LD. Since $(\alpha = \text{dthat}[\alpha])$ is valid (see Remark 3), it is surely capable of being known a priori. But if α lacks a Stable Content (in some context c), $\Box(\alpha = \text{dthat}[\alpha])$ will be false.

Remark 11:   Our 0-0-place *i*-functors are not proper names, in the sense of Kripke, since they do not have a Stable Content. But they can easily be converted by means of stabilizing influence of 'dthat'. Even dthat[α] lacks a Stable Character. The process by which such expressions are converted into expressions with a Stable Character is 'dubbing'—a form of definition in which context may play an essential role. The means to deal with such context-indexed definitions is not available in our object language.

There would, of course, be no difficulty in supplementing our language with a syntactically distinctive set of 0-0-place *i*-functors whose semantics requires them to have both a Stable Character and a Stable Content in every context. Variables already behave this way, what is wanted is a class of constants that behave, in these respects, like variables.

The difficulty comes in expressing the definition. My thought is that when a name, like 'Bozo', is introduced by someone saying, in some context c^*, "Let's call the Governor, 'Bozo'", we have a context-indexed definition of the form: $A =_{c^*} \alpha$, where A is a new constant (here, 'Bozo') and α is some term whose denotation depends on context (here, 'the Governor'). The intention of such a dubbing is, presumably, to induce the semantical clause: for all c, $\{A\}^{\mathfrak{A}}_{cf} = \{\alpha\}_{c^*f}$. Such a clause gives A a Stable Character. The context-indexing is required by the fact that the Content of α (the 'definiens') may vary from context to context. Thus the same semantical clause is not induced by taking either $A = \alpha$ or even $A = $ dthat[α] as an axiom .

I think it is likely that such definitions play a practically (and perhaps theoretically) indispensable role in the growth of language, allowing us to introduce a vast stock of names on the basis of a meager stock of demonstratives and some ingenuity in the staging of demonstrations.

Perhaps such introductions should not be called 'definitions' at all, since they essentially enrich the expressive power of the language. What a nameless man may express by 'I am hungry' may be inexpressible in remote contexts. But once he says "Let's call me 'Bozo'", his Content is accessible to us all.

Remark 12:   The strongest form of logical equivalence between two formulas ϕ and ϕ' is sameness of Character, $\{\phi\} = \{\phi'\}$. This form of synonymy is expressible in terms of validity.

$$\{\phi\} = \{\phi'\} \quad \text{iff} \quad \models \Box[\neg F\neg(\phi \leftrightarrow \phi') \wedge \neg P\neg(\phi \leftrightarrow \phi') \wedge (\phi \leftrightarrow \phi')]$$

[Using Remark 9 (iii) and dropping the condition, which was stated only to express the intended range of applicability of $\models_T$, we have: $\{\phi\} = \{\phi'\}$ iff $\models_T (\phi \leftrightarrow \phi')$.] Since definitions of the usual kind (as opposed to dubbings) are intended to introduce a short expression as a mere abbreviation of a longer one, the Character of the defined sign should be the same as the Character of the definiens. Thus, within LD, definitional axioms must take the unusual form indicated above.

Remark 13: If β is a variable of the same sort as the term α but is not free in α, then $\{\text{dthat}[\alpha]\} = \{\text{the } \beta \ AN(\beta = \alpha)\}$. Thus for every formula ϕ, there can be constructed a formula ϕ' such that ϕ' contains no occurrence of 'dthat' and $\{\phi\} = \{\phi'\}$.

Remark 14: Y (yesterday) and G (one day ago) superficially resemble one another in view of the fact that $\models (Y\phi \leftrightarrow G\phi)$. But the former is a demonstrative whereas the latter is an iterative temporal operator. "One day ago it was the case that one day ago it was the case that John yawned" means that John yawned the day before yesterday. But "Yesterday it was the case that yesterday it was the case that John yawned" is only a stutter.

Notes on Possible Refinements

1. The primitive predicates and functors of first-order predicate logic are all taken to be extensional. Alternatives are possible.

2. Many conditions might be added on $\mathcal{P}$; many alternatives might be chosen for $\mathcal{T}$. If the elements of $\mathcal{T}$ do not have a natural relation to play the role of $<$, such a relation must be added to the structure.

3. When K is a set of LD formulas, $K \models \phi$ is easily defined in any of the usual ways.

4. Aspects of the contexts other than c_A, c_P, c_T, and c_W would be used if new demonstratives (e.g., pointings, You, etc.) were added to the language. (Note that the subscripts A, P, T, W are external parameters. They may be thought of as functions applying to contexts, with c_A being the value of A for the context c.)

5. Special continuity conditions through time might be added for the predicate 'Exist'.

6. If individuals lacking positions are admitted as agents of contexts, 3(iii) of page 543 should be weakened to: $c_P \in \mathcal{P} \cup \{\dagger\}$. It would no longer be the case that: $\models$ Located I, Here. If individuals also lacking temporal location (disembodied minds?) are admitted as agents of contexts, a similar weakening is required of 3(ii). In any case it would still be true that $\models$ Exist I.

XX. Adding 'Says'

[This section is not yet written. What follows is a rough outline of what is to come.]

The point of this section is to show, in a controlled experiment, that what Quine called *the relational sense* of certain intensional operators is unavoidable, and to explore the *logical*, as opposed to epistemological, features of language which lead to this result.

I have already mentioned, in connection with Dr. Lauben, that when x says 'I have been wounded' and y wishes to report in indirect discourse exactly what x said, y has a problem. It will not do for y to say 'x said that I have been wounded'. According to our earlier remarks, it should be correct for y to report x's *content* using a character appropriate to the context of the report. For example, accusingly: 'You said that you had been wounded', or quantificationally: '$(\exists z)(Fz \wedge x$ said that z had been wounded)' where x alone satisfied 'Fz'. I will try to show that such constructions are the inevitable result of the attempt to make (third person) *indirect discourse* reports of the first person *direct discourse* sayings when those sayings involve indexicals.

The situation regarding the usual epistemic verbs—'believes', 'hopes', 'knows', 'desires', 'fears', etc.—is, I believe, essentially similar to that of 'says'. Each has, or might have, a *direct discourse* sense in which the character which stands for the cognitive significance of the thought is given (he thinks, 'My God! It is *my* pants that are on fire.') as well as an *indirect discourse* sense in which only the content need be given (he thinks that it is *his* pants that are on fire).[68] If this is correct, and if indexicals are featured in the language of thought (as suggested

---

[68] My notion of 'indirect discourse' forms of language is linked to Frege's notion of an 'ungerade' (often translated 'oblique') context. My terminology is intended to echo his.

earlier), then any *indirect* discourse reports of someone's thought (other than first person on the spot reports) must contain those features—*de re* constructions, referential occurrences, quantification in, relational senses—that have so puzzled me, and some others, since the appearance of "Quantifiers and Propositional Attitudes."[69]

What is special and different about the present approach is the attempt to use the distinction between direct and indirect discourse to match the distinction between character and content. Thus when you wonder, 'Is that me?', it is correct to report you as having wondered whether you are yourself. These transformations are traced to the indexical form of your inner direct discourse rather than to any particular referential intentions. The idea is that the full analysis of indirect discourse includes mention of the suppressed character of the direct discourse event which the indirect discourse reports, thus:

$\exists c, C$ [c is a context $\land$ C is a character $\land$ x is the agent of c $\land$ x direct-discourse-verb C at the time t of c $\land$ the content of C in c is that...]

approximates a full analysis of

x indirect-discourse-verb that ... at t.

Rather than try to include all these semantical ideas in an object language which includes the direct discourse forms of the verbs, the object language will include, *as is usual*, only the indirect discourse forms. The information about the character of the direct discourse event will provide the metalinguistic data against which the truth of object language sentences is tested.[70]

---

[69] Quine, in his "Reply to Kaplan" in *Words and Objections*, ed. D. Davidson et al. (Dordrecht: Reidel, 1969), raises the question—in the idiom of "Quantifiers and Propositional Attitudes" (*Journal of Philosophy* 53 (1956); reprinted in Martinich, op. cit.)—which of the names of a thing are to count as exportable? My point here is that the indexical names must be exportable, not because of some special justification for the transformation from a *de dicto* occurrence to a *de re* occurrence, but because indexicals are devices of direct reference and have no *de dicto* occurrences. I am reminded of the Zen ko-an: How do you get the goose out of the bottle? Answer: It's out!

[70] If this analysis is correct, the suppressed character should wreak its mischief in cases of suspension of belief (I believe, 'that man's pants are on fire' but at the moment neither assent to nor deny 'my pants are on fire') as does its counterpart in section XI of "Quantifying In." Burge, in "Kaplan, Quine, and Suspended Belief," *Philosophical Studies* 31 (1977): 197–203, proposes a solution to the problem of section XI which he believes is in the spirit of Quine's formulations. A similar

What is not yet clear to me is whether all directly referential occurrences of terms within the scope of indirect discourse epistemic verbs are to be justified *solely* on the basis of a like (though generally distinct) term in the direct discourse event or whether in some cases the English idioms which we symbolize with quantification in (for example, 'There is someone whom Holmes believes to have shot himself') involve some element of *knowing-who* or *believing-who*. To put the question another way: are all the cases that Quine describes, and others similar, which irresistibly suggest the symbolic idiom of quantification in, accounted for by the semantics of direct reference (including indexicals and possibly other expressions as well) as applied to the (putative) direct discourse events? "Quantifying In" suffers from the lack of an adequate semantics of direct reference, but its explicandum includes the epistemological idea of knowing-who, which goes beyond what can be analyzed simply in terms of direct reference. When Ingrid hears someone approaching through the fog and knows 'Someone is approaching' and even knows 'That person is approaching', is it justified to say that there is someone whom Ingrid knows to be approaching? Or must we have, in addition to the indexical 'that person', *recognition* on Ingrid's part of who it is that is approaching? My present thought is that the cases which irresistibly suggest the symbolic idiom of quantification in involve, in an ambiguous way, two elements: *direct reference* (on which we are close to getting clear, I hope) and *recognition*.[71] (The latter is my new term

---

proposal in the present context would seem starkly inappropriate. But there has been a shift in task from "Quantifying In" to the present attempt. In large part the shift is to a course outlined by Burge in the last two pages of the above-mentioned article and urged by him, in conversation, for several years. The point only began to sink in when I came on it myself from a different angle.

[71] There is another form of common speech which may be thought to suggest formalization by quantification in. I call this form the *pseudo de re*. A typical example is, "John says that the lying S.O.B. who took my car is honest." It is clear that John does not say, "The lying S.O.B. who took your car is honest." Does John say $\ulcorner \delta$ is honest$\urcorner$ for some directly referential term δ which the reporter believes to refer to the lying S.O.B. who took his car? Not necessarily. John may say something as simple as, "The man I sent to you yesterday is honest." The reporter has simply substituted his description for John's. What justifies this shocking falsification of John's speech? Nothing! But we do it, and often recognize—or don't care—when it is being done. The form lends itself to strikingly distorted reports. As Church has shown, in his *Introduction to Mathematical Logic* (Princeton: Princeton University Press, 1956), on page 25, when John says "Sir Walter Scott is the author of *Waverley*" use of the *pseudo de re* form (plus a quite plausible synonymy transformation) allows the report, "John says that there are twenty-nine counties in Utah"! I do not see that the existence of the *pseudo de re* form of report poses

for knowing-(or believing)-who.) The term is chosen to reflect the idea that the individual in question is identified with respect to some prior or independent information—*re*-cognition—not immediately connected with the current attribution.) Of the two elements the former is semantical; the latter, frankly epistemological. The English idiom 'There is someone such that Ingrid indirect-discourse-propositional-attitude-verb that ...he ...' always implies that a singular proposition is the object of Ingrid's thought (and thus that some directly referential term α occurred in her inner direct discourse) and may sometimes imply (or only suggest?) that Ingrid recognized, *who α is*. I offer no analysis of the latter notion.[72]

In the first paragraph, I referred to a controlled experiment. By that I mean the following. Accepting the metaphor of "inner direct discourse events" and "indirect discourse reports" in connection with the usual epistemic verbs, I want to examine the logical relations between these two. But the study is complicated by at least three factors which obscure the issues I wish to bring to light. First, there is no real syntax to the language of thought. Thus, even in the case of the simplest thoughts the relation between the syntax of the sentential complement to the epistemic verb and the structure of the original thought is obscure. Second, in containing images, sounds, odors, etc., thought is richer than the language of the report. Might these perceptual elements play a role in determining logical relations? Third, thought ranges from the completely explicit (inner speech) to the entirely implicit (unconscious beliefs which explain actions) and through a variety of occurrent and dispositional forms. This makes it hard to pin down the whole direct discourse event. These three factors suggest taking as a paradigm of the relation between direct and indirect discourse—direct and indirect discourse!

Even when reporting the (outer) discourse of another, at least three obscure irrelevancies (for our purposes) remain. First, if Christopher speaks in a language different from that of the report, we have again the problem of translation (analogous to, though perhaps less severe than,

---

any issues of sufficient theoretical interest to make it worth pursuing.

[72]There is a considerable literature on this subject with important contributions by Hintikka, Castañeda and others. In connection with the proposal that $\ulcorner a$ knows who α is$\urcorner$ can be symbolized $\ulcorner \exists x(a$ knows that $x = \alpha)\urcorner$, it should be noted that a's knowledge of the logical truth $\ulcorner \text{dthat}[\alpha] = \alpha\urcorner$ leads, simply by the semantics of direct reference, to $\ulcorner \exists x(a$ knows that $x = \alpha)\urcorner$. This shows only that a *recognition* sense of knowing a singular proposition is not definable, in the obvious way, in terms of a purely *direct reference* sense of knowing a singular proposition.

that of translating the language of thought). We control this by assuming the direct discourse to be in the language of the indirect discourse report. Second, as Carnap once pointed out to me, if Christopher's discourse had the form $\ulcorner \phi \wedge \psi \urcorner$ even the strictest court would accept as true the testimony, $\ulcorner$Christopher said that $\psi \wedge \phi \urcorner$. What logical transformations on the original discourse would be allowed in the report? (If Christopher says '$\exists x$ x is round', may we report him as saying that $\exists y$ y is round?) We control this by allowing no logical transformations (we are explicating *literal* indirect discourse). Third, if in saying 'The circle can't be squared' Christopher thought that 'can't' was synonymous with 'should not' rather than 'cannot', should he be reported as having said that the circle can't be squared? We control this by assuming that our speakers make no linguistic errors.

What then remains of the logic? Is the move from direct discourse to literal indirect discourse not simply the result of disquotation (and decapitaliztion) plus the addition of 'that', as in:

> Christopher says 'the world is round'
> ∴ Christopher says that the world is round   ?

But how then are we to report Dr. Lauben's saying, 'I have been wounded'? Certainly not as, 'Dr. Lauben says that I have been wounded'!

Even in this highly antiseptic environment, the logic of *says* should provide us with a full measure of that baffling and fascinating *de re* versus *de dicto*, notional versus relational, etc., behavior. And here, using the conceptual apparatus of the semantics of direct reference, we may hope to identify the source of these antics.

[I also hope to distinguish, in discussing reports of self-attribution, *x says that x is a fool*, from *x says-himself to be a fool*.]

XXI. Russell on Egocentric Particulars and Their Dispensability

In chapter VII of *Inquiry Into Meaning and Truth*,[73] Russell gives a series of atrocious arguments for the conclusion that "[indexicals] are not needed in any part of the description of the world, whether physical or psychological." This is a happy no-nonsense conclusion for an argument that begins by remarking "A physicist will not say 'I saw a table', but like Neurath or Julius Caesar, 'Otto saw a table'." [Why Julius Caesar would be provoked to say 'Otto saw a table', is unexplained.]

---

[73] Bertrand Russell (London: Allen & Unwin, 1940).

Let us examine Russell's conclusion without prejudice to his argument. [What follows is an outline.]

In brief, there are essentially two points. First: if we have both the indexicals and an unlimited supply of unused directly referential proper names, and we can do instantaneous dubbing, then in each context c for any sentence ϕ containing indexicals we can produce a sentence ϕ^* whose character is fixed and whose content is the same as that of ϕ in c. In this sense, if you can describe it with indexicals you can describe it without.[74] There are problems: (i) things can change fast and dubbings take time, (ii) the indexicals retain a kind of epistemic priority.

The second point is: given any *prior* collection of proper names, there will be things, times, places, etc., without a name. How do I say something about these unnamed entities? (E.g., how do I tell you that your pants are on fire—now? It may be that nothing in sight, including us, and no nearby time has a name.)

There are two cases. It seems most likely that without indexicals some entities cannot even be uniquely *described*. In this case we are really in trouble (unless Russell believes in the identity of indescribables —objects lacking uniquely characterizing descriptions) because without indexicals we cannot freely introduce new names. If every entity *can* be uniquely described, there is still the problem of not presenting the right content under the right character required to motivate the right action (recall the discussion on pages 532–33). The proposition expressed by 'the pants belonging to *the x Fx* are on fire at *the t Gt*' is not the proposition I want to express, and certainly does not have the character I wish to convey.[75]

XXII. On Proper Names

[Some thoughts on proper names from the perspective of the formal system are contained in Remark 11, page 551. What follows is the most hastily written section of this draft. I sketch a view that is mainly

---

[74] I assume here that proper names are not indexicals. I argue the point in section XXII.

[75] Some interesting arguments of a different sort for the indispensability of indexicals are given by Burge in "Belief De Re," *Journal of Philosophy* 74 (1977): 338–62, and by Bar-Hillel in his pioneering work, "Indexical Expressions," *Mind* (1954). In connection with the arguments of Burge and Bar-Hillel it would be interesting to check on some related empirical issues involving linguistic universals. Do all languages have a first person singular form? Do they all have all of the standard indexicals?

negative, without including much supporting argumentation (several of the omitted arguments seem both tedious and tendentious). My current inclination is to drop this whole section from the final draft.]

A *word* is an expression along with its meaning. When two expressions have the same meaning, as with "can't" and "cannot", we call the two words *synonyms*. When two meanings have the same expression, we call the two words *homonyms*. In the latter case we also say that the expression is *ambiguous*. (Probably we would say that the *word* is ambiguous, but accept my terminology for what follows.) In a disambiguated language, semantics can associate meanings with expressions. Even in a language containing ambiguities, semantics can associate a set of meanings with an expression. But given an utterance, semantics cannot tell us what expression was uttered or what language it was uttered in. This is a presemantic task. When I utter a particular vocable, for example, the one characteristic of the first person pronoun of English, you must decide what *word* I have spoken or indeed, if I have spoken any word at all (it may have been a cry of anguish). In associating a word with my utterance you take account of a variety of features of the context of utterance that help to *determine* what I have said but that need not be any *part* of what I have said. My egotism, my intonation, my demeanor, may all support the hypothesis that it was the first person pronoun of English. But these aspects of personality, fluency, and mood are no part of any semantic theory of the first person pronoun. The factors I have cited are not, of course, *criterial* for the use of the first person pronoun. What are the criteria? What would definitively settle the question? I don't know. I think this is a very difficult question. But among the criteria there must be some that touch on the utterer's intention to use a word in conformity with the conventions of a particular linguistic community. For proper name words, in part because they are so easily introduced, this aspect of the presemantic determination is especially important.

According to the causal chain or chain of communication theory, there are two critical intentions associated with the use of the proper name word. One is the intention to use the word with the meaning given it by the person from whom you learned the word. The other is the contrary intention to create (and perhaps simultaneously use) a proper name word to refer to a given object irrespective of any prior meanings associated with the expression chosen as a vehicle. One who uses a proper name word with the first intention generally (but not always) believes that someone originated the word by using it with the second intention, and—according to the causal chain theory—intends to refer to the given object.[76]

In "Bob and Carol and Ted and Alice," appendix IX, I introduce the notion of a *dubbing* for what I took to be the standard form of introduction of a proper name word. That notion has been mistakenly taken to imply—what I deliberately sought to evoke—a formal public ceremony. What I actually had in mind was a use of a proper name word with the second intention: the intention to originate a word rather than conform to a prior usage. Thus a fleeting "Hi-ya, Beautiful" incorporates all the intentional elements required for me to say that a dubbing has taken place. I believe that my notion here is closely related to Donnellan's notion of a *referential use* of a definite description. Donnellan's distinction between referential and attributive uses of definite descriptions is easily and naturally extended to referential and attributive uses of proper names. When the intention to conform to a preestablished convention is absent we have the pure referential use. In this case, when a proper name is in question, I take it that an internal, subjective, dubbing has occurred. When a definite description is in question, again the speaker does not intend to give the expression its conventional meaning although he may intend to *make use* of the conventional meaning in conveying who it is that is being referred to or for some other purpose associated with

---

[76]There is disagreement as to how the given object must be given to one who introduces a proper name word with the second intention. Must he be acquainted with the object, directly acquainted, *en rapport*, perceiving it, causally connected, or what? My liberality with respect to the introduction of directly referring terms by means of 'dthat' extends to proper names, and I would allow an arbitrary definite description to *give* us the object we name. "Let's call the first child to be born in the twenty-first century 'Newman 1'." But I am aware that this is a very controversial position. Perhaps some of the sting can be removed by adopting an idea of Gilbert Harman. Normally one would not introduce a proper name or a dthat-term to correspond to each definite description one uses. But we have the means to do so if we wish. Should we do so, we are enabled to apprehend singular propositions concerning remote individuals (those formerly known only by description). Recognizing this, we refrain. What purpose—other than to confound the skeptics—is served by direct reference to whosoever may be the next president of Brazil? The introduction of a new proper name by means of a dubbing in terms of description and the active contemplation of characters involving dthat-terms—two mechanisms for providing direct reference to the denotation of an arbitrary definite description—constitute a form of cognitive restructuring; they broaden our range of thought. To take such a step is an action normally not performed at all, and rarely, if ever, done capriciously. The fact that we have the means—without special experience, knowledge, or whatever—to refer directly to the myriad individuals we can describe, does not imply that we will do so. And if we should have reason to do so, why not?

the act of utterance (as in "Hi-ya, Beautiful"). What is important here is that the speaker intends to be creating a meaning for the expression in question rather than following conventions. Dubbings, whether aimed at introducing a relatively permanent sense for the expression or only aimed at attaching a nonce-sense to the expression, are unconventional uses of language. Dubbings create words.

In many, perhaps most, uses of definite descriptions there is a mixture of the intention to follow convention with the intention to refer to a preconceived individual. The same mixture of 'attributive' and 'referential' intentions can occur with a proper name. If I introduce a name into your vocabulary by means of false introduction ("This is Jaakko Hintikka", but it isn't), you are left with an undiscriminated tangle of attributive (to refer to Jaakko Hintikka) and referential (to refer to the person to whom you were introduced) intentions associated with your subsequent uses of the expression 'Jaakko Hintikka'. There are several ways in which one might attempt to account for these mixed intentions in a general theory of language. First, we might distinguish two notions: speaker's-reference and semantic-reference. The presence of an attributive intention justifies giving the expressions a conventional meaning and thus allows us to claim that preexisting *words* were used. Whereas the presence of a referential intention (not just a *belief* that the semantic referent is the given object, but an independent intention to refer to the given object) justifies the claim that the speaker is referring to the given object independent of any particular interpretation of the expressions he used as words and independent of whether the utterance has an interpretation as words. A second way of accounting for mixed intentions of this kind is to assume that one of the two intentions must be dominant. If the referential intention dominates, we regard the utterance, on the model of "Hi-ya, Beautiful," as an apt (or inept, as the case may be) introduction of a proper name word (or phrase). Thus, as essentially involving a dubbing. On this way of accounting for mixed intentions, a referential use of an expression would endow the expression with a semantic referent identical with the speaker's referent.[77]

---

[77] This is not an unnatural way to account for the use of the proper name word in the false introduction case, but it does seem a bit strange in the case of a definite description. In that case it involves hypothesizing that the speaker intended the description expression to have a meaning which made the given object its semantic referent, and only *believed* that the conventional meaning would do this, a belief that he is prepared to give up rather than acknowledge that the semantic referent of his words was not the given object. Something like this seems to happen when descriptions grow capitals, as in 'The Holy Roman Empire', and in other cases as

My aim in the foregoing is to emphasize how delicate and subtle our analysis of the context of utterance must be for the presemantic purpose of determining what words, if any, were spoken. I do this to make plausible my view that—assuming the causal chain theory of reference—proper names are not indexicals. The contextual feature which consists of the causal history of a particular proper name expression in the agent's idiolect seems more naturally to be regarded as determining what word was used than as fixing the content of a single context-sensitive word. Although it is true that two utterances of 'Aristotle' in different contexts may have different contents, I am inclined to attribute this difference to the fact that distinct homonymous words were uttered rather than a context sensitivity in the character of a single word 'Aristotle'. Unlike indexicals like 'I', proper names really are ambiguous. The causal theory of reference tells us, in terms of contextual features (including the speaker's intentions) which word is being used in a given utterance. Each such word is directly referential (thus it has a fixed content), and it also has a fixed character. Therefore, in the case of proper name words, all three kinds of meaning—referent, content, and character—collapse. In this, proper name words are unique. They have the direct reference of indexicals, but they are not context-sensitive. Proper name words are like indexicals that you can carry away from their original context without affecting their content. Because of the collapse of character, content, and referent, it is not unnatural to say of proper names that they have no meaning other than their referent.

Some may claim that they simply use 'indexical' in a wider sense than I (perhaps to mean something like 'contextual'). But we must be wary of an overbroad usage. Is every ambiguous expression an indexical because we look to utterer's intentions to disambiguate? Indeed, is every expression an indexical because it might have been a groan?

If the character and content of proper name words is as I have described it (according to the causal theory), then the informativeness of $\ulcorner \alpha = \beta \urcorner$, with α and β proper names, is not accounted for in terms of differences in either content or character. The problem is that proper names do not seem to fit into the whole semantical and epistemological scheme as I have developed it. I claimed that a competent speaker knows the character of words. This suggests (even if it does not imply) that if two proper names have the same character, the competent speaker

---

well, for example Russell's 'denoting phrases' which do not denote. But it still seems strange.

knows that. But he doesn't. What is perhaps even more astounding is that I may introduce a new proper name word and send it on its journey. When it returns to me—perhaps slightly distorted phonologically by its trip through other dialects—I can competently take it into my vocabulary without recognizing it as the very same word! Shocking!

In earlier sections of this paper I have tried to show that many of the metaphysical and epistemological anomalies involving proper names had counterparts involving indexicals, and further that in the case of indexicals these wonders are easily explained by an obvious theory. Insofar as I am correct in regarding the anomalies as counterparts, the theory of indexicals may help to break down unwarranted resistance to the causal chain theory. It may also suggest the form of a general semantical and epistemological scheme comprehending both indexicals and proper names. This is not the place to attempt the latter task; my purpose here is simply to show that it is not trivial.[78] Those who suggest that proper names are merely one species of indexical depreciate the power and the mystery of the causal chain theory.

---

[78] The issues to be resolved by "a general semantical and epistemological scheme comprehending ... proper names" are such as these. Is the work of the causal chain theory presemantic, as I have claimed? Do proper names have a kind of meaning other than reference? Does the causal chain theory itself constitute a kind of meaning for proper names that is analogous to character for indexicals (but which, perhaps, gives all proper names the same meaning in this sense)? Are proper names words of any particular language? Is there synonymy between proper names that are expressed differently (as there is between 'can't' and 'cannot')? How should we describe the linguistic competence of one who does not know that Hesperus is Phosphorus? Is he guilty of linguistic error? Should we say he does not know what words he speaks? Does he know that 'Hesperus' and 'Phosphorus' are different words? Are they? Is it really possible, as I claim, to account for the semantics of indexicals without making use of the full conceptual resources required to account for the semantics of proper names? I raise these issues—and there are others—within the framework of a hypothetical acceptance of the causal chain theory. There are other issues, of a quite different kind, involved in trying to fill out some details of the causal chain theory itself. For example, if one who has received some particular proper name expression, say, "James", hundreds of times, uses that expression attributively as a proper name, and has in mind no particular source, how do we decide which branch to follow back? The first set of issues seems to me to be largely independent of the details of the relevant causal chains.

18

Afterthoughts

David Kaplan[1]

Demonstratives is now being published, after all these years, in the form in which it was written and circulated for all these years.[2] It is manifestly unfinished. It still retains bracketed metacomments like "[My current inclination is to drop this whole section from the final draft.]." So why have I not cleaned it up and finished it?

Two reasons: a small one and a big one. First and least, I don't know exactly how to fix some of the sections that now seem wrong, and I don't yet see exactly how to connect my current thinking, about propositional attitudes and proper names, with indexicals. Last and most, the spirit

[1] © 1989 by David Kaplan.

I am deeply grateful to John Perry, Howard Wettstein, and Joseph Almog, not only for their efforts in planning and executing the conference that resulted in the present volume, but for their patient encouragement of the publication of *Demonstratives* and their good-natured tolerance of the time it has taken me to gather my afterthoughts. Throughout my life, I have had the uncommonly good fortune to fall under the influence of persons of great intelligence, good humor, and tolerance. Principal among these are my wonderful parents, Martha and Irv Kaplan, my inspiring teachers, Rudolf Carnap and Donald Kalish, and my remarkable wife, Renée Kaplan, the *ne plus ultra* of all three qualities.

[2] I have made the following changes to the circulated text of draft #2. Bibliographical references have been added and the footnotes renumbered. In a few places, a word or a bit of punctuation has been added or a phrase has been moved. I have also corrected a few typographical errors. None of the philosophical errors have been touched. (Thanks to Edward Zalta for his logician's help with the corrections, and thanks to Ingrid Deiwiks for her typographical skills.)

of the work—the enthusiasm, the confidence, the hesitations—has an integrity that I regard fondly. It reflects its time, the time described in the preface. My own concerns have moved to other topics. I have even felt a resurgence of atavistic Fregeanism. For me to revise *Demonstratives* now would be the intrusion of a third party between the author and his audience.

I had thought of responding to criticisms, of which there have been many over the past decade, several in this very volume, and some quite technically challenging. Unfortunately, I do not have the space to agree in detail with all of them. So instead I have decided to try to look more closely at a few of *Demonstratives'* central concepts.

My reflections are divided into four sections, each of which is intended to be more or less coherent (though I must confess that tangent avoidance has never been my strong suit). The separate sections are somewhat disconnected, as one's afterthoughts tend to be.

Table of Contents

I. What is Direct Reference?

Demonstratives was written against my own Fregean upbringing, as was its progenitor "Dthat".[3] I aimed to challenge several tenets of Fregean semantics. In particular, I argued that Fregean *Sinn* conflates elements of two quite different notions of meaning. One, which I called *character*, is close to the intuitive idea of linguistic meaning (and perhaps of cognitive content). Another, which I called *content*, is what is said or expressed by an expression in a particular context of use. The *content* of an utterance of a complete sentence is a truth-bearing proposition. Where indexicals are involved, the difference between character and content is quite clear. The *content* of the sentence "Today is my birthday" will vary with speaker and day of utterance. The *character* of the sentence is the common meaning which each language user can deploy to speak of himself and of the day of utterance. It is this common character that determines how the content adapts in the varying contexts of use.

The idea of Content—the what-is-said on a particular occasion—is central to my account. It is this notion that I saw, and continue to see, as the primary idea behind Frege's *Sinn*.[4] For what I call *directly referential* expressions, among which are indexicals and demonstratives, I argue that the Fregean picture of the relation between *Sinn* (content) and *Bedeutung* (referent) is entirely wrong.

Directly referential expressions are said to refer directly without the mediation of a Fregean *Sinn*. What does this mean? There are two things it might mean. It might mean that the relation between the linguistic expression and the referent is not mediated by the corresponding propositional component, the content or what-is-said. This would be directly contrary to Frege, and it *is* what I meant. But it also might mean that *nothing* mediates the relation between the linguistic expression and the individual. So stated, this second interpretation is a wildly implausible idea. And it is contrary to the development of the notion of character which occurs in the text. This is *not* what I meant.[5]

---

[3] "Dthat" was written and read in 1970, published in *Syntax and Semantics*, vol. 9, ed. P. Cole (New York: Academic Press, 1978); and reprinted in *The Philosophy of Language*, ed. A. P. Martinich (Oxford: Oxford University Press, 1985).

[4] My own analysis of the notion, however, is closer to Russell's *signification*, than to Frege's *Sinn*. I have written more recently on the difference between the semantics of Russell and Frege in section VII of "Opacity" (in *The Philosophy of W. V. Quine*, ed. L. E. Hahn and P. A. Schilpp (Illinois: Open Court, 1986)).

[5] Nor did I mean that whatever mediation takes place is nondescriptional. The question whether some sort of description can be fashioned to give the correct reference for a term is not decisive for direct reference (but see footnote 24 below).

The "direct" of "direct reference" means unmediated by any propositional component, not unmediated *simpliciter*. The directly referential term goes directly to its referent, *directly* in the sense that it does not first pass through the proposition. Whatever rules, procedures, or mechanisms there are that govern the search for the referent, they are irrelevant to the propositional component, to content. When the individual is determined (when *the reference is fixed*, in the language of Saul Kripke[6]), it is loaded into the proposition. It is this that makes the referent prior to the propositional component, and it is this that reverses the arrow from propositional component to individual in the Direct Reference Picture of the Preface to *Demonstratives*.

How does rigid designation come in?

If the individual is loaded into the proposition (to serve as the propositional component) before the proposition begins its round-the-worlds journey, it is hardly surprising that the proposition manages to find that same individual at all of its stops, even those in which the individual had no prior, native presence. The proposition conducted no search for a native who meets propositional specifications; it simply 'discovered' what it had carried in. In this way we achieve rigid designation. Indeed, we achieve the characteristic, direct reference, form of rigid designation, in which it is irrelevant whether the individual exists in the world at which the proposition is evaluated. In *Demonstratives* I took this to be the fundamental form of rigid designation.

So certain was I that this *was* the fundamental form of rigid designation, that I argued (from "systematic considerations") that it must be what Kripke had *intended* despite contrary indications in his writing.[7]

It was not. In a letter (asking that I take his remarks into account in these afterthoughts), Kripke states that the notion of rigid designation he intended is that "a designator d of an object x is *rigid*, if it designates x with respect to all possible worlds where x exists, and *never designates an object other than x with respect to any possible world*." This definition is designed to be neutral with regard to the question

---

[6] Saul Kripke, "Naming and Necessity," in *Semantics of Natural Language*, ed. G. Harman and D. Davidson (Dordrecht: Reidel, 1972); revised edition published as a separate monograph, *Naming and Necessity* (Oxford: Basil Blackwell, 1980). References are to the revised edition. Also see Saul Kripke, "Identity and Necessity," in *Identity and Individuation*, ed. M. K. Munitz (New York: New York University Press, 1971).

[7] Footnote 16, *Demonstratives*.

whether a designator can designate an object at a world in which the object doesn't exist. It was motivated, he says, by the desire to avoid getting bogged down in irrelevant discussions of the existence question.[8]

My own discussion of rigid designation was motivated by the desire to highlight the features of rigidity that are associated with direct reference. In the first draft of *Demonstratives* I had actually used the expression "rigid designation" where I now use "direct reference". I thought of my work as delving into the phenomena identified by Donnellan, Putnam, Kripke, and by me in "Dthat". Direct reference was supposed to provide the deep structure for rigid designation, to underlie rigid designation, to explain it. It would never have occurred to me to be 'neutral' about existence.[9] Existence problems would simply disappear

---

[8] The view I thought of as manifest in his texts, what I called "the more widely held view," is stated on page 146 of "Identity and Necessity" (I&N) in the words, "In a situation where the object does not exist, then we should say that the [rigid] designator has no referent and that the object in question so designated does not exist." Kripke asserts that this view should not be attributed to him and that it occurs nowhere, explicitly or implicitly, in *Naming and Necessity* (N&N). Regarding the statement in I&N, he writes that it would be somewhat odd if "there was a mysterious change of position between my explicit view in *Naming and Necessity* and 'Identity and Necessity', delivered a month or so later." (This was the reason I used the remark in I&N to resolve the uncertainties of N&N.) He then questions the accuracy of the language of I&N (quoted above), writing "It is also possible, I think, that the sentence is mistranscribed from the tape of the talk. A simple change of 'and' to 'or' in the sentence would make it entirely consistent with what I said in *Naming and Necessity*.... The corrected version would read even better if 'so' were changed to 'though' (an easy mistake in the transcription of an oral presentation)."

It is good to know his mind on this matter, and I regret misrepresenting his views. I cannot, however, feel embarrassed by my reading of the textual evidence. In the course of my discussion of rigid designation in *Demonstratives*, I was careful to cite all the relevant passages. The neutral definition he intended, containing the clause "and never designates an object other than x," does not occur in N&N, I&N, or the new preface to N&N written ten years after the lectures were given. I continue to think that 'the more widely held view', now seen not to be *Kripke's view*, *is* the more widely held view.

Proper names are the main topic of N&N. Regarding the rigid designation of proper names, Kripke tells us in the new preface that "a proper name rigidly designates its referent even when we speak of counterfactual situations where that referent would not have existed." It is this view of rigid designation that I had thought he intended all along.

[9] That is, to be neutral on such questions as whether a designator can designate an object at a world in which the object doesn't exist or whether a name from fiction such as "Pegasus" might designate a merely possible object that exists in another possible world. I had stated my views strongly on these issues in appendices X and XI of "Bob and Carol and Ted and Alice," in *Approaches to Natural Language*,

when the underlying, direct reference structure was seen. How could rigid designation not be based on some deeper semantical property like direct reference? It couldn't be an *accident* that names were rigid and descriptions were not.[10]

It all seemed of a piece to me: the singular propositions, the direct reference, the rigid designation. And all of it could be illustrated by the case of indexicals, in which the mechanism of direct reference was understood. When I set out to revise the section distinguishing Kripke's notion from mine, I realized that it is easier to explain the difference between A and B if they are not both named "A". I therefore determined to introduce a new expression, and so coined the phrase "direct reference".

If we call a designator that designates the same object at all worlds, irrespective of whether the object exists there or not, an *obstinately* rigid designator,[11] then in the usual modal semantics, all directly referential terms will be obstinately rigid (though not every obstinately rigid term need be directly referential).[12] It is obstinate rigidity that I took as the fundamental form of rigidity in *Demonstratives*.

The paradigm of the variable

This conception of direct reference takes the variable under an assignment of value as its paradigm.[13] In evaluating "Fx" at a world w, we do not ask whether its value exists in w, we only ask what value was *assigned* to the variable before the process of evaluation at w began. Until a value is *assigned* we have nothing to evaluate.[14] Furthermore, and this is important, it is irrelevant *how* "x" gets its value, *how* the

---

ed. J. Hintikka et al. (Dordrecht: Reidel, 1973).

[10] It should be noted, of course, that even an accidental difference between the modal behavior of names and descriptions is sufficient to establish that names are not simply abbreviated descriptions.

[11] Following a suggestion of Nathan Salmon in *Reference and Essence* (Princeton: Princeton University Press, 1981) p. 34.

[12] An example of an obstinately rigid designator that is not directly referential is given in *Demonstratives*, section IV. It has the form:

$$\text{The } n[(P \wedge n^2 = 9) \vee (\sim P \wedge 2^2 = n + 1)].$$

[13] See paragraph 3 of the Preface to *Demonstratives*.

[14] Until a value is assigned, the entity that is to be evaluated at the possible worlds, whether it be thought of as an open formula or as the content of an open formula, is incomplete. There may not yet be enough information available for it to bear a truth-value.

assignment is made, how the value of "x" is *described* when it is assigned to "x". All that matters to the evaluation is that "x" *has* a particular value.

Pronouns in natural language have often been analogized to variables. Pronouns are lexically ambiguous, having both an anaphoric and a demonstrative use.[15] An anaphoric use of a pronoun is *syntactically bound* to another phrase occurring elsewhere in the discourse. In meaningful discourse, a pronoun not used anaphorically is used demonstratively. As I saw the matter, a demonstrative use of a pronoun was simply a *syntactically free* use. Like a free occurrence of a variable, it requires something extralinguistic, a *demonstration* as I then termed it, to *assign* it a value. Demonstrative and anaphoric occurrences of pronouns can thus be seen to corresponded to free and bound occurrences of variables. What I want to stress is that the difference between demonstrative and anaphoric uses of pronouns need not be conceptualized primarily in terms of lexical ambiguity; it can also be seen in terms of the syntactical distinction between free and bound occurrences of terms. I saw the analogy between variables and pronouns as even closer than had been thought.

I believe that the case of the free pronoun, the demonstrative, can take a lesson from the case of the free variable. As in the case of the free variable, the mechanism by which a value is assigned to a demonstrative, *how* a particular demonstration demonstrates its object, is extralinguistic and thus off-the-record, so to speak. It should not figure in the *content* of what was said. (This, of course, still leaves open the possibility that it might figure in the *cognitive value* of the utterance.) All that matters to the evaluation of what is said (content) is that the demonstrative has a particular value.

Thus my vivid talk about loading the referent into the proposition comes down to this: when using a directly referential term, the *mode of presentation of the referent* (if you will allow a lapse into the Frege idiom) is no part of what is said. Only the referent itself figures in content. Directly referential expressions are *transparent*.[16] Though there may be

---

[15] In "Nomoto inscribed his book" and "Each author inscribed his book," we would ordinarily take "his" to be syntactically bound to "Nomoto" and "Each author". Such syntactically bound uses of pronouns are called *anaphoric*. The same form of words can be used with "his" occurring as a demonstrative, for example, if we were to point at a third party when uttering "his".

[16] The sense of transparency I wish to evoke has nothing to do with the contrast between Quinean opacity and Russellian transparency (for which see footnote 30 of my "Opacity"). Rather, it is that of the well-designed computer program in

a complex semantical mechanism that mediates the connection between linguistic expression and referent, that mechanism is unseen in what is said.

Taxonomy: semantics and metasemantics

The inspiration for direct reference was, as reported in "Dthat", the true demonstratives. One does feel initially that in the use of a true demonstrative, not only is one trying to put the object itself into the proposition (direct reference), but that the connection between demonstrative and object, call this *reference*, is also extraordinarily direct as compared with the connection between a definite description and its denotation. Demonstratives are transparent, whereas descriptions are visibly at work, searching, searching, searching. Despite this, there is an elaborate theory of reference for demonstratives in *Demonstratives*.

How should we organize our total semantical theory so as to take account of the mechanisms of direct reference? Some have questioned whether these mechanisms even belong to semantics. I think that it is quite important to get clear on this and certain related taxonomic questions if we are to improve our understanding of the relation of semantics to thought.[17] And I am quite unclear on the subject.

There are several interesting issues concerning what belongs to semantics. The fact that a word or phrase *has* a certain meaning clearly belongs to semantics. On the other hand, a claim about the *basis* for ascribing a certain meaning to a word or phrase does not belong to semantics. "Ohsnay" means *snow* in Pig-Latin. That's a semantic fact about Pig-Latin. The *reason* why "ohsnay" means *snow* is not a semantic fact; it is some kind of historical or sociological fact about Pig-Latin. Perhaps, because it relates to how the language is *used*, it should be categorized as part of the *pragmatics* of Pig-Latin (though I am not really comfortable with this nomenclature), or perhaps, because it is a

---

which the commands are 'obvious' and the user need not take account of, indeed is usually unaware of, *how* a command is executed. He knows only that to delete you press "Delete". What else?

[17] On my understanding of the controversy between Donnellan and Kripke, just such a taxonomic question is one of the central points at issue. See Keith Donnellan, "Reference and Definite Descriptions," *Philosophical Review* 75 (1966): 281–304; reprinted in Martinich, op. cit.; Saul Kripke, "Speaker's Reference and Semantic Reference," in *Contemporary Perspectives in the Philosophy of Language*, ed. P. French, T. Uehling, Jr., and H. Wettstein (Minneapolis: University of Minnesota Press, 1977); Keith Donnellan, "Speaker Reference, Descriptions, and Anaphora," also in *Contemporary Perspectives in the Philosophy of Language*.

fact *about* semantics, as part of the *Metasemantics* of Pig-Latin (or perhaps, for those who prefer working from below to working from above, as part of the *Foundations of semantics* of Pig-Latin). Again, the fact that "nauseous" used to mean *nauseating* but is coming to mean *nauseated* is a historical, semantic fact about contemporary American English. But neither the reason why the change in semantic value has taken place nor the theory that gives the basis for claiming that there has been a change in meaning belongs to semantics. For present purposes let us settle on *metasemantics*.

Does the historical chain theory (or 'picture' as some are wont to say) of what determines the referent of a proper name belong to semantics or to metasemantics? The critical question seems to be: does the theory state a semantic value of proper names, or does it rather tell us the basis for determining a semantic value for a proper name. Those who believe that the semantic function of a name is completely exhausted by the fact that it *has* a particular referent will regard the historical chain theory as a part of metasemantics. Those who believe that a name *means* something like *the individual who lies at the other end of the historical chain that brought this token to me* will regard the historical chain theory as a part of semantics, as *giving* the meaning rather than as telling us how to discover it. In general, if a referent is all the meaning a name has, then any information used to *fix* the referent is metasemantical. *If* names have another kind of meaning, another kind of semantic value (mere cognitive value, if not identified with *Sinn* or with *character*, won't do), then the fact that certain information is used to fix the referent may well belong to semantics.[18]

Now what about the mechanisms of direct reference? In the case of an indexical, it seems clear that the rule that tells us how the referent varies from one context of use to another, for example the rule that tells us that "yesterday" always refers to the day before the day of utterance, is a part of the meaning of the indexical. It is this kind of meaning that I call *character*. To argue that character belongs to metasemantics, one would have to regard indexicals as systematically ambiguous and as having no meaning at all outside a particular context of use. This is a view that seems reasonable for *generic names*, the kind of name that all us Davids have in common. But it is decidedly implausible for indexicals.

---

[18] It is interesting to note that historical chains also have a use in what we might call *metasyntax*. They give the basis for saying that various utterances are utterances of the same word. I will return to historical chains in section IV.

There is also the fact that there is a *logic* of indexicals, a logic whose semantically valid arguments deviate from the classically valid. This in itself seems to argue that the mechanisms by which directly referential expressions determine their referents belong to semantics?[19]

Demonstratives seem to me a less certain case, perhaps because my views about their semantics is less certain. However, I do think that the indexical model—a common meaning for all uses of, say, "you", which then determines a referent in a particular context of use—is closer to the truth than the generic name model according to which "you" would be a meaningless symbol available to use in dubbing whoever one addresses.

This suggests a related reason for wanting to place the mechanisms of direct reference outside of semantics. It is the analogy between these mechanisms, which determine the referent of expressions that already bear meaning, and the methods available to *create* meaningful expressions from empty syntactical forms, by dubbings, definitions, and the like. Especially in the case of a true demonstrative, one may feel— wrongly, I believe—that one is *assigning* a meaning to an otherwise empty form. If content were all there is to meaning, then, since the mechanisms of direct reference do determine content, it would be reasonable to claim that such mechanisms belong to metasemantics. But in general, it is incorrect to equate meaning with content, and it is certainly incorrect in the case of indexicals.[20]

So, as between semantics and metasemantics, I remain of the view that the theory of the mechanisms of direct reference, at least as that theory is developed in *Demonstratives*, in terms of character and content, belongs to semantics.

A second interesting question is whether to call the theory of these mechanisms *semantics* or *pragmatics*. The central role of the notion *context of use* in determining content might incline one to say that the theory of character is semantics, and the theory of content is pragmatics. But *truth* is a property of contents, and one wouldn't want to be caught advocating a pragmatic theory of truth. The problem is that on my analysis, the mechanisms of direct reference operate *before* the familiar semantical notions of truth and denotation come into play. If I continue

---

[19] Or does it? What *does* the fact that there is an interesting logic of indexicals tell us about the taxonomic place of character? If there is no interesting logic of names, does that tell us something?

[20] It may be correct in the case of proper names, though even there I would be more inclined to equate meaning with referent and to say that referent determines content. I will return to the distinction between the assignment of meaning and the evaluation of meaning in the final section.

to think, as Carnap taught me,[21] that the overall theory of a language should be constructed with syntax at the base, semantics built upon that, and pragmatics built upon semantics, I am faced with a dilemma. The mechanisms of direct reference certainly are not *post*semantical. But equally surely they are not syntactical. Thus I put them in the bottom layer of semantics.[22]

Whether semantics or pragmatics, it is important to emphasize that there are two roads from singular terms to individuals. The road through what is said, through the propositional component, through content. And the direct road, outside of what is said, outside content. Both roads belong to the *rules* of the language, and not to the vagaries of individual difference among language users. Both connect language to the world.

How do the two roads figure in names?

In *Demonstratives* I inquire into the semantic mechanisms whereby indexicals and demonstratives are connected to their referents. How might an analogous discussion of names proceed? Without prejudice to any ultimate issues of semantics versus metasemantics, we might begin with a frankly metasemantical inquiry into naming (what I elsewhere[23] call "dubbing") and the process by which a given name can change its referent over time (if, as seems to be the case, it can). These are matters on which, in theory, Fregeans and Direct Reference theorists might agree.

There is a second question: Does the mechanism whereby the referent of a name is determined belong to semantics, as does character, or to metasemantics, as does the mechanism of meaning change? And if the answer is "semantics", there is the third question: Is the mechanism a part of what is said when the name is used? Or, are names transparent so that only the referent itself figures in what is said? It is on this question that direct reference theorists confront Fregeans.[24]

---

[21] *Introduction to Semantics* (Cambridge, Mass.: Harvard University Press, 1942), p. 9.

[22] The time may have come to rethink what I think Carnap taught me.

[23] In "Bob and Carol and Ted and Alice."

[24] Note that the outcome of the initial discussion may prejudice this tertiary question. Even if the mechanism by which a name is connected to its referent is taken to be a part of semantics, if the mechanism characterizes the referent from the perspective of the context of use, as does the character of an indexical, rather than from a world perspective, it may not be suitable to play the role of propositional constituent. Thus the result of the first inquiry may argue for a direct reference answer to the third question.

Finally, there is the question: Is the expression a rigid designator? This again is a matter on which we may all agree.

In this last connection it is important to see, as I earlier did not consistently see, that even one who believes that a name is connected to its referent by a description that the speaker associates with the name and who further believes that this description is *included as part of what is said when the name is used* can achieve rigidity, even obstinate rigidity, through the use of rigidifying operators. Thus, a Fregean who takes the name "Aristotle" to have as its sense *the pupil of Plato and teacher of Alexander the Great* need only add something like *actuality* to the content in order to account for the rigidity of proper names. We then have something like *the actual pupil of Plato and teacher of Alexander the Great* as the propositional component. Rigid designation without direct reference.[25] Well ... not quite *entirely* without direct reference, since the rigidifying operator seems to involve some form of direct reference. But certainly the *name* has not come out directly referential.

But are names merely rigid and not transparent? I, of course, believe not. In some cases arguments that have been given for rigidity can be shown actually to support the stronger claim of transparency, but I will not take up those arguments here.

A generic argument for transparency

There is, however, one generic argument for transparency which seems to apply in many cases of alleged direct reference. It is not a *decisive* argument. Rather, it is a challenge to those who maintain a contrary view.

Many users of the so-called directly referential expressions lack a real understanding of the exact mechanism or rule of reference by which the referent is determined. Though we act *in conformity* with some such rule, we do not invariably know the rule in the sense of being able to articulate it.[26] If one could articulate all the cultural rules one conformed

---

[25] I think that this form of rigidity, logical rather than mathematical or metaphysical, falls under what Kripke now calls *de jure* rigidity, which he describes as "the reference of a designator [being] *stipulated* to be a single object, whether we are speaking of the actual world or of a counterfactual situation" (*Naming and Necessity*, footnote 21 to the new Preface). Note that such descriptions can be used to stipulate the constituents of a possible world, as in "Suppose that the actual author had plagiarized the actual plagiarizer."

[26] This is contrary to my claim in *Demonstratives* that the character of pure indexicals is known to every competent speaker. There I claimed that Character = Linguistic Meaning. I still believe that Character captures an important sense of

to, anthropology would be a much easier discipline. In the case of syntax, it is even more obvious that we act in accordance with a complex set of rules which most of us could not even begin to articulate. Children certainly master the use of indexicals, demonstratives, and proper names well before they develop the rather sophisticated conceptual apparatus needed to undertake explicit semantical investigations. If we don't know what the semantical rule is, how could it be part of what we say when we use the relevant expression?

So long as we were able to cling to the illusion that words like "I" and "Aristotle" abbreviate simple descriptions that are immediately available to introspection, we could think that anyone who used such an expression knew how it secured its reference and might express this knowledge in using the word. But who still thinks that nowadays?

The notion of Content is central to my account

To recapitulate: the issue is not whether the information used to determine the referent is descriptive or not. It is rather whether the relevant information, of whatever form, is a part of what is said. Opening an alternative semantic road to reference, one that does not run through content but may nevertheless play a role in the analysis of cognition (belief, knowledge, etc.), may in the end help us all, Fregean and non-Fregean alike, to reach a deeper understanding of the puzzling phenomena that challenged Frege.

As is apparent, the notion of content is central to my way of explaining direct reference. I know that there are some who reject the notion of content. I can't prove that my way of organizing the theoretical apparatus is indispensable. Surely it isn't. But there are observations, intuitions if you will, both in the text of *Demonstratives* and in the formal logic, for which every theory must account. This *is* indispensable.

Are dthat-terms directly referential?

Some semi-technical meditations on dthat-terms may help to illuminate the notions of content and of direct reference.

As parents soon realize, any worthwhile creation quickly becomes autonomous. Recently I have found myself bemused by my own uses of "dthat".

Linguistic Meaning, but I have become more sceptical about the competence of competent speakers and about our access to what our words mean.

Two interpretations of the syntax and semantics of "dthat"

The penultimate paragraph of section IV of *Demonstratives* warns that the possible world semantics of the formal system in section XVIII obscures the distinction between direct reference and rigid designation. The representation of content as a function from possible worlds does not allow us to distinguish between a directly referential expression and one that is merely obstinately rigid. Both cases are represented by the same function, a constant function. There are two separate reasons for this. First, in this representation the content of a syntactically complex expression does not reflect that complexity. I call this the problem of *multiplying through*, as when the content of "4×(5+4)+8×(7-2)+6" is represented by a constant function to 82. Second, even for syntactically simple expressions, the functional representation captures only the obstinately rigid designation, there is no further distinction among obstinately rigid designators that marks the directly referential ones.[27]

The representation in possible world semantics tempts us to confuse direct reference and obstinately rigid designation.[28] Could anyone have confused them after the clear warning of section IV? Could I have? Yes.

This is very unfortunate, because I coined the term "direct reference" just in order to keep the distinction clear. I find the confusion most evident in connection with dthat-terms, about whose syntax and interpretation I seem to equivocate. On one interpretation, "dthat" is a directly referential singular term and the content of the associated description is no part of the content of the dthat-term. On another interpretation, "dthat" is syntactically an operator that requires syntactical completion by a description in order to form a singular term.[29]

---

[27] If, as some have hypothesized, an expression is directly referential if and only if it is syntactically simple and obstinately rigid, then the second problem is spurious.

[28] If so, why use it? First, because the functional representation is *sufficient to do the work* of *Demonstratives*, namely to show that character and content must be distinguished and to develop a coherent theory within which some unconventional claims about logic, belief, and modality could be grounded. Second, because it is a precise and reliable tool, within the scope of its representational limitations.

[29] Properly speaking, since descriptions are singular terms rather than formulas, "dthat" would be a functional expression rather than an operator. But I wish I *had* made "dthat" into an operator for *this* usage. I wish I had made it into a variable binding operator for which I would write "dthat $x\,Fx$" instead of writing "dthat[the $x\,Fx$]". Then there would have been a much clearer distinction between the two uses of "dthat", and I would not have been led into temptation.

In *Demonstratives* dthat-terms are eliminable in favor of definite descriptions plus the Actually and Now operators (Remark 13, section XIX). It should be noted that this result is not fundamental. It is dependent on the possibilist treatment

If "dthat" is an operator

If "dthat" is an operator, and if the description, which constitutes the operand and thus syntactically completes the singular term, induces a complex element into content, then the correct way to describe "dthat" is as a rigidifier. Complete dthat-terms would be rigid, in fact *obstinately* rigid. In this case the proposition would not carry the individual itself into a possible world but rather would carry instructions to run back home and get the individual who there satisfies certain specifications. The complete dthat-term would then be a rigid description which induces a complex 'representation' of the referent into the content; it would not be directly referential. The *operator* "dthat" might still be regarded as *involving* direct reference, though its own referent would not be the individual denoted by the complete dthat-term, but, like that of all operators, would be of an abstract, higher-order functional type.[30]

---

of variables in the formal semantics. The variables range over all possible individuals, and a primitive predicate of existence is introduced to represent the varying domains of the different possible worlds. This form of language is more expressive than one in which at each world, the variables range only over the individuals of that world and $\ulcorner \beta \, exists \urcorner$ is expressed by $\ulcorner \exists x \, x = \beta \urcorner$. I now incline toward a form of language which preserves the distinction between what *is* (i.e., what the variables range over) and what *exists*, but which does not automatically assume that all possible individuals have *being* (i.e., does not assume that the variables range over all possible individuals).

[30] The operators "it is actually the case that" and "it is now the case that" could also be thought of as rigidifiers on this model. In all three cases I am somewhat uncomfortable calling the *operator* directly referential, though they certainly seem to contain a directly referential *element*. Perhaps, in view of the highly abstract nature of their content, the content should be thought of as a complex, only one part of which is induced by direct reference. The operator "it is now the case that" would then be seen as a syntactically complex application of the grammatical formative, "it is the case at __ that" to the directly referential term "now". And similarly for the operator "it is actually the case that", which would be seen as a syntactical combination involving application of the same grammatical formative to the term "actuality". Such a treatment would comport better with the suggestion that only names, including "now", "actuality", etc., are directly referential.

Nathan Salmon points out that if one wished to treat species names like "horse" as directly referential, and as having the species *Equus caballus* as referent, it would be required to adopt a similar device regarding the predicate "is a horse", treating it as a syntactically complex application of the grammatical formative "is a" (a kind of copula) to the directly referential term "horse". Salmon is sceptical, but to me this seems natural. The content of the predicate "is a horse" would then be a complex formed of copulation with the species *E. caballus*.

The desire to treat a variety of lexical items as directly referential requires more attention to the distinction between grammatical formatives and those 'pure'

If "dthat" is a demonstrative surrogate

The operator interpretation is not what I originally intended. The word "dthat" was intended to be a surrogate for a true demonstrative, and the description which completes it was intended to be a surrogate for the completing demonstration. On this interpretation "dthat" is a syntactically complete singular term that requires no *syntactical* completion by an operand. (A 'pointing', being extralinguistic, could hardly be a part of syntax.) The description completes the *character* of the associated occurrence of "dthat", but makes no contribution to content. Like a whispered aside[31] or a gesture, the description is thought of as off-the-record (i.e., off the *content* record). It determines and directs attention to what is being said, but the manner in which it does so is not strictly *part* of what is asserted. The semantic role of the *description* is pre-propositional; it induces no complex, descriptive element into content. "Dthat" is no more an operator than is "I", though neither has a referent unless semantically 'completed' by a context in the one case and a demonstration in the other. The referent of "dthat" is the individual described (rather than an abstract, higher-order function). It is directly referential.

The operator interpretation is more 'natural' for the formal system

The predominant interpretation of "dthat" in the text seems to be as demonstrative surrogate except, I am sorry to say, in the formal system. There, the natural interpretation is as rigidifying operator. The reason for this is that the 'completing' description has a syntactical reality within the formal language. It plays an essential role in the logic, for example in the theorem of Remark 13 showing that dthat-terms are eliminable. Although Frege claimed that the context of use was part of

---

lexical items that might be regarded as naming an abstract object, like a species or a color. I would treat "is a bachelor" in the same way as "is a horse". While acknowledging the *metaphysical* differences between a species and *bachelorhood*, the syntactical unity of "horse" and "bachelor" suggests an analogous *semantical* treatment. Keith Donnellan makes this point in "Putnam and Kripke on Natural Kinds," in *Knowledge and Mind*, ed. C. Ginet and S. Shoemaker (Oxford: Oxford University Press, 1983), pp. 84–104, especially section III. Also, I would go further in syntactical decomposition and first form the complex denoting phrase "a horse" (with appropriate content) before forming the predicate "is a horse".

[31] This is how Kripke characterized the description which completes a dthat-term in his lecture at the conference.

"the means of expression" of a thought,[32] he never, to my knowledge, attempted to incorporate "the pointing of fingers, hand movements, glances" into logical syntax. Can an expression such as the description in a dthat-term appear in logical syntax but make no contribution to semantical form? It would seem strange if it did. But there is, I suppose, no strict contradiction in such a language form.

If there are two different interpretations of "dthat" in *Demonstratives*, they seem to be run together in footnote 72. But maybe there aren't. *Probably* there aren't. Probably, I was just farsighted in envisioning yet-to-be-realized forms of formal semantics. I earlier held that my views were inconsistent. I now deny that my views are inconsistent![33]

II. Do Demonstrations Complete Demonstratives?

In *Demonstratives* I took the demonstration, "typically, a (visual) presentation of a local object discriminated by a pointing," to be criterial for determining the referent of a demonstrative. While recognizing the teleological character of most pointing—it is typically directed by the speaker's intention to point at a perceived individual on whom he has focused—I claimed that the *demonstration* rather than the *directing intention* determined the referent.[34]

I am now inclined to regard the directing intention, at least in the case of perceptual demonstratives, as criterial, and to regard the demonstration as a mere *externalization* of this inner intention. The externalization is an aid to communication, like speaking more slowly and loudly, but is of no semantic significance.[35]

---

[32] Gottlob Frege "The Thought: A Logical Inquiry," *Mind* 65 (1956): p. 296. Original German publication in *Beiträge zur Philosophie des Deutschen Idealismus* (1918–19).

[33] Thanks to Nathan Salmon and Joseph Almog for help with this section.

[34] This view goes back to the case, discussed in "Dthat", of Carnap's picture. I now regard this as a rather complex, atypical case.

[35] I contrast *no* semantic significance with the fundamental idea of direct reference: that there are matters of semantic significance which do not appear in content. In my earlier treatment, I regarded demonstrations as off-the-record in terms of *content*, but as semantically relevant in determining *character*. I now regard them as totally off-the-record in regard to the semantics of demonstratives. I now see demonstrations as playing the same role for true demonstratives as does pointing at oneself when using the first-person pronoun.

We might think of the demonstration on the model of a term in *apposition* to the demonstrative. Such a term appears to duplicate the demonstrative syntactically, but its semantic contribution is to a subordinate, side remark; its semantic contribution to the main clause seems to be only to hold targets for anaphora. (I know

I had rejected this view earlier, in part because it seemed to confound what Donnellan might call the *referential* and the *attributive* uses of a demonstrative. It seemed to me that this should not happen in a proper semantical theory. I recently realized that the distinction still held. In the case of a perceptual demonstrative, the directing intention is aimed at a perceived object. This object may or may not be the object the speaker has in mind. We can distinguish between Donnellan's kind of having-in-mind and perceptual focus.[36]

A benefit of the view that the demonstration is a mere externalization of the perceptual intention, which determines the referent, is that it offers a new perspective on one of Donnellan's most compelling cases of referential use.

> Suppose someone is at a party and, seeing an interesting looking person holding a martini glass, one asks, "Who is the man drinking a martini?" If it should turn out that there is only water in the glass, one has nevertheless asked a question about a particular person.[37]

Because of the importance of the perceptual element it is tempting to think of this case in terms of demonstratives. Here the directing intention is aimed at the interesting looking person seen holding a martini glass. Had the speaker pointed and said "Who is that man?", the case would have raised no question of referential use. But suppose, having been taught that it is rude to point at people, the normal mode of externalizing the intention is unavailable. What to do? He cannot simply say, "Who is that man?" with *no* externalization. This would baffle his auditor, who would say, "Which man?". To which the original speaker would have to reply, "The man with the martini." So he shortens the dialogue and uses the description "the man with the martini" as a substitute for the demonstration. Here the speaker might equally well have said, "Who is that man with the martini?" or, "Who is that?" followed by an appositive, parenthetical, whispered "(the man with the martini)."

Now according to my new view of what determines the referent of a demonstrative, the demonstration (here, the description) is there only to

---

of no well-developed semantics of apposition; it seems a topic worth pursuing.)

[36] Just as it is possible to mis*describe* a perceived object, for example, as a martini when it is really only water in a martini glass, so it is also possible to mis*recognize* one. For example, I may have you in mind, and believing that it is you whom I see hiding under the bed, begin berating you. Even if it was not you under the bed, might it not still be you whom I criticized?

[37] Keith Donnellan, "Reference and Definite Descriptions".

help *convey* an intention and plays no *semantical* role at all. We might sum up the case by saying the speaker had a demonstrative intention and, constrained by the conventions of polite behavior, substituted a description for the usual pointing.[38] The slight misdescription has no more effect on the determination of the referent of the tacit demonstrative than would a slight error in aim have had on the determination of the referent of a vocalized demonstrative accompanied by a pointing. In both cases the referent is properly determined by the perceptual intention. In neither case is anything semantical at stake in the description or the pointing. All that is at stake is the accuracy of *communicating* what was said.

What makes this analysis especially intriguing is that this classical case of the referential use of a description can be seen as an *attributive* use of a tacit perceptual demonstrative.

Not all of Donnellan's cases can be accounted for in this way. And in any case, as I have already stated, I believe the distinction between referential and attributive uses is fundamental. But still the idea of finding a role for nonsemantic, communication facilitators, and accounting for referential uses of definite descriptions in this way, is appealing. The theory of direct reference, with its prepropositional semantics, seems especially open to such off-the-record elements in language.

Occurrences

As I carefully noted in *Demonstratives*,[39] my notion of an *occurrence* of an expression in a context—the mere combination of the expression with the context—is not the same as the notion, from the theory of speech acts, of an *utterance* of an expression by the agent of a context. An occurrence requires no utterance. Utterances take time, and are produced one at a time; this will not do for the analysis of validity. By the time an agent finished uttering a very, very long true premise and began uttering the conclusion, the premise may have gone false. Thus even the most trivial of inferences, P therefore P, may appear invalid. Also, there are sentences which express a truth in certain contexts, but not if uttered. For example, "I say nothing." Logic and semantics

---

[38] A quite different summary would deny the demonstrative element and say that the conventions of polite behavior constrain the speaker to use descriptions and not to use demonstratives. This yields Donnellan's original analysis. Accept my summary. (Is there a basis in the speaker's intentions for claiming that a description is, or is not, being used in apposition to a tacit demonstrative?)

[39] Section XIII.

are concerned not with the vagaries of actions, but with the verities of meanings.[40]

Problems with occurrences of true demonstratives

On the theory of true demonstratives in *Demonstratives*, a demonstration accompanies every demonstrative and determines its referent. On my current view, the referent of a true demonstrative is determined by the utterer's intention. But if occurrences don't require utterances, how can we be sure that the requisite intention exists in every possible context? We can't!

A version of this problem already existed in a proposal considered in *Demonstratives* for the formal treatment of "you".[41] The idea is that the context simply be enriched by adding a new feature, which we might call the *addressee*. But suppose there is no addressee. Suppose the agent intends no one, e.g., Thomas Jefferson, dining alone, or surrounded by friends but not *addressing* any of them. Or, suppose the agent is hallucinatory and, though addressing 'someone', no one is there.[42] The problem is that there is no *natural* addressee in such contexts, and thus no natural feature to provide within a formal semantics.

A refined conception of Context for true demonstratives

There are really two problems here, calling for separate solutions. The first is the case of the absent intention. In this case one would want to mark the context as *inappropriate* for an occurrence of "you", and rede-

---

[40] I am unclear even as to what arguments *ought* to come out as utterance-valid (as opposed to occurrence-valid). There are different notions of utterance-validity corresponding to different assumptions and idealizations. With no idealizations, the rules of repetition and double negation become invalid. This seems hopeless. Should we assume then that utterances take no time? (We might imagine writing out premises and conclusion ahead of time and holding up the paper at the moment of assertion.) Should we assume that the agent knows the language? Should we assume that the agent *asserts* the premises and conclusion, that he *believes* them? This last is related to the question: should "*P*, but I don't believe it" (Moore's paradox) come out to be an utterance-contradiction? It certainly is not an occurrence-contradiction.

[41] Possible Refinement #4 of section XIX combined with the 'indexical theory of demonstratives' of section XVI. The idea is considered, not advocated.

[42] I have in mind the classic hallucination involving an imagined person, not a hallucination *of* an actual person who happens not to be present.

fine validity as truth-in-all-*appropriate*-possible-contexts.[43] The second
is the case of the hallucinatory agent. Here the context seems appropriate enough, the agent is making no *linguistic* mistake in using "you".
But the occurrence should be given a 'null' referent.[44]

Another proposal I have heard is just to *impose* an intention on
the agent whether he has it or not. Put more gently, this is a logician's
proposal; just *assign* a referent. There are two problems with this. First,
if it is *possible* for the agent to intend the proposed addressee, there will
already be a possible context in which he does. So nothing is lost by
ignoring the context in which he doesn't. And if it is *not* possible for
the agent to intend the proposed addressee, the imposition seems much
too heavy handed. (We don't want an impossibility to come out true.)
Second, if we are impatient with intention and just want to *assign* away
and get on with the logic, we could formulate the expression with free
variables instead of demonstratives. And we should. Why pretend that
real demonstratives are nothing more than free variables? If the logic
of real demonstratives turns out to be identical with the logic of free
variables, well ... that's something that should *turn out*. It shouldn't
be presupposed.[45]

We must make one further refinement in our conception of a context
for a true demonstrative. The same demonstrative can be repeated, with
a distinct directing intention for each repetition of the demonstrative.
This can occur in a single sentence, "You, you, you, and you can leave,
but you stay", or in a single discourse, "You can leave. You must stay."
Such cases seem to me to involve an exotic kind of ambiguity, perhaps
unique to demonstratives (see below). Where different intentions are
associated with different syntactic occurrences[46] of a true demonstrative,
we would want to use distinct symbols in our formal language in order
to avoid equivocation.

Why do we not need distinct symbols to represent different syntactic occurrences of "today"?[47] If we speak slowly enough (or start just

---

[43] The idea, once broached, of defining validity in terms of *appropriate* contexts
might also be used to approach utterance-validity.

[44] There are several ways to accommodate this in a formal semantics. I am imagining
a treatment along the lines of my use of † in section XVIII of *Demonstratives*.

[45] There are morals to be drawn from these arguments. I urge the young author of
Demonstratives to take them to heart if he wishes to do serious work.

[46] I say *syntactic* occurrence to differentiate from my expression-in-a-context sense
of "occurrence".

[47] I choose "today" rather than "now" to avoid the distracting issue of the vagueness
of "now".

before midnight), a repetition of "today" will refer to a different day. But this is only because the context has changed. It is a mere technicality that utterances take time, a technicality that we avoid by studying expressions-in-a-context, and one that might also be avoided by tricks like writing it out ahead of time and then presenting it all at once. It is no part of the *meaning* of "today" that multiple syntactic occurrences must be associated with different contexts. In contrast, the meaning of a demonstrative requires that each syntactic occurrence be associated with a directing intention, several of which may be simultaneous. And if it happened to be true that we never held more than one such intention simultaneously, *that* would be the mere technicality. In fact, it is not true. In the aforementioned cases ("You, you, you, and you ..."), in which there is simultaneous perception of all addressees, I think it correct to say that are several distinct, simultaneous, directing intentions, indexed to distinct intended utterances of the demonstrative "you" (which are then voiced one at a time).

The basic fact here is that although we must face life one *day* at a time, we are not condemned to perceive or direct our attention to one *object* at a time. (If we were, the language of thought would be monadic predicate logic.)

Thus within the formal syntax we must have not one demonstrative "you", but a sequence of demonstratives, "you_1", "you_2", etc., and within the formal semantics the context must supply not a single addressee, but a sequence of addressees, some of which may be 'null' and all but a finite number of which would presumably be marked *inappropriate*.

We will need to be able to formulate sentences of the formal language in which different intentions are associated with different syntactic occurrences of a demonstrative, if we are to face the looming challenge of Frege's Problem, in which one who is simultaneously perceiving two parts of what may or may not be a single object asserts, "$That_1$ is $that_2$".[48]

The semantic role of directing intentions

What should we think of as the contextual feature relevant to the evaluation of a demonstrative? In the formal semantics, it may be taken to

---

[48] Consider, for example, a magician performing the 'sawing a woman in half' illusion. The audience sees someone's head sticking out of one end of a box and what appear to be someone's feet sticking out of the other end. "Is that person really *that* person?" they wonder.

be the demonstratum. But at the preformal level, I think of it as the *directing intention*. The directing intention is the element that differentiates the 'meaning' of one syntactic occurrence of a demonstrative from another, creating the *potential* for distinct referents, and creating the *actuality* of equivocation.[49] It also seems critical for the 'cognitive value' of a syntactic occurrence of a demonstrative, at least for the speaker. Note however that it is neither character, content, nor referent. In the case of the pure indexicals, "today", "here", etc., the relevant contextual feature is always the referent, and there doesn't seem to be any role, let alone a semantic role, for a comparable entity. Curiouser and curiouser!

In *Demonstratives* I accepted "tentatively and cautiously" what I called *the Fregean theory of demonstrations*. The demonstration—a 'manner of presentation' of an individual that was separable from any particular context and could be evaluated at other contexts and circumstances—supplied the character for the associated demonstrative.[50] A reason why I favored the Fregean theory of demonstrations was that the need for a completing demonstration distinguished the true demonstratives from the pure indexicals. A second reason was that the Fregean idea that *that very demonstration* might have picked out a different demonstratum, an idea that depended on the separability of a demonstration from a particular context, seemed to track very closely the cognitive uncertainties of "$that_1$ is $that_2$". This cognitive value appears in character, and thus as an aspect of meaning.

The need for a directing intention to determine the referent of a demonstrative still allows us to distinguish the true demonstratives from the pure indexicals. The parameters for the latter are brute facts of the context, like location and time. But if directing intentions are not separable and evaluable at other points (perhaps they are), the cognitive uncertainties of "$that_1$ is $that_2$" may no longer be an aspect of meaning. Should they be?

Linking true demonstratives

It is interesting to note that in natural language every new syntactic occurrence of a true demonstrative requires not just a referent-determining intention, but a *new* referent-determining intention. When two syntactic occurrences of a demonstrative appear to be linked to a single intention,

---

[49] I regard it as an equivocation whenever a new directing intention is involved, even if it directs a second syntactic occurrence of a demonstrative to the same referent.

[50] See sections XV and XVI of *Demonstratives*.

at least one must be anaphoric. When we wish to refer to the referent of an earlier demonstrative, we do not repeat the demonstrative, we use an anaphoric pronoun, "He [pointing] won't pass unless he [anaphoric pronoun] studies." The fact that demonstrative and anaphoric pronouns are homonyms may have led to confusion on this point. The case is clearer when the demonstrative is not homonymous with the anaphoric pronoun. Contrast, "This student [pointing] won't pass unless he [anaphoric pronoun] studies" with "This student [pointing] won't pass unless this student [pointing a second time at what is believed to be the same person] studies." The awkwardness of the second, shows that the way to *secure* a second reference to the referent of a demonstrative, is to use an anaphor.

This implies that it is impossible to utter an instance of the rule of Double Negation using a premise containing a demonstrative, "You stay. Therefore, it is not the case that you do not stay." We have a Hobson's choice. We can intend the "you" of the conclusion as anaphoric across the sentential barrier to the "You" of the premise (something we readily do in ordinary discourse, but are ill-prepared to do in formal logic).[51] In which case, the argument is valid, but not really an instance of Double Negation (at least not as we know and love it). Or, we can concentrate, try not to blink, and try to hold our attention on the same addressee, in the hope that we will succeed in targeting the same individual with the second demonstrative. (Can we ever be *certain* that they haven't pulled the old switcheroo?) In this case, the form of argument is really something like, "You$_1$ stay. Therefore, it is not the case that you$_2$ do not stay", and hence not valid. Even if we idealize the speed of speech, so that we are certain that they haven't pulled a switcheroo, the *form* of the argument is still not that of Double Negation because of the equivocation involved in the use of a second demonstrative.

Perhaps we should give up on Double Negation, and claim that the argument is a valid enthymeme with the implicit premise "You$_1$ = you$_2$", the premise we strove to make true by fixing our attention. "All right," said the tortoise to Achilles, "repeat the argument and this time remember to utter the additional premise."

The source of the difficulty is the principle, the correct principle,

---

[51] It would be good if our formal language allowed variables to be bound to arbitrary terms both within the sentence and across the sentential barrier in the way in which anaphoric reference takes place in natural language. The problem of how to do this in a suitably smooth way seems quite interesting.

that every new syntactic occurrence of a demonstrative (one that is not a disguised anaphoric pronoun) requires its own determining intention. The problem, in a nutshell, is that where demonstratives are involved, it doesn't seem possible to *avoid* equivocation. There is an understood, harmless, systematic equivocation built into the semantics of demonstratives in natural language. It is this that I termed "an exotic kind of ambiguity, perhaps unique to demonstratives."

For purposes of logic, on the other hand, it seems essential both to avoid equivocation and to allow any well-formed expression to have multiple syntactic occurrences (in antecedent and consequent, or in premise and conclusion) *without changing its semantical analysis.* The validity of the sentence "If you stay, you stay" (with no anaphors) depends on using the same intention to determine the referent of both occurrences of the demonstrative "you". Just as multiple occurrences of "now" in a single argument must be referenced to the same time parameter, so multiple occurrences of the same demonstrative must be referenced to the same directing intention. Otherwise the language would suffer the same systemic equivocation that natural language does, and there would be no logic, at least none with Double Negation and Repetition and the like. Using the refined conception of context described above, it is easy to write semantical rules that give the same analysis to recurrences of the same demonstrative (what is hard is to write rules that don't). It seems certain that this is how we ought to proceed.

But does it leave our logic vulnerable to a charge of misrepresentation? What is it that we hope to learn from such a logic? I don't think we can regard this as an idealization comparable to that involved in referencing all occurrences of "now" to a single instant. To assume that one intention can drive two occurrences of a demonstrative seems more falsification than idealization.

I hope that there is a key to this problem in my earlier remark that logic and semantics are concerned not with the vagaries of actions, but with the verities of meanings. There is something I'm not understanding here, and it may be something very fundamental about the subject matter of logic.

III. What is Context?

Context provides parameters

Some directly referential expressions, most notably the indexicals, require that the value of a certain parameter be given before a determinate element of content is generated. Context of Use is this parameter. For example, the content of the word "today" is a function of the time of the context of use. If we think of the formal role played by context within the model-theoretic semantics, then we should say that context *provides* whatever parameters are needed.[52] From this point of view, context is a package of whatever parameters are needed to determine the referent, and thus the content, of the directly referential expressions of the language.

An assignment of values to variables is the parameter needed to determine the referent of a variable

Taking context in this more abstract, formal way, as providing the parameters needed to generate content, it is natural to treat the assignment of values to free occurrences of variables as simply one more aspect of context. My point is taxonomic. The element of content associated with a free occurrence of a variable is generated by an assignment. Thus, for variables, the assignment supplies the parameters that determines content just as the context supplies the time and place parameters that determine content for the indexicals "now" and "here".

The assignment, as I am arguing we should conceive of it, is not 'evaluating' the variable at a world, rather it is generating an element of content, and it is the content which is then evaluated at a world.[53] Content is generated at a context, and each context is associated with a particular possible world.[54] The agent, time, and place are all drawn from that world. Similarly, an assignment associated with a particular

---

[52] This, rather than saying that context *is* the needed parameter, which seems more natural for the pretheoretical notion of a *context of use*, in which each parameter has an interpretation as a natural feature of a certain region of the world.

[53] I know, I know! There are other ways to treat assignments, but they obscure my point. Having returned to the semantics of free variables, it may seem that I am obsessed with the topic, but bear with me.

[54] When I revert to the standard "possible worlds" nomenclature rather than the "possible circumstance of evaluation" terminology of *Demonstratives*, it is in order to connect certain points I wish to make with the standard literature. I use the two phrases synonymously.

context may be taken to assign only values that exist in the world of the context. Once such a value is assigned, that is, once a content is determined, the content can, of course, be evaluated at worlds in which the value does not exist.

In arguing that assignments of values to variables play a theoretical role analogous to contexts, I harp upon my theme that free variable can be taken as paradigms of direct reference. Though the theme was stated in *Demonstratives*, I did not then recognize how thoroughgoing it was, because I did not then think of free variables in the robust way I now do, as demonstrative uses of pronouns. Not as real demonstratives, which require a directing intention from the agent of the context, but as a kind of *faux demonstrative*, one which looks real until you check into the origin of its value.

As remarked above, free occurrences of pronouns in meaningful discourse are demonstratives. But a free occurrence of an *anaphoric* pronoun would literally be meaningless. In our logical formalisms, variables play the anaphoric role. Thus a free occurrence of a variable is the mark of an incompletely interpreted expression. The case we are dealing with here is the free occurrence of a variable in a premise or conclusion of an argument. Do not confuse this case, the case with the interpretational gap, with the case in which a *bound* occurrence of a variable *appears* free because we are focusing attention on a subformula. It is the second case, the case of *bound* variables, for which the Tarski apparatus of *satisfaction* and *assignments* was originally designed. In that case there is no interpretational gap; it is the *quantifier* (or other variable binder) that is being interpreted, and we must get it right. So the rules for evaluating *bound* occurrences of variables are another story entirely, and an irrelevant one.

That which is interpretively unconstrained is available for office, and those familiar with logic will be aware that authors of deductive systems have chosen varying paths in their treatment of free variables. Some prohibit them entirely. Some treat them as if they were bound by invisible, outer, universal quantifiers, what is sometimes called the *generality* interpretation. Some treat them as if they were individual constants. My own treatment uses the familiar idea of an *assignment*, taken from the Tarski apparatus for the treatment of bound variables. I even confine the values of the variables to the domain of quantification (assuming the domain of quantification consists of what exists). This seems natural enough. But it does, as will be seen, have surprising consequences.

The discussion of parameters completes the analogy between free variables and indexicals. From an abstract formal point of view, they are highly analogous. Both are *parametric*, their content varies as the parameter varies. If we package all parameters under the heading *context*, an odd but interesting thing to do, we could even claim that content varies with context, the mark of indexicality. (Note that not all directly referential expressions are parametric; proper names are not.)[55]

These formal analogies should not cause us to lose sight of the fundamental difference between free variables and indexicals.[56] Indexicals are real, meaning-bearing elements of language. Free variables are not; they are artifacts of our formalism. Assignments are *stipulative*; they have no fact-of-the-matter parameter as do the pure indexicals and true demonstratives. Indexicals are *perspectival*, their content is dependent on the speaker's point of view, the context of utterance. Free variables are not *perspectival* in any but the most attenuated metaphorical sense. It is for these reasons that I use the term *parametric* for what indexicals and free variables have in common.[57]

The rule of Necessitation fails for free variables

One of the things that delighted me about indexicals was the convincingly deviant modal logic. As shown in *Demonstratives*, the rule of Necessitation:

If ϕ is valid, then $\Box\phi$ is also valid.

fails in the presence of indexicals.[58] The same rule also fails in the presence of free variables. If our assignments to free variables draw their values from the domain of quantification, then

$$\exists y\ y=x$$

is valid, but if the domain of quantification varies from possible world to world,

---

[55] Not, at least on my interpretation. One who thought of proper names as *generic* (as standing for any individual so named) until set into a context of use would be thinking of them as parametric.

[56] It should be clear that I am exploring the notion of a content-generating parameter, not insisting on one way of developing the semantics of free variables.

[57] Perhaps the closest analogy is that developed above (in the subsection: "The paradigm of the variable") between the free variable, the 'free' pronoun, and the demonstrative, whose referent must be stipulated by a directing intention. Even in this case, however, there remains the puzzling problem of the seeming semantic role of the directing intention. In the case of an assignment, it is surely only the value that matters.

[58] For example, take ϕ to be "I am here now" or "I exist."

$$\Box \exists y \ y = x$$

is not valid.[59]

Harry Deutsch points out a related feature of the logic of free variables. On the present interpretation, although the basic *quantifier* logic for variables is classical, a free logic is simulated within the scope of the necessity operator. Thus, although

$$(\forall x F x \rightarrow F y)$$

is valid,

$$\Box(\forall x F x \rightarrow F y)$$

is not. An additional antecedent that is characteristic of free logic is required within the scope of $\Box$:

$$\Box((\exists x \ x = y \land \forall x F x) \rightarrow F y).$$

The failure of the rule of Necessitation in the presence of free variables results from the play between context (if the assignment parameter is taken as part of context) and point of evaluation. I view it as indicating that a parametric expression, likely to be directly referential, is at work.[60]

The actual-world as an aspect of Context

The world of the context of use—what is taken for model-theoretic purposes to be the *actual-world*—plays a dual role in the logic. It is the parameter that the context provides for the indexical operator "it is actually the case that." It is thus a *generation parameter* required to fix

---

[59] Using a domain of quantification that varies from world to world deviates from the formulation in *Demonstratives*. As noted earlier, in *Demonstratives* I used a fixed domain, thought of as including all 'possible' individuals, along with a predicate "*exists*" whose extension could vary from world to world.

[60] There is another, more sceptical, way to view failures of the rule—as an indicator of unclarity regarding the interpretation of free variables. This may be Kripke's outlook in his pellucid discussion of the Barcan formula in "Semantical Considerations on Modal Logic," *Acta Philosophica Fennica* (1963): 83–94. His analysis assumes the generality interpretation of free variables (on which the rule of Necessitation does in fact hold). He then shows that an apparent counterinstance to the rule is based on an incorrect formulation of the rule in this environment. As a corrective he proposes to formulate the system of derivation in a way that prohibits free variables in asserted formulas. He does not question the validity of the rule. I, being familiar with other counterinstances to the rule, have no difficulty with an interpretation of free variables that simply makes the rule invalid.

a determinate content for sentences containing the indexical operator. At the same time, and quite independently, it is also an *evaluation parameter* that plays a special role in the notion of validity. The latter is its more fundamental role, a role that would be required even if the language contained no indexicals for which the actual-world was needed as a generation parameter.[61]

Validity is truth-no-matter-what-the-circumstances-were-*in-which-the-sentence-was-used*. As I would put it, *validity* is universal truth in all *contexts* rather than universal truth in all possible worlds. Where indexicals are involved we cannot even speak of truth until the sentence has been set in a context. But it may appear that for a modal language *without* indexicals, without expressions that require a parameter, the notion of a context of use has no bearing. This is not correct. Truth in every model means truth in the 'designated' world of every model. This 'designated' world, the world at which truth is assessed, plays the role of actual-world. It is all that remains of context when the generation parameters are stripped away. But it does remain.

Perhaps this is more easily seen if we add the indexical operator "it is actually the case that" to the language. It is then apparent that the 'actuality' referenced by this operator is what we have become accustomed to refer to as the "designated" world.

The notion of the *actual-world* can be obtained in either of two ways. As I did, by starting from a full-blown language containing indexicals, deriving the notion of a context of use from its role in the semantics of indexicals, and then recognizing that truth, absolute truth in a model, is assessed at the world-of-the-context, i.e., the actual-world; or alternatively, by starting from a modal language *without* indexicals, recognizing that truth, absolute truth in a model, is assessed at the 'designated' world, and noticing that if we *were* to add the actuality operator this designated world would be the actual-world. Briefly, we can come upon the notion either in its guise as 'world of the context of use' or in its guise as 'designated world'. On either approach, the notion of actual-world plays a special role in validity. It is the indispensable residue of the notion of *context*.

The terminology "context of use" evokes agents and utterances; the terminology "it is actually the case that" does not. There is, however, this common, underlying idea, one which I continue to think of as

---

[61] Within the formal system of *Demonstratives*, a content is evaluated at both a world and a time. Within that system, what is said here of the world of the context also holds of the time of the context.

perspectival—the actual world is where we actually are . . . now. Recognizing that there are these two faces to the one notion makes me want to differentiate the possible worlds that can play the role of actual-world from those that are 'merely' possible, for example, by requiring that the former but not the latter not be empty; but not all will agree that there should be such differentiation. It is, in the end, a question of what you want to *do* with your logic.

Why the deviant logic?

The intuitive distinction between the actual-world, in which the content is generated, and all those possible-worlds in which the content can be evaluated,[62] lies at the heart of such interesting logical phenomena as the failure of Necessitation. Any feature of a possible world which flows from the fact that it contains the context of use may yield validity without necessity. Such features need not depend on the contingent existence of individuals. For example, in the actual-world, the speaker, referred to by "I", must be located at the place referred to by "here" at the time referred to by "now". Hence "I am here now" is valid. But this requirement holds *only* in the actual-world, the world in which the content is expressed. Hence, what is expressed by the sentence need not be necessary. No 'existence questions' cloud this case.

I find it useful to think of validity and necessity as *never* applying to the same entity. Keeping in mind that an actual-world is simply the circumstance of a context of use, consider the distinction between:

(V)   No matter what the context were, ϕ would express a truth in the circumstances of that context

and:

(N)   The content that ϕ expresses in a given context would be true no matter what the circumstances were.

The former states a property of sentences (or perhaps characters): validity; the latter states a property of the content of a sentence (a proposition): necessity.

The nonstandard logic of *Demonstratives* follows from two features of the semantics of context and circumstance. The first is the possibility

---

[62] Joseph Almog emphasizes this distinction in "Naming without Necessity," *Journal of Philosophy* (1986): 210–42.

that a given sentence might have a different content in different contexts. It is this that makes "I am here now" a valid *sentence*. And the second is the fact that not every possible circumstance of evaluation is associated with an (appropriate) possible context of use, in other words, not every possible-world is a possible actual-world. Though there may be circumstances in which no one exists, no possible context of use can occur in such circumstances. It is this that makes "Something exists" a valid sentence. Even if no indexical occurs in the language, the second feature puts bite into the notion of the actual-world.

These two features correspond to two kinds of a priori knowledge regarding the actual-world, knowledge that we lack for all other possible worlds. Corresponding to the first feature, there is our knowledge that certain *sentences* always express a truth regarding the world in which they are expressed. Corresponding to the second feature, there is our knowledge that certain *facts* always hold at a world containing a context. The latter is independent of the indexical resources of the language.[63]

A word for cognitive value

The contexts of *Demonstratives* are metaphysical, not cognitive. They reach well beyond the cognitive range of the agent. Any difference in world history, no matter how remote, requires a difference in context.[64]

In *Demonstratives* I tried to get at cognitive value through the notion of character.[65] When the twins, Castor and Pollux, each sincerely say, "My brother was born before I was," they are said to be in the same cognitive state but to believe different things.[66] Though the utterances of the twins have the same cognitive value (same character), they do not bear the same truth-value (nor have the same content). I found it attractive to follow Frege in using a strictly semantical concept (character), needed for other semantical purposes, to try to capture his idea of cognitive value.[67]

---

[63] The preceding material of this section resulted from a conversation with Harry Deutsch and Kit Fine.

[64] As noted, the entire world history is an aspect of context; it is the parameter for the indexical "Actually".

[65] I have been told that "cognitive" is not the right word for what I have in mind. (I have also been told that what I have in mind is not the right idea for what I am trying to do.) I am not committed to the word; I take it from Frege (who probably never used it.)

[66] As indicated in *Demonstratives*, my views on this have been influenced by John Perry.

[67] Even granting that we cannot *articulate* the rules of character for all directly

As in the case of content, the possible-worlds style of formal semantics in *Demonstratives* represents character as a function, in this case as a function from possible contexts of use. I continue to believe that proper names are not parametric, i.e., the *same name*[68] does not vary in referent from context to context.[69] Thus, the characters of two distinct proper names of the same individual would be represented by the same constant function, and thus, under the functional interpretation, coreferential names would not differ in character. Since it is indisputable that distinct proper names have distinct cognitive values,[70] the project of discriminating cognitive values of proper names by character is immediately defeated.[71]

Lately, I have been thinking that it may be a mistake to follow Frege in trying to account for differences in cognitive values strictly in terms of *semantic* values. Can distinctions in cognitive value be made in terms of the message without taking account of the medium? Or does the medium play a central role? On my view, the message—the *content*—of a proper name is just the referent. But the *medium* is the name itself.[72]

---

referring expressions, we may still recognize a difference in cognitive value when presented with a pair of terms of different character, there may still be a correlation between distinct characters and distinct cognitive values. Joseph Almog suggests that we might express the point by saying that cognitive value *supervenes* on character.

[68] A less obvious notion than may appear.

[69] A proposed counterinstance: If a name can change its referent over time, as "Madagascar" is said to have done, then would not that very name have had one referent in an early context and another in a recent context? (For a partial response see the discussion below of logically proper names.)

[70] It is on the rock of distinct cognitive values for distinct names that Frege erected his gossamer theory. Note that Frege's initial argument makes use only of the uninterpreted forms "a=a" and "a=b". The distinction between repetition of a single name and the use of two distinct names is already sufficient to make the points about *cognition* even before any examples (or even the notion of *Sinn*) are introduced.

[71] One could, of course, argue that distinct names do differ in character and abandon the idea that character represents only the *parametric* determination of reference, i.e., how content varies from context to context. The fact that *indexicals* are parametric, that their character can be represented as a function from possible contexts, would then be regarded as a special case. The danger of trying to find characterological differences in distinct proper names is that the notion of *character* either will slip over from semantics to metasemantics or will become an ad hoc pastiche. In either case the dignified reality of character as the fundamental semantical value for indexicals would be seriously diluted.

[2] In the case of indexicals, the character, which I took to represent cognitive value in *Demonstratives* may also be thought of as the medium by which content is generated (though character is semantic rather than syntactic in nature).

There are *linguistic* differences between "Hesperus" and "Phosphorus" even if there are no *semantic* differences. Note also that the syntactic properties of "Hesperus" and "Phosphorus", for example, their distinctness as *words*, are surer components of cognition than any purported semantic values, whether objectual or descriptional.

If words are properly individuated, by their world histories rather than by their sound or spelling, a name might almost serve as its own Fregean *Sinn*. The linguistic difference between "Hesperus" and "Phosphorus"—the simple difference between thinking of Venus qua *Hesperus* and thinking of it qua *Phosphorus*—may be all the difference in mode of presentation one needs in order to derive the benefits of sense and denotation theory. Words are undoubtedly denizens of cognition. If, through their history, they also provide the worldly link that determines the referent, then except for serving as content, they do all that Fregean *Sinn* is charged with. But they do it off-the-record, transparently and nondescriptively.[73]

IV. Who Can Say What?

To complete my afterthoughts regarding the semantics of direct reference, I must address certain issues on the border between metasemantics and epistemology.[74] My reflections were driven by a puzzle about Russellian 'logically proper names'. In the end I concluded that the puzzle has a simple answer (to which I will return in the end).[75] But it prompted thoughts on the more controversial issue of constraints on what an agent in a particular epistemological situation can express.

What we can't do with words: the Autonomy of Apprehension

As I understand Frege and Russell, both believed that the realm of propositions accessible to thought, i.e., those capable of being *apprehended*, is independent of and epistemologically *prior to* the acquisition of language. In using language we merely encode what was already

---

[73] Here I echo an idea urged by Felicia (then Diana) Ackerman in "Proper Names, Propositional Attitudes, and Nondescriptive Connotations," *Philosophical Studies* 35 (1979): 55–69.

[74] I am indebted to Keith Donnellan for several formative discussions of this material.

[75] It has at least one simple answer; it also has several less simple answers.

thinkable.[76] Therefore, whatever can be expressed using language was already, prelinguistically, an available object of thought.[77]

I see this view of the *autonomy of apprehension* in Russell's claim that

> in every proposition that we can apprehend (i.e., not only in those whose truth and falsity we can judge of, but in all that we can think about), all the constituents are really entities with which we have immediate acquaintance.[78]

Perhaps it accounts for the feeling one has in reading Russell on logically proper names, and even more so in reading Frege, that, like Humpty Dumpty, everyone runs their own language. When we speak, we *assign* meanings to our words; the words themselves do not *have* meanings. These assignments are, in theory, unconstrained (except by whatever limitations our epistemic situation places on what we can apprehend). In practice, it may be prudent to try to *coordinate* with the meanings others have assigned, but this is only a practical matter.[79]

Subjectivist semantics

We may term this view, *subjectivist* semantics. Although the *entities* which serve as possible meanings may be regarded as objective, in the sense that the same possible meanings are accessible to more than one person,[80] the *assignment* of meanings is subjective, and thus the *semantics* is subjective. Since each individual user must *assign* meanings rather than receiving them with the words, each user's semantics is autonomous. What the language community does make available to each

---

[76] Here we may have the foundation for the view that meaning is all in the head, or at least all already directly accessible by the head.

[77] Language, of course, aids communication, and also makes it easier, perhaps even possible, to *reason* using very complex thoughts. But the *manipulation* of thoughts is not what I am getting at here. My interest is in what can be apprehended and what can be expressed.

[78] Bertrand Russell, "On Denoting," *Mind* 14 (1905): 479–93.

[79] Prudential considerations of this kind will not, of course, affect a free spirit like H. Dumpty. An analogy: the concept of driving a car in traffic does not imply obedience to the conventions (sometimes called "rules" or "laws") whereby the movement of different drivers is coordinated. But it is usually (often?, occasionally?) prudent to so act. Dumpty's friend Dodgson appears to have shared his views. See Lewis Carroll (with an Introduction and Notes by Martin Gardner), *The Annotated Alice* (Cleveland: World Publishing Company, 1963), especially the notes on pages 268–69.

[80] This was certainly the view of Frege and sometime the view of Russell.

of its members is a syntax, an *empty* syntax to which each user must add his own semantics.

The individual can express only those propositions that were already available to him as thoughts before receiving the benefits of linguistic communion. We cannot enlarge the stock of possible meanings that are available to us by drawing on the total stock of meanings extant in the language community. In this sense there is no semantic sharing. What each user can express is independent of the resources of other members of the language community, and in this sense what each user can express is *independent of language*.

There are differences between Frege and Russell in the way in which one's epistemic situation is seen to influence the propositions one can apprehend. Frege suggests that all mankind has access to the same thoughts. Thus that differences in our experience, our location in space and time, our culture (including in particular our linguistic community), do not affect what propositions we can apprehend.[81]

Russell's view was plainly different. He believed that our idiosyncratic experiences *do* affect what propositions we can apprehend. For Russell one can apprehend a proposition containing an individual x as a component if and only if one is directly acquainted with x. And it is clear that what one is directly acquainted with is a function of one's experience.[82]

A fixed point of all such Russellian theories is that we may be so situated as to be able to *describe* a certain individual x but not to *apprehend* it; whereas a friend may be able to *apprehend* that selfsame individual. The friend can dub x with a logically proper name n, and try to communicate his thought using n. No use. We cannot just accept n with his meaning, we must assign it our own meaning, and in this case his meaning (namely, x) is not available to us for assignment. Sigh![83]

---

[81] In "The Thought: A Logical Inquiry," his discussion of the first-person pronoun indicates some ambivalence regarding this view. His suggestion that context of use is a partial determinant of the *Sinn* of an indexical may also indicate ambivalence if it implies (what I believe to be true) that persons in different contexts have access to different (indexical) thoughts.

[82] Let different views of how direct *direct acquaintance* must be reflect different *Theories of Apprehension*. Russell suggests in the beginning of "On Denoting" that we may be acquainted with other people's *bodies* though we are not acquainted with other people's minds "seeing that these are not directly perceived." This suggestion does not accord with Russell's later views, and some think that this was not his *true* view even at the time of "On Denoting".

[83] This is the situation in which we are forced to assign a descriptive meaning to the word our friend used as a name. Bad coordination, but unavoidable accord-

Consumerist semantics

Contrast the view of subjectivist semantics with the view that we are, for the most part, language *consumers*. Words come to us prepackaged with a semantic value. If we are to use *those words*, the words we have received, the words of our linguistic community, then we must defer to *their* meaning. Otherwise we play the role of language *creators*.[84] In our culture, the role of language creators is largely reserved to parents, scientists, and headline writers for *Variety*; it is by no means the typical use of language as the subjectivist semanticists believe. To use language as language, to express something, requires an intentional act. But the intention that is required involves the typical consumer's attitude of compliance, not the producer's assertiveness.[85]

There are two senses of "naming": dubbing and referring. To the consumerist, subjectivist semanticists have not adequately distinguished them.

To some, subjectivist semantics will seem a right and proper conservatism: Practice self-reliance—there is no such thing as a free thought! But it should be recognized that the view is incompatible with one of the most important contributions of contemporary theory of reference: the historical chain picture of the reference of names.

The notion of a historical chain of acquisition by which a name is passed from user to user, was first used to facilitate abandonment of the classical, description theory of proper names found in Frege and Russell.[86] The notion of a historical chain does this by offering an al-

---

ing to Russell. Frege's theory of apprehension seems to *permit* perfect coordination, which he urges for scientific discourse while recognizing that we don't always achieve it in ordinary discourse.

[84] We may, like the prudent subjectivist semanticist, always attempt to give a known word the same meaning as that *commonly given* to it. We would still be playing the role of language creators, though without the creativity of someone like H. Dumpty.

[85] I would like to formulate the relevant intention as one to use the word with *its* meaning, rather than with the meaning *assigned* by the person from whom the consumer heard (first heard?) the word. The immediate source from which the word was received seems to me to be primarily relevant to question of which word it is (among homonyms), rather than to the question of what meaning it has.

[86] The idea, and its use in the argument against description theory, first appears in print in Keith Donnellan's "Proper Names and Identifying Descriptions," *Synthese* 21 (1970): 335–58; reprinted in *Semantics of Natural Language*, ed. D. Davidson and G. Harman (Humanities Press, 1972). It then appears in Kripke's *Naming and Necessity*, which, coincidentally, was first published in the same collection in which Donnellan's article is reprinted (*Semantics of Natural Language*). Kripke notes, "the historical acquisition picture of naming advocated here is apparently

ternative explanation of how a name in local use can be connected with
a remote referent, an explanation that does not require that the mechanism of reference is already in the head of the local user in the form
of a self-assigned description. In determining the referent of the name
"Aristotle", we need not look to the biography's *text*, instead we look
to its *bibliography*.

A role for language in thought: Vocabulary Power as an epistemological enhancement

There is another, possibly more fundamental, use of the notion: to tilt
our perspective on the *epistemology* of language away from the subjectivist views of Frege and Russell and toward a more communitarian
outlook.[87] The notion that a referent can be carried by a name from
early past to present suggests that the language itself carries meanings, and thus that we can *acquire* meanings through the instrument
of language. This frees us from the constraints of subjectivist semantics and provides the opportunity for an *instrumental* use of language to
broaden the realm of what can be expressed and to broaden the horizons
of thought itself.

On my view, our connection with a linguistic community in which
names and other meaning-bearing elements are passed down to us enables us to entertain thoughts *through the language* that would not otherwise be accessible to us. Call this the *Instrumental Thesis*.[88]

The Instrumental Thesis seems to me a quite important, though
often tacit, feature of contemporary theories of reference, and one that
distinguishes them from many earlier views. It urges us to see language,

---

very similar to views of Keith Donnellan" (addenda to *Naming and Necessity*,
p. 164).

[87] The two uses of the notion of a historical chain of communication are related. It
is hard to see how to avoid some version of a description theory of proper names,
at least for names of individuals we are not acquainted with, if one maintains a
subjectivist semantics. Thus the attack on description theory (by which I mean
not just the attack on *classical* description theory but the claim that descriptions
are not even required as reference fixers) is *a fortiori* an attack on subjectivist
semantics.

[88] Given the wide acceptance of some version of the historical chain explanation for
the mechanism of reference for proper names, it is surprising that there has been
so little explicit discussion of the epistemological issues to which the Instrumental
Thesis is addressed. A notable exception is the discussion of Leverrier's original use
of "Neptune" in Keith Donnellan's "The Contingent *A Priori* and Rigid Designation," in *Contemporary Perspectives in the Philosophy of Language*, ed. P. French,
H. Uehling, and H. Wettstein (Minneapolis: University of Minnesota Press, 1979).

and in particular semantics, as more autonomous, more independent of the thought of individual users, and to see our powers of apprehension as less autonomous and more dependent on our vocabulary.[89]

Contrary to Russell, I think we succeed in thinking about things in the world not only through the mental residue of that which we ourselves experience, but also vicariously, through the symbolic resources that come to us through our language. It is the latter—*vocabulary power*— that gives us our apprehensive advantage over the nonlinguistic animals. My dog, being color-blind, cannot entertain the thought that I am wearing a red shirt. But my color-blind colleague can entertain even the thought that Aristotle wore a red shirt.

One need not fall in love to speak of love. One need not have grieved to speak of grief. The poet who has never felt or observed love may yet speak of it *if he has heard of it*. The fact that the language to speak of it and to enable us to have heard of it exists may show that *someone* once felt love. But it need not be the poet. And as with love, so with Samarkand (and red, and Aristotle). Our own individual experience may play a dominant role in providing the conceptual resources with which we address the world, but it does not play the whole role.[90]

So how shall I apprehend thee? Let me count the ways. I may apprehend you by (more or less) direct perception. I may apprehend you by memory of (more or less) direct perception. And finally, I may apprehend you through a sign that has been created to signify you.

Does a name put us in causal contact with the referent?

I should add that I do not believe that the third category can be subsumed under the first. Apprehension through the language is not a very indirect form of perception that yields a very indirect form of acquaintance—like hearing a scratchy recording of Caruso or perhaps viewing his letters to his manager. Names are not, in general, among the causal effects of their referents. Perhaps a name should be regarded as among the causal effects of the person who *dubbed* the referent, but only in unusual cases will this *be* the referent.

---

[89] How could Putnam have apprehended the dismaying thought that he couldn't tell a Beech from an Elm, without the help of his linguistic community? Could one *have* such a thought without having the *words*?

[90] My grand instrumentalist views regarding red and love go beyond a more cautious version of the Instrumental Thesis that would be limited to names like "Aristotle" and "Samarkand". I note this at the urging of friends who characterize the cautious view as "persuasive" and my view as "shocking".

Even if we granted the referent a causal role in a typical dubbing by ostension, we can introduce a name by *describing* the referent (e.g., as the ratio of the circumference of a circle to its diameter). Such names are still directly referential and, in my view, still have the capacity to enlarge what we can express and apprehend. If we were to discover that Aristotle had been predicted and dubbed one year before his birth, or had been dubbed "Aristotle" only in medieval times, the name, like "π", would still be a *name*, with all its attendant powers.[91]

I recognize that some will find my tolerance for nonostensive dubbings unacceptable, and may insist that the mere reception of a name *is* the reception of a causal signal from the referent. The name is likened to a lock of hair, a glimpse of one far distant, uninformative, but evocative. If names were like this, if there were a simple, natural (i.e., nonintentional) relation between name and named as there is between hair and behaired, the theory of reference for proper names would be a simple thing ... and it isn't.[92]

On my view, acquisition of a name does not, in general, put us *en rapport* (in the language of "Quantifying In") with the referent. But this is not required for us to use the name in the standard way as a device of direct reference. Nor is it required for us to apprehend, to believe, to doubt, to assert, or to hold other *de dicto* attitudes toward the propositions we express using the name.[93]

The *de dicto* hedge reflects my current view that *de dicto* attitudes, even those toward propositions expressed using directly referential terms, cannot easily be translated into *de re* attitudes.[94] The reason for this lies in part with the problems that led to my original claim that we need to be *en rapport* with those toward whom we hold *de re* attitudes and in part with technical problems involving reflexivity.[95]

---

[91] Howard Wettstein points out that whereas dubbing by ostension has a special Russellian flavor, dubbing by description seems the paradigm for Frege. Since both adhere to subjectivist semantics, *they* believe that their dubbings are strictly for home use and will never go on the open market. (Did either have children?)

[92] Those who see names as among the causal effects of the thing named seem to me to be insufficiently appreciative of Grice's distinction between nonnatural and natural meaning. H. P. Grice, "Meaning," *Philosophical Review* 66 (1957): 377–88.

[93] It is required, however, that we *use* the name. I would suppose that with some very exotic names we might forbear their use in favor of their mention, and conceive of the referent only as *the referent of that name*.

[94] This represents a change from the view expressed in footnote 69 of *Demonstratives*.

[95] The first sort of problem involves understanding the conditions under which we correctly ascribe to Holmes, for example, the *de re* attitude that there is someone whom he believes to have committed the murder. It seems clear that the mere fact

The proponents of connectivity urge that although the language enables us to *express* contents that would otherwise be inaccessible (thus contradicting subjectivist semantics), something more, something like being *en rapport* with the components of the content, is required to *apprehend* the content (and thus to hold attitudes toward it).[96] I think of the proposal as a requirement that we have *knowledge of* the components. This certainly does not require direct acquaintance with the components, but it may require a natural connection to the components that is stronger than that provided by a name introduced into the language by one who did not himself have *knowledge of* the object (for example, a name now introduced for the first child to be born in the twenty-first century, or for the next president of Brazil, whosoever that may be).[97] The suggestion seems to be that all names (including perhaps names of colors, natural and unnatural kinds, etc.), however introduced, carry their referent as meaning; but not all names carry *knowledge of* their referent. Those names that were properly introduced, by ostension or based on some other form of knowledge of the referent, carry and transmit the requisite epistemic connection. But in a tiny fraction of cases the connection is absent—semantics (or metasemantics) does not require it—and in these cases we have direct reference, and expressibility, but no apprehension.[98]

In theory, this is a dramatic weakening of the Instrumental Thesis, since it urges that more than a *semantic* connection needs to be established between a name and its referent before a name can attain its full powers. In practice, because only a tiny fraction of our vocabulary would lack the requisite connection, it may be almost no weakening at

---

that the murderer has given himself a *nom de crime* and leaves a message using this name should not suffice. (In fact, I suspect that there are no fixed conditions, only conditions relative to the topic, interests, aims, and presuppositions of a particular discourse.)

The second sort of problem is discussed in "Opacity", appendix B: The Syntactically *De Re*.

[96] A version of this view can be found in my "Quantifying In," *Synthese* 19 (1968): 175–214; reprinted in A. P. Martinich, op. cit. Others have espoused more sophisticated versions.

[97] The second example shows that what is required is that the *knowledge of* the individual play a special role in the dubbing. It must be intended to dub the individual *as known*. If someone I know well were to turn out, to my astonishment, to be the next president of Brazil, that would not qualify. Donnellan might say that in a dubbing by description, the description must be used referentially to dub an individual that one *has in mind*.

[98] A name may later take on the required epistemic connection when the referent appears upon the scene and is recognized as the named object.

all.[99]

I am not entirely unsympathetic to this view.[100] We do distinguish knowledge from belief in part by the way in which we are connected to the object of knowledge. And thus insofar as one needs *to know what it is* that one apprehends, *to know what it is* that one believes, doubts, asserts, etc., the demand for epistemic connection may seem reasonable in analogy to that demanded for knowledge of facts (knowing-that). Note that on this view what gives us *knowledge of* the content of a name is *just* the connection, not any (new) beliefs. In fact, in this sense of knowing-what-we-apprehend, no beliefs at all are involved, only a well-connected name. In any case, a caveat must be added. To know what one apprehends is not to be able to *individuate* it. The Babylonians knew what Hesperus was, and knew what Phosphorus was, but didn't know that they were the same. Similarly, one might apprehend the proposition that Hesperus is a planet, and apprehend the proposition that Phosphorus is a planet, without knowing that they are the same proposition (if they are).

Naming the nonexistent

There are certain categories of objects which clearly have no causal effects upon us. If such objects can be given names, the view that names are among the causal effects of their referents cannot be correct. I have in mind future individuals and merely possible individuals. Such putative entities are *nonexistent*.[101]

If we can give a name to the person who *once* occupied this body ("John Doe #256"), why should we not be able to give a name to the person who *will*, in fact, arise from this fertilized egg? And if we possess an actual knock-down lectern kit, containing instructions for assembly

---

[99] My own hesitations regarding *de re* attitudes (the *de dicto* hedge) can also be seen as a limit on the scope of the Instrumental Thesis, a limit comparable to that proposed by those who suggest that an epistemic connection is required. If those who demand an epistemic connection identify *de dicto* attitudes toward propositions expressed using names (singular propositions) with *de re* attitudes (as I did in *Demonstratives*), it may even be that their qualms are really qualms about *de re* attitudes. But I had better not speak for others' qualms.

[100] Not *entirely*, though I do still maintain the view of footnote 76 of *Demonstratives*.

[101] We certainly can't get *en rapport* with such individuals. Past individuals are also, in my view, nonexistent, but they do affect us causally. Some abstract objects, like numbers, do not, I think, affect us causally (in the appropriate sense), and they surely can be given names. I do not consider them because of qualms about the objectivity of such objects.

and all materials (form and matter), why should we not be able to name the unique, merely possible lectern that *would have* been assembled, if only we had not procrastinated until the need was past.

The sceptics, who take the position that an individual cannot be dubbed until it comes into existence, would insist that there is no naming the baby until the end of the first trimester (or whenever the current metaphysical pronouncements from the Supreme Court may indicate). One may, of course, express an intention to dub *whatever first satisfies certain conditions* with a particular name. Perhaps one may even *launch* the dubbing before the referent arrives. But the naming doesn't *take*, the name doesn't *name* it, one cannot *use* the name to refer to it (at least not to refer directly to it in the way names are said to refer by direct reference theorists) until the referent comes into existence.

A difficulty in the sceptical position is that in planning and in other forward-looking activities, we often wish to speak *about* such unnameables, perhaps through the use of descriptions.[102] In my experience, those who protest the possibility of *naming* the first child to be born in the twenty-first century often accept the view that the description is—how shall I put it—not *vacuous*.

Perhaps they accept quantification over such entities and just object to the practice of introducing *names* on the basis of arbitrary descriptions (for names they want connectivity). It would then be natural to add a *narrow existence predicate* to distinguish the robust being of true local existents, like you and me, from the more attenuated being of the nonexistents.

If such quantification is *not* accepted, the position seems odd. Is it assumed that there are clever ways to reformulate any sentence in which such descriptions occur so as to 'eliminate' those that appear outside the scope of a temporal operator?[103] It is not obvious to me how to do this. How would the *de dicto* sentence, "Katie owes her first- (to be) born child to Rumpelstiltskin" be reformulated?[104]

---

[102] Or other 'denoting phrases' as Russell termed them.

[103] I note that if there is such a method, then there is probably a similar method for eliminating descriptions of past individuals that no longer exist.

[104] Using "Fy" for "y is a first-born child of Katie", and "Ox" for "Katie owes x to Rumpelstiltskin", we might try the following 'elimination' of the definite description from what is roughly "$O(the\ x)Fx$" (ignoring the 'if any' aspect of the description "her first-born"),

$$Future\ \exists x(Always\forall y(Fy \leftrightarrow y = x) \wedge Now\ Ox).$$

This symbolization would be correct for "Katie *will give* her first-born child to

What sounds like scepticism with regard to naming the nonexistent, may merely be the quite different concern that the description of the intended dubbee is insufficiently specific to select a unique nonexistent individual. Such may be the case of the possible fat man in the doorway.

Insufficient specificity seems to be Kripke's qualm in *Naming and Necessity* regarding the merely possible species Unicorn and a merely possible referent for "Sherlock Holmes".[105] However, his discussion of what he calls "the epistemological thesis" (that the discovery that there were animals with all the features attributed to Unicorns in the myth does not establish that there were Unicorns) suggests an entirely different argument, namely that *the way in which these particular names arose* (from pure myth and pure fiction) makes it impossible for *them* to name merely possible entities.[106] This argument is independent of the degree of specificity in the myth or in the fiction.[107]

Rumpelstiltskin", but not for "*owes*". The problem is that "owes" (like "needs" and "seeks") is an intensional verb with respect to its grammatical object. Even if it turns out that Katie's first-born child is her ugliest child, $Always \; \forall \; y(Fy \leftrightarrow Uy)$, she does not now owe Rumpelstiltskin her ugliest child. (However, if she *will give* her first-born child, then she will give her ugliest child.) The 'elimination' of the definite description transforms the predication from *de dicto* to a quantification in. And this leads to incorrect results for intensional verbs. (Note that the same sort of 'elimination' occurs automatically whenever we use first-order logic to symbolize a sentence with an indefinite description as grammatical object. Compare the symbolizations of "Katie owes a bushel of gold to Rumpelstiltskin" and "Katie will give a bushel of gold to Rumpelstiltskin". The interesting problem about indefinite descriptions as grammatical objects of intensional verbs is how to 'uneliminate' them.)

So long as there are no intensional verbs, the eliminations are not plainly incorrect. Intensional *operators*, so long as they are *sentential* operators, do not create a problem, because definite and indefinite descriptions can be eliminated from predicates while remaining within the scope of the operator.

Some think that "*owes*" can be paraphrased to produce a sentential complement where the grammatical object of "owes" appears, for example, as "Katie is now obligated that at some future time she gives her first- (to have been) born child to Rumpelstiltskin". This allows a tense operator ("at some future time") to be inserted between the new sentential operator and the old grammatical object of "owes". If you are of this view, try "Katie is thinking about her first (to be) born child", and read appendix A: Paraphrasing Into Propositional Attitudes from "Opacity".

My aim here is to indicate that there is a substantial technical problem faced by those who hope to achieve the effect of quantification over future individuals through the use of temporal operators.

[105] Addenda, pp. 156–58.

[106] As Harry Deutsch puts it, *reference is no coincidence*.

[107] In lecture, Kripke has made the intriguing suggestion that there are abstract but actual (not merely possible) *fictional individuals* that serve as the referents of

Neither insufficient specificity nor the objections concerning extant names from fiction or myth apply to the case of the first child to be born in the twenty-first century or to the case of the possible lectern, in both of which a frank attempt is made to dub what is recognized as a nonexistent object.

Logically proper names

The question that prompted all my thoughts on subjectivist semantics, the Instrumental Thesis, and vocabulary power is this: How should Russellian 'logically proper names' be accommodated in the semantics of Context and Circumstance?

Using "name" for what he sometimes called a "logically proper name," Russell writes,

> a *name* ... is a simple symbol, directly designating an individual which is its meaning, and having this meaning in

names like "Sherlock Holmes". The admission of such entities might be accompanied by a narrow existence predicate to distinguish the fictional from the non. I am not aware of Russell's views on future individuals, but he expressed himself in opposition to fictional entities in *Introduction to Mathematical Philosophy*,

> If no one thought about Hamlet, there would be nothing left of him; if no one thought about Napoleon, he would have soon seen to it that someone did. The sense of reality is vital in logic, and whoever juggles with it by pretending that Hamlet has another kind of reality is doing a disservice to thought.

Despite Russell's rhetorical power, I must confess to having been persuaded by Kripke's analysis. (As Joseph Almog points out, it is not clear that Russell's insistence that Hamlet does not have "another kind of reality" would apply to what I take to be Kripke's view that Hamlet, though not a *person*, exists as a *fictional character* in *our* reality.)

If Kripke is correct, it would seem to settle the case in which an author creates a fiction 'out of whole cloth' but specifies one of the characters, which he names "Woody", to have particular characteristics which, though nothing does in fact *have* the characteristics, our favorite theory of essentialism tells us that there is exactly one possible object that *could* have them (e.g., the characteristic of having been assembled from a certain lectern kit). "Woody" would name an actual fictional entity, not a merely possible nonfictional entity.

Or should we say instead that the author made up a story *about* a particular merely possible nonfictional entity? The fairly plain distinction between an individual, *x*, *having the properties* of a character in a story and the story being *about x*, grows dim when *x* is merely possible. And if we add the difficulties of the distinction between being *about x* and being *modeled on x* (a hard enough distinction for real *x*), I lose discriminability.

its own right, independently of the meanings of all other words.[108]

It is hard to resist the idea that for Russell, such names are directly referential. However, his ideas about the existence predicate are baffling. He continues,

> The proposition "the so-and-so exists" is significant, whether true or false: but if *a* is the so-and-so (where "*a*" is a name), the words "*a* exists" are meaningless. It is only of descriptions—definite or indefinite—that existence can be significantly asserted; for, if "*a*" is a name, it *must* name something: what does not name anything is not a name, and therefore, if intended to be a name, is a symbol devoid of meaning.

His claim that it is meaningless to predicate existence of a logically proper name is plainly a mistake.[109] Far from being meaningless, such propositions are required as the objects of what Russell called *propositional attitudes*, "I regret that this pain exists", "I am pleased that Nixon exists" (taking "Nixon" and "this pain" to be logically proper names). These assertions are by no means either trivial or meaningless.

The requirement that a logically proper name *name* something seems to have the result that "*a* exists" ("*a*" a logically proper name) cannot be used to express a proposition that is false. But unless "*a*" names a necessary existent, the proposition expressed would not be necessary. Thus we have a seeming failure of the rule of Necessitation. This, along

---

[108] From chapter 15 of *Introduction to Mathematical Philosophy* (London: Allen & Unwin, 1919), reprinted in Martinich, op. cit.

[109] I do not understand why Russell did not recognize that the intolerable existence predicate could be defined by forming the indefinite description, "an individual identical with *a*", and then predicating existence of the indefinite description in the way Russell finds so commendable, "∃*x* *x* = *a*".

The problem with empty names should not have dissuaded him. If such names are taken to be (disguised) definite descriptions, as he usually claimed they were, then (where *a* is now a definite description), "∃*x* *x* = *a*" is again equivalent to "*a* exists" according to Russell's own theory of descriptions. (As a sidelight, it is interesting to note that even if an empty name is taken to be "a symbol devoid of meaning," it is possible to develop a rigorous semantics according to which "∃*x* *x* = *a*" is again equivalent to "*a* exists". Russell was not aware of this.)

It is not my claim that the notion of *existence* is captured by the existential quantifier; variables can have any domain. My argument is *ex concessis*. Insofar as existence can be "significantly asserted" of indefinite descriptions, it can be significantly asserted of names.

with Russell's epistemological ideas, which emphasize the special situation of the agent who uses the name, is highly reminiscent of my analysis of indexicals.

These reflections made logically proper names seem a natural topic for the apparatus I had developed in *Demonstratives*, and this drew me in deeper.

When I attempted to apply the apparatus, I was surprised by the results. I was faced with a puzzle. The principles governing logically proper names seemed to imply that a logically proper name *must* name something that exists in its context of use, but need not name a *necessary* existent. But if the referent is not a necessary existent, then there must be a world and time at which it does not exist, and if *c* is a context of use in such a world at such a time, what would be named by an "occurrence" of the name in the context *c*? Briefly, how can every possible occurrence of a name have an existent referent, if the referent isn't a necessary existent?

To make things definite, consider the puzzling case of Nixon. Suppose that I name a certain pain with which I am directly acquainted, "Nixon". We agree that Nixon does not have necessary existence. So there must be a happier world (or time) in which Nixon does not exist.[110] If I were to utter "Nixon" in this happier circumstance, what existent would I be referring to? If "Nixon exists" cannot be used to express a proposition that is false, an occurrence of "Nixon" in such circumstances must name something that exists there. This cannot be Nixon, *ex hypothesi*. What could it be?

Be clear that I am not raising questions about how to *evaluate* at the happier circumstance what is expressed by an occurrence of "Nixon exists" in the painful context of dubbing. No problem there; it's false (again, *ex hypothesi*). The question is: What is *expressed* by an occurrence of "Nixon exists" in a context in the happier circumstance? And how can it be true there?

So what *is* the referent of "Nixon" when it occurs in a context in a world and time in which Nixon doesn't exist?

We can be certain that names do not enter vocabularies through a trans-world chain of communication. If the world is one in which Nixon never exists, how is the agent of the context able to use the term

---

[110]For example, the next day, when Nixon has subsided into nonexistence. Or, if you think that pains like Nixon never cease to 'exist' (in some sense) once they appear, take the day *before* Nixon came into existence. Or, better yet, take some possible world in which Nixon *never* comes into existence.

"Nixon"; was the name introduced there to dub a merely possible entity? Not likely.

The solution to the puzzle is, I think, independent of all the issues surrounding subjectivist versus consumerist semantics. As was emphasized earlier, our notion of an *occurrence* of an expression in a context does not require an *utterance* of the expression nor even that the agent of the context have the use of the expression. The apparatus of Context, Character, and Circumstance is designed to help articulate the semantics of an *interpreted* language, one for which meanings, *however derived*, are already associated with the expressions. It takes account of what the meanings are, not of how they came about. Given an interpreted language, a sentence is valid if it expresses a truth in every context, including those contexts in which the language doesn't or couldn't exist, or doesn't or couldn't have that interpretation. Thus the objection that certain meanings *could not arise* or *could not be used* in certain contexts is, strictly speaking, irrelevant to our issue: What is the content in such contexts of an expression which already carries a certain meaning?

So the answer is: Nixon. (Just as you knew all along.) The intuition that "Nixon exists" must be logically valid whenever "Nixon" is a logically proper name, is in error in tacitly assuming that to *evaluate* our language in a foreign context, the language, with its interpretation, must exist there.[111]

I see here a reaffirmation of the importance of a central distinction that I have tried to build into my very nomenclature, the distinction between what *exists* at a given point and what can be 'carried in' to be *evaluated* at that point, though it may *exist* only elsewhere. My 'Circumstances of Evaluation' evaluate contents that may have no native existence at the circumstance but can be expressed elsewhere and carried in for evaluation. What is crucial to the puzzle about "Nixon" is that my 'Contexts of Use' are also points of evaluation, they evaluate characters (meanings) that may have no native existence at the context but can also be created elsewhere and carried in for evaluation.

Where within the formal theory do I take account of the locus of *creation of character*, the *assignment* of meanings that is presupposed

---

[111] This, however, suggests that there may be another interesting analysis of the puzzle about logically proper names in terms of utterance-validity. And another using the notion, from the discussion of contexts for demonstratives, of a context *appropriate* for a particular expression. These considerations may throw light on a kind of metasemantical analyticity, not the usual: truth solely in virtue of what the meaning is, but instead: truth in virtue of having come to have that meaning.

in the notion of an interpreted language? Where within the formal theory do I take account of such metasemantical matters as constraints on the kinds of dubbings allowed? I do not.[112]

[112] In addition to assistance specifically acknowledged, I have been much helped (provided one includes expressions of dismay as *help*) by Joseph Almog, Harry Deutsch, Keith Donnellan, Kit Fine, John Perry, Elisabetta Fava, Nathan Salmon, and Howard Wettstein.